OUTSIDE READINGS IN PSYCHOLOGY

OUTSIDE READINGS IN PSYCHOLOGY

SECOND EDITION

EUGENE L. HARTLEY

RUTH E. HARTLEY

College of the City of New York

THOMAS Y. CROWELL COMPANY

New York — 1957

Library of Congress Catalog Card Number 56-12627

(b. 7. 57)

Manufactured in the United States of America
by The Vail-Ballou Press, Inc., Binghamton, N.Y.

PREFACE

IN THE YEARS since publication of the first edition of this book, psychological research, theory, and applications have made notable progress. Yet the time allotted to introductory courses in psychology remains severely limited. In spite of new teaching aids and methods, the problem of encompassing a rapidly expanding field of knowledge within a fixed time challenges the teacher's ingenuity.

The purpose of this volume, like that of its predecessor, is to make easily available a wide selection of good teaching material, beyond the textbook, that will help students learn, consolidate, and remember the subject matter of their course. With a copy of the book in the hands of each student, the teacher can assign source materials that will quicken the student's understanding of the textbook. One article may reinforce a textbook chapter by stating its thesis in slightly different terms; another may integrate and clarify a theoretical concept; and still another may amplify the treatment in the text. Many of the readings will provoke class discussion. The sudden flash of understanding, the new point of view, or the heightened interest in the subject that can result from such outside reading will lighten the student's task of learning and ease the teacher's burden of presentation.

While the aim of the book is unchanged, the contents of this edition are almost entirely new. Some articles in the first edition have been dropped because their subject areas are covered in the newer textbooks. In general, the present book places greater emphasis upon a broad psychological point of view rather than on physiology or psychiatry, and substitutes new clinical materials for the traditional examples. Many of these changes have followed closely the suggestions so generously offered by users of the first edition.

Also in line with the experience of users, as well as of the editors, is the increased emphasis upon this edition as a learning aid. Brief introductions to each of the major sections relate the articles to each other and to the text materials. In addition, a headnote for each article provides a setting for that particular selection.

Such merit as may inhere in this volume is, of course, the result of the scholarship and skill of the original authors of these papers. Individual acknowledgment of these contributions is made in footnotes at the beginning of each selection. Here, however, we should like to thank them collectively for their gracious permission to include their writings in this volume. Similarly, we wish to express our gratitude to the original publishers who granted permission to reprint. This courtesy, generosity, and cooperativeness, which make it possible to bring these selections before a wider audience than the more specialized ones for which they were for the most part originally presented, should result in extended awareness, interest, and endeavors. Our personal appreciation cannot be more directly expressed than by the earnest hope that this expectation will be fulfilled.

We take particular pleasure in acknowledging the aid of Wendy Ellen Hartley in the preparation of the manuscript.

EUGENE L. HARTLEY
RUTH E. HARTLEY

New York, N.Y.
January, 1957

CONTENTS

OUTSIDE READINGS IN PSYCHOLOGY

NOTE TO STUDENTS

THIS BOOK has been designed to make readily available to you source materials that will help you in your study of psychology. Many of the articles can be readily enjoyed in their own right. A few may require careful reading in part. Each, however, has been included because we believe it will contribute something valuable to your knowledge of psychology.

As teachers we would encourage you to use your own initiative—browse through this book reading those articles that appeal to you. When you read one that is particularly interesting, go to the library and look up the source from which it came (the full reference is given in the footnote at the beginning of the article). Some of the readings are from books, and you may want to read the rest of the volumes in which they appear; others are from magazines and journals, and you may want to read other articles appearing in these publications. Moreover, in their original sources many of the readings have bibliographical references that direct you to interesting related writings, references that have been omitted here in order to conserve space.

Further, this single volume cannot provide complete coverage for the subject matter of the field and should be read in conjunction with a textbook or series of lectures. The list on pages 486–88 indicates parallels between chapters in some of the more widely read texts and the articles included here.

We sincerely hope that you will find your reading here and in related channels suggested by these articles both pleasant and profitable.

EUGENE L. HARTLEY
RUTH E. HARTLEY

I

INTRODUCTION

THE WORD "psychology" is widely used in everyday speech, with many different meanings. Introductory courses in Psychology at the college level, however, tend primarily to treat psychology as a science. Surveying the field of psychology broadly, they usually include basic principles, a selection of some of the findings, an introduction to the current methods of investigation, and an illustration of some of the applications. The training of students in practical, professional skills is usually deferred until graduate study.

The two selections that follow provide a contemporary orientation toward two basic aspects of psychology important for the beginning student: the quality of *scientific functioning* it shares with other sciences, and some of the recent advances in its own specific area.

1. How Scientists Work and Think *

IN THIS selection a physical scientist outlines the potential role of scientific thinking in everyday life. Scientific thinking is a way of thinking and as such can be applied to many kinds of materials—its application is not restricted only to scientific facts. If we can learn to think in this way, psychology as a science that deals with human beings can help us to be more accurate and effective in handling the human relations that are a part of all our activities.

THE WAYS by which scientists have learned, through a gradual evolution, to form sound judgments are exerting great influence on human affairs.

* Joel H. Hildebrand, "How scientists work and think," Office of Naval Research *Research Reviews,* February, 1956, pp. 33–34. By permission of the author and the *Research Reviews.*

This influence would become far wider and more beneficial, however, if these scientific methods could play a greater role in the education of everybody, including scientists themselves.

Let us consider a few examples. When Lenin stated that "Politics is a structure erected upon an economic foundation," he was using a pure analogy, having no value whatever as proof. Plato's assumption that heavenly bodies move in circles because "the circle is the most perfect geometrical figure" may have been pretty good for Plato, but we have learned in the meantime that the stars are not governed by man's notions of perfection. A scientist knows that "the law of averages" does not influence the weather to strive to follow a dry year with a wet one. He distinguishes between events which are predictable, like the death rate, and those that are not, like the death of an individual. He should know that it is not scientific to expect that the stock market will either fall or continue to rise simply because it has been rising, and, similarly, that the prediction of a "historicist" that "some sort or other of totalitarianism is inevitable" is a quite unwarranted extrapolation.

No mathematician now defines an axiom as "a self-evident truth," and no intelligent scientist accepts a conclusion based upon the assertion, "it stands to reason. . . ." He knows that the value of a battery additive is not determined by the testimony of satisfied users (the method of lawyers) and that getting well after taking an alleged remedy is not proof that the medicine caused the cure. He knows that foaming is not the proper measure of detergency; that advertising claims of "better," "faster," "bigger," are meaningless. He is aware of the danger of oversimplifying, and likely to be skeptical regarding such simple models as "the economic man," "the average citizen," "the typical Englishman," and of the simple solutions offered by politicians for complex national problems.

Our people would profit by a much larger infusion of scientific thinking into their personal and collective life.

Science is not a lot of book-learning; it is an active enterprise. It is what scientists do and how they do it. They do not wave magic wands, neither do they proceed by a series of rigid logical steps to sure conclusions. Instead, they keep their eyes open for discrepancies between actual phenomena and the current explanations for them, and they try to improve them in order better to understand, control, and predict. They devise instruments for observation and measurement. They use imagination to set up hypotheses, which they test by carefully designed and controlled experiments. Results found to occur so uniformly as to have high probability of recurrence are formulated as "laws," although it is understood that, unlike statute laws, they do not control.

These laws are explained, where possible, by theories and models. Mathematics often plays an important role, but its limitations must be kept in mind.

A science develops beyond the initial stages of observing, naming, and classifying by aid of unifying ideas or concepts, such as energy, entropy, quantum theory, and organic evolution.

The rich rewards of these methods in terms of economic prosperity and the health and well-being of the people are fairly well appreciated; what is not realized are their profound effects upon the ways in which we form judgments in general. Science is the great antidote to superstition, prejudice, wishful and emotional thinking. Its findings have, therefore, great influence upon social and ethical evaluations. It refutes, for example, the myth of racial superiority, responsible for so much of the world's injustice and cruelty. In the words of the philosopher, William R. Dennes, "Of all the servants of morality, science is the greatest; for it is the one serious way we have to discover what means are likeliest to lead to the realization of the ends we cherish."

---

2. *Implications of Recent Advances in Prediction and Control of Behavior* *

IN MODERN psychology the point that each individual is unique is often stressed. Nevertheless, there are many generalizations that may validly be made about people and their behavior. This paper is concerned with the selected recent advances in the scientific study of human behavior that have special significance for educators. It provides a good illustration of scientific thinking in psychology through the author's consistent use of the results of objective research in framing his generalizations. It also gives the reader an introduction to an important segment of the field he is studying.

THE SCIENCE of psychology, in spite of its immaturities and its brashness, has advanced mightily in recent decades. From a concern with observation and measurement, it has moved toward becoming an "if-then" science. By this I mean it has become more concerned with the discernment and discovery of lawful relationships such as that *if*

* Carl R. Rogers, "Implications of recent advances in prediction and control of behavior," *Teachers College Record,* LVII (February, 1956), 316–22. By permission of the author and the Bureau of Publications, Teachers College, Columbia University.

certain conditions exist, *then* certain behaviors will predictably follow.

I believe that few people are aware of the breadth, depth, and extent of the advances in psychology and the behavioral sciences, and still fewer seem to be aware of the profound social, political, economic, ethical, philosophical, and educational problems posed by these advances. In this discussion I should like to focus on the educational implications of these advances in the science of psychology (which inevitably will involve me in some concern with the philosophical implications as well) and to review a few selected examples of what I mean by the increased ability of psychology to understand and predict or control behavior. Each illustration I will give is supported by reasonably rigorous and adequate research, though like all scientific findings, each is open to modification or correction through more exact or imaginative future studies.

What, then, are some of the behaviors or learnings for which we now know how to supply the antecedent conditions?

We know how to set up the conditions under which many members of a group will report judgments which are contrary to the evidence of their senses. They will, for example, report that Figure A covers a larger area than Figure B, when the evidence of their senses *plainly* indicates that the reverse is true. Experiments by Asch, later refined and improved by Crutchfield, show that when a person is led to believe that everyone else in the group sees B as larger than A, then he has a strong tendency to go along with this judgment, and in many instances does so with a real belief in his false report.

We know a great deal about how to establish conditions which will influence consumer responses and/or public opinion. I refer you to the advertisements in any magazine, or to the TV program, "The $64,000 Question," and the sales of the sponsor's lipsticks.

We know how to influence the buying behavior of individuals by setting up conditions which provide satisfaction for needs of which they are unconscious, but which we have been able to determine. It has been shown that some women who do not buy instant coffee because of "a dislike for its flavor" actually dislike it at a subconscious level because it is associated in their minds with laziness, spendthrift qualities, and being a poor housekeeper. This type of study has led to sales campaigns based upon appealing to the unconscious motives of the individual —his unknown sexual, aggressive, or dependent desires.

We know how to predict which members of an organization will be troublesome and delinquent. On the basis of a paper and pencil test, Gough has predicted which department store employees will be unreliable and dishonest or otherwise difficult. He freely states that it is quite possible to identify, with a good deal of accuracy, the potential troublemakers of any organized group.

This ability to identify troublemakers is only an extension of the knowledge we have about prediction in other fields—predicting which individual is most likely to become a good salesman, or typesetter, or physician, or student in college.

We know how to provide conditions in a work group, whether in industry or in education, which will be followed by increased productivity, originality, and morale. Conversely we know how to provide the conditions which lead to low productivity and low morale. Studies by Coch and French and by Katz, Maccoby, and Morse show in general that when workers in industry participate in planning and decisions, and when they are not supervised in a suspicious or authoritarian way, production and morale increase. The reverse conditions produce a reverse effect. A study reported by Corey indicates that when the leader of a teacher group acts in a manner which is understanding, and which facilitates participation, the group is more productive in making and carrying through plans.

We know how to provide the conditions of leadership which will be followed by personality growth in the members of the group, as well as by increased productivity and improved group spirit. Richard, in his experience as manager of an industrial plant, and Gordon, in his study of leadership of a workshop, have shown that where the leader or leaders hold the attitudes customarily thought of as therapeutic, the results are good. In other words, if the leader is understanding, acceptant, and permissive toward his group and also acceptant of his own feelings in the situation, then the members of the group show evidence of personality growth and function more effectively and with better spirit.

We know how to provide the psychological conditions in the classroom which will result not only in the usual learning of academic content, but in improved personal adjustment as well. Studies by Asch and Faw show that if the attitudes of the teacher are similar to those described above for the leader, and hence responsible participation by the student is permitted and encouraged, then academic learning proceeds about as usual as measured by conventional tests, and personal growth and adjustment improve significantly.

We know how to provide an interpersonal relationship with qualities such that it enables the individual to meet stress with more serenity, less anxiety. Thetford, in an experiment with group therapy, and Faw, in a recent study of teacher-pupil relationships in the classroom, came to similar conclusions, though using very different methods and instruments. When individuals—clients or students—have experienced for a time a relationship of warmth, understanding, and acceptance, they are able to meet stress situations with less physiological upset and quicker recovery of physiological balance [Thetford] and are less upset psychologically by the stress [Faw].

We know the attitudes which, if provided by a counselor or a therapist, will be predictably followed by certain constructive personality and behavior changes in the client. Studies which in recent years have been completed in the field of psychotherapy justify this statement. The findings from these studies may be very briefly summarized in the following terms:

If the therapist provides a relationship in which he is (a) genuine, internally consistent; (b) acceptant, prizing the client as a person of worth; (c) empathically understanding of the client's private world; then the client becomes (a) more realistic in his self-perceptions; (b) more confident and self-directing; (c) more positively valued by himself; (d) less likely to repress elements of his experience; (e) more mature, socialized, and adaptive in his behavior; (f) more like the healthy, integrated, well-functioning person in his personality structure.

It is obvious that the essence of these findings in the field of therapy is closely related to the three previous illustrations.

We now know how, I believe, to disintegrate a man's personality structure, dissolving his self-confidence, destroying the concept he has of himself, and making him completely dependent upon another. This example has not been, so far as I know, verified by objective research. I make this statement after having studied, as far as one is able, the methods used in preparing prisoners for confession in various purge trials in Russia, and the brainwashing procedures applied in Communist China. It seems rather evident that these methods use many of the principles of psychotherapy, but use them in reverse fashion to bring about the disintegration of the autonomous personality, rather than integration. In a curious and abhorrent way this tends to validate the principles of psychotherapy mentioned above, because it indicates that the lawfulness of the process of therapy may be used to build or destroy personality.

We know how to provide psychological conditions which will produce vivid hallucinations and other abnormal reactions in the thoroughly normal individual in the waking state. This knowledge came about as the unexpected by-product of research at McGill University. It was discovered that if all channels of sensory stimulation are cut off or muffled, abnormal reactions follow. If healthy subjects lie relatively motionless, to reduce kinaesthetic stimuli, with eyes shielded by translucent goggles which do not permit perception, with hearing largely stifled by foam-rubber pillows as well as by being in a quiet cubicle, and with tactile sensations reduced by cuffs over the hands, then hallucinations and ideation bearing some resemblance to that of the psychotic occur within forty-eight hours in many of these subjects. What the results would be if the sensory stifling were continued longer is not known.

We know how to influence psychological moods, attitudes, and behaviors through drugs. For this illustration we have stepped over into the rapidly developing borderline area between chemistry and psychology. From "truth serum," to the chemotherapy now practiced in psychiatric wards, to drugs for the normal citizen there are many ways of changing psychological states. We may take a drug to mobilize our energy to cram for an exam, or a drug to allay our anxiety about the exam. Drugs have reportedly been given to soldiers before a battle to eliminate fear. While much is still unknown in this field, Dr. Skinner of Harvard states that "In the not-too-distant future, the motivational and emotional conditions of normal life will probably be maintained in any desired state through the use of drugs."

We know the psychological conditions of family life which, if established in a home, will tend to produce emotionally secure children with many socially valuable characteristics. Here we go to a very different field, that of personality development in children, for our example. We can measure the attitudes and emotional climate which parents are creating for their children, and from these measurements we can predict that Home A will in all probability produce children who will grow somewhat brighter over the years, will be emotionally secure, original, relatively unexcitable; who will be liked by their peers, likely to be leaders, and well-adjusted to adults. On the other hand we can predict that Home B will be likely to produce emotional, excitable children, with little emotional control, and with less of originality than the children from Home A. The studies done by Baldwin and others at the Fels Research Institute are the basis for these statements. Home A is the home in which the parents' attitudes and behaviors cluster in what the investigators have termed the "democratic" category, and parental attitudes and behaviors in Home B cluster in what they term the "actively rejectant" group.

My purpose in the above examples has been to point up the wide-ranging power, the very diverse potentialities for control and prediction, which psychological knowledge is giving us. When we project ourselves into the future, and try to imagine the further developments which will inevitably come, the prospect arouses uneasiness. Small wonder that Dr. Robert Oppenheimer, in speaking of the points of similarity between his own profession, physics, and the profession of psychology, says that one of these points "is the extent to which our progress will create profound problems of decision in the public domain. The physicists have been quite noisy about their contributions in the last decade. The time may well come—as psychology acquires a sound objective corpus of knowledge about human behavior and feeling—when the powers of control thus made available will pose far graver problems than any the physicists have posed."

Inherent in this development of the psychological or behavioral sciences are, I believe, two profound questions for educators. They are: How do educators propose to use these rapidly increasing potentialities for influencing and altering human learning and human behavior? How shall we prepare students to live in a world where the possibilities for such control of human behavior exist?

I shall not attempt to answer either of these questions, but shall only comment on each one. As to how educators propose to use this accumulating knowledge, I believe it is clear that it will depend entirely on their philosophy of education, as that philosophy is operationally defined in action. We are rapidly acquiring the knowledge and the skills which will enable us to turn out passive followers or independent citizens. Many teachers and educators, if we take account of their actions rather than their words, have the former as their goal. They will be able to implement this purpose much more adequately in the future. On the other hand, if the aim is to turn out self-directing, inquiring minds which will form their own judgments as to the truth, then knowledge exists which can facilitate this purpose also. It will be up to the educators, and even more broadly, up to the community, to choose the direction in which we shall go.

With regard to how we shall prepare students to live in this fearsome future world, I believe some of the research I have cited suggests possible answers.

In the investigation by Crutchfield, it was found that about one-third of the responses made by a group of individuals were strongly influenced by the majority opinion, even when that majority opinion was clearly false. However, not all individuals were equally influenced. Some persons were swayed on almost every item by what they thought to be a solid group opinion, but others were influenced scarcely at all. They "called the shots as they saw them," regardless of what others might think.

When Crutchfield analyzed the personality characteristics of these two groups on the basis of extensive personality assessment, the differences were sharp. The conforming group, who were swayed by the majority opinion, tended to be individuals who had little understanding of themselves, were defensive, had to put up a good "front." They were rigid, moralistic, and had great respect for authority. They were somewhat anxious, guilty, suggestible, and unable to tolerate ambiguity. They lacked self-confidence, were vacillating, and tended to become confused under stress.

The independent group, on the other hand, were active, effective, persuasive leaders. They were individuals in whom others felt confidence, and they had confidence in themselves. They were natural, unaffected, non-defensive, and expressive. They were unconventional and adventurous.

To generalize somewhat speculatively from Crutchfield's study to some of the others, I believe it may be tentatively said that the individuals who may be most easily "managed" through the psychological know-how I have tried to sketch in this paper are those who are passive, rigid, insecure, and authoritarian. On the other hand, those who resist being "managed," who are able to deal intelligently with these possible influences, are confident, open, secure, independent, and spontaneous.

But here again we face an exciting fact. The individuals who were not overwhelmed by the majority opinion in Crutchfield's experiment bear a very strong resemblance to individuals produced in a democratic home atmosphere, to workers who have developed in a group-centered industrial situation, to students who have been exposed to an acceptant teacher-pupil relationship, to clients who have experienced a warm and empathic relationship in therapy. In other words, we already know to a considerable degree how to provide the conditions in which such individuals develop. And though the reverse evidence is not quite so clear, I believe it may be said that in large measure we also know how to provide the conditions in which the passive, insecure followers develop.

What I have been trying to say is that the growing body of knowledge in the behavioral sciences gives to our modern culture an astonishing power of choice. We know how to influence and mold behavior and personality in a great many significant ways. We also have available the choice of whether to set the conditions which develop a suggestible, submissive, unsure individual who can be easily influenced to behave in any way that "we" think wise, or the conditions which will develop an open, adaptive, independent, free-thinking, self-respecting individual. It is this latter person who will perhaps be able to use with intelligence and sensitivity to human values the enormous powers which the physical and behavioral sciences are putting at his disposal. The issue of what choice to make in this regard constitutes, I believe, the challenge of tomorrow both for education and for our whole culture.

It might well be pointed out that with few exceptions the psychological know-how which I have sketched has not been widely used or exploited by society. Hence it might seem that the challenge as I have described it is greatly exaggerated.

It is quite true that this knowledge has not been widely used. In this respect the status of the physical sciences is very different from that of the behavioral sciences. The physical sciences have become so greatly respected that if scientists from these fields report that they can create a satellite in space, the only question in the public mind is, How soon will it be done? There is no tendency to scoff at the possibility, as the public in 1906 scoffed at the Wright brothers' "ridiculous" predictions that a machine could fly. As of 1955 the behavioral sciences occupy, in the public mind, a status similar to that of the physical sciences in 1906. The community does not as yet believe that the behavioral sciences can achieve results. Yet this attitude is changing with remarkable rapidity. Who would have supposed, a few years ago, that our military forces would invest millions of dollars in research in the behavioral sciences, that industrial leaders would employ consultants whose main task is to provide a therapeutic relationship for the executives, that research in consumer attitudes would be a big business?

So I conclude that knowledge in the science of psychology will in the near future be used and exploited as fully as knowledge in the physical sciences is used today. The challenge for educators is unreal only if we are looking a year or two ahead. From the long view I know of no problem holding greater potentiality of growth and of destruction than the question of how to live with the increasing power the behavioral sciences will place in our hands and the hands of our children.

II

DEVELOPMENT

MORE AND MORE widely used, as an approach to the study of behavior, is the question, "How do individuals, or the different kinds of behavior shown by them, develop?" Sometimes this is the only approach that enables us to detect the biological influences on man's functioning. This knowledge is important because the integration of an organism's biological potentialities with the experiences and opportunities to which it is exposed is the basis for the resultant individual, a bio-social unit.

Opening this section is a report of an experimental study with dogs that shows the far-reaching effects of very early environmental conditions of growth. The next selection emphasizes the importance of the *timing* of experience in relation to the development of the individual. The succeeding three papers are devoted to the developmental process with respect to motivation, intellect, and emotions, three of the most significant aspects of psychological functioning. The concluding selection, particularly, helps us realize that the maturational process continues long after birth and early childhood.

3. Individual Differences in Dogs: Preliminary Report on the Effects of Early Experience *

STUDENTS OFTEN raise the question, "What would a man be like if he were raised completely alone, perhaps on a desert island, with-

* R. S. Clarke, W. Heron, M. L. Fetherstonhaugh, D. G. Forgays, and D. O. Hebb, "Individual differences in dogs: preliminary report on the effects of early experi-

out any people around him?" Obviously, no modern psychologist would undertake an experiment of this kind with human beings, but experiments along these lines can be done with animals—and studying animals has many advantages. Not only can stricter control of experimental conditions be imposed on animals than on humans, but subjects can be selected whose genetic composition is fairly homogeneous (compared with pure-bred cattle and mice and dogs, man is decidedly a mongrel specimen). For example, in the experiment reported below, only litter-mates were used. These were divided into two groups, one to be raised under conditions of restricted stimulation and experience, and the other more freely as pets. The genetic backgrounds of the individuals in the two groups could be considered as roughly equivalent. With the final observations made under identical conditions for all, differences found could be assigned to the experimental variable: the external conditions under which development took place.

WE REPORT here the preliminary results of a study of temperamental and intellectual differences among dogs. The development of methods for the study of emotion, motivation, problem-solving, and differences of capacity for learning motor skills is a logically prior objective, important in itself because of the opportunities it would create for a number of useful investigations. But it is probably chimerical to think of first devising adequate methods, and only then beginning research. We have therefore attempted to combine our search for methods with a first study of the effects of the infant environment upon adult behaviour, as one source of individual differences.

The starting point was the earlier study of the rat, made in this laboratory by Hymovitch and Forgays who showed that the animal's opportunities for exploration and complex visual experience during growth were closely related to its problem-solving at maturity. This does not, of course, deny the importance of heredity in intelligence. It indicates a role of the environment in developing the inherited, *potential* capacity for problem-solving. Such a result is not an isolated one, unrelated to other aspects of behaviour, nor peculiar to a single species. A good deal of work in the last decade or two, summarized by Hebb, indicates that the whole question of the relationship of adult behaviour to the infant environment should be examined. For such a purpose the dog has great advantages. He has a relatively short period

---

ence." Reprinted from the *Canadian Journal of Psychology,* 1951, 5, 150–56, by permission of The Canadian Psychological Association and The University of Toronto Press, and of the authors. This research was supported in part by grants from the Defence Research Board, National Research Council of Canada, and the Dominion-Provincial Mental Health Project.

of growth, permitting experimental control of the environment during growth, which would hardly be practicable during the five to ten years' period required by monkey or ape; yet he has a complexity of temperament and of intelligence that the rat does not have.

SUBJECTS AND REARING

A litter of six animals of an inbred Scottish terrier strain from the Jackson Memorial Laboratory was divided into two groups. Three pups, two males and one female, were raised as pets (two in the laboratory, one in a private home), and had considerable handling. The rest, all males, were brought up together in a cage 3 by 6 feet which was specially designed so that the dogs could not see outside, but which admitted light. The dogs were never removed from the cage during this time, and their only contact with humans occurred during the daily feeding and cleaning period. At the age of 7½ months they were removed, and with their littermates were allowed the run of a large room in the laboratory. At this time there were no noticeable differences in weight or general health between the two groups.

TEMPERAMENTAL DIFFERENCES

Peculiarities in the behaviour of the restricted (cage-reared) animals were very marked for the first few days after removal from isolation. They would not go through a doorway without coaxing, and though they appeared to be eager for human attention, they strongly avoided handling. When an observer extended his hand to them or otherwise attracted their attention, they would approach and vigorously lick his hand or feet; but at the first attempt to pat or grasp one of them, the whole group would draw back sharply.

The most striking peculiarity on the part of the restricted animals was the "freezing" behaviour which they displayed when they were placed in unfamiliar surroundings, or handled by an experimenter. The animal would hug the floor, forelegs apart, ears back, and eyes staring forward. This state was apparently accompanied by some degree of anaesthesia; when subjected to injections, for example, the restricted animals "froze" and made no protest when the needle entered. The animals who were reared as pets (free-environment), on the contrary, objected vociferously to the whole procedure.

It was possible, for three or four months, to observe gross differences of responses to human attention between the two groups. For example, if the dogs were kept in cages overnight, the first experimenter to open the cage doors in the morning would find that the free-environment dogs would approach him and be quite eager to be allowed out of the cages. The restricted animals, on the other hand, would withdraw to the back of the cage, and it was difficult to get them out. This avoidance behaviour took place even when both groups of dogs were present in the same cage.

Some of the peculiarities of behaviour on the part of the restricted animals were greatly diminished after about a week; at the time of writing (six months later) they can be elicited under certain conditions, but only in a vestigial form.

When the dogs were 10 months old, 2½ months after the restricted group had been removed from isolation, a more systematic study of temperament and social behaviour was undertaken. Test situations were devised in which a quantitative description of the results was possible.

In the first test, a competitive situation (fighting for a bone) in which each dog was compared with every other dog, all of the restricted animals were markedly subordinate to all the free-environment animals. When pitted against each other, two restricted dogs would show a tendency to "share" the bone, both gnawing at it for some time before the less dominant animal was driven away. This type of behaviour was never noticed in the free-environment dog, who, when dominant, would immediately drive off the other contending animal.

When two dogs, one from each group, were placed together in an environment with which they were unfamiliar, a "following" score was recorded. "Following" either is defined literally as the running of one dog behind the other, or, when two animals move together side by side, means that one dog (the leader) initiates movement and changes of direction. In much of the activity there was no obvious leader or follower; but where following could be determined, the mean number of "follows" by the restricted group was 12 (range: 7–16), while that of the free-environment animals was 3 (range: 1–6). This difference between the groups, however, was not observed when the animals were in familiar surroundings; that is, the room in which they were normally kept when not undergoing testing, or a room with which they had become familiar because of its frequent use as a testing room.

A test of reaction to unfamiliar dogs was carried out in an area 20 by 40 feet, in one section of which there was a wire pen 8 by 8 feet. A strange dog was placed in this pen, and two experimental animals, one from each group, were brought into the main test area. A record was kept of the number of times each experimental animal went over to the pen and "paid attention to" the test dog inside, and also of the amount of time so spent. The criteria of paying attention were pausing and looking in the direction of the test dog, and more marked social responses such as barking, rolling over, and trying to enter the pen. After five minutes, the strange dog was let out into the main test area, and a record kept of the amount of time that each experimental animal showed interest in it by sniffing, barking at, or rolling over in front of it. This observation period lasted five minutes. The whole test was repeated four times, using a different test animal on each occasion.

The restricted animals were very indifferent to the test dog, and on the whole tended to ignore it, while the free-environment dogs were highly responsive. The restricted dogs went, on the average, 8 times (range: 4–12) to the pen, spending there a mean time of 44 seconds (range: 9–77); the free-environment dogs went an average of 22 times (range: 13–30) and spent there a mean time of 271 seconds (range: 136–368). In addition, the free-environment animals spent about four times as much time displaying interest in the test dog when it was released from the pen. This behaviour is consistent with what was displayed when both groups were placed in the same room for the first time after the restricted animals had been removed from their cage. Then, the cage-reared animals tended to avoid the free-environment dogs, who on the contrary displayed a lively interest in the cage-reared, sniffing at and following them.

An attempt was made to investigate the reaction of both groups to a mild stress situation by using a modification of a test described in the Bar Harbor Manual, which involves a certain degree of hunger frustration. The animals, deprived of food for 24 hours, were placed two at a time in a wire enclosure 8 by 15 feet. They were observed for five minutes, and then a dish of food was placed outside the pen where it was visible to the experimental animals. At the end of another five-minute interval, another dog was allowed to eat the food for one minute, and was then removed. This was followed by a final five-minute observation period. Scoring was on the basis described in the manual, a check being placed every 30 seconds in the column of the score sheet which most aptly described the animals' behaviour at that particular moment, such as sitting, jumping, walking, and so on.

The free-environment animals showed a consistently higher level of activity throughout the test, and made more attempts to get out of the pen. One interesting result was that as the situation became more stressful (when the food dish was placed outside the pen) the activity of the restricted decreased, while that of the free-environment animals increased.

The final temperament test was one that investigated another aspect of motivation. The amount of time each dog spent sitting and lying down under various conditions was recorded. It was found that in unfamiliar rooms, generally, there was no difference in the level of activity between the groups. If taken into an unfamiliar room repeatedly, however, there was a steeper falling-off in the activity level of the free-environment animals. These dogs spent a significantly greater amount of time sitting and lying down after a number of exposures to the room than did the restricted. A parallel observation is that the restricted dogs would continue to tear up and play with or chew sheets of newspaper for a longer period of time than would the normally reared animals.

One other noticeable difference between the groups was that when the animals were taken outside for "intelligence testing," as described in the following section, the restricted dogs soon learned to run directly to the testing area ahead of the experimenters. The free-environment animals, on the other hand, very often would run off in some other direction, galloping vigorously about. The experimenters would occasionally have considerable difficulty getting them into the test area. These observations indicate differences in stimulation-value with the repetition of a relatively simple situation (or conversely, differences in capacity for "boredom").

INTELLECTUAL DIFFERENCES

Four days after the restricted group was first brought out into the wider environment, both groups of animals were given a "barrier" umweg-type test. A series of maze problems and a motor learning test followed between the fourth and eighth weeks, and a "ramp" umweg-type test at nine weeks.

The barrier test apparatus consisted of three sides of a 4-foot square, 2 feet high, with wooden side walls and a wire mesh front. The animal was placed in this, and fed three morsels of food under the wire. On the five test trials food was placed 6 inches outside the wire, and a correct run was scored if the dog ran around the sides of the apparatus directly to the food without attempting to get through the mesh barrier. The time of each trial was recorded.

None of the restricted group made a single correct run on this problem. The free-environment animals averaged 3 correct solutions, with a range of 1 to 5. Moreover, the responses of the former group were more stereotyped; though it was possible to reach food by going round either the right or left side of the barrier, only one restricted dog changed its direction during the five test trials, and then only once.

The free-environment animals all changed their direction on at least one run, the mean number of changes for the group being 2. The restricted group spent a much longer period of time per run than the free-environment group.

The most elaborate test used was a modification of the "closed-field" test originally designed to measure intelligence in the rat. For the present study, it was set up outdoors in a space 15 by 26 feet, and the problems used were more complex than those used in testing the rat. The dogs were given preliminary training on 11 problems, with 8 trials on each. The test series consisted of 18 problems, given at the rate of one per day. Errors were defined as entry into predetermined error zones.

The mean error score for the restricted animals was 309 (range: 305–313), and for the free-environment group 236 (range: 219–268). Most of the errors of the restricted dogs resulted from the fact that they continued to follow the path which had been correct in the test of the previous day, although the situation had changed.

Each day after the dogs had been tested in the maze, training in a simple motor habit was carried out. The animals were taken one at a time into a quiet room and taught to roll over, using a pellet of food as reward. On the first day 25 trials were given, with 10 trials per day subsequently. The restricted dogs took an average of 34.3 (range: 30–39) trials to learn the habit, the free-environment an average of 16 (range: 7–26).

The final problem used was the ramp test. A table 42 inches high and 30 inches square was placed in the centre of an enclosure which was 18 feet square. By running up a wooden ramp, or runway, the dog could reach the top of the table, where it was given food. The starting place was constant, and the ramp was moved through four positions corresponding to the four sides of the table. Each time that the ramp was moved, it was replaced by a false ramp, which was similar to the bottom half of the true ramp but did not reach to the table top. Soon after the restricted animals had been brought out of their cages, all the dogs had been trained to go up to the table for food with the ramp in position 1. One month later they were tested on all four positions, eight trials being given on each. The enclosure was marked off into squares, and an error was scored when the dog entered a square off the direct path to the correct ramp.

The mean error score for the restricted animals was 192.3 (range: 170–219), that for the free-environment 144.3 (range: 113–167). In addition, qualitative differences were observed. The restricted animals tended to persist in going to the position of the ramp which had previously been correct. They had a greater tendency than the free-environment dogs to run up and leap or fall off the end of the false ramp, behaving as if it were the correct one; and after the ramp had been moved to a new position they might sniff it occasionally, or take a few steps up, then leave it to run across the enclosure to one of the false ramps.

CONCLUSIONS

This work can be considered only a beginning in the analysis of the differences which exist between animals reared under different conditions. Even though the present data were obtained over a number of months, we do not know at present how permanent the observed differences are. Our methods of study are as yet crude, and we are not able to state the essential features underlying the singular behaviour of the restricted animals. However, these results clearly confirm the previous findings with rats in showing that animals reared under restricted conditions are inferior in problem-solving ability to those reared in a more complex environment. In addition, they suggest that marked disturbances of social behaviour and motivation may occur in the restricted animals.

---

4. Critical Periods in Socialization and Overdependency *

REPORTS OF the effects of different kinds of experiences on human development have often been contradictory. It is now believed that this situation may have resulted from a failure to consider fully the *timing* of events. We have recently begun to recognize the occurrence of "critical periods" in the development of different kinds of functioning. The same experience may have quite different consequences, depending on whether it comes before, during, or after a "critical period." This paper focuses on the tendency toward overdependency in children, and two critical periods are suggested for its beginnings. Mrs. Stendler offers a theoretical formulation

* Celia Burns Stendler, "Critical periods in socialization and overdependency," *Child Development,* XXIII (March, 1952), 3–12. By permission of the author and the Child Development Publications of the Society for Research in Child Development, Inc.

that tries to integrate observations on development with learning theory and the concept of "critical periods." This selection demonstrates the need for relating data from different areas of research for an understanding of more general aspects of psychological functioning. It also helps call attention to the quality of experience from the child's point of view as he matures biologically and is exposed to differing and often antagonistic pressures by the people who are important to him.

THE PROCESS of socialization during the child's early years has been described by many writers. They usually agree that during the first months of an infant's life there are few demands made upon him. The infant leads an irresponsible kind of life where his every whim is gratified and where he need do nothing in return—except grow and develop as a normal healthy baby. He cries and sooner or later he is fed, he sleeps when he is sleepy, evacuates at will, and is indulged and waited upon by loving relatives who make him the center of the household. As a result the child's first concept of himself is not that of a helpless infant, but rather of an omnipotent being whose mother and others are at his beck and call. Freud has described this period as one of "infantile omnipotence."

But although from the infant's standpoint this period may be referred to as one of infantile omnipotence, actually during this period the infant is learning, not to be all-powerful, but to be dependent. He is not born with dependency needs, but acquires them, if we follow learning theory, in accordance with certain known principles. The baby is hungry or is in pain; he cries and his mother (or other socializing agent) helps him. Soon he learns to depend upon his mother for reduction of his hunger drive or for alleviation of his pain. Whiting describes how dependency learning occurs in Kwoma society:

Kwoma infants are cared for almost exclusively by their mothers. For approximately the first three years of his life a Kwoma infant sits in the lap of his mother during the day and lies by her side at night. It is the Kwoma mother's duty to care for all the needs of her child during this period. When, despite this constant care, Kwoma infants suffer frustration, crying is the response which becomes most firmly fixed. A Kwoma mother, whenever her infant cries, does her best to comfort him. If he is hungry she feeds him; if he is cold she warms him; if he is sick or in pain she tries to soothe him. Thus by removing the source of frustration or pain the Kwoma mother rewards crying as a response to these conditions. Toward the end of infancy, when the child begins to talk, he responds to frustration or pain by asking for help, and his mother complies with his request whenever it is possible for her to do so. Thus during infancy a frustration-dependence sequence is established.[1]

Actually, it may not be necessary for frustration (defined as interference with a habit) to occur for the child to learn to be dependent upon the mother. The mother can acquire secondary reward value simply because she becomes associated with the reduction of the hunger drive and the elimination of pain. Gradually the child builds up an association of mother as the giver of love and approval and comes to be dependent upon her for emotional succorance as well as for satisfaction of physical needs.

Five aspects of the socializing agent come to have reward value for the child. Perhaps the first aspect of the parent that acquires such value is that of physical contact; the infant learns to associate being picked up with reduction of the hunger drive, or being burped with reduction of pain. Thus the three-months-old baby can be soothed by being picked up and will stop his crying momentarily even though hunger or pain still persist. Next, proximity of the parent may become reinforced as the infant comes to associate the mere presence of the socializing agent with drive reduction. This may come at the point when the child actually recognizes the mother and distinguishes her from other adults in his environment. Now the mother does not have to pick the baby up; she merely has to enter the room to stop his flow of tears, while leaving the room may be enough to induce crying or a fear reaction.

Two other aspects of the parent that come to be rewarding to the child are paying attention and verbal praise or approval. Actually these represent a lessening of dependency; they come at a time when independence is on the rise. As the child comes to do more and more things by himself, he depends upon his parent not so much for help as for attention to what he is doing, or for verbal praise and approval.

A fifth aspect of the parent, the helping aspect, also comes when independence is on the rise. As the word "helping" implies, the parent no longer does everything for the child but now only "helps" when the child has begun a task and has encountered difficulties in completing it. Thus the three-year-old may put on his own shoes but his mother helps

[1] Dr. Whiting has indicated in recent correspondence a modification of his theory of dependency. He now makes what seems to this writer to be a helpful distinction between dependency as a habit and dependency as a drive. I interpret the above quotation as a description of the learning of a dependency habit. Whether a dependency habit develops depends upon the mother's rewarding or punishing the child's demands. The drive which is behind the habit comes about as a result of the child's learning to associate reduction of the hunger drive and elimination of pain with one person.

by pointing out which shoe goes on which foot and by tying the laces.

Dependency needs build up first and fast while independency training begins later and proceeds at a much slower tempo. Nevertheless some six-months-old babies hold their own bottles and are rewarded by being able to regulate the intake of milk to their own liking. The nine-months-old baby may get satisfaction from finger-feeding because his hunger drive can be more readily appeased in that fashion. And as the proud mother exclaims over the baby's achievement he eventually finds enough reward in her approval to want to repeat his independent behavior. Paradoxically, he learns to be independent because he has learned to be dependent upon his mother for acceptance and approval. It is only when he is sufficiently dependent to be pleased at parental approbation that he can make rapid strides in independence.

Independence, like dependence, must be culturally trained, however. It is not enough for the child to be independent in those areas he chooses for himself; he must learn to be independent and dependent in ways of which the culture approves. Therefore the early period of indulgence must end and child training begin. Typically parents in our society begin to make demands upon the child when he is old enough to be dangerous to himself or destructive to objects in his environment. The nine-months infant is restrained from standing in his carriage, the fourteen-months toddler is not permitted to climb stairs by himself but only when accompanied by an adult, the eighteen-months baby must eat with his spoon and not with his fingers, the two-year-old must tell his mother when he needs the bathroom. Over and over again, former habits are interfered with. As one group of writers has put it:

> It must learn to walk where it has formerly been carried; . . . it learns not to be picked up when it has experienced some small disaster. It must give up much of the cuddling, holding and petting which is the prerogative of the smallest darling. Childish approximations of table manners and etiquette must be altered in favor of the customs preferred by adults. The child must learn to wait for its food, to keep its face clean, to submit to having its hair combed, to eat in the regular stages designated by our table techniques. At some time or another all of these lengthened sequences invoke frustrations and elicit protest from the child.

During this early period of child training, considerable resistant or negative behavior appears. Various psychological explanations of negativism have been advanced. From one standpoint the period may be viewed as one where the child is learning culturally accepted ways of being dependent and independent, where dependent behavior begins to wane and independent behavior is on the rise. At this point conflicts may arise because the child's conception of independent behavior is at variance with the parent's; that is, the child wants to be independent in ways of which the parent does not or cannot approve. Or conflicts may arise because the parent wants the child to give up his dependence in certain areas, and the child rebels. A satisfactory resolution of the crisis results when the child has learned those areas in which he is expected to be dependent and those in which he is to be independent.

Not all children arrive at a satisfactory dependency-independence ratio, however. Some children become overdependent, some too independent. It is with the overdependent child that we are concerned in this paper.

Reinforcement theory lends itself very well to an explanation of how *over*dependency may originate with some children. Where the child from birth is consistently rewarded for being dependent and non-rewarded or punished for being independent, he becomes a dependent, submissive individual. This kind of treatment is typically afforded the child by overprotecting mothers. Levy has described extreme cases where this development has taken place. His overprotected children had excessive contact with the mother; they were still being indulged and waited upon as if they were babies; their attempts at independent behavior were discouraged. Such children may be said to be overdependent because of a deficiency in independence training and because dependent behavior is constantly rewarded.

Not all children who are overdependent conform to Levy's description, however. Some overdependent children have mothers who are not overprotecting, as were the mothers Levy described. Levy's parents might be said to be the instigators of the overdependency. In some parent-child relationships, however, the mother *unwillingly* accedes to the child's excessive dependency demands and because of her unwillingness is inconsistent in her treatment of the child. The child is the instigator of extreme dependency demands. Also, the child's overdependency does not extend to all areas but is limited to selected ones. Thus the child of the non-overprotecting mother may insist upon his mother's accompanying him back and forth to school but accomplish such tasks as tying shoe laces at six years of age without demanding help.

It is necessary to elaborate on reinforcement theory to explain how this type of overdependency begins. In a study of ordinal position in the family as a psychological variable, Sears found among other things that the oldest child in the family was more likely to have experienced anxiety in the nursing and weaning situations, and at the same time more nurturance at bedtime and more cautioning about sickness and danger than second and later children. Older children were also rated as the more dependent. Sears suggests that the anxiety produced in the nursing and weaning frustration would serve as the facilitating instigator to whatever behavior had been predominant in those infant situations in which the anxiety was aroused. Thus, since dependency behavior is likely to be predominant at the time of nursing and weaning, anxiety produced in nursing and weaning situations will strengthen the dependency needs.

Extending Sears' hypothesis, we might suggest certain critical periods in the socialization process for the formation of *over*dependency. These are the periods when shifts in awareness of his position in relationship to the socializing agent occur in the child. A child builds up a set of expectations with regard to how his dependency needs are to be met. From time to time these expectations change as the child matures in his perceptions and as his culture makes demands upon him. If there is a disturbance during one of these times of change, of such a nature that the child must quickly and radically change his expectations, anxiety will arise. The child will attempt to resolve the anxiety by the method he has learned to resolve anxiety, i.e., demands upon the mother for nurturance.

In order to produce overdependency, however, the anxiety must occur not when one goal response is interfered with, but when whole sets that seriously threaten dependency needs are disturbed. Thus a baby may seem "anxious" if the living room furniture is changed around but he does not become overdependent as a result. But consider a baby whose grandmother has been the important gratifier of his dependency needs and whose mother has been the reinforcing agent for any independence training. If grandmother dies during this critical period in socialization, the child's expectancy of how his dependency needs are to be filled is forced to change. Or an absent father may return, with the result that a mother now plays the role of wife as well as mother, whereas the child had learned to expect her to act only as mother. Or a mother may take on the role of wage-earner and a new socializing agent be introduced. Or the physical environment may be changed by moving about; one's favorite toys, crib, blankets, eating utensils may disappear and only the one stable figure of mother be left. In such cases as these anxiety results in increasing the strength of the already established dependency drive.

Two critical periods for the formation of overdependency are proposed. The first critical period begins when the child begins to test out the mother to see if he can depend upon her. For most children this occurs toward the end of the first year of life. Earlier the infant has been learning to be dependent upon the mother. Now he shows his sudden recognition of the importance of his mother by his demands upon her and especially for his mother's proximity. In effect, he tests out his mother, to see if he really can depend upon her and to see if he can control her. He cries when she leaves his presence and demands that she be in sight or readily available when he needs help. Gesell reports that as early as 28 weeks the baby "demands more of the one who feeds him." Bowlby suggests that the most critical time for the production of anxiety concerning the mother is after eight months, "when the child's first object relationship (to his mother) is developing in a specific way."

Severe traumatic experiences involving separation from the socializing agent are important to consider, then, during this period when the child has become aware of his dependency upon the mother and is testing his control of her. During this critical period it is necessary that the infant have his dependency needs met in the manner to which he has become accustomed. As Bowlby says, "Once a clearly differentiated relationship with the mother has developed at about nine months, mothering from anyone will not do and it is imperative that the child have an opportunity of forming a continuous affectional attachment to one person." If proximity of the socializing agent is denied the infant at this time for long periods of his waking hours (i.e., if the child is hospitalized, or if the mother becomes ill, or goes back to work), anxiety will be aroused which the child will attempt to resolve by excessive demands upon the mother when he does have her. His dependency drive will be strengthened by the anxiety and overdependency may result.

The next critical period for the formation of *over*dependency comes during the two- to three-year-old period. As we have already indicated, this is the time in our society when demands upon the child to change his old ways of doing things increase tremendously. Now the child must give up his control of his mother and come to accept his dependence upon her, yet at the same time learn to be independent in culturally approved ways. Again, anxiety arises because important goal responses are being interfered with. In normal socialization the anxiety generated produces the right amount of dependency. But where disturbances of a traumatic nature occur so that important habits must be suddenly and drastically changed, so much anxiety may be generated that overdependency will result.

A case where a break in continuity with regard to dependency needs occurred at this critical period is described below:

Randy was the first child of a young mother and father, born while the father was overseas. His mother had moved back with her own folks while her husband was away and Randy's first two years were spent in an environment where he was the stellar attraction. He was the first grandchild on both sides of the family; paternal grandparents lived in the same community and vied with maternal grandparents in lavishing love and material things upon Randy. The mother had little to do in the household and so she was free to devote herself almost exclusively to Randy. Her major role in the household was that of daughter, however, rather than mother.

At the age of two Randy's father was returned to the States but was hospitalized for a year, during which time he was able to visit his family on a few occasions. Just before Randy's third birthday, a baby brother was born, the father was discharged and the reunited family left the grandparents' roof to set up a home of their own.

In the two years that followed, Randy had several serious accidents. He caught his arm in the wringer of the washing machine; he overturned a pan of boiling water on himself; he was run over by a car. The mother reported that during this period he was continually demanding of her time and attention. "He wouldn't let me leave him, even to go to the store," she said.

When Randy entered school, he made a scene each morning over leaving home. His parents insisted that he go, whereupon he developed stomach aches and vomited each day after breakfast. His mother found it hard to send him off following these spells, but his father broke the cycle one day by carting him off, still retching, to school, where the father requested the teacher to keep Randy even though he continued to vomit. Randy next developed ear aches but again the father firmly but kindly drove him to school in the car when the mother would have permitted him to stay home. It was not until Randy's second year in school that he became resigned to leaving his mother each day.

Randy's case illustrates how a combination of circumstances during a critical period in his socialization prevented the development of certain habits of independence and strengthened habits of dependence. In his early life Randy had learned an expectancy of how his dependency needs would be satisfied. Then Randy lost: (1) the love and affection his grandparents had showered upon him; (2) almost exclusive possession of his mother who took on additional roles as wife, mother of a new baby, and homemaker; (3) a familiar physical setting. At the same time his mother and a stranger called father began to make demands upon him to be a big boy. Randy's reaction was to demand harder than ever what he had once had and was now being denied, and to refuse to grow in independence.

What we have been saying is that there are critical periods in the child's life for the formation of overdependent behavior. These critical periods are normally anxiety-producing for all children because they involve interference with goal responses; disturbances which occur during one of these periods and which arouse excessive anxiety may so strengthen the dependency drive that overdependency will result.

We would like to hypothesize further that the timing of disturbances which affect the dependency drive will also be a factor in determining how other aspects of personality will be affected. That is, the dependency drive is so related to other aspects of personality that a disturbance during one of the critical periods will affect other aspects of personality and that the effects will differ according to the timing of the disturbance. A disturbance during the first critical period will have a different impact upon personality development than will a disturbance during the second critical period.

To clarify our hypothesis we might draw an analogy to what happens in prenatal development. There is a special time in the prenatal timetable for the development of each organ. If an organ does not develop at the proper time "it will never be able to express itself fully, since the moment for the rapid outgrowth of some other part will have arrived." Thus if something occurs in the prenatal environment at the time when the skull is being formed, then humans with incompletely formed skulls will result. Disturbances of the prenatal environment are tremendously significant and the *timing* of disturbances is the crucial factor.

While we cannot push our analogy too far (for we cannot postulate a timetable of personality development after birth on the basis of any innate factor alone), nevertheless what is proposed here is that disturbances with regard to dependency needs at a particular time will have particular effects upon personality development.

During the first eight or nine months of life the child is building up a set of expectations with regard to how his needs will be met; he is learning dependency. Translated into Erikson's language, he is learning basic trust in another human being. He learns to depend upon others, as we have pointed out, by having his physical needs met consistently by one person. If he does not learn that he can depend upon others, however, serious personality difficulties arise. Lauretta Bender has described children who have not had continuous affectionate care of one person up to the age of nine months:

> These children impress us with their diffusely impulsive unpatterned behavior. At all levels the behavior is unorganized and remains unorganized. It is exceedingly difficult to find any educational or psychotherapeutic method whereby it can be modified into organized or patterned behavior. The child is driven by inner impulses which demand immediate satisfaction; these impulses or needs show the usual changes with physical and chronological growth of the child, but even this does not add much pattern to the behavior. Motivation, discipline, punishment and insight therapy have little effect.
>
> The behavior remains always infantile. It is true that there are some

differences as to the level of the infantile fixation, but it is always pre-oedipal and pre-superego. It is as though a newborn infant had urgent needs which must be satisfied. Screaming, kicking or temper tantrums or disturbed behavior of which the larger child is capable continue when frustration occurs, as it must a good deal of the time. All kinds of oral activity, clinging, wetting, soiling, senseless motor activity, genital manipulation may be observed. These are not neurotic traits and do not indicate regression but retardation in personality development. Psychopathic behavior-disordered children are often attention-seeking, clinging, passively dependent, seductive and amiable. This may be mistaken for an attachment or interpersonal relationship. Actually, there is no warmth, and the relationship can stand no separation or disappointments or demands; it shifts to the nearest new object as soon as the recipient is out of sight.

These are children who, in our terminology, have not learned dependency behavior. We are not concerned in this paper with cases such as these, but rather with those children who have built up a set of expectations with regard to how dependency needs are to be met and then suddenly and radically have to change them. What I am proposing is that overdependent children who become so as a result of disturbance during the first critical period will differ from overdependent children who become so as a result of a disturbance during the second critical period. The first group of children is more likely to be affected with regard to ego-aspects of personality whereas the second group is more likely to be affected with regard to superego-aspects of personality.

To make clear the reasoning behind this distinction we need to understand the different nature of the frustration involved during the two critical periods. In discussing the process of identification, Mowrer differentiates between two types of frustration. He says:

It is true that in both developmental and defensive identification the subject is "frustrated," but the different nature of the frustration in the two instances is noteworthy. In the one case it arises from a sense of helplessness and loneliness: the parent or parent-person is *absent,* and the infant wishes he were *present.* In the other case, the frustration arises from interference and punishment: the parent or parent-person is *present,* and the infant wishes he were *absent.* But the latter wish brings the average child into intolerable conflict: while he hates the parent for his disciplinary actions, he also loves the parent and experiences acute anxiety at the prospect of his really being separated, physically or emotionally, from him (or her).

Developmental identification, we may suppose, is a milder and simpler experience than is defensive identification, which has a violent, crisis-like nature. The one is powered mainly by biologically given drives ("fear of loss of love," in the analytic sense) and the other by socially inflicted discomforts ("castration fear" or, less dramatically, simply fear of punishment). The first presumably involves relatively little conflict; but in the latter case, conflict and attendant anxiety are outstanding.

The first type of frustration we see as occurring during the first critical period and, as a result, affecting the developmental or ego-aspects of identification. The second type of frustration occurs during the second critical period and as a result affects the defensive or superego-aspects of identification.

Overdependent children produced during the first critical period will be children who have experienced helplessness; who have not been able to control the socializing agent at the time when recognition of the importance of that agent for one's own well-being was dawning. Therefore we can expect such children to be low in ego-strength, with resulting low level of aspiration and low frustration tolerance. Also, such children, while they cling to the socializing agent will tend to see that agent as a punishing figure rather than a helpful one. These things may not be true of overdependent children produced during the second critical period. These children are more likely to be affected in the area of conscience. They will tend to resolve the anxiety generated by the frustration by overdoing the job of building a punishing voice inside. They will be rigid in their ideas of right and wrong, overconforming in behavior, unduly disturbed by the wrongdoings of other children. They will prefer well-defined structured situations to those which allow for more freedom of choice.

This is a sketchy picture of possible developments during critical periods in socialization. A necessary task for the future is spelling out in detail the relationship between dependency needs and other aspects of personality development during these critical periods.

SUMMARY

This paper examines some theoretical questions with regard to the origin of overdependency. According to the proposed theory, there may be two critical periods in the socialization process for the beginnings of overdependency. One of these may be toward the end of the child's first year of life; the other when his parents begin to increase their demands upon the child. Disturbances of a serious nature during either of these periods may result in overdependency. It is suggested that the timing of the disturbance with regard to dependency needs may influence ego and superego development in particular ways.

5. *The Fundamental Needs of the Child* *

CONTEMPORARY RESEARCH into the origins of maladjustment (mainly conducted within the last two decades) has emphasized that the childhood period of the human organism is the time during which the difficulties begin. This conclusion has inspired many studies of the psychological functioning of newborn infants and young children, and the findings have forced a reconsideration of educational practices. Mr. Frank's article summarizes the implications of a large number of separate investigations into the varying physiological and psychological needs of children. It states succinctly the present position of many pediatric, psychiatric, and educational specialists in child development. Because this paper was originally addressed to nursery school teachers, it contains references to practical procedures that might implement its point of view in a realistic fashion.

• • • • •

PROBABLY THE most general statement that we can make about the child's needs is that he should be protected from distortions, from unnecessary deprivations and exploitations by adults—parents, teachers and nurses, physicians, psychologists, and others engaged in dealing with children.

It is difficult to realize the extent of these often subtle coercions and pressures exerted upon the child. Before the infant is born, the parents may have built up a picture of the kind of child he or she is to be, with a pronounced bias toward the male or the female sex, or toward a certain kind of temperament, physique, and ability. The infant, having within him the genes of countless previous generations as well as the characteristics of his parents, enters into a family situation that even at birth may be threatening and out of harmony with his peculiar, idiosyncratic temperamental make-up and needs. Parents who are eager to minister to the infant's need for warmth, food, and safety may be doggedly determined to deny the child's sex and his many personal, temperamental characteristics, which give rise to needs as important and urgent as the need for physical care.

It is not without reason, therefore, that we stress this primary and inalienable need of the child to be accepted as a unique individual, or, if the parents cannot or will not accord that acceptance, the need to

* L. K. Frank, *Mental Hygiene,* XXII (1938), 353–79. Reproduced in slightly shortened form by permission of the author and the publisher.

be protected and reinforced against the destructive, warping influence of these parental biases. Every child suffers to a greater or less extent from this denial of his own personal, temperamental individuality, because even the most emancipated parents are not wholly free from the desire to see their children conform to the images they have constructed. Moreover, every teacher has these partialities, often unconscious, which incline her toward one child and away from another. Further, the child himself is subject to the strong desire to be like the parents, however out of harmony with his own make-up such an identification may be. It is interesting to see how the recognition of individual differences is resisted even by professionally trained persons, such as teachers, who will accept the fact of such differences with respect to mental capacity, as shown by standardized mental tests, but deny it with respect to personality, temperament, physical maturity, and other obvious characteristics.

The infant, as he grows into childhood and youth, faces a series of life tasks that cannot be evaded or denied. The way in which he meets those life tasks and his attempts to master them give rise to the various needs for which we today believe his nurture and education should provide. It is obvious that we have only a fragmentary knowledge of those needs, since we have studied so briefly the process of growth and development and the life tasks presented by our culture. But it is highly significant, as we suggested earlier, that we are genuinely concerned with understanding child growth and development and are trying to discover the child's needs, as a basis for his education and nurture.

The processes involved in living and growing create needs for warmth, nutrition, and bodily care concerning which we are gaining more knowledge and technical competence. Much of the research in the field of nutrition and its results are still in terms of uniform standardized rules based on pure-strain rat colonies, with no allowance made for individual differences in vitamin and mineral requirements, so that, in the name of scientific standards, we may create serious deficiencies in the individual child as contrasted with the standardized laboratory animal. Even rats in the same litter differ, as Streeter has recently shown, in their susceptibility to rickets. The nutritional and other physical needs of the individual child are to be viewed dynamically, not statically, in terms of continuing growth and development rather than fixed height-weight standards which are purely statistical averages. Moreover, these needs should be viewed in terms of physiological functioning, not merely of structural size and shape, since it is functional efficiency, not structure, that is important.

How many problem children, hypochondriacs, and psychoneurotics have been created by blind adherence to these standardized tables which physicians and nurses, health educators, and teachers have given to mothers as scientific laws and which mothers have then used on their children! Surely we should allow for individual differences in children and not increase parental anxiety in this area of physical needs by insisting upon these standardized height and weight tables for chronological-age groups. The child's need is for food, rest, sleep, and play, so that he will continue to grow and develop *at his own rate*. The emphasis should be upon the growing, not upon fixed dimensions for chronological ages based upon the assumption that all children grow at the same rate.

The same criticism may be made of other chronological-age standards, such as prescribed hours for sleeping, where again failure to make allowance for individual differences has created many distraught mothers and problem children. The sleep needs of children vary greatly, and the loss of a nap is often much less undesirable than conflict, rebellion, punishment, and other consequences of a rigid sleep regimen.

If we are to gain a better understanding of the child's needs in terms of the life tasks he faces, we should envisage the physiological processes involved in what we call socialization. First in order of impact upon the infant is the regularization of feeding, involving a fixed interval of three or four hours between food intake, to which the infant must adapt despite individual differences in the reduction of blood sugar that creates hunger and in the capacity to endure hunger. Prolonged hunger and crying, often while the mother keeps her eye on the clock to see when the precise minute for feeding arrives, create in the child a condition of tension that may in some cases initiate persistent personality difficulties.

In feeding we are confronted with something more than just a need for nourishment. In early infancy, the whole body of the infant is receptive and in need of comforting, cuddling warmth and opportunity to suckle. In breast-feeding these needs may be adequately filled, through the warmth of the mother and the close tactual contact with her through nourishment and suckling, wherein the baby receives much of his needed sense of security and feeling of being protected. Tactual contacts and soothing are primitive, but highly necessary forms of reassurance. We never outgrow the need of them, but it is especially great in infancy and childhood. In this respect the human infant is like the young of all mammals, who thrive when nursed and cuddled and derive much needed emotional security from the oral activity of sucking and the close contact with the mother.

By many students of personality, it is said that if the infant is given adequate breast-feeding and affectionate cuddling, his future attitude toward the world will be outgoing, generous, and trusting, whereas if he is denied these satisfactions, he will be suspicious, niggardly, and resentful. Dr. David Levy is quoted with approval by Dr. James S. Plant as stating "that satisfactory breast-feeding [cuddling] experiences do more than whole dictionaries of later words in the establishment of security in the family group"—what Dr. Plant calls "belongingness." Since so many children nowadays are deprived of breast-feeding, it is necessary to consider the acceptance of that deprivation as a life task that is imposed upon the dependent infant, thereby creating specific needs which may persist throughout life. The seriousness of this deprivation could be diminished if the bottle-fed infant were held by the mother and cuddled while taking the bottle, so as to receive the warmth and security of her close presence during the feeding.

But even the breast-fed infant must sooner or later lose that happiness and comfort and face the process of weaning, which may create anxiety and irritability if too abruptly or roughly handled. During weaning the child needs additional reassurances and comforting to prevent acute feelings of insecurity and anxiety and to lessen the loss of sucking. Every deprivation is a threat to the child, a source of anxiety which can be mitigated by affectionate reassurance which makes him feel that the deprivation is not a punishment and that he is still loved. The important question for nursery schools to ask is what can they do for the children who have been deprived of breast-feeding or unwisely weaned, and who need to be reassured and protected, helped to outgrow their anxiety, and aided with affectionate reassurance.

Eliminations and their regularization present two more life tasks that may create persistent needs. In discussing and teaching toilet training, we are apt to forget what a profound physiological disturbance we are imposing on the child. The physiological processes of elimination of urine and feces are marvelously well organized, so that automatically the sphincters of the bladder and the rectum respond to accumulated pressure within. This physiological autonomy the child is asked to surrender when toilet training begins. Instead of functioning in accordance with his physiological needs, he is asked to inhibit the sphincter response to pressure, responding instead to an external stimulus—vessel, place, and so on—presented by the adult. Furthermore, he is asked to respond at a fixed time, whether or not he needs to do so physiologically. In this training, the child is expected to subordinate his processes to outside events and times, giving up his own physiological autonomy, often months before he is sufficiently mature to make such an adjustment. Maturity does not mean chronological age or size or weight; it means that the child has had enough of an activity, such as sucking or unrestricted elimination, to be able to go on to something else without a persistent feeling of deprivation or an unsatisfied infantile longing.

The widespread prevalence of enuresis and of constipation are not unrelated to the way in which toilet training has been imposed upon children who find in this process a serious nervous and emotional strain. During toilet training the child needs constant reassurance and comforting to stand the anxiety he so often feels. When failure to be continent elicits scoldings and punishment, the emotional stresses are increased and reinforced by feelings of guilt and inadequacy, often expressed in various symptoms of misbehavior. Evidence of how precariously the little child is balanced during toilet training is seen in the relapses that follow any emotional shock or family disturbance, or in the appearance of misconduct suddenly in the midst of peaceful, engrossing play, when the child is made uneasy and restless by a full bladder of which he is not yet fully aware. The evident over-concern of parents and nurses with toilet training raises for nursery schools the question what they can do to provide reassurance for the anxious child, and to make toilet functions an unemotional subject and action. It is probable that some nursery schools themselves are guilty of aggravating the child's insecurity by their rigid overemphasis upon toilet training and the fuss made over "slips" or the teachers' unconscious reaction toward feces.

Here it is necessary to point out that the emotional tone or attitude of parents, nurses, and teachers toward toilet training is the important thing, not their actions, for the child reacts to the tone or attitude and feels the tenseness or overemphasis or dislike in the adult's voice and handling. The importance of the manner and tone of voice lies in the child's feeling that he is being deprived by his training. Any anger or impatience, then, may become an occasion for anxiety and feelings of guilt. How else is the child to understand and interpret the adult's treatment of him? Since many adults carry over from their own childhood a feeling of anxiety or disgust at feces, it is clear that they are not able to treat the child under their care without emotional stress when faced with this process, which for the child is entirely normal and unconnected with emotion until adult interference begins. Since few children pass through toilet training without some stress, we may include among the needs of the child the need for reassurance and often for release from the effects of this process upon the personality. It is appropriate to raise the question about toilet training: Are we concerned only with character training and the conformity it implies, or are we concerned with personality development and the kind of human being we are helping to foster? We can instill good habits or foster a personality; in the latter case, the habits will usually be established without difficulty. Weaning and toilet training, as often handled, are important sources of personality twists and biases, and may give rise to persistent needs in the child.

The arrival of a younger child in the family also may create acute anxiety when the older child has not been prepared for it. The shock of waking up one morning to find the mother absent, to be told that she has gone to the hospital to have a baby, and then to have her return with an infant who engrosses her time and attention, is the unhappy fate of many children whose parents either ignore their need for preparation and reassurance or else deny it because they cannot face the questions about sex and procreation involved. So many children suffer unnecessarily from the arrival of a younger brother or sister when that arrival could be the occasion for happy expectations and enjoyment! Here we have an excellent illustration of how children are sacrificed to religious and moral traditions that insist upon denying sex and hiding procreation as something shameful and obscene.

The symptoms of sibling rivalry, often aggravated by overt favoritism for the new baby and rejection of the older child, are many and various. The young child is faced with the necessity of accepting a place and a rôle for which he needs much affection and reassurance, which he may not receive at home or at school. Often this shock comes just as the child is striving to learn toilet habits, so that he is under a double load of anxiety which may lead to "slips" or persistent enuresis.

The frequency of rejected children—children not wanted or not acceptable as personalities or temperaments to the parents—is so great that special mention should be made of the need of such children for something to compensate for their unhappy fate. In this group must be numbered the children of oversolicitous mothers who are hiding their rejection of the child under an effusive care and atoning for their guilty feeling by "smothering" the child. Nursery schools have a great opportunity to meet the acute needs of these children.

The little child is frequently disturbed physiologically by emotional reactions such as anger, rage, and grief which clamor for expression or release in overt behavior. In a very real sense these physiological disturbances or upheavals seize control of the child and often impel him to act violently and destructively against things and people and even himself. One of the most important of life tasks for the young child is to learn how to manage these emotional reactions and thereby to free himself from this overwhelming experience. It is difficult for adults to conceive or to understand the panic that these emotional reactions may arouse in the child, who finds himself helplessly carried on a tide of feeling so strong that he cannot resist it unaided. If at the same time he meets with a violent response from adults, who strike him or forcibly restrain him, the emotional disturbance may be aggravated cumulatively until terminated by exhaustion. Such an experience teaches the child nothing constructive or helpful, and it may make him so afraid of himself that he begins to be anxious about this behavior and less and less prepared to meet the next provocation. Although the adult may forcibly control the child at the moment, what the child needs is help in controlling the emotional disturbance himself, so that, instead of a persistent conflict within the child between himself and his emotions, he can bring these emotional reactions into the pattern of his own living. The situation is in many respects like that in the case of hunger and elimination, where physiological processes are initially dominant, but are gradually transformed into regulated functional activities over which the individual has, as we say, control, because those functional processes are subject to the culturally sanctioned times, places, and objects.

In other words, the emotional reactions of the child are normal physiological functions that call for regulation and patterning, so that the child may be freed from their urgency and disturbance. They are not, as our tradition teaches, moral or ethical problems, and when handled as such, they only increase the child's guilt and resentment and serve to fixate him at that infantile level, as in toilet training when it is made a moral issue. Anger and rage, like fear, have had a great biological value in the past, but in group living they may, as persistent infantile reactions, seriously interfere with the individual's capacity for peaceful, co-operative adult living, just as persistent incontinence of feces will restrict an individual's activities.

The child, then, needs help in bringing his emotional responsiveness under regulation. Some children are more prone to anger and rage, others to fear and pain, so that each child requires highly individualized help in meeting his peculiar personal reactions. Unfortunately we have little knowledge of how to provide this help in a constructive, rather than a repressive, manner, because we have treated the problems as moral issues, meeting them with threats, punishment, shame, and often equally violent emotional reactions. There is need for much experimentation here in terms of physiological processes that need to be regulated and integrated into the child's total personality make-up through the help we can give him in his handling of these internal upheavals.

Perhaps the greatest need in these situations is for sympathetic reassurance that will allay the child's panic and so help him to meet the situation more effectively. If not helped early in life, the child may go forward with a capacity for violent reaction that his increasing size and strength make potentially dangerous, especially since he may, at the same time, be developing an increasing resentment toward others because of the way frustrations and deprivations are being inflicted upon him—a resentment that may later take the form of a persistent hostility and aggression, repeatedly reinforced by the revival of the infantile emotional reactions.

Fear and grief are also difficult reactions for the child to handle, but again we usually fail to provide really constructive help and only too often aggravate these feelings by our clumsy or careless attempts to dissipate them. Both fear and grief are physiological reactions that more or less paralyze or restrict activity, unless the fear activates flight. The child needs reassurance and reinforcement in meeting the strange, unknown, and apparently threatening experiences that confront him, and if we will accept the child's view that a situation is terrifying, even if we see that it is not, we can avoid the usual mistakes. Nothing is so helpful as learning some effective method of dealing with a fear-producing situation, since a learned motor response displaces the panicky fear of helplessness, as we see in the training of firemen, policemen, soldiers, and others. But many of the fears of children are not really physiological fears, but rather a disguise for other needs which the child cannot or does not reveal. It is the insecure, anxious child, the child who is not sure of himself or his place in the family or group, who appears fearful of situations that have no terrifying character, so that our earnest explanations and reassurances of safety are wholly irrelevant. Then, too, many children are reared under a constant threat of danger, the parents instilling fear before the situation arises in their efforts to protect the child, or the environment itself may be constantly terrifying. Again, many children have suffered really shocking accidents or exposures to danger which have been indelibly impressed upon them, so that they are ever apprehensive of a repetition and live in dread. Children from such a background need a long experience of peace, of safety and security, to escape from the terror that dominates their lives. In some cases only repeated rehearsals of the shock will enable them to escape from their hysterical reactions.

. . . . .

Another task of the child that is a source of anxiety, creating an acute need for reassurance and understanding help, is that of accepting his or her own sex and the many taboos that surround this subject. The traditional view of childhood is that children have no awareness of sex differences and no concern over their genitals, while the cumulative clinical evidence indicates that they are often greatly worried about sex differences and puzzled, if not greatly preoccupied, by their genitals. It is hard for a child to envisage the process of procreation, to accept his maleness or her femaleness, and to see any meaning or sense in the confusing "explanations" given, at the same time striving to understand the violent reactions of adults to exposure of the genitals, manipulation, and so forth.

Little children need constant reassurance and simplified enlightenment on questions of sex and procreation if they are to escape prolonged anxiety and possible lifelong unhappiness. In so far as nursery schools and other schools can provide children with an understanding and wholesome attitude here, we can see how the education of children may change our whole culture, for undoubtedly our culture is warped and distorted by our inherited traditions of uncleanliness, obscenity, and wickedness in regard to sex. We cannot expect to dispose of the child's curiosity and concern by purely biological explanations, since, as Otto Rank has pointed out, adults themselves are not satisfied with merely biological answers. Moreover, the exigent questions about sex, for the child and the adult, are not concerned with gestation, but with the uses of sex in living, in feeling, in intimacy and affection.

It is not too much to say that the ability of men and women to marry and to find happiness in marriage and family life is largely conditioned by their experience and acceptance of their masculine or feminine rôles and sex differences during the pre-school years. If the boy is to grow up as a psychologically potent male, he must during the pre-school years develop his maleness and focus his future sex interests and needs in the genitals, since failure to do so at that time, as clinical evidence amply shows, will compromise his adolescence and prevent his achievement of a wholesome heterosexual adjustment toward women. Likewise it is clear that the little girl, during the pre-school years, must get a clear idea of her future feminine rôle, must accept her essential biological, physiological, and anatomic difference from the male and begin to look forward to her psychological differentiation as a female, with unique capacities for mating, procreation, lactation, and maternal and feminine rôles.

• • • • •

Another life task confronting the child is that of learning to recognize and observe the inviolabilities that every culture establishes with respect to objects, persons, places, and times. We are so accustomed to think of private property in things and animals, of the sanctity of the physical person of individuals, of the great number of special places and days consecrated to particular purposes which must not be profaned, that we fail to realize that private property and the sanctity of the person are not entities or mysterious powers, but learned ways of behaving toward things and persons, taught to children often with severe penalties for evasion or violation. These lessons as to the inviolability of things and persons are painfully learned by the young child as he begins to explore the world about him, seeking occasions for satisfying his needs and expressing his impulses, and being more or less forcibly restrained, rebuffed, and frustrated. He finds that everything and every person is protected by an invisible barrier of inviolability ("don't touch," "don't look," "don't eat," "don't go near," "don't handle") which he may not disregard except in duly sanctioned ways, such as buying and selling and making contracts or agreements. He must also learn to uphold the inviolability of his own person and property.

These lessons are not simple, since there are many fine distinctions to be made. What is freely accessible in the home is taboo outside; certain persons may be freely invaded, as in fighting with siblings, while others, such as strangers, are inviolable; certain persons are receptive to physical contact, such as parents or near relatives, while others not in the family group are untouchable; actions that may be performed in one place or at one time are forbidden in other places and at other times. Then, too, the child confronts the magical power of money, whereby small pieces of metal or paper render freely accessible what is otherwise inviolable.

These lessons are indeed formidable, and the young child struggling with the complicated customs of group life faces a heavy task for which he needs endless patience and sympathetic teaching. How often a little mistake over private property, which he is just beginning to understand, evokes sudden and immediate punishment, with accusations of "thief" and "liar" and other terrifying characterizations. When we realize that these early lessons in observing the inviolabilities are the most essential steps in preparation for group living, perhaps we shall devise more desirable and effective methods of teaching them, and shall remember to provide toleration and reassurance for the bewildered child who is attempting to assimilate the cumulative customs of thousands of years. It is little wonder that the learning of these inviolabilities, involving as they do repeated frustrations and a form of negative conditioning that inhibits the response to biologically adequate stimuli of objects and persons, should so frequently impair the child's whole adult life, causing him to face every encounter and every negotiation with timidity or anxiety, or to be intensely preoccupied with getting the better of every one in all situations.

Besides learning to inhibit his responses to things and persons who are inviolable, the child must also learn to perform those acts which his parents insist upon as the required actions in various situations. These actions include the traditional manners and customs, the etiquette and the moral duties which the parents especially cherish and respect and which they are compelled to teach their children as the essentials of life. These lessons are difficult for the child because, like the inviolability of things and persons, the required conduct has no natural, biological relation to the situations in which it is demanded of the child. He must, therefore, be repeatedly shown what to do, and prompted and compelled to do it, with a greater or less amount of verbal and often physical punishment. The outcome of this training is the establishment of more or less automatic conduct, according to the required pattern, which is always a variation, peculiar to the family, of the general socially approved pattern.

As in the teaching of inviolabilities, parental instruction as to the performance of these required actions involves the exercise of authority, often by the father, who rarely has as close and affectionate a tie with the child as the mother and who, therefore, relies more upon coercion to exact obedience, while the mother relies upon the child's desire for her love and approval. Thus the child experiences authority and coercion for the first time, and only too often it is administered severely and arbitrarily, arousing in the child fear, resentment, and hostility toward the father.

These disturbing emotional reactions toward the parents, especially the father, are of crucial importance for the future of the child. As a member of a group, he has to learn to acknowledge and to accept authority, to recognize outside himself a regulator, controller, and arbiter of conduct that is largely traditional, not reasonable or based upon anything but custom. He must learn to observe in his conduct the repressions and frustrations required by the inviolability of things and persons; and equally he must learn to perform various acts, from small courtesies to the greater, more important duties appropriate to his sex, status, class, position, and so on, accepting all these complicated and largely ritualized acts as necessary and desirable and as duly sanctioned by the law and the prescribed rules of social living. The development of such conduct involves the constant recognition and willing acceptance of the authority of the state, which, to be really effective, must function, not in physical coercion and police supervision, but within the individual himself. Authority, then, like private property, is merely a way of behaving toward individuals and situations; it is an attitude or effective reaction toward what is expected or demanded.

Now if the young child experiences authority for the first time as coercive, severe, and brutal, as something that arouses fear, anxiety, and resentment, his socialization will be compromised. He cannot calmly and gracefully accept that which is expected or demanded, performing acts or refraining from responses, but rather he will feel tension, will resent the parental authority, and will develop a persistent hostility toward the parents, especially the father, and all others who attempt to direct his conduct.

Instead, then, of accepting the inviolabilities or the required performances, the child who has been thus treated will fail to build those conduct patterns into an integrated whole, in which his behavior and his personality are at one. He may outwardly conform to what is demanded or prohibited, but only because of fear and anxiety. The learned conduct, essential to group life, is never assimilated or made wholly automatic, and so the child becomes preoccupied with the conflict between what he must do and not do and what he feels. Often he releases his feelings in misbehavior that is difficult to understand, for it gives the child nothing of value or advantage and usually is wholly incongruous with the situation. These aberrant actions are symptoms of conflict, modes of expressing resentment or hostility against authority that has made him fearful and unhappy.

With so many children exposed to this destructive experience of authority, destined by their persistent feelings of fear and resentment to unhappy adult lives, if not to more serious outcomes in mental disorders and criminality, the nursery schools are confronted by the urgent need of these children for help in accepting authority and in escaping these initial disturbances. Can we devise experiences in the nursery school that will enable the child to accept authority and to find freedom from the emotional conflicts and resentments that his previous experiences have engendered? The need is for ways of inculcating acceptance of authority without aggravating the already serious conflicts so many children have when they come to nursery schools; and this calls for reformulation of the problem, as discussed above, so that the authority will be transferred to the situation and divested of the personal element that evokes the resentment and conflict. Paradoxically, this depersonalization of authority depends upon a personal relation of the parent to the child wherein the exercise of authority is benevolent and helpful, not antagonistic and repressive.

• • • • •

One of the most important problems facing students of personality today is this question whether hostility and aggression are inborn characteristics of all individuals or whether they are the reactions of individuals who, as infants and pre-school children, were deprived of needed love and affection and security and so were driven by the unrelieved pressure for socialization to hostile, aggressive, destructive conduct. This question is of the utmost importance socially and educationally, since the answer involves the future of our society and of the civilized world. If man is innately hostile and aggressive, prone to destructive antagonisms and rivalries, then the prospects for a better, more humanly desirable society are not very bright. If human nature, as theological tradition and many of our contemporary students of personality tell us, is born wicked, sinful, and hostile and must be forced to be social, co-operative, and altruistic, the task of education is essentially a coercive one, that of curbing the hostility, of teaching individuals to "handle their aggressiveness." If, on the other hand, human nature is essentially plastic, subject to educational direction toward friendliness, co-operativeness, gentleness, and genuine group or social activity, then the task of education is to prevent the early distortions and unnecessary deprivations that arouse resentment and aggressiveness, by providing as much affectionate reassurance and toleration of individual, temperamental differences as possible for the children who have been ill treated or neglected by their parents. . . .

But here we must ask whether we know enough now to meet this issue of resentment and aggressiveness wisely. The policy of restraint and repression in many schools may prevent fighting and disorder for the moment, but it does nothing to release the child from the inner tensions and frustrations of which his aggressions are but symptoms. Perhaps we have to face a mixed answer to the earlier question and realize that tensions and resentment are probably present in all children in the early years, as a necessary consequence of the process of deprivations and coercions they undergo during socialization. Whether these tensions will become persistent, lifelong hostile attitudes toward the world, or be replaced by friendly, co-operative attitudes, may be the critical issue of pre-school education. No permanent good is achieved by a repressive policy, nor is any constructive end attained by permitting the children to fight it out, with the risk of damage to all concerned. What is needed is an imaginative, insightful handling of conflicts and aggressions on an experimental basis, addressed to the underlying anxiety, guilt, and frustrations and the need for reassurance and security. There is also need for methods of handling situations in such a way that the initial hostility or aggression of the child may be rendered unnecessary by opportunities for friendly, helpful responses. Many children do not know how to act co-operatively and need the skillful guidance of an adult to encourage them in friendly conduct and sympathetic actions. It must be realized that repeated rebuffs and frustrations may transform love into hatred and aggression, so that the child can only attack what he has most desired.

This brings us to the exigent question of freedom and self-expression, over which there has been so much controversy and often hasty action. It may help us to obtain some perspective on this question if we will remember again that the child faces a series of unavoidable life tasks, including the persistent problem of how to get along in an organized group life. To the young child the world around him is indeed precarious and ambiguous. He faces a natural world often dangerous and always puzzling even to adults; his own organism, with its many functions and needs which must conform to parental and social patterning; obscure, often unconscious, impulses that impel him to actions that frequently he cannot understand, and that others usually resent, rebuke, and often retaliate for; a social or cultural world organized into patterns of behavior and regulated by symbols, such as language, that are subtly differentiated and variable; a constellation of human relationships, in the immediate family, the wider kinship group, the neighborhood, and the school, among which he must find personality fulfillment and security despite the capricious and disparate character of all these impinging personalities; and finally an immense body of tradition and folklore, knowledge, skills, and play.

Faced with such a welter of confusing, conflicting adjustments, the young child desperately needs the security of stable, persistently uniform situations, of dependable human relations, and of endless patience and tolerance. The frequent cry against any repression of the child involves a confusion that is often tragic for the child. Every culture involves deprivations and repression, the patterning and regulation of physiological functions and human behavior, which, if wisely handled, are only redirections and modulations of impulses. The young child especially needs a wisely administered regulation or direction because he cannot sustain the immense burden of making individual decisions on all the aspects of life and of learning unaided to manage his impulses. Few adults can do this, as we see in the overwhelming need for guidance, for precepts, for legal, ethical, and religious direction. Moreover, the regularization of hunger and elimination and the respecting of the inviolabilities leaves the individual free for other activities and interests that would not be possible if he were continually driven by hunger, beset by impulses to elimination, and at the mercy of every provocative personal contact or sexual stimulus. These learned patterns and repressions are the chief factors in man's ability to go beyond a purely organic existence. It is not the ordering of life that damages the child, but the distortion, the fears, anxieties, and permanent frustrations and inhibitions that parental and educational practices unnecessarily inflict upon the child in the process of establishing these socially and individually necessary repressions.

It is also the confusion and anxiety and insecurity of capricious, vacillating teaching that damages the personality in search of something stable and constant to build upon. Children love order, regularity, repetition of the same pattern endlessly, and they need consistent adult guidance and help in learning these patterns of what is essential to their adult life and social living. But they do not need, nor can they safely endure, the fears, the anxieties, the feelings of inadequacy and of guilt that so many parents and teachers instill during this socialization process. Indeed fear seems to be the chief psychological instrument in early child-rearing—either the arousal of fears by cruel and coercive treatment or the inculcation of fears of experience, of people, of living, which cripple the child for life. Fear, and the resentment or hostility it often generates, are indeed the major emotional drives in our social life and give rise to much unsocial and antisocial behavior. What the child needs, but seldom receives, is a clear-cut definition of the situation and of the conduct appropriate therein, so that he can and will learn what conduct is permitted and what is not permitted without the emotional disturbances he now experiences during these lessons. . . .

---

6. Principal Factors Determining Intellectual Evolution from Childhood to Adult Life *

SOME OF the most illuminating data concerning the nature of the child's mental processes have come from the ingenious studies conducted by Jean Piaget and his collaborators. In this paper Dr. Piaget summarizes the results of several studies of intellectual development. He describes a series of successive modes of function-

* Jean Piaget, "Principal factors determining intellectual evolution from childhood to adult life," in *Factors Determining Human Behavior* (Harvard Tercentenary Publications, Cambridge: Harvard University Press, 1937), pp. 32–48. Reprinted by permission of the author and the publisher.

> ing that might be thought of as stages in development. First, the organism adjusts to the world with an elementary sensory-motor reactive system, which, with growth and experience, becomes more complex and differentiated. Later, as language is learned, the use of verbal symbols in thinking becomes possible, and new forms of mental organization emerge. These forms of mental organization seem to parallel some aspects of the earlier sensorimotor development. In the beginning all thinking is based on the experiences and needs of the individual—the possibility of a different point of view does not occur to him. This kind of functioning is called "egocentric." Later, some appreciation of relativity develops and the child can conceive of the world as it might be perceived from another perspective. Rational, logical thinking, which depends on an awareness of the existence of objects and relationships apart from the individual observing them, emerges still later, and permits the individual to develop a more realistic social and intellectual approach to the world.

THE SUBJECT of our investigations is intellectual evolution—that is, the development of knowledge and of its different modes, the genesis of the forms of thought, of their adaptation to experience, and the rules which they obey.

In its point of departure this evolution raises a problem which is essentially biological; the relationship between understanding or perception and its objects is a particular case of adaptation—that is, a combination of assimilation and accommodation—which unites the organism with its external environment. The first question which the theory of the development of the understanding must investigate is how this relationship results from biological organization and adaptation. For example, it is impossible to determine how the elementary forms of spatial perception are evolved without seeing how they are related to the mode of inheritance of the organs of perception and of equilibrium, and to the different modes of organic adaptation.

But in the last analysis the evolution of individual thought is closely enmeshed in collective systems of knowledge, especially in those great systems of rational collaboration which deductive and experimental science has produced. The genetic theory of knowledge must therefore reach out into an historico-critical analysis of scientific thought, and also into genetic logic. For instance, to understand the evolution of the idea of space in the mind of a child, it is not enough to know how this idea is first born. One must also determine how the so-called "displacement groups" which form it follow one another in succession from the motor level to that of the most abstract conceptions; one must establish the respective parts of the scheme of logic and of the intuition in this formation; one must define exactly the relationship between the ideas of space and those of time, object, number, movement, speed, et cetera. In short, truly to understand the psychological aspect of the development of space, one must attack all the problems which this idea and related ideas suggest in the realm of mathematics and physics; but not from a point of view which is purely reflective and abstract, rather from one which is genetic and experimental. A comparative analysis must intervene between the psychological development of thought and the history of science.

The psychology of intellectual evolution leans therefore upon the biological theories of adaptation, the psychological theories of understanding, the sociological theories of signs and norms (the rules of socialized thought), the history of science, and upon comparative logic. One can then consider this special branch of psychology as a genetic theory of knowledge, a broad theory which must borrow its elements from a very great number of fields of research, thus partially synthesizing them, but withal an exact and well-defined theory, which has its own method, namely, the envisaging of intellectual realities only from the point of view of their development and genetic construction.

In fact, the best method for the psychological theory of the development of the understanding will always be the analysis of the intellectual evolution of the child. The thought of the child alone constitutes a continuous process which by a normal evolution links the initial sensorimotor adaptations to the socialized and scientific forms of understanding. In so far as the development of individual thought from birth to adult life can be observed directly and by experiment, and in so far as it is also open to the influences which various adult social groups have on the formation of the reason, this development forms an ideal field on which to set up all the biological, psychological, sociological, and logical problems of understanding in order to examine their genetic construction. A genetic and experimental epistemology is thus conceivable as a special branch of psychology.

We should like in what follows to give an example of this method and its results in studying—on the three planes of sensorimotor activity, egocentric thought, and rational thought—the genesis of some of those ideas of conservation (continuity) which play such a great role in scientific thought. As we trace this growth we shall also have the opportunity of following, on these three successive levels, the steps of one of the most important processes in the development of thought, namely, the passage from egocentric perception and thought to objective reasoning.

For the following hypotheses may be made in this matter. At the beginning of mental life, the world appears to the child as a series of pictures which are centered about activity and lack any intrinsic stability. The absence of permanent objects and of the objective organization of space seems thus to go hand in hand with a radical and unconscious egocentricity, so that the subject does not consider himself as one thing among many, but only conceives of things in relation to his own actions. Yet at the other extremity of the development the universe is considered as being formed of permanent objects whose movements take place in a space independent of us, and whose many relationships form a series of invariables which prolong the conservation of the object itself; invariables of number, quantity, matter, weight, et cetera. One may therefore say then that, in so far as egocentricity is reduced by the co-ordination of the individual point of view with other possible ones, the co-ordination which explains this reduction explains also the formation of logical instruments of conservation (ideas of "groups," systems of relations, et cetera) and the formation of invariables in the world of reality (ideas of the permanence of the object, of quantities, weights, et cetera).

I. SENSORIMOTOR INTELLIGENCE

Even in the most elementary sensorimotor activities with which the intellectual development of the child begins, it is possible to discern certain of the processes of conservation. Because of the final richness of these processes, as well as their initial limitations, it is necessary to analyze them in detail.

It is evident that the reflex mechanisms (for example, sucking), the habits grafted on these reflexes (thumb sucking, et cetera), or the more complex "circular reactions" which tend to reproduce an interesting result (to swing suspended toys, et cetera) all lead essentially to repetition, and consequently imply a tendency toward persistence. On the one side these factors assume that movements are so organized that they are always capable of returning to their point of departure. From the point of view of space, these motor units form what the geometricians call "displacement groups," closed systems of operations which tend to continuance. On the other side, the elementary psychological activity which is characteristic of them is essentially an "assimilation" of external realities, so that these realities are not considered as entities in themselves, but only as functional elements (things are conceived merely as something to be sucked, something to be swung or handled, et cetera). Now this assimilation is also a factor in conservation, since it implies a certain practical recognition and a certain identifying generalization based on habitual repetition. Thus, when the baby of five or six months sees his usual rattle, or even a new plaything, dangling before him, he will swing it at once, assimilating it (by an assimilation which reproduces, recognizes, and generalizes) into the scheme of objects to be swung.

But, if these elementary sensorimotor organizations thus introduce from the very start a certain permanence into the primitive universe by constructing space in practical "groups" and by an assimilation of the things perceived into schemes of action, this conservation and this permanence emanate from the subject himself, and hence begin by presenting a purely egocentric character. In other words, there is not yet any conservation of objects as such, nor any permanence in the external world, not even in the space which forms its framework.

First of all, as far as objects are concerned, it is easy to establish the fact that, although the baby is capable of recognizing differences in things at a very early age, almost to the end of his first year he behaves as if the objects which disappeared from his field of perception momentarily ceased to exist. For instance, between the ages of five and eight months, when the child already knows enough to seize any solid objects which he sees, one has only to cover them with a cloth, or place a screen in front of them at the moment when the baby's hand is directed toward them, and he will give up looking for them and immediately lose his interest. I have even observed this in systematically hiding the bottle when my six months old son was about to take it. But one can see a still more curious reaction around nine or ten months, when the child is capable of seeking the object behind the screen and the notion of real exterior permanence begins to put in an appearance. For example, when the baby is placed between two pillows and he has succeeded in finding an object hidden under the right one, the object can be taken from his hands and placed under the left pillow before his very eyes, but he will look for it under the right pillow where he has already found it once before, as if the permanence of the objective were connected with the success of the former action, and not with a system of external displacements in space.

In short, the primitive world is not made up of permanent objects with autonomous trajectories, but of moving perceptive pictures which return periodically into nonexistence and come back again as the functional result of the proper action. It is easy to prove still more clearly that this world is centered in the activity of the self by an analysis of the egocentric character of space which determines its configuration.

If the movements of the child are immediately capable of organization into "groups," closed and reversible systems, those "groups" are in the beginning centered entirely on the subject himself, and afford no room for any objective spatial construction. The clearest example of these egocentric "groups" is seen in the way in which a baby, before nine or ten months, rotates objects, a movement which finally forms the idea of the "wrong side" of objects. Everyone has observed a child handling things and turning them over and over to explore their various sides. Now do these rotary movements give way immediately to the formation of objective groups? A very simple experiment shows us that this is not so. One has only to give a five or six months old baby his bottle with the nipple away from him, and turn it around slowly before his very eyes. If the child can see a bit of the rubber nipple at the other end of the bottle, he immediately turns the object around, but if he doesn't see the nipple, he doesn't even attempt to turn it, but sucks the wrong end! A series of other experiments with other "displacement groups" has shown the same centering on the subject and not on the object.

How then is the baby going to construct a world of permanent objects situated in a real space, and thus escape from his primitive egocentric universe? It is the work of the sensorimotor or practical intelligence, which precedes language, to set up a system of relations to co-ordinate this series of various perspectives which the baby has and thus cause him to locate himself among objects instead of illusively bringing them to him.

In other words, as the activity of the baby develops and the causal, temporal, and spatial sequences which this activity creates become more complex, objects are detached more and more from the action itself, and the body of the subject becomes one element among others in an ordered ensemble. Thus a total reversal of perspective takes place, which marks the beginning of the objectification of the external world, and of the idea of its permanence. The interplay of practical relationships in the world of reality teaches the child to shift the center of space and its objects from his action to himself, and thus locate himself at the middle point of this world which is being born. In this way the permanence of objects appears as the product of this formation of objective "groups" of displacements, and these groups themselves depend for their creation upon the way in which the sensorimotor or practical intelligence allows the child to free himself from his initial egocentricity and gives him power to act on things, thanks to a system of co-ordinated relationships.

But, if the co-ordination of practical relationships leads to a first victory over egocentricity and to the beginning of the objective idea of conservation, this external permanence remains limited to the plane of action and immediate perception, and cannot extend at once to the level of conceptual representation in general. In fact, it is in a sense an "ontological egocentricity" from which the practical intelligence delivers the individual, and not social and representative egocentricity, which will remain very important even after the appearance of language, and all through infancy. In other words, the co-ordination of practical relationships teaches the child that his body is one thing among many, and that he is thus part of a world of stable objects, whereas at the beginning the baby saw only a world of inconsistent pictures gravitating about his own activity. But the sensorimotor intelligence is not enough to teach the child that the perspective he has of this world is not absolute but relative, and must be co-ordinated with the perspectives of other people to attain a general and truly objective picture of reality.

II. EGOCENTRIC THOUGHT

Just at the moment when the practical world of which we have been speaking has been created, the child comes into possession of language, and henceforth is called upon to adapt himself to the thoughts of others as well as to the external material world. Now on this new plane of thought which the social world creates, the child finds difficulties similar to those he has already overcome on the plane of the practical universe, and so he passes through stages similar to those of his escape from initial egocentricity and his progressive co-ordination. Hence the principles of conservation remain unchanged, only this time they are on the plane of abstract concepts. Although the child admits the permanence of concrete objects in the world of immediate experience, he really has no idea of the conservation of matter, weight, or movement, nor even any conception of logical or numerical groups. If he fails, it is because he lacks an intellectual instrument with which to construct the "invariables of groups" which are formed by physical realities. This instrument is called "the logic of relations" by the logicians, and is really the tool of co-ordination par excellence, both from the social and from the rational point of view. It is created only as it succeeds in stemming the egocentricity which constantly opposes it.

In order to make the link between ontological egocentricity of the first sensorimotor stage and the social and logical egocentricity of the beginnings of conceptual thought perfectly clear, let us briefly turn again to the example of space. We have already seen that on the practical plane the child of two or three years is capable of using a certain number of "groups" of displacements: he knows how to turn an object over, to hide it behind one screen, or a series of two, and find it in the right place, et cetera. But what will happen when it is a question not only of acting upon the object, but of imagining distant objects, and of co-ordinating the perspective of different observers?

One of our assistants, Mlle. E. Meyer, has investigated this in the following experiment: the child is placed opposite a small model of three mountains, and given a certain number of colored pictures of these mountains; he is then asked which of the pictures show the mountains from the positions occupied successively by a doll on the mountains in the model. The function of age in the development of these reactions is very clear. The little ones do not understand that the observer sees the same mountains quite differently from various points of view, and hence they consider their own perspective absolute. But the older ones gradually discover the relativity necessary to objectivity, after a number of systematic errors due to the difficulty of co-ordinating the relationships in question. Here then on this social and logical plane of the co-ordination of perspectives we have a passing from egocentricity to an objective "group" of changes, exactly parallel to the passage one has observed on the sensorimotor level in the relationships between the baby and the objects handled, only this time the necessity of considering the point of view of other people has created a new difficulty.

Now this process also influences very closely the idea of the conservation or continuity of the mechanical and physical characteristics of objects as well as of their spatial peculiarities. In fact, since the child considers a mountain as being just what it appears to be in his own perspective, it could not possibly have either form or stable dimensions—that is, no "invariables of groups" are constructed. That is actually what observation shows to be true. I have been able to determine in experimenting on my own children, by going about real mountains with them, that at about four or five years of age they still considered the apparent changes due to our own changes of position as quite real. For every mountain they admitted the existence of changes of form and dimensions absolutely contrary to the idea of the permanence of objects. It would be easy to generalize these results for all objects in distant space (stars, clouds, et cetera).

But we must show how this preoccupation with the problem of the proper perspective—that is to say, of "immediate experience" as opposed to experience based on rational deduction—hinders the mind from co-ordinating relationships, and finally forming ideas of the permanence of matter, weight, movement, et cetera. It is clear that every principle of conservation implies a system of relationships which explains real permanence through apparent change. Now in so far as the mind is dominated by "immediate experience," it is not capable of recognizing this relativity, nor the "invariables" which it implies.

Here is an example dealing with the ideas of the conservation of matter and weight. We show children of different ages two paste balls of the same dimensions and weight. Then we change the shape of one of them to a cylinder (a sausage), and we ask if the two objects still have the same weight. Now the little ones think that the weight of the cylinder is less than that of the ball (because a ball appears to concentrate more matter in itself than an elongated cylinder), and they even state that the quantity of paste has diminished because of the change in form! But the older ones believe in the conservation of weight and matter; and between the two one finds a stage at which children think that weight alone varies with form, matter remaining constant.

In the same way, one of our pupils, Mlle. B. Inhelder, has shown that sugar dissolved in a glass of water is not conserved, in the minds of young children: the level which rises at the immersion of the sugar is considered as being lowered as before, after the sugar is dissolved; the sugar is conceived of as gradually vanishing, and even the sweet taste, which is all that remains of the dissolved piece, is supposed to disappear after several hours. But older children, by a series of steps it is useless to describe here, succeed in attaining the idea of the conservation of the sugar, its weight, and even the volume it occupied in the liquid. Some even go so far as to construct a kind of rude atomic theory, like that which the pre-Socratic physicists had, to account for these phenomena.

It is the same *a fortiori* in the case of more subtle ideas, such as that of the conservation of movement, or the principle of inertia. It is, indeed, easy to show that the physics of the child begins by being impregnated with an animistic dynamism, which is the direct opposite of the idea of inertia. Things are endowed with active forces, spontaneous and untransmittible, formed on the model of voluntary muscular activity. Later, before arriving at more mechanistic ideas, the child passes through an intermediate period which recalls in many respects the physics of Aristotle. Thus the trajectory of a projectile is explained, not by the conservation of the impulse received, but by an ʼαντιπερίστασις in the real sense of the word, the projectile being pushed by the air it displaces in its progress. The clouds move in the same way, by the wind which their displacement arouses, et cetera.

It seems to us easy to show that all these ideas which are so contrary to the ideas of conservation are explained by the same causes, by an egocentric relationship, not yet reciprocal or rational, between the subject and the objects of the external world. On the one hand, objects are assimilated to the ego, and conceived on the model of its own activity. Hence the anthropocentric ideas of force, weight, et cetera, which are common in the physics of the little ones. On the other hand, experience remains "immediate," dominated by a series of successive impressions which have not yet been co-ordinated. It is not formed by that logic of relationships which alone will impress upon it an objective form by co-ordinating the many relationships which are perceived or conceived. Thus, in the case of the pellets which change their form, the child does not succeed in freeing his judgment from the illusions caused by habitual perceptions (we know the point at which the evaluations of weight are dependent on factors of form), that he may co-ordinate the relationships into a coherent ensemble which can support the deduction of real permanence. In short, the absence of permanence is the result of the pre-eminence of immediate experience over rational deduction, and immediate experience is the ensemble of subjective impressions, successively registered and not yet co-ordinated into a system of relationships which encloses the subject in an objective world.

III. RATIONAL CO-ORDINATION

We saw first of all how the sensorimotor co-ordinations led the child from an unstable world centered about his own activity to an idea of the permanence of objects, based on the formation of "displacement groups" which ordered space into an objective practical universe. On the other hand, we have just established the fact that when thought and abstract concepts are imposed on this sensorimotor world, egocentricity reappears on this new plane, and the world of concepts also begins to be centered in the ego, and is thus stripped of the basic permanence which reason demands. How is the child to surmount this second group of obstacles and reach the idea of rational permanence?

The process of reasoning on this plane of conceptual thought is exactly the same as on the sensorimotor level, with this difference, that it is a question henceforth of the co-ordination of the perspectives of different individuals, as well as the co-ordination of the different aspects of individual experience. This social co-ordination, which adds a new dimension to those which are already a part of rational co-ordination, creates in the intellectual realm what one might call "logic," in contrast to the sensorimotor or practical intelligence, which makes only perceptions and motions into systems. Logic is then the "group" of operations which co-ordinates the inter-individual relationships with the intra-individual ones into a system capable of assuring the permanence which is necessary to the invariables of experience.

The essence of rational co-ordination is then to be sought in the "logic of relations"—that is, in this fundamental group of operations which assures the reciprocity of individual perspectives and the relativity of the facts of experience. To refer again to the example of space, on which we have already insisted, it is the logic of relations which makes the child come gradually to understand, between seven and eleven years, that the left and the right are not absolute, but that his own left corresponds to the right of an individual opposite him, and that an object between two others is at one and the same time at the left of the first and the right of the third. It is then the logic of relationships which permits the formation of the idea of a conceptual space by the co-ordination of the different perspectives possible, and which also allows the imposition of this upon practical space, whose relationships, however well co-ordinated they may be among themselves, are always limited to one's own perspective.

Now this logic of relations, which thus maintains on the level of thought the "groups" of operations outlined by sensorimotor intelligence, and which gradually eliminates intellectual egocentricity, finally succeeds, in the realm we are trying to analyze here, in forming invariables which represent for the reasoning mind so many principles of permanence applicable to the physical world.

In the field of the permanence of quantity, for instance, it is easy to show how the grouping of relationships involves in each case the construction of formal invariables which, when applied to reality, correct the illusions of nonpermanence. In her investigations into the genesis of the ideas of quantity and number, our assistant, Mlle. A. Szeminska, brought to light a number of facts which make this change clear.

When one fills a large glass with some continuous substance, such as colored water, or a discontinuous one, such as beads, and then separates these into two or four small glasses, or into some narrow and elongated or short and fat ones, et cetera, the quantities appear to increase or diminish for the child below seven years of age according to whether the subject considers the level of the substance in the receptacles, their size, or their number. Moreover, when one makes two groups correspond piece by piece (for example, the beads in two rectilinear rows), the child considers at first that the two quantities are equal; but this is only an illusion, because one has only to place the elements in one of these groups nearer or farther apart (to put the beads in a heap, or make one row longer and more widely spaced than the other) and the two quantities are no longer considered as equal; a row of ten beads is conceived as increasing in number if they are spaced more widely, and a pile is considered as containing more or fewer beads according to whether one heaps it up or spreads it out before the eyes of the child, et cetera.

In short, before the age of six or seven there is no idea of the permanence of continuous quantities, nor of discontinuous groups, nor any necessary equivalence between two groups which correspond piece by piece, et cetera, whatever the active operations may be which the subject himself performs in the course of the experiments. For this reason up to this age the child has not yet formed any idea of cardinal or ordinal numbers which are capable of indefinite extension; nor has he yet elaborated any idea of classes of things in extension, which depends upon the inclusion of parts in a permanent whole. The essential forms which number and logical class give to the mind are thus, after all, bound up closely with the processes of conservation, and one might say in general that if the thought of the child remains pre-logical during infancy, it is because of the lack of these very principles of permanence.

Now how does the child proceed from this pre-logical state to the discovery of the permanence of groups and quantities? By the co-ordination of the relationships involved; that is, by those operations of "multiplication of relations" which are essential to the logic of relationships. As soon as he ceases to envisage as separate unities the level, size, and number of the columns of liquid, the length of the rows, and the space between the objects, et cetera, the child succeeds in co-ordinating these relationships, in understanding their relative positions in a system of independent variables, and thus he forms units which are capable of permanence. It is therefore the logic of relationships which transforms immediate experience, with its illusions of perception, into a rational system, the changes of which depend on necessary invariables. It would be easy to show that the idea of the permanence of matter, weight, and movement, which we were speaking of above, is the result of similar processes. In the thought of the child, as in the evolution of the sciences, rational permanence always results from the union of a deduction based on the co-ordination of relationships with an experience similarly formed; and every invariable implies a "group" which creates it—that is, a system of related and reversible changes.

But you will say that the problem is not yet solved, that there still remains the question of how this "logic of relations" which explains the genesis of the principles of conservation and of the "invariables of groups" is itself originated. Now it is first necessary to understand the epistemological character of what we call the egocentricity of the child (i.e., a quite unconscious and natural illusion of perspective, which precedes moral egoism and conscious egocentricity). Then one will understand that this process of co-ordination, at once social and intellectual, by which the child escapes from his self-centered point of view to find his place among other people, is actually the rational instrument which makes up this logic of relations. For, in any field, the faculty of knowing is a process of co-ordination in which the ego is subordinated to some objective system of references, and the logic of relationships is nothing but a tool and a result of this co-ordination; a tool in that it guides the ego in its escape from itself, and a result since it is a grouping of systematic operations and an ensemble of successive invariables.

In conclusion, one sees how the genetic analysis of any aspect of the thought of a child necessarily corresponds to the analysis of scientific thought. Indeed, the effort by which the child, by means of that social and rational instrument which the logic of relationships gives him, escapes from his egocentricity and creates a universe is the very beginning of that ever-present gigantic effort of science to free man from himself by putting him within the relativity of the objective world.

---

7. Senescence and the Emotions: A Genetic Theory *

THE MARKED INCREASE in the number of senior citizens in our population, paralleling the rapid extension of man's life expectancy over recent decades, has given rise to a new appreciation of the science of gerontology, the study of aging. The psychological aspects of gerontology constitute a newly emphasized branch of developmental psychology.

Dr. Banham reviews some of the major findings from recent studies of aging and outlines a theory of emotional development that embraces the total life span. Starting with the random behavior and undifferentiated responses of infancy, this account progresses through increasing differentiation and integration to maturity. It postulates then a period of consolidation, followed by some disintegration, and a final stage of constricted response and

* Katharine M. Banham, "Senescence and the emotions: a genetic theory," *Journal of Genetic Psychology,* LXXVIII (1951), 175–83. Reprinted by permission of the author and of The Journal Press.

perseverative behavior. Though this outline is based primarily on emotional functioning, it is suggestive of the developmental pattern for other psychological processes as well.

RECENT STUDIES of the psychological aspects of aging have revealed similarities between the emotional behavior of aged persons and that of neurotic individuals irrespective of age. In a monograph entitled *Social Adjustment in Old Age,* Otto Pollak says:

> There is general agreement among both laymen and students of old age that a number of traits indicating maladjustments are more frequently found among old people than among younger groups in the general population. A partial list of these traits follows:
>
> 1. Feelings of inadequacy.
> 2. Feelings of rejection, of being unwanted.
> 3. Feelings of depression, of self-pity.
> 4. Hypochondria, including overvaluing genuine physical symptoms.
> 5. Anxiety, worry.
> 6. Emotional sensitivity (irritability, querulousness, tearfulness).
> 7. Boredom, restlessness.
> 8. Apathy, passivity.
> 9. Negativism.
> 10. Guilt feelings.
> 11. Narrowing of interests.
> 12. Social withdrawal.
> 13. Rigidity, difficulty in adjusting to new conditions.
> 14. Conservatism.
> 15. Loss of social inhibitions (vulgarity, untidiness, uncleanliness, overtalkativeness).
> 16. Regressive tendencies, especially sex (autoerotism, voyeurism).

Pollak attributes these maladjustments partly to environmental frustrations and the limited opportunities of old people for the satisfaction of thwarted needs, and partly to changes in mental and physical capacities and functions.

Most observers have agreed that there seems to be a decline in mental functioning with old age. Thinking becomes slower; memory patchy and incomplete; ideas become confused; motivation, ambition, and range of interests are reduced; speech is repetitive; and attention tends to wander. This wandering of attention on the part of old folk, though apparently similar to that of the inattentive child, has certain qualitative differences. The young child is usually keenly aware of a number of things, and he does not concentrate or fixate his attention on any one of them for more than a few seconds. The old person, on the other hand, is blithely indifferent to many aspects of his environment or psychological situation. His attention fixes on one aspect and then upon another, in a fashion related in his past experience by contiguous occurrence, emotional bond, or conceptual thinking. His attention is narrowed and specific rather than diffuse or dispersed. But it may be no more concentrated and actively engaged in a process of mental organization than that of a restless and inattentive child.

The older person has been observed to fatigue more easily than the younger, physically as well as mentally. Speed of movement, strength, and endurance become reduced, and motor coördination becomes increasingly difficult. Possibly it is by way of adapting to this reduction in vitality that he tends to economize rather than squander his resources in excess activity. He sits quietly for hours at a stretch. He "cuts corners," does things the easiest way, sometimes carelessly and untidily. In handwriting his letters are often poorly formed and illegible, as much from carelessness as poor eye-hand coördination. Sometimes he appears to take the longest route in the pursuance of a task, as when clearing a desk of accumulated papers, he puts away one at a time instead of classifying and grouping them. Such organization would require more concentration and mental effort, it would involve new learning which he finds difficult to do.

Two characteristics of behavior frequently associated with old age are those of rigidity and difficulty in adjusting to new conditions. The former is expressed in perseverative and repetitive behavior, in prejudiced attitudes, and fixation of feeling tone. A variety of techniques have been devised, and reported in the literature, for the measurement of different forms of rigidity. Scatter pattern analyses of results on intelligence scales, such as the Wechsler Bellevue, have revealed slowness and difficulty in new learning of a cognitive nature by old people, i.e., those over 65 years of age. Attitude inventories have provided evidence of poor emotional adjustment on the part of elderly people, possibly due in some measure to lack of affective adaptability.

In old age it would seem that there is a decreasing ability to form new associative bonds or new Gestalt patterns in acts of cognition, including perception and thought, in motor coördination and in feelingful attitudes. The older person misperceives objects and spoken words, translating them into what is familiar to him. His thinking and speech are repetitive, determined by past associations rather than present purpose or relevance. He has an inability to reject or eliminate the inessential in thought as well as in action. The elderly person forms new concepts and abstractions with great difficulty, but he makes use of old established ones quite freely in his conversation, thus giving the impression that he is more intellectually agile than he is. He uses vague general terms, abstract symbols and clichés quite glibly, although he may have forgotten the full significance of their meaning which he had known at one time. Old people, moreover, cling to their prejudices. Their emotional attitudes, like their habits of thought, persist with but slight bearing upon changed circumstances.

Schrier and Boyd, in their studies of rigidity, using the Bender Gestalt test and an arithmetical technique, obtained results which indicated some positive relationship (significant multiple correlation .556) between different rigidity measures. Rokeach suggests that there may be a "general rigidity factor." Thus, a person showing rigidity in one form of behavior may be expected to show it in another. There is a growing amount of evidence in the literature that a rigid "inability to shift" may apply to goal objectives and feelingful attitudes or prejudices as well as to cognitive and motor learning.

Angyal, Shakow, and Rosenzweig have conducted investigations, the findings from which indicate that there is some relationship between rigidity of behavior and the functional neuroses and psychoses. Since rigidity is also one of the traits associated with old age, it may be the common factor relating behavior of mentally disordered persons with that of the aged. It may be true that, as Pollak has suggested, there are more maladjusted persons among the aged than among younger folk. But it is also possible that rigidity is merely a characteristic of the normal process of aging. According to this view, persons suffering from some forms of psychoneurosis or psychosis, who behave in a rigid manner are showing signs of senility in this respect. Neurotics are by no means all rigid in their behavior. Some are exceedingly flexible and pliable. But all old people show a certain amount of rigidity, inflexibility, and narrowing of range of response. Individuals vary as to the specific nature and degree of their inflexibility, but, by and large, as they become older they become more set in their ways, their beliefs, attitudes, and emotional moods.

In order to explain the apparent diminution of affective adaptability in old age, the theory is here postulated that emotional organization undergoes a certain amount of consolidation, constriction, and disintegration in later life. When an old person is stimulated by an exciting or a terrifying event, instead of becoming hyperactive or generally inhibited and tense in his responses like a young child, he acts in a specific, repetitive fashion. The excited child's behavior may be inappropriate because of its violent or random nature, but the disturbed older person behaves inappropriately because of the limited nature of his behavior and its unchangeability.

The young child, when recovering from the intense excitement or shock prompted by a startling event, such as a thunderstorm, has at his disposal a considerable amount of mobilized energy, which he may expend in diversified play or constructive pursuits. The old person, on the contrary, may be exhausted by the emotional shock, less able to turn to other things, and he may remain anxious or depressed for a long time. The emotions of old people are characterized by paucity rather than over-abundance of affective energy. The form of their behavior tends to narrow, like a stream in drought, into one channel rather than brim over into general hyperactivity or tension.

A commonly accepted theory of explanation of neurotic behavior, among psychiatrists and psychologists, is that it is regressive in nature. It represents either a fixation at, or return to more childish and primitive ways of behaving in a difficult and emotionally disturbing situation. Neurotic adults are considered to be manifesting emotional immaturity. The writer considers that this explanation may be adequate for some cases, particularly overexcitable and anxious types. But certain obsessive and compulsive neurotics exhibit behavior more characteristic of elderly persons than of young children. They are rigid and inflexible in their behavior. They might be described as prematurely senile in their reactions to distressing situations, rather than emotionally immature.

It is a tenable hypothesis, then, in the absence of adequate proof, that older persons are no more apt to be neurotic than younger ones. The data so far accumulated, which indicates that more old people show signs of maladjustment than younger groups, may be accounted for largely by the fact that they have more frustrations to face both in social restrictions and their own personal limitations. The evidences of rigidity in the behavior of older people may be normal characteristics of advancing age, and not necessarily signs of neurotic personality.

Indeed, the great majority of elderly people are happily adjusted to their social environment and personal limitations. Partly on account of the wisdom of experience, habits based on successful solution of difficulties in the past, and partly on account of reduced emotional excitability, the older person is much less disturbed by discomfort, frustrations, and inconveniences than young children. He knows more, is better prepared to meet an emergency, and so is less easily frightened. His tendency to "single track" thinking and action make him less likely to experience the anxiety that accompanies conflicting impulses. In some ways his reduced affective sensitivity and changeability may actually be helpful factors in adjustment, rather than drawbacks. Unkind treatment by others, economic privations, and diminished physical and mental capacities are often accepted with resignation, and without the emotional turmoil that such conditions would provoke in younger people.

Accepting the hypothesis that repetitiveness in behavior and lack of affective adaptability, two of the manifestations of rigidity, are normal attributes of aging, it follows that younger people who exhibit these traits are showing signs of senility rather than immaturity. This holds for "normal" individuals restricted in their outlook on life as well as for mentally disordered persons. Feebleminded persons, also, regardless of age, are apt to be rigid in their performance and inflexible in their emotional attachments. In these respects they may be considered to be more senile than childlike in behavior.

Just as there appears to be a process of maturation of behavior in early infancy, with a neurological counterpart in myelination of axon sheaths, so also there seems to be a process of psychobiological senescence in the later years of life. This maturation and senescence shows in affective behavior as well as in motor coördination and processes of thought. The behavior of an infant in an emotionally disturbing situation is general and random in nature. It is undifferentiated and undiscriminating. In terms of Gestalt psychology, the part is confused with the whole. The child reacts vaguely to the total situation. Gradually during the first few months of life emotional reactions become more differentiated and specific in nature, and related to certain definite events, such as threatening dangers, interfering restrictions, or refreshing movement. Thus the emotions of fear, anger, and joy evolve. Actual experiences in life determine largely the pattern of emotions and the form of their expression which each individual develops (Table 1).

During the years of maturity emotional behavior is at its most adaptive level. Certain situations, for example, such as the loss of a pocket book or an invitation to a banquet, are dealt with appropriately and in a variety of different ways by the same individual on different occasions. Some emotion may be expressed in visceral and behavioral response, but not too much, and none is wasted in useless movement or tension as in the case of young children and emotionally immature persons. There is maximum sensitivity to environmental conditions and refinement of aesthetic appreciation in emotional maturity. Behavior responses are most varied, but purposefully and adaptively related to the stimulating event, to individual and social needs.

The aged person, when emotionally stimulated, is generally less responsive than a younger one. He shows less enthusiastic zest and less emotional concern in his later years. His responses to a disturbing situation are specific, like those of any mature adult, but they are less varied and sometimes less appropriate than those of a younger person. The older person tends to react to the part rather than the whole situa-

TABLE 1

Schematic Presentation of a Genetic Theory of Life-Span Emotional Changes

Infancy		*Maturity*		*Old Age*
Undifferentiated response. Random behavior.	Processes of differentiation and integration.	Mature emotional sensitivity and control. Maximum differentiation of response and aesthetic feeling.	Processes of consolidation and some disintegration.	Constricted response. Perseverative behavior.
Excitement: Distress	Anxiety, Fear, Shame, Anger, Disgust, Jealousy, Disappointment, Restless uneasiness		Grief, Worry, Self pity, Guilt feelings, Querulousness, Irritability, Boredom	Depression → Apathy and Passivity
Excitement: Delight	Joy, Elation, Hopeful anticipation, Affection, Sex love		Mystical ecstasy, Possessive satisfaction, Benevolence, Gustatory sensuousness	Content → Apathy and Passivity

tion. When emotional maladjustment occurs in old age, the writer suggests, it may be an outcome of too great specificity and constriction, a paucity of affective energy and lack of flexibility in behavior. Emotional responses of old people are inadequate because they are not comprehensive and varied enough to deal with a new situation. There is insufficient drive or desire to experiment. The maladjusted child's behavior, on the other hand, is inappropriate because of its all-or-none nature, its lack of discrimination, over-exuberance or active general resistance.

As many observers have already pointed out, there are regressive tendencies in older people, and on occasion their behavior may show signs of emotional immaturity. But all neurotic maladjustments whether in old or young people cannot be accounted for in this way. Some so-called emotionally immature adolescents manifest in their behavior an inflexible specificity, characteristic of senescence. Elderly people, on the other hand, at times regress to child-like negativistic or excited behavior. They show explosive temper, become immobile with fear, or hyper-active and talkative with excitement. For the most part, however, their emotions are attenuated, and are stimulated only through a few ideational associative patterns.

The foregoing theory may be applied in consideration of the problem presented by the psychoses. It may, for example, offer a psychological explanation of what occurs in the mental functioning of a patient who improves in adjustment after shock treatment or after a pre-frontal lobotomy operation. It is suggested that the effect of a shock, whether electric, insulin, heat or other form, is to reactivate many old pattern reactions that have fallen into disuse during the psychotic periods. In this way, a greater variety of responses becomes available for use by the patient in dealing with current situations. Among these reactivated patterns may be the grosser and less differentiated emotional responses of early childhood that serve to further mobilize mental energy. Shock may also broaden the perceptions, thus making the individual more keenly aware of the total external and internal situation, and this in turn helps him to act appropriately and to deal more adequately with life's daily problems.

Psychotic patients who show improvement in their social relations and emotional expression after pre-frontal lobotomy may do so for a different reason from that explaining general improvement after shock. It is suggested that during the psychosis the person's emotional responses have become narrowly specific and stereotyped, associatively tied to one ideational system. When certain nerve connections are cut between the cerebrum and thalamus which controls bodily response in emotion, the stereotyped emotional patterns are broken up and the individual is freer to act in a more general way. While affective responses were being channeled into the patient's psychotic symptoms, other emotional responses were inhibited or dormant. The release of inhibited responses, and reactivation of dormant ones, after operation frees the patient's attention to perceive more of his environment and allows him to vary his behavior. He has still, however, to build up new sentiments and affective patterns to deal with emergencies as they arise.

If there is any truth in the foregoing theory that premature senile rigidity and inflexibility are dynamic factors in certain psychoneuroses and psychoses, checks could be made by means of treatment calculated to increase flexibility of behavior, motivation and versatility of response, applied to patients in different age groups. Physical treatments which would improve blood circulation in the brain and other organs, physiotherapy, and endocrine therapy to regulate metabolism, might all have some effect in reducing rigidity. Psychological treatment should also be even more effective, in the form of perceptual and motor stimulation, through color, sound, rhythmic movement, manual and creative activities. If these were accompanied by play or analytic therapy to release the tied and channeled emotion, old stereotypes might be broken down, and more integrated and appropriate behavior developed. Improvement, however, would not be anticipated in the case of very deteriorated psychotics, feebleminded, and aged and demented patients.

SUMMARY

The relationship of certain characteristics of the behavior of elderly persons and of maladjusted persons has been briefly discussed. The theory has been presented that a tendency to rigidity, i.e., to perseveration and inflexibility, is part of the normal process of aging. The rigidity is manifest in affective behavior as well as motor performance and thought. It may appear in extreme form or prematurely early in cases of mental disorder and maladjustment. A genetic theory of emotional changes that take place during the life span of an individual has been outlined. These changes include increasing differentiation and integration of affective response from infancy to maturity, and reduction in intensity, variety and flexibility of response towards old age. Suggestions for a psychological explanation of improvement in emotional adjustment following shock and lobotomy treatment of psychotic patients have been given, using as a basis the genetic theory and its implications. A schematic diagram, representing the genetic theory of life-span emotional changes, is given in Table 1.

III

PERCEPTION

THE TOPIC Perception covers a group of problems that are central for the study of psychology. Some of the questions that might be asked in connection with this topic are: How do external energies that impinge upon the organism become transformed into energy changes within the individual, the stuff of which psychological processes are formed? How are internal changes coordinated to provide the organism with direction? How do we organize the variety of stimuli that bombard us, and establish order and meaning in our world? How do we observe things, what attracts our attention, or how do we establish and maintain attention? These and many other questions that may be seen as interrelated are approached through the study of the process of perception.

Of the thousands of papers that have been written in this field, we have selected only seven. Six illustrate the influence on perception of some physical, individual, or social factor, and one shows the relation of perceptual to other processes.

8. The Peculiar State of Weightlessness *

WE USUALLY take the operation of our senses for granted, and most of us assume that they provide a direct and true representation of the world as it really exists. We are seldom aware that their functioning poses any problems. The following paper should disillusion us on that score. In addition, it is an interesting peep into the fu-

* Siegfried J. Gerathewohl, "The peculiar state of weightlessness," *Instructors Journal,* USAF Air Training Command, V (1954), 290–96; and in *Medical Problems of Space Flight,* USAF School of Aviation Medicine, Randolph AFB, Texas, 1955. Reprinted by permission of the author and the *Instructors Journal.*

ture, highlighting an area for research that has barely been touched upon until now. It also serves to emphasize the relation between physical conditions and perception, the interrelation within the organism of the various sense modalities, and the multiplicity of cues that contribute to our normal adjustments to the world. Finally, considered thoughtfully, it suggests capacities in the organism to react with unsuspected resources to the new environments in which technological advances may require man to function.

OF ALL THE strange sensations that men may soon encounter in sustained rocket flight, the strangest is the condition of zero gravity, in which they will have no feeling of weight. It is psychologically the most fascinating problem of space flight, because it has no parallel in human experience on the ground or in most conventional flying. It is the most difficult to investigate, because it can be produced only in circumstances approximating those of actual flight in space.

At first glance, it might seem that weightlessness would be a very simple, pleasant experience—rather like floating through the air as we do sometimes in dreams, or like drifting on the surface of a pool of water. But this is not necessarily the case. On earth we are never free from weight. The dream condition is only a wish fulfillment which in itself recognizes the consciousness of weight. The swimmer is still subjected to the full force of gravity, but is supported on the water as he would be on a solid object like a bed.

Actual weightlessness can be experienced only when the force of gravity itself is removed—or, to be more specific, when it is counterbalanced by an opposite force. Then no gravitational pull whatever acts upon the body's organs. The result is a condition which may seriously affect the flyer's behavior and his orientation—that is, his ability to locate his position in space by his own subjective feelings and perceptions.

In such a state the directions which we call "down" and "up" cease to have any meaning. The automatic compensation of the muscles for the body's normal weight produces erratic and exaggerated movements. And there is a possibility that the mind's response to this eerie situation might be one of befuddlement and uneasiness, if not of actual terror.

The phenomenon which we know as weight is the result of the gravitational tug of the earth's mass, drawing us toward its center. We are only aware of the force because of the support provided by the earth's surface—or, in an aircraft, by the lift of the wings—that prevents us from falling freely. If the support is removed, and we do fall freely, then there is no longer any sensation of weight. But this never happens in the lower regions of the earth's atmosphere, up to an altitude of about twenty miles, because the resistance of the air itself provides a substantial measure of support.

It has been calculated that a body falling through the lower atmosphere cannot attain a greater speed than about 90 knots. But, in a free fall in space, the body is constantly accelerated. Without any mechanical restraint, the only force that could be opposed to gravitation is the body's own inertia. However, its inertia responds freely to gravitation, and so the body is weightless. No one has yet bailed out of a craft above 100,000 feet, and so no one has ever been subjected to a free fall in the full sense of the term.

Another case of weightlessness, or zero gravity, is provided when a body moves in a so-called Keplerian trajectory. This is the kind of arc whose most familiar examples are the orbits of celestial objects like the Moon or the earth itself. The speed of the body then creates a centrifugal force that exactly balances the pull of the gravitational field through which it moves, and the body has no weight. It may be thought of as falling freely through space, but in a curving path that never brings it downward toward the center of the mass that attracts it.

Such a trajectory need not be confined to the outer reaches of space. A craft with sufficient speed could fly a Keplerian orbit a few feet off the ground. And a jet plane a few miles up can fly an arc in such a way that for a number of seconds, it follows a Keplerian trajectory. In this case, thrust counteracts drag and centrifugal force counterbalances gravity, so that for a time the plane and its occupants are weightless.

In jets, because of their limitations in speed and altitude, zero gravity can be achieved for only about 30 to 45 seconds. But with rocket propulsion the situation is quite different. After a relatively high initial acceleration, the rocket attains such velocity that it can coast for the rest of its flight, without any additional power except possibly in landing. By this means, after the rocket has penetrated the bulk of the atmosphere, it cruises entirely unsupported by the forces of lift that sustain conventional aircraft.

In this cruising state, both the missile and the passengers become weightless, and remain so until they reenter the denser air below. Thus it can be said that weightlessness is the normal gravitational condition in rocket flight, whether we speak of the relatively brief ascents that may be made before long for tactical and observational purposes, or of the prolonged flights that may some day be made into outer space.

It is important to realize that this condition has nothing to do with the craft's distance from the earth, except to the extent that distance affects the density of the air. Weightlessness is simply a function of speed and trajectory, produced by the equilibrium of gravity and centrifugal force. In practice, it can occur anywhere outside the atmosphere, or within it if the craft is properly flown along a parabolic course.

A German professor, Dr. Heinz von Diringshofen, first observed the phenomenon of weightlessness during World War II in experimental flights. Just after the War, Drs. Otto Gauer and Heinz Haber, then performing research at the Aeromedical Center in Heidelberg, Germany, noted the rapid advance of rocketry and drew some hypothetical conclusions about the effects of zero gravity on the flyer's mind and body.

Briefly, they postulated that the brain receives its information on the position, direction, and support of the body from four perceptual mechanisms: pressure on the nerves and organs, muscle tone, posture, and the labyrinth of the inner ear, which contains a number of small, calcareous particles called otoliths that indicate changes in acceleration and direction by exerting pressure on their hair cells. Drs. Gauer and Haber theorized that the first three of these mechanisms would cease to function properly when weight is removed from the body, and that the otoliths might send signals to the brain which would actually confuse the rocket traveler.

The possibility was serious enough to convince several investigators for the United States Air Force that some means should be found to study the effects of weightlessness under experimental conditions. In June, 1951, Dr. Heinz Haber and his brother, Dr. Fritz Haber, both of whom had by then joined the Department of Space Medicine at the USAF School of Aviation Medicine, published a paper in the *Journal of Aviation Medicine* on "Possible Methods of Producing the Gravity-Free State for Medical Research." They recommended flying a Keplerian trajectory as the only practicable method. Later Dr. Heinz Haber joined this author in a discussion of the "Physics and Psychophysics of Weightlessness," also published in the *Journal of Aviation Medicine*.

In 1951, at Edwards Air Force Base, California, the noted test pilot, Scott Crossfield, made fifty flights in an F-84, following Keplerian trajectories, for the National Advisory Committee on Aeronautics. About thirty of these flights produced zero-gravity conditions for 15 to 40 seconds. The results were inconclusive in some respects. Crossfield reported a feeling of "befuddlement" during the transition into weightlessness, but this feeling disappeared after the fifth flight. He had no sensation of falling, and no loss of muscular coordination other than a tendency to overreach with his arm. He did experience some vertigo occasionally on the pullout after a run.

Crossfield himself conceded that true zero gravity might not have been attained, because in almost every flight considerable drag was felt, indicating a longitudinal deceleration during the trajectory. The pilot of course was strapped to his seat, and had no lack of visual references to compensate for any tendency to disorientation. The period of weightlessness was perhaps too brief to establish any definitive findings.

Similar flights were made at about the same time by Maj. Charles E. Yeager at Edwards Air Force Base and by Dr. E. R. Ballinger with the cooperation of the Fighter Test Branch at Wright-Patterson Air Force Base, Ohio. Dr. Ballinger's observations coincided with Mr. Crossfield's. His subjects expressed the opinion that, if they had not been restrained by seat belts and had been blindfolded, "disorientation might have been extreme." Major Yeager experienced a brief sensation of falling in the transition to the weightless phase. Also he noted some orientational difficulty, which was later described as follows by Dr. Heinz Haber:

> In his thirteenth second of weightlessness, he got the impression that he was spinning around slowly in no particularly defined direction. After 15 seconds he became lost in space, and he pulled out of the parabola. With returning weight, his badly-needed orientation was restored too.

Still, these subjective impressions did not fully confirm or deny the possibility of physiological and psychological disturbances with the prolonged removal of gravity.

A group of researchers, headed by Dr. James P. Henry of the Aero Medical Laboratory at Wright-Patterson Air Force Base, then attacked the problem in a different way. They sent mice up in three test-rocket launchings, with cameras to record their behavior during weightlessness. A V-2 and two Aerobees were used in these experiments.

In the first test, with the V-2, a single animal was carried in a small compartment with a wire-mesh floor. Still photographs were taken at four-second intervals throughout the flight. It was difficult to analyze the subject's reactions by this technique. Signs of disorientation were observed, but the mouse was able to maintain his coordination by clinging to the wire mesh. During the weightless phase, he appeared as comfortable in an inverted position as in any other.

In the later studies, with the Aerobees, cylindrical drums were placed in the rockets, rotating laterally about their axes. Motion pictures were taken during the weightless period of two to three minutes, and again as parachutes braked the rockets' descent, restoring normal weight. In each test the drum was divided by a smooth plexiglas wall into two compartments, with an animal in each, for comparison.

Both compartments in the first Aerobee were equipped with small hurdles, over which the mice had to jump in order to remain on the "bottom" of the drum. The floor of the drum was smooth. One of the animals was normal; the other had lost the labyrinths of the ear, with their directional otoliths.

The normal mouse was much confused by the removal of weight, clutching desperately for some kind of foothold as he floated freely in the compartment. The labyrinthectomized mouse was less disturbed. He received no clues, either true or false, from the otoliths, and was accustomed to his lack of orientation.

In the second Aerobee both mice were normal, but only one was provided with a hurdle on the floor of the rotating drum. This animal clung to the barrier and managed to keep some kind of equilibrium. The other moved violently about the compartment, not only confused by the loss of weight but also seemingly unable to adjust his muscular tension to the small amount of effort required for motion.

Another striking series of animal studies were reported recently by Dr. H. J. A. von Beckh in the *Journal of Aviation Medicine*. For some time Dr. von Beckh has been studying orientation and coordination with a species of South American water turtles. They are particularly suitable for research of this kind, because they move in three dimensions in the water. Ordinarily they strike with deadly accuracy at their food, projecting their long, S-shaped necks like snakes toward the target.

Dr. von Beckh went away for a few days, leaving a caretaker to watch over his laboratory. He returned to find that the water in the turtles' tank was far above a tolerable temperature. Several of the animals were dead. One had lost the use of his labyrinth, which is the main organ of orientation in turtles, as in human beings.

For several weeks the injured turtle was unable to coordinate his movements properly. In striking for his food, he would miss the bait, and had to be hand-fed. Then the animal learned to compensate for the damage to his otoliths by visual orientation. Presently he was as adept as the other turtles in seizing a bait.

At this point Dr. von Beckh placed several of the animals, including the injured one, in a small, open tank, and took them up in a fast two-seater aircraft. He put the plane into a series of dives, securing brief periods of zero gravity. During these periods he tested the coordination of the animals.

One difficulty in the dives was that the water, with the turtles in it, would rise up out of the tank and float above it. Several times it was necessary to lift the tank and fit it around the water again. This was a graphic demonstration of the physical effect of weightlessness.

As von Beckh had expected, the damaged animal was able to snap at his food without trouble during these weightless moments, using the visual cues that he had learned. The normal animals behaved as the turtle with the useless labyrinths had behaved immediately after his accident. In the course of some twenty or thirty flights, however, they too began to regain their coordination.

Von Beckh also did a group of experiments in flight with human subjects. In these he was associated with Dr. von Diringshofen, who first raised the question of the effects of weightlessness in Germany, and who had gone to the Argentine after the War. The subjects were required to draw crosses in seven small squares arranged diagonally across a sheet of paper. The tests were made during weightlessness, sometimes with the eyes open and sometimes when they were closed.

Extreme difficulty was exhibited by the subjects in drawing the crosses under zero-gravity conditions. When their eyes were shut, they lost all sense of orientation. However, as with the turtles, after a considerable number of flights their accuracy improved.

Von Beckh has pointed out another effect of weightlessness that applies in tactical evolutions with conventional planes. He had the pilot dive from about 10,000 to 7,000 feet and pull out rather abruptly, afterwards rising on the ascending arc of a parabola. In this maneuver, after an acceleration of about 6.5-g, the pilot found that his blackout lasted longer, his responses were delayed, and he had the sensation of flying upside down.

Situations of this kind may occur in aerial combat, when fighters dive on a bomber from above, pull up to make the gunnery pass from below, and then dive again to evade the bomber's fire. In such maneuvers the flyer may experience a few moments of weightlessness after high acceleration at the critical point of the attack. The result may be to impair his vision and coordination when he needs them most.

These preliminary studies—all covering weightless conditions of short duration—seem to show that there is a definite tendency to disorientation in a flyer when normal gravity is removed. On the other hand, it appears that the effects can be overcome in time by an experienced pilot, especially if he can fall back on visual points of reference.

In the rocket craft of tomorrow he may have fewer such reference points. Because of the intense and confusing contrasts between light and darkness at very high altitudes, because of the craft's tremendous velocity, and because of the need to shield the flyer against various types of radiation, it may be necessary to close the cabin altogether and to fly solely by instruments. As every pilot knows, instrument flight lends itself more readily than VFR to orientational disturbances.

Beyond that, we have to ask ourselves what may be the effects of a prolonged period of weightlessness, lasting from several minutes to several hours or more. Difficulties which are readily overcome in a few moments of intense concentration may develop subtler and more serious manifestations over an extended time of comparative idleness.

In weightlessness we face a condition which man has never experienced before. We have no precedents on which to predict its effects, and no means of producing it artificially for experimental purposes on the ground. We know that the sensation will be novel and perhaps weird, but we cannot determine in advance just how the psychological symptoms will reveal themselves. We can only explore the subject cautiously as the science of rocket flight advances, and hope that the lifting of this age-old burden from men's bodies will not raise problems so extreme as to incapacitate them.

---

9. Arrested Vision *

WE RARELY stop to ask how much of man's capacity to see is inborn and how much is to be attributed to learning. Yet, for real understanding of how we function, these are important questions. The role of maturation in vision, the variety of cues on which visual perception depends, are still not completely known, but the studies reported in the following paper take us a long step forward. It would be difficult, if not impossible, to get experimental evidence on some aspects of these problems from human subjects. The use of chimpanzees and the ingenuity of these experiments are striking demonstrations of how difficult methodological problems can be solved.

MANY PRIMITIVE ORGANISMS show immediate and highly uniform reactions to light from the moment of birth. In man vision is a much more complex skill that develops gradually through the years of infancy and childhood. How much of this capacity is innate and how much is acquired by learning or through the natural maturation of the eyes during the child's early years? What are the factors that determine visual perception? If we knew the answers to these questions we could do a great deal more than we can now to improve defective vision.

The task of separating the hereditary factors from the effects of experience in human vision obviously is not easy. For example, a new-

* Austin H. Riesen, "Arrested vision," *Scientific American,* CLXXXIII (July, 1950), 16–19. By permission of the author and the publisher.

born infant at first shows no clear indication of any response to a bright disk presented before its eyes. Only after several weeks does the growing infant begin to look at the disk. Is this the result of growth, of experience or of both? Does the change in response come about through practice in the use of the eyes, or through a natural maturation that occurs, quite independently of use, in the retina of the eye, in the eye or neck muscles, in fiber tracts of the central nervous system or in several of these parts combined?

Scientific studies of the growth of behavior have shown that certain abilities do develop without use as animals mature. Thus tadpoles raised under anesthesia to prevent swimming movements nevertheless improve in swimming ability. Chicks and rats kept in darkness for a time show some progress in vision-controlled behavior. Children also demonstrate a basic rate of maturation in some capacities: there is a limit to the degree of retardation or acceleration of these abilities that can be effected by restricting or expanding their training.

But some of these studies have revealed curious contradictions. Wendell Cruze at North Carolina State College found that after newly hatched chicks had been kept in darkness for five days, they were generally able to peck at and hit 24 of the first 25 grains presented to them; this score was 12 per cent better than the average of hits by chicks immediately after hatching. On the other hand, S. G. Padilla at the University of Michigan showed that if the period of darkness was extended to 14 days, the pecking response failed to appear, presumably because the instinct to peck at spots on the ground died out through disuse. The chicks began to starve in the midst of plenty. So it appears that lack of practice, at least if sufficiently prolonged, can interfere with the development of behavior which is basically instinctive or reflex in nature.

In human beings the most nearly pertinent evidence on this problem has come from studies of patients operated upon at advanced ages for congenital cataracts. These patients, who have passed all their lives in near-blindness, ranging from the bare ability to tell day from night to some ability to distinguish colors and localize light, invariably report an immediate awareness of a change after a successful operation. They begin at once to distinguish differences in the parts of the visual field, although they cannot identify an object or describe its shape. After a few days' practice they can name colors. From this point on progress is slow, often highly discouraging, and some patients never get beyond the ability to distinguish brightness and color. Others, over a period of months and even years, develop the ability to identify simple geometric figures, read letters and numbers and, in rare cases, to identify complex patterns such as words, outline drawings and faces. During their efforts to improve their visual skill the patients go through a long period of picking out elements in an object and inferring the nature of the object from these elements—often erroneously. For example, a child of 12, some months after her operation, is reported by her doctor to have pointed to a picture and called it "a camel, because it has a hump." What she identified as a hump was the dorsal fin of a fish.

But such cases of congenital cataract do not give us very satisfactory evidence on the elementary problem of how disuse affects the development of visual behavior. There are too many other variables; we must take into account (1) the degree of the patient's previous blindness, since he was not in total darkness, (2) the limit that is imposed on his potentialities for improvement by the fact that the eye operated on lacks a lens, and (3) the circumstance that in all these cases there appears to be another visual handicap—jerky movements of the eyeballs known as spontaneous nystagmus. The effects of these combined difficulties are not readily calculable. For a more meaningful study it is highly desirable to eliminate these variables by setting up a controlled experiment that will determine the effects of disuse on normal eyes. Obviously such an experiment cannot be risked in human beings; no one would wish to impose permanent reading difficulties on any person having to adjust himself to a civilized society. The most logical subject for the experiments is another higher primate. The chimpanzee was chosen, because its behavior, like man's, is dominated by vision, and because it is intelligent and tractable.

In 1942 at the Yerkes Laboratories of Primate Biology in Orange Park, Fla., an infant male chimpanzee was separated from its mother on the day of birth and blindfolded with a gauze bandage and adhesive tape. This animal defeated the experimenters by loosening the tape at the side of his left nostril and habitually peeking down his nose with his left eye. By the age of 16 weeks he gained full freedom from facial bandages. Although he did not recognize his feeding bottle at this time, nor show fixation of persons or objects, he developed fairly adequate visual behavior within a few weeks.

In 1945 the experimenters tried again. This time two newborn chimpanzee infants, a male and a female respectively named Snark and Alfalfa, were housed in a completely darkened room. During the first 16 months the only light these infants experienced was an electric lamp turned on for intervals of 45 seconds several times daily for their routine care and feeding. When they were first tested for visual perception at the age of 16 months, both chimpanzees showed extreme incompetence. Their reflex responses indicated that their eyes were sensitive to light—the pupils constricted; sudden changes of illumination startled the animals; they responded to a slowly waving flashlight with jerky pursuit movements of the eyes and side to side following motions of the head. But both chimpanzees failed to show any visual responses to complex patterns of light until after they had spent many hours in illuminated surroundings. They did not respond to play objects or their feeding bottles unless these touched some part of the body. They did not blink at a threatening motion toward the face. When an object was advanced slowly toward the face, there was no reaction until the object actually touched the face, and then the animal gave a startled jump.

After the 16-month period of darkness, Alfalfa was placed on a limited light schedule until the age of 21 months and Snark until 33 months. When Alfalfa was later moved into a normal daylight environment, in the course of many months she developed normal recognition of objects, began to blink in response to threats and ceased to be startled by a touch. Snark was much more retarded. Between the ages of 20 and 27 months, while he was still on rationed light, he learned after many hundreds of trials to tell the difference between contrasting signs, differing in color or pattern, which indicated either food or a mild electric shock. His visual acuity, as measured by ability to discriminate between horizontal and vertical lines, was well below that of normally raised animals. At the end of 33 months he began to live in the normally lighted chimpanzee nursery and later out of doors with chimpanzees of his own age. It was expected that he would rapidly acquire normal visual behavior. He did improve slightly at first, but after this small initial improvement he actually lost ground in visual responsiveness, until even reflex activity began to die away.

What is the explanation of this deterioration? Had the development of his eyes been permanently arrested by the absence of light? There had been no previous evidence that stimulation by light is essential for the normal growth of the primate retina or optic nerve. It was a surprise to find that, while the eyes of these chimpanzees remained sensitive to light after 16 months in darkness, the retina and optic disk in both animals did not reflect as much light as normal chimpanzee eyes do. Snark later developed a marked pallor of the optic disk in both eyes. There is other evidence suggesting that fish and amphibians, at least, need light-stimulation for normal eye development. So the physiological effects of the lack of light may be part of the explanation for Snark's loss of visual function. But it is not the whole explanation for all the visual abnormalities in these two chimpanzees, nor does it explain the visual difficulties of the cataract patients. These patients have excellent color discrimination, and, incidentally, do not show pallor of the optic disk. Moreover, we now have clear evidence from further experiments with chimpanzees that not merely light itself but stimulation by visual patterns is essential to normal visual development.

In these experiments three other newborn chimpanzees, two females and a male, were put into the darkroom. Debi was raised for seven months in complete darkness, even during her feedings and other care. Kora was raised for the same period on a ration of an average of one and a half hours of light daily, but the light, admitted through a white Plexiglas mask, was diffuse and unpatterned. Lad was given one and a half hours of patterned light daily: he could observe the edges of his crib, the variations in pattern introduced by movements of his own body and appendages, and all the accompaniments of bottle-feeding, including the moving about of persons in the moderately lighted room.

At seven months, when the three subjects were removed to normal daylight surroundings, Lad's visual performance was indistinguishable from that of chimpanzees raised normally. Kora and Debi, however, showed the same kinds of retardation as had Snark and Alfalfa, with some minor exceptions. Kora did not develop the blink response to a moving object until six days after her removal from darkness, and Debi not until 15 days. It took Kora 13 days and Debi 30 days to acquire the ability to pursue a moving person with the eyes, and they did this by a series of refixations instead of following smoothly as normal animals of comparable age do; it took Kora 20 days and Debi 16 days to pursue visually a moving feeding bottle; Kora 13 days and Debi 30 days to fixate the image of a stationary person.

These differences between Debi and Kora may lie within the range of variation that would occur in a group of animals treated exactly the same as either Debi or Kora. This question could be checked only by repeating the experiment many times.

Between seven and 10 months of age Debi and Kora both showed a moderate and intermittent outward (wall-eyed) deviation of the eyes. This gradually was overcome. Both infants also showed an initial spontaneous nystagmus, *i.e.,* jerky eye movements. It appeared only sporadically, and was more pronounced under general excitement than when the animals were well relaxed.

Normal animals of seven months learned to avoid a large yellow and black striped disk after receiving one or two mild electric shocks from it. Debi and Kora, however, were shocked by the disk twice a day for six and nine days, respectively, before they so much as whimpered when it was shown. Only after 13 days in Kora's case and 15 days in Debi's did they consistently indicate by some sort of avoidance response that they saw the disk within five seconds of the time that it was raised in front of their eyes.

In still another study an infant chimpanzee named Kandy was put in the darkroom for only the first three months of life. After she was removed to daylight surroundings, her progress on the same tests was approximately parallel to that of Debi and Kora. There were three interesting differences: 1) Kandy showed a convergent squint (cross-eyes), which cleared up in a little less than two months; 2) she did not have spontaneous nystagmus; 3) she required 24 days, as compared with 13 or 15, to develop consistent avoidance of the black and yellow shock-disk. The last difference suggests that Kandy learned more slowly because of her younger age; in other words, that the development of visual discrimination was a matter of maturity as well as learning. This conclusion was strongly supported by the finding that an infant chimpanzee started through the same training at the age of two days failed to show avoidance in a month's time.

All these observations demonstrate that vision must be put to use if it is to develop normally, but they also indicate that during the first few months of an infant's life visual development is advanced by growth factors which are entirely independent of practice. Normally reared animals, for example, do not blink in response to the movement of objects across the visual field until they have reached the age of two months; the older darkroom animals, despite previous lack of experience, began to show this response within about two weeks after they were transferred to daylight surroundings.

The development and maintenance of normal visual functions in higher primates depends on a whole complex of interrelated factors, hereditary and environmental, and it can readily be disturbed at any stage of the individual's growth. This was shown in an experiment with a chimpanzee named Faik. Faik was raised in the normal light of the laboratory's nursery until the age of seven months. At that time the standard series of tests described above showed that he had excellent use of vision. Then from the age of eight to 24 months he was kept in the darkroom. He lived an active life filled with tactile, auditory, olfactory, gustatory and kinesthetic stimulation. He invited rough-house play from his caretakers at feeding times, and his general state of health remained entirely satisfactory.

When Faik was returned to daylight living quarters at 24 months, he had lost all ability to utilize vision in his interplay with the environment. He no longer recognized the feeding bottle, and failed to look at objects or persons, either stationary or moving. More than this, he possessed a strong spontaneous nystagmus and was even unable to follow a moving light in a darkroom until the fifth day after he was put back into a lighted environment. His first visual following movements, like those of all the darkroom-raised subjects, were not smooth but a series of jerky refixations, made even more jerky by the pronounced spontaneous nystagmus.

Even in direct sunlight Faik failed to grimace or close his eyelids; he gave no indication of the slightest discomfort when the sun shone in his eyes. (The chimpanzees raised in the darkroom from birth did close their lids in intense light.) Faik showed pallor similar to that of Snark and Alfalfa in his optic disks. His recovery of vision has been slow and is still only partial. Explanation of his case, and that of Snark, remains a challenge to further research.

These chimpanzee studies have established several fundamental points. They show that newborn animals, and older infants that have been kept in darkness for a time, exhibit visual reflexes when they are first subjected to light. Some responses that bear a close resemblance to reflex behavior, such as blinking at something rapidly approaching the face, become automatic only after considerable practice. Visual pursuit of moving objects, the coordination of the two eyes and convergent fixation, and the first recognition of objects come only after many hours or weeks of experience in use of the eyes. It takes the chimpanzee hundreds of hours of active utilization of the eyes to develop its vision to the stage where it can adequately guide locomotion and complex manipulations. The findings in the cases of two subjects that were kept in darkness for long periods indicate that the postponement of light exposure for too long can result in making the development of normal visual mechanisms extremely difficult if not impossible.

---

10. The Role of Set in Perceptual Judgment *

THIS STUDY is an example of a well-controlled demonstration of the importance of "set" in making perceptual judgments. The results of the experiment clearly show that routinization of response, habit, and expectancy all tend to influence our perceptions and the judgments and inferences we draw from them.

A. THE PROBLEM

RECENT psychological literature witnesses an ever increasing emphasis upon the role of the perceiver in the process of perception. This well merited accord has been the result of a long overdue recognition of the

* Ludwig Immergluck, "The role of set in perceptual judgment," *The Journal of Psychology,* XXXIV (1952), 181–89. By permission of the author and The Journal Press.

importance of variables other than those inherent in the structure of the stimulus for the total process of perceiving. The distinction between the structure of the perceiver, as it were, and the structure of the stimulus is by no means a new one. Accounts of "subjective factors," "private meanings," "individual differences," or "situational conditions" are to be found in the oldest writings in this field. To be sure, they are most likely to appear in footnotes, or else are dismissed by some as annoying deviations, a kind of nuisance by-product of the experiment but, nevertheless, they do make their stubborn appearance. Gestaltists, too, who have perhaps paid most of the attention to stimulus characteristics, distinguish between a "behavioral" and a "geographic" environment, although they have not brought forth much work concerned with systematic investigations of the "behavioral environment." What has emerged, however, that is new on the horizon of experimental work on perception is the recognition of the necessity to change these "subjective factors" and "individual differences" from hardly audible asides into lines of the major plot and, furthermore, to study these variables with systematic, experimental rigor.

Although much of the recent experimental work in perception is being produced under the slogan of "Perception and Personality," one should be reminded that "factors other than those inherent in the structure of the stimulus" encompass really a variety of areas and sources of variables not all of which are direct expressions of personality, at least not as the term is generally understood. Some studies deal, for example, with the influence of the immediate experimental situation, such as verbal instructions, tension, tension release, frustration, to name but a few, upon the perception of presented stimuli. Others investigate the importance of physiological drives; still others have as their concern social attitudes and values as perceptual determiners. The relationship between more basic personality traits and perceptual stimuli is, of course, exemplified by most projective technique studies. In spite of the numerous and often very divergent theoretical orientations, the common element underlying all these investigations is their desire to lay bare, in systematic fashion, the variables or hierarchy of variables that enter into the complex make-up of a perceptual response. Certainly, the distinction between the autistic and the veridical aspect of perception characterizing the current experimental orientation, emerges as a very fruitful one and promises to lead not only to greater understanding of the perceptual process as such, but perhaps to badly needed new conceptualizations in personality theory as well.

Among the vast array of studies concerned with the effect of antecedent conditions upon perception, the rôle of *mental sets* has been given intense attention. Typically, early investigators in this area have attempted to demonstrate that specified attitudes on part of the subject result in *selective perception,* i.e., accentuate certain aspects of the stimulus while neglecting others. A classical experiment by Kuelpe may be cited as an example of this type of study, where subjects who were confronted with tachistoscopic presentation of a sequence of colored letters were unable to report the colors if they were *set* to count the letters or to describe their spatial relationship. More recent studies, employing reversible figures, showed similar results by demonstrating that a subject's preparatory set will tend to favor the perception of one of the figures to the relative exclusion of other perceptual possibilities. Great popularity has been enjoyed, particularly recently, by studies exploring the influence of preparatory attitudes upon the perception of ambiguous stimuli. Carmichael, Hogan, and Walter's experiment constitutes a representative study of this nature. These investigators showed that the perceptual responses of subjects who were presented with a series of ambiguous drawings (such as a drawing that could be interpreted either as a "boat" or a "kidney bean") would conform to previously given experimental instructions. A multitude of other studies, utilizing vaguely structured material, dim illumination, or tachistoscopic exposures have been yielding data that begin to spell out pertinent variables underlying the rôle of perceiver attitudes in perceptual responses.

Even in a cursory survey of research writings on the functions of mental sets, one is immediately struck by the loose usage of the term and by the great variety of different behavior and attitudes that fall under its label. Actually, any predisposing factors operating at the moment a perceptual response takes place may be subsumed under a broad definition of *set.* In this sense, social attitudes, needs, values, complex personality traits may all be conceived as "preparatory sets" influencing or determining an individual's perceptions at a given moment. Such broad definition, however, loses its heuristic usefulness and probably obscures more than it clarifies our understanding of perceptual determiners. Gibson, in a very comprehensive critical review of the rôle of set in psychological experimentation, comments on the wide variety of meanings with which this term has become imbued and pleads for greater clarity.

B. THE DEFINITION

The present report addresses itself to a study of the effect of set on perceptual judgment. In the light of the above considerations, it becomes imperative to state at the outset the specific meaning this term is given here: *Set, as used in the present investigation, denotes a perseveration tendency of a response. It implies the establishment of a response-mechanism which is maintained even though environmental conditions or changes in the structure of stimuli demand a different or a new type of behavior.*

Many investigations, particularly in the area of human problem solving, adhere, at least implicitly, to this type of definition. Although it is not possible within the confines of this paper to review even briefly studies in this area, it will prove very fruitful to consider some aspects of one particular set of experiments which, in its methodology and general design, is very pertinent for the present investigation. The series of experiments under consideration concern A. S. Luchins' studies on the effect of *Einstellung* or set upon problem solving behavior. The subjects in Luchins' investigation were required to reason out on paper how to obtain a specified volume of water, given certain empty jars for measure. A typical problem was: "Given jars with gallon capacity 21 127 3, obtain 100 gallons." To solve this problem, the center jar has to be filled first, then from it the jar to the right filled twice and the jar to the left once, leaving the correct amount of water in the center jar. Subsequently, the subjects were presented with a series of similar problems, all of which could be solved by the very same method. When later in the series a problem was introduced which could be solved in a much more direct way, the subjects tended to carry over into the new situation the rather involved habituated solution process. The set effect seemed to "blind" them to seeing *other* possibilities involving different methods. In this connection, it is interesting to observe that the habituation and mechanical application of such problem solving responses are less dependent upon intelligence than one might suspect. Among the subjects who fell prey to such mechanizations were included college and graduate students and many holders of the Ph.D. and M.D. degrees.

Examining the characteristics of the mechanization process in Luchins' subjects, we notice first of all that their responses to the presented stimuli underwent a *qualitative change*. The behavior elicited by the first problem was different from that exhibited later on. Thus, first contact with the task evoked responses that had the familiar attributes of problem solving activity (e.g., exploration, searching for relationships, etc.). Further intercourse with subsequent similar tasks, however, appeared to be accompanied by a *diminishing* of these attributes until the behavior became finally transformed from the original problem solving activity into the observed mechanized or *routinized* response.

The tendency towards this type of routinization can be demonstrated in wide areas of human behavior [1] as well as in the findings of a number of experimental studies. Its exact nature and operation remain, from a conceptual viewpoint, largely in the dark. What are the specific functions of routinization? What adaptive purposes (if any) does it serve? What factors, including personality variables, will tend to favor its occurrence? These are questions that still await research based answers. In a careful scrutiny, however, of the multitude of conditions under which such routinized behavior occurs, as well as in consideration of the experimental data available, a starting hypothesis regarding the nature of set suggests itself. In the light of this hypothesis, *set* is assumed to be an expression of a postulated *Principle of Economy* characterizing a response. According to this principle, behavior is viewed as possessing a tendency to express itself in the most simple, in the most *economical* fashion. Routinization of a response is one such expression of economy. In Luchins' experiment it was more economical, in the sense of requiring less energy expenditure than would be involved in more active problem solving activity, to apply mechanically a once found solution that has repeatedly proved satisfactory to new situations. The hypothesis implies further that the tendency towards routinization will become behaviorally pronounced whenever environmental conditions make the application of a mechanized response possible. Turning to Luchins' investigation again, repeated presentation of problems that *could* be solved by a rote response made the exhibited mechanization possible. Similar propitious environmental conditions, whether they go under the label of "pre-training," "past experience," "channelization" or other titles, underlie all comparable set experiments.

The present study is concerned with an examination of some aspects of the rôle of *set* in the area of perceptual judgment. Specifically, the experimental questions raised are:

(a) To what extent are simple perceptual responses subject to routinization?

(b) How will such routinization affect perceptual judgment?

In terms of the present experimental design, the questions may be restated: Will a series of perceptual responses that were adequate in previous situations be carried over to new perceptual tasks in which they are no longer valid?

[1] In a sense, certain rigidly maintained social attitudes and prejudices may be conceived as a function of routinization. Social responses that may have been adequate in a number of highly specific situations and are now mechanically carried over into new situations constitute such examples.

C. THE EXPERIMENT

Thirty-two female college students ranging in age from 17.5 to 21.5 years constituted the total subject group. The subjects were divided into two groups, an Experimental and a Control Group, each consisting of 16 individuals.

The experimental material consisted of two series of 6″ × 4″ cards, each containing a pair of simple geometric designs. The figures on

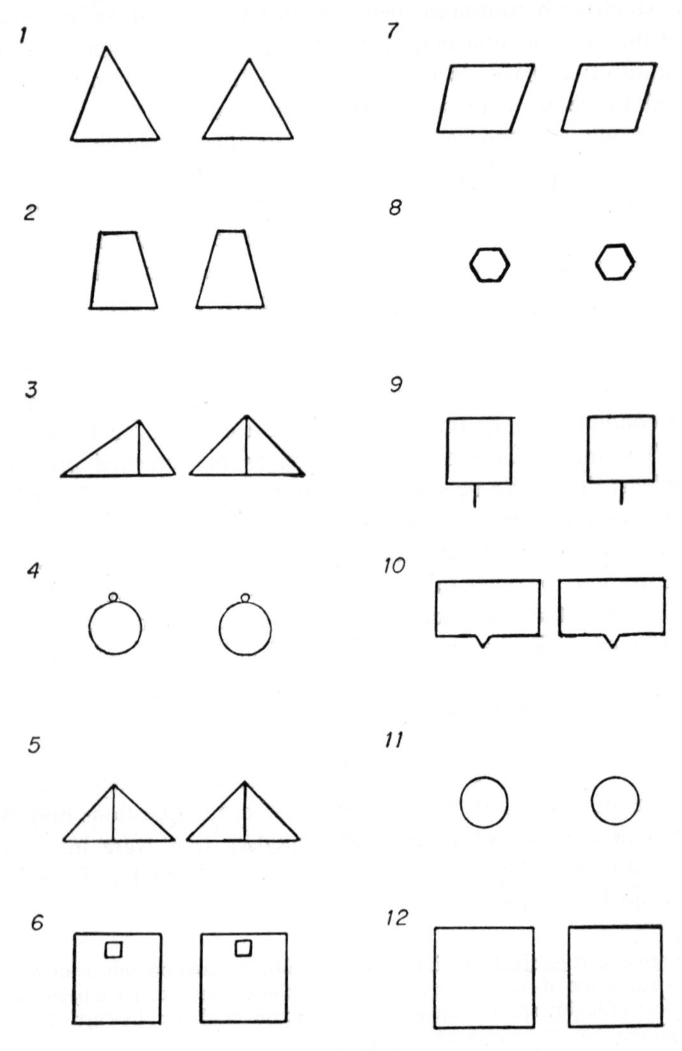

FIGURE 1

every card, although very similar to each other, were of such nature that one of them constituted a better, a more perfect geometric design. The cards were divided into two series, the *Set Series* in which the more perfect figures were always on the *right* side, and the *Mixed Series* in which the better figure appeared on the right on some cards and on the left on others, in mixed order. The twelfth card constituted the *Test Card* and was identical for both groups. This card contained two designs with the *left* figure representing a perfect geometric square (58mm^2) and the right a rectangle approaching squareness (54mm $\times$ 58mm). The experimental series, including the Test Card, is shown in Figure 1 approximately 1/10 of the actual size. The Mixed Series contained the identical figures except that on Cards 2, 5, 7, 9, 10 the geometrically better figure appeared on the left side.

The design of the experimental procedure was as follows: The Experimental Group was given a sequence presentation of the Set Series with the Test Card offered last; the Control Group was presented with the Mixed Series also followed by the last card. The procedure of presenting the cards was the following: The cards were placed in a stack, face down, in front of each subject and approximately 12 inches away. Each card was then exposed separately for 4 seconds.[2] The subjects were instructed to indicate by saying either "right" or "left" on which side the better figure occurred. Care was taken in instructing them to use only the specific geometric criterion asked for rather than any esthetic or other values in their judgment of the "better" or "more perfect" figure. Then, before each card was presented, the subjects were asked a specific pertinent question, such as: Which is the more symmetrical figure? or, Which is the better circle?, and in the final Test Card: Which is the better square? Responses to all presented designs were recorded.

D. RESULTS AND DISCUSSION

The judgments with regard to the position of the correct square on the Test Card given by both subject groups are summarized in Table 1. The statistical significance of the difference of the position judgments between the two groups, as determined by the difference of the Standard Errors of the percentage of correct judgments for each group, is greater than at the one per cent level of confidence.

[2] The 4-second exposure was chosen because some exploratory work in which the test figures were presented to a group of individuals drawn from the same population, showed that approximately this exposure time represented the maximum time needed for correct identification of the square.

TABLE 1

Comparison of Test Card Judgments Between Experimental and Control Groups

	Experimental group	*Control group*
N	*16*	*16*
Correct placement of square	3	14
Per cent of incorrect judgments	81.2	12.5

It can be seen very readily that exposure of the Set Series resulted in the establishment of a *positional set* in the subjects of the Experimental Group which distorted their judgment of the Test Figures. Repeated presentation of a better figure on the right side of the card established a "right side" expectancy which was carried over to the Test Card where the *rectangle was perceived as a square* (and by implication the square as a rectangle). In terms, then, of the original experimental questions posed, the results indicate that (*a*) perceptual responses are subject to routinization and (*b*) such sets have a significant influence upon perceptual judgment; in the present situation, they resulted in an alteration of perceptual judgment.

An evaluation of the implications of the present data demands that two points be borne in mind. First, *set,* within the definitional framework of this study, implies that the exhibited routinization tendency is a response attribute which has emerged behaviorally as a result of the structure of the experimental conditions. In that sense, it has to be distinguished from other perceptually predisposing conditions that are primarily an outgrowth of specific personality variables, basic needs, social values, etc. The choice of geometric designs as the experimental material for the present study was made precisely to preclude, as much as possible, any stimulus implications of such values or needs.[3] There was no such "need" or "emotional predisposition" to perceive the rectangle as a square. It is postulated that this perceptual distortion occurred because the preceding conditions made the tendency towards routinization behaviorally possible. In terms of the suggested hypothesis, after the position "right" has proved repeatedly adequate, it became more *economical* to perceive in mechanical fashion figures on the right as the better ones.

The second important point to be kept in mind concerns the structure of the stimulus material. It should be remembered that in most

[3] This does, of course, not imply that emotional and personality factors are not operant in set. However, in order to isolate the routinization process as such, emotional and personality variables have to be experimentally minimized.

of the studies dealing with the influence of personality factors upon perception, the stimulus objects presented are usually *ambiguous*. Ambiguity may be achieved in different ways, such as a particular structuring or lack of structuring of the stimulus material, dim illumination, etc. Tachistoscopic exposure, too, represents an ambiguous situation, even when more structured material is presented, in the sense that it does not permit the subject to come to full grips with the material offered. Ambiguity implies that the stimulus itself possesses intrinsic characteristics that make it possible for its being perceived in more than one way. Thus, in reversible figures both perceptual possibilities are part of the stimulus structure; Hogan, Carmichael, and Walter's drawings did look like a number of different objects, and inkblots have almost unlimited *intrinsic* perceptual possibilities. In the present study, however, the intrinsic characteristics of the test figures possessed no such multiperceptual possibilities and subjects not influenced by a positional set showed no difficulty in distinguishing between the square and rectangle.[4] The present findings, then, suggest an interpretation not so much in terms of a perceptual selection or accentuation of properties resident in the structure of the stimulus, but rather as a *perceptual distortion* of the presented stimulus material. It must be emphasized, of course, that the terms "ambiguity" or "lack of ambiguity" denote *relative* degrees of structuredness or *relatively* small or wide latitudes of perceptual possibilities. Our rectangle was relatively ambiguous in the sense that it did resemble a square, and it was relatively unambiguous in the sense that subjects uninfluenced by set conducive conditions recognized its objective characteristics very readily.

The question regarding the extent to which set behavior will be carried into situations characterized by increasing degrees of structuredness constitutes an experimental challenge and invites further investigation.

The importance of individual differences influencing the establishment of sets is underlined by the three members of the Experimental Group who did not exhibit the observed positional set effect. In another paper data will be presented which is specifically concerned with identifying the interrelationship of some personality and motivational factors and the ease with which perceptual routinization responses are established as well as the tenaciousness with which they are maintained.

[4] It should be noted that the two members of the control group who did give a wrong judgment of the square also misjudged other figures in antecedent cards, among them some that involved exceedingly easy discrimination. It seems, therefore, that their failure to identify the correct square can be interpreted as the result of a general poor perceptual judgment or some other factors rather than in terms of structural ambiguity inherent in the test figures.

The present study was specifically aimed to demonstrate the nature of some factors underlying perceptual routinization.

---

11. The Effects of Attitudes on Descriptions of Pictures *

THIS IS an experimental demonstration that perception can be influenced by attitudes. The attitudes in this case—happiness, criticalness, and anxiety—were induced by hypnosis for the experiment. (Though there are still many unsolved problems concerning hypnotism, they need not interfere with our acceptance of the findings of this research.) The conclusion of the study that moods, feelings, and attitudes play an important role in our perceptions and general intellectual life are supported by a wealth of case material in the psychological literature and anecdotal accounts from everyday life.

THIS PAPER deals with the effects of three hypnotically induced attitudes —happiness, criticalness, and anxiety—upon observation and thought. Three *S*s described a series of pictures when under the influence of each of these attitudes.

INTRODUCTION

Laymen as well as psychologists are well aware that attitudes, sets, moods, and other internal conditions may greatly affect both perception and thought. Nevertheless, it is only in recent years that a few experimental psychologists have brought the intellectual effects of these internal conditions under scientific scrutiny. When perception, memory, and intelligence are studied in the laboratory under simplified, objective, unemotional—almost inhuman—circumstances, factors like anxiety or resentment, which are of the highest importance in the everyday functioning of these processes, are overlooked. Gardner Murphy brings this out forcefully in his 1944 presidential address to the American Psychological Association.

A new trend is indicated by Bartlett's and Rapaport's studies of the

* Clarence Leuba and Charles Lucas, "The effects of attitudes on descriptions of pictures," *Journal of Experimental Psychology,* XXXV (1945), 517–24. By permission of the authors and the American Psychological Association.

effects of attitudes and emotions on remembering, by Murray's study of the influence of fear upon children's estimates of the maliciousness of other personalities, and by Sanford's and Levine, Chein, and Murphy's investigations of the perceptual distortions produced by various degrees of hunger.

Though projective techniques were originally developed to discover an individual's attitudes and other characteristics, they can also be useful for discovering the influence of known attitudes on perception and thought. Proshansky in a recent experiment found that liberals and conservatives, as determined by an attitude scale, could be reliably detected from their descriptions of suitably chosen pictures. In an unpublished experiment we found that, according to three judges, there were three times as many indications of anti-labor sentiments in the descriptions of six photographs of economic scenes by two anti-labor *S*s as in those by two pro-labor *S*s.

In these studies, the experimenters limited themselves to investigating the effects of already present attitudes on the description of pictures. Under ordinary circumstances the creation in the laboratory of the particular attitudes one wishes to study is difficult if not almost impossible. By using hypnosis, however, almost any attitude, set, or mood can be very readily created. In hypnosis the experimental psychologist has a technique for controlling variables in situations otherwise beyond the reach of psychological experimentation. Erickson's investigations provide many illustrations of the successful use of post-hypnotic suggestions for the creation and study of such moods as resentment or jealousy. Other investigators have been able to study the effects of hypnotically induced elation, depression, and hypochondria upon Rorschach records.

PROCEDURE

The present experiment involved the description of six pictures by three *S*s when in each of three different moods: happy, critical, and anxious. The *S*s—upperclass students in their early twenties, one man and two girls—were picked from a number of volunteers because of the ease with which they could be made to pass into the deepest stages of hypnosis.

The six photographs were chosen from current magazines. They showed young people of college age in a variety of situations, such as attending a seminar, digging in a swampy area, jitterbugging, engaging in battle activities, and lying on a sunny campus.

Each of the three *S*s completed his portion of the experiment at one sitting and independently of the others. Each knew nothing of the experiment's purpose. The process of creating each of the three moods was done gradually, after the *S* had been deeply hypnotized. The final suggestion for the happy mood was as follows: "Now you are feeling very happy and you are in a cheerful and joyous mood. You feel as if everything is rosy and you are very optimistic. You have a comfortable feeling of well-being; nothing is worrying you. You feel perfectly at peace with everything and everyone. You are in a very happy, cheerful, and optimistic mood." It was noticed incidentally that facial expression tended to change with each mood.

After the *S* had described all six pictures, he was told to relax, close his eyes, and rest awhile. The happy mood was removed and the *S* was brought back to his "normal" hypnotic state. He was told that he would forget having seen the pictures just shown and that he would also forget what he had said about them. Then the *S* was gradually put into a critical mood. The final suggestion was: "Now you are very critical; you are quick to find fault and to condemn unfavorably. Your judgment of others is very harsh and severe. You see failings and faults very clearly. You are very critical and fault finding." The procedure of showing the six pictures, taking down the descriptions, then wiping out the induced mood, and suggesting amnesia for the pictures and for what had been said, was the same as for the happy mood.

The final suggestion in producing the last or anxious mood was: "Now you are quite anxious. You are disturbed over some possible misfortunes. You are disquieted and concerned as to something in the future. You are a little fearful and mildly alarmed. You have a feeling as if you were expecting something disagreeable to happen, yet were not sure that it would. You are quite anxious."

In each mood, Subject A was told to tell something about what was seen, as well as exactly what he saw in each picture. As a result A's reports tend toward accounts of what he thought about the situation pictured, or of what it reminded him. Subjects B and C were told to tell only what they saw in each picture; consequently they limited themselves more to what was actually in the picture and added less interpretative material. The pictures had no titles and were shown one by one always in the same order. None of the *S*s showed any recollection of having seen the pictures while in the preceding mood. The *E* wrote down each *S*'s description of each picture as he gave it (see Table I on pages 90–93).

RESULTS AND CONCLUSIONS

The induced attitudes are influential in determining what the *S* observes. In the happy mood, A describes picture IV as "a wonderful faculty group"; but in the anxious mood A's attention is focused entirely upon one recently deceased member of that group. The moods are much more noticeable, however, in their effects on the interpretation of what is observed. The meanings and feelings attached to the activities shown in the pictures and the probable causes and results of those activities are usually very different from mood to mood. In a happy frame of mind the *S*s see the soldier in picture III "as being well taken care of," and as being taken "back to safety," or to a "transport plane." When in an anxious mood these same *S*s say the soldier "is in bad shape," "may not live," "an emergency case," "it frightens me." After viewing picture VI, when in a happy mood, A says the boys are "lying on campus . . . having a good time." But when in a critical mood, A describes the boys as "loafing"; and when in an anxious mood, A thinks of them as maybe "overseas, or wounded, or dead." Attitudes exert a directive influence both on what is observed and on the train of thoughts suggested by the observations.

To gain a more objective appraisal of the extent to which the three attitudes actually influenced observation and thought, the 54 statements shown in the charts were typed on slips of paper and, after being thoroughly shuffled, were submitted to three judges. The instructions given the judges were: "The statements you have been given are brief descriptions of pictures. Indicate how many times, if any, each of these three attitudes or moods is expressed or implied in each statement: (1) HAPPINESS—cheerfulness, joy, optimism, well-being, satisfaction, approval of things as they are, contentment; (2) CRITICALNESS—faultfinding, condemnation, disapproval, dissatisfaction with things as they are; (3) ANXIETY—concern over the outcome of events, foreseeing unfavorable outcomes."

Descriptions made by the *S*s when in a happy mood averaged, according to the three judges, 2.33 indications of happiness, .24 indications of criticalness and .13 indications of anxiety (Table II). Under the critical mood, the average statement had three indications of criticalness and negligible indications of each of the other two attitudes. The effect of the anxious mood was not quite so clearcut: anxiety was indicated 1.44 times per statement, happiness .17 times, and criticalness .50 times. In every case the difference between the mean number of indications of the induced mood and the mean number of indications of each of the other two moods was statistically significant.

TABLE 1

Descriptions of Pictures Given by Subjects in Different Moods

Pictures	*Subject A*	*Subject B*	*Subject C*
		HAPPY ATTITUDE	
I. Young people digging in a swampy area.	It looks like fun; reminds me of summer. That's what life is for: working out in the open, really living—digging in the dirt, planting, watching things growing.	Nice summer day. Working. Cool feet in water. Nice lot of food when they get through.	Boys and girls digging. Trees, stream, shovel. Mud all over them. Corn or wheat and shadow of a mountain in the background. Digging for irrigation or maybe planting something.
II. Colored people jitterbugging.	Having a good time. No matter what people say, they have a sense of rhythm. We whites miss that enjoyment; we worry too much.	Village—some night when they're really hot and having a good time. Just hilariousness.	Men and women jitterbugging. Zoot suit. Satin shorts on girl. They're having a good time; maybe a play of some sort.
III. Wounded man being carried on litter by soldiers to aeroplane.	Wounded soldier. Good thing men were there to help him and get him to a hospital. The men in this war are well taken care of.	Restfulness after a hard day's fight. Taking a guy back to safety from a battlefield.	Man being carried by litter bearers. Clouds and palms, canteen and flying jackets. Wounded being taken to a transport plane. Maybe Florida.
IV. Seminar around fireplace at faculty home.	Wonderful faculty group—it's wonderful, you don't find it everywhere. That's what's important in college; less book-learning.	Fireplace, home. All relaxed. Just a feeling of mellowness.	Woman reading to a group of people. Fireplace, clock, figures on mantle, books, fire. I like this. Very comfortable looking. Looks like fireplace at home.
V. Waist gunner in action in a bomber.	It's funny how they dress them up—protected from injury by machine. Now, they care more about the individual. Best possible working conditions.	Lot of work and exertion. Firing a gun in the heat of battle.	Looks like a monkey. Machine gun, empty cartridges. Oxygen mask, heavy clothing. Excellent composition, good photography.

VI. Four college men on sunny lawn typing, reading, listening to radio.	Before the war. Boys lying on campus listening to radio and reading. Not getting much done but having a good time. That's fun though.	Complete relaxation. Not much to do—just sit, listen, and relax. Not much at all to think about.	Sunbathers, radio, books, studying and typing in the sunshine. It must be a very warm and restful place.
	CRITICAL ATTITUDE		
I. Young people digging in a swampy area.	Pretty horrible land. There ought to be something more useful for kids of that age to do instead of digging in that stuff. It's filthy and dirty and good for nothing.	Digging a ditch in slimy mud. Girls working there too, tsk, tsk. Looks like pretty hard work.	People digging and getting all dirty. The spade is not being held right. Don't look very clean. Stalks all battered down.
II. Colored people jitterbugging.	Negroes jitterbugging as usual; that's all they do. Unaesthetic; no one enjoys looking at it. Nothing good about it. They should be directed into other than useless activity.	One guy looks deformed. Seems to be having a good time though. Kid looks pretty young. Savoy or New York City. Probably all lit.	Bunch of crazy jitterbugs. He looks like a runt. Sort of silly because of the clothes and the movements they're making. All night binge. Don't like checks with stripes. Only one looks half decent.
III. Wounded man being carried on litter by soldiers to aeroplane.	Wounded or killed soldier; one more in a million who are just killing each other off. That's war, I guess. We must think it's fun or we wouldn't do something so useless as murder and destruction.	Wounded man being taken to safety, but a lot of good it does now. Looks as if they're in a hurry—must be pretty badly hurt. Must have been a tough scrap.	Fellows carrying away sleeping man. Movie set. Hands don't look natural or as if they're carrying something. The picture is artificial and was posed for.
IV. Seminar around fireplace at faculty home.	People sitting around talking. Sometimes we run up blind alleys arguing for the sake of argument.	Guy here looks disgusted. Grandmother looks bored. One gal is looking daggers. Grandpa doesn't look comfortable.	Woman reading to a bunch of unhappy people. Everything in the room is too formal. Reader is not comfortable. Girl with middy looks droopy. White-haired woman has a long face. I don't like picture.

TABLE I (*continued*)

Pictures	*Subject A*	*Subject B*	*Subject C*
	CRITICAL ATTITUDE (*continued*)		
V. Waist gunner in action in a bomber.	Typical example of man hiding away from himself. Closing himself in a factory. He doesn't know where he is going. Same thing every day and for what!	Having a hard time. Has been fighting steady for quite a while. Looks mean with goggles and maybe the guy he is shooting at looks just as mean.	Oh God! Man shooting gun. Why don't they pick up the shells? Messy. No room to move around.
VI. Four college men on sunny lawn typing, reading, listening to radio.	Typical college campus. Everybody loafing. Typing a letter he doesn't need to type. Slacking on their work.	Someone ruining a good pair of pressed pants by lying down like that. They're unsuccessfully trying to study.	Somebody trying to get a tan, wasting time. Not comfortable. Tie coming undone, sole of shoe worn out. Messy. Leaves unraked.
	ANXIOUS ATTITUDE		
I. Young people digging in a swampy area.	They're going to get hurt or cut. There should be someone older there who knows what to do in case of accident. I wonder how deep the water is.	Digging in a hurry to get rid of flood waters. Must be pretty important to get it done.	Burying something or digging something. Wide open field and mountain in the distance.
II. Colored people jitterbugging.	Look as though they're having a good time; it seems as though they shouldn't be because something may happen to their families.	Good time. I wonder how they'll feel tomorrow. Probably back to driving trucks.	People jitterbugging. I hope we don't look that way when we jitterbug. I don't like the picture.
III. Wounded man being carried on litter by soldiers to aeroplane.	He is wounded and they're taking him to a plane but he's in bad shape and may not live even though the plane will rush him to a hospital.	Everybody in a hurry to get him back to safety. Must be emergency case, more so than usual. Man trying to act not too far gone but that doesn't mean he isn't.	Wounded man being carried off by buddies. Fliers, lots of boys like that. The man on the litter has a sweet face. I hate to have something like this happen; it frightens me.

IV. Seminar around fireplace at faculty home.	Mr. G. and some students. The picture is not right because Mr. G. isn't living anymore. You never know when tragedy is going to hit.	Solving a big family problem. Everybody looking on. Anxious look on Grandmother and Sister. Thoughtful look on Grandpop's face.	Lot of people discussing. Lady reading to them. Somber atmosphere. It makes me feel as if I don't want to go to anyone's house.
V. Waist gunner in action in a bomber.	I wonder if it is safe—seems like the floor is badly cluttered. If anything happened I wonder if anyone would know. He might become tangled up in the rigging and be helpless.	Having a hard battle. Wonder if he'll win it. I bet he wonders what is going to happen to him.	Like monster from Mars. He's in a battle and perhaps he'll be killed. Don't like it because it reminds me of the war. Depressing.
VI. Four college men on sunny lawn typing, reading, listening to radio.	Boys relaxing on college campus. By now they may be overseas or wounded or dead. They never know whether they'll come through alive.	They're listening to a football game or world series. Probably a tight game. One guy looks as if his side wasn't winning.	Lot of men. Peaceful enough. I wonder if they want to come back, and what's going on in their minds. Are they fighting now?

TABLE II

Effects of Three Moods (Happy, Critical, and Anxious) on the Descriptions of Six Pictures by Three Subjects

	Happy			*Critical*			*Anxious*		
	Happy	Critical	Anxious	Happy	Critical	Anxious	Happy	Critical	Anxious
Mean number of times each mood was indicated per picture	2.33	.24	.13	.09	3.15	.11	.17	.50	1.44
	$\sigma = .96$	$\sigma = .39$	$\sigma = .17$	$\sigma = .30$	$\sigma = 1.41$	$\sigma = .23$	$\sigma = .22$	$\sigma = .57$	$\sigma = .78$
Statistical reliability of the differences between the means	$M_h - M_c = 2.09$			$M_c - M_h = 3.06$			$M_a - M_h = 1.27$		
	S.E.$_{dif.}$ = .24; $C.R. = 8.7$			S.E.$_{dif.}$ = .35; $C.R. = 8.7$			S.E.$_{dif.}$ = .21; $C.R. = 6.1$		
	$M_h - M_a = 2.20$			$M_c - M_a = 3.04$			$M_a - M_c = .94$		
	S.E.$_{dif.}$ = .23; $C.R. = 9.5$			S.E.$_{dif.}$ = .35; $C.R. = 8.6$			S.E.$_{dif.}$ = .25; $C.R. = 3.8$		

An anxious mood, as developed in this experiment, apparently tends to produce an appreciable number of remarks which three judges label as indicators of criticalness. The judges sometimes found it difficult to decide whether the remarks made during the anxious mood were critical, anxious, or neutral. The great majority of the descriptions written in the happy or critical moods, however, did not contain even a single remark which, according to the judges, was indicative of a mood other than the induced one. In some instances the mood exercised such a profound influence on perception that the picture would not be recognized from the description as the same one described in the other two moods.

These results would seem to indicate that (1) common sense and clinical insight are correct in assigning a major role to moods, feelings, and attitudes in the determination of intellectual processes; and that (2) even very brief descriptions of suitably chosen pictures show clearly the effects of a dominant attitude. Further experiments might be designed to discover what incidents typical of everyday life can create such powerful, directive attitudes, how these attitudes exercise their effects on perception and thought, and how these effects might be controlled. Hypnosis should prove an invaluable tool in creating the conditions necessary for such experiments.

---

12. They Saw a Game: A Case Study *

THIS RESEARCH STUDY, using material from everyday living, demonstrates the influence on perception and judgment of the loyalties and identifications evoked by group memberships. In addition, the discussion provides an introduction to the point of view and emphasis in psychology known as *transactional.* This point of view, which has been advanced only recently in psychology, may be examined a bit more fully in Selection 46.

ON A BRISK Saturday afternoon, November 23, 1951, the Dartmouth football team played Princeton in Princeton's Palmer Stadium. It was the last game of the season for both teams and of rather special significance because the Princeton team had won all its games so far and one of its players, Kazmaier, was receiving All-American mention and had

* Albert H. Hastorf and Hadley Cantril, "They saw a game: a case study," *Journal of Abnormal and Social Psychology,* XLIX (1954), 129–34. By permission of the authors and the American Psychological Association.

just appeared as the cover man on *Time* magazine, and was playing his last game.

A few minutes after the opening kick-off, it became apparent that the game was going to be a rough one. The referees were kept busy blowing their whistles and penalizing both sides. In the second quarter, Princeton's star left the game with a broken nose. In the third quarter, a Dartmouth player was taken off the field with a broken leg. Tempers flared both during and after the game. The official statistics of the game, which Princeton won, showed that Dartmouth was penalized 70 yards, Princeton 25, not counting more than a few plays in which both sides were penalized.

Needless to say, accusations soon began to fly. The game immediately became a matter of concern to players, students, coaches, and the administrative officials of the two institutions, as well as to alumni and the general public who had not seen the game but had become sensitive to the problem of big-time football through the recent exposures of subsidized players, commercialism, etc. Discussion of the game continued for several weeks.

One of the contributing factors to the extended discussion of the game was the extensive space given to it by both campus and metropolitan newspapers. An indication of the fervor with which the discussions were carried on is shown by a few excerpts from the campus dailies.

For example, on November 27 (four days after the game), the *Daily Princetonian* (Princeton's student newspaper) said:

> This observer has never seen quite such a disgusting exhibition of so-called "sport." Both teams were guilty but the blame must be laid primarily on Dartmouth's doorstep. Princeton, obviously the better team, had no reason to rough up Dartmouth. Looking at the situation rationally, we don't see why the Indians should make a deliberate attempt to cripple Dick Kazmaïer or any other Princeton player. The Dartmouth psychology, however, is not rational itself.

The November 30th edition of the *Princeton Alumni Weekly* said:

> But certain memories of what occurred will not be easily erased. Into the record books will go in indelible fashion the fact that the last game of Dick Kazmaier's career was cut short by more than half when he was forced out with a broken nose and a mild concussion, sustained from a tackle that came well after he had thrown a pass.
>
> This second-period development was followed by a third quarter outbreak of roughness that was climaxed when a Dartmouth player deliberately kicked Brad Glass in the ribs while the latter was on his back. Throughout the often unpleasant afternoon, there was undeniable evidence that the losers'

tactics were the result of an actual style of play, and reports on other games they have played this season substantiate this.

Dartmouth students were "seeing" an entirely different version of the game through the editorial eyes of the *Dartmouth* (Dartmouth's undergraduate newspaper). For example, on November 27 the *Dartmouth* said:

> However, the Dartmouth-Princeton game set the stage for the other type of dirty football. A type which may be termed as an unjustifiable accusation.
>
> Dick Kazmaier was injured early in the game. Kazmaier was the star, an All-American. Other stars have been injured before, but Kazmaier had been built to represent a Princeton idol. When an idol is hurt there is only one recourse—the tag of dirty football. So what did the Tiger Coach Charley Caldwell do? He announced to the world that the Big Green had been out to extinguish the Princeton star. His purpose was achieved.
>
> After this incident, Caldwell instilled the old see-what-they-did-go-get-them attitude into his players. His talk got results. Gene Howard and Jim Miller were both injured. Both had dropped back to pass, had passed, and were standing unprotected in the backfield. Result: one bad leg and one leg broken.
>
> The game was rough and did get a bit out of hand in the third quarter. Yet most of the roughing penalties were called against Princeton while Dartmouth received more of the illegal-use-of-the-hands variety.

On November 28 the *Dartmouth* said:

> Dick Kazmaier of Princeton admittedly is an unusually able football player. Many Dartmouth men traveled to Princeton, not expecting to win—only hoping to see an All-American in action. Dick Kazmaier was hurt in the second period, and played only a token part in the remainder of the game. For this, spectators were sorry.
>
> But there were no such feelings for Dick Kazmaier's health. Medical authorities have confirmed that as a relatively unprotected passing and running star in a contact sport, he is quite liable to injury. Also, his particular injuries—a broken nose and slight concussion—were no more serious than is experienced almost any day in any football practice, where there is no more serious stake than playing the following Saturday. Up to the Princeton game, Dartmouth players suffered about 10 known nose fractures and face injuries, not to mention several slight concussions.
>
> Did Princeton players feel so badly about losing their star? They shouldn't have. During the past undefeated campaign they stopped several individual stars by a concentrated effort, including such mainstays as Frank Hauff of Navy, Glenn Adams of Pennsylvania and Rocco Calvo of Cornell.
>
> In other words, the same brand of football condemned by the *Prince*—that of stopping the big man—is practiced quite successfully by the Tigers.

Basically, then, there was disagreement as to what had happened during the "game." Hence we took the opportunity presented by the occasion to make a "real life" study of a perceptual problem.[1]

PROCEDURE

Two steps were involved in gathering data. The first consisted of answers to a questionnaire designed to get reactions to the game and to learn something of the climate of opinion in each institution. This questionnaire was administered a week after the game to both Dartmouth and Princeton undergraduates who were taking introductory and intermediate psychology courses.

The second step consisted of showing the same motion picture of the game to a sample of undergraduates in each school and having them check on another questionnaire, as they watched the film, any infraction of the rules they saw and whether these infractions were "mild" or "flagrant."[2] At Dartmouth, members of two fraternities were asked to view the film on December 7; at Princeton, members of two undergraduate clubs saw the film early in January.

The answers to both questionnaires were carefully coded and transferred to punch cards.[3]

RESULTS

Table 1 shows the questions which received different replies from the two student populations on the first questionnaire.

Questions asking if the students had friends on the team, if they had ever played football themselves, if they felt they knew the rules of the game well, etc., showed no differences in either school and no relation to answers given to other questions. This is not surprising since the students in both schools come from essentially the same type of educational, economic, and ethnic background.

Summarizing the data of Tables 1 and 2, we find a marked contrast between the two student groups.

[1] We are not concerned here with the problem of guilt or responsibility for infractions, and nothing here implies any judgment as to who was to blame.

[2] The film shown was kindly loaned for the purpose of the experiment by the Dartmouth College Athletic Council. It should be pointed out that a movie of a football game follows the ball, is thus selective, and omits a good deal of the total action on the field. Also, of course, in viewing only a film of a game, the possibilities of participation as spectator are greatly limited.

[3] We gratefully acknowledge the assistance of Virginia Zerega, Office of Public Opinion Research, and J. L. McCandless, Princeton University, and E. S. Horton, Dartmouth College, in the gathering and collation of the data.

TABLE 1

Data from First Questionnaire

Question	Dartmouth Students (N = 163)	Princeton Students (N = 161)
	(per cent)	
1. Did you happen to see the actual game between Dartmouth and Princeton in Palmer Stadium this year?		
Yes	33	71
No	67	29
2. Have you seen a movie of the game or seen it on television?		
Yes, movie	33	2
Yes, television	0	1
No, neither	67	97
3. (Asked of those who answered "yes" to either or both of above questions.) From your observations of what went on at the game, do you believe the game was clean and fairly played, or that it was unnecessarily rough and dirty?		
Clean and fair	6	0
Rough and dirty	24	69
Rough and fair *	25	2
No answer	45	29
4. (Asked of those who answered "no" on both of the first questions.) From what you have heard and read about the game, do you feel it was clean and fairly played, or that it was unnecessarily rough and dirty?		
Clean and fair	7	0
Rough and dirty	18	24
Rough and fair *	14	1
Don't know	6	4
No answer	55	71

Nearly all *Princeton* students judged the game as "rough and dirty" —not one of them thought it "clean and fair." And almost nine-tenths of them thought the other side started the rough play. By and large they felt that the charges they understood were being made were true; most of them felt the charges were made in order to avoid similar situations in the future.

When Princeton students looked at the movie of the game, they saw the Dartmouth team make over twice as many infractions as their own team made. And they saw the Dartmouth team make over twice as many infractions as were seen by Dartmouth students. When Princeton students judged these infractions as "flagrant" or "mild," the ratio was about two "flagrant" to one "mild" on the Dartmouth team, and about one "flagrant" to three "mild" on the Princeton team.

TABLE 1 (*continued*)

Question	*Dartmouth Students* (*N* = 163) (*per cent*)	*Princeton Students* (*N* = 161)
(Combined answers to questions 3 and 4 above)		
Clean and fair	13	0
Rough and dirty	42	93
Rough and fair *	39	3
Don't know	6	4
5. From what you saw in the game or the movies, or from what you have read, which team do you feel started the rough play?		
Dartmouth started it	36	86
Princeton started it	2	0
Both started it	53	11
Neither	6	1
No answer	3	2
6. What is your understanding of the charges being made? **		
Dartmouth tried to get Kazmaier	71	47
Dartmouth intentionally dirty	52	44
Dartmouth unnecessarily rough	8	35
7. Do you feel there is any truth to these charges?		
Yes	10	55
No	57	4
Partly	29	35
Don't know	4	6
8. Why do you think the charges were made?		
Injury to Princeton star	70	23
To prevent repetition	2	46
No answer	28	31

* This answer was not included on the checklist but was written in by the percentage of students indicated.

** Replies do not add to 100% since more than one charge could be given.

As for the *Dartmouth* students, while the plurality of answers fell in the "rough and dirty" category, over one-tenth thought the game was "clean and fair" and over a third introduced their own category of "rough and fair" to describe the action. Although a third of the Dartmouth students felt that Dartmouth was to blame for starting the rough play, the majority of Dartmouth students thought both sides were to blame. By and large, Dartmouth men felt that the charges they understood were being made were not true, and most of them thought the reason for the charges was Princeton's concern for its football star.

When Dartmouth students looked at the movie of the game they saw both teams make about the same number of infractions. And

TABLE 2

Data from Second Questionnaire Checked While Seeing Film

Group	*N*	*Total Number of Infractions Checked Against— Dartmouth Team*		*Princeton Team*	
		Mean	*SD*	*Mean*	*SD*
Dartmouth students	48	4.3 *	2.7	4.4	2.8
Princeton students	49	9.8 *	5.7	4.2	3.5

* Significant at the .01 level.

they saw their own team make only half the number of infractions the Princeton students saw them make. The ratio of "flagrant" to "mild" infractions was about one to one when Dartmouth students judged the Dartmouth team, and about one "flagrant" to two "mild" when Dartmouth students judged infractions made by the Princeton team.

It should be noted that Dartmouth and Princeton students were thinking of different charges in judging their validity and in assigning reasons as to why the charges were made. It should also be noted that whether or not students were spectators of the game in the stadium made little difference in their responses.

INTERPRETATION: THE NATURE OF A SOCIAL EVENT [4]

It seems clear that the "game" actually was many different games and that each version of the events that transpired was just as "real" to a particular person as other versions were to other people. A consideration of the experiential phenomena that constitute a "football game" for the spectator may help us both to account for the results obtained and illustrate something of the nature of any social event.

Like any other complex social occurrence, a "football game" consists of a whole host of happenings. Many different events are occurring simultaneously. Furthermore, each happening is a link in a chain of happenings, so that one follows another in sequence. The "football game," as well as other complex social situations, consists of a whole matrix of events. In the game situation, this matrix of events consists of the actions of all the players, together with the behavior of the referees and linesmen, the action on the sidelines, in the grandstands, over the loud-speaker, etc.

Of crucial importance is the fact that an "occurrence" on the football field or in any other social situation does not become an experiential

[4] The interpretation of the nature of a social event sketched here is in part based on discussions with Adelbert Ames, Jr., and is being elaborated in more detail elsewhere.

"event" unless and until some significance is given to it: an "occurrence" becomes an *"event"* only when the happening has significance. And a happening generally has significance only if it reactivates learned significances already registered in what we have called a person's assumptive form-world.

Hence the particular occurrences that different people experienced in the football game were a limited series of events from the total matrix of events *potentially* available to them. People experienced those occurrences that reactivated significances they brought to the occasion; they failed to experience those occurrences which did not reactivate past significances. We do not need to introduce "attention" as an "intervening third" (to paraphrase James on memory) to account for the selectivity of the experiential process.

In this particular study, one of the most interesting examples of this phenomenon was a telegram sent to an officer of Dartmouth College by a member of a Dartmouth alumni group in the Midwest. He had viewed the film which had been shipped to his alumni group from Princeton after its use with Princeton students, who saw, as we noted, an average of over nine infractions by Dartmouth players during the game. The alumnus, who couldn't see the infractions he had heard publicized, wired:

> Preview of Princeton movies indicates considerable cutting of important part please wire explanation and possibly air mail missing part before showing scheduled for January 25 we have splicing equipment.

The "same" sensory impingements emanating from the football field, transmitted through the visual mechanism to the brain, also obviously gave rise to different experiences in different people. The significances assumed by different happenings for different people depend in large part on the purposes people bring to the occasion and the assumptions they have of the purposes and probable behavior of other people involved. This was amusingly pointed out by the New York *Herald Tribune's* sports columnist, Red Smith, in describing a prize fight between Chico Vejar and Carmine Fiore in his column of December 21, 1951. Among other things, he wrote:

> You see, Steve Ellis is the proprietor of Chico Vejar, who is a highly desirable tract of Stamford, Conn., welterweight. Steve is also a radio announcer. Ordinarily there is no conflict between Ellis the Brain and Ellis the Voice because Steve is an uncommonly substantial lump of meat who can support both halves of a split personality and give away weight on each end without missing it.
>
> This time, though, the two Ellises met head-on, with a sickening, rending

crash. Steve the Manager sat at ringside in the guise of Steve the Announcer broadcasting a dispassionate, unbiased, objective report of Chico's adventures in the ring. . . .

Clear as mountain water, his words came through, winning big for Chico. Winning? Hell, Steve was slaughtering poor Fiore.

Watching and listening, you could see what a valiant effort the reporter was making to remain cool and detached. At the same time you had an illustration of the old, established truth that when anybody with a preference watches a fight, he sees only what he prefers to see.

That is always so. That is why, after any fight that doesn't end in a clean knockout, there always are at least a few hoots when the decision is announced. A guy from, say, Billy Graham's neighborhood goes to see Billy fight and he watches Graham all the time. He sees all the punches Billy throws, and hardly any of the punches Billy catches. So it was with Steve.

"Fiore feints with a left," he would say, honestly believing that Fiore hadn't caught Chico full on the chops. "Fiore's knees buckle," he said, "and Chico backs away." Steve didn't see the hook that had driven Chico back. . . .

In brief, the data here indicate that there is no such "thing" as a "game" existing "out there" in its own right which people merely "observe." The "game" "exists" for a person and is experienced by him only in so far as certain happenings have significances in terms of his purpose. Out of all the occurrences going on in the environment, a person selects those that have some significance for him from his own egocentric position in the total matrix.

Obviously in the case of a football game, the value of the experience of watching the game is enhanced if the purpose of "your" team is accomplished, that is, if the happening of the desired consequence is experienced—i.e., if your team wins. But the value attribute of the experience can, of course, be spoiled if the desire to win crowds out behavior we value and have come to call sportsmanlike.

The sharing of significances provides the links except for which a "social" event would not be experienced and would not exist for anyone.

A "football game" would be impossible except for the rules of the game which we bring to the situation and which enable us to share with others the significances of various happenings. These rules make possible a certain repeatability of events such as first downs, touchdowns, etc. If a person is unfamiliar with the rules of the game, the behavior he sees lacks repeatability and consistent significance and hence "doesn't make sense."

And only because there is the possibility of repetition is there the possibility that a happening has a significance. For example, the balls used in games are designed to give a high degree of repeatability. While a football is about the only ball used in games which is not a sphere, the shape of the modern football has apparently evolved in order to achieve a higher degree of accuracy and speed in forward passing than would be obtained with a spherical ball, thus increasing the repeatability of an important phase of the game.

The rules of a football game, like laws, rituals, customs, and mores, are registered and preserved forms of sequential significances enabling people to share the significances of occurrences. The sharing of sequential significances which have value for us provides the links that operationally make social events possible. They are analogous to the forces of attraction that hold parts of an atom together, keeping each part from following its individual, independent course.

From this point of view it is inaccurate and misleading to say that different people have different "attitudes" concerning the same "thing." For the "thing" simply is *not* the same for different people whether the "thing" is a football game, a presidential candidate, Communism, or spinach. We do not simply "react to" a happening or to some impingement from the environment in a determined way (except in behavior that has become reflexive or habitual). We behave according to what we bring to the occasion, and what each of us brings to the occasion is more or less unique. And except for these significances which we bring to the occasion, the happenings around us would be meaningless occurrences, would be "inconsequential."

From the transactional view, an attitude is not a predisposition to react in a certain way to an occurrence or stimulus "out there" that exists in its own right with certain fixed characteristics which we "color" according to our predisposition. That is, a subject does not simply "react to" an "object." An attitude would rather seem to be a complex of registered significances reactivated by some stimulus which assumes its own particular significances for us in terms of our purposes. That is, the object as experienced would not exist for us except for the reactivated aspects of the form-world which provide particular significance to the hieroglyphics of sensory impingements.

---

13. Time Orientation and Social Class *

STUDIES OF modern communities have confirmed the existence of stratifications in society related to socio-economic status. The different strata, or classes, have different customs and values. In the

* Lawrence L. LeShan, "Time orientation and social class," *Journal of Abnormal and Social Psychology,* XLVII (1952), 589–92. By permission of the author and the American Psychological Association.

present paper, Dr. LeShan develops the hypothesis that there should be different time perspectives in the different classes corresponding to the differences in dominant values. By the analysis of stories told by children drawn from different classes, he confirms the hypothesis that members of each class operate according to specific temporal frames of reference. By slight extension of these findings, as well as other more direct studies, it is readily seen that class membership also influences other processes in the perceptual field.

ONE OF THE most fruitful areas of research in modern sociology has been the investigation of the various levels of social class in America. An extensive literature on this subject has arisen in the past ten years. Volumes such as Havighurst and Taba's *Adolescent Character and Personality,* Gardner and Davis' *Deep South,* and Warner, Meeker, and Eell's *Social Class in America* have summed up some of the major studies.[1] Out of the vast amount of data collected, many of the important implications have been extracted and reported. However, in as rich and new a field as this, there are always new implications to be explored and tested.

This paper is an attempt to examine one of the possible differences between members of social classes in America. This variable might be termed "collective-ego-space-time" after Erickson. It concerns the perceived relationship of the individual and his goals in time. How far ahead is the time span with which the individual is concerned? What is the crucial time limit during which he will frustrate himself in order to attain a goal? Does he relate his behavior primarily to the far future, the immediate future, the present, or the past? Bateson has pointed out that this orientation seems to differ widely between Balinese culture and the culture of the (middle class) United States. There would be important implications in knowing if it differed in various classes within the United States itself.

THE HYPOTHESIS

The general hypothesis of this paper is that there are various temporal goal orientations in the various levels of social class. Very briefly, these temporal orientations may be described as follows:

1. In the lower-lower class, the orientation is one of quick sequences of tension and relief. One does not frustrate oneself for long periods or plan action with goals far in the future. The future generally is an

[1] Clear definitions of the various social classes may be found in any of the above-mentioned volumes. In the interest of space saving, these definitions are not included here.

indefinite, vague, diffuse region and its rewards and punishments are too uncertain to have much motivating value. In this social class, one eats when he is hungry; there are no regular meal hours and each member of the family takes food when he feels like it if food is available.

2. In the upper-lower, middle, and lower-upper classes, the orientation is one of much longer tension-relief sequences. As the individual grows older, he plans further and further into the future and acts on these plans. As an adult, he may start planning for retirement when he is in his twenties. In these classes, one eats at regular "clock" hours. One quickly learns to inhibit activity leading to the relief of a basic tension (food-getting behavior) until a watch shows that it is time to eat.

3. In the upper-upper class, the individual sees himself as part of a sequence of several or more generations, and the orientation is backward to the past. One eats at traditional hours and lives out the traditions set up in the past.

This hypothesis has been implied in many of the books and articles on social class. A few quotations may serve to demonstrate this.

> . . . in a lower class family . . . the disciplinarian . . . is certain to believe that the way to make a child learn is to beat him. . . . It seems clear . . . that a child cannot be trained in this fashion to undergo the long periods of renunciation which the middle class ideal of socialization demands of him.
>
> Every individual in the upper class has a series of duties and privileges associated with . . . his direct lineal ancestors, symbols of the past.
>
> The greatest possible insult to an upper-upper class person is the defamation of his "original ancestor," the founder of his local line.
>
> Both upper-middle-class and lower-middle-class husbands and wives recognize the raising of a family as the primary function of their relationship, more important than the sexual enjoyment of their partners, their economic security or their general physical comfort.

EVIDENCES FROM CHILD-REARING PRACTICES

We would expect these various temporal orientations to be demonstrated in the techniques with which parents from these social classes train children. We would expect this for the double reason (a) that the parents themselves possess this orientation and (b) that we believe that children will, by and large, also have it when they mature. In studying training techniques as revealed in the various books and articles on social class, we find this expectation confirmed. In the third group (upper-upper) as postulated in this paper, we find training techniques such as: "What would your grandmother say?" or "Your grandfather would rather see you dead." In the second group (upper-middle, middle, and upper-lower), stress is on the future. Children are exhorted to do well in school, for example, by threats that they will not be able to get a good job, that they will not get a good spouse, or that they will not get into college. In the first group (lower-lower), training techniques are more in terms of immediate punishment and reward. Children are made to do (or stop doing) things by the threat that something will happen to them immediately if they do not obey. In this class, thumb-sucking and masturbation are stopped by threats of an immediate beating, physical punishment, or by physical restraint. A reference to moral or developmental reasons for doing or not doing something is rarely if ever made.

In one lower-lower case studied a ten-year-old son has "found" some ice skates and brought them home. The father looks at them and says: "Now, listen, Johnny, I don't want you keepin' them if there's going to be any trouble with them."

TABLE 1

Parental Control Methods in a Lower-Lower Class Family, an Analysis of the Items in an Unpublished Case Study

Type of Control	*Example*	*Number of Attempts Observed*
1. Flat declarative statements	"Put down that bottle."	35
2. Immediate punishment or reward threatened	"You go back to bed or I'll beat you with this leather strap."	57
3. Reward or punishment to follow within 24 hours	(Taking a dirty toy from a child) "Wait until Tootsie comes home and we'll wash it and you can play with it."	7
4. Reward or punishment to follow within the week	(2 days before Xmas) "Santa Claus won't come if you're bad."	1
5. Reward or punishment after 1 week or at an indefinite time	"I'll never take you any place again."	1

This same case history of a lower-lower family was analyzed for the methods that the parents used to control the children. The interviewer became a close friend and confidant of the family and spent a great deal of time at their home. She observed very frequent attempts of the parents directly to make the child do, or not do, something. These can be broken down into categories as can be seen in Table 1. This table seems to indicate an orientation in the parents such as we have postulated, which one would suspect would be likely to produce a similar orientation in the children. Also of interest is the fact that 28 of the parental responses were unpredictable from the point of view of the child—as well as the point of view of the interviewer! As an example, we mention the following incident: The father had brought a three-year-old daughter some candy cigarettes. The child pretended to smoke them, flicking off the ashes, etc. When she did this, the father took them away from her and spanked her for "putting on the dog."

Children of the lower-lower class soon learn that major changes in their lives often occur suddenly and unpredictably. The mother in the case history mentioned above describes the weaning of one child: "Yeah, one day she threw the bottle out of her crib and I gave it back to her and she didn't want it so I never gave it to her again." This is a far cry indeed from the careful, long-term weaning of the middle classes. With the lower-lower type of experience one might speculate that children would grow up not at all certain of the basic stability of the universe.[2]

Food, shelter, heat in the winter (and even personal safety) are also unpredictable. Food is present and eaten when father gets a pay check *if* he brings it home. There is never enough over a long period of time and one can never tell whether or not there will be food when he is next hungry.

In the lower-lower group there seems to be a circular phenomenon at work. The parents' training is inconsistent because of their inability to work for long-range goals, and this prevents them from breaking out of the economic trap they are in. Economic pressures further decrease stability. Children who go through this training will also emerge unable to work for long-range goals and so on.

Other factors add to the inconsistency of training of children in the lower-lower class in relation to that of children in the middle and upper-upper classes. The lower-lower class child plays on the streets away from adult supervision. Here he is to a large degree at the mercy of his own impulses with reward or punishment following immediately on his actions. Rewards here may be in terms of motor activity, physical gratification, etc. The parents are at work or are usually unaware of what he is doing.

In the other social classes, the play situation tends to be quite different. Children play near the house or near the house of a neighbor and are, a large percentage of the time, under some adult supervision. Less often do both parents work and there is much more watching and controlling the children's play. Figuratively, they tend to play "in front of the

[2] With such a frame of reference, planning for a distant future would not seem to be an intelligent procedure.

house." The child has more training in controlling his own impulses because of the help in control he receives from older figures.

According to psychoanalytic theory, the individual must have a strong superego if he is to frustrate himself and renounce present pleasure for future gains. This is built up out of the child's image of the parents in his early years. It rewards him for self-control and punishes him for transgressions. In the second and third groups set up in this paper, the parents and families tend to remain constant for years at a time. In the first group, families are much more flexible: adults move in with other adults; children may be switched from one family to another for a while if this arrangement seems to be more convenient. Under this situation, it would be improbable that a strong and stable ego-ideal could be built up. There would be many shifting adults, all too inconsistent in their behavior for the child to build a model.

PROCEDURE

To test partially this time orientation hypothesis, the stories of 117 children of 8 to 10 years old were examined. These stories were told in response to the stimulus "Tell me a story." Seventy-four of the children were lower class and 43 were middle class. The groups were equated for age. The stories were examined in terms of the period of time covered by the action of the story. In line with the hypothesis, one might expect that the middle-class group would produce stories covering a longer time-period from beginning (the starting of action) to the end (final action) than would the lower-class group. This expectation was confirmed statistically (Table 2). A chi-square test indicated

TABLE 2

Length of Time Covered by Action of Stories Told by 117 Children In Response to Stimulus "Tell Me A Story"

Class	*Under 1 Hr.*	*1–12 Hrs.*	*12–24 Hrs.*	*1 Day–7 Days*	*1–2 Wks.*	*2 Wks.–1 Yr.*	*1 Yr. Plus*
74 Lower-Class Children	43% (32)	32% (24)	5% (4)	8% (6)	5% (4)	4% (3)	1% (1)
43 Middle-Class Children	28% (12)	23% (10)	9% (4)	23% (10)	9% (4)	2% (1)	5% (2)
	($df = 6$)				($p = .001$)		

that the two groups were not from the same population insofar as this variable was concerned. There is a statistically significant difference between the length of time covered in stories told by children of these two social classes. If one accepts the hypothesis that in unstructured situations of this sort, individuals tend to project the world as they see it onto the stimulus, then our major hypothesis of different time orientations in different social classes is strengthened.

DISCUSSION

If our hypothesis of different time orientations for different social classes is valid, there are various implications which may be of importance, such as the need to think through again the problem of goals and methods in the public schools, and re-education in old age when a time span which includes planning for the future may lose its meaningfulness. It appears worth while to consider two such implications in a little more detail.

One of the trickiest problems in modern psychopathology has been the concept of the psychopath. Whether or not psychopaths exist, and if so what the symptoms and etiology are, has been discussed in a great many articles with no real agreement or even pragmatically useful results. The essence of the various definitions advanced seems to rest on two general symptoms: low frustration tolerance and marked hostility turned inward and/or outward. It may be of value to examine the psychopath category in terms of personal time orientation as discussed above. One might speculate that an individual raised in an environment where (a) reward and punishment generally follow immediately on action and (b) where these results are unpredictable a large part of the time would have a low frustration tolerance. He would not have learned to act in terms of future reward and would, indeed, have learned the opposite since the future would be an unpredictable region and to work in terms of it would be nonsensical for him. Further, this orientation in a world that is primarily run on longer sequences might well produce conflicts, failures, and resulting hostility. This training factor has not, to the author's knowledge, been investigated and it may be that here lies one of the roots of psychopathy.

A further implication of the concept of personal time orientation is in the general area of the prevention of delinquency. A reform school will be neither a deterrent in the future nor a lesson from the past in an individual who has learned to respond only in terms of what is immediately present. It may well be that in order to control delinquency it will be necessary first to change the time orientations of the delinquents. At present, very little is known concerning the management of such learning and it would appear to be a fruitful subject for research.

CONCLUSION

The hypothesis that there are different personal time orientations in different social classes is advanced. Data are presented (a) from child-rearing practices in the various classes of American society and (b) from the greater time span of the action in stories told by middle-class children as compared with those told by lower-class children which tend to confirm this hypothesis. Some further implications of the hypothesis are discussed briefly.

---

14. Attention and Involuntary Movement *

In the analysis of the way man observes the world about him, the study of attention is of central importance. This selection presents an experiment that adds to our understanding of attention by examining performance under distraction in two different conditions of attention. Dr. Edwards emphasizes the connection between laboratory experiment and everyday living by relating his findings to some problems involved in safe driving.

In a situation such as automobile driving, how important is involuntary movement? To what extent is uncontrolled movement different with fixed and with shifting attention? To what extent is two-armed driving more steady and controlled than is one-armed driving? It is not sufficient to know that certain conditions are important for safety. It is desirable to know as accurately as possible to what extent certain conditions modify the control of activities in the total behavior of individuals who are involved in skilled work or in what may be dangerous occupations. Although inferences cannot be made directly from laboratory experiments to such activities as automobile driving, it is believed that the following experiments may throw some light upon the problems.

Two experiments have been performed for the purpose of discovering quantitatively the effect of certain conditions upon involuntary movement. The involuntary movement chosen was finger tremor, arm extended with no rest, since that can be accurately measured in three dimensions with the writer's finger tromometer. The two conditions

* Austin S. Edwards, "Attention and involuntary movement," *Journal of Applied Psychology*, XXXIII (1949), 503–9. By permission of the author and the American Psychological Association.

especially used were distractions with attention held upon a fixation spot without any shifting, and, second, the effect of distractions when the attention shifted.

EXPERIMENT 1. INVOLUNTARY MOVEMENT WITH FIXED ATTENTION

This experiment was performed in the dark room with the light dimmed to one foot-candle. The distractions were an automobile horn from a Ford automobile, actuated by six volts, and the bright light from a Plymouth automobile, actuated by a current of six volts. The horn was in a box about five feet in front of the *S*, where it could not be seen. The light was placed about ten feet in front of the *S* slightly to the left and arranged so that it could easily be moved in any direction and shone into the eyes of the *S*. The finger tromometer was on the table directly in front of the *S* and a fixation spot about six feet in front so that the *S* could look over the top of the tromometer and fixate the spot.

Procedure

Standard procedure was used with the tromometer, the *S* being allowed to rest before the measurements began, and the measurements consisting of the sum of the three readings—front-back, right-left, up-down. The time of measurement was thirty seconds.

The first control measurement was made before any distractions were used, and then measurements were taken while either the light or the horn, or both, were used as distractions. Following these three experimental measurements, a second control measurement was made. When the light was directed into the eyes of the *S*, or the horn was blown, the time consumed by the distraction was approximately twenty of the thirty seconds. Order of stimuli was varied so that each stimulus—light, sound, or both together—appeared with varying *S*s as either first, second, or third stimulus. The order of stimulation was recorded for each *S* so that not only could the results of each stimulating condition be studied, but also the effect of the stimuli as regards order, namely, first, second, or third, could be studied.

Subjects

One hundred *S*s, unselected college students, half men and half women, were used in this experiment. The ages were 17 to 25. The *S*s were asked whether they had been in any accidents, automobile or other, and notes were made as to such accidents, their number and seriousness.

Instruction

The following instruction was used: "Lean back comfortably; both feet on the floor; hold your hand as steady as you can, and watch fixation spot during the testing."

The sound of the horn was probably somewhat louder and more disturbing than is found in traffic, and the automobile light shining into the *S*'s eyes was closer and probably brighter than is usually found in actual driving situations. *S*s sat about five minutes before the experiment began.

Since it might soon become known among students that sound and light distractions were being used, conditions were made as equal as possible for all *S*s by telling them at the beginning of each series of measurements that there would be a control measurement, light and sound distractions, one or both; after the last measurement with distraction another control measurement was taken to compare with the first control.

Results

Detailed results were worked out with means, medians, standard deviations, sigma of the mean, Q_1 and Q_3. Analyses were made for men and women separately, both for the light stimulus and sound stimulus, and both together, and for the first, second, and third stimulus. This permitted finding out first whether greater effect might be found in finger tremor because of the sound, the light, or both, and second, whether the first, the second, or the third stimulus had more effect.

It was somewhat surprising to find that on the average there was no statistically significant increase in finger tremor. Both stimuli together had no appreciable effect greater than one of the distractions alone. Whereas it might be expected that the first distraction might be more disturbing and the later ones less, or, that with the second and third distractions the *S* might become more upset, neither result appeared. With all the averages running from about 37 to not quite 43 mm., the greatest increase in finger tremor caused by the distractions was for the men 8 per cent and for the women 9 per cent. None of the critical ratios between the means was significant for the entire experiment, the highest being 0.66, which indicates results not much better than chance.

It might be expected that those students who had been in automobile wrecks or who had had serious traumatic experiences would be more disturbed than the others. No such evidence was found. Some of those who had been in the worst accidents had the lowest finger tremor throughout the experiment.

The only positive results that can be stated are in the cases of a few exceptional students who were very greatly disturbed and who showed greatly increased finger tremor during one or all of the experimental measurements. Of these *S*s, and considering those whose finger tremor was increased 50 per cent to more than 100 per cent, there were 16 men and 12 women.

Of the 16 men considerably affected by sound, light, or both distractions together, it appeared that both distractions together affected the men most and most frequently, 12 of the 50; sound affected very considerably 6, and light 4 of the 50 men.

Of the 12 women considerably affected by the distractions, only 5 were greatly affected by both distractions together; 9 by sound, and 6 by light. It is to be noted that some of the 16 men and some of the 12 women were greatly affected by more than one of the distracting stimuli.

Considering the order of distractions, first, second or third, for the 16 men and 12 women greatly affected, 6 men were most affected by the first distraction, 6 by the second, and 4 by the third. Of the 12 women, 5 were most affected by the first distraction, 6 by the second, and only 1 by the third.

Taking these cases and our averages for the 100 *S*s altogether, there is no evidence that two distracting stimuli cause more involuntary movement than one of them alone; or that a series of distractions cause more disturbance in involuntary movement than do a first or second disturbing distraction.

It may also be noted that there is no evidence of a general build-up of disturbing influence caused by a series of three disturbing stimulus situations. This is, of course, not without exceptions in certain of the *S*s. But the first control average was 38.29 mm. and the second control average following the distractions was only 39.46, an insignificant difference of only 1.18 mm.

Conclusions

It appears from this experiment with steadily fixed attention that, with certain exceptions (16 of the 50 men, and 12 of the 50 women), students selected at random and irrespective of experience with accidents showed on the average no statistically significant increase in finger movement under conditions which were assumed to be considerably distracting and might have been expected to be quite disturbing.

On the other hand, 32 per cent of the men and 24 per cent of the women had very considerable increases of involuntary movement.

Considering all of the cases and the specially disturbed *S*s altogether, there is no evidence that the two disturbing stimuli were more disturbing than was one at a time; nor that the third distraction had any more effect than the first or second.

There was no build-up of disturbing effect since the first control experiments and the last showed no significant difference in average.

Some suggestion appears from this experiment to corroborate what we already know, namely, the importance of fixed attention in connection with motor control.

EXPERIMENT 2. INVOLUNTARY MOVEMENT WITH SHIFTING ATTENTION

In this experiment conditions were changed in several ways. Preliminary tests were made with the same set-up described in Experiment 1, but with the instruction to *S* to shift attention and to look sideways during the measurements. The preliminary experiments indicated decidedly different results and led to the development of an experiment in which the steering wheel of an automobile was fastened to two units (front-back, right-left) of the tromometer. The steering wheel was mounted so that it was at the height and angle of the steering wheel in a car. The tromometer was placed so that the top of the steering wheel was between the two units of the tromometer that were used for measurements. Movement of the wheel thus moved one of the riders on the tromometer. Movement in the opposite direction moved the other rider. In this set-up the control experiment might have practically or almost zero recorded, because with both hands on the wheel it was possible to hold it very steady. Also, two riders instead of three were engaged. All measurements, both control and experimental, were thus very much reduced.

Procedure

S was given time to rest before the control measurements were taken. He was told that during the experiment he was to remain as steady as possible, to keep his feet flat on the floor, and to keep his eyes on the fixation point unless told otherwise. He was to be as comfortable as possible in the chair which was placed at a comfortable position for the *S* for holding the wheel. The first control measurement was made with *S* placing both hands on the wheel and holding his attention steadily on the fixation spot, which was three feet in front of him. Time of measurement was thirty seconds. After *S* had rested, the first experimental measurement was taken; *S* was in the same position as in the control measurement, but after fifteen seconds he was told to look out of the window, which was six feet to his right. After four seconds *S* was told to look back at the fixation spot. The second control measurement was taken with only one hand on the steering wheel. *S* was told to use the hand with which he wrote, and to hold attention steadily on the fixation spot. The next experimental measurement was made with one hand on the wheel, but after fifteen seconds *S* was told to look out of the window. After four seconds *S* was told to look back at the fixation spot. The third experimental measurement was made by having *S* hold both hands on the wheel, but after fifteen seconds *S* was told to take the pencil which was handed to him by *E* and then to put his hand back on the wheel. The pencil was handed to him at a distance of two feet. There were thus two control and three experimental measurements.

Subjects

In this experiment there were 60 men, aged 18–35, and 40 women, aged 18–24, all college students selected at random.

Results

The results in this experiment are in direct contrast with those of Experiment 1. For the 100 students, with the men and women studied separately, the effect of shifting attention was great and consistent, all differences with definitely significant critical ratios, 2.526 to 9.71. For the men, the means showed an increase from the first control to the first experimental situation on the average from 3 mm. to 4.6 mm. The second control was 6.18; the second and third experimental ratings 9.05 and 14.48 respectively. For the women, the increase from control to first experiment was from 2.38 mm. to 2.85, and from the second control of 4.53 mm. to third and fourth experimental measurements 6.93 and 11.7. The smallest percentage increase was 40 and the largest percentage increase was 158. The average percentage increase for all *S*s was 80.9; for men, 82.25, for women, 79.5. See Figure 1.

But compared with the first controls (both hands on the wheel and fixed attention) other conditions showed increases of uncontrolled movement of 300 to 400 per cent. On the basis of the averages, and taking the first control series for the men and for the women, shifting the attention to reach and take a pencil increased involuntary movement for the men, 4.46 times, and for the women, 4.91 times. If so great increase of involuntary movement takes place in the relative quiet of the laboratory, how much is to be found under the more disturbing conditions of actual automobile driving?

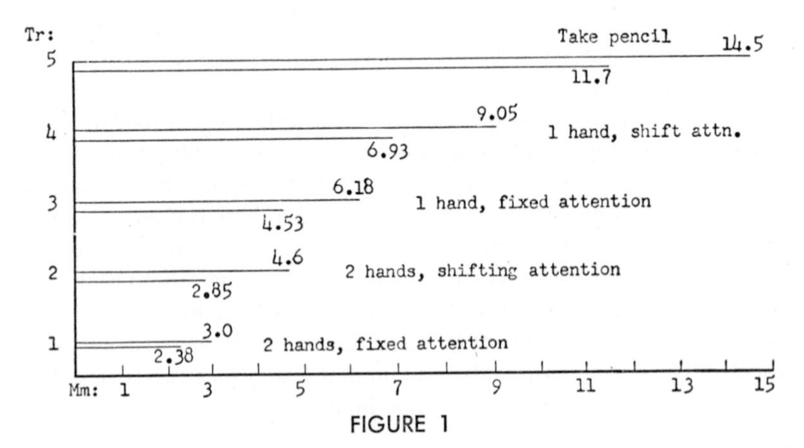

FIGURE 1

Increased hand and arm movement with shifting attention. Tr indicates the series of trials: 1, the first control series; 2, the first experimental series; 3, the second control series; 4 and 5, the experimental series that followed 3. Horizontal lines are in mm., the upper line for men, the lower for women. There were 60 men and 40 women. The C.R.'s between means were all from 2.526 to 9.71.

Reference to Figure 1 also shows a very significant difference in control, when only one hand is used instead of two. The uncontrolled movement is about twice as great.

Conclusions

With shifting attention and slight distraction (no bright lights or loud sounds), the increase in involuntary hand and arm movement was large, consistent, and statistically significant. Although one cannot draw conclusions directly from these experiments to what may be expected to happen in such a situation as driving an automobile, the question is raised as to how much danger exists in driving on account of involuntary movement over which the driver has no control. We may perhaps surmise that with the varying conditions of driving or of similar occupations, the varying amounts of monotony, emotional excitement, and various distractions might produce much more uncontrolled movement than we have found in the laboratory.

Considering the two experiments together it appears that hand and arm steadiness are relatively great with fixed attention; and that involuntary movement is relatively great when attention is shifting, especially when one is using one hand for a second operation.

It also appears that in a considerable number of cases involuntary movement of considerable amount may occur even when there is steadily fixed attention.

The great increase of uncontrolled movement when only one hand is used is of no small significance for automobile driving in traffic.

PRACTICAL IMPLICATIONS

Although it is clear to those who are informed that individuals suffering from certain abnormal conditions such as epilepsy and general paresis should not be permitted to engage in occupations where uncontrolled movements might happen, it has not been clear that there are so-called normal individuals and so-called normal situations that should require limitation of occupation in the interest of safety to self and to others. A more accurate and thorough knowledge of the involuntary movements that may occur with easily disturbed individuals and for practically all "normal" people under certain disturbing conditions may well find place in connection with our industries, automobile driving, and in other situations which demand steady neuro-muscular control. Too little is known and known accurately about the relation of involuntary movement to the total behavior pattern.

The question is forcibly raised: How dangerous is the one-arm driving of automobiles?

IV

LEARNING

One of the major characteristics of living matter is that it is modifiable through experience: it adapts, it learns. The precise nature of the learning process, despite a great deal of study, is not completely clear. Psychologists are still concerned with problems like the following: Is there only one basic process or are there several? How many kinds of conditioning are there? What about canalization, learning through familiarization, illustrated by a narrowing of the range within which a motive may be satisfied? Is learning best conceived as perceptual reorganization? How do the laws of association relate to the laws of conditioning? And so on, ad infinitum.

The topic Learning may be thought of as embracing the full range of acquisition (true learning), retention, and reproduction of the learned material. A scientist cannot observe the true learning process, acquisition, without having his subjects retain the material being learned for at least a little time. Nor can we have evidence of learning without having the change of the organism manifested in some way, which involves the process of reproduction of material. It seems reasonable, therefore, to include remembering (retention) and recall, recognition, and other forms of demonstrating learning along with acquisition in one major unit.

Just as some psychologists make a "perception" approach to the study of personality, and some make a "motivation" approach, many rely on learning theory as the basis for understanding the nature of man. The study of learning has been stimulated by practical as well as theoretical considerations.

Our first selection in this section suggests a stimulating general perspective on the problems involved, and is calculated to upset any complacency the reader may have on the subject. The three theoretical papers (Selections 16, 17, and 19) include discussions of studies, but make their greatest contribution in the radically different approaches they take to the problem. The single experimental report (Selection 18) and the clinical paper (Selection 20) illustrate the variety of methodologies that have been applied to study in this field. These selections do not readily add up to a simple whole since the field itself is complex, but they should help the reader appreciate more fully a variety of different aspects of the problem being studied and acquaint him with some of the approaches currently being made to its solution.

15. Learning—"They Ain't No Such Animal" *

JUST WHAT is meant by learning? If we go to the library we will find many books that open to a particular page because so many students have sought out the special passages. Should we say that a book has learned to open to that page? Even if we restrict our consideration to living subjects, can we differentiate between learning and fatigue or muscular growth or even disease without involving a value system of goals and concepts of "improvement" and "efficiency" in performance?

We recognize that in science real advances depend upon the way we put our questions to Nature. "If you ask a silly question you get a silly answer" applies in research as well as in social relations. Here Dr. English suggests that we may have been asking the wrong questions.

IT IS ONLY within the memory of men now living that psychologists began explicitly to postulate a specific and unitary construct by means of which to explain the universal fact that organisms learn. A theory of learning is a product of the very recent past.

The earlier psychologists, you remember, spoke of memory and of association. Baldwin's big two-volume *Dictionary of Psychology* in 1902 does not even list the term learning. Warren's *Dictionary* in 1934 gave learning a place but only as a term belonging to applied psychology. My own little *Dictionary* in the same year defined learning in terms of improvement—thus making it a technological concept—but also attempted to define it in scientific terms. It is not until the era of Thorndike—say around 1910—that learning came into widespread use

* Horace B. English, "Learning—'They ain't no such animal,'" *Journal of Educational Psychology*, XLIII (1952), 321–30. By permission of the author and the publisher. A portion of the Presidential Address, the Division of Educational Psychology of the American Psychological Association, 1951.

as a basic psychological construct. Now, however, learning crowds association and even memory clear out of the indexes of our textbooks.

Yet the new construct did not spring full-grown from the Jovian brow of Thorndike like Athena from the head of Zeus. Learning came into psychology as the child of associationism and wittingly or unwittingly we all conceive learning in terms which we have inherited from that ancient doctrine.[1] Research on learning has been almost wholly dominated by the view that it consists in acquiring and retaining something—usually a "stimulus-response bond." This research has, I believe, made notable contributions to the general theory of behavior, but, curiously enough, has given us almost no light on the specific problems of how organisms learn; that is, of how they come to improve their behavior.

There have been various proposals for correcting the narrowness of the associationist position. One of the earliest was set forth by McDougall and May Smith. It proposed a two-factor theory—one a fairly strict contiguity factor, the other concerned with the apprehension of meaning. I have carried out a considerable number of investigations designed to test this hypothesis. My experiments, though still inconclusive, include over a quarter-million distinct, measured responses.[2] The Gestalters and neo-Gestalters (e.g. Katona) have brought forward evidence for a kind of learning which cannot be reduced to contiguity-conditioning. And Tolman and more recently Mowrer have proposed bi- or multi-factor theories of learning.

But the search in all these cases was still for the process or processes which are specific to learning—i.e., for processes always present when learning is taking place, absent when learning is not taking place. Now it is my suggestion that there are no such processes and therefore the construct of learning and of the learning process is scientifically invalid. Note that I do not deny that there are learning "phenomena." My point is that they belong together under one heading only on a purely formal basis.

[1] It is very interesting to trace the way in which associationism was shaped at each era by the kind of thinking prevalent in the scientific world. Hume sought laws of association to parallel the laws of gravitation; later association became mental chemistry; later still, telephony. Nowadays it is more acceptable or "advanced" to conceive of association in "field theoretical" terms. Except for the last view, which has not yet managed to alter the vocabulary and hence the thinking of the man in the street, all these views may be fairly characterized as "atomistic."

[2] I cannot quite forbear remarking that I am unimpressed with experiments which measure only twenty or thirty responses in any given category, even when the found differences meet small-sample criteria of significance. Surely the day is not too far off when we shall recognize small-sample studies as pilot experiments only.

All psychophysical or organic activity leads inevitably to a change in performance. You can call this change learning if you like, but to segregate the aspect of change from the totality of organic activity is an abstraction. When we perceive, when we think, when we emote, we certainly change in our capacity for later behavior; but the laws or explanatory principles are those of perceiving or thinking or emoting. There is no set of laws specific to the changing of performance, hence there is no valid construct of learning in the science of psychology.

I would not on that account abandon all talk of learning, but I would restore to the term its original meaning. Try as we will, we cannot for long avoid bringing in the notion of learning as "improvement." Now that means that we leave the field of science for the field of psychotechnology, and that is where the concept of learning belongs.

In making this distinction I am not seeking to drive a broad wedge between psychology as science and as technology. The relationships and interactions between them are many and significant. For one thing, the whole broad range of scientific method is entirely common ground. Nonetheless the two disciplines have distinct goals and tend, therefore, to develop different concepts and working tools.

Science works with such a division or classification of all intrinsically related phenomena as will enable us to explain nature in the simplest possible terms (or, what comes to the same thing, in the fewest or most universal laws). This Principle of Parsimony is a basic regulator of all science. Technology, on the other hand, works with groupings of phenomena which have been segregated because their manipulation and control serves a human or social purpose. The phenomena brought together in a technology may have few intrinsic relations with each other; consider, for example, the variety of phenomena grouped together in oil geology! [3] Science, then, seeks parsimonious explanation, technology practical control.

It must be said at once that the distinction just made is not absolute: control over nature is the ultimate goal of even the purest science. And even the narrowest technology demands that its rules be as few and as inclusive as possible—within limits of the practical purposes from which it starts. But each practical purpose leads to its own set of rules, and these may overlap in complex fashion with the rules or working principles developed for other purposes. A tremendous number of rules and explanatory principles is thus generated for technological use. Few

[3] We are here including applied science under the term technology. If desired, distinction may be made between the search for general principles with immediately practical ends in view (applied science), and the manipulation of a specific or concrete situation (technology). When pushed, however, the distinction appears one of degree.

of these principles fit into the pattern of scientific law or even suggest these laws. Thus the rules for building a brick wall do not pointedly suggest the laws of physics and chemistry, although of course such laws apply. Nor could one derive the practical rules for building a wall from the law of gravitation and the chemistry of mortar.

A simple illustration will suffice to show how psychological technology may proceed in ways which cut across the lines of scientific theory. It is commonly accepted that persons suffering from "feelings of inadequacy" tend to learn slowly. The technologist would wish to learn as exactly as possible the extent of this correlation—what kinds of things they learn slowly, for example. And he would seek to find methods of teaching which are adapted to different levels and areas of "feelings of inadequacy." [4] Now such an investigation is not very likely to add to psychological theory, though of course it might bring to light facts which in another context would magnificently serve theory. (The most unlikely-looking fact sometimes yields scientific illumination.) Certainly such investigation is very unlikely to add to our understanding of what "learning really is." Yet there are many concrete situations where classifying learners in terms of "feelings of inadequacy" is of great help in the effort to produce the greatest degree of learning.

The frank recognition that "learning" is a concept which deals with improvement, that is with practical ends, seems to promise considerable advantage both to the science of psychology, from which the term would be excluded, and to psychotechnology, to which the concept would be assigned. Take pure science first. Bringing together, under the one concept of learning, phenomena which do not belong together has led to over-generalization on the one hand and to a frustrating failure to find generalizations on the other. In the laboratory and in the study we have made valiant effort to find common principles of explanation for all the many and diverse personal activities which have been brought together under the single rubric of learning. So far we seem to have failed. Abandonment of that effort, at least until more is known of the apparently distinct activities, will release the energies of investigators for the study of more specifically conceived problems, will lead to better experimental designs.

What are these problems? It would be presumptuous of me to attempt a complete list. Certainly, however, many of the problems studied as if they were learning problems are problems of perceptual

[4] We need not, for the purpose of this illustration, raise the question as to whether, even for technological purposes, the concept of "inadequacy" is happily constructed. And of course we do not assume that feelings of inadequacy are in all cases unalterable barriers to learning, but merely that we may often have to proceed as if they were.

discrimination; nothing is added by roundly proclaiming that their study is a contribution to learning theory. These problems grade over into problems of so-called insight, of conceptualization, of thinking and of judgment. Other problems are perhaps more appropriately categorized as those of motivation—at least this construct, while still confused, seems to have promise for the ordering of the data of our science. There are many other proposed conceptualizations of the facts of behavior—you need not fear that I shall attempt here and now to review them. What I am suggesting is that they have been less fruitfully attacked because conceived as subproblems of learning. As scientific problems they are more profitably attacked independently of any alleged relationship with a superordinate concept of learning. That has been in fact the actual procedure in many cases; it should be in all.

As these specific problems are vigorously attacked, we shall have a better chance to discover whether there is indeed an "element" common to them all which justifies the construct of learning, and if so what its nature may be. The hypothesis that there is such a common process is currently beset by so many apparent discrepancies that it is, at the least, premature, and our attachment to this hypothesis is a hindrance to a clear envisagement of our actual problems in pure and systematic psychology. My suggestion is, therefore, that "learning" is not a construct which brings order to the facts of psychology; rather it imposes a spurious, and in the end confusing, unity upon diverse phenomena.

Even if, however, it shall eventually prove that there is a proper place for the concept of learning in pure science, we must recognize the validity of considering learning as an independent psychotechnological problem. We have, as a matter of fact, always been insistent that learning had practical implications. The whole approach has been characteristically American, and as such influenced by the dominant characteristics of American scholarship, especially by a passion to be practical and an almost fanatical devotion to facts. The student of learning, however much he designed his experiments as a venture in pure science using rats as his subjects, almost always had one eye cocked on practical conclusions. And he often found them.

But psychology is dominated also by another American characteristic, the yearning for a relatively simple and all-inclusive formula. And the effort to impose such an all-inclusive formula upon the data has tended to restrict our vision. Facts which do not fit the formula are too often "filed and forgot." Thus much of great importance which deals with the improvement of behavior is neglected.

When, however, we put aside the desire for the all-inclusive formula, and face learning as a technological concept, a whole nest of facts and problems comes to light. The variables and dimensions to be considered are seen as far more diversified than those of traditional learning experimentation. Thus, both the enduring and the temporary condition or state of the learner, instead of being ignored or treated as a source of constant or variable "errors," come to life as by far the most significant among the determiners of learning. The integrated organism ("the whole child" so beloved of some educators) also is seen as having a vital rôle. The social norms and frames of references within which learning tasks are set up, are recognized as more potent influences than, for example, serial position, in controlling the speed and direction of learning. Indeed from the standpoint of practical life the traditional learning experiment looks like a demonstration of the way "trivial" influences can be made to affect improvement when all the more "vital" influences have been eliminated from the experimental design.

It is true that for pure science, "trivial" and "vital" are irrelevant characterizations of the variables. An influence too small to be worth counting in practice may help to reveal what the basic psychological processes are. We do not, therefore, criticize the use of such variables as part of a theoretically-oriented experimental design. The error comes when we overestimate the value of such findings for the practical control of learning to the neglect of others more important. Specifically, in not one task in a thousand is such a typical laboratory variable as "serial position" a material influence on the rate of learning. Even when the task is to learn unrelated items in a given serial order (auto licence numbers, for example) our learning or failing to learn the item will far more often be determined by other factors than by where the item is placed in the series. For all that, the facts of serial position may be important for behavior theory and should be studied for that purpose. They are not much more than a footnote in applied psychology of learning.

For contrast, take the extended and careful studies of learning in arithmetic made by William Brownell. These studies are not suggested, so far as I can see, by any theory of learning nor can they be assimilated into any general theory of learning now current. Yet in my opinion they have revolutionary significance. Or consider the principles formulated by F. P. Robinson under the rubric of the higher study skills. They certainly do not derive from the traditional doctrines of learning and the more one examines the principles of higher study skills the more they appear as almost entirely independent of learning theory. Yet these empirically discovered principles make enormously more difference to the improvement of study performance than any application of what we know about serial position or forward association.

Or take the relationship between a child's learning and his liking for his teacher. We lack experimental evidence that liking for a person can directly influence the rate with which conditioned responses are formed, though some of Razran's evidence about the CR and eating together looks in that direction; and Mowrer's theory of two kinds of learning may yet throw light on this situation. The facts, however, are too complex to be put down as merely autonomic-based, emotional learning. Mowrer tells us how emotions get learned; yet to come is the theory and the evidence as to how emotion and the learning of geography interact. This, however, we know from direct observation; the child perceives, imagines, thinks and feels differently in respect to geography when he likes his teacher. And as a result, he learns differently, generally better.

The increased learning which comes from group membership must also be reckoned with. Which variable, do you think, makes more difference to the child's change in attitudes towards sex: the variable of the serial order in which the facts are presented; or the variable of teacher versus peer groups as the source of information? Or, if you don't like serial order, choose absolutely any principle of learning based upon trying to make connections more efficient. Would you select frequency of repetition? But in the field of sex information we seldom employ repetition. I'll still stick at any rate to the social factors as making more difference. Or let me contrast Jost's law—one of the best established of connectionist principles—with a principle for which I can, more's the pity, as yet cite you very little experimental evidence.[5] I state it, however, in the form of a testable law. First, Jost's law, in case you have forgotten it: "When two associations or S-R bonds are of equal strength but of unequal age, repetition strengthens the older more than it does the younger." And now the proposed "law of group identification": "A person will modify his attitudes, feelings and actions more quickly in the direction of conformity with those of a group with which he strongly identifies himself than in the direction of conformity with those of a group with which he weakly identifies himself."

Which, ladies and gentlemen, will you take as your guide when you next enter a grade-school classroom, the political arena or even your graduate seminar?

What I am trying to say is that our current learning theories, and probably any conceivable learning theories, are too restricted to cover the many facts which we must consider when we try to control or direct the improvement of behavior. The belief in the fundamental character of this or that learning construct puts blinders on us, keeps us from a flexible empirical approach to our technological problems, inhibits re-

[5] T. M. Newcomb in *Social Psychology* (1950, p. 259) cites evidence from Lewin and Bales. Actually there is a great deal of factual evidence which suggests this theorem.

search because it is not "fundamental," and above all interferes with our finding the widest possible generalizations which will serve practical ends.

So I am urging first that pure theory will make more rapid advance if it abandons concern with the unfruitful construct of learning, and second that the term learning be returned to psychotechnology whence it came and where it is of use. Before psychology took it over, the verb "to learn" was used in common speech to designate the whole complex process of reorganizing, improving, adjusting one's behavior. The term has its semantic rights and privileges to continue to be used in this inclusive fashion. We must not try to confine learning within the strait-jacket of connectionism or of any other monolithic theory. To limit consideration of the factors which facilitate learning to those which directly facilitate or depress an alleged nuclear process of conditioning or connection-forming, is to sterilize them, to render them barren for the practical world from which the notion of learning originally came and to which it must ultimately return having issue as a result of its relations with psychology. A systematic technology of learning, however, freed from the necessity of trying to interpret miscellaneous facts in terms of a unitary scientific principle, can rescue the enormous range of facts which bear on practical problems, can put these facts in order for the use of teachers, foremen, and all others who in one way or another seek to help people improve their behavior.

If learning is thus a technological concept, does it belong to psychology? Not exclusively. There are considerations germane to learning which are non-psychological: philosophical, sociological, physiological or merely administrative. But the heart of learning as technology has always been and will continue to be psychological. To deal adequately with a practical problem of learning one may have to mobilize resources from the psychology of perception, of social norms, of motivation, of individual differences—almost anything, it may seem, but the "psychology of learning" as usually conceived. To modify the attitudes and views of forewomen toward the employment of older women—that is, to get them to learn a new attitude—the technologist may need, as Marrow and French have illustrated for us, the techniques of non-directive interviewing in order to discover the specific attitudinal barriers, may need the psychology of "catharsis" in order to clear the emotional atmosphere, or the psychology of participation in order to insure a problem-solving approach. To insure retention of material learned in school, the technologist may need to find ways of providing that the material shall be ego-related for the particular learners.

These, clearly, are highly psychological principles; and the research which leads to their discovery and to the elucidation of their rôle in learning, the whole development of a systematic technology, is a task for the applied psychologist interested in actual learning activities for their practical value. That it will have fruitful relations with pure psychology goes without saying.

Such a technology of learning will make a direct attack upon significant practical problems. It will deal as closely as possible with the actual conditions under which the learner must work. Thus work with animals must be regarded as, at best, merely suggestive. A study of the effect of "tuition" upon the way rats run the maze may or may not yield data for scientific theory; it yields practical conclusions only about how rats run mazes. Experiments with the pursuitmeter or with nonsense syllables have similar potential value for pure theory and, surely, similar limitations for application. If we wish to learn how children spell, as technologists we must study just that; we must conduct our experiments in schools, under the real conditions of school life, or as nearly so as possible.

I grant that such an approach has its limitations. The generalizations discovered lack "spread" and, as indicated earlier, technological generalizations often overlap with each other in a way which for science would be exceedingly untidy and unparsimonious. When the organizing principle is that of use, there is apt to be much duplication and repetition.

But it is possible to bring order and system into the rules and principles of practical use in the field of learning just as it has been in engineering. The psychotechnology of learning will therefore have its theories. But they will be the theories which arise out of the problems of everyday living and they will be theories which lead us back into the field of application—i.e., where we help persons to reorganize their behavior for readier and more effective response to the conditions of life.

---

*16. The Operant, from Rat to Man: An Introduction to Some Recent Experiments on Human Behavior **

THE CLASSICAL APPROACH to studies of the conditioned response follows in the tradition of Pavlov. In these studies an unconditioned stimulus is presented together with another that is to become the

* William S. Verplanck, "The operant, from rat to man: an introduction to some recent experiments on human behavior," *Transactions* of The New York Academy of Sciences, XVII, Series II (1955), 594–601. By permission of the author and The New York Academy of Sciences.

conditioned stimulus. In time, with repeated presentations together, the conditioned stimulus alone is sufficient to elicit the response formerly given to the unconditioned stimulus. Note that in this outline, both of the stimuli are exposed *before* the subject responds.

Recent extensions of this research, however, have stressed the importance of the results of particular behaviors rather than what preceded them. We do something, it is rewarded or reinforced by what happens afterwards, so we tend to repeat the performance. This kind of learning situation has been called "operant conditioning," and much recent research has concentrated on clarifying the principles governing its operation. Most of the work has been done with animal subjects. The present paper, however, reports some studies with human subjects that show more clearly the relevance of these principles to normal social functioning.

VIRTUALLY ALL PSYCHOLOGISTS accept the premise that human behavior is orderly. The order that they see, however, varies considerably from group to group, and the aspects of behavior in which these orders appear differ as well. The clinician and the personality psychologist observe their fellow men and see need-presses, repressions, and aggressive drives. The experimental psychologist finds his order in the rates at which nonsense syllables are learned, or at which conditioned eyelid reflexes are acquired. If he is physiologically oriented, he is apt to concern himself with muscle twitches and even with the secretion of saliva. It is in terms of such variables that psychologists have set their descriptions of, and their predictions about, the actions of people.

All of us, whether psychologists or not, observe people acting. We learn rules of "practical psychology." Some of us, especially the novelists and playwrights, do a remarkably good job of giving plausible accounts of behavior, often in terms that seem pertinent. These writers, however, do not employ the language used by psychologists at either end of the spectrum. They describe ordinary, everyday behavior, and describe it well, but not by using the conceptualizations that psychologists seem to have found useful, nor even terms that can be readily translated into such conceptualizations.

The psychologist's efforts tend to be limited in their usefulness to the description and prediction of the behavior of people whose behavior is awry, or of people who are engaged in the strange and unusual activities demanded of them in a laboratory of experimental psychology. Dale Carnegie, practical politicians, and, perhaps, everybody *but* psychologists, concern themselves with simple, ordinary, everyday behavior. One reason for this situation is, perhaps, the lack of methods of conceptualizing behavior, or of abstracting relevant aspects of behavior for study that are not clinic- or laboratory-bound. This lack of methods is due, perhaps, to a conviction that ordinary behavior is too complex and is determined by too many variables to make possible the discovery of any order except by the application of theory.

What I desire to do here is to introduce some concepts, and to describe some experiments derived from them, that suggest that the orderliness of human behavior may be more accessible than has been hitherto assumed. These experiments may accordingly suggest new directions for research on human behavior.

A number of years ago, in a series of articles that were summarized in his book, *The Behavior of Organisms* (1938), B. F. Skinner introduced two new concepts into the behavioral sciences. These concepts had familiar names, but their experimental and theoretical content represented a sharp break with the past, a break that had been foreshadowed only in the writings of Kantor (1924).

The first of these concepts is that of the operant response, defined as a part of behavior (a) that is recurrently identifiable and hence enumerable; and (b) whose rate of occurrence can be determined as a systematic function of certain classes of environmental variables. These parts of behavior, or actions, are what we can see an animal perform repeatedly. They are not simple muscle twitches or limb movements. Rather, they are meaningful, repeated actions. They constitute bar presses rather than leg extensions, the picking up of food rather than digital flexions, the speaking of words rather than laryngeal contractions. One class of environmental variable of which such responses are functions represents the second new concept. This is the reinforcing stimulus, defined as a recurrently identifiable and experimentally manipulable part of the environment that has the property of modifying the rate of occurrence of those operant responses that have produced it. Like responses, they are parts of the environment that are meaningful to the animal, not abstract physical events. They are doors, spoken words, food, not the energy patterns that concern sense physiologists. The two concepts are closely related to one another, so much so, in fact, that many writers, including Skinner himself, often state that operant responses are defined by their consequences, that is, by their production of a given reinforcement. Without going into detail on the experimental and theoretical questions involved in this statement, let me single out for elaboration certain properties of these concepts that distinguish them sharply from those other concepts of stimulus and response that have been widely understood—and even more widely misunderstood—by both psychologists and laymen.

The first of these properties is this: it is not possible to determine arbitrarily and a priori what recurrently identifiable parts of behavior will prove to be responses—that is, what parts of behavior will obey the empirically established laws of behavior. True, within limits, an experimenter may "shape" a part of behavior by differential reinforcement, and thus may be able to introduce a new response into the animal's repertoire, but his ability to do so is sharply limited by the animal itself. Animals of each species, each with its own individual history, come to the experimenter with a repertoire of operant responses that the experimenter can analyze and, within limits, modify. By and large, however, the experimenter must work with those responses that he finds in the animal's behavior. Not all recurrently identifiable behaviors are responses. After observation, the sophisticated experimenter will often be able to guess which identifiable parts of the animal's behavior will prove to be responses, that is, will vary as particular functions of reinforcing stimuli.

Similarly, the experimenter does not have unlimited latitude in determining a priori what environmental events he can use as reinforcing stimuli for an animal. As with responses, he can convert, to a limited degree, originally neutral events into reinforcing stimuli. To do this, he must follow certain experimental procedures. There still remains, however, the empirical problem of determining the whole class of events that will reinforce an already identified response of his experimental subject. Again, as with response, the sophisticated experimenter often will be able to guess which of the environmental events that he can make dependent on a response will produce changes in the rate of occurrence of that response in the period following the occurrence of the environmental event.

With some reason, operant responses have been characterized as "spontaneous" or "voluntary." They are what the animal does "by himself." This is not to say that operants are independent of the ordinary laws of elicitation (and hence of our usual conceptions of causality in behavior) but rather that, for all practical purposes, the only control the experimenter has over them is the one he exerts by the operation of reinforcement, that is, by presenting the animal with a reinforcing stimulus following the occurrence of the response.

In tackling any new piece of behavior experimentally, or in starting to study the behavior of a previously uninvestigated species, the experimenter has a double problem. He must find responses, and he must find reinforcing stimuli that control their occurrence. More often than not, he designs experiments that involve the simultaneous identification both of the operant responses and of the reinforcing stimuli by demonstrating orderly changes in the rate of some part of behavior that are contingent upon the association between that part of behavior and a specific environmental change. A bar press is a response, and food is a reinforcing stimulus, because when bar presses produce food, the rat presses the bar more frequently. By the same rules, water is a reinforcing stimulus for a thirsty rat, whose response may be the sticking of its nose in one corner of the cage.

In view of these systematic restrictions, one is not surprised that almost all studies of operant conditioning have been made on two responses and on two species. The bar pressing of hungry rats and the key-pecking of hungry pigeons, both with reinforcement by food, have been experimentally studied on a scale that, to put it mildly, is intensive. A few other responses from a few other species, involving a few other reinforcing stimuli, have been studied, but not very extensively. In any case, a very large body of experimental evidence has been amassed on the operant, and behavioral psychologists may take some pride in the number of stimulus-response laws that have been found.

The problem arises, however, of the relationship of this body of experimental data, and the laws derived from it, to human behavior. For those investigators interested in men, wherein lies the relevance of these laws? Several kinds of attempts have been made to exhibit such relevance. The first of these may be termed "extrapolation by analogy." The theorist hypothesizes that certain kinds of human behavior are responses and that certain kinds of events are reinforcing stimuli for humans. The rat- and pigeon-derived laws are then assumed to apply, and a set of statements about human behavior are generated that satisfy the writer and his friends, and that horrify others or (what is worse) leave them cold. This has been the history of Skinner's *Walden Two* (1949), and of his *Science and Human Behavior* (1953).

The second tactic is to elaborate a rather complex theoretical structure and then to spell out predictions of human behavior that may or may not be experimentally testable. This, too, has produced books that edify or horrify, depending on the reader.

A third procedure is an experimental one. In this, one studies human behavior in the laboratory under conditions that parallel as closely as possible the experimental procedures followed for the lower animals. Very simple responses are studied, and very simple reinforcers are used. In 1942, Warren and Brown conditioned children to press a lever, using candy as a reinforcing stimulus. Since then, a number of responses have been conditioned, usually involving tapping a telegraph key or the like as response and, with food, the registration of a number, or the playing of music as reinforcer. The studies have shown clearly the reproducibility in human subjects of the laws of operant conditioning found to obtain in rats. These methods, however, leave something to be demanded. The relevance of pressing-a-key-for-a-piece-of-candy to most everyday human behavior may be questioned, and the vexing problem of "awareness" enters, so that a variety of "interpretations of the results" are possible. It may reasonably be questioned whether a human subject, under observation and engaged in unfamiliar activities in a laboratory, will behave as he would if he were not in such a special situation.

The fourth tactic is the one that is the subject of this paper. This is the identification of responses and of reinforcing stimuli, and the verification and eduction of laws relating them to one another in human behavior under conditions where the subject is acting as naturally as possible, and where, insofar as possible, he is not "aware" of what is going on. The approach is characterized by a broad increase in the classes of both responses and reinforcing stimuli investigated, and by a controlled relaxation of the rigorous (and very probably irrelevant) environmental controls exerted in the laboratory.

The first such investigation was that of Greenspoon (1950). From his observations of "nondirective" therapy, Greenspoon suspected that the therapist's "mmm-hmm" was a reinforcing stimulus and, hence, that it modified the verbal behavior of the client undergoing therapy. He proceeded to test this notion in the laboratory by instructing each of his large (separately run) number of subjects to say as many different words as they could. He further assumed that *saying plural nouns* was a response, and proceeded to show that the relative frequency of plural nouns in the subject's verbal behavior was a function of the experimenter's manipulations in reinforcing the subject by casually murmuring "mmm-hmm" each time he said one. Greenspoon went on to discover several other reinforcing stimuli. In the data he reported, none of his subjects was aware that his behavior had changed as a function of reinforcement. None seemed to notice the experimenter's "mmm-hmm's," even though his behavior changed as a function of them.

In 1951, we tried to repeat the Greenspoon experiment in a class at Harvard. The experimenters had had very little previous work with human conditioning. They were game, however, and cornered their subjects in a variety of places. The results were interesting and instructive. A few experimenters obtained unequivocally positive results, but not always without the subject becoming aware of the reinforcements. The successful experimenters were the most prestigeful, socially adept individuals, and the unsuccessful ones tended to be those of what might be termed lower prestige. At the same time, attempts were made to condition simple motor behavior, using reinforcers such as "mmmhmms," smiles, and "good." The results, as with verbal behavior, were indifferent.

Therefore, a new tack in the research was taken. In an attempt to pin down the relevant variables, we reverted to the study of simple motor behavior, and modified the procedure to ensure that subjects responded to the reinforcing stimuli (the experiments described here are more fully reported in a paper now in press). Subjects were instructed explicitly as to the environmental changes that the experimenter would manipulate, although no information was given them as to the behavior the experimenter would reinforce. After finding a fellow student who was willing to be a subject, the experimenter instructed him as follows: "Your job is to work for points. You get a point every time I tap the table with my pencil. As soon as you get a point, record it on your sheet of paper. Keep track of your own points." With these instructions, it seemed likely that a pencil tap, a "point," would prove to be a reinforcing stimulus. The method worked very well. Indeed, the experimenters were now able to condition a wide variety of simple motor behaviors, such as slapping the ankle, tapping the chin, raising an arm, picking up a fountain pen, and so on. They were further able to differentiate out, or shape, more complex parts of behavior, and then to manipulate them as responses. The data they obtained included the results on the manipulation of many of the variables whose effects were familiar in operant conditioning of rats and pigeons. Despite the fact that the experiments were carried out in a variety of situations, the experimenters were able to obtain graphical functions that could not be distinguished from functions obtained on the rat or the pigeon in a Skinner box.

To be sure, the responses studied in humans were very different from the key pecking of a pigeon, or the bar pressing of a rat, and a point is a very different event from the arrival of a pellet of food in a food hopper. But the general laws relating those parts of behavior demonstrated to be responses to those environmental events shown to be reinforcing stimuli were the same.

More interesting, there appeared to be no fixed relationship between the conditioning effects and the subject's ability to state verbally the response that the experimenter was reinforcing. That is, the subjects were responding in a lawful and orderly way without necessarily being aware of what they were doing. They were not necessarily "figuring it out."

With these results, we were encouraged to proceed in two directions. First, we returned to the Greenspoon experiment and repeated it with certain refinements of design, and with experimenters who had acquired considerable experience in the conditioning of human motor behavior. These results are reported elsewhere, but they may be summarized briefly here: experienced experimenters had no difficulty in reproducing the changes in rate of saying words of particular classes that Greenspoon reported. The experimenters' "mmm-hmm," although uttered without instructions and introduced as if unintentionally, modified the subject's behavior, whether or not the subject noticed it. Subjects usually were aware of the reinforcing stimuli, however, and, at the end of the experiment, would tend to report something such as, "I noticed that you seemed to like nouns for a while, and that then you didn't care."

The second direction was forward, and it took a long step beyond the chin tappings and word sayings that had been shown to be responses. For a number of reasons (not the least of which was a set of encouraging results from an exploratory experiment), we hypothesized that in an ordinary conversation, saying sentences of a particular class would act as a response, and that agreement by a hearer, or paraphrasing back to the speaker by a hearer, would prove to be reinforcing stimuli to the speaker.

Two experiments were done. In the first, the response reinforced was *stating opinions,* where opinions were defined as sentences beginning "I think that," "I believe that," and the like. In the second, the response reinforced was *making any statement on a preselected topic,* the topic being chosen by the experimenter and introduced into the conversation by him in a sentence requiring no answer.

The experiments were carried out in a series of 44 conversations that took place on a wide variety of topics and in a variety of circumstances. The sole restriction on the experimenter was that he carry out the experiment with only himself and the subject present, and under conditions where he could keep accurate but camouflaged records of the subject's behavior. He was also under instructions to terminate the experiment if the subject gave any indication that he suspected that this was anything other than an ordinary conversation.

The results of these experiments were unequivocal. In the first experiment, on opinion-statements, every one of 23 subjects showed a higher rate of giving opinion-statements during the 10-minute period when the experimenter reinforced each of them by agreeing with it, or by repeating it back to him in paraphrase, than he showed in the first 10-minute period, when the experimenter did not reinforce. In a final 10-minute period, 21 of 23 subjects showed the converse effect, termed extinction, that is, they decreased in their rate of stating opinions when reinforcement was withdrawn. Irrespective of topic of conversation, or of the situation in which the conversation took place, the expected changes in rate occurred, under conditions where not one subject gave any indication, at any time, that he was "aware" of the experimental manipulation. The subjects' behavior, an orderly function of the experimenters' actions, followed the laws of reinforcement without any awareness by the subject, even of the fact that he was in an experiment.

In the second experiment, the experimenter introduced the experimental topic at the end of the first 10 minutes of conversation. Some subjects (N = 6) were controls, and were not reinforced through the following 10-minute period. The others (N = 15) were regularly reinforced. Under these conditions, every subject but one replied to the experimenter's sentence introducing the topic. Those who were not reinforced dropped the topic quickly (within 2 or 3 minutes), whereas those who were reinforced shifted their speech so that almost everything they said through the next 10 minutes of conversation fell into the specified response-class. In all cases, on the withdrawal of reinforcement, and without respect to whether statements on other topics were reinforced, the subjects dropped to a rate of zero on the previously introduced and reinforced topic.

Again, no subject gave evidence of being aware in any way that this was not an ordinary conversation.

These experimental results indicate that our hypotheses with respect to the analysis of conversational speech into response and reinforcing stimuli were justified. One example of complicated, superficially variable human behavior proves simple under experimental analysis. Order is readily demonstrable. The time may hence be ripe for an extension of experimental analysis into other areas of human behavior that have been considered unsusceptible to direct experimental investigation.

Orderly, significant data *can* be collected in situations devoid of the elaborate environmental controls exerted in the laboratory if significant variables are manipulated, if measures of that behavior are possible, and if experimental designs are clear-cut. Experiments can be performed on human subjects "in the field" and under conditions where the subject will not be able to discriminate either his own or the experimenter's behavior as dependent on an experimental procedure. Hence we can study human behavior with good reason to hope that the mere fact that it is being investigated will not modify it. This alone has seriously limited the generality of the many results of laboratory experiments.

One can now conceive of a broad experimental program designed to determine what other parts of behavior have the functional properties of responses, and how broad a class of environmental events will prove to be reinforcing stimuli for one or another subject. The conceptual tools are at hand. The experimental methodology, involving a number of sophisticated and skilled experimenters, is at hand. A very rapid development in this field may be expected. We may hope for an experimental, rather than an "intuitive," understanding of many of the things that people do.

---

17. A Restatement of the Problem of Learning *

THIS STATEMENT offers an examination of the learning process from the "field theoretical" viewpoint, or field theory. Although prepared more than twenty-five years ago, it represents an approach that still leads to many significant contributions in this and other areas of psychology. Note that this formulation proposes that learning be regarded as a reorganization of the field, almost in perceptual terms. The approach is very different from that taken by those emphasizing conditioned responses, and Dr. Adams makes the difference quite clear in his discussion.

I. INTRODUCTION

THE PRESENT chaotic state of the psychology of learning affords an ample demonstration of the urgent need for a re-examination of current formulations of the problem.

The best introduction to the restatement here to be advanced is a brief critical consideration of certain general properties of the class animals, with some mention of those facts which are known as the "laws of learning." For the purposes of this critique the discussion will be more or less limited to the relatively unambiguous types of learning which, incidentally, are those upon which the "laws" are for the most part based, and of which the learning of animals in puzzle boxes, mazes, *détour* problems and the like is typical. It will be a relatively simple matter later to indicate the position in this formulation of the more equivocal forms of modifiability,[1] such as adaptation, conditioned reflexes, etc. It will also not be difficult to extend these considerations from apes, cats and rats to both ends of the animal kingdom. So when the reader has an impulse in the following introductory critique to insist:

* Donald K. Adams, "A restatement of the problem of learning," *British Journal of Psychology,* XXII (1931), 150–76. By permission of the author and the *British Journal of Psychology.*

[1] The term "modifiability" seems to be a lumping or confusion of the four properties discussed in the next section.

"But here is a type of learning to which these considerations do not apply," I can but ask him to be patient and to reserve his objections for a later section, with the assurance that this temporary limitation is adopted only in the interests of clarity and brevity of exposition.

II. CERTAIN PROPERTIES OF ORGANISMS

In my opinion, learning is a *real* process (the exact nature of which will be defined in due course) and not the superficial and merely technologically defined concept for which it is so generally mistaken. Further, learning is not only a real, but a *psychological* process, a fact that psychology seems to have forgotten. Finally, it is a *process,* and not to be confused with certain *properties* which we shall have to discuss. Failure to make this distinction is one of the important factors in the present confusion of thinking about learning.

(a) *Needs*

The first property of organisms to which attention must be called is the obvious one that they need things, *i.e.* they have *needs*. This admits of no argument. Sticks and stones do not need things, but organisms do. These may be air, water, light, wealth, pearl necklaces, motor cars or what not. Some of these needs, namely those that are common to or characteristic of large groups (*e.g.* species) of organisms and that recur frequently through fairly large parts of their life cycle, have been called instincts.

This is, I believe, the essential basis of the distinction made by Lewin when he speaks of "real" needs and "quasi-needs." The former I take to be what are usually called instinctive needs, and the latter the less common ones. Perhaps they could better be characterized as specific (*i.e.* common to a species) and individual needs, but the distinction has, at least for our present purpose, no great importance. Certainly the difference between them is not one of reality or genuineness.

The needs of organisms have no necessary relation to consciousness. They may or may not be represented in consciousness by wishes, desires, etc. Behaviourists especially talk a great deal about their doctrine as being a branch of biology, which of course it is not. Psychology, however, *is* a biological field, and one of its fundamental premises must be the recognition that a tree's need for light, a cat's need to escape from the puzzle box and a psychologist's need to put her into it are but different manifestations of the fundamental biological fact that organisms need things.

(*b*) *Parsimony*

The second property of the class animals which we have to discuss is not so easily described. Although a fundamental property, co-ordinate with that of needs, it has been only partially recognized, and even that by only a few investigators. Consequently we shall have to approach it in a more roundabout way.

In attempting several years ago to give a general description of the adaptive behaviour of cats in a considerable variety of situations, the following appeared to be the essential features of the process:

1. There is a cat.
2. There is something the cat wants.[2] The thing wanted may be a state of affairs, such as freedom from constraint, and the thing may be wanted very much or very little.
3. There are other things too. Nearly everybody calls these the situation. The disposition of these other things may be such as to facilitate or to impede the cat's getting what it wants.
4. In one way or another, after certain movements [3] with respect to the situation and the thing wanted, the cat gets what it wants.
5. There is the cat again.
6. There is something the cat wants.
7. There is another situation, *more or less* like the first. This similarity may be very great [the "same" situation] or very slight.
8. The cat gets what it wants more readily than it did before, that is, with greater economy of movement.[4] This economy may be small or great.

Now this economy is, under certain conditions (*i.e.* repetition), a characteristic *behaviour sign* of learning in just the same way that

[2] Prof. McDougall suggested shortly after the appearance of the above formulation that the word "need" would be more accurate and comprehensive and less ambiguous than "want." He was right, and the word "need" is here used throughout. It is necessary also to mention Wallace Craig's very acute studies of the dynamics of behaviour. These studies, especially that on appetites and aversions, seem never to have commanded the hearing they deserve, perhaps because our ears were filled with the sound and fury of behaviourism. Lewin's ingenuity has more recently opened up this whole field (in humans) to experimental investigation.

[3] In man actual movement may not be involved, and the whole field, including the needed objects, may be purely ideational or symbolic. We make no real error and have the advantage of concreteness if discussion is restricted for the moment to non-human animals and actual movement. As will be abundantly evident, the same considerations hold for both species.

[4] Unless anticipated, the objection will probably be raised that this economy upon repetition does not always occur, that the second trial may take longer than the first, that the tenth may display more movement than the ninth. These are "accidental" in the truest sense of the word: that is, they are due to undetected differences in the animal or the situation. Either the situation or the need is not the same as in the preceding trial.

spherical shape is, under certain conditions, a sign of surface tension in a drop of fluid. Moreover it is *merely* a sign of learning. It is not necessary for the act ever to be repeated in order that the learning process should take place, any more than it is necessary for a drop of liquid to be in the situation in which it assumes a spherical shape in order that the process of exposing the least possible surface may occur. The spherical shape of raindrops or of molten lead, in falling, may very well have been the sign that led to the discovery of the fact of surface tension; and the economy of movement upon repetition of an act may serve in the same way to draw our attention to the fact of learning. But to consider that this economy *is* learning, as is usually done, introduces at the very outset a fundamental confusion between the process and one of its contingent or conditional behaviour signs.

Economy upon repetition is the most convenient and accessible and perhaps also the least unreliable sign of learning. Under certain conditions it may even be, and has been, used as a "measure" of learning, but it must be used with extreme caution. Measuring this economy in terms of elapsed time required to execute an act is notoriously unsatisfactory; measuring it in terms of "errors" is somewhat less so. In any case what is measured is not learning but economy, which is no more than a contingent behaviour sign of learning. This is often, to be sure, the best we can do, but it must be remembered that learning is not being measured directly and that it occurs in the absence of the condition usually used to demonstrate its sign, namely, of repetition.

Further, this economy upon repetition or, better, the property (we shall call it *parsimony*) of which it is simply one manifestation, is a fundamental property of a certain class of bodies (namely, animals and probably all organisms [5]) in just the same way that surface tension is a property of another class of bodies (liquids). *We need not and cannot profitably inquire further.*

Thorndike included among his classical experiments on cats some in which the door of the puzzle box was opened by the experimenter when the cat licked or, in some cases, scratched herself. He found, in spite of the crude measure (time) of economy used, marked differences between the learning curves of these cats and those of the cats that learned to escape from puzzle boxes the doors of which were opened by some effort of the cat herself, such as pulling a loop, pressing a pedal or turning a button. We are not here primarily concerned with this difference,

[5] I think that parsimony is a property of all organisms, but the point is not sufficiently important to the problem of learning to warrant the extended treatment that would be required to demonstrate it. Some interesting *Umweg* experiments might be made with potato sprouts in cellars.

to which we shall have later to return, but with another even more significant. He observed that "there is in all these cases a noticeable tendency, of the cause of which I am ignorant, to diminish the act until it becomes a mere vestige of a lick or a scratch. . . ."

Now Thorndike had the insight to recognize an ultimate fact when he saw it and did not attempt an "explanation." In the more than thirty years since his observation was first published it has never been explained, and I suggest that we proceed for a while on the assumption that it never will be. In discussing this valuable observation in the monograph previously quoted I wrote:

> As to the tendency for the act to diminish into a mere vestige and not to be immediately repeated if the door is not opened the first time: in the loop box the animal experiences something that resists, then gives way and more or less immediately thereafter, the release. (This may be the clatter of the falling door or the sight of the hole in the wall, or both.) Further, the release does not occur unless the other experience occurs. Now to the experimenter who releases the cat from the other box, a lick is a lick and a scratch is a scratch, no matter of what energy or what degree of attention by the animal. There is no irreducible minimum of effort as there is in pulling the loop. The animal achieves the same end with a little lick as with a big one, and behaviour is parsimonious.

That is all that can be said about it. Behaviour *is* parsimonious and there is nothing (at least for the present) that we can do about it. It may profitably be regarded as a fundamental property of animals that we must learn to use in the formulation of our problems. One manifestation of this property of parsimony has been recognized by a number of investigators for a long time, but always, so far as I know, in confusion with another property. This derivative fact, about economy upon repetition, has been given various names such as the "law of least action" or of "least effort." Szymanski called it *"das Prinzip der kürzesten Bahn."* Gengerelli, who has recently supplied some good illustrations of it, calls it "the principle of maxima and minima" and tries to make it do too much. His formulation, in addition to being the most recent, is one of the clearest that I know. It is as follows:

> The behaviour of an organism elicited by a given stimulating situation which affords relief to an internal need of that organism tends, *with repetition,*[6] to approach, in terms of time, space and effort involved, the minimal limit compatible with the relief of that need; the nature of the limit being defined by the structure of the organism and of the external situation.

[6] Italics mine. Several pages earlier Gengerelli says, in italics, that *"the organism, under the stress of a need, tends in consequence of repetition, to relieve that need by the process of least effort."*

This, as a generalization of observed fact, can hardly be challenged, for it is corroborated by every learning curve ever drawn. Gengerelli considers it self-evident enough and all-embracing enough to be taken as one of those facts "which do not stand in need of explanation," to serve as the "cornerstone of our explanation" of learning. Its self-evidence is not likely to be questioned, but whether it is "capable of embracing all of the varied phenomena with which we have to deal" is another matter. Perhaps it would be useful to sacrifice a little self-evidence for greater extension. Certainly any candidate for a postulate should have some implications beyond the phenomena it is designed to "explain."

What has "repetition" to do with this matter? We have seen that it is primarily merely a means of detecting economy. Its inclusion in the above formulation probably derives from the notion that repetition is a causal factor in learning, and inasmuch as this postulate is not required to do more than explain learning (which is apparently the phenomenon described by the postulate itself!), it embodies that traditional misconception. That there is no causal relation between "repetition" and learning is clear from the fact that each may occur in the absence of the other. Learning occurs without repetition and repetition occurs without learning. The relation between them is accidental and wholly contingent upon a variety of special conditions, some of which we shall have later to mention.

If, instead, we consider that *all* behaviour is parsimonious, as I have already proposed, we shall have an instrument of considerably wider utility. Accordingly, I shall consider parsimony a property of the class animals, co-ordinate with needs and the others to be discussed. It may be described briefly as follows: animals approach a needed object or state of affairs by the shortest route or most economical means functionally possible. Now "functionally possible" may be taken to mean "possible for that particular animal at that particular time (*i.e.* point in its history or experience, physical condition, etc.) in that particular situation." It is thus differentiated both from the "physically" possible and from the potentially possible for that animal. (This qualification is made only for temporary convenience of exposition and loses its significance when the matter is properly regarded.) Now this property of parsimony is not so "self-evident" as the "principle of maxima and minima." It can be observed most clearly in situations and under conditions (inside and outside the animal) such that what I have called the functional and the physical routes of least roundaboutness coincide.[7] This occurs under certain conditions when only one need is involved as

[7] Cf. Bingham's "principle of the readiest means."

in certain "tropisms," where the structural or physiological factors that limit parsimony are usually fairly evident. In much the same way surface tension can be observed most clearly under certain special conditions, *i.e.* when a drop of one fluid is suspended in a quantity of another of like specific gravity. But there is no reason to suppose that parsimony ceases to hold when more needs than one are involved, as is usually the case in psychology. Physical laws can be verified only in specially constructed "pure" cases, but we do not suppose that they lose their validity in the everyday world.

The recognition of parsimony as a property of animals (organisms) thus substitutes for the sterile question, "Why, or how, does the 'correct response' get selected?" the much more profitable and answerable one, "Why is it (the *potentially* most economical) not always selected at once?" The behaviour of the paramoecium bumping his way round an obstruction does not look very parsimonious until we consider his peculiar structure. In the case of Gengerelli's rats, for example, we must ask why they did not take the diagonal—the physically and potentially shortest—path at once. Part of the answer is that the animals were satisfying different needs at different times. The naive assumption that they were always satisfying the need for food is entirely unwarranted and a direct consequence of insufficient and insufficiently critical anthropomorphism. Thus, at first, the field was largely determined by the need to get information (Pavlov's "exploratory reflex"). Later it was jointly determined by the need for food and the need to stick to the wall ("stereotropism"), and eventually by the need for food (practically) alone. If the other needs had been satisfied first, it would have been evident that repetition has nothing to do with the property of parsimony. But here again the confusion of this property with the learning process has vitiated both the experiment and the "postulate."

We find then that parsimony is a universal property of the class animals as surface tension is a property of the class liquids; that *one* manifestation of this property is economy upon repetition of an act; that this particular manifestation of the property of parsimony is often used as a behaviour sign or even as a "measure" of learning; that this sign is practically always mistaken for the process of learning itself. It will be apparent by now that the "law of least action" involves a confusion between the property of parsimony here described and the next property to be mentioned, *i.e.* retentivity.

What then becomes of the "law" of exercise or repetition or frequency? We have seen that parsimony is a property of the class animals, comparable to growth. Now growth takes place in time and requires time to become evident. Economy (usually) requires repetition to become evident. But how far would we get in understanding the biology of growth if we solemnly proclaimed that the sole law of growth is that size increases, within limits, with time? Yet that is essentially what the "law" of repetition or frequency asserts with regard to the psychology of learning: *i.e.* that learning or efficiency, within limits, increases with frequency of repetition.[8] In either case, a condition necessary to, or useful in, the detection of a process is considered its cause. When the role of repetition as a rather clumsy but still very useful instrument for detecting the economy that is a sign of learning is once clearly seen, the point requires no further elaboration, and the "law" of repetition is seen to be meaningless.

The familiar fact of insight *alone* is sufficient to demonstrate once and for all that there is no real or necessary or causal relation between learning and repetition or frequency of repetition. Whatever else insight may or may not be, it is a kind of learning which does not require repetition in order that its expression should attain maximal economy. In spite of its familiarity we managed, with sufficient determination, consistently to ignore [9] the fact of insight in our thinking about learning until Köhler forced it upon our attention by exhibiting it in apes. Even then there was, and is, an uncomfortable feeling that a fact so disturbing to our revered "laws" of learning ought either to be argued out of existence or to be repealed by edict of the Behaviourist.[10] One thing at least is finally established by the mere occurrence of insight, and that is that learning is *not* caused by repetition. Certain special conditions under which repetition may seem upon superficial examination to have a causal relation to learning will be discussed in a later section.

(c) *Retentivity*

Another property of organisms, more generally recognized than parsimony, and consequently requiring less extended treatment, is *retentivity*. This has been called by various names, *e.g.* Semon's *Mneme.* One of its particular manifestations is called "memory." Now for some obscure reason this *property* of retentivity has, like that of parsimony, usually been confused with the *process* of learning. Perhaps this confusion may be traced to the fact that the detection of retentivity always, and the detection of learning often, requires repetition.

The physiological or physico-chemical basis of this property is nat-

[8] It is not necessary here to criticize particular formulations of this "law." These considerations are believed to apply to the idea in all its varied expressions.

[9] Or else to throw it into the catch-all of "meaning," another problem in urgent need of restatement.

[10] Or the Anthroponomist.

urally a matter of very great interest to psychologists: but it is not primarily a psychological question. We do not need, and cannot afford, to wait for the chemist's explanation (if indeed one ever becomes possible) in order to recognize the property and its importance to psychology. Certain animal protoplasms (nervous) or organizations thereof seem to possess the property of retentivity in greater degree than others. That also is interesting and important, but the more essential fact is that it is a fundamental property of the class animals, entirely co-ordinate with and distinct from the previously described property of parsimony. The fact that both of these may be displayed by means of repetition does not in the least affect their mutual independence.

The "laws" of disuse and of recency are expressions of the fact that this retention has temporal limits. They do not deal with the learning process at all.

This property, like all those mentioned, has no necessary relation to consciousness. It may or may not be manifested by conscious processes.

(d) *Sensitivity*

The fourth and, for the present purpose, the last of the general properties of organisms that requires to be mentioned is that of *sensitivity*. It too is generally recognized for what it is (namely a *property* of organisms co-ordinate with needs, parsimony and retentivity) thanks largely to the insight of Verworn, who called it "irritability."

The property of sensitivity may be briefly characterized as that in virtue of which an organism acquires information about its environment. Now this "information" may be anything, from that received by a paramoecium when it enters a drop of acid to that received by a physicist when he reads a differential equation. The property of sensitivity, like all the others here discussed, has no general or necessary relation to consciousness. The "information" received by an organism in virtue of this property may or may not be represented in consciousness by sensations, perceptions, or ideas.

III. ON THE NATURE OF THE LEARNING PROCESS

Before defining the nature of the learning process it is desirable to inquire what are the necessary and sufficient conditions of learning. To this end it will be useful to refer again to the previously quoted general description of adaptive behaviour in very diverse situations (page 138). It contains a serious possibility of confusion in the third proposition, which states that the situation may be so disposed as "to facilitate or to impede the cat's getting what it wants." These two possibilities are by no means co-ordinate. "Facilitating" factors may indeed be present in the *situation, i.e.* among the "other things" than the cat and what it wants. In some experimental situations they constitute very important factors indeed. But they are usually at the outset "facilitating" factors *only for the experimenter and not for the animal.*

This brings us to a far-reaching and vitally important distinction that I have elsewhere discussed at considerable length in criticizing Thorndike's neglect of it. This is the distinction between the *situation* and what I shall call the *field.* By "situation" is meant the physical environment, the "other things" of the quoted description. The "field" is the *real* situation in the customary non-psychological use of the word: it is the situation *as it is for the animal.* Again, the field is the situation as it *is* (has existence) for the animal, as it is "sensed" or "received" or "recepted" (must I repeat, without any implication of consciousness?) by the animal by virtue of its property of sensitivity (as well as *all* the other properties we have described). Factors in the *field* may be anything, from an amoeba that has just escaped from another amoeba, to prohibition, economic depression and delusions of persecution.

With the distinction between situation and field clearly in mind it is evident that while the *situation* may contain both facilitating and impeding factors, the *field* of an animal "in" that situation may contain (of these two) only the impediment. The two types of factors are *not,* as their collocation in the quoted proposition might suggest, co-ordinate.

The presence in the field of an impediment, or obstruction, or obstacle, constitutes a necessary condition of learning in general, for obvious reasons. If there is no obstruction in the field learning cannot occur, because the need is satisfied with maximal potential parsimony at once.

The obstruction may be anything, from a barbed-wire fence when the need is to pick up a shot grouse on the other side, to the weight of tradition when the need is to reformulate a scientific problem. The impediment in the field may coincide with a physical barrier in the situation, as in some *détour* (*Umweg*) situations (which incidentally present the simplest possible concrete realization of the conditions of learning), or it may have no counterpart at all in the situation.

The next step is obvious: given the four described properties of organisms, a need, parsimony, retentivity and sensitivity, the presence of an obstruction in the field is the sole and sufficient, as well as the necessary, condition of learning.

The "law" of effect will now be seen to contain (beside its implications for retentivity) the propositions that in all cases of learning there is a need and there is an obstacle to its satisfaction. It thus makes considerably more sense than some of the other "laws." The fact that more or less irrelevant "punishments" and "rewards" are sometimes efficacious is due to the particular (and more complicated) structure of the *field* in those instances.

Discerning psychologists have seen for a long time that learning is a species of adaptation. Yerkes has for years been calling learning "adaptive behaviour." A behaviouristic colleague once criticized the use of this term by Yerkes and the writer, by saying that if adaptive meant anything *all* behaviour was adaptive.

Adaptation certainly means something very concrete and important. It is a collective name for the class of all those processes which are conditioned by any need, specific or individual, of any animal. It is, so to speak, what gets done about a need. Adaptive behaviour is any behaviour conditioned by any need of any animal.

This conception of adaptation and adaptive behaviour obviously is more inclusive than the notion that they mean a class of events or behaviour that is in some way useful or beneficial or pleasant to the animal. It is equally devoid of any implication of value, teleology or hedonism. As McDougall has pointed out in criticism of hedonism, many specific needs, notably those of a female with young, are directly opposed to the pleasure or even to the survival of the animal. The satisfaction of a neurotic compulsion may be accompanied by no pleasure whatever, yet it is a real if only an individual need.

Satisfaction of a need does not at all imply a subjective satisfaction, or pleasantness, or pleasure. It should be repeated that needs have no general relation to consciousness. Whether a need, in any particular case, has a conscious correlate is relatively unimportant.

My behaviourist critic was right, though he did not believe it, when he said that *all* behaviour was adaptive. All behaviour is conditioned by a need, or by needs. It might seem at first that an exception should be made in the case of diffuse discharge such as emotional behaviour, laughter and restless behaviour, but this is not the case. A behaviourist might urge that an exception should be made in the case of the reflexes, but this also is not the case. At the time of the conversation mentioned (1927) I too thought it necessary to distinguish two coordinate sorts of behaviour, *responses* and *acts,* the latter alone being characterized by reference to a need. They may perhaps still be usefully distinguished, but not on that basis. Responses (reflexes, motor habits, etc.) are always either one of two things. They may be acts in themselves, that is, they may be the functionally most parsimonious means to the satisfaction of a particular need, *e.g.* pupillary, wink, or scratch reflexes, etc.[11] Or they may be integral and dependent *parts* of acts. In either case the units of all behaviour are *acts,* and these are *always* determined by a need or needs.

As previously noted, a few psychologists have known for a long time that learning is a species of adaptation. If we recall the definition of adaptation and the property of parsimony it is evident that this is the case. So far as I know, however, the exact nature of the relation, the differentia of the species learning in the genus adaptation have never been clearly stated. They are as follows.

Adaptation has two species. In other words, the processes conditioned by any need of any animal may be of two kinds: (1) changes in the need itself, and (2) changes in the field. It is the second of these that is usually called learning.

This may become clearer through a consideration of the type of learning which, since Köhler, is generally called *insight.* Now insight possesses the extremely valuable characteristic of occurring sufficiently rapidly to permit us to see the true nature of the process of which it is an extreme case. Some processes in nature occur too rapidly to be seen and some occur too slowly. Learning is one of the latter. It is quite possible that if it required a much longer time than it does for the signs of surface tension to become visible the physicists might have been led to ask all manner of foolish questions about it. Learning usually, and always under the conditions customarily established in experiments on the subject (*i.e.* puzzle boxes, nonsense syllables, and particularly mazes), occurs too slowly for its real nature to be evident.[12] Thus behaviourists have even asserted that the conditioned reflex is

[11] It is perhaps necessary here again to remind the reader of the truism that a need does not have to be conscious in order to be an effective determinant of behaviour. A moment's reflection will show that the foregoing applies equally well to such reflex responses as heart beat, which adjusts to meet the need for oxygen, etc., under such varied conditions as temporary violent exercise and permanent arteriosclerosis.

[12] There have been some very ingenious and valuable uses of the maze (in many of these cases it ceases to be a maze), but for the most part it has proved an unmitigated nuisance. It has filled the literature with elaborate investigations of pseudo-problems. It has provided an easy satisfaction for the need of many psychologists to do something "experimental" without forcing them to set a real problem. Its use has become so ingrained and recourse to it so automatic that it short-circuits even conscientious attempts to formulate a problem with decent precision. Its "reliability," or lack of it, has furnished many opportunities for a flight from the difficulties of psychology into statistical virtuosity. It has paralysed or stultified current thinking about learning to an extent that we are not yet in a position even to estimate.

the type of all learning, though they do not seem to have attempted the task of showing precisely *how* other types of learning, more properly so called, may be related to it. The fact is that the conditioned reflex is the one type of learning that manages, even more completely than maze learning, to conceal the true nature of the learning process in a mass of special conditions.

In the case of insight, however, the learning process occurs fast enough for its essential character to become clear. Inasmuch as the term has been somewhat abused in recent years it is perhaps desirable to adduce some specific instances. The case of Köhler's ape who, being in need of a stick, sees a branch of a tree for the first time as a stick, is an excellent one. In this case, an instant earlier the branches of the tree were merely something to be played with: he was sucking them as a matter of fact. His attention was drawn to the bananas outside the cage, and a need for the banana came into existence. With this animal, by reason of his earlier use of sticks, the primary need for the banana implied immediately a need for a stick. With the existence of this need the field was completely reorganized, and what a moment before was a tree became a treasury of sticks. In this case the reorganization of the field took place immediately upon the coming into existence of the need. (Incidentally, the need in turn did not arise until the animal was in a new field, that of the bananas. This instance thus exemplifies also the interdependence of needs and fields which is so characteristic of behaviour.)

It is in some respects still more illuminating to take a case in which the reorganization of the *field* is occasioned by an "accidental" change in the *situation*. The following is one that can very easily be duplicated. A piece of liver is placed on a small pan in a large square cage, enclosed on three sides by wire mesh and on the fourth by a horizontal grill through which the can can be pulled by the attached string. The string is laid in a loose right angle so that about a metre of it must be pulled out before the pan will be moved by the pulling. A cat which has never pulled, played with, or even seen a string is admitted to the room. She soon finds the liver and claws energetically at the wire *nearest* it. She persists in this for a while but eventually gives up: *i.e.* the need subsides with failure, other needs arise. In Freud's language, she suppresses the need: in Lewin's, which, though also designed for human problems, here fits admirably as a description of the behaviour, she "goes out of the field." [13] She may return from time to time to claw

[13] This is equally true when the cat in the puzzle box stops trying to get out and washes and purrs contentedly. While still physically "in the puzzle box" it is no longer there psychologically.

directly at the liver but eventually gives up for good. Under these circumstances, possibly as a "substitute activity," of which I have noted many instances, she may play with the string. In the course of this play the string is eventually pulled straight and the next pull moves the pan. This "accidental" (*i.e.* occurring in the course of activity determined by a different need) change in the situation, and ultimately in the field (the cat hears the pan move and feels its inertia), brings about a still greater one. The need for the liver, which was in abeyance or non-existent, recurs, and the string is no longer a plaything but something that brings the liver nearer. The cat goes to the cage, this time where the string comes out; not (as before) at the point *physically* nearest the desired object but at that which is now *functionally* nearest. She pulls the string again, this time with intent and with gaze fixed upon the pan. She may pull it again, watching instead her foot and the near end of the string. Then she pulls out the liver without further ado.

It is probably not necessary to mention other instances of insight to make the point clear. Though the particular reorganizations of the field involved will vary tremendously, some sort of reorganization occurs in every instance of insight. In the *détour* or *Umweg* problems which, as we have seen, present the simplest possible realization of the conditions of learning, the reorganization consists in the metamorphosis of the first part of the *détour* from a "going away" into an integral part of a "going toward."

There will probably be no serious objection to the proposition that insight consists in a (rapid) reorganization of the field, since that may fairly be called self-evident. It is not at first glance so obvious that *all* learning consists in the reorganization of a field, since in many cases the process occurs very slowly. It is possible in every case, however, to show that the "end-product" of the learning process is a *reorganized* field, and in many cases to determine the nature of the reorganization at once. Where the latter is not at once evident, there is a real problem for experiment. But before considering these problems in greater detail it is necessary to note the conditions, beyond the obvious ones of the situation, that determine fields in general.

We have seen that animals have four properties of importance to learning: needs, parsimony, retentivity and sensitivity. Sensitivity may be very highly differentiated, as in man and the higher animals, or it may be very slightly differentiated, as in the protozoa. The field will naturally be determined in part by the sensitivity of the animal. Visual objects do not occur in the field of an animal without photoreceptors.

The constitution of the field depends also upon retentivity, which likewise varies greatly in different animals. To an animal that has once used a stick as a tool, sticks may retain their tool character for a considerable time. Within this time a situation containing sticks presents quite another field than that which the animal has in the same situation before he has used sticks and after they have lost their tool character.

Parsimony and needs may be considered together. The ultimate dynamic factors in all fields are the needs. Parsimony determines the direction of the movements toward the needed object. Where in other respects equal possibilities for various fields exist, the need that is strongest will determine which potential field is realized.[14] On the other hand, as we have seen, an "accidental" change in the field may occasion a new need.

These four properties are conditions of all fields. The particular type of field which gets reorganized, the type, that is, with which learning is concerned, has one additional condition, namely, an *obstruction* to the satisfaction of the need, as we have already seen. Now in all fields containing an obstruction there occurs a phenomenon of paramount importance, namely, that an obstructed need *distorts* the field in which it occurs to an extent proportional to the strength of the need and the completeness of the obstruction. The precise determination of the kinds of this distortion and of the conditions under which each occurs constitutes, in my opinion, the fundamental task of the psychology of learning. At present we know practically nothing about it. I have a little evidence that, under the influence of a very strong and completely obstructed need, the field contracts spatially. I should be inclined to guess that, under certain conditions, it would also contract temporally, but that again can only be settled by experiment. We shall have occasion later to make several other hypotheses about the varieties of distortion which an obstructed need may produce in a field.

We may be entirely certain of only one thing: that *some* kind of distortion of the field is caused by obstructed needs. The most striking example of this occurs in man in autistic thinking. Here the *field* is so distorted by a strong and frustrated need (self-assertion, sex, or what not) that it no longer bears any resemblance to the *situation*. (Such a field is still *determined* in part by the situation, *e.g.* by the type of obstruction it contains, even when it least resembles the latter.) Somewhat less remote from the "real" situation, but still diverging materially from it, is the field in what is known as "wishful thinking."

In general, of course, imaginal or ideational fields offer much less resistance to distortion, are much more plastic and pliable than other

[14] In the conscious fields of humans and the higher animals this fact is called "attention."

fields, and consequently furnish the most extreme examples of distortion. The manifestations in consciousness of this distortion of the field may also be observed in *perceptual* fields. One of the most valuable of the observations reported in Köhler's book on apes was made upon himself. The following is his description:

> Even before the chimpanzee has happened on the use of sticks, etc., one expects him to do so. When he is occupied energetically but, so far, without success, in overcoming the critical distance, anxiety causes one's view of the field of action [what is here called the situation] to suffer a phenomenological change. Long-shaped and movable objects are no longer beheld with strict and static impartiality, but always in a "vector" as if with a drive toward the critical point.

We constantly see the same and other varieties of distortion of perceptual fields by obstructed needs in everyday life. The impatient motorist for whom red is green, the anxious hunter for whom any moving object in the brush becomes a buck, and countless other instances indicate the universality and versatility of distortion in perceptually present fields.

It must not be supposed that *conscious* fields alone are distorted by needs. They simply provide the clearest and most familiar examples. The distortion of the field of a tree in a dense forest by its need for light is reflected in the distortion of the tree itself. Isolated, it would branch and spread. When the light is obstructed by other trees, it becomes a straight bare trunk with a few branches at the top. The particular mechanism of any such phenomenon (*e.g.* "selection," the fact that collateral branches do bud and die) must not be allowed to obscure the fact that the field is distorted by an obstructed need.

As has been noted, given the properties of organisms, the sole additional condition of learning is an obstruction. An obstructed need always distorts the field. The determination of the varieties of this distortion and of the conditions under which each occurs constitutes the proper task of the experimental psychology of learning. Learning is the process of reorganization sometimes undergone by fields distorted by an obstructed need. When in such fields learning does not occur, the other sort of adaptation (change in the need) must occur.

IV. VARIETIES OF ADAPTATION

(a) Changes in the Need

For the present purpose this group of problems does not require extended treatment. The dynamics of needs in general are being very successfully investigated by Lewin and his collaborators.

We have here only to mention some varieties of changes in needs that have a more or less intimate and obvious relation to the general (*i.e.* not specifically human) problems of learning.

One of the most striking changes that needs undergo is that consequent upon their satisfaction or (under compulsion) supersatiation. Dodge has dealt with a related phenomenon in conjunction with the refractory phase of nervous tissue, and the two phenomena may be very closely related indeed. Karsten has made the most extensive study of satiation. The change undergone by a need in this process amounts to a complete transformation. The need for food may be satisfied to such an extent that it becomes (or there occurs) a need to get away from food even to the point of regurgitation. Incidentally it is here that, for the first time, we find repetition really functioning in a psychological process. It *does* produce satiation (indifference) and, under compulsion, supersatiation (repulsion), which is a complete transformation of the need.

An extreme case of this is the familiar one of the new operative in the chocolate factory or the new girl in the candy shop. According to tradition the needs of these people for sweets are quickly supersatiated to such a degree that they *never* recur. But we need not depend on tradition. It was this very phenomenon, the only one of which repetition may properly be considered a cause, that led Dunlap to question the "law" of repetition. The cases reported by him and by Holsopple and Vanouse of correcting a constant typing error by "practising" the error are cases of the supersatiation, under compulsion, of a weak lower-order need which was already in conflict with a strong higher-order need. By a first-order need I mean the need that determines the whole field. By a lower-order need I mean a need that occurs only in a field determined by another need. Thus Dunlap's need to spell "the" "hte" occurred only in the field determined by the need to type something intelligible. I think this is probably a more useful distinction at least for our purpose, than Lewin's between *"echte"* and *"quasi-Bedürfnisse."* Thus Dunlap's "gamma" hypothesis is more nearly correct than the "beta" hypothesis, and it is not a matter of "probability."

A second way in which needs get changed occurs when an obstruction makes their satisfaction functionally impossible. The Freudians call this *compensation,* but it might more properly be called *substitution.* Its mechanism is not clearly understood, but the phenomenon consists essentially in the fact that when the satisfaction of a strong need is *completely* obstructed, another need becomes still stronger. The only principle of selection of this substitute need that I have been able to observe is the obvious one that the substituted need must be one for which satisfaction is relatively *unobstructed.* The cats, for example, that failed entirely to escape from the puzzle boxes generally washed themselves most assiduously, as if nothing else in the world had any importance. This substituted need may eventually be so well satisfied that they will lie in their cages and purr.

A phenomenon very frequent in human beings but also occurring in many other animals is that of the *induction* of needs. A need may occur in an animal upon the occurrence within its field of the satisfaction or approach to satisfaction of a like need in another animal. The Smiths need a new car, though their old one is in excellent condition, because the Joneses have purchased one. The ape that was quite indifferent to the banana outside his cage needs it so badly when another ape approaches it that he invents a method of getting it. Kuo has recently reported some very painstaking experiments, on the genesis of rat killing in cats, which gain measurably in significance when regarded as experiments on the induction of needs, and which should be extended with this question in mind.

(b) Changes in the Field: Learning

Any doubts that *all* learning is a reorganization of a field determined by an obstructed need may be dispelled, even in those cases where the process itself is too slow to be observed, by examining the "end-product" of the process and comparing it with the original field. The keyboard of a typewriter presents quite another field to the experienced typist than it did when she first made its acquaintance. The maze is very different to the rat after he has been through it. The buzzer has a wholly new place in the field of the "conditioned" dog. The "end-product" of all learning, even in the technological sense, is always a reorganized field.

These examples are of the kind that behaviourism would bring forward in objection to the proposition that repetition has no causal relation to learning. We must therefore consider why, in these and similar instances, repetition may appear to possess great importance.

We may choose typewriting as the representative of the whole group of skills, because the *situation,* the "physical" correlate of the field, so to speak, is more obvious and concrete in this instance than in most of the others, and the exposition will consequently be clearer to those who insist upon a visible physical correlate for the field. In the higher animals the property of sensitivity is developed to an extraordinary degree in certain tissues, but in each for only one particular kind of physical event, *e.g.* light waves, periodic pressures, aperiodic pressures, etc. Now some of these tissues, especially the eye, *including* its phylogenetically more recent parts in the central nervous system, yield, for reasons into which we need not here inquire, a very wide and highly organized field.[15] Others, notably the somaesthetic, including the kinaesthetic, yield in isolation relatively small and unorganized fields.

But there are other important differences among the various senses, failure to note which has contributed largely to the behaviouristic fallacy. Among these must be mentioned the fact that the adequate stimulus for some of these specialized tissues is movement, or strain, or pressure, as in kinaesthesis. In other words, there *is* no (perceptual) kinaesthetic field unless something is being done. In order merely to *produce* a kinaesthetic field something must be done. Now this "doing" may be called a "repetition," but the fact remains that it is a necessary condition to the *existence* of a (perceptual) kinaesthetic field, just as opening the eyes is necessary for the existence of a visual (perceptual) field. Thus a "repetition" has the same relation to a kinaesthetic field that a "glance" has to a visual field. To say that it requires so many "repetitions" for a kinaesthetic field [16] to be reorganized corresponds exactly to saying that it requires so many one sigma exposures for a visual field to be reorganized into something recognizable.

The important psychological fact that there is in either case an optimal temporal distance between successive doings or exposures ("repetitions") concerns only the property of *retentivity,* which varies in different animals, tissues in the same animal, etc. It has nothing whatever to do with the learning process as a scientific concept. This confusion of retention and learning, which is almost universal, is another factor that has militated against a proper understanding of the problem. Such facts as that mentioned do have some significance for "learning" when the latter is conceived teleologically and anthropocentrically as a practical utilitarian, technological *improvement* in a desirable performance. It need hardly be pointed out that such concepts, however serviceable they may be in the various technologies that draw upon psychology, have no place in science. The behaviouristic attempt to make "laws" about such matters is characteristic of the teleological bent of that doctrine.

Neglect of this obvious difference in the type of stimulus adequate to the various sensory tissues (including always their central parts) has misled behaviourists into an attempt to argue the fact of insight out of existence because it does not occur in kinaesthetic fields. They do this in spite of the fact that they usually accept Stricker's theory that human thought is generally a kinaesthetic field, and hence, in most

[15] It seems practically impossible in uninjured animals to produce a visual field without a considerable degree of organization.

[16] Throughout, the expressions "kinaesthetic field," "visual field," etc., are used to mean *predominantly* kinaesthetic, visual, etc. Probably no field is entirely restricted to one modality in animals with differentiated sensitive tissues.

people, the type of field in which insight most commonly occurs. Incidentally, it may be remarked that it is at least at present much more illuminating to ask, not why insight occurs, but *why it does not always occur.*

It should be noted also that kinaesthetic fields are usually more extended in time than are visual or auditory fields. This is in part a necessary consequence of their limitation in scope. To use again the example of typewriting, the operator has only ten fingers and some thirty or forty keys. She cannot touch all the keys at once. Similar considerations hold for all skills. This fact of greater temporal extent combined with less "spatial" extent of kinaesthetic fields has doubtless contributed to the confusion inherent in the notion that repetition has a causal relation to learning. The matter is further complicated by the fact that the reorganization undergone by a kinaesthetic field while and after it runs its temporal course can usually be *detected* only upon repetition.

If now, to recapitulate, we ask why repetition has ever been thought to have anything directly to do with learning we must answer: (1) The learning *process* has been confused with the *properties* of sensitivity and retentivity. (2) Attention has been confined to learning under such conditions that it occurs too slowly to be evident without some such indirect sign as economy upon repetition. (3) Consideration has been limited largely to kinaesthetic learning, *i.e.* to the reorganization of kinaesthetic fields, in which, owing to the peculiar nature of the adequate stimulus, namely, "doing," phenomena which in other senses would be called exposures are called repetitions.

These considerations obviously apply with equal force to learning in the maze. In this case, however, the possibility of other than a kinaesthetic field is more or less excluded by means of walls, which are made as visually homogeneous as possible, and by various other measures. Similar considerations, which will be evident to the reader, apply to nonsense syllables and to rote memorizing.

The special conditions which might give repetition the appearance of a causal factor in the learning of multiple choice problems will be discussed in a later paper reporting some hitherto unpublished experiments with cats.

Somewhat similar conditions obtain in the case of discrimination habits in animals. Every experimenter knows that in the establishment of such habits the battle is won as soon as the objects to be discriminated become parts of a single structure. In some recent experiments (soon to be published) on weight discrimination in rats, the differences used were so large that the heavier weight obviously taxed the rat's strength to the limit while the lighter required very slight effort. In spite of these large physical differences, until the two were organized into one field, they were functionally equal. With human subjects we "structure" the field from the start by means of verbal instructions. For other animals there is first an inductive problem to be solved.

The case, however, which most successfully conceals the nature of the learning process by means of *very* special conditions is that of the conditioned reflex. This important and interesting phenomenon has unfortunately been degraded by its enthusiastic devotees to the level of a catchword or a magic formula. It is indicative of the bankruptcy of the psychology of learning that the conditioned reflex could seriously be considered representative of learning in general and even hailed as the key to all its mysteries. The conditioned reflex is another of those types of learning that, unless analysed, seem to suggest a causal relation of some sort between repetition and learning, and here again the special conditions that permit of this appearance should be exhibited. To do this adequately would require much more space than is available, but some of these special conditions may be indicated.

Here as everywhere else the "end-product" of learning is patently a reorganized field. The point at issue is how this reorganization comes about. The current "laws" of learning state or imply that repetition *per se* does it. That this is not the case is established by the occurrence of one case of insight. How it does come about we do not know, but we can at least ask sensible questions about it and make hypotheses which may be tested.

It should be noted first that the field of the animal in the conditioned reflex situation is determined by a need. If the dog is not hungry there will be no salivary reflex. Second, it must, as in all learning, be an *obstructed* need. The to-be-conditioned stimulus must occur before the unconditioned or preconditioned stimulus. If it occur simultaneously with or after the latter, the need is no longer obstructed and there is consequently no dynamic factor to bring about a reorganization of the field.[17] Third, the need must, as always, be the strongest need of the organism at that time. "Thus, for example, if the dog has been so fastened up that anything causes severe irritation, it does not matter how many times the combination of stimuli is repeated we shall not be able to obtain a conditioned reflex." In such a case the "stimuli" simply are not in the field. With the same physical energy as when under

[17] Beritoff and Switzer have supplied evidence that in the case of strong "defence reflexes" with very small latencies an originally indifferent stimulus may be conditioned even when it follows the unconditioned stimulus by a very short interval. It is of course not surprising that a very strong need should continue to distort the field for a brief interval after its satisfaction.

other conditions they are effective, they are not really stimuli at all. When the field is determined by the need to escape the irritation, instead of by the need for food, they have no existence.

That the field is determined by the strongest of several competing needs is even more clearly indicated by certain experiments reported by Pavlov. He found that it was possible to take a strong stimulus (*e.g.* electric shock) which evoked a strong unconditioned response of its own (*e.g.* the "defence reflex") and make it a conditioned stimulus to the salivary reflex. "This, we consider, was due to the fact that the alimentary reflex is in such cases stronger than the defence reflex." But if the shock were applied over bone, the defence reflex was stronger than the alimentary, and conditioning could not be obtained! "Successful transformation of the unconditioned stimulus for one reflex into the conditioned stimulus for another reflex can be brought about only when the former reflex is physiologically weaker and *biologically of less importance* [italics mine] than the latter." This "biological importance" is exactly what I mean by degree of intensity of a need.[18]

"Conditioned reflexes are quite readily formed to stimuli to which the animal is more or less indifferent at the outset, although, strictly speaking, no stimulus within the animal's range of perception exists to which it would be absolutely indifferent." Here again is recognition of the fact that the field is determined by a need or needs and that nothing exists in the field that has not some relation to some need, if it be only that which Pavlov calls the "investigatory reflex."

It should further be noted that conditioning is facilitated by the exclusion of other stimuli and apparently to the extent that they are excluded. The presumption is warranted by extrapolation that if this desideratum were completely attained (*i.e.* if there were only *one* event in the field prior to the unconditioned stimulus, which is impossible because of internal stimulation if for no other reason) one "repetition" would suffice to establish a conditioned reflex. Pavlov reports many cases in which one was established in three to five trials, and at least one which was set up in one trial. In general, it would seem that the more "prominent" the to-be-conditioned stimulus in the field (whether this prominence be produced by the exclusion of other stimuli or by

[18] Pavlov's use of the term "reflex" is so loose that the term had better be dropped for scientific purposes. He calls movements and activities *a* reflex (as *the* "defence reflex," *the* "freedom reflex," *the* "investigatory reflex," *the* "reflex of self-preservation," etc.), which have nothing in common except the need which determines them. Both the "stimulus" and the "response" may be utterly different, as *e.g.*, in the "investigatory reflex," yet so long as the need is the same he considers them one reflex. Evidently he is really talking not about reflexes but about *needs*.

"biological importance"), *so long as it does not arouse a stronger need* and hence create a new field, the more rapidly conditioning occurs.

Another very important circumstance is implied in the following: "Similarly, while with the help of a very strong [19] unconditioned stimulus it is possible to convert a very unsuitable stimulus—for example, one which naturally evokes a different unconditioned reflex—into a conditioned stimulus, it is exceedingly difficult or even impossible with the help of only a weak unconditioned stimulus to transform even a very favourable neutral stimulus into a conditioned stimulus." This remark indicates that what the field lacks in structure must be compensated by the strength of the need. In other words, it requires a *very* strong obstructed need to distort the field sufficiently for two such otherwise irrelevant events as a buzzer noise and a piece of meat to form one object or structure. The only structuring factor in the typical conditioned reflex situation is temporal contiguity, which alone does not normally provide much structure, but which, when accentuated by a very strong need, is sufficient to make one object of two events that have nothing else in common.

We constantly observe the same thing in men when very strong needs are involved. The football coach whose team won an important game when he happened to have eaten macaroni (which he loathed) for luncheon, thereafter always eats it before a game. The fact that he detested it, *i.e.* that it "naturally evoked a different unconditioned reflex," merely gives it additional prominence and accounts for the game's having been won by the macaroni instead of by the tie he wore. The angler who lost his tobacco and had to smoke his friend's particularly bad brand throughout a most successful day thereafter buys that kind —but only when he goes fishing! In all of these, two events which have the same very slight structuring factor as the two stimuli in the conditioned reflex situation (*i.e.* contiguity in time) may become one object or figure if the field is distorted by a strong enough need.

I am not clear as to when Pavlov considers a conditioned reflex established. Sometimes it seems as if it were when the new stimulus provokes about the same amount and rate of secretion as the original stimulus, but most of his conditioned reflexes never reach this point. In any case the amount of secretion that shall be considered indicative of a

[19] A "strong stimulus" here means a piece of meat when the dog is very hungry; a "weak stimulus" means the same piece of meat when the dog is not so hungry. This is a good example, not only of the dependence of the field upon the needs, but of typical objectivist obscurantism. We have seen above that Pavlov usually calls a need a "reflex," and here we find him confusing it with "stimulus." It is by means of this sort of paralogism, which H. M. Johnson has aptly termed the "method of equivocance," that behaviourism makes its specious appeal of simplicity and shirks the necessary analysis.

conditioned reflex is just as arbitrary as "three errorless trials" in a maze or a grade of *C* in calculus. *All* of these reflect the technological or utilitarian concept of learning already mentioned. The endless and sterile discussions of "criteria" of learning (*e.g.* in the maze) show how futile such concepts are in science. For learning in the true scientific sense occurs whether it is ever demonstrated by repetition or not. The field is actually undergoing reorganization from the first; whether in the particular "favourable" direction desired by the experimenter or whether the field is the one that the teacher hopes it is, is quite irrelevant to the *psychological* problem.

We have seen that the only fields that get reorganized are those in which a need is obstructed, and we must make hypotheses about the nature of the distortion that brings about reorganization. Now while all fields are determined by *more or less* obstructed needs, not all are sufficiently obstructed for appreciable distortion to occur. Yet all fields are in greater or less degree organized. There must then be some factors of organization that are more or less independent of the needs, and determined primarily by the nature and organization of the sensitive tissues (central as well as peripheral).

There are such factors. Some of them have been known for two millennia and have been called "laws of association" for two centuries. Some have been unearthed in the last two decades by the *Gestalt* psychologists who have called them *Gestaltfaktoren.* Most of them, both old and new, still require more precise characterization.

Owing to a curious and interesting combination of circumstances (the complete unravelling of which must be left to the historian), some of these principles, those called the laws of association, were long thought to be factors of *retentivity* only and not factors of *sensitivity,* of the organization of *present* sensory fields. This was partly because the latter was taken for granted,[20] and partly because of too much anthropocentrism and insufficient (or, sometimes, insufficiently critical) anthropomorphism. At all events, this confusion is not now so prevalent, and the realization is becoming quite general that these factors of organization operate in all fields.

Now in most of the fields that occur in nature at least several and often all of the structural factors, contiguity (spatial and temporal),

[20] In its relatively brief history psychology has exhibited a notable capacity for taking the wrong (*i.e.* the least useful) things for granted. General physiology escapes most of these difficulties and the necessity of clear definition by dealing only with (1) very constant needs, (2) stimuli which may be more or less purely physically defined, such as light, gravity, etc., and (3) sensitive tissues such that the field has a simple relation to one or two aspects of (4) a very simple situation. For these reasons it can get along with such crude and unanalysed concepts as that of tropisms.

similarity, closure, continuity (*"objektive Einstellung"*), etc., are given in the situation. It is only or chiefly when man intervenes with artificial constraints that only *one* of these factors is present and operative. Thus, in the usual conditioned reflex situation the sole organizing factor is temporal contiguity.[21] This is, to be sure, not an unimportant one, but by itself it is probably one of the weakest. There is no other factor uniting the buzzer and the food in the conditioned reflex situation, but even so, if these are the *only* events in the field and the need is very strong, a conditioned reflex may be established in one "repetition."

The foregoing considerations do not by any means exhaust the special conditions that give repetition the appearance of a causal factor in "conditioning" a "reflex," but the more important ones have been indicated. Others will be inferable from the discussion of those obtaining in skills. The general fact that repetition is used to provide a sign of reorganization (of both acts and fields) is here also an additional source of confusion, as is the inclusion of retentivity in the technological concept of learning as learning *enough*—enough for some practical human purpose.

We have seen that repetition is incapable of bringing about the reorganization of a field, that it has no general causal relation to learning, and that in the absence of a need no amount of it would bring about learning. I have already suggested in discussing the conditioned reflex that the "distortion" of a field by an obstructed need is what brings about this organization or reorganization. The hypothesis is now advanced more precisely and explicitly that *whatever structural factors* (contiguity in space and time, similarity, continuity, closure, etc.) *a field may contain are enhanced by an obstructed need in proportion to the strength* (*within limits*) *of the need and to the extent to which it is obstructed.*

Experiments to test this hypothesis with respect to certain of the structural factors are now in progress. Others will have to wait upon a clearer formulation of the factors themselves. Wertheimer has made a bold and ingenious beginning upon this task, but there is still much necessary analysis to be done. Some of the factors as currently described seem to overlap others, and some—even Aristotle's similarity—

[21] As Köhler has pointed out, this does not need to be the case. The adequate and the inadequate stimuli might have any degree of organization from the very slight one customarily used to a quite irresistible unity. Investigation of the influence of "objective" organization on the formation of conditioned reflexes should be very useful in the analysis of the structural factors. The only experiment I know of that approximates an attack on the problem, of which this would be a strategic special case, is that of Warden and Hamilton. These investigators found that varying the factor of temporal contiguity had a marked influence upon the rate of reorganization of the field. Unfortunately they also varied other factors.

need more precise characterization. To this extent the psychology of learning must wait upon the psychology of perception, although the investigation of the former along the lines here described may well help to clarify the latter. Perhaps Wertheimer's method (of opposing one factor with another) applied to animals would yield the cleanest analysis.

I have said that the fundamental problem of learning is the determination of the kinds of distortion undergone by a field in which a need is obstructed and of the conditions under which each kind occurs, and have advanced certain hypotheses. The validity of this statement of the problem of learning does not, of course, depend upon the correctness of the particular hypotheses here advanced. Further, the hypotheses themselves (that at least some of the varieties of distortion consist in the enhancement or accentuation of the given structural factors) do not imply that our present conceptions of the structural factors are either exhaustive or correct.

This formulation of the problem of course makes no pretensions to finality. More precise ones can and will be made, but they may have to wait for a changed intellectual climate. Perhaps the term "learning" is so saturated with non-scientific connotations that it will ultimately be found useful to leave it entirely to technology, but we cannot hurry such matters. That some change is imperative in the type of question we ask about learning can hardly be denied. The utility of any proposed change in direction can be determined only by trying it.

V. SUMMARY

Animals (and probably all organisms) have four properties which are of direct importance to learning: needs, parsimony of movement in their satisfaction, sensitivity and retentivity. "Repetition" has only a contingent relation to learning. Some of the conditions under which it might seem to have a causal relation are given when: (1) the learning process is confused with the property of retentivity; (2) repetition is used to exhibit economy which, in turn, is used as a behaviour sign of learning; (3) consideration is restricted to fields (especially kinaesthetic or predominantly kinaesthetic) in which a "repetition" is really an instantaneous exposure; (4) the field is for some reason temporally extended; (5) the situation is for some reason, usually the intervention of man, very weakly structured, *e.g.* presents only one or two of the structural factors which have been called the laws of association, the principles of grouping, etc., some of which possibly remain to be discovered, and all of which need more precise description.

Adaptation is what gets done about a need. It is of two kinds: the first, usually called adaptation, consists in a change in the need. This may take place in several ways, *e.g.* by satiation or supersatiation, by substitution, by induction, etc. The second kind of adaptation is called learning, and it consists in the organization or reorganization of a field. A field is a situation as it biologically *is* for a specific animal at a specific time. All fields are determined by needs and contain a functional minimum of entities. An obstructed need *distorts the field* (thus facilitating reorganization) in proportion to the strength of the need and to the completeness of the obstruction. The fundamental task of the experimental psychology of learning is the determination of the kinds of this distortion and the conditions under which each occurs. The hypothesis is made that at least some of the ways in which fields are distorted by obstructed needs consist in the enhancement or accentuation of the structural factors given in the situation.

---

18. An Experimental Study of Early Childhood Memory: Final Report *

How LONG does learning last? Have you lost all the effects of training when you can no longer consciously "remember" what you once knew? In this article Professor Burtt attempts to answer both of these questions. His experiment leads one to the tentative conclusion that some residual effects of learning persist for years after even the memory of having learned has disappeared.

THE PRESENT STUDY is a continuation of one reported earlier in which nonsense material presented systematically to the subject in infancy was relearned at a later age and the rate of relearning compared with the rate of learning new material of similar nature. The previously reported relearning experiments began at the ages of 8½ and 14, respectively; the present one at the age of 18. The material consisted of selections from Sophocles *Oedipus Tyrannus* in the original Greek which was tantamount to nonsense material. Each selection included approximately 20 lines or 240 syllables of iambic hexameter. The subject was a boy with an IQ of approximately 130. Beginning at the

* Harold E. Burtt, "An experimental study of early childhood memory: final report," *Journal of Genetic Psychology,* LVIII (1941), 435–39. By permission of the author and The Journal Press.

age of 15 months three of these selections were read to him once daily for a period of three months—a total of 90 repetitions. At the age of 18 months these selections were discontinued and three others read daily for three months. This procedure was continued until the subject was three years old and 21 selections had been presented. The 8-year experiment utilized one-third (seven selections—one from each three-month period) of the available material which had been presented in infancy plus three new selections for control. The 14-year experiment utilized another third, and the present and final experiment used the last seven selections plus three new controls. It was thus possible to compare the "saving" at the three ages.

The procedure in the present case was practically identical with that in the previous experiments. Two trials were given daily and this schedule was maintained with very little variation. A minor difference was the relearning of two selections which had served as controls in the two previous series. The 12 selections under comparison were always given in one trial and their order from trial to trial was rotated systematically. The selections as in the earlier experiment, were merely read to the subject for the first 18 trials. Beginning with the nineteenth, every third trial used the prompting method in which the selection was read slowly and the subject anticipated any syllables which he could. These syllables were underlined in the text and the date noted at which they had first been anticipated correctly. This procedure was continued until every syllable in a selection, except for the initial cue words, had been anticipated and the requisite number of trials constituted one item of score. The repetitions were continued as necessary until the subject could recite the entire selection without prompting and the number of trials up to this point constituted the other item of score. Motivation in the present instance was apparently about the same as in the second experiment. A variable which could not be controlled, of course, was the occasional tendency to think of words or phrases between trials. This was marked with reference to Selection *D* (infra) but otherwise the tendency was negligible. In a few instances while listening to a selection when he was not supposed to recite, the subject did speak it softly to himself. On the occasions when there was an apparent tendency to depart from the regular program in the way of reciting between trials, no comment was made and the practice seldom persisted. With the exception of Selections *A* and *D,* which had served as controls in the two earlier series, the subject apparently had no notion as to which were original and which were control selections.

The main results together with some data from the earlier experiment by way of comparison are given in Table 1. The first column gives the age at which the original reading took place. The Roman numerals in the next column are the arbitrary designations of the selections used in the 8-year experiment. The next column gives the number of repetitions necessary before the subject recited the selection verbatim without prompting. The data were analyzed from two standpoints, the number of repetitions necessary before each word in the selection had been anticipated and the number of repetitions required for reciting it verbatim without prompting. Previous analysis indicated, however, that there was little choice between these two methods of scoring and for the remainder of the discussion the data will be confined to the last method, viz., the number of trials necessary for a complete verbatim recital without prompting. Such scores for the 8-year experiment occur in the third column. The next two columns give similar data for the 14-year experiment and the last two columns for the present experiment. The lower portion of the table gives data for the control selections, i.e., those which were learned *de novo*. These were arbitrarily designated by letters rather than by Roman numerals. In the last two columns Selections *A* and *D* appear a second time. They were included at the 18-year level to determine the difficulty of relearning a selection of this type which had been mastered ten or four years previously.

TABLE 1

Trials Necessary for Correct Recitation

Age in Mos. at Original Reading	*Eight-Year Selection*	*Trials*	*Fourteen-Year Selection*	*Trials*	*Eighteen-Year Selection*	*Trials*
15–18	III	382	II	142	I	202
18–21	VI	253	V	139	IV	190
21–24	IX	385	VIII	169	VII	181
24–27	XII	379	XI	151	X	220
27–30	XV	328	XIV	145	XIII	160
30–33	XVIII	226	XVII	169	XVI	175
33–36	XXI	265	XX	127	XIX	193
Av. of all		317		149		189
Av. 3 early		340		150		191
Av. 4 later		299		148		187
Control	*A*	409	*D*	169	*G*	205
	B	451	*E*	151	*H*	193
	C	445	*F*	166	*J*	175
Av. control		435		162		191
					A	112
					D	37

The most general notion of the results may be obtained from the averages. It required 189 repetitions for a correct recital of the average selection in the present relearning experiment whereas for the corresponding control selections the average is 191. The difference obviously is negligible and of no statistical significance. By the other method of scoring (supra—not shown in table) the corresponding averages are 172 and 175. The absence of any saving in the present case may be compared with the 27 per cent at 8 years (30 per cent by the other method of scoring—supra) and 8 per cent at 14 years by either scoring method. Apparently the last four years were sufficient to eradicate completely any trace of the original stimulation in infancy.

As in the previous experiments, the selections were grouped and averaged so that the three which were presented earliest in infancy constituted one group and the four in later infancy a second group. The difference between these averages obviously is not significant in the present series.

Learning curves were plotted as in the previous series. The two curves for average relearning selection and average control selection are practically indistinguishable and not worth presenting here.

The gross number of repetitions necessary in the present study was much less than in the 8-year but slightly greater than in the 14-year experiment. The former difference is presumably due to greater maturity, better motivation and an appreciation of the scientific importance of the experiment. The reason for the latter is less clear. It cannot be attributed to the mere lapse of time since the reading in infancy, because it characterized control as well as experimental selections. The subject reported occasional confusion of groups of syllables with similar groups which he remembered vaguely. It is quite possible that such similar groups were carried over from the 14-year experiment and caused this confusion. Indications of this carry-over may be seen in the fact that Selection *D* which had been learned to the point of complete recitation at age 14 was relearned at age 18 in 37 repetitions, and on the 19th trial which was the first one on which he was allowed to attempt recitation the subject repeated 182 out of the 240 syllables. Incidentally on the second trial with that selection the subject stated that it sounded familiar and thereafter was suspicious that he had experienced it more recently than infancy. However quite early with Selection *G* (control) he stated that some words were vaguely familiar.

On the whole the experiment suggests that the effect of presenting nonsense material in infancy was very clearly manifest in relearning experiments at the age of 8½, traces were still apparent at the age of 14, but by the age of 18 the effect had completely disappeared.

SUMMARY

Meaningless material (20-line selections of Greek drama) was read aloud to the subject daily beginning at the age of 15 months. Every three months a different set of similar selections was used as material and this procedure was continued till the age of three. When the subject was 8½ years old he learned some of the original material by a modified prompting method in comparison with other material which he learned *de novo*. Similar experiments were conducted with still other material from the original selections and further controls at ages of 14 and 18.

At the age of 8½ the relearning required on the average 27 or 30 per cent (depending on the method of scoring) fewer repetitions than were needed to learn new (control) material. At the age of 14 the corresponding saving was 8 per cent. At the age of 18 there was no saving at all. At the age of 8½ the original selections which had been presented later in infancy were relearned more readily than those presented earlier in infancy. No tendency of this sort was manifest in the two later series. Learning curves for experimental and for control selections were appreciably discrete in the first two series with the experimental curves rising more rapidly than their controls. In the 18-year series the curves were indistinguishable. The effect of the presentation in infancy was clearly manifest at the age of 8½, was still present but markedly less at the age of 14, and was completely gone at the age of 18.

---

19. Individual and Social Determination in Remembering *

The naive view of memory assumes that as a result of a particular experience "something is engraved on the brain" and stays there until it decays from disuse. Professor Bartlett offers a very different conception, which he has developed as the result of a long series of highly original investigations of remembering. These investigations demonstrated that memory is not automatic but is, rather, selective and organized. It should be noted that, where the author

* F. C. Bartlett, *Remembering* (Cambridge University Press, 1932), Chapter 19, pp. 301–14. Reprinted by permission of the author and the publisher.

uses the word "scheme" here, he has in mind his own definition, given earlier in his writing, that it is "an active organization of past reactions, or of past experiences, which must always be supposed to be operating in any well-adapted organic response."

1. A RE-STATEMENT OF THE GENERAL POSITION

THE DETAIL and conclusions of both parts of this study have now been presented. At the risk of some repetition, it seems desirable to bring together the main results, since these touch upon a very large number of problems, but nevertheless present a coherent picture of the development of human response to the demands of external environment.

The picture is one of human beings confronted by a world in which they can live and be masters only as they learn to match its infinite diversity by increasing delicacy of response, and as they discover ways of escape from the complete sway of immediate circumstances. The psychologist who is concerned with the processes of recall comes to his problems only when an immense amount of this necessary development has already been achieved. Already the long struggle which results in the specialization of the senses has attained its main ends, already the organism with which the psychologist is concerned has discovered how to utilize the past in such phenomena as those of lowered threshold, of chain and conditioned reflexes, of "schematic" determination, and in the sequences of relatively fixed habit. But these, all necessary in their way, still cramp and confine man's activities. For in them all the past operates *en masse,* and the series is of greater weight than its elements. Moreover in many of them the past retains its constraining capacity in the form of relatively fixed sequences which cannot readily be broken.

If any marked further advance is to be achieved, man must learn how to resolve the "scheme" into elements, and how to transcend the original order of occurrence of these elements. This he does, for he learns how to utilize the constituents of his own "schemes," instead of being determined to action by the "schemes" themselves, functioning as unbroken units. He finds how to "turn round upon his own schemata," as I have said—a reaction literally rendered possible by consciousness, and the one which gives to consciousness its pre-eminent function.

When, as psychologists, we try to understand how this critical step in organic development becomes possible, our attention must turn away from the fact of "schematic" organization to the conditions which direct the formation of these active settings. Here, also, the bulk of the work has been done long before the psychologist comes upon the scene at all. It seems likely, however, that the earliest "schemes" follow the lines of demarcation of the special senses. Then certain reactions which are of special biological significance, such as all those having to do with appetites, like food-seeking, sex and sleep; or with instincts, like those of the danger reactions, or of assertiveness and submissiveness, are of particular importance in relating together the modes of adaptive response that arise when they are active. Again, differences in the weighting of special sensorial reactions and of appetitive and instinctive tendencies set up what I have called "individual difference tendencies," the combinations of which define a particular organism's "temperament." All these, and perhaps others within the special sense distinctions—especially those connected with spatial and temporal relations—are involved in the formation of active "schematic" settings. They are supplemented by other influences arising from the interplay of reactions which occurs during the lifetime of the individual—that is, by that mass of reaction tendencies which together constitute "character"—and particularly by social conditions consequent upon group life. This complexity of "schematic" formation means that many objects, many stimuli, many reactions, get organized simultaneously into different "schemes," so that when they recur, as, in the world we know they are bound to do, they tend to set into activity various cross-streams of organizing influence.

For the next point we have definite evidence from experiment at the psychological level proper. In all these "schemes" there is operating that kind of unwitting analysis which gives the weight to certain elements of the whole. In many cases, as in my own percept, image and recall experiments, it is possible to see exactly to what particular detail the weight goes. Sometimes the weighting is determined directly by sensorial dominance—usually by vision in man, by smell in certain of the other animals—and often by spatial distinctions within the predominant sense. Sometimes it is settled by appetitive or instinctive dominance. Most often of all, in human adult reaction, it is a matter of the operation of persistent "interests."

Even before the capacity to "turn round upon one's own schemata" is acquired, there are probably instances in which outstanding details play a predominant part when reaction threatens to be determined in many ways at once, and a consequent risk of harmful indecision arises. When the "schematic" content itself comes to be used as a guide to reaction, the predominant, weighted details tend to stand out as images. Images are, then, literally details picked out of "schemes" and used to facilitate some necessary response to immediate environmental conditions. They are essentially individual and concrete in their character, and, since the typical case for their occurrence is the arousal of cross-streams of interest, they often bring together psychological material and reactions which had diverse origins. Thus they increase the possible range of diversity of responses, and they mark a further step forward in the general development of distance reactions. They share the chronological character of everything that goes to make up "schematic" organization, and hence have special significance in relation to detailed and dated recall.

Again turning to our experiments, we find that in many cases the main conditions for the occurrence of images appear to be found in their affective setting. This functions as an "attitude," and the attitude is best described as an orientation of the agent toward the image and its less articulated "schematic" surroundings. If, then, as in specific recall, we are called upon to justify the image, we do so by constructing, or reconstructing, its setting. Thereupon the attitude requires a rationalization. Social grouping, with its accompaniment of conventionalized and relatively permanent traditions, institutions and customs, has been shown to play a great part in the development of interests, in the determination of the affective setting which is often at the basis of image formation, and in the provision of material for the constructive processes of recall.

With all this, the image method has its serious drawbacks. The most important of these are: that the image, with its sensorial character, is apt to go farther in the direction of the individualization of situations than is biologically useful; that the principles of the combination of images have their own peculiarities, resulting in constructions which appear jerky, irregular and a matter of personal idiosyncrasy, and that the applicability of the image to the situation in which it occurs remains either unformulated or, at best, inadequately expressed. Thus, although the image method in general increases the possible range and diversity of response, it contains within itself characters that are precisely opposed to this development. However, the social demand for the description of images, necessary in order that their occurrence and character should be appreciated by more than one person, has already linked up the word with the image method. Words are essentially more explicitly analytic than images: they are compelled to deal with situations in a piecemeal fashion. Moreover, they can indicate qualitative and relational factors in a general aspect just as well as they are able to describe particular features. They supplement the deficiencies of images and at the same time, being in some respects antagonistic to the particularity of the image, they appear in the experiments as a kind of alternative form in recall. They are the main instruments of the thinking process, for in the latter we find the effort to deal with situations independently of the place and time of their occurrence carried through to its most successful issue. Words are the best of all human inventions for perfecting distance reactions.

Alike with images and with words, the old "schematic" modes of determination which they serve to break up tend to return once more. So we get image and word habits, persistent individual automatisms of word and image formation, and persistent social conventions of descriptive expression.

Such, in outline, is the picture which I have drawn from the materials contributed by my experiments. Many details have been filled in; many gaps call for further work. Meanwhile, it is once more clear that a study of remembering, its conditions and its conventionalizations, leads directly to the most persistent general problems of psychology. All research must be given an arbitrary end somewhere. So I will choose three only of these long-standing topics of dispute, all of which I have touched upon already, for some additional consideration. These three are: the principles of association; the self, individual and social; constructive imagination and thinking.

2. THE PRINCIPLES OF ASSOCIATION

Everything in this book has been written from the point of view of a study of the conditions of organic and mental functions, rather than from that of an analysis of mental structure. It was, however, the latter standpoint which developed the traditional principles of association. The confusion of the two is responsible for very much unnecessary difficulty in psychological discussion.

Let us consider any type of response such as that involved in my *Picture Sign* experiments or in *Repeated Reproduction*. In the clearest and most definitely articulated cases, there first occurs the arousal of an attitude, an orientation, an interest. Then specific detail, either in image or in direct word form, tends to be set up. Finally there is a construction of other detail in such a way as to provide a rational, or satisfactory setting for the attitude. Now we may take the whole completed recall and submit it to analysis. We say: "This detail stands next to that one and that to the other." Then we may take the neighbouring details, and we may see whether we can classify the marks which, being next one another, they possess. If we adopt this plan, we are almost sure to arrive at those broad principles of association which have been the stand-by of associationists at all times: contiguity and similarity. We say: "This, being next to that, is similar to it in some respect, or was contiguous to it in some assignable way when they were first presented." If these principles appear to be too wide, we can very easily develop them in detail by taking into consideration all the kinds of similarity and contiguity that can logically occur. We may then arrive at a detailed scheme such as the following:

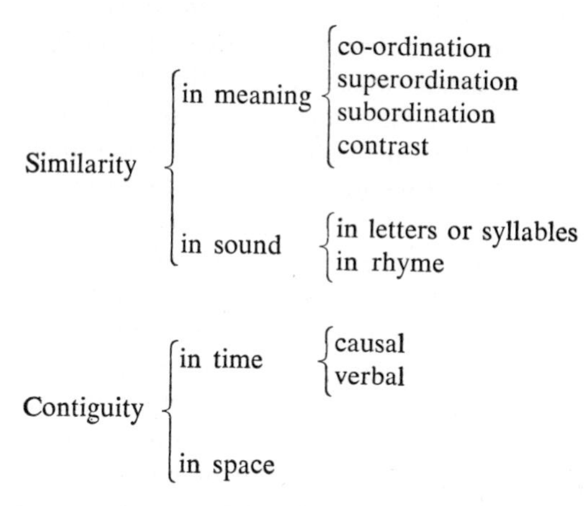

Such schemes can be extended almost indefinitely until they include every possible relationship of objects or of names. All this is on the plane of descriptive analysis; and, so long as it is kept on that plane, is not only harmless but valuable.

Then we may suddenly change our point of view. We may transform the statement: "These details, being together, are similar," into: "These details are together *because* they are similar." Trouble at once arises.

There are three main difficulties. Similarity appears to necessitate inspection, and before the similarity of any details that are associated can be noticed it would seem as if they must already in some way be together, for only then can the necessary inspection be carried out. This difficulty is not, in fact, a very serious one, and it has been much magnified by some writers who do not sufficiently recognize that qualities and characteristics may stimulate functional activities long before their precise nature is known. The young child, for example, reacts differentially to colors some time before he can possibly be said to be able to identify, and especially to name, color differences.

Secondly, similarity obviously has a host of divergent forms. Not all of these are equally potent in association. A difference of attitude on different occasions may bring about a great change in the relative influence of the different types of similarity. For example, in association experiments "The percentage of answers returned for the various classes are found to be influenced by fatigue, by drugs, and by pathological disorders of the nervous system. Broadly speaking, the effect of these conditions is to produce an increase in the proportion of associations by similarity of sound and a decrease in the proportion of those by similarity of meaning." That is to say, if similarity is to be regarded as of any explanatory importance, it has to be supplemented by various other considerations which cannot be discovered merely by an inspection of the characteristics of the details which are associated.

Thirdly, if we try to use these few broad associative categories as explanatory principles, there naturally arises a belief that the essential course by which mental structure is gradually built up is by the adding together of innumerable details which originally had no connection whatever one with another. When we are engaged upon an analytical description of completed structure we can undoubtedly view the matter in this way; but no sooner had psychology altered its point of view, under the influence of biological science, from that of description to that of explanation, than the typical associationist method was found radically faulty. The first English psychologist fully to recognize this was James Ward, and the brilliance and originality of his psychological writings were mainly due to this recognition. He made a devastatingly triumphant attack upon associationism; but, largely, I think, because his interests remained dominantly epistemological, he never completely cut adrift from the traditional methods, and consequently more recent writers have often been able to assume the credit for the revolution which he, in fact, led. Ward would have nothing to do with similarity as a principle of association, and he replaced contiguity by succession. This is most significant, for succession is seen to be a principle of association, not in consequence of a study of the characteristics of the detail or content associated, but by a consideration of how the associative *reactions* appear to be determined.

We have seen several times that succession does appear to be a genuine factor relating together reactions, and the psychological material with which they deal. But once we reach the "post-schematic" method, the image or the word method, of utilizing what is not now immediately present, very special pleading is needed to square the facts with any simple principle of succession. The event of today may recall at once, without any discoverable mediation, an event of years ago. The image, or the words, indicating the distant event are there as soon as the perception of the current event is complete. The principle of the combination of successive reactions is cut across in many ways. If we are to treat the problems of association as functional, we have to use attitudes, orientation, appetitive and instinctive tendencies and interests as our active, organizing factors. Whatever material is dealt with by persistent reaction tendencies of these types will tend to be associated. No doubt this is to bring back in some sense the notions of similarity and identity. It is not, however, a similarity, or an identity, that can be discovered by any amount of inspection of the material associated. The similarity or identity involved is one of the functions of the underlying organizing tendencies, and it may account for the association of materials possessing surprisingly diverse characteristics. My experiments also suggest that, in many cases, it is some accompanying quality of affect, which almost always goes with these active tendencies, that largely accounts for the functional coincidence of interests dealing with descriptively different realms of material.

Stout, developing the original suggestion of Ward, proposed to take "continuity of interest" as the primary associative principle, and this was a legitimate and necessary step along the road which Ward had begun to travel. But modern psychological developments have made it undesirable to lump all the organizing tendencies together as "interests," and "continuity" is a less accurate term than "persistence," for the latter is consistent with that intermittence and re-arousal of reaction tendencies which the facts seem to demand.

Why is it that, although everybody now admits the force of the criticism of associationism, the associationist principles still hold their ground and are constantly employed?

First, it is because the force of the rejection of associationism depends mainly upon the adoption of a functional point of view; but the attitude of analytic description is just as important within its own sphere. For a study of the characters of any completed structure of knowledge, the achievements of the associationist psychologists have a high and lasting value.

Secondly, it is demonstrable that every situation, in perceiving, in imaging, in remembering, and in all constructive effort, possesses outstanding detail, and that in many cases of association the outstanding detail of one situation is taken directly out of that, and organized together with the outstanding detail of a different situation. It is no more right to suppose that the mental life develops and works solely by the expanding articulation of a "whole," or of many "wholes," than it is to suppose that it grows and operates solely through the gradual accretion of originally distinct elements.

Thirdly, we have seen how to some extent images, and to a great extent words, both of them expressions often of associative tendencies, slip readily into habit series and conventional formations. They do this mainly in the interests of intercommunication within the social group, and in doing it they inevitably take upon themselves common characteristics which render them amenable to the general descriptive phrases of the traditional doctrines of association.

In various senses, therefore, associationism is likely to remain, though its outlook is foreign to the demands of modern psychological science. It tells us something about the characteristics of associated details, when they are associated, but it explains nothing whatever of the activity of the conditions by which they are brought together.

3. THE SELF, INDIVIDUAL AND SOCIAL

Most psychologists who have written about recall have pointed out that memory, in its full sense, always contains a peculiarly personal reference. Already we have seen the main reason for this. The materials dealt with by different "schemata" overlap, and both the "schemata" and the appetites, instinctive tendencies, attitudes, interests and ideals which build them up display an order of predominance among themselves. Moreover, this order remains relatively persistent for a given organism. This is equivalent to saying that recall is inevitably determined by temperament and character. All these considerations, however, give us no justification for speaking of some intangible and hypothetical Self which receives and maintains innumerable traces and re-stimulates them whenever the need arises. All that we can say for certain is that the mechanism of adult human remembering demands an organization of "schemata" which depends upon an interplay of appetites, instincts, interests and ideals peculiar to any given subject.

Equally, of course, we have so far no ground for denying the existence of a substantial, unitary Self, lurking behind all experience, and expressing itself in all reactions. We know only that the evidence of the experiments which have been considered does not necessitate such a hypothesis.

This was the position reached at the end of the first part of our study. The same problems must now be reconsidered in the light of our study of the social functions in remembering. It is certain that practically all the processes of individual repeated recall have their precise parallels in those of social conventionalization. There are the same types of change in original material: of blending, condensation, omission, invention and the like. There is the same strong tendency to reduplication of detail in certain circumstances. In both cases, the final product approaches stability, that of the determined and relatively fixed individual memory in the one case, and that of the social conventionalization in the other. Alike with the individual and with the group, the past is being continually re-made, reconstructed in the interests of the present, and in both cases certain outstanding events or details may play a leading part in setting the course of reaction. Just as individual recall takes on a peculiar personal tinge, owing to the play of temperament and character; so that kind of recall which is directed and dominated by social conditions takes a coloring which is characteristic of the special social organization concerned, owing to the play of preferred persistent tendencies in the group.

It is curious that the analogy between the individual and social organization has most frequently been used by those who, having already decided what individual characteristics are important, wish to transfer these to the group. Obviously it could equally well be turned round and, for whatever the argument is worth, we could use it just as well to urge that the individual is nothing more than a special sort of group, as to maintain that the group possesses all the characters of the individual. The common prejudice is in favor of a hypothetical, substantial self for the individual, and against one for the group. Both alike remain prejudices, so far as all these parallels go, and are wholly lacking in demonstration.

Yet it may be said that I am guilty of an inconsistency, for I have freely written of "individual recall," and have urged that the evidence does not justify the use of the phrase "group memory." I have not, it must be noticed, dogmatically denied group memory, but I think we can never be certain that it veritably exists. This arises from an inevitable limitation due to our position in the group. When we say "I remember," all that we literally mean by the "I" is that the reactions concerned are determined directly by temperament and character, defined as I have defined them above, peculiar to this case and to numerous other cases described by us in the same language. With the individual, temperament and character work directly upon the materials organized into the "schemata" which they have built up. Now I am, for my part, certain, as I have said, that every stable and persistent social group possesses both temperament and character. But, owing to our own position within the group, we can never be sure that its temperament and character can work in any other way than through those of the individuals who constitute the group. They do this, and that is enough to give to recall within the group a specific group coloring. There is only one way by which we could be satisfied that they do more, namely that the group, as a psychological unit, should be able to tell us. So far as we know, no group, as a group, possesses a language, or if it does our position in the group debars us from knowing it. Thus we may speak of individual recall, refuse to speak of group memory, and still consistently deny that *this* difference justifies our belief in a substantial self in the one case and our disbelief in a substantial self in the other.

It is tempting to use an intriguing, but highly speculative illustration. The temperament and character by which individual remembering is effected involve a large group of co-ordinated and organized "schemata," much as a social group involves a number of individuals organized together. Suppose that each "schema" had some mode of language. Then the visual-spatial "scheme," for example, finding itself in some more or less familiar environment, and helping out its orientation by the aid of visual images, might put this into language by saying its equivalent of "I remember." The other "schemata" might do likewise, each on its own appropriate occasion. Moreover, each "scheme" might be able to see that it formed an integral part of various larger groups, and that specific determining conditions belonged to each group. Still the "schema," if it were sufficiently psychological and sufficiently cautious, would say: "I cannot be sure that the larger group remembers, though it has its own specific part to play in my remembering."

The "I" in this illustration stands for the relatively separate "schema," or group of "schemata," and the "larger group" in the illustration is precisely the "I" of the ordinary phrase "I remember." Moreover, the position of the "schema" in the larger group is exactly that of the individual in the social group. Perhaps, after all, this is not quite so fanciful an illustration as might appear. It seems to be just what does happen in some cases of multiple personality, where groups of organizing tendencies and "schemes" escape from mutual control. Then the actions and experiences which are the expression of every considerable group claim the sanction of the "I," and some reject the claims of the others. Probably all such cases may be so treated that they yield a re-synthesis in which the memories and actions now claimed to belong to the "I" are once again very different. But this only serves to show afresh that when we say "I remember" we merely assert that there is recall which is primarily the work of those reaction tendencies and their accompanying organized psychological material which are most persistent and constant for the organism concerned. And when we say that perhaps the group does not remember, we mean only that, so far as we can see, the group temperament and character can produce their effects only through the mediation of individual reaction tendencies, these latter alone dealing directly with the external environment.

The position reached at the end of the first part of our study needs no modification. There may be a substantial self, but this cannot be established by experiments on individual and social recall, or by any amount of reflection on the results of such experiments. Anyone who still feels a great need to demonstrate such a self must therefore seek arguments elsewhere, or else fall back upon a blank affirmation of immediate knowledge.

4. CONSTRUCTIVE IMAGINATION AND THINKING

If there be one thing upon which I have insisted more than another throughout all the discussions of this book, it is that the description of memories as "fixed and lifeless" is merely an unpleasant fiction. That views implying this are still very common is evidence of the astonishing way in which many psychologists, even the most deservedly eminent, often appear to decide what are the characteristic marks of the process they set out to study, before ever they begin actually to study it. Prof. Stout, for example, writing of memory, says: "It is better to confine it to ideal revival, so far as ideal revival is merely reproductive, and does not involve transformation of what is revived in accordance with present conditions." It should now be sufficiently clear that, so far as all ordinary processes of recall go, this, if it were literally to be accepted, would leave to memory an exceedingly small and rather unimportant field.

Yet, if we say that memory is itself constructive, how are we to differentiate it from constructive imagination and thinking? The easy way is to say that the difference is merely one of "degree." This particular mark of differentiation is, in psychology, as confusing as it is common. In this context it must mean that recall, imagination and thinking differ only as regards the fixity of the detail with which they deal. But our studies have shown us that all manner of changes in detail constantly occur in instances which every normal person would admit to be genuine instances of remembering. There are changes in order of sequence, changes of direction, of complexity of structure, of significance, which are not only consistent with subjectively satisfactory recall, but are also perfectly able to meet the objective demands of the immediate situation. Degree of fixity is here a criterion which it would assuredly be hard to apply.

I suggest that the chief differentiating marks between constructive recall, constructive imagination and constructive thinking are to be found in the range of material over which they move and the precise manner of their control. According to the general theory of this book, remembering is "schematically" determined. The circumstances that arouse memory orientations, whether they occur in the laboratory or in everyday life, always set up an attitude that is primarily towards a particular "schematic" organization. The construction, or reconstruction, which is effected is, in the most typical cases, always within the range of this special organization, and in any case the material which is central purports to be drawn from this. It is, for example, verbal material, or pictorial material, sensory material, material occurring over a particular chronological stretch, always material that has been dealt with by a specific and more or less defined interest, that we set to work upon when we remember. As I have shown, to serve the needs of biological adaptation interests are all the while increasing in diversity, in narrowness and in definiteness. So our range of search, when we have to attempt recall, tends to get more and more defined. Always it is material from some specially organized mass which has to be central, and about this the constructions and reconstructions of memory cluster. The overlap of "schematic" organization and the crossing of interests no doubt come to mean that items from one "scheme" may, more and more, be utilized in the recall of material from another. But the other "schemes" are here ancillary, always subordinate, and merely serving the interests of the one which is central.

With constructive imagination this is not so. The central "scheme" is not, so to speak, predetermined by the initial orientation. There is a freer range from setting to setting, and from interest to interest. The construction develops as it proceeds, and the points of emphasis grow with it. Material from any one "scheme" may be set next to material from any other "scheme," and there is only that amount of control which means that any item must be capable of carrying enough significance to prevent its falling wholly away from the rest, and so leaving a mere gap. This apart, the more unexpected and unusual the juxtaposition, the more the final product satisfies the demands by which it is produced. It is not in constructiveness that constructive imagination is peculiar, but in the range and play of its activity, and in the determination of its points of emphasis.

In constructive thinking, we come back to a greater rigidity of control once more. It is, however, not a control which makes us seek material organized within a single "scheme," or a single "schematic" group. On the contrary, constructive thinking demands the bringing together of realms of interest which ordinarily, so far, have not been connected. Again, it must not merely bring them together and exhibit them in juxtaposition. It has so to work out and express the connection that the relation may be apparent to everyone who can understand its language. Even this is not all. It has to investigate what follows from this juxtaposition, so as to attempt the solution of a problem set within the limits of the topic with which it deals. Hence it must submit to whatever kind of control the nature of the topic demands. Such control may be of objective and experimental fact as in science; it may be of standards which claim to be independent of individual idiosyncrasy, as in literature, art and philosophy. What may be seen in a flash and exhibited, in constructive imagination, may slowly gain general assent by the effort of constructive thinking. Much constructive imagination, however, never gets so far, and no doubt some never could; for the initial orientation and the initial control are different in the two cases.

I have written a book preoccupied, in the main, with problems of remembering and its individual and social determination. But I have never regarded memory as a faculty, as a reaction narrowed and ringed round, containing all its peculiarities and all their explanations within itself. I have regarded it rather as one achievement in the line of the ceaseless struggle to master and enjoy a world full of variety and rapid change. Memory, and all the life of images and words which goes with it, is one with the age-old acquisition of the distance senses, and with that development of constructive imagination and constructive thought wherein at length we find the most complete release from the narrowness of presented time and place.

---

20. Cases Illustrating Psychoanalytic Contributions to the Problems of Reading Disabilities *

EVEN THOUGH the major body of research in the principles of learning has focused on external conditions for learning, much clinical evidence has been uncovered that points to the importance of the personality of the learner as a factor in the learning process. The following illustrations of reading difficulties and the accompanying discussions expose the intimate connection between the nature of the material to be learned, the learning process, and the motivational dynamics of the individual.

FOR PURPOSES OF BREVITY, the following illustrations will not be complete case summaries but will consist of material selected chiefly to clarify points made in the preceding general discussion. Since the selection has been made for research purposes and to illustrate theoret-

* Phyllis Blanchard, "Cases illustrating psychoanalytic contributions to the problems of reading disabilities," *The Psychoanalytic Study of the Child,* II (1946), 174–85. By permission of the author and the publisher, International Universities Press, Inc.

ical concepts, no implications as to therapeutic methods and techniques are intended. In some instances, longer case reports have been published previously (in papers referred to in reviewing the literature on reading disabilities). Perhaps it should be stated that the children were seen at the clinics, appointments being once or twice weekly for varied periods of time. When the children were living in their own homes, case work with the parents was quite as important as psychotherapy for the children.

The first case illustrates a chronically unfavorable parent-child relationship in which the child was under constant emotional strain. For some three years prior to his referral to clinic, the boy had been the object of his father's anxiety and criticism, focused upon the subject of reading. Why the boy developed difficulty in reading and other neurotic symptoms should be self-evident from the case material presented below.

Case 1. Matthew was a twelve-year-old boy who was repeating fifth grade and still failing the work. He was considered mentally deficient by parents, teachers and classmates but psychological examination showed that he actually was of superior intelligence, with an IQ of 133.

The boy's father had had considerable difficulty in his vocational adjustments and had often been unemployed. He displaced anxiety from himself onto worry about the boy's future, stressing success in school as a preparation for later vocational success. When the boy was in third grade, the father began to supervise his school work. Although Matthew's teachers gave him good marks in reading, his father decided that he was poor in this subject. The father came to this conclusion after asking Matthew to read matter that was far too advanced for a third grade pupil. From that time, however, the father centered his anxiety upon the boy's reading and began to tutor him in it. Invariably, he scolded and criticized the boy during these home lessons, so that they always ended with Matthew in tears and his father in a temper. It is not strange, therefore, that the boy made no further progress in reading between the third and fifth grades or that by the time he was in fifth grade, he had a serious reading disability. By then, also, he was so sensitive to criticism that he would burst into tears at the slightest reprimand from a teacher and would fight with any child who said a teasing word to him.

Neither remedial teaching nor psychotherapy helped in this case so long as the boy remained at home, for the father was unable to change in his relationship to the boy, continued to displace anxiety onto him, and could not be induced to forego tutoring him. When the boy went to a boarding school and was thus freed from his father's anxiety and criticisms, he was able to learn to read with the help of individual remedial teaching.

Unfavorable comparisons with a brother or sister have been mentioned in the literature as another type of chronic family situation leading to neurotic conflicts and trouble with reading, in some instances. In the next case, comparisons between a living child and brother who had died were intimately associated with the reading disability.

CASE 2. Patrick was a nine-year-old boy, of normal intelligence (IQ 105) but was unable to read. Remedial teaching provided at school was unsuccessful in helping him to learn reading. There had been three children in the family—a first son who had died, Patrick, and a younger sister.

In his interviews with the therapist, Patrick soon spoke of the death of his older brother as having occurred shortly before he himself started first grade. A little more than a year later, Patrick said, he received a book as a birthday gift but he had not liked it, for when the stories were read to him, they proved to be about people who were killed. He had hated the stories and cried whenever he saw the book. After hearing those stories, he felt that he never wanted to hear a book read again nor did he ever want to read one himself.

At first, during his interviews, he stressed his love for his mother and his dead brother and dwelt upon wishes always to be good and kind to people. However, he soon became jealous of other patients, was angry with them for coming and with the therapist for seeing them. He complained that the therapist was just like his teachers, preferring other boys to him. After awhile, he began to accuse his mother of never having loved him as much as his dead brother. He told how she often talked about the dead child, saying that he had learned to read very quickly and criticizing Patrick for not being as apt at reading. "I wouldn't want to be like my brother," Patrick asserted contemptuously, "maybe he could read but he couldn't stand up for himself with the other kids. I'm a good fighter. They don't dare pick on me."

Patrick also told of his mother's weekly visits to his brother's grave and the tears that she shed each time she went there. Discarding his desire to be good and kind, he went on to express his wishes to dig up the brother's body and bury it somewhere so far away that his mother would never be able to find the grave and visit it. Or better yet, he would burn the body, destroying it completely. He then told how he hated his mother when he believed that she was behaving as if she wished his brother had lived and he had died. Similarly, he hated his teachers and his therapist when he thought that they might prefer other boys to him.

The mother, in the above case, had brought the boy to the clinic at the insistence of the school; she rarely kept her appointments with the social worker but sent the boy alone for his interviews with the therapist; finally, she withdrew him from therapy before it was completed. The material is therefore of interest only in connection with the etiology of the boy's reading disability. Obviously, when he first came to therapy, his conflicts about his mother and brother had been unconscious and he had repressed his resentment and hostility. His wishes to be good and kind were defenses by which he maintained the repression. The book with stories about people being killed naturally stirred up the repressed aggressive drives and threatened to bring them into his conscious experience. In turn, this aroused feelings of guilt and anxiety (shown in his weeping whenever he saw the book) as he came closer to awareness of his hostility toward his mother and his dead brother. Thus another defense and way of maintaining the repressions was refusal to learn to read, for he feared that reading content might release aggressive impulses. Self-assertion through being different from his brother was indicated by his stating his preference for being a good fighter rather than a good reader and his desire not to be like his brother. This was another motive influencing his negative attitude toward reading. Again, not learning to read was a disguised expression of hostility toward the mother who wanted him to be clever in this respect.[1] He identified the teachers who wanted him to read with the mother and also rebelled against learning to read to please them. Indeed he transferred his jealousy of his mother and brother to the teacher and other pupils at school, and to the therapist and other patients at the clinic, always neurotically recreating for himself the unpleasant and painful family situation which he was trying to repress from consciousness.

In the following case, we see how a later event may reactivate the unconscious feelings that surrounded an earlier traumatic one.

CASE 3. Thomas was an eleven-year-old boy, failing fifth grade for the second time. He had made low ratings on group tests given at school. Individual tests showed that he had an IQ of 108 but was handicapped in doing both group tests and school work by a reading disability. He dated the start of his trouble with reading from the first part of third grade, when a teacher whom he liked very much had to go to the hospital for an operation. Since she did not return to school, Thomas assumed she had died. He explained that he was so worried over the teacher's absence and her supposed death that he could not keep his mind on his work and so fell behind in reading.

This preoccupation with the question of the teacher's possible death becomes more intelligible if we know that when the boy was five years old, his mother had been away in a hospital, for an operation. He did not recall these circumstances about his mother's hospitalization, even when they were mentioned to him; he only remembered about the teacher.

In some of his therapeutic interviews, Thomas wanted to read aloud. It then became obvious that the content of reading often brought up his unconscious emotional conflicts. He would be reading fairly well when suddenly he would begin to make many errors until he stopped and talked of personal matters suggested to him by something he had read. After speaking out what had come into his mind, he could resume reading without excessive mistakes. For example, in reading a story about a dog, Thomas began making errors and continued to do so until he had paused to talk about a dog he once had owned. He had loved his dog very much indeed, he said, but he had not been permitted to keep it. After his dog was given away, he was very lonely; he cried and cried because he wanted his dog back and because he did

[1] I am indebted to Dr. F. H. Allen for calling to my attention the motive of wishing to be different from his brother in connection with the boy's reading disability. Failure in reading as a covert form of hostility to a parent was mentioned by Pearson and English.

not know what might be happening to it. "I was afraid my dog might die without my knowing about it," he explained. "It is awful to be wondering whether someone you love is alive or dead."

By the time his therapy ended, he could read without breaking down as described above. According to follow-up reports, during the next two years, his school progress was satisfactory.

The circumstances of the teacher's going to a hospital for an operation evidently revived the boy's feelings about his mother's hospitalization even though he had repressed the memory of his mother's operation and his anxiety about it. Reactivation of the emotional trauma was not the only reason for his trouble with reading, however, for from his interviews it was evident that reading content too frequently tended to stir up his unconscious conflicts. It does not take a very vivid imagination to realize that his feelings about his dog, for instance, were like those he had experienced when his mother was in the hospital. These feelings quite obviously were brought closer to consciousness when he read the story about the dog, even though it was a very cheerful one, just because the content contained the word dog many times repeated.

Both case 2 and case 3 illustrate the statements in the preceding general theoretical formulation concerning the case with which reading content becomes associated with a child's unconscious emotional conflicts, leading to a break-down in reading skill, or to an aversion to reading.

An immediate effect of an emotional trauma connected with separation from the mother at a time when the child is entering school is illustrated by the next case.

CASE 4. When Ethel was nearly six years old, her mother was forced to place her in a boarding school. Ethel's father had died two years previously and now the mother had to go to work so that she could no longer keep the child with her. At the school, Ethel seemed to have little appetite and would refuse to eat very much except when her mother visited and brought her food, which she would eat heartily. She did not learn to read during two years in first grade. She was brought to the clinic at the age of eight years, unable to read, still refusing food and having lost weight to the point where she seemed weak and ill and had to be kept in bed for considerable periods. Medical examinations could detect no physical basis for her symptoms.

In her interviews at the clinic, both her refusal to eat and her failure in learning to read soon appeared as symptoms of her unconscious conflicts over being sent away to school by her mother. At first she spoke of how much she loved her mother but soon in her play she began to dramatize her other attitudes of anger and hostility. She portrayed a mother doll sending her little girl doll away to school. The little girl doll was then angry with the mother, would not let the mother have anything to eat because she wanted to starve her mother to death, a fate that would serve her right for sending the little girl away to school. Immediately afterward, however, the little girl was punished for being so bad to her mother and also was described as being unable to eat and feeling weak and ill. Another drama with the dolls showed the little girl refusing to study or to read at school. Her poor school reports were sent to the mother doll, who decided that the school was no good and came to take the little girl home.

After this play with the dolls, Ethel could talk about how she felt when her mother placed her in the boarding school. She became aware of her idea that if she became ill or did not do well in her school work, she could force her mother to take her home again. At this point, she went on to explain that in reality, her mother could not take her because she no longer had a home. Since her father was no longer alive to take care of her mother and herself, her mother had to work to support them. She worked hard to earn money to pay for Ethel's school and her clothing. Ethel then felt very sympathetic toward her mother, who was tired from her hard work, and she was sorry that she had worried her mother by not eating and not learning to read. She announced that she was eating all right now but she had not been able to learn to read at school and she wished she could have someone to help her with reading. This request was seen as indicative of a change in attitude toward reading and special teaching was provided. Ethel worked hard with her tutor. She learned to read and began to make regular progress in school. At the time of the last follow-up report she was in seventh grade. None of her symptoms had recurred.

We might ask why this girl reacted so much more violently to being placed in boarding school by her mother than to her father's death. We can only guess at the possible reasons. Many children have less conflict over the loss of a parent through death than over separation from a parent through placement. Apparently placement is often taken as an act of aggression and rejection from the parent and therefore stimulates anger and resentment as well as grief. When a parent dies, love and grief over the loss need not necessarily come into conflict with other attitudes of anger and resentment. Serious conflicts over the death of a parent of course do occur when there was so much hostility toward the parent that a child feels guilty because of the hostile wishes before the parent died, as if they were responsible for the event. Thus a parent's death may or may not be a source of conflict to a child, depending upon the relationship that preceded it. On the other hand, placement often arouses conflict because it engenders hostility toward the parent while at the same time love and wishes to be reunited with the parent still persist.

While the next case also involves a child's conflicts over placement by the mother, it was selected for presentation primarily because it illustrates how errors in reading may provide a disguised expression and gratification of repressed wishes and drives, as was suggested in the more theoretical explanations of reading difficulties.

CASE 5. Benjamin was an eight-year-old boy who had remained for two years in the first half of first grade without learning to write or read words. His efforts to write them consisted of reversals of letters or sequence, seemingly meaningless combinations of letters, or a series of peculiar marks. Other symptoms were a solitary withdrawal from social relationships and wetting and soiling himself, although when still living with his own mother, he had established bladder and bowel control. Regression to wetting and soiling began when he was about three years of age after the mother placed him.

Repeated medical examinations revealed no physical basis for his symptoms. There was no left-handedness nor left or mixed eye-hand dominance connected with his tendency to reversals in writing words. At the age of three years, before his neurotic symptoms appeared, he achieved an IQ of 95. When tested by the same psychologist at five and seven years of age, he achieved IQ's of 75 and 74. At the end of therapy, after he had recovered from his severe neurosis, he was retested and his IQ then was 95.

Benjamin was placed in a foster home after the birth of a sister. Both children were illegitimate but the mother married the father of the second one. He did not wish to take the child by a former lover into their home, so the mother turned the boy over to a placement agency and then deserted him completely.

Benjamin was seen for nearly a year and a half, mostly twice a week. During these appointments, emotional conflicts about having been deserted by his mother were very evident. His feelings toward the mother were transferred to the therapist, whom he often reproached for sending him to live with strange people and causing his illness symptoms, saying, "I hate you for what you have done to me." He had various fantasy explanations of why his mother had deserted him. Since she placed him at the time of his sister's birth, he sometimes imagined that she had given him away because she loved girls better than boys. At other times, he suspected that she stopped loving him when she began to love the man she married, for it was after she had known this man that she gave up Benjamin. He hated his mother because he felt that placement was a proof of her ceasing to love him more than because of the placement per se. His hatred was expressed in certain fantasies associated with the symptoms of wetting and soiling; for example, he pictured burning up his mother with his hot urine or poisoning her by making her eat his feces. On the other hand, fantasies of being a baby, living with his mother and cared for tenderly by her, were also closely connected with his enuresis and soiling. Thus these symptoms concealed his love as well as his hostility and afforded gratification of ambivalent feelings toward his mother. Both his resentment toward his mother and his longing for her love had been repressed and were permitted an outlet only through his symptoms.

Benjamin regarded reading as evidence of being grown-up, but was blocked in his wishes to grow up because of fantasies that this could be achieved only by eating the father to gain his traits in magic manner. He was very guilty about such aggressive desires. But Benjamin's errors in writing words, like his other symptoms, were similarly disguised expressions of feelings toward his mother. He sometimes explained his mother's desertion as due to her not being Jewish, like himself, for he had heard that Christians were cruel to Jews. If his mother was not Jewish, the English language that they wanted him to write at school must be her language and he hated her so much that he did not want to learn it; instead, he wished to learn Hebrew, the language of Jewish people. He was unable to write Hebrew but he knew that it is written in the opposite direction to English; he explained that he tried to turn the English taught at school into Hebrew by writing it backwards. This was the reason for his reversals in writing words.

He called the peculiar marks that he sometimes made for words his "Chinese writing." He knew that the Chinese made peculiar marks to represent words; he had heard that Chinese tortured people whom they hated. When he hated his mother for deserting him, he elaborated, he felt like torturing her the way she had tortured him by letting him love her and then sending him away from her. His "Chinese writing" was a magic spell that would cause his mother to be tortured with sharp knives or in other ways and to be eaten by fierce animals.

These two types of errors in writing words—the reversals and the peculiar marks—were thus symbolic of his anger toward his mother, and his wish to hurt her. His other errors, in which he combined letters into what seemed nonsense, were symbolic of the love he still felt for his mother. For instance, he once wrote the following letter combinations—"As ur mor," which stood for the words, "Ask your mother." It developed that what he wanted to ask her (and the therapist, too) was to have a baby for him, as a proof that his love was returned. Then he need no longer fear that his mother loved the man she had married better than him.

It was only after he had produced all his imaginary explanations for his mother's having placed him and had become conscious of his repressed ambivalent feelings toward her, that he could realize there might be a different reason for the placement than those he had fantasied. Finally he accepted the reality that his mother had placed him because she could no longer take care of him. He then decided that he no longer needed to hate his mother, adding that this permitted him to love other women, too—his foster mother and his teachers at school. He explained that when he hated his own mother, he had hated all women, and so he had never wanted to do a single thing that his foster mother or his teachers asked of him. Now that he could love women, he wanted to do as they expected, so he would not have any more trouble with school work.

In thus describing how he felt about doing things for people because he loved them, this boy was confirming the psychoanalytic theory that the child first learns to please adults whom he loves. Of special interest was the fact that the reversals in writing words, often explained on a physical basis, in this instance were symbolic expressions of hostility and aggression. In two more recent clinic cases, reversals in reading and writing were similarly disguised forms of negative attitudes toward parents and teachers, accompanied by aggressive, destructive fantasies.

In reviewing the literature, there was a reference to a statement by Pearson and English concerning an inhibition of reading after a child had been forbidden peeping activities by parents. Our last case is that of a boy whose expressions of sexual curiosity and also of aggression had been stringently restricted. This case shows a reading disability developing from too severe limitations of instinctive drives.

CASE 6. Jonathan, eight years old when referred to the clinic, had been living in the same foster home since infancy. He had for some time been a tense, hyperactive child, hardly ever still. After two years in school, he had not learned to read. At first it was difficult to maintain contact with him or carry on any connected conversation because of his extreme motor restlessness. He was always running around the room and never continued any one play activity or topic of conversation for more than a few minutes. It was soon observed that he often hunted among the therapist's books, as if searching for something in particular, but he never would tell what he was looking for, saying that he did not know, which was probably quite true. One day as he rummaged through the books, he came upon *Growing Up*. He seized it with the exclamation, "That's what I wanted," but immediately replaced it upon the shelf, saying he could not read it. When asked if he would like it read to him, he hastily disclaimed any such wish.

For some time after this episode, the interviews were taken up with some of his conflicts about living in a foster home and having no parents of his own. At first he tried to protect himself from the anxiety aroused by the knowledge that his own parents had died when he was a small child, by fantasies that the foster parents were his own. After a while he gave up this defense and admitted the insecurity he felt at having no "real" parents like other children at school. Instead of running aimlessly around the room, he now began to do carpentry, liking to fashion swords, knives and guns out of wood. From his talk about these weapons, it was clear that they were symbols of both masculinity and aggressive tendencies, but he often had to leave them with the therapist because he was sure that his foster mother would object to his having them. Actually, when he did get courage to take home a sword he had made, his foster mother took it away from him. As he complained, she wanted him to act like a girl. His complaint had foundation in the fact, for the foster mother told us that she had wanted the placement agency to give her a girl (although she had never mentioned this to the agency) and when receiving a boy instead, she had dressed him like a girl as long as he would tolerate it and still expected him to be feminine in his behavior.

After he had found some relief from the repression of aggression and masculinity imposed by the foster mother, he again sought out the book *Growing Up* and looked at the pictures, asking the therapist to read some of the pages. He was guilty about this until he had talked over how his foster father once read him this book—but behind locked doors and with a stern warning that Jonathan must never talk about these sex education matters with the foster mother or anyone else except the foster father himself. This was only one aspect of the foster father's need to assure himself the sole intimate relationship with the boy; he did not permit Jonathan to play after school with other children, visit them or invite them to his home. Once Jonathan had thrown aside the restriction his foster father had placed upon his speaking of sex matters to other people, his next interviews with the therapist were full of questions and talk about sex and babies, including repetition of all the slang words and phrases he had heard. He concluded this series of interviews by saying, "I wish I could have asked my mother these things and talked about them with her, but I didn't dare because it would have made my father so angry that maybe he wouldn't have kept me. I was afraid he would give me back to the agency." He also told how he had been eager to learn to read when he first went to school, so that he could read *Growing Up* by himself, only he was fearful that the foster father would not have liked his reading it, for he always kept the book locked in his desk.

After the therapy was completed, Jonathan was able to learn to read at school without remedial teaching. By then, too, he was ready for a move to another foster home where masculine and aggressive strivings were acceptable. Follow-up reports from the agency indicated that he was developing along normal masculine lines thereafter and when a young adolescent, he was seen for educational guidance tests and interview. At this later date, he could never have been recognized as the same repressed, effeminate boy who had come to the clinic years earlier.

It is interesting to raise a question as to whether this boy would have developed his reading disability as the result of limitation of sexual curiosity alone. To be sure, he was so guilty over wanting to read *Growing Up* and talk about it with his foster mother that he had to resist all reading, but it would seem that repression of aggression was also involved in his avoidance of reading. At least, it was plain in the therapeutic interviews that he could only admit his interest in sex questions, in defiance of his foster father's prohibitions, after relaxation of the repression of masculine, aggressive strivings. Apparently reading was not simply a way of acquiring knowledge but also was an activity that represented aggressive rebellion against the foster father's restrictions, and against his desire to keep the boy to himself.[2] The boy realized that aggression of any kind would meet with disapproval from the foster mother, on whom he had been very dependent as a young child. He

[2] In this connection, it is interesting to recall that Freud mentioned the sadistic nature of desire for knowledge in the obsessional neuroses.

was afraid also that the foster father might punish rebellious resistance to his domination by refusing to give him a home any longer. Hence it is little wonder that the boy had to repress aggression so completely.

CONCLUSION

In the clinical cases just presented to illustrate reading disabilities of a psychogenic nature, it seems possible to interpret the material in the light of psychoanalytic theories of reading and learning. But it also appears that there is no single situation or personality maladjustment which can be isolated to explain the development of a reading disability as one of the child's neurotic symptoms. The background may be either traumatic or may reveal chronically unfavorable experiences; the personality difficulties may be severe (as in the case of Ethel who made herself ill by refusing food, or Benjamin who was withdrawn from social relationships and had other serious neurotic symptoms, or Jonathan who was inhibited, passive and effeminate); or maladjustments other than the trouble with reading may be mild enough to be masked from ordinary observation and may become fully apparent only to the professional eye in therapeutic work with the child. These statements might not seem warranted as generalizations on the basis of the comparatively small number of cases included in this paper or reported in previous ones, except for the fact that other investigators have arrived independently at the same conclusions by accumulating statistical data on large numbers of cases.[3]

Both our individual case studies and the statistical findings of other psychologists suggest that a complexity of factors came together in a focal point around reading, particularly where the disability is of emotional origin. In this respect, the neurotic reading disability conforms to the psychoanalytic concept of neurotic symptoms generally as being over-determined. It also conforms otherwise to psychoanalytic theories of symptom-formation: for the repression of instinctive drives and existence of emotional conflicts forms the setting for the reading disability as well as for other neurotic symptoms; errors in reading may serve as disguised ways of gratifying repressed impulses just as illness-symp-

[3] Bell speaks of research in this field as indicating that reading is related to many different factors and is a highly complex function of the personality; Jackson reaches a similar conclusion on the basis of his own statistical findings. Gates states that there is no single personality pattern among pupils of adequate intelligence coexistent with reading disability but that difficulty in reading may occur in all sorts of personalities, emotional patterns and parental relationships. Moreover, Gates points out, citing examples, that a factor which seems to be a chief cause of a reading disability in one individual may even be a strong motivation for learning to read well in another.

toms serve this purpose; failure in reading may represent a hidden antagonism to adults expressed in passive resistance rather than in openly rebellious behavior, and thus may also conceal repressed attitudes. To be sure, at other times the failure may result from a wish to avoid reading because it has previously stirred up feelings of guilt or anxiety, but here, too, it closely resembles a well-known neurotic tendency toward avoidance of imaginary dangers.

In considering that reading disabilities tend to appear as a center of convergence for several emotional factors, we probably need to take into account the timing of this occurrence. It is reasonable to believe that reading is most apt to become involved in a child's emotional conflicts when these concur with the period of learning the fundamentals of the reading process in the early school grades. Once a firm foundation has been acquired, further proficiency in reading depends more upon enlarging the reading vocabulary than learning new processes so that disability for this subject is less likely to begin in higher grades, although it may have remained undetected until then. It is possible, therefore, that the time element may have a bearing on whether a special educational disability will be for reading or for some other subject. Since in many cases personality maladjustments of children begin by the time they enter school or soon afterward, this may be one reason why reading disabilities are more frequent than others. But an equally valid reason, already mentioned, is the ease with which reading content, either directly or symbolically, can become associated with unconscious emotional conflicts.

V

MOTIVATION AND EMOTION

PERCEPTION, LEARNING, AND MOTIVATION seem to be the important basic psychological processes. Partly because they are interrelated, their operation affects almost everything we do. As we have seen in Section III, perceptual function involves learning and motivation; learning, similarly, is related to perception and motivation: and a thorough study of motivation must take account of perception and learning. However, many psychologists insist that only a man's motives furnish the real key to understanding him. The work of many psychotherapists rests upon an analysis of their clients' motivational patterns.

In studying motivation we find terms like *instincts, needs, drives,* and *goals* as well as *motives*. Sometimes these terms are carefully defined and differentiated; more often they are not. Because, in general, the study of motivation is concerned with the inner springs of man's behavior, emotions and feelings are generally included in discussions of the subject, for they, too, are instrumental in initiating and guiding behavior.

In this section there are five selections. The first is an attempt by representatives of three different disciplines—a zoologist, a psychologist, and a sociologist—to pool their thinking on the subject of instincts and to interrelate their conceptions of man's basic motivational and behavioral patternings. Other papers examine some anticipated developments in motivation theory and the role of early experience as a determiner of motivating patterns.

The selections focusing on emotions include material that should help the reader develop an integrated conception of the biological and psychological functioning of the individual we know as a person. Together, they make a strong case for the necessity of considering these two aspects of functioning a dynamic unity.

21. *A Re-examination of the Concept of Instinct* *

THE TERM "instinct" is used with so many different meanings in everyday speech that many psychologists have stopped using the word. Nevertheless, it is clear that there *are* some unlearned drives and patterns of behavior that depend on the genetic makeup of a species. Many significant researches have been done to help identify the particular factors that are involved in a number of instincts.

In this selection we find a zoologist, the late Dr. Allee; a psychologist, Dr. Nissen; and a sociologist, Dr. Nimkoff, trying to clarify, from their different points of view, the true nature of instincts.

. . . . .

INSTINCT FROM THE ZOOLOGIST'S STANDPOINT

A SIMPLE OUTLINE of different phases of animal behavior may help orient this discussion of instinct. One such outline recognizes a primary division of all behavior into (I) unlearned, and (II) learned behavior patterns. The former can be broken into smaller categories as follows: (a) poorly organized responses of animals lacking nervous systems, e.g., sponges, or early embryos; (b) reflex-arc reactions; (c) kineses, meaning a speeding or slowing of unoriented responses of whole organisms; (d) the oriented tropisms of sessile plants and animals and the tactic reactions of motile forms consisting, when shown in purest form, of oriented forced movements which seem to resemble reflex actions of entire organisms; (e) instincts, the most complex of all phases of unlearned behavior, including many levels of behavior from variable appetitive responses to more rigid consummatory actions.

The great confusion about instincts results in part from the fact that much so-called instinctive action of man and other vertebrates, and, perhaps, of some invertebrates also is really behavior based on very early training. The training has been forgotten; the definite activity pattern remains. Sometimes the learning may be based on a single exposure to a given situation.

There are a great many definitions of instinct. These fall into two main types: (a) those that are primarily objective, the biologically behavioristic definitions; (b) the subjective ones.

Existence of the subjective emphasis is a part of the cause of justi-

* W. C. Allee, H. W. Nissen, and M. F. Nimkoff, "A re-examination of the concept of instinct," *Psychological Review,* LX (1953), 287–97. By permission of the American Psychological Association and of H. W. Nissen and M. F. Nimkoff.

fiable skepticism regarding instincts among biologists, including, of course, psychologists. Parenthetically, the scientific part of psychology obviously is a branch of biology. The subjective definitions may be illustrated by the statement that if birds migrate south early in the fall, earlier than they are normally expected to do, this may be taken as a sign that an uncommonly cold winter is coming. The migrating birds are supposed to have a supernatural instinctive insight in the matter. Such fantasies are similar to folktales about whiteness of chicken bones foretelling the severity of the coming winter.

Good definitions of instinct are hard come by. Most of them, even of the objective, biologically behavioristic sort, are involved and difficult to interpret. There are two I wish to present. One is adapted from W. M. Wheeler, who said, approximately, that an instinct is a relatively complicated activity of an organism that is acting (a) as a whole rather than as a part; (b) as a representative of the species rather than as an individual; (c) without previous experience or without modification caused by experience; and (d) with an end or purpose of which the reacting animal has no knowledge. More recently, in 1951, N. Tinbergen, in his book entitled *The Study of Instinct,* gives his definition only after he is more than halfway through the book. Even then, the definition is offered almost apologetically in loose association with his admittedly somewhat imprecise discussion of neurophysiological relationships. His statement is: "I will tentatively define an instinct as a hierarchically organized nervous mechanism which is susceptible to certain priming, releasing, and directing impulses, of internal as well as of external origin, and which responds to these impulses by coordinated movements that contribute to the maintenance of the individual and the species." These two objective definitions supplement each other more than they overlap. They may be tested against such activity patterns as breathing, swallowing, gland secretion, muscle contraction, all of which may be shown to occur without learning. Some types of glandular secretion, for example, can be effected by learning only with great difficulty, if at all. On casual inspection, such activities as breathing, etc. come more nearly to fitting Tinbergen's definition than they do that advanced by Wheeler, although they run aground there only on the first idea that the organism should be acting as a whole rather than as a part when displaying instinctive behavior.

Instinctive reactions represent examples of prolongation of development exhibited as behavior rather than as formation of new structure. Contrast, for example, the difference between a chrysalid and a cocoon. Each is found at pupation time in the life history of certain members of the Lepidoptera. The butterflies form a chrysalid which consists essentially of a thickening of the hypodermis to form a protective covering. This thickened chrysalid is frequently attached to the walls of some crevice by a gluelike secretion. Inside its protecting covering the pupation processes take place. In contrast, the moths, as pupation time approaches, spin a more or less elaborate silk cocoon. Inside the cocoon the moth larva also develops a somewhat thickened hypodermis, which serves as an additional protection. There is no essential difference in these activities being examples of prolongation of development. One is limited primarily to the hardening of the hypodermis; the other is complicated by the presence of silk-spinning activities which represent instinctive behavior. The moth larva cannot form the cocoon until the silk glands are matured; that is, this spinning activity is also a deferred activity that cannot be expressed until the moth larva has developed functioning silk glands. Instincts and development are inextricably bound together.

Many writers speak of instinctive and intelligent actions as though these two types of behavior differ fundamentally from one another. Against this view it may be asserted that a large instinctive element enters into every form of intellectual activity; whereas instinctive actions do not usually run their courses altogether automatically and mechanically but contain in addition to fixed and unchanging components a variable element, more or less adapted to the particular situation.

An act, A, is at one and the same time normally a function of the constant, C, and a variable, V; expressed as a formula this becomes

$$A = \int (C \leftrightarrow V).$$

The constant is the instinctive biologically inherited element. The variable is the element which produces, in some cases, an appropriate modified reaction, in others, an unforeseen response to a situation. Analysis of the action into these two components is purely an abstract analysis. V and C must not be taken as two more or less opposed natural agencies pulling the organism now in this direction, now in that, as they battle for supremacy. They are merely two different aspects of the same reality. In inherited, innate, instinctive reactions C is greater than V; in intelligent action the relationship is reversed. I first read this analysis in a book by Alverdes; Yerkes gave a part of the same idea in his 1943 book on chimpanzees.

Two instances of instinctive behavior that I personally observed may be interesting, and, in addition, helpful for the discussion.

Years ago, near the Marine Biological Laboratory at Woods Hole, Massachusetts, I was trotting back from a noontime swim in a hurry for dinner when I saw a solitary wasp dragging an immobilized caterpillar across the uneven surface of the dusty road. I stopped to watch. The wasp turned before she reached the sidewalk. She passed near a low sturdy weed up which she climbed and balanced the caterpillar over a low fork some few inches from the ground. All this time the wasp and her prey had been followed by a small tachina fly, which would lay her own egg or eggs on the egg of the wasp larva. The tachina larva on hatching would feed on the larva of the wasp, while it, in turn was feeding on the paralyzed, living caterpillar.

The wasp descended from the weed, proceeded a few feet to a small burrow, which was a fraction of an inch wide and about that deep. She entered, and enlarged the burrow, digging vigorously.

After a short time the wasp left the enlarged burrow, returned along the way she had come, but did not remember the weed-climbing incident, and did not locate the caterpillar immediately. Meantime the tachina fly had stayed near the caterpillar in place of following the wasp on her digging activities. Finally the wasp located the weed, climbed it, brought down the caterpillar and renewed her slow progress to the burrow. Now the tachina fly followed, keeping, again, about a foot to the rear.

The wasp dug a bit more, dragged the caterpillar into the burrow, and deposited her egg. Just then the tachina fly darted forward, dove into the burrow, presumably laid her own egg or eggs, emerged, and flew away. The wasp filled in the hole, leveled off the ground, and she, too, flew away. All these complicated patterns were examples of innate, unlearned behavior, both by wasp and tachina fly. There was evidence of adjustment to existing irregularities in the surface of the dust, to the size of the burrow, and, also, to the whole weed incident. However, C loomed much larger than V.

Years later I saw a more elaborate instance of essentially the same behavior—this time out in the mountains in Utah north of Great Salt Lake. There were three of us, including a poet and a psychologist, coming down the mountain trail. We disturbed a wasp carrying her numbed caterpillar enough so that she dropped her prey. We stopped, and she soon actively quartered the region, a few feet from the caterpillar. When she was beginning to waver in her quartering, I picked up the limp caterpillar and deposited it near the wasp, which soon was carrying it on to the partly excavated burrow a short distance away. She repeated the digging and burying routine. The poet sprawling with his eye close to the opening of the burrow saw the glistening egg deposited on the paralyzed caterpillar. Then the wasp filled and leveled off the burrow so that to us the spot was indistinguishable from the bare ground elsewhere except for its being darker from the moisture, which would soon dry. Still the wasp hovered near giving us the impression that she had not yet finished the operation. After a short while she settled down on a fallen cluster of three pine needles still wrapped together as they grew on the tree, transported these to the site of the burrow, and deposited them there. Then that spot looked to us as casually littered as the ground nearby, and the wasp flew away as though entirely finished.

Lorenz, Tinbergen, Baerends, and the other present-day European students of instinct study such behavior patterns by fragmenting them into smaller and smaller units, striving towards breaking them down to their reflex-arc components. At each step they attempt to discover the releasing stimuli, which they call simply releasers. In this they use passive and moving models. They report considerable and promising progress, for example, with the mating activities of grayling butterflies, stickleback fish, and various birds. The analysis of several sorts of instinctive behavior of fishes and birds has been carried fairly far in the identification of sign stimuli that serve as releasing mechanisms, finding, for example, that a bunch of red feathers is the effective releaser of territorial defense for an English robin.

Tinbergen states that the reason why dependence of innate behavior on sign stimuli has not yet been generally recognized notably lies in the fact that so many laboratory psychologists have been studying conditioned reactions. He thinks that conditioned reactions are not usually dependent on a limited set of sign stimuli, but seem to depend on more complicated stimulus situations. The progress these men are making in an obscure phase of behavior is stimulating. It is particularly heartening to see the long stagnant field of instinctive behavior, freighted with "oh my" stories such as I attempted to use in telling about the solitary wasps, beginning to yield to methods of objective analysis.

INSTINCT AS SEEN BY A PSYCHOLOGIST

As Dr. Allee has shown, many animals exhibit complex patterns of behavior, constant for the species and apparently unlearned, which need a name to set them off descriptively from other behaviors. In the first part of my discussion I shall try to relate the term "instinct," as designation for these uniformities, to certain other concepts, such as reflex, habit, and drive. These considerations will lead to the conclusion that "instinct" has real but limited usefulness, and to the suggestion that all behaviors may be ordered on a continuum of possible associations which are more and less readily learned.

My second point will be a criticism of the current tendency to oversimplify the problem of motivation by organizing all behavior under half a dozen biogenic drives or instincts plus a few psychogenic or secondary drives. This part of the discussion will be illustrated by recent observations of the development of sex behavior in chimpanzees.

Terms referring to the dynamic or energizing aspect of behavior must be kept sharply separate from those pertaining to the form or pattern of the behavior itself. Confusion between the two has been responsible for much of the misunderstanding and controversy about instinct and persists even today: Tinbergen presents a diagram of "the hierarchical organization of instincts" which looks like the flow chart of a military chain of command. The top brass—that is, the top instinct—decides the strategy, lower centers direct the tactics, and the lowest-level instincts do the work. The "instinct of pugnacity" refers both to the motivation to fight, and to the manner or pattern of fighting. The term is useful only in the latter sense, which is the way I shall use it here.

The dynamic factor in behavior has been given various names, the most common one, perhaps, being "drive." Morgan has termed it "the central motive state," or CMS, and I have called it the "sensitizing component of behavior determination." The drive or sensitizing factor elicits behavior which is often such as to increase or decrease the amount of a certain kind of stimulation. Thus the earthworm may orient away from the source of light, whereas the Euglena may swim towards the light. Instead of deriving from the external environment, the stimulation may arise internally: the organism sneezes, defecates, or urinates. In other cases, the effective condition is a surplus or deficiency of chemicals in the bloodstream, presumably sensitizing certain parts of the nervous system. In still other cases, the mechanism of the energizing factor is completely unknown. You will note that I am postulating a sensitizing factor in all behavior, whether it is of external or internal origin, and whether it leads to behavior as simple as a reflex or as complicated as nest-building.

Now the behavior which ensues when a sensitizing factor is active may differ in various ways. Most obviously, it may be all over in a moment, or it may last a long time. When the goal or situation which brings relief is immediately present, the response is prompt and brief; we call it an unconditioned or conditioned reflex, tropism or taxis, or automatized habit. When the goal object or situation is not at hand, a more or less prolonged series of acts occurs. Duration in time is therefore one differentiating criterion. Further, a reflex typically is elicited by a specific, localized stimulus, whereas an instinct is usually determined by a combination of internal factors plus a *class* of external stimulus patterns which, in their details, may vary considerably. On the response side, a reflex implies contraction of a particular muscle or muscle group, whereas instinctive behavior allows considerable leeway in the effector mechanisms by which a common effect is achieved.

In the absence of the goal or drive-reducing situation, the organism is forced to an indirect, extended series of acts. These longer sequences may be classified into five categories, in accordance with information available to us regarding *how* the form of that behavior was determined: (a) When little or no direction or selectivity is in evidence, we speak of "random" or "spontaneous" activity. (b) When innately determined components are conspicuous, we call the sequence an "instinct." (c) When learning has determined the pattern, we call it a "complex habit." (d) When there is evidence of reasoning and foresight, we speak of "purposive striving" or "goal-directed" activity. (e) When we want to remain neutral about the role of the innate, experiential, and central factors involved, we call it simply "drive behavior."

Together with the other terms designating prolonged behavior sequences, "instinct" implies the sensitizing effect of neural stimulation. An animal behaves differently when hungry than when thirsty. The drive or motivating factor sensitizes the animal to some stimuli and makes it obtuse to others. It both filters and intensifies. This selective action does *not* differentiate among the five classes of long sequences. Nor does the consummatory response, which usually gives the behavior its name, and which may be the same for random, instinctive, rational, and habitual responses. It is in the etiology of the behavior preceding the consummatory response, in the past history of the animal, that the differentiating criteria are to be sought. This demands experimental analysis. Sometimes the data are unambiguous, as when the isolated bird sings the song which is characteristic of its species. Both birds and chimpanzees build tree nests; in the former the behavior pattern is often innate, but in the apes it is evidently learned, being transmitted from one generation to the next. Often the answer is complicated, because the behavior sequence contains both innately determined and learned components. Instinct and intelligence are *not* mutually exclusive. Some of the fastest and most efficient learning that we know of is intimately related to instinctive behavior: the foraging insect must learn and remember, on the basis of a single flight, the direction or the landmarks which guide it back home. According to Baerends, the digger wasp even remembers from day to day how well each of its eight or ten burrows is stocked with provisions.

Finally, I should like to suggest that reflexes, instincts, and the inherited capacity to learn may be distributed on a continuum. What is inherited may be *a more or less specific readiness to learn.* The concept of learning implies that such readiness is rather nonspecific. But often, as in the case of the wasp, there is a readiness to learn very specific things. When such selective readiness is common to the species, the resulting behavior can hardly be distinguished from instinct or reflex.

We come, now, to a criticism of the tendency to ascribe all or most behavior to a few drives or instincts. During the past two years I have been observing the behavior of male-female pairings of late-adolescent chimpanzees. As youngsters these animals lived together, but well before puberty they were separated by sexes. Starting at least a year after the first menstruation, and at a higher chronological age for the males, these animals were put together for periods of observation at times when the female was in swelling, that is, during the periods of physiological receptivity. All possible pairings of five sexually naive males and a like number of females were made. The observations total over 100 in number. If I had used experienced, rather than inexperienced, chimpanzees under like conditions, a conservative estimate of the number of copulations which would have occurred is 200. In my observations there were no copulations.

However, except for what Carpenter has delicately called "primary sex activity," the chimpanzees were very active during these hours of observation. These primates are notoriously inventive and varied in their behavior, and practically everything that a caged ape *can* do these animals *did* do in the course of my observations. The behaviors which occurred were both individual and social. The former included self-grooming, solo gymnastics such as somersaulting and doing cartwheels, sucking a thumb, or just sitting and thinking. Among the social interactions there were a few instances of serious aggression, many occurrences of bluffing or exhibitionistic behavior, a great deal of play-fighting, wrestling, playful slapping or boxing, tag or follow-the-leader, and mutual grooming. The point to be stressed is that, although there was no copulation, there was a great deal of social behavior, including most of the constituent acts which enter into the mating pattern.

The question now arises whether the observed behavior which did occur is properly and appropriately designated as sex behavior, as expression of the sex drive or instinct. The only excuse for doing so is *our* knowledge (a) that with other, experienced, male-female pairings the sex act would occur, and (b) that, with continuation of the prevailing conditions for a long enough time, the sex act most probably *will* occur, eventually, in each of these 25 pairings. But this is not adequate justification for ascribing these long sequences of variable behavior to the "sex drive." There was no consummatory act and no drive reduction; the reactions were not "preparatory" (except in a far-fetched teleological sense) for mating.

What, then, did motivate the great variety of behavior which was observed? There are several theoretical possibilities. The old concept of youthful play as being the incomplete, nonserious expression of later biologically significant behavior patterns is particularly unsatisfactory here because, structurally and physiologically, these animals *are* ready for actual mating and its consequences. A second possibility is to postulate an independent drive, such as activity, exploration, play, or curiosity. The conceptualizations are too glib and facile—they "explain" too much too easily, and give no "handle" for experimental testing. Still another possibility is the idea of displacement reactions, as proposed by the German neonaturalists. They suggest that when the environment does not provide the stimuli or objects necessary for the development of the currently dominant instinct, reactions belonging to some other instinct will occur. This also is an *ad hoc* explanation which can be brought in as necessary to "explain" almost anything.

Instead of starting with a dozen or so drives, instincts, or propensities, under one or another of which all behavior is ordered, we may, instead, postulate a multiplicity of self-motivated activities. What were conceived of as part-activities, all contributing towards some one definite end, are thought of, instead, as a series of independently motivated acts. Every postural adjustment, every approach to or avoidance of a given object, each episode of grooming, has its own, intrinsic motivation. To explain the vast number of movements and acts, extending over hours, and sometimes over weeks and months, as all being determined and guided by one drive, whose direct and identifiable expression can be seen only in a brief consummatory act, is pure anthropomorphism. The acrobatics, wrestling, and grooming seen in my male-female pairs of chimpanzees cover a longer period of time, and involve a greater variety of precise coordinations, than does the act of mating which takes less than a minute. But mating is all that may be strictly designated as sex behavior.

Mutual grooming by chimpanzees contains elements which, in human behavior, we call foreplay or petting and which we ascribe to the sex drive. Could it be suggested that petting is, sometimes, an end in itself, with no sinister motive towards a further ulterior goal? In chimpanzees, grooming occurs as frequently in preadolescent animals, who have had no sex experience, as it does in adults; it occurs in female-female pairs as much as in male-female pairs; and it occurs more often after mating than before. Looked at from the outside and as a whole, the goal-directedness of the behavior sequence is obvious, but that is the view seen by the human mind, not the view of the organism doing the behaving. To suppose that it is, is to endow the animal, anthropomorphically, with the foresight which characterizes the deliberate, devious, and planful behavior of man.

The behaviors legitimately and descriptively named sex, hunger, thirst, and so on, are relatively infrequent, isolated events in the flow of behavior; their motivation demands explanation no more, and no less, than do the many activities appearing in each of various sequences. To say that a given act is sometimes motivated by sex, another time by hunger, is to slur over the basic question of motivation. Differential sensitization, determining the probability of occurrence of various reactions, needs explanation. But more fundamental than the problem of frequency of elicitation, is *why* grooming and wrestling and play-biting occur at all. Since they appear when there is no copulatory drive, and more often after reduction of the sex drive than before, they must be independently motivated.

The theme of the view which I am advocating might be summarized in the words of a once-popular song, whose title is, "Every little movement has a meaning all its own." I should perhaps restate this to read, "Every little action has a motive all its own." My point, of course, is not that sex has been overrated, but rather that it already has enough to account for, without our burdening it with more than its fair share of responsibility.

A SOCIOLOGIST'S VIEW OF INSTINCT

Since Dr. Allee, a zoologist, has dealt mainly with the lower animals, and Dr. Nissen, a psychologist, with chimpanzees, my function is to consider the question of instinct in relation to man. Although sociologists concern themselves primarily with man, they need for proper perspective on this question of instinct some knowledge of the motivations of other animals. This knowledge comes largely from zoology and psychology. Sociologists may, of course, properly study the social life of animals other than man, although few do so.

To avoid semantic difficulties, it is desirable at the outset to clarify the concept of instinct, which the two preceding discussants have done. Central to the concept are the ideas that the behavior is complex, common to the species, and unlearned. An example is the building of nests by birds. A bird that has never seen any other bird build a nest will still build a nest if the conditions are right. There is, in fact, an inner compulsion that forces certain animals through the motions of nest-building even when the necessary materials are lacking. The nests of different species of birds may vary much more than do the nests of any one species.

Does man have any instincts? The early psychologists, William James, William McDougall, and E. L. Thorndike, drew up long lists of instincts. James said man had more instincts than any other animal. His list included sucking, crying, locomotion, curiosity, shyness, cleanliness, pugnacity, fear of dark places, acquisitiveness, love, jealousy.

About 1924 the reaction set in with the publication of *Instinct* by L. L. Bernard, a sociologist, who showed how confused was the use of the term. Covering some 400 authors, he disclosed that about six thousand urges had been called instinctive. These were of two kinds, those of a general nature like sex and social behavior, and those that were more specific like "an instinct for the piano" and "an instinct to avoid eating the apples of one's own orchard." From our perspective today, Bernard's analysis seems like a caricature. Instinct in human psychology was buried, and Knight Dunlap and John B. Watson added their nails to the coffin with their accent on conditioning and learning.

The tendency in recent years has been to reserve the term instinct to the lower animals. Man's nervous system is not as imperious in dictating behavior because it is more complex than that of other animals and is less fully coordinated at birth. For instance, it takes a human being longer to learn to walk than it does an ape. This complexity and plasticity of the human organism makes possible more and richer learning. So, in the case of human beings, we drop the term instincts and speak of organic drives, which are more general. There are also drives of a purely social origin which have been termed wishes or motives. Most of man's behavior is learned, whereas most of a bird's behavior is not learned.

The problem of instinct appears to be a matter of differences in the degree of the learning capacity of organisms. Some students object to the use of the term instinct even in reference to the lower animals because they, too, may be capable of learning and are not mechanistically repetitive in their behavior. Even the lowly amoeba can, apparently, learn to alter its behavior in response to new stimuli. Birds improve the quality of their nests with practice, and learn from other birds. So the differences between man and the lower animals can be exaggerated. The anthropomorphic danger is ever present, and man must beware of his bias in favor of himself. The evolutionary viewpoint is a wholesome corrective, emphasizing as it does differences in degree as well as differences in kind.

We can stress the fact that differences in learning ability fall along a continuum, but this need not cause us to lose sight of the fact that differences in degree may be very considerable indeed. The ants have complex behavior patterns based on the division of labor, differentiation of status, and different classes of workers. These patterns are inherent in the structure of each ant and show little change except as the ant may change. Professor W. M. Wheeler examined ants embedded in Baltic amber fifty to seventy-five million years ago and concluded that these ants had developed all their various castes just as they exist today. The larvae and the pupae were the same. They kept guest beetles in their nests and had parasitic mites attached to their legs in the same special positions as do our species today. Apparently the ants have learned very little in fifty million years. On the other hand, man has learned much. A community like New York City with its eight million inhabitants and complex social organization is very different indeed from an Eskimo band of 10 to 100 individuals or thereabouts, a change which represents a cultural span of about 15,000 years. So we may say that while other animals may have some culture, the amount is negligible, and man is the only animal with a substantial and significant culture. The differences in cultural level among animals reflect differences in learning capacity, a biological phenomenon. Among large groups of men, like races and nations, differences in learning are the result of differences in opportunities for building culture, not differences in inherited learning ability.

Sociology depends on biology and psychology for knowledge of the inherited biological nature of man. What can sociology itself contribute to our understanding of this problem? Sociology is interested in the structure and function of social systems: that is, the total cultural organization that constitutes man's social environment. We cannot control the human environment experimentally, like that of birds or chimpanzees, to observe how individuals behave when reared in isolation. The folkways and mores, which are so important to human learning, nowhere permit this.

While it does not seem possible to hold the human environment constant by isolating individuals and denying them the opportunity of learning from the group, we can in a sense reverse the situation and observe what happens when the genetic factor is held constant, as it is when very large groups of human beings are involved. Individual differences in genetic traits are minimized or cancelled out under these conditions.

What we find in different human societies is a considerable diversity of customs. Some cultures are strictly monogamous, others polyandrous, still others polygamous. Some societies do not permit divorce, most societies frown on it but permit it, and a few encourage it. The folkways are marked by variety. This is thought to demonstrate man's highly flexible inherited tendencies.

Underlying the diversities, however, are certain uniformities. Whether it be monogamous, polyandrous, or polygamous, the family is everywhere to be found. So it is natural to ask: do the uniformities in culture the world over reflect certain common human drives that are genetically determined? Are the cultural universals an expression of man's unique biological nature?

In the case of the family, the answer seems clearly to be in the affirmative. The universality of the human family as a social institution rests on the fact that there are two sexes endowed with a sex drive and that the human infant is highly dependent on others for survival. The family is omnipresent, but the organization of the family varies greatly. So we conclude that the presence and broad outlines of this institution are determined by man's biology, but not the details of structure and function.

Cultural universals are not the only indicators of man's innate biological nature. Cultural preferences may be indicators, too. While culture patterns vary widely, some patterns are more common than others. Polygamy, the marriage of one male and several females, is much more frequent than polyandry, the mating of several males and one female. Does this suggest that polygamy is more compatible with the biological nature of man than polyandry? The evidence from the primates supports this interpretation. The male, generally larger than the female, often shows signs of jealousy and possessiveness. The organization of a baboon family is described by Zuckerman as consisting of a male overlord, his female or females, together with their young, and sometimes including one or more "bachelors" or unmated males.

It is not safe, however, to infer that behavior is genetically determined simply because it is found to be widespread, or even universal. Take, for example, the taboo against incest. Every society enjoins incest, although the definition varies, as does that of the family. Violation of the incest taboo is severely punished, and few if any offenses are regarded as more serious. Is the horror of incest "instinctive," as some have argued? If so, it would hardly seem necessary to have a taboo against it. The explanation of the taboo is not clear, as may be gathered by an examination of the voluminous literature on the subject. A more plausible explanation for the incest taboo is that it is the result of universal social factors and that it helps to promote social organization. It is difficult, for instance, to see how authority patterns could be maintained in the family without it. Therefore we are unable to conclude that human behavior which is universal must, by virtue of this fact, be biologically motivated. There may be universal considerations in the acquired social situation which prompt the behavior.

Moreover, behavior which is biologically induced may be modified by the culture so that its usual or normal expressions are not evident. The sex drive, for instance, can be repressed. People can be persuaded to fast and even starve to death, although it is difficult to see how the latter behavior could be universalized if society is to persist.

In short, there does not seem to be any easy formula which we can use for determining what is learned and what is genetically motivated in human behavior.

---

22. The Trend in Motivational Theory *

THIS PAPER opens with a review of projective tests, those tests that permit the subject to interpret stimulus material (ink blots, vague pictures, incomplete sentences) according to his personal reaction patterns. These tests are widely used for personality diagnoses and often are used to give insights into the motivational patterning of an individual. Dr. Allport then proceeds to a critical review of psychodynamics, essentially "a general science of motivation," and takes issue with a number of postulates stemming from the study of neurotics that are frequently applied uncritically to normal people. This is a provocative article that should help the reader maintain a scientific, critical attitude in the face of temptations to extend personality theories beyond the justifying data.

MOTIVATIONAL THEORY today seems to be turning a corner in the road of scientific progress. In attempting to characterize this change in direction I wish to pay special attention to the problem of psychodiagnostic methods. For the successes and failures of these methods can teach us much about psychodynamic theory.

Let us start by asking why projective methods are so popular in both diagnostic practice and research. The answer, I think, is to be found in the history of motivational theory during the past century. All of the major influences have pressed in a single direction. Schopenhauer, with his doctrine of the primacy of the blind will, had little

* Gordon W. Allport, "The trend in motivational theory," *American Journal of Orthopsychiatry,* XXIII (1953), 107–19. By permission of the author and the *American Journal of Orthopsychiatry.*

respect for the rationalizations invented by the individual's intellect to account for his conduct. Motives, he was sure, could not be taken at their face value. Darwin followed with his similar anti-intellectual emphasis on primordial struggle. McDougall refined the Darwinian stress on instinct, retaining in his horme the flavor of Schopenhauer's will, Darwin's struggle for survival, Bergson's *élan,* and Freud's libido. All these writers were irrationalists—confident that underlying genotypes in motivation should be sought rather than the surface phenotypes. All of them were reacting against the naïve intellectualism of their predecessors and against the rationalizations offered by self-justifying mortals when called on to account for their conduct. Among these irrationalists who have dominated western psychology for the past century Freud, of course, has been the leading figure. He, like the others, correctly perceived that the mainsprings of conduct may be hidden from the searchlight of consciousness.

In addition to irrationalism modern dynamic psychology has developed another earmark: geneticism. The original instincts laid down in our nature are regarded as decisive, or if not, then the experiences of early childhood are held to be crucial. At this point, the leading nondynamic school of thought, stimulus-response psychology, joins forces with geneticism. Stimulus-response theorists agree with instinct psychologists and psychoanalysts in viewing adult motives as conditioned, reinforced, sublimated, or otherwise elaborated editions of instincts, drives, or of an id whose structure, Freud said, "never changes."

Not one of these dominating theories of motivation allows for an essential transformation of motives in the course of life. McDougall explicitly denied the possibility; for our motivational structure is laid down once and for all in our equipment of instincts. New objects may become attached to an instinct through learning, but the motive power is always the same. Freud's position was essentially identical. The concept of "sublimation" and of shifting object "cathexis" chiefly accounted for whatever apparent alterations occur. Stimulus-response psychology is likewise geared to the assumption of remote control operating out of the past. We respond only to objects that have been associated with primary drives in the past, and we do so only in proportion to the degree that our responses have been rewarded or gratified in the past. From the stimulus-response point of view the individual can hardly be said to be *trying* to do anything at all. He is simply *responding* with a complex array of habits that somehow were rewarded year before last. The prevailing dictum that motivation is always a matter of "tension reduction" or of "seeking equilibrium" is consistent with this point of view, but scarcely consistent, I think, with all the known facts.

This prevailing atmosphere of theory has engendered a kind of contempt for the "psychic surface" of life. The individual's conscious report is rejected as untrustworthy, and the contemporary thrust of his motives is disregarded in favor of a backward tracing of his conduct to earlier formative stages. The individual loses his right to be believed. And while he is busy leading his life in the present with a forward thrust into the future, most psychologists have become busy tracing it backward into the past.

It is now easy to understand why the special methods invented by Jung (forty years ago), Rorschach (thirty years ago) and Murray (twenty years ago) were seized upon with enthusiasm by psychodiagnosticians. At no point do these methods ask the subject what his interests are, what he wants to do, or what he is trying to do. Nor do the methods ask directly concerning the subject's relation to his parents or to authority figures. They infer this relationship entirely by assumed identifications. So popular is this indirect, undercover approach to motivation that many clinicians and many university centers spend far more time on this type of diagnostic method than on any other.

Occasionally, however, a client may cause the projective tester consternation by intruding his unwanted conscious report. The story is told of a patient who remarked that a Rorschach card made him think of sexual relations. The clinician, thinking to tap a buried complex, asked him why. "Oh, because," said the patient, "I think of sexual relations all the time anyway." The clinician scarcely needed a Rorschach card to find out this motivational fact.

Still it is probably true that most psychologists prefer to assess a person's needs and conflicts by going the long way around. The argument, of course, is that everyone, even a neurotic, will accommodate himself fairly well to the demands placed upon him by reality. Only in an unstructured projective situation will he reveal his anxieties and unmasked needs. "Projective tests," writes Stagner, "are more useful than reality situations for diagnostic purposes." To my mind this uncompromising statement seems to mark the culmination of a century-long era of irrationalism, and therefore of distrust. Has the subject no right to be believed?

Fortunately, the extensive use of projective methods at the present time is yielding results that enable us to place this technique in proper perspective, and to correct the one-sided theory of motivation upon which their popularity rests.

Let us consider first the wartime research conducted with 36 conscientious objectors who lived for six months on a semistarvation diet. Their diet was so rigorously meager that on the average they lost one quarter of their initial body weight in the course of the six months. The food need was agonizingly great; their incessant hunger most poignant. Unless occupied with laboratory or other tasks they found themselves thinking of food almost constantly. Typical daydreaming is reported by one subject as follows: "Today we'll have Menu No. 1. Gee, that's the smallest menu, it seems. How shall I fix the potatoes? If I use my spoon to eat them I'll be able to add more water. . . . If I eat a little faster the food would stay warm longer—and I like it warm. But then it's gone so quickly." Now the curious thing is that while these men were clearly obsessed by their food drive, and all their energy seemed directed toward its fulfillment, yet on projective tests the need failed to appear. The investigators report that among the tests used (free word association, first letters test, analysis of dreams, Rorschach, and Rosenzweig's P-F Study) only one gave a limited evidence of the preoccupation with food, viz., the free association test.

Here is a finding of grave significance. *The most urgent, the most absorbing motive in life failed completely to reveal itself by indirect methods.* It was, however, entirely accessible to conscious report. Part of the explanation may be that the subjects turned in relief to laboratory tasks to forget for a while their obsessive motive. They responded to the projective tests with heaven knows what available, habitual associational material. The failure of night dreams to reveal a significant amount of wish fulfillment is somewhat more perplexing. It can scarcely be ascribed to a defensive mental set. But both types of result suggest a possible law: Unless a motive is repressed it is unlikely to affect distinctively the perception of, and responses to, a projective test. It is too early to tell whether this is a valid generalization, but it is a hypothesis well worth testing.

Other studies on hunger seem to yield supporting evidence. Their trend suggests that on projective tests the number of explicit food associations actually declines in longer periods of fasting, apparently because the motive itself gradually becomes completely conscious and is not repressed. It is true that instrumental associations (ways of obtaining food) continue to appear in the subject's word-responses as the state of hunger grows. This finding, however, is quite consistent with the hypothesis, since while hunger is fully conscious, the subject in the experimental situation is prevented from seeking satisfaction, and thus is still repressing his instrumental action-tendencies.

Another revealing line of evidence comes from the research of J. W.

Getzels. This investigator utilized two forms of a sentence completion test—one couched in the first person and one in the third. His pairs are of the following type:

> When they asked Frank to be in charge he . . . .
> When they asked me to be in charge I . . . .
>
> When Joe meets a person for the first time he usually . . . .
> When I meet a person for the first time I usually . . . .

In this experiment, of course, the items were randomized. In all there were 20 diagnostic items of each type. The subjects were 65 veterans, 25 diagnosed as well adjusted; 40 were psychoneurotic cases discharged from service with disability involving personality disorder.

It turned out that to a highly significant degree the well-adjusted men gave *identical* responses to the first and to the third person completions. If we assume that the third-person sentence is a "projective method" then the results obtained by this method for well-adjusted subjects squared almost perfectly with the results obtained from the direct, first-person questioning. The psychoneurotics, on the other hand, to a highly significant degree varied their responses. They said one thing when queried directly (e.g., "When they asked me to be in charge I agreed") and another on the projective item (e.g., "When they asked John to be in charge he was afraid"). The first-person completion is so direct that in the psychoneurotic it invokes the mask of defense and elicits a merely conventionally correct response.

Thus the direct responses of the psychoneurotic cannot be taken at their face value. The defenses are high, the true motives are hidden and are betrayed only by a projective technique. The normal subjects, on the other hand, tell you by the direct method precisely what they tell you by the projective method. They are all of a piece. You may therefore take their motivational statements at their face value, for even if you probe you will not find anything substantially different.

This research adds weight to the tentative judgment we formed in the case of the starving subjects. It is not the well-integrated subject, aware of his motivations, who reveals himself in projective testing. It is rather the neurotic personality, whose façade belies the repressed fears and hostilities within. Such a subject is caught off guard by projective devices; but the well-adjusted subject gives no significantly different response.

There is, however, one difference between the two researches. The starving subjects actually *avoided* any betrayal of their dominant motive in the projective tests. The well-adjusted veterans, on the other hand, gave essentially the *same* type of response in both direct and in projective testing. It may be that the dissimilar nature of the tests used in the two situations accounts for this difference in results. But this detailed difference need not detain us here. What seems to be important is the implication of these researches that *a psychodiagnostician should never employ projective methods in the study of motivation without at the same time employing direct methods.* If he does not do so he will never be able to distinguish a well-integrated personality from one that is not. Nor will he be able to tell whether there are strong conscious streams of motivation that are entirely evading the projective situation (as in the case of the starving subjects).

The trend of evidence that I have presented seems to indicate that a normal, well-adjusted individual with strong goal-directedness may on projective tests do one of two things: (1) either give material identical with that of conscious report—in which case the projective method is not needed; or (2) give no evidence whatever of his dominant motives. It is only when emotionally laden material comes forth in projective responses that is contradictory to conscious report, or to other results of direct assessment, that we find special value in projective testing. And we shall never know whether or not a neurotic situation prevails unless we use both diagnostic approaches and compare the yield.

Consider for a moment the diagnosis of anxiety. Using various responses on the Rorschach and TAT cards the clinician might infer a high level of anxiety. Now this finding taken by itself tells us little. The subject may be the sort of person who is enormously effective in life because he harnesses his anxiety to performance. He may know perfectly well that he is a harried, worried, bedeviled overachiever. Anxiety is an asset in his life, and he has enough insight to know the fact. In this case the yield by projective methods is matched by the yield from direct methods. The projective technique was not really needed, but it does no harm to use it. Or, as in our starvation cases, we might find that projective protocols reveal no anxiety while in actuality we are dealing with a person who is as harried, worried and bedeviled as our first subject, but who effectively controls his jitters. In this case we assume that his large measure of control enables him to tackle the projective tests with some mental set unrelated to his anxious nature. But we may also find—and here is where projective methods have their uses—that an apparently bland and calm individual, denying all anxiety, reveals profound disturbance and fear in projective performances. It is this type of dissociated nature that projective tests help to diagnose. Yet they cannot do so unless direct methods also are employed.

In speaking so frequently of "direct" methods I have referred chiefly to "conscious report." To ask a man his motives, however, is not the only type of "direct" method that we may employ. It is, however, a good one—especially to start with.

When we set out to study a person's motives we are seeking to find out what that person is trying to do in this life, including of course what he is trying to avoid, and what he is trying to be. I see no reason why we should not start our investigation by asking him to tell us the answers as he sees them. If the questions in this form seem too abstract they can be recast. Particularly revealing are people's answers to the question, "What do you want to be doing five years from now?" Similar direct questions can be framed to elicit anxieties, loyalties and hostilities. Most people, I suspect, can tell what they are trying to do in this life with a high degree of validity, certainly not less on the average than the prevailing validity of projective instruments. Yet some clinicians disdain to ask direct questions.

But by "direct methods" I mean also to include standard pencil-and-paper measures, such as the Strong Interest Inventory and the recently revised Allport-Vernon-Lindzey Study of Values. Now it often happens that the yield on such instruments is not what would come from the subject's conscious report. The subject may not have known, for example, that compared with most people his pattern of values is, say, markedly theoretical and aesthetic, or far below average in economic and religious interest. Yet the final score on the Study of Values is itself merely a summation of a series of separate conscious choices that he has made in 45 hypothetical situations. While his verbal report on the pattern as a whole may be faulty, yet this pattern not only squares with all his separate choices, but is known on the average to have good external validity. People with certain patterns of interests as measured by the test do in fact make characteristic vocational choices and do in their daily behavior act in ways that are demonstrably consistent with the test results.

To sum up: direct methods include the kind of report that is elicited in careful interviewing, whether it be of the simple psychiatric variety, the sort employed in vocational or personal counseling, or in nondirective interviewing. Autobiographic methods when employed at their face value are likewise direct. So too are the results of any kind of testing where the final scores represent a sum or pattern of a series of conscious choices on the part of the subject.[1]

[1] For the purposes of the present argument this simplified discussion of "direct" and "indirect" techniques is adequate. Psychodiagnosis requires, however, a much more discriminating classification of the methods currently employed, and of the

The currently fashionable term *psychodynamics* is often equated explicitly with psychoanalytic theory. Projective techniques are considered psychodynamic because they are thought to tap deepest layers of structure and functioning. We have already indicated reasons for doubting the sufficiency of this assumption. Many of the most dynamic of motives are more accurately tapped by direct methods. At the very least the discoveries by projective techniques cannot be properly interpreted unless they are compared with discoveries yielded by direct methods.

Devotees of psychodynamics often say that no discoveries are of value unless the unconscious is explored. This dictum we find in the valuable book by Kardiner and Ovesey, *The Mark of Oppression,* dealing with the seriously disordered and conflictful motivational systems of Negroes in a northern city. Unless I am greatly mistaken, however, the authors discover little or nothing about their cases through psychoanalytic probes that is not evident in the manifest situation. The conscious handicaps of a Negro in our society, the economic misery, the deteriorated family situations, the bitterness and despair, constitute a painful psychodynamic situation in individual lives that in most instances receives no further illumination when depth analysis is employed.

Most of the psychodynamic evidence given by Kardiner and Ovesey concerning their cases is, in fact, drawn from straightforward autobiographical report. Their use of this method is acceptable and their findings highly instructive. But their theory seems to me out of line with both the method actually used and the findings obtained. Psychodynamics is not necessarily a hidden dynamics.

This point is well made by the psychiatrist J. C. Whitehorn, who correctly holds that psychodynamics is a general science of motivation. Into its broad principles one may fit the specific contributions and insights of psychoanalysis. But psychoanalysis itself is by no means the sum and substance of psychodynamics. Whitehorn insists that the

---

"levels" of organization that each normally taps. An excellent beginning is Rosenzweig's proposal that three classes of methods be distinguished, each adapted in principle to tapping three levels of behavior. What he calls *subjective* methods require the subject to take himself as a direct object of observation (questionnaires, autobiographies). *Objective* methods require the observer to report on overt conduct. *Projective* methods require both subject and observer to "look the other way" and to base the diagnosis on the subject's reaction to apparently "ego-neutral" material. Broadly speaking, Rosenzweig's subjective and objective procedures correspond to what I here call "direct" methods, and projective procedures to "indirect" methods.

Especially noteworthy is the author's statement that the significance of projective methods (e.g., his own P-F Study) cannot be determined unless the subject's projective responses are examined in the light of his subjective and objective responses.

proper approach to psychotic patients, especially to those suffering from schizophrenic or depressive disorder, is through such channels of their normal interest systems as remain open. It is not the region of their disorder that requires primary attention, but those psychodynamic systems that still represent sturdy and healthy adaptations to reality. In Whitehorn's words, the therapist should seek "to activate and utilize the resources of the patient and to help him thereby to work out a more satisfying way of life with a less circumscribed emphasis upon these special issues."

Sometimes we hear it said that psychoanalytic theory does not do justice to psychoanalytic practice. What is meant is that in the course of therapy an analyst will devote much of his time to a direct discussion with his patient of his manifest interests and values. The analyst will listen respectfully, accept, counsel and advise concerning these important, and *not* buried, psychodynamic systems. In many instances, as in the cases presented by Kardiner and Ovesey, the motives and conflicts are taken at their face value. Thus the method of psychoanalysis as employed is not fully sustained by the theory that is affirmed.

Nothing that I have said denies the existence of infantile systems, troublesome repressions, or neurotic formations. Nor does it deny the possibility of self-deception, rationalization and ego defense. My point is merely that methods and theories dealing with these aberrant conditions should be set in a broad conception of psychodynamics. The patient should be assumed insightful until he is proved otherwise. If you asked a hundred people who go to the icebox for a snack why they did so, probably all would answer, "Because I was hungry." In ninety-nine of these cases we may—no matter how deeply we explore—discover that this simple, conscious report is the whole truth. It can be taken at its face value. In the hundredth case, however, our probing shows that we are dealing with a compulsive overeater, with an obese seeker after infantile security who, unlike the majority of cases, does not know what he is trying to do. It is peace and comfort he is seeking—perhaps his mother's bosom—and not the leftover roast. In this case—and in a minority of all cases—I grant we cannot take the evidence of his overt behavior, nor his account of it, at their face value.

Freud was a specialist in precisely those motives that cannot be taken at their face value. To him motivation resided in the id. The conscious, accessible region of personality that carries on direct transactions with the world, namely the ego, he regarded as devoid of dynamic power.

It is a misfortune that Freud died before he had remedied this one-sidedness in his theory. Even his most faithful followers tell us now that he left his ego psychology incomplete. In recent years many of them have labored to redress the balance. Without doubt the principal current in psychoanalytic theory today is moving in the direction of a more dynamic ego. This trend in theory is apparent in the work of Anna Freud, Hartmann, French, Horney, Fromm, Kris, and many others. In a communication to the American Psychoanalytic Association, Kris points out that the attempt to restrict interpretations of motivation to the id aspect only "represents the older procedure." Modern concern with the ego does not confine itself to an analysis of defense mechanisms alone. Rather it gives more respect to what he calls the "psychic surface." Present psychoanalytic techniques, he tells us, tend to link "surface" with "depth." In a similar vein Rapaport has argued that a measure of true autonomy must now be ascribed to the ego.

To illustrate the point at issue, we might take any psychogenic interest of maturity, for example, the religious sentiment. Freud's handling of the matter is well known. To him religion is essentially a neurosis in the individual, a formula for personal escape. The father image lies at the root of the matter. One cannot therefore take the religious sentiment, when it exists in a personality, at its face value. A more balanced view of the matter would seem to be this: *sometimes* one cannot take this sentiment at its face value, and *sometimes* one can. Only a careful study of the individual will tell. In a person in whom the religious factor serves an obviously egocentric purpose—talismanic, bigoted, self-justificatory—we can infer that it is a neurotic, or at least immature, formation in the personality. Its infantile and escapist character is not recognized by the subject. On the other hand, in a person who has gradually evolved a guiding philosophy of life where the religious sentiment exerts a generally normative force upon behavior and confers intelligibility to life as a whole, we infer that this particular ego formation is not only a dominant motive, but that it must be accepted at its face value. It is a master motive and an ego ideal whose shape and substance are essentially what appear in consciousness.

Let us consider a final example. It is well known that most boys around the age of four to seven identify with their fathers. They imitate them in many ways. Among other things they may express vocational aspirations for daddy's job. Many boys when grown do in fact follow their fathers' footsteps.

Take politics. Father and son have been politicians in many families: the Tafts, Lodges, Kennedys, La Follettes, Roosevelts, to mention only a few. When the son is at a mature age, say 50 or 60, what is his motivation? Is he working through his early father identification or is he not? Taken at its face value the interest of the son in politics now seems to be absorbing, self-contained, a prominent factor in his own ego structure. In short, it seems to be a mature and normal motive. But the strict geneticist would say: "No, he is now a politician because of a father fixation." Does the geneticist mean that an early father identification started him in a political direction of interest? If so, the answer is yes, of course. All motives have their origin somewhere. Or does he mean, "This early fixation now, today, sustains the son's political conduct"? If so, the answer is normally, no. The political interest is now a prominent part of the ego structure, and the ego is the healthy man's source of energy. To be sure, there may be cases where a person mature in years is still trying to curry father's favor, to step into his shoes, to displace him with the mother. A clinical study of a second-generation politician may conceivably show that his behavior is compulsively father-identified. In such a case his daily conduct is in all probability so compulsive, so ungeared to realistic situational needs, so excessive, that the diagnosis can be suspected by any skilled clinical observer. But such instances are relatively rare.

To sum up: we need in our motivational theory to make a sharper distinction between infantilisms and motivation that is strictly contemporary and at age.

I am fully aware of my heterodoxy in suggesting that there is in a restricted sense a discontinuity between normal and abnormal motivation, and that we need a theory that will recognize this fact. Discontinuities are distinctly unpopular in psychological science. One theory of abnormality tells us that we are merely pleased to regard the extremes on our linear continuum as abnormal. Further, some culture theorists insist that abnormality is a relative concept, shifting from culture to culture, and from one historical period to another. Likewise, there are many borderline cases which even the most experienced clinician could not with confidence classify as normal or as abnormal. Finally, and most important, is the fact that in many normal people one can by scratching deeply enough find *some* infantilism in their motivation.

Granted all these familiar arguments, there is still a world of difference—if not between normal and abnormal people—then between the healthy and unhealthy mechanisms involved in the development of motivation. What we call integrative action of the nervous system is basically a wholesome mechanism that keeps motivation up to date. It tends to bring about both an internal consistency and a reality testing among the elements entering into motivational patterning. Effective suppression is another healthy mechanism, not only harmless to the individual, but making possible the arrangement of motives in an orderly hierarchy. With the aid of effective suppression the individual ceases to act out infantile dramas. Insight, a clear self-image, and the little understood factor of homeostasis may be mentioned among the balancing mechanisms.

As Getzels' experiment shows, direct and projective performances in healthy people are all of a piece. A further test of normality—unfortunately one psychologists have not yet developed—may lie in the harmony of expressive behavior (facial expression, gestures, handwriting) with the individual's fundamental motivational structure. There is evidence that discoordination between conscious motives and expressive movement is an ominous sign. This lead for research should be followed through.

In unhealthy motivation, unbalancing mechanisms have the upper hand. There is always some species of dissociation at work. The individual represses ineffectively; repressed motives erupt in autistic gestures, in tantrums, in nightmares, in compulsions, perhaps in paranoid thinking. Above all, self-knowledge is lacking in large regions of the life.

My point is that normally the balancing mechanisms have the upper hand. Sometimes, in certain badly disordered lives, the unbalancing mechanisms take over. Occasionally too, we find them operating in a segmental way in lives that are otherwise healthy. When the clash in mechanisms is marked, diagnosis is then aided by the use of projective techniques. But when there is essential harmony within the personality system projective methods will teach us little or nothing about the course of motivation.

From what has been said it is clear that a satisfactory conception of psychodynamics will have the following characteristics. (1) It will never employ projective methods nor depth analysis without allowing for a full diagnosis of motives by direct methods as well. (2) It will assume that in a healthy personality the great bulk of motivation can be taken at its face value. (3) It will assume that normal motivation of this order has a present and future significance for the individual that is by no means adequately represented by a study of his past life. In other words, it will allow that the present psychodynamics of a life may in large part be functionally autonomous, even though continuous with early motivational formations. (4) It will at the same time retain the epochal insights of Freud and others to the effect that infantile fixations frequently occur, and that we do well to check on conscious report and to supplement direct methods by indirect.

Before such an adequate conceptualization can be achieved there is one current dogma in motivational theory that demands re-examination. I refer to the oft-encountered statement that all motives aim at "the reduction of tensions." This doctrine—found in instinctivism, psychoanalysis, and in stimulus-response psychology—operates to keep us on a primitive level of theorizing.

We cannot, of course, deny that basic drives seem to seek "reduction of tension." Oxygen need, hunger, thirst, elimination are examples. But these drives are not a trustworthy model for all normal adult motivation. Goldstein remarks that patients who seek only tension reduction are clearly pathological. They are preoccupied with segmental irritations from which they seek relief. There is nothing creative about their interests. They cannot take suffering, or delay, or frustration as a mere incident in their pursuit of values. Normal people, by contrast, are dominated by their "preferred patterns" of self-actualization. Their psychogenic interests are modes of sustaining and directing tension rather than escaping it.

We should, I think, agree with Goldstein that tension reduction is not an adequate statement of the functioning of mature psychogenic motives. At the time of his inauguration as president of Harvard, James Bryant Conant remarked that he was undertaking his duties "with a heavy heart but gladly." He knew he would reduce no tensions by committing himself to the new job. Tensions would mount and mount, and at many times become almost unbearable. While he would in the course of his daily work dispatch many tasks and feel relief, still the over-all commitment—his total investment of energy—would never result in any equilibrium. Psychogenic interests are of this order: they lead us to complicate and strain our lives indefinitely. "Striving for equilibrium," "tension reduction," "death wish" seem trivial and erroneous representations of normal adult motivation.

Recent years, as I have said, have brought a wholesome turn in theorizing. Few authorities on war neuroses, for example, wrote in terms of tension reduction. They spoke rather of "firm ego structure" or "weak ego structure." Grinker and Spiegel say, "As the ego becomes stronger the therapist demands increasing independence and activity from the patient."

After successful therapy these and other writers sometimes remark, "The ego now seems in full control." In such expressions as these—and one encounters them with increasing frequency—we meet post-Freudian ego psychology again. True, the flavor of these theoretical statements varies. Sometimes they still seem close to the conception of the ego as rationalizer, rider and steersman. But often, as in the statements just quoted, they go far beyond. They imply that the ego is not only normally able to avoid malignant repression, chronicity and rigidity, but that it is also a differentiated dynamism—a fusion of healthy psychogenic motives that can be taken at their face value.

There is no need to take fright at the conception of an "active ego." As I see the matter, the term "ego" does not refer to a homunculus, but is merely a shorthand expression for what Goldstein calls "preferred patterns." The term means that normally healthy personalities have various systems of psychogenic motives. They are not limitless in number. Indeed in a well-integrated adult they may be adequately indicated on the fingers of two hands, perhaps one. What a person is trying to do persistently, recurrently, as a function of his own internal nature, is often surprisingly well focused and well patterned. Whether these leading motives are called desires, interests, values, traits or sentiments does not greatly matter. What is important is that motivational theory—in guiding diagnosis, therapy and research—should take these structures fully into account.

---

23. Competition: The Effects of Infantile Experience upon Adult Behavior *

COMPETITIVE BEHAVIOR in human adults has been given so much attention that many people feel it is based on inborn, instinctive tendencies. In this study of mice, Dr. Fredericson demonstrates that learning may play a major role in much competitiveness. Using two groups of subjects of similar heredity, the experimenter subjected one group to special training in infancy. All the subjects were then raised to adulthood without any opportunity for competing. When they reached adulthood, all were tested under similar conditions. The results showed clearly that the infantile experience influenced adult behavior.

VARIOUS THEORIES OF PERSONALITY and especially psychoanalysis emphasize the role of infantile experience in determining adult behavior. At present only a beginning has been made toward securing controlled experimental evidence supporting such theories. Hunt has shown that food deprivation during infancy will increase the amount of hoarding by adult rats. The purpose of the present experiment is to investigate the effects of infantile experience on a different type of behavior, namely,

* Emil Fredericson, "Competition: the effects of infantile experience upon adult behavior," *Journal of Abnormal and Social Psychology,* XLVI (1951), 406–9. By permission of the author and the American Psychological Association.

This investigation was supported by a research grant from the National Institute of Mental Health, U.S. Public Health Service.

competition. The social importance of competitive behavior is obvious. An attempt will be made to test the hypothesis that a limited period of hunger-motivated competition for food during the infancy of mice will cause them in adulthood to show increased competition for food even when not motivated by hunger.

A pilot study which preceded the experiment to be reported here, and other published results, indicated that the experience in deprivation per se was primarily responsible for the development of competitive fighting over food.

PROBLEM

In the present experiment an attempt has been made to test the hypothesis that a limited period of competition for food during infancy will result in competitive behavior at a later stage in development, despite the absence of hunger.

METHOD

Population

A total of 50 inbred mice were used. These mice were the offspring of brother-sister matings well beyond 30 generations, and it may consequently be assumed that within a given strain the individuals were (except for sex differences) almost identical.

This group consisted of eight black mice of subline 10 from strain C57; twenty-two C57 blacks, subline 6; sixteen C Bagg albinos, and four C3H mice.

Each strain had an approximately equal sex representation. The animals were weaned at 21 days of age and lived in pairs, males with males, and females with females.

Procedure

The technique which elicited competition over food consisted of presenting a given pair of hungry mice with a single piece of hard laboratory food. The types of competitive response varied with the strain. Several strains were included in this study because pilot studies exploring the competitive behavior of these strains revealed characteristic differences in competition.

The albinos exhibit a primarily mild type of competitive response which consists of a huddling together and taking the food away from the competitor when needed. The C3H mouse (agouti) is an intense fighter but slow in becoming aroused. Both sublines of the C57 black mouse are vigorous fighters and also extremely possessive. A typical fight consists of a chasing of the opponent that has the food, culminating in vigorous wrestling, biting, and loud squealing. The writer has isolated another form of fighting which is spontaneous in nature and apparently not a function of frustration.

The experimental design consisted of two separate experiments, each with its own littermate controls.

EXPERIMENT 1. The experimental group was given seven one-a-day trials in competition beginning at 29 days of age. This group was retested when 72 days old. The first and crucial trial at this time occurred when the mice were not hungry. Presumably, these sexually mature adult mice would, according to the proposed hypothesis, fight over food though not hungry because of their experiences in competition during early life.

The control group, consisting of the littermates of the experimental group, received no experience in competition over food or food deprivation during infancy, but was tested when not hungry at 72 days of age. These mice should not fight over food because of the absence of previous experience in this kind of behavior.

EXPERIMENT 2. This experiment differs from Experiment 1 in that the experimental group received only a single experience in competition over food at 33 days of age. This group was also retested when 72 days old.

The control group for this experiment was tested at 72 days, having had no previous experience in competition over food. In order to prevent the possibility of conflict altogether, these mice literally lived and ate upon a cage floor padded with food. Presumably they should not compete over food when not hungry because of the lack of previous experience. In contrast to this, the control group in Experiment 1 was fed from food hoppers which permitted the eating of food but not its acquisition.

In both experiments competition, once started, was permitted to last for ten seconds after its onset; the mice were then separated by *E* to prevent dominance. The length of a trial was five minutes.

These two experiments can actually be considered as one, since the emphasis is on what the mice in both groups do in comparison with a control group at 72 days of age and not hungry.

RESULTS

Tables 1 and 2 indicate the experimental design, as well as the results for Experiments 1 and 2, respectively. Upon combining the

TABLE 1

Behavior * of Mice on Tests in Infancy and Adulthood, Experiment 1

	Age (in Days)								
Subject	29 *D.* †	30 *N.D.* †	31 *D.*	32 *N.D.*	33 *D.*	34 *N.D.*	35 *D.*	72 *N.D.*	73 *N.F. 24* †
EXPERIMENTAL GROUP									
1 C m	1	1	1	1	1	1	1	1	2
2 C f	1	1	1	1	1	1	1	1	3
3 C f	1	1	3	1	1	3	1	2	2
4 C m	1	1	3	1	1	1	1	1	2
5 C f	1	1	3	1	1	1	1	1	2
6 C3H f	0	1	3	3	3	3	3	2	2
7 C 57–10 f	3	2	3	3	3	3	3	2	2
8 C 57–10 f	3	3	3	3	3	3	3	3	3
9 C 57–10 m	3	2	2	2	2	2	2	3	3
CONTROL GROUP									
(No experience in competition over food during infancy; never deprived of food.)									
11 C f								0	3
22 C m								0	3
33 C f								0	1
44 C3H f								0	3
55 C57–10 m								0	3

* KEY: 0, disinterested; 1, mild competition; 2, possessive; 3, vigorous fighting over food.

† *D.* means that mice were deprived of 1 gram of food for 24 hours, out of a total of 3 grams, which is the average amount of food consumed by mice at this age. *N.D.* means not deprived in this manner. *N.F. 24* means no food at all for 24 hours.

results as shown in the tables, we find that the critical test involves 14 experimental and 11 control pairs. The results indicate that the experimental *S*s competed over food when 72 days old, although they were not hungry at the time. The *S*s in the control group, on the other hand, did not show any evidence of competitive behavior. Attention should be directed to the fact that the numbers as found in both tables, namely 0, 1, 2, and 3, are not rating scores; they represent levels of competitive behavior which characterize the different mouse strains. The crucial point is whether competitive behavior, regardless of its specific behavioral form, does or does not occur. From a general point of view, the differences between mouse strains in terms of competitive behavior point to hereditary differences in the management and expression of aggressiveness.

A statistical evaluation of these results has been made by the X^2 test. Specifically, a test was made here in terms of testing the divergence of the obtained results from values computed on the null hypothesis. Thus, when the results in Tables 1 and 2 are combined, the proportion of competition obtained in the total population, namely, 14/25, is used as the proportion to be expected by chance in each cell. This procedure allows a test of the null hypothesis which considers the experimental and control groups as randomly selected from the total population. Computation shows the results for both experimental and control groups to be significant well beyond the .01 level of confidence. The customary correction for continuity as it applies to small table entries has been made. One can, therefore, discard the null hypothesis and state that the results obtained are not due to chance, and probably indicate the effects of an infantile experience.

The advantages and disadvantages of sampling homogeneous populations are clearly revealed by these results. On the one hand, it is not actually surprising to find a literally 100 per cent conformity of experimental results with the originally postulated hypothesis, namely, that the effects of an infantile experience make themselves known at a later stage in development despite the absence of the originally existing need.

From a genetic point of view, one would, of course, expect a population sample with little or no hereditary variability to show homogeneous effects in behavior as well. The fact, therefore, that no exceptions oc-

TABLE 2

Behavior * of Mice on Tests in Infancy and Adulthood, Experiment 2

	Age (in Days)					
Subject	33 *N.H.* †	34 24 h. †	72 *N.H.*	73 *N.H.*	74 24 h.	75 *N.H.*
EXPERIMENTAL GROUP						
20 C 57–6 m	0	3	3			
21 C 57–6 m	0	3	3			
22 C 57–6 f	0	3	3			
23 C 57–6 f	0	3	2			
24 C 57–6 f	0	3	2			
CONTROL GROUP (No experience in competition over food during infancy; never deprived of food.)						
10 C 57–6 f			0	0	0	2
11 C 57–6 f			0	0	3	3
12 C 57–6 m			0	0	3	3
13 C 57–6 m			0	0	2	3
14 C 57–6 f			0	0	3	2
15 C 57–6 m			0	0	3	3

* KEY: 0, disinterested; 1, mild competition; 2, possessive; 3, vigorous fighting over food.

† *N.H.* means not hungry; *24 h.* means 24 hours without food.

curred merely reflects the actual use of several inbred strains with restricted behavior responses. The experimental data may, however, for this reason represent an artifact, because some other mouse strains as yet unknown to us might have given completely different results. Several strains were used, specifically in order to test this possibility in a limited fashion. In general, the above considerations show the necessity for a meticulous account not only of environmental but of hereditary variables as well.

Tables 1 and 2 reveal, as an additional check of the experiment as a whole, that the control groups began to compete for food as soon as they were deprived of it, but not before that time. The importance of frustration for the elicitation of competitive behavior is also shown by the fact that the experimental group (Table 2) when first tested at 33 days of age, did not compete over food during the first "not-hungry" trial. In other words, all of the *S*s that were used showed that they were capable of competing in one way or another over food, but that an experience in competition during infancy caused the experimentals to compete later on, even when it was not necessary for them to do so.

DISCUSSION

The fact that a single infantile experience produced results which persisted into adult life seems to support Guthrie's contention that important learning can occur in one trial. The exact nature of the reinforcement for such learning is a problem. Can the present concepts of reinforcement theorists such as Hull deal adequately with (1) the reinforcement of such behavior on a single trial, and (2) the performance of such behavior by adult animals in the absence of the primary drive of hunger?

SUMMARY

The present study explored the importance of early experience in competition with respect to adult behavior. Hungry infant mice were trained to compete over food for a few days shortly after weaning. Following this experience they were allowed to grow into adulthood without having to compete. This experience in competition during infancy turned out to cause them to fight over food on a retest many weeks later when they were sexually mature; they were not hungry at this time. The littermates of the experimental *S*s were raised without competitive experience during infancy. This control group did not compete for food when adult and not hungry. It is believed that these results support theories of personality which emphasize the importance of infantile experience.

---

24. *The Physiology of Fear and Anger* *

RECENT RESEARCHES seem to have identified the physiological correlates of the psychological experiences of fear and anger. Although we can all testify to the differences in the psychological experiences of these emotions, their physiological patterns have only recently been differentiated. Identification of these patterns may clarify the relationship between these emotions and some chronic states of illness in which the body shows similar patterns. Together with recent developments in the use of chemotherapy, this information may serve as a guide to more effective treatment of psychiatric disorders.

WHEN THE LATE Walter B. Cannon, by his historic experiments nearly half a century ago, showed a connection between emotions and certain physiological changes in the body, he opened a new frontier for psychology and medicine. His work, coupled with that of Sigmund Freud, led to psychosomatic medicine. It also made the emotions accessible to laboratory measurement and analysis. Within the last few years there has been a keen revival of interest in this research, because of some important new discoveries which have sharpened our understanding of specific emotions and their bodily expressions. It has been learned, for instance, that anger and fear produce different physiological reactions and can be distinguished from each other. The findings have given us a fresh outlook from which to study mental illnesses.

The best way to begin the account of this recent work is to start with Cannon's own summary of what he learned. Cannon found that when an animal was confronted with a situation which evoked pain, rage or fear, it responded with a set of physiological reactions which prepared it to meet the threat with "fight" or "flight." These reactions, said Cannon, were mobilized by the secretion of adrenalin: when the cortex of the brain perceived the threat, it sent a stimulus down the sympathetic branch of the autonomic nervous system to the adrenal glands and they secreted the hormone. Cannon graphically described the results as follows:

* Daniel H. Funkenstein, "The physiology of fear and anger," *Scientific American,* CXCII (May, 1955), 74–80. By permission of the author and the publisher.

Respiration deepens; the heart beats more rapidly; the arterial pressure rises; the blood is shifted away from the stomach and intestines to the heart and central nervous system and the muscles; the processes in the alimentary canal cease; sugar is freed from the reserves in the liver; the spleen contracts and discharges its content of concentrated corpuscles, and adrenin is secreted from the adrenal medulla. The key to these marvelous transformations in the body is found in relating them to the natural accompaniments of fear and rage—running away in order to escape from danger, and attacking in order to be dominant. Whichever the action, a life-or-death struggle may ensue.

The emotional responses just listed may reasonably be regarded as preparatory for struggle. They are adjustments which, so far as possible, put the organism in readiness for meeting the demands which will be made upon it. The secreted adrenin cooperates with sympathetic nerve impulses in calling forth stored glycogen from the liver, thus flooding the blood with sugar for the use of laboring muscles; it helps in distributing the blood in abundance to the heart, the brain, and the limbs (*i.e.*, to the parts essential for intense physical effort) while taking it away from the inhibited organs in the abdomen; it quickly abolishes the effects of muscular fatigue so that the organism which can muster adrenin in the blood can restore to its tired muscles the same readiness to act which they had when fresh; and it renders the blood more rapidly coagulable. The increased respiration, the redistributed blood running at high pressure, and the more numerous red corpuscles set free from the spleen provide for essential oxygen and for riddance of acid waste, and make a setting for instantaneous and supreme action. In short, all these changes are directly serviceable in rendering the organism more effective in the violent display of energy which fear or rage may involve.

Cannon recognized that among all these physiological changes there were a few which could not be ascribed directly to the action of adrenalin. He therefore postulated that the hormone was supplemented by two additional substances from the sympathetic nerves. An active agent, distinguishable from adrenalin, was eventually identified in 1948, when B. F. Tullar and M. L. Tainter at length succeeded in preparing the optically active form of the substance. It proved to be a second hormone secreted by the adrenal medulla. Called nor-adrenalin, it differs markedly from adrenalin in its physiological effects. Whereas adrenalin elicits profound physiological changes in almost every system in the body, nor-adrenalin apparently has only one important primary effect: namely, it stimulates the contraction of small blood vessels and increases the resistance to the flow of blood.

An animal exhibits only two major emotions in response to a threatening situation: namely, rage and fear. A man, however, may experience three: anger directed outward (the counterpart of rage), anger directed toward himself (depression) and anxiety, or fear. In studies of physiological changes accompanying various emotional states among patients at the New York Hospital, H. G. Wolff and his co-workers noticed that anger produced effects quite different from those of depression or fear. For example, when a subject was angry, the stomach lining became red and there was an increase in its rhythmic contractions and in the secretion of hydrochloric acid. When the same subject was depressed or frightened, the stomach lining was pale in color and there was a decrease in peristaltic movements and in the hydrochloric acid secretion.

The experiments of Wolff, the evidence that the adrenal medulla secreted two substances rather than one and certain clinical observations led our group at the Harvard Medical School to investigate whether adrenalin and nor-adrenalin might be specific indicators which distinguished one emotion from another. The clinical observations had to do with the effects of a drug, mecholyl, on psychotic patients. We had been studying their blood-pressure responses to injections of adrenalin, which acts on the sympathetic nervous system, and mecholyl, which stimulates the parasympathetic system. On the basis of their blood-pressure reactions, psychotic patients could be classified into seven groups. This test had proved of value in predicting patients' responses to psychiatric treatments, such as electric shock and insulin: certain groups responded better to the treatments than others. But more interesting was the fact that psychotic patients with high blood pressure reacted to the injection of mecholyl in two distinctly different ways. In one group there was only a small drop in the blood pressure after the injection, and the pressure returned to the usually high level within three to eight minutes. In the other group the blood pressure dropped markedly after the injection and remained below the pre-injection level even after 25 minutes. Not only were the physiological reactions quite different, but the two groups of patients also differed in personality and in response to treatment. Thirty-nine of 42 patients whose blood pressure was sharply lowered by mecholyl improved with electric shock treatment, whereas only three of 21 in the other group improved with the same treatment. Further, the two groups showed distinctly different results in projective psychological tests such as the Rorschach.

All this suggested that the two groups of patients might be differentiated on the basis of emotions. Most psychotic patients in emotional turmoil express the same emotion constantly over a period of days, weeks, or months. Psychiatrists determined the predominant emotion expressed by each of 63 patients who had been tested with mecholyl, without knowing in which physiological group they had been classified. When the subjects' emotional and physiological ratings were compared, it turned out that almost all of the patients who were generally angry at other people fell in Group N (a small, temporary reduction of blood pressure by mecholyl), while almost all those who were usually depressed or frightened were in Group E (sharp response to mecholyl). In other words, the physiological reactions were significantly related to the emotional content of the patients' psychoses.

The next step was to find out whether the same test could distinguish emotions in normal, healthy people, using medical students as subjects. They were studied at a time when they were under stress—while they were awaiting the decisions of hospitals on their applications for internships. As the competition among the students for the hospitals of their choice is keen, the period just prior to such announcements is a time of emotional turmoil for the men. A group of students who responded to this situation with elevated blood pressure was given the standard dose of mecholyl. The results were the same as for the psychotic patients: students who were angry at others for the situation in which they found themselves had a Type N physiological reaction; those who felt depressed (angry at themselves) or anxious showed a Type E physiological reaction. The reaction was related only to their temporary emotional state; after the internships were settled and their blood pressures had returned to pre-stress levels, all the students reacted the same way to the injection of mecholyl.

It was at this point that we undertook to investigate the comparative effects of adrenalin and nor-adrenalin. A group of workers at the Presbyterian Hospital in New York had shown that injections of nor-adrenalin and adrenalin produced two different types of rise in blood pressure, one due to contraction of blood vessels and the other to faster pumping by the heart. Upon learning of this work, we designed experiments to test the hypothesis that the two types of elevated blood pressure, differentiated by us on the basis of mecholyl tests, indicated in one instance excessive secretion of nor-adrenalin and in the other excessive secretion of adrenalin. Healthy college students were first given a series of intravenous injections of salt water to accustom them to the procedure so that it would not disturb them. Then each subject was tested in the following way. He was given an injection of nor-adrenalin sufficient to raise his blood pressure by 25 per cent. Then, while his blood pressure was elevated, he received the standard dose of mecholyl, and its effects on the blood pressure were noted. The next day the subject was put through the same procedure except that adrenalin was given instead of nor-adrenalin to raise the blood pressure.

Ten students were studied in this way, and in every instance the effect of nor-adrenalin was different from that of adrenalin. When the blood pressure was elevated by nor-adrenalin, mecholyl produced only a small drop in pressure, with a return to the previous level in seven to

10 minutes. This reaction was similar to the Type N response in psychotic patients and healthy students under stress. In contrast, when the blood pressure was elevated by adrenalin, mecholyl produced the Type E response: the pressure dropped markedly and did not return to the previous level during the 25-minute observation period.

These results suggested, in the light of the earlier experiments, that anger directed outward was associated with secretion of nor-adrenalin, while depression and anxiety were associated with secretion of adrenalin. To check this hypothesis, another series of experiments was carried out.

A group of 125 college students were subjected to stress-inducing situations in the laboratory. The situations, involving frustration, were contrived to bring out each student's habitual reaction to stresses in real life; that the reactions actually were characteristic of the subjects' usual responses was confirmed by interviews with their college roommates. While the subjects were under stress, observers recorded their emotional reactions and certain physiological changes—in the blood pressure, the pulse and the so-called IJ waves stemming from the action of the heart. This test showed that students who responded to the stress with anger directed outward had physiological reactions similar to those produced by injection of nor-adrenalin, while students who responded with depression or anxiety had physiological reactions like those to adrenalin.

There remained the question: Does the same individual secrete unusual amounts of nor-adrenalin when angry and of adrenalin when frightened? Albert F. Ax, working in another laboratory in our hospital, designed experiments to study this question. He contrived laboratory stressful situations which were successful in producing on one occasion anger and on another occasion fear in the same subjects. His results showed that when a subject was angry at others, the physiological reactions were like those induced by the injection of nor-adrenalin; when the same subject was frightened, the reactions were like those to adrenalin. This indicated that the physiology was specific for the emotion rather than for the person.

In all these experiments the evidence for excessive secretion of nor-adrenalin and adrenalin was based on the physiological changes being similar to those which can be produced by the intravenous injection of nor-adrenalin and adrenalin. Since the substances involved have not been identified chemically, and the evidence is entirely physiological, at the present time we prefer to limit ourselves to the statement that the reactions are *like* those to the two hormones. However, nothing in our experiments would contradict the hypothesis that these substances are actually adrenalin and nor-adrenalin.

What is the neurophysiological mechanism whereby different emotions evoke different adrenal secretions? Although no conclusive work in this area is yet available, some recent investigations suggest a possible answer. U. S. von Euler in Sweden found that stimulation of certain areas of the hypothalamus caused the adrenal gland to secrete nor-adrenalin, whereas stimulation of other areas caused it to secrete adrenalin. These areas may correspond to those which the Nobel prize winner W. R. Hess of Zurich stimulated to produce aggressive behavior and flight, respectively, in animals. The experiments suggest that anger and fear may activate different areas in the hypothalamus, leading to production of nor-adrenalin in the second. Until more experiments are made, these possibilities must remain suppositions.

Some of the most intriguing work in this field was recently reported by von Euler. He compared adrenal secretions found in a number of different animals. The research material was supplied by a friend who flew to Africa to obtain the adrenal medullae of wild animals. Interpreting his findings, J. Ruesch pointed out that aggressive animals such as the lion had a relatively high amount of nor-adrenalin, while in animals such as the rabbit, which depend for survival primarily on flight, adrenalin predominated. Domestic animals, and wild animals that live very social lives (*e.g.* the baboon), also have a high ratio of adrenalin to nor-adrenalin.

These provocative findings suggest the theory that man is born with the capacity to react with a variety of emotions (has within him the lion and the rabbit), and that his early childhood experiences largely determine in which of these ways he will react under stress. Stated in another way, the evolutional process of man's emotional development is completed in the bosom of the family. We have found in other studies that individuals' habitual emotional reactions have a high correlation with their perceptions of psychological factors in their families.

This entire series of experiments yielded data which can be understood in the frame of reference of psychoanalytical observations. According to theory, anger directed outward is characteristic of an earlier stage of childhood than is anger directed toward the self or anxiety (conflicts over hostility). The latter two emotions are the result of the acculturation of the child. If the physiological development of the child parallels its psychological development, then we should expect to find that the ratio of nor-adrenalin to adrenalin is higher in infants than in older children. Bernt Hokfelt and G. B. West established that this is indeed the case: at an early age the adrenal medulla has more nor-adrenalin, but later adrenalin becomes dominant.

Paranoid patients show a greater degree of regression to infantile behavior than do patients with depression or anxiety neurosis. And it will be recalled that in our tests paranoid patients showed signs of excessive secretion of nor-adrenalin, while depressed and anxious patients exhibited symptoms of adrenalin secretion.

These parallels between psychological and physiological development suggest further studies and some theories for testing. Standing on the shoulders of Cannon and Freud, we have extended our view of human behavior and discovered fertile new fields for exploration.

---

25. Physical Complaints of Neurotic Origin *

MOST DISCUSSIONS of emotion emphasize the overt expressions and consciously recognized states. Dr. Weiss discusses another aspect of emotional functioning—its covert and unrecognized operation—and makes clear that when emotions are not permitted direct expression, they tend to become chronic and may find indirect expression through physical symptoms.

PHYSICAL COMPLAINTS can be of neurotic origin; they are bodily expressions of psychological conflict. Our term, "psycho-somatic medicine," now used to describe such symptoms, is recent; but our knowledge that the *psyche*—the mind—can affect the *soma*—the body—is of considerable antiquity. Two and a half thousand years ago Socrates stated: "The body cannot be cured without the mind." Observation since that time has piled up a steadily increasing confirmation of Socrates' opinion, and the experience of this present war shows once more the enormous importance of the problem.

Between 4 and 5 million men in the war were rejected or discharged as unfit for service; more than a third of the rejections, and over 40 per cent of the medical discharges have been for neuro-psychiatric reasons. Among the leading psychosomatic disorders involved are: asthma, peptic

* F. A. Weiss, Summary of Lecture No. 11, delivered before the Auxiliary Council of the Association for the Advancement of Psychoanalysis. By permission of the author and the Association for the Advancement of Psychoanalysis. This article is one of a series on psychoanalytic subjects, printed individually in pamphlet form. Information and copies, at 10¢ each, may be obtained from ACAAP, 220 West 98th St., New York 25, N.Y.

ulcer, gastro-intestinal disturbances, and neurocirculatory asthenia—a condition formerly described as "effort syndrome," or disordered action of the heart.

In the last fifty years medicine has made gigantic strides. X-ray and electrocardiogram, bacteriology, and blood chemistry, enable the physician of today to treat many diseases much more successfully than in the past. Medicine has reached its machine age. Every organ of the body can be investigated after death, each cell examined under the microscope; new and better weapons are constantly being invented to enable the doctor to look deeply into all parts of the living body also.

But, unfortunately, this great mechanical progress all too often causes the physician to forget that behind the cells and organs exists the individual as a whole, in whom mind and body form an inseparable unit. Before each opening of the body stands a specialist ready to diagnose the most minute physical changes with gastroscope, bronchoscope, cystoscope, or rectoscope; but the most observant specialist may nevertheless fail to realize that he is looking, not merely at a stomach or a bronchus, but at the stomach or bronchus of a specific individual who is living in a specific total life situation.

Any doctor's office will provide endless examples of the person who brings physical symptoms that can be relieved only through an understanding of the patient's total situation.

There is, for example, the excited woman of 50 who comes to have her blood pressure checked. It is above 200, and she naturally thinks of heart trouble, and fears a stroke. But the very first interview reveals a cause for the high pressure: the woman's son has recently married, and his mother-in-law now tries to influence him to regard his parents as people of a lower social level. His mother feels both deserted and enraged, but she represses her anger and hurt, and says nothing; instead, her blood pressure speaks for her, a very clear language.

Following the first visit, weekly readings of the blood pressure were taken, and at such times the woman was given an opportunity to talk. We describe such talks as "cathartic" for they allow a person to express his grievances fully. In about six weeks the blood pressure was down to 120, and the grateful patient remarked: "Doctor, could you not continue treatment with this wonderful apparatus? It has helped me so much." The "wonderful apparatus" was, of course, the manometer, which did nothing but register the pressure.

Another example is the diabetic shopkeeper; variations in the amount of sugar in his urine reflect almost exactly the weekly state of his business, but reflect it in reverse—a high tide in his sugar excretion indicating a low tide in his income.

Then there is the down-trodden husband whose stomach ulcer invariably speaks whenever he would like to "speak up" to his wife, but dares not. And there is the patient with asthma; he goes away to a health resort to escape the pollens to which he is allergic at home, but he nevertheless comes down with a severe attack of asthma after receiving a letter from his mother. His specialist has carefully eliminated all sources of allergy, but has failed to consider the possibility that his patient is allergic to—his almost sadistically dominating mother.

These instances are, of course, still very simple examples of psychosomatic action. But they illustrate the importance of viewing the disturbed function of a bodily organ as part of the disturbed function of the whole body-mind unit; and of viewing the patient as part of a still greater social unit of interpersonal relations.

TRANSMITTING EMOTIONAL TENSION

During the past twenty years we have learned to understand the vital function of the so-called autonomous nervous system—"autonomous" because it is not dependent on our conscious will, nor controlled by it. This vital system has well been named "the nerves of life." By means of its two antagonistic branches it reaches and controls all organs of the body from the hair on top of the head to the sweat glands on the soles of the feet. It regulates the action of heart and blood-vessels, and the whole process of circulation, the function of the bronchi and the process of respiration, the function of stomach and intestines and the process of digestion and, in addition, all other viscera such as liver, kidney and bladder, and particularly the hormone glands such as the thyroid, the pituitary in the brain, the sex glands, and the adrenals above the kidneys.

The extensive network of the autonomous nervous system acts as a kind of keyboard; on it the emotions play and through it neurotic conflicts, and strong emotions such as hostility and anxiety, are under certain conditions *converted* into bodily symptoms.

A great variety of single tones and mighty chords can be sounded on this keyboard, but the loudest discords are produced by the powerful emotions of fear, rage, anxiety, and hostility. Under their stimulus the respiration deepens, the heart beats more rapidly, the blood pressure rises, the function of stomach and intestines become intensely disturbed; sugar is shifted from its storage room, the liver, into the blood; the spleen contracts and sends its blood reserve into the body like a powerful blood transfusion; sweat may be poured out on the body surface.

Such an extreme total response of the whole organism was interpreted by Dr. Walter B. Cannon as the body's original reaction to vital danger —a preparation for life-saving fight or flight.

> The forces of the organism [Dr. Cannon says] are put upon a war footing. But if there is no war to be waged, if the emotion has its natural mobilizing effects on the viscera when there is nothing to be done . . . obviously this very mechanism will upset the whole organism. It is not surprising, therefore, that fear and worry and hate can lead to harmful and profoundly disturbing consequences.

Anxiety, conflict, and physical symptoms: What fear and external danger mean to primitive man, anxiety and internal danger mean to us who live in the present. In order to explain what anxiety and internal danger are, psychiatry had to develop beyond its earlier and limited approach, which confined it to a mere classification of the end results of emotional conflicts—the psychoses. It had to follow each step in the development *from* the so-called normal *to* the psychotic, and include in its investigation the large neglected field of neurotic disturbances, which for centuries had been regarded as only meaningless deviations from normal behavior. To find the meaning of neurotic symptoms the static system of psychiatry had to be changed to the dynamic method of psychoanalysis.

We owe it to the genius of Sigmund Freud that today we are closer to the answer of this problem. Freud discovered that disturbances of our psychological as well as our physiological functions could be caused by anxiety or an unconscious conflict. Many of Freud's basic discoveries remain valid; but considered from the viewpoint which emphasizes the character as a whole, his concept of anxiety appears limited.

Freud's concept of the role of conflict in neurosis, though very constructive in itself, is also limited because of his introduction of congenital instincts as the main factor in this fight, a fight which is understood by him as a struggle between the instinctual impulses of the Id, and the relentless coercive demands of the Superego—with the Ego the victim of the insoluble conflict.

Conflicts do play a decisive role in the structure of neurosis, but they are *human* conflicts caused by the clash between contradictory neurotic trends which had been formed as safety devices during an insecure childhood. The compulsive need for affection may clash, for example, with the compulsive need for power.

Any vital threat to the safety of the individual may set in motion the whole powerful response of the autonomous nervous system. Safety, to the neurotic, is based on the satisfaction of his neurotic needs. His safety also depends on preserving intact the ideal image he has formed of himself—an image composed of the less questionable aspects of his conflicting trends so unified that contradictions are hidden and appear as part of a "superior" or "unique" personality.

This image is essential to his feeling of safety, for it enables him to harbor and protect in himself completely conflicting trends. The strongest threat to a neurotic individual is the breakdown of this image, for it faces him with full awareness of his conflict. But any frustration of his neurotic needs is also felt as danger. Anxiety and hostility result.

Such is Dr. Karen Horney's creative concept of anxiety, and it enables us to use Dr. Cannon's viewpoint for an understanding of psychosomatic medicine.

FUNCTIONS AND MEANINGS OF PHYSICAL SYMPTOMS

The neurotic tries to escape anxiety. Four ways are open to him: (1) he may *rationalize* it—turn anxiety into a seemingly rational fear; (2) he may *deny* it—exclude it from consciousness; (3) he may *narcoticize* it—drown it in alcohol, drugs, work, sex, or sleep; and finally, (4) he may *avoid* all situations, thoughts, or feelings which arouse anxiety. When this last mechanism is well-established and operates automatically we have the phenomenon known as *inhibition*.

It happens with particular frequency on escape roads 2 and 4 that the partial or total dissociation of anxiety from consciousness leads to the formation of physical symptoms. Sometimes a person banishes the whole existence of neurotic conflict from his mind; but more often he represses only one of the conflicting trends. Any drive, need, feeling can be repressed if it endangers another drive, need, feeling, which for the individual is of vital importance.

On road 2 anxiety is merely denied, and nothing else is done about it. All that shows is the physical accompaniment of anxiety such as shivering, sweating, accelerated heart beat, choking sensations, frequent urge to urinate, diarrhea, vomiting, and in the mental sphere a feeling of restlessness, of being rushed or paralyzed. We may experience these same feelings and sensations when we are afraid and know that we are afraid. When we are afraid and do not know it, then the feelings and sensations are the only expression of repressed anxiety, and in that case *all that the individual knows* about his condition is this outward evidence of disturbance—symptoms with no apparent physical cause.

On road 4 a person escapes anxiety because the mechanism of inhibition takes away his ability to do, think or feel, anything that might produce anxiety. He is usually unaware of feeling any anxiety, and has no capacity for overcoming inhibition by conscious effort. We meet the most extreme physical symptoms resulting from this mechanism in the various so-called *hysterical* losses of body function.

"Hysteria" is derived from "hystera," the Greek word for womb, but the condition it describes is no longer connected specifically with the womb, or other sex organs, and its occurrence is just as frequent in men as in the owner of the womb—women. The neurotic personality in which we are most likely to find this condition is that characterized by excessive needs for affection and approval. Hysterical symptoms—such as hysterical blindness or deafness—have a double meaning, and the individual experiencing them is unaware of either meaning: they protect him from the perception of an unacceptable reality, and they bring him special attention and affection. Hysterical speechlessness may represent an attempted solution of two conflicting drives: the desire to express hostility openly, and the conflicting need to preserve a relationship of dependency toward the object of one's hostility. In a similar way the paralysis of a leg allows a patient to avoid taking certain necessary "steps" in the direction of a possibly dangerous decision.

We can easily observe such visible psychosomatic reactions as blushing or trembling, but we have only limited opportunity to see psychosomatic changes *within* the body. We can follow the reactions of internal organs to emotional conflict with such instruments as the fluoroscope, and see that position, shape, and movement of stomach and intestine change completely if, under hypnosis, emotional conflicts are produced and released. A stomach may be found several inches lower than usual under emotional tension, and the contour of the bowels—usually rather smooth—may look so ragged that a specialist in such matters can easily diagnose repressed rage from this picture. Or—to take another example—the gall bladder contracts visibly in emotional tension, so that less and thicker, darker bile is secreted. Some kind of intuition must have enabled the Greeks to guess at this phenomenon, for their word *melancholia* means "black bile."

A patient had burned his esophagus with hot clam chowder at the age of 9. This tragic accident allowed medical science to observe what happens in the stomach of a person in a state of anxiety or rage. Through the permanent opening into his stomach which had to be created to feed him we have seen that when he represses hostility—due to inner conflict—his stomach becomes dark red, and blushes like his face; the glands also produce excessive hydrochloric acid, and the stomach's motility increases. It is well known that these conditions, occurring together, will lead to severe inflammation of the stomach wall and, if they continue over a long period, to the formation of a gastric ulcer.

In this particular patient the most extreme gastric reactions occurred whenever anything threatened his idealized image of himself as a very special and privileged person, or whenever he had to repress a need toward aggression, or toward fighting back.

War experience has confirmed on a great scale the importance of repressed hostility as a cause for ulcers, and other psychosomatic disorders. In a large percentage of cases it was not those at the front who developed ulcers, but those who experienced bombings without being able to fight back. In Leningrad many people developed a disease named "sequel of bombing"—a specific kind of high blood pressure that ends in ruptured blood vessels and cerebral hemorrhage.

We can now interpret the exact function in the neurotic conflict of some symptoms, but others do not yet permit such specific interpretation. We can say, however, that they are the expression of emotional tension produced by repressed anxiety or conflict.

Some of this "language of the body" is astonishingly well described in popular phrases. We speak, for example, of not being able to "swallow" an insult or belittling remark; we have a "load on our chest" when worried or depressed; we "breathe more easily" after an anxiety state is over; we warn our neighbor against anger with—"Don't get your blood pressure up!" People may indeed have difficulty in swallowing when confronted with unwelcome life situations, and vomiting may express rejection not only of food but of some unacceptable fact—Napoleon vomited when told that he must go to St. Helena.

It is often the chronic repetition of relatively slight traumatic experiences which leads to functional disturbance, and finally to organic change.

CHOICE OF ORGAN

We cannot yet answer in all cases why a given organ becomes the seat of neurotic disturbance; but we do know some of the factors that determine the choice:

1. The choice may be what we describe as *"symbolic"*: that is, the symptom may play a symbolic role in the unconscious attempt at a solution of conflict. For example, the paralysis of an arm may be the neurotic solution of a conflict between a desire to express hostility by physical action, and the opposed desire to preserve the ideal picture of a good relationship.

2. *The medical history of the patient* may play a significant role; the neurotic mechanism may occasionally select and use a biologically in-

ferior organ, but it is more apt to follow the way prepared by an earlier organic disease. A neurotic may develop, for example, a swollen wrist, which symptom the body had "learned" during a previous attack of rheumatic arthritis; or asthma may first show during a severe bronchitis, but reappear later under emotional tension.

3. *Identification* represents another mechanism that may influence the choice. If, for instance, a domineering mother has heart trouble, migraine, or asthma, her dependent daughter may unconsciously respond to conflict situations with the same symptoms; or a girl who has a repressed wish for pregnancy may imitate a pregnant friend's "morning sickness."

4. Finally a kind of *conditioned reflex* may operate—as in the famous case reported by the French Dr. Trousseau, in which a woman who was sensitive to roses had an asthmatic attack when she saw an artificial rose in Trousseau's buttonhole.

SEXUAL SYMPTOMS OF NEUROTIC ORIGIN

Since the neuroses affect interpersonal relationships, it is not surprising that we meet a great many neurotic disturbances in the field of sex —the closest interpersonal relation. Partial or total impotence and premature ejaculation in the man, partial or total frigidity and vaginal spasms in the woman, are all definitely neurotic symptoms. Conflicts between a need for affection and a need for domination are frequently found as a background for such disturbances.

To relieve the symptoms the conflicts have to be analyzed and resolved, instead of the medieval treatments of prostate massage in the male, or stretching the vagina in the woman. Frigidity, the passive resistance, and vaginal spasm, the active resistance against the full acceptance of the relationship, cannot be cured with instruments, nor can they be analyzed as isolated symptoms. Sterility, which seems so far removed from psychoanalytic considerations, also belongs to our subject. Not only is a woman who has no orgasm less likely to conceive, but emotional conflict may prevent ovulation—the formation and expulsion of the egg—and may cause spastic contraction of the tube and block the passage of the egg. Menstrual disorders too, irregularities, absence or increase of menstruation, and particularly premenstrual pain, may have their function in the subconscious mechanism of the conflict.

SECONDARY GAINS

In addition to its main function of protecting the neurotic from the full impact of anxiety and hostility, and from the full awareness of his basic conflict, the psychosomatic symptom provides him with several important secondary gains: his symptoms may gain him special consideration from friends and relatives, or special public esteem, and may provide him with an escape from difficult tasks or responsibilities, and particularly from those situations that endanger his idealized image, that involve competition or risk, or that simply entail his growing up emotionally.

These secondary gains are NOT the cause of the neurosis, but represent an added "bonus" derived from it, and the fear of losing this seeming advantage can increase the patient's resistance during analysis.

Finally, the psychosomatic symptom has a special value in one type of neurotic—or pseudo—solution: a mechanism we name "externalization," whereby internal difficulties are projected onto the external world. As a neurotic will invariably prefer to blame his condition on others, or on external circumstances, so he will usually prefer the *somatic* interpretation of his symptoms to the psychoanalytic one. He correctly regards it as much easier to change his diet or climate, or even to undergo one or more operations, than to change his personality.

PHYSICAL SYMPTOMS AND PSYCHOANALYSIS

From the viewpoint of psychoanalysis, we have always to keep in mind that psychosomatic disturbances are only *symptoms* of neurotic conflict. In the course of an analysis, physical symptoms often go through three more or less distinct phases. During the *first* period, simple symptoms like sweating or vomiting may disappear rather quickly, due not to the analytic process itself, but to the general feeling of support, and the relief of tension produced by the "catharsis" of being able to express oneself freely. During the *second* period symptoms may reappear at moments when the neurotic trends are threatened by increase of insight, or by the break-down of defense mechanisms. Such an increase in symptoms may therefore be a sign of progress, as it may show that the neurotic pseudo-equilibrium is shaking, and the conflict entering awareness.

Only in the *final* period of analysis—when the neurotic trends are no longer needed to give a false sense of security—will the psychosomatic symptoms really disappear. An analysis should approach the awareness of conflict with full consideration for the patient's psychological tolerance. When the timing is carefully handled, the patient will be able to recognize his conflicting needs—as for example, needs for dependency and aggression; his real security will grow until he becomes strong enough to do without his ideal image, to *accept* reality or *change* it.

NEUROTIC CONFLICTS AND PHYSICAL ILLNESS

During the last three decades such scourges as tuberculosis, diphtheria, scarlet fever and typhoid have greatly diminished, but circulatory and digestive diseases, asthma and goitre, have tremendously increased; angina pectoris has nearly trebled. The increase is in just those diseases which are typical results of psychosomatic action, and due to inner conflict.

Which conflict? There are, of course, many, but one in particular has become the basic conflict of the neurotic of our time: that between the neurotic need for dependency and for competitive aggression. Elements in our present society tend to foster this conflict.

The development of our mechanized and specialized system is characterized by a growing interdependence. More and more of us—bookkeepers, clerks, accountants, factory hands—are confined to a routine of fixed hours and often monotonous tasks, and become entangled in a great web of dependency. But at the same time we are forced to compete and be aggressive in a steadily-increasing degree. In this social *compression chamber* the neurotic individual is much more apt to be confronted with a sudden awareness of his inner conflict. He resents the dependency, and feels hostility coming up; but this hostility is repressed, not only for reasons of external security, but because it contradicts his ideal image of himself as a good, socially-minded citizen. So he swallows his resentment, and this swallowing is more important in the causation of gastric ulcers than the swallowing of rough or hard food.

The word "anxiety" has the same root as has the Latin word "angina," which means narrowness, a narrow pass. The neurotic feels hopelessly caught in the narrow pass between his conflicting trends. Only a successful analysis can resolve his conflict.

VI

INTELLIGENCE

Popular conceptions of intelligence, like those of other topics we have studied, do not accurately describe the functions involved. Though we may start with the belief that intelligence is inborn, we soon find that its actual operation is measurably influenced by environmental conditions and that it consists of several different factors.

Research workers in the past have treated intelligence as separate from other functions of the individual. Recent work, however, has shown a tendency to re-examine the nature of intelligence and to include within the concept the total behavior of the individual. Some workers in this field are beginning to suggest that "intelligence" may be defined by what the observer is looking for rather than something existing within the performer. Others are saying that we ought perhaps to assess intelligent behavior as an aspect of the total personality of the individual rather than as an independent though related item; although not yet universally accepted, this point of view seems to point a significant direction for the future.

Three of the four papers in this section deal with some of the newer directions in studying intelligence. The first attempts a complete recasting of the conception of the nature of intelligence. The second reports on a single child followed over a 7½-year period, relating the variation in his test performance to changes in his life situation. The fourth selection suggests the possibility of increasing the national supply of "genius" by appropriate social and educational devices. Selection 28 briefly distinguishes among the related, and often confused, concepts of aptitude, intelligence, and achievement as used in testing programs.

26. *Intelligence from a Perceptual Point of View* *

IN A NOVEL approach to the problem of defining intelligence Dr. Combs takes the *experience* of the individual, rather than his *behavior,* as a point of departure. In many other fields of psychology an inside-the-individual, or phenomenological, point of view has been introduced to supplement the limited data possible through the purely objective, external approach. Here we see how this approach can develop provocative leads to further study and new applications of theory.

THERE IS a growing trend in psychology toward viewing behavior as a function of perception. More and more we have come to understand that the individual's behavior is not so much a function of the physical stimulus as it is a function of his perceptions of the events to which he is exposed. It is the meaning of events to the individual rather than the externally observed nature of events which seems crucial in behavior. As a result, psychologists in increasing numbers are turning their attention to the problems of human perception and are attempting to observe behavior, not from an external point of view, but from the point of view of the individual who is behaving. This paper is an attempt to relate this method of observation to the problem of intelligence. The question we wish to explore in this paper is: "What is the nature of intelligence viewed from a perceptual or phenomenological frame of reference?"

INTELLIGENCE AS A PROBLEM OF PERCEPTION

By the term *intelligence* we ordinarily refer to the effectiveness of the individual's behavior. In a personal frame of reference the individual's behavior is described in terms of the perceptions that he can make in his own unique perceptive field. This perceptive field has been called by Snygg and Combs *The Phenomenal Field* and has been defined by them as "the universe of experience open to the individual at the moment of his behavior." In other words, the behavior of the individual will be dependent upon the perceptions that the individual makes in his phenomenal field at the moment of action. The effectiveness of his

* Arthur W. Combs, "Intelligence from a perceptual point of view," *Journal of Abnormal and Social Psychology,* XLVII (1952), 662–73. By permission of the author and the American Psychological Association.

behavior will necessarily be a function of the adequacy of those perceptions.

If an entity in the perceptive field is vague and ill defined, the behavior of the individual will be correspondingly vague and lacking in precision. Until the child has clearly differentiated that 2 plus 2 equals 4, this function is comparatively meaningless and his behavior in arithmetic is correspondingly inaccurate and ineffective. Thus, the precision and effectiveness of the individual's behavior will be dependent upon the scope and clarity of his personal field of awareness. Intelligence, then, from a perceptual point of view becomes a function of the factors which limit the scope and clarity of an individual's phenomenal field.

The perceptions that could be made of any given situation, such as looking at a stone wall, for example, are, theoretically, practically infinite in number and quality. As a matter of fact, however, we are strictly limited in our perceptions of a stone wall to those which we, as human beings, can make. The perceptions possible to us are only those that people can make. We cannot, for instance, perceive the wall as it would appear to a man from Mars, or from the interior of an atom, or as it would appear to a centipede. What is more, we cannot even perceive it as it would appear to all people. Different people will perceive different aspects of the wall differently, even at the same instant. I can only perceive the wall, and hence behave toward it, in terms of the perceptions that I, as an individual, can make regarding it. I may, for instance, perceive it as a fine, sturdy fence enclosing my property, while a stone mason friend might perceive it as having been poorly designed or as having been built with too little cement in the mortar mixture. The perceptions open to my mason friend are the result of his unique experience. I, not having such experience, am incapable of those perceptions at this moment.

POTENTIAL AND FUNCTIONAL PERCEPTIONS

Before proceeding further with our discussion of the limiting factors in perception, it is necessary for us to pause for a moment to distinguish between potential and functional perceptions. By potential perceptions I mean those perceptions that exist in the individual's unique field of awareness and that, given the right circumstances at any particular moment, *could* occur. The fact that a perception is potentially possible to any individual, by no means, however, means that it will occur at the moment of action. Even those perceptions that I can make potentially may not be active for me at any given moment. Potentially, I might be able, for instance, to perceive the wall that we have just been using as an example as a barrier to be gotten over, as an eyesore to be beautified, as composed of 687 bricks costing me $80.27, or as providing pleasant shade on a hot day. These are all potential perceptions I am capable of making about the wall. They will affect my behavior, however, only when they are active or functioning in my field of perceptions. When I am beating a hasty retreat pursued by a neighbor's angry dog, perceptions about the shade, beauty, or cost of the wall, though potential, are not functional in affecting my behavior. I behave only in terms of my functioning perception of the wall as something to get over—and quickly. The fact that particular perceptions may exist potentially in the phenomenal field of an individual is by no means a guarantee that they may exist functionally at the moment of action.

While the potential intelligence of the individual is of interest in judging his capacities, it is practically always a matter impossible to measure with any degree of accuracy. We can only sample those parts of a phenomenal field that *we* happen to feel are important. Obviously the measurement of a person's potential perceptions in these terms is open to extremely grave sampling error and improves in accuracy only as the individuals tested have common experience in the materials chosen for testing. It seems probable that an intelligence test cannot accurately measure the potential differentiations that the individual can make in his phenomenal field. Rather, what we usually measure are the subject's functional perceptions. That is, we measure what differentiations he can make when confronted with the necessity to do so for one reason or another. We may define these functional perceptions as: those perceptions in the field experienced by the individual at the moment of behaving.

From a perceptual viewpoint, if intelligence is the capacity for effective behavior, *the intelligence of an individual will be dependent upon the richness and variety of perceptions possible to him at a given moment.* To understand and effectively to foster intelligent behavior, it will be necessary for us to be concerned with the limiting factors upon the perceptions of an individual. We need to know not only what the individual *could* perceive, but what he *would* perceive at a given moment of behaving.

SOME LIMITING FACTORS UPON PERCEPTION

Physiologic Limitations on Perception

Certainly the physical limitations upon the organism affect the differentiations possible in the phenomenal field. Some forms of prenatal anomalies, like mongolism, microcephalia, and similar disorders, indubitably reduce the level of operation at which the individual can function and seriously impair the ability of the organism to make adequate perceptions. Similarly, there seems good reason to believe that some types of mechanical or disease injury to the central nervous system may result in impaired functioning, such as occurs in cerebral palsy, birth injuries, prefrontal lobotomy, the aftermath of such diseases as encephalitis or, even, in common childhood diseases accompanied by prolonged high fever. Various forms of endocrinopathies, particularly cretinism, also appear to have limiting effects upon differentiational capacity for some individuals. Such physical or biological limitations upon the organism have been widely studied but account for only a small proportion of those persons operating at impaired intelligence levels.

Other less dramatic forms of physical handicaps may also have important effects upon the perceptions possible to the individual, however. This is particularly true of individuals suffering impairment of various sense modalities which may inhibit the clarity or even the existence of some perceptions. We need to remind ourselves, however, that such persons may have as rich and varied a perceptive field within their own limitations as we have within ours. Testing persons living in one frame of reference with tests based on those of another can easily lead us astray, a fact well known to the makers of some tests for the handicapped. The limitations imposed upon perception by such physical handicaps as the loss or impairment of locomotion or the use of arms or hands are also important in limiting certain kinds of perceptions. These people experience different, but not necessarily fewer or poorer perceptions of events than so-called "normals."

Perhaps less well recognized in their effects upon perception are such factors as malnutrition, focal infections, and chronic fatigue, which may reduce both the need for and the ability to make adequate perceptions. It is well known in industrial psychology, for example, that fatigued workers are more likely to have accidents, perhaps because of failure to make the right differentiations at the right time. It is conceivable that persons suffering from chronic fatigue over long periods similarly fail to make differentiations useful to them on later occasions.

Certainly such physical factors as these have important effects upon the ability of the individual to make adequate differentiations in his perceptive field. The more dramatic of these have often been recognized and studied. Others, such as the effects of malnutrition, fatigue, and the like, have been less adequately explored. In spite of the lack of research in respect to some of the physical limitations upon intelligence, far more work has been done in this area, however, than in some of those to be discussed below.

Environment and Opportunity as a Limitation upon Perception

The differentiations in the phenomenal field that an individual can make will, of course, be affected by the opportunities for perception to which he has been exposed. To appear in the perceptive field an event must have been, in some manner, experienced by the person who perceives it. Environmental effects upon perception appear to be of two types, actual or concrete and symbolic or vicarious.

Exposure to Actual Environmental Events. In the first place the perceptions possible to any individual will be limited, in part, by the actual environmental factors to which he has been exposed. Eskimos ordinarily do not comprehend bananas, nor African Bushmen snow, since neither has had the opportunity to experience these events in their respective environments. It is not necessary to go so far afield for illustration, however. In our own country our experience with the testing of children in various parts of the nation has shown that perceptions are highly limited by the environmental conditions surrounding the individual. Mountain children, for example, often give bizarre responses on intelligence tests. Sherman and Henry found intelligence test results on such children arranged themselves in order of the opportunities provided by their environment.

There are differences also between the perceptions of rural and urban children, children from the North and children from the South, mountain and valley, seaboard and plains. Nor are such differences confined only to children. Adults, too, are limited in their perceptions by environmental factors. During the war I worked for a time in an induction station receiving men from the mountains of Kentucky, West Virginia, and southern Ohio. An intelligence test in use at this station was composed of a series of five pictures with instructions to the subject to cross out that one of each series of five objects that did not belong with the others. One set of five pictures showed four stringed instruments, a guitar, harp, violin, bass fiddle, and a trumpet. Large numbers of these back country men crossed out the harp because they had never seen one or because "all the others are things in our band." We cannot assume that these men were less able to make differentiations or had perceptive fields less rich than their examiner on the basis of these tests. We can only suggest that their perceptions are different from those who made the test. Presumably, had they made the test and administered it to the psychologist, the psychologist would have appeared rather dull!

Exposure to Symbolic or Vicarious Events. Differentiations may occur in the perceptive field upon a symbolic basis as well as from exposure to an actual event. That is, perceptions may occur in the individual's field through indirect exposure to experience as in reading, conversation, movies, and other means of communication. Although I cannot directly perceive that it is dangerous to expose myself to rays from an atomic pile, for example, I can differentiate this notion through what others whom I respect have told me. Ideas and concepts are largely differentiations of this sort and it is probable that many of our perceptions are acquired through a symbolic rather than an actual exposure. Certainly most of our formal schooling falls in this category, which may explain, in part, why so little of it is effective in our behavior.

It will be recognized at once that exposure to events in no sense completely determines the perceptions that the individual will make. Exposure to events is only one of the factors involved in determining whether or not an event will be differentiated. Even with equivalent exposure, the perceptions we make are not alike. Perception is not an all or none proposition but a selective process. The same person in the same situation at different times may perceive quite different aspects of the situation and behave accordingly. The provision of opportunity to perceive is by no means a guarantee that a particular perception will occur, a phenomenon of which teachers are only too aware. The personal field of the individual is always organized and meaningful and, even with exposure to events, only those aspects that have meaning for the individual in his own unique economy will be differentiated with permanence.

The individual in a particular culture perceives those aspects of his environment that, from his point of view, he needs to perceive to maintain and enhance his self in the world in which he lives. This does not mean he makes fewer perceptions than an individual in another culture; he makes only *different* perceptions. Thus, intelligence tests made in one culture and applied in another do not measure the ability to differentiate, nor do they measure the richness of the individual's field. Perhaps what they really measure is no more than the difference between cultures. American-made intelligence tests applied to other cultures generally show the following arrangement of nationality groups in decreasing order; British Isles, Germany, France, Italy, the Balkans, Asiatic countries. It will be noted that these nationality groups are also roughly arranged in order of the degree of commonality with our own culture.

Time as a Limitation of Perception

Differentiation requires time. The richness of perception, therefore, will be in part a function of how long the individual has been in touch with experiences. While it is true that a perception is possible only when confronted by an experience, it is also true that this exposure must be long enough to make differentiation possible. This principle is familiar to anyone who has looked at a painting for a period of time. The perceptions which can be made are almost limitless if one looks long enough.

In thinking of the effect of time upon differentiation, it is necessary for us to keep in mind that we are speaking of the duration of the individual's experience with an event and not of the observer's experience. Thus, while it may appear to an outside observer that an individual is confronted by an experience, from the individual's own point of view, he may have no contact with it whatever. A child may sit in school all day, apparently exposed to the curriculum, but may actually be experiencing and perceiving quite different aspects of the situation. Perception is an internal, individual phenomenon and may be quite different from that of another person, even in the same situation.

Most perceptions that the individual makes are functions of previous differentiations he has made in his phenomenal field. For example, before one can perceive the mechanics of multiplication he must have perceived addition. In the same way, before he can perceive the function of a sand dome on top of the locomotive he must differentiate the fact that locomotive wheels sometimes slip. Clearly this process of differentiation takes time. It seems axiomatic that to make differentiations an individual must have lived long enough to do so, a fact we recognize in the construction of intelligence tests calibrated for various age levels, and which teachers recognize in the concept of readiness.

Differentiations in the phenomenal field seem to be occurring continuously as the organism seeks to satisfy its needs in the myriad situations of life. In this sense, intelligence never ceases to develop but is continuously increasing so long as the individual remains alive and operating. That intelligence seems to level off at age sixteen or later is probably a mere artifact of our method of observation. So long as the individual remains in school we have at least a modicum of comparable experience which can be tested in different persons. After the school years, when individuals are free to go their separate ways, this modicum of comparable experience rapidly disappears. The older one gets, the more diverse is his experience. Intelligence tests based upon comparability of experience may thus fail to evaluate properly the effectiveness of adults.

The Individual's Goals and Values as a Limiting Factor in Perception

Up to this point in our discussion we have been dealing with factors affecting perception that are widely discussed in the literature and for the most part are well understood. In the remainder of this paper let us turn our attention to several factors less well explored as they appear in a phenomenological setting. The first of these has to do with the effects of the individual's own goals and values as a limiting factor on perception.

From a phenomenological view the individual is forever engaged in a ceaseless attempt to achieve satisfaction of his need through the goals and values he has differentiated as leading to that end. These goals and values may be explicit or implicit, simple or complex, but they are always unique to the personality itself. The goals of an individual will vary in another respect as well. The individual's goals and values may be either positive or negative. That is, in the course of his experience, the person may differentiate some things as matters to be sought, while other things may be differentiated as matters to be avoided. What is more, although there is a considerable degree of stability in the major goals and values of a particular individual, there may be great fluctuations in how some goals are perceived from time to time, depending upon the total organization of the perceptual field at any moment.

The goals and values an individual seeks have a most important effect upon the perceptions he can make. Once goals have been established by the individual they continue to affect his every experience. Thus, the person who has differentiated good music as a goal to be sought, perceives music more frequently. His entire experience with music is likely to be affected. Certainly his experience will differ markedly from the person who has formulated a goal to avoid music at all costs. In the same way the experiences of children who perceive schooling as something to be sought are vastly different from those of children who try to avoid all aspects of schooling. If the fundamental thesis of this paper is accurate, that intelligence is a function of the variety and richness of the perceptive field, then the individual's goals must have a most important effect upon intelligence. A considerable body of research has been accumulating over the past several years, demonstrating this controlling effect of goals and values on the individual's perceptive experience. . . .

This effect of goals on perception is by no means limited to the subject whose intelligence we wish to measure. It is equally true of the intelligence test constructor. It leads to the very confusing situation wherein the test constructor with one organization of goals perceives certain experiences to be marks of intelligence for another person who may or may not have similar goals. Indeed, the likelihood is that he, almost certainly, does not have similar goals. Intelligence tests thus become highly selected samplings of perception in terms of what the testers consider important. Low scores do not necessarily mean less rich and varied fields of perception; they may mean only fields of perception more widely divergent from those of the examiner. A young man whom the writer tested at an induction center during the war illustrates the point very well. This young man was a newsboy on the streets of a West Virginia city. Although he had failed repeatedly in grammar school and was generally regarded as "not bright," he appeared on a national radio hook-up as "The Human Adding Machine." He was a wizard at figures. He could multiply correctly such figures as 6235941×397 almost as fast as the problem could be written down. He astounded our induction center for half a day with his numerical feats. Yet, on the Binet Test given by the writer he achieved an IQ of less than 60! People in his home town, who bought his papers, amused themselves by giving him problems to figure constantly. When not so occupied this young man entertained himself by adding up the license numbers of cars that passed his corner. He was a specialist in numbers. Apparently as a result of some early success in this field, he had been led to practice numbers constantly, eventually to the exclusion of all else. This was one area in which a poor colored boy could succeed and he made the most of it. His number perceptions were certainly rich and varied but other things were not. Although he was capable of arithmetic feats not achieved by one in millions, he was classified as dull! I do not mean to argue that variety of perception is unimportant in effective behavior. I do mean to suggest the importance of goals in determining perception.

Cultural Effects on Goals and Perceptions

We have stated here that the richness of the individual's perceptive field is in part a function of the goals he has differentiated as important or threatening to him. But, clearly these goals are themselves the result of the individual's experience. The culture one grows up in deeply affects the goals one holds. Cultures both restrict and encourage, approve and disapprove the formulation of goals in the individual. This selective effect of the culture in large measure determines the goals sought and avoided by the individual. These goals in turn must exert important effects upon the perceptions that become part of the individual's perceptive field.

I remember the Kentucky moonshiner to whom I once administered the Wechsler-Bellevue. This man could not tell me "how many pints in a quart" although he had certainly been taught this fact in his early schooling. Knowing that my client did a considerable business in bootleg liquor, I framed the question differently and asked "Well, how do you sell your liquor?" He smiled tolerantly and replied, "Oh Boss, I just sell it by the jug full!" In his community to have done otherwise would have been to risk bankruptcy! In a culture where a jug is standard container for spirits, what need to know about quarts?

It is conceivable that low intelligence may be, at least in part, no more than a function of the goals an individual is striving to reach in achieving his need satisfaction. The well-known phenomenon in which intelligence tests give best results in the school years, when experience and goals have a degree of commonality, and break down badly following those years would seem to corroborate this point. Perhaps by concerning ourselves with human goals we can affect perception, and thus intelligence, much more than we believed possible. Can it be that the child of low apparent intelligence is not so much a problem of an unfortunate heredity as an unfortunate constellation of goals or values? We could do a great deal about intelligence if that were true.

The Self-Concept as a Factor Limiting Perception

We are just beginning to understand the tremendous effects of the individual's concept of self upon his perceptions and behavior. Lecky, for instance, reports the effect of a change in self-concept in improving the ability of children to spell. Other researches have reported similar effects of the self-concept upon the perceptions which the individual may make. Clinical experience would tend to bear out such observations. Any clinician is familiar with numerous instances in which a child's conception of his abilities severely limited his achievement, even though his real abilities may have been superior to his perception of them. One needs but to go shopping with one's spouse to discover again how one's conception of himself as a male or female affects the things he sees and the things he hears.

Perception is a selective process and the conception one holds of himself is a vital factor in determining the richness and the variety of perception selected. It makes a great deal of difference, for example, how one perceives the president of our country if one conceives of himself as a democrat, a republican, or a communist. One needs but to observe a group of children to become aware that little boys perceive things quite differently from little girls. Professors do not perceive like truck drivers, although when I have had to ride with professor automobile-drivers, I have often wished they did. Thousands of people in our society avoid perceptions having to do with mathematical functions by their firm concept of themselves as people who "cannot do mathematics." The self-concepts we hold have a very vital effect in selecting the perceptions which become part of our perceptive fields. If the effectiveness of behavior is dependent on our perceptive fields, it follows that the self-concepts we hold must affect the "intelligence" of our behavior.

There is another factor in the effect of the self-concept upon perception that makes it even more important as a selector of experience. That factor is the circular effect of a given concept of self. Let us take, as an example, the child who has developed a concept of himself as "unable to read." Such a child is likely to avoid reading and thus the very experience which might change his concept of self is by-passed. Worse still, the child who believes himself unable to read, confronted with the necessity for reading, is more likely than not to do badly. The external evaluation of his teachers and fellow pupils, as well as his own observations of his performance, all provide proof to the child of how right he was in the first place! The possession of a particular concept of self tends to produce behavior that corroborates the self-concept with which the behavior originated.

Every clinician has had experience with children of ability who conceive of themselves as unable, unliked, unwanted, or inacceptable and perceive and behave in accordance with their perceptions. And this effect is not limited to children alone. It seems to me one of the great tragedies of our society that millions of people in our society perceiving themselves as able to produce only *X* amount, behave in these terms. Society, in turn, evaluates them in terms of this behavior and so lends proof to what is already conceived by the individual. Compared to this waste of human potential in our society, our losses in automobile accidents seem like a mere drop in the bucket. It is even conceivable in these terms that we create losses in intelligence. If, in our schools, we teach a child that he is unable and if he believes us and behaves in these terms, we need not be surprised when we test his intelligence to discover that he produces at the level at which we taught him!

It is conceivable that psychology has unwittingly contributed to this situation by the widespread publication of a static conception of intelligence and human capacities. The concept of severe limits upon the capacities of the organism simply corroborates the self-concept of the man in the street and decreases the likelihood of change in his concept of self. Even more important must be the effect upon our educational system. Teachers who believe in an unchanging character of child capacities provide the attitudes and experiences that produce and maintain a child's conception of self and his abilities. It is notorious that children's grades vary very little from year to year through the course of schooling. This continuous and little-changing evaluation must have important effects on the self-concept of the child. If the school system in which the child lives is thoroughly imbued with the notion that a child's capacities are comparatively fixed, it is even conceivable that the system may in large measure produce a child's intelligence level by the circular effect we have mentioned above.

Threat as Factor in Perception

The last of the factors I should like to discuss as a possible factor in intelligence is the effect of threat upon the perceptive field. If our fundamental assumption that intelligence is a function of the richness and breadth of the phenomenal field is correct, the effect of threat on this field becomes a most important consideration. Although these effects have been so widely understood by the layman that they have been made a part of his everyday speech, it is interesting that until very recently the phenomenon has been given little attention by psychologists. The perception by the individual of threat to himself seems to have at least two major effects upon the perceptive field.

Restriction of the Perceptive Field under Threat. The first of these effects is the restrictive effect that the perception of threat to self seems to have on the individual's perception. When he feels himself threatened, there appears to be a narrowing of the perceptive field to the object of threat. This has often been described in the psychology of vision as "tunnel vision." The phenomenon is extremely common and almost everyone has experienced it at some moment of crisis in his lifetime. One hears it described in such comments as "All I could see was the truck coming at us," or, "I was so scared I couldn't think of a thing." There seems reason to believe that this effect is not limited to traumatic experiences alone, but exists in lesser degree in response to milder threats as well. Combs and Taylor, for example, have demonstrated the effect under extremely mild forms of threat.

Such limiting effects on perception must certainly have a bearing upon perceptions available to the individual in his phenomenal field. Subjects who have participated in food deprivation experiments report uniformly that when threatened by hunger, food becomes an obsession. Recently, at the dinner table, I asked my young daughter what she had learned at school that day. "Oh nothing," said she with much feeling, "but was our teacher mad! Wow!" It would appear from her remarks that, feeling threatened by an angry teacher, it was difficult for her to perceive much else. Her perceptions of the day were apparently entirely concerned with the nature of anger. No doubt these are valuable perceptions to possess, but I know of no intelligence test which measures them.

I recall, too, the behavior of two little girls whose mother was taken to a mental hospital at the beginning of the summer. The matter was kept a deep secret from these two children for fear they "would not understand." The children spent most of the summer with the writer's daughter in an incessant game of "hospital." From morning to night this game went on outside our living room window. Apparently, this preoccupation was the direct outcome of the threat they felt in the loss of their mother, for with the mother's return the game ceased as suddenly as it had begun. To the best of my knowledge it has not occurred since. Under threat there seem to be severe limits imposed upon the breadth and character of perception.

Defense of the Perceptive Field under Threat. There is a second effect of threat upon the individual's perceptions. This effect has to do with the defense reactions induced in the individual on perceiving himself to be threatened. The perception of threat not only narrows the field and reduces the possibility of wide perceptions, but causes the individual to protect and cling to the perceptions he already holds. Thus, the possibility of perceptual changes is reduced and the opportunities for new perceptions or learning are decreased. Under threat, behavior becomes rigid. The fluidity and adaptation which we generally associate with intelligent behavior are vastly decreased. A number of interesting experiments in the past few years have demonstrated this phenomenon. Cowen, for example, illustrated this effect in problem solving.

Our own experiment previously mentioned also demonstrated this effect with even very mild forms of threat. This rigidity or resistance of perception to change under threat is well known to the layman and is well illustrated in some of the sayings of our culture. Such aphorisms as "Nobody ever wins an argument" or "You can lead a horse to water but you cannot make him drink" seem to be illustrations of a vague understanding of the phenomenon in the public mind. It is surprising that this principle has been so long overlooked.

I think it will be generally agreed that intelligent behavior is quite the antithesis of rigidity. In the terms we have used in this article, intelligent behavior is a function of the variety and richness of perception in the phenomenal field. Whatever produces narrowness and rigidity of perception becomes an important factor in limiting intelligence. If this reasoning is accurate, or even partly so, one is led to wonder about the effects of long continued threat upon the development of intelligence. What of the child who has suffered serious threats to himself for long periods of his life, as in the case of the delinquent, for example? Or what of the child who has been seriously deprived of affection and warmth from those who surround him over a period of years? Is it possible that we have created low intelligence in such children? Axline has reported a number of cases in which intelligence scores improved considerably under therapy. We have observed similar changes in our own clinical practice.

It may be argued that, although threat seems to reduce perception, some people under threat apparently produce more effectively. I think, however, it is necessary for us to distinguish between "threat" and "challenge." In threat, the individual perceives himself in jeopardy and feels, in addition, a degree of inadequacy to deal effectively with the threat perceived. In challenge, the individual perceives himself threatened but feels at the same time a degree of adequacy to deal with the threat. It would appear that whether an event is perceived as threatening or challenging is a function of the individual's feeling of competence to deal with it. If this analysis is correct, it would explain why a situation that appears threatening to a person, from the viewpoint of an outside observer, might one time produce rigidity and another highly effective behavior. This description of events seems characteristic of the history of civilization as well as of individuals, if Toynbee's explanation can be given credence. He points out that the most productive (more intelligent?) societies are those in which the society faces some crisis within its capacities to cope with the situation (challenge), while societies without crisis or in which the crisis is overwhelming produce very little or collapse entirely.

SOME IMPLICATIONS OF THIS CONCEPTION OF INTELLIGENT BEHAVIOR

If the conception of intelligence we have been discussing in this paper should prove accurate, it seems to me to raise serious questions about some of our common assumptions with respect to intelligence and, at the same time, opens some exciting new possibilities for the treatment or education of persons we have often assumed to be beyond help. It implies that our conception of the limiting factors of intelligence may have been too narrow. It would suggest perhaps that our very point of view with respect to intelligence may have resulted in our own tunnel vision, such that we have not been able to perceive other factors given little attention to this point. Perhaps we have been too impressed with the limitations upon growth and development which we observe in physical maturation. We may, for instance, have jumped too quickly to the assumption that intelligent behavior was limited as severely as physical growth and that we have explored to exhaustion other factors that may limit intelligence.

I am not suggesting that physiologic limits do not exist in respect to intelligence. I am suggesting that we may have conceded too early that we had approached those limits. There is no doubt that we can demonstrate in some cases, such as mongolism, cretinism, and the like, that physical factors severely limit intelligence. But these cases are comparatively few compared to the so-called "familial" cases of low intelligence that we often assume are hereditary in origin. What evidence do we really possess that would lead us to the position that an individual of "normal" physical condition and vigor may be limited in his capacity for effective behavior by some physical condition? We assume there must be such factors operating because we cannot explain his handicap otherwise. That biological science has not yet been able to demonstrate such physical bases has not deterred us in this. On the contrary, we have simply deplored the lack of sufficient advance in that discipline to demonstrate our conclusion! I should like to suggest that this may not be their failure but ours. Until it can be definitely established that limitations exist as biological functions, our task as psychologists is to assume that they may just as well be social or psychological in character and to work just as hard exploring the matter in our discipline as we expect the biologist to work in his.

Let us, for example, explore to the very fullest the possibility that in those cases where we cannot demonstrate biologic impairment, the limitations upon intelligence may be psychological. If it turns out not to be true, we shall find out in time. I do not believe we can afford to limit the places where we look by the pre-perceptions we have about the matter. Our responsibility here is too great. Education, to name but the most obvious of our social institutions, has in large measure predicated its goals and methods on a concept of humanity with certain static limitations on intelligence. If these limitations are not static, it is up to us as psychologists to find out. The task of the scientist is to question, not to be content with answers. We cannot afford to accept an undemonstrated point of view that prevents us from asking questions.

Some Implications for Intelligence Testing

If the concepts of intelligence we have been discussing prove accurate, another area of psychological thought toward which we must cast a quizzical eye is the area of intelligence testing. This is particularly important at a time when our culture has come to accept these instruments as trustingly as the family doctor's prescription. If our approach to intelligent behavior as a function of the variety and richness of the perceptual field is a valid consideration, we need to ask regarding these tests at least the following questions:

1. Is our sampling of the perceptive field truly adequate? If I lived for years in a prison cell, I presume I should become expert in perceptions about that cell. Unfortunately, they would be of little value outside the prison walls, but can it truthfully be said that my perceptions are less rich or varied, or only that they are less rich and varied about things I have not had opportunity to experience? Is the delinquent, with rich and varied perceptions on how to elude the police, less intelligent or has he simply not perceived things society wishes he had?

2. Since perceptions are always closely affected by need, by whose need shall we sample perceptions—yours, mine, society's, the subject's own? I suspect that in terms of his own needs and perceptions the subject might be deemed quite brilliant, though he might or might not appear so from the point of view of society. For the most part our tests are based on the assumption that academic, upper middle-class, intellectual perceptions are important. But are they? Can we assume that the expert machinist, who can perceive things "out of this world" for most of the rest of us about a piece of stock on his lathe, is less intelligent than a diplomat who perceives many things about foreign affairs? Can we be so sure of our values as to call one bright and the other dull? Can we blame the machinist for his lack of perception about foreign affairs without asking the diplomat to be equally skilled in the machinist's field of perceptions?

3. Finally, if perceptions are affected by the factors we have discussed in this paper, is it fair to sample intelligence irrespective of the control of such factors? Shall we, for example, examine the child who has lacked opportunity to perceive, has possessed a concept of self or been so threatened over a long period of time so as to have been unable to perceive what we wish to sample without consideration of those factors? Shall we overlook such factors and be satisfied that the perceptions important to us are not there, or shall we seek for ways to make it possible for the child to have them? Shall we assume that

our failure to discover a particular perception present in the field is, *ipso facto,* evidence of lack of capacity; or seek to discover why it is not? On the positive side of the picture, if the concepts we have here been discussing are sound, there is reason to believe that intelligence may be far less immutable than we have thought. It may be that we can do far more than we have dreamed we could. Perhaps we may even be able to create intelligence!

Implications for Constructive Action

Who can say, for example, what results we might be able to achieve by a systematic effort to remove or decrease the effectiveness of the limitations on perception discussed in this paper? It is fascinating to speculate on the possibilities one might try in constructing a situation for a child, or adult, consciously designed to minimize the limitations imposed on perception by physical condition, environment, goals, the individual's self-concept, and the effects of perceived personal threat.

If the position we have taken is accurate, it would suggest that there is much we can do (a) to free individuals from the restraints upon perception and (b) to provide the opportunities for perception to occur.

1. First and most obviously, we should be able to discover and make available to far more people the means to achieve better physical condition. We have already done a good deal in this area but much needs yet to be done. Who can say, for instance, what completely adequate medical care for all our people might mean a generation hence?

2. If this discussion has merit, there lies the possibility of providing experiences for people that will make adequate perceptions possible. We have tried to do this in our schools, but have not always accomplished it. We have succeeded very well in gathering information and in making it available to students. We have not succeeded too well in making such information meaningful. Can it be that the decreases in school success with advance through the school years is more a function of lack of meaning for students than lack of intelligence? Is it enough to assume that experience provided by us to the student is truly provided when he is free to experience it? Has the child in school, who is so worried about his relationship with his peers that he cannot perceive what his book is saying, truly been provided opportunity to perceive?

In our training of children of "low intelligence," we often provide situations wherein they are carefully taught to perform repeatedly a simple act. Is it possible that in so doing we may be further narrowing their fields of perception and building self-concepts that produce even narrower perceptive fields?

What kinds of environments could we construct that might more effectively result in increased perception? Such experiments as Lippitt and White have carried on with democratic and autocratic environments suggest some possibilities, but we need to know much more. Perhaps we could learn to build such environments from observing with greater care and understanding the methods of good teachers.

3. Who can say what possible effects might occur from a systematic release of the individual's perceptions by the satisfaction of his most pressing needs or goals? We college professors insist we can produce more, which is another way of saying perceive more, when we have the leisure time to do so, when we are freed from the necessity of spending our time satisfying our needs for sheer existence. Can this be less true of others? It is possible that the child with needs of love, affection, status, prestige, or a girl friend might also be freed to perceive more widely and richly, if we could but find ways of helping him satisfy his needs. Ordinarily, we pay a good deal of attention to the physical needs of a child, understanding that with these needs unfulfilled, he makes a poor student. Is there any good reason to suppose his psychological needs are less pressing or less important in freeing him to perceive widely and accurately? We spend much time and energy trying to find ways of "motivating" people or blaming them for not being motivated to do what we need them to do. We assume that if permitted to seek their own needs, people will not satisfy ours. Perhaps we should get further by helping them satisfy their needs; they might then be free to satisfy ours.

4. Most of our educational methods are directed at the provision of perceptions for the student. He is lectured, required, shown, exhorted, and coerced to perceive what someone thinks he should. It seems possible that with equal energy devoted to the matter of creating needs, goals, and values in students, rich and varied perceptions might be more efficiently produced.

What effects might we be able to produce by providing experiences that build adequate concepts of self in children and adults? What differences in the richness and variety of perception might result from a generation of people with "I can" rather than "I can't" conceptions of themselves? What possibilities of increased perceptions and hence of increased intelligence might accrue to such a program? Clinical experience has demonstrated frequently how a changed perception of self as a more adequate personality can free children for improved school performance, for example.

What would happen if we were consciously and carefully to set about the task of providing experiences that would lead people to conceptions of themselves as adequate, worthy, self-respecting people? If freedom to perceive is a function of adequate perceptions of self, it should not surprise us that the child who perceives himself as unwanted, inacceptable, unable, or unliked behaves in rigid fashion. It should be possible, too, to reverse this process and produce more adequate perceptions by systematic efforts at producing more adequate definitions of self. The possibilities seem tremendous but we have scarcely scratched the surface of this problem.

Finally, if threat to the individual has as important effects as seem indicated in this discussion, the removal of threat would seem a most important factor to consider in the release of the individual to perceive more adequately. The work of Rogers and his students in client centered therapy has already illustrated to some degree what possibilities freeing the individual to perceive more adequately may accomplish through the provision of a permissive nonthreatening relationship between counselor and client. We have already mentioned the effects Axline has reported following a permissive, nonthreatening form of play therapy.

Such effects do not seem limited to the therapeutic situation, however. A number of workers have applied this principle of permissiveness to the classroom situation with equally gratifying results. Experiments in student centered teaching at Syracuse have led many of us to believe in the tremendous educational possibilities in the removal of threat.

This paper has asked many questions. Indeed, it has asked far more questions than it has presumed to answer. That, it seems to me, is the function of theory. The picture of intelligence presented here as it seems from a phenomenological viewpoint may be accurate or false or, more likely, partly true and partly false. Only time and the industry of many observers can check its adequacy or inadequacy. It seems to me to pose problems that are both exciting and challenging. If it proves as stimulating to the reader as it has to the author, I shall rest content that a theory has achieved its purpose.

---

27. *Mental Test Performance as a Reflection of the Child's Current Life Situation: A Methodological Study* *

VARIATIONS IN the performance of some individuals on standardized intelligence tests have long intrigued and baffled psychologists. Some variation may be attributed to the unreliability of the tests themselves, of course. Often, however, the changes are too great to be explained in this way. The following paper suggests some answers to this puzzle, as it traces the development of a single individual, and parallels the changes in his test scores with reports of other aspects of his life and personality that could relate to his ups and downs in performance. (As some of the case reporting is based on projective tests—the Rorschach ink-blot test and the Thematic Apperception Test—the reader would do well to read his text's discussion of these tests if they have not already been taken up in class.) This study is a good example of the intensive long-term follow-up work needed to improve our use of cross-sectional group studies as predictive indicators in individual cases.

THOSE WHO WORK with children clinically are sensitive to the possibility that the child's symptoms or test performance on a given occasion may reflect his current and perhaps temporary adjustment more than they do his usual or "constitutional" potentiality. While this may be particularly true of psychological testing (as contrasted with pediatric examination, for example), psychologists are inclined to attribute the vagaries of performance on a single test as due, possibly, to "unreliability" of the test, or "probable error." Most testers suppose that the I.Q., for example, has a probable error of five points, so that an I.Q. of 82 should read, 77–87. In other words, chance factors might depress or enhance the I.Q. by five points in either direction.

In this report it is the intention to present, together with the I.Q. curve of one child over a seven and one-half year period, all the data that were recorded in regard to all aspects of his life in a rather intensive longitudinal study. The data will be presented chronologically, so that the reader may draw his own conclusions as to correspondence (or lack of it) between fluctuations in the curve and other incidents, trends, influences, pressures, or forces in the child's life.

* T. W. Richards, "Mental test performance as a reflection of the child's current life situation: a methodological study," *Child Development,* XXII (1951), 221–33. By permission of the author and the Child Development Publications of the Society for Research in Child Development, Inc.

The child who is the subject of this case study was one of some 175 children in the Fels research program [1] whose I.Q. curves were plotted in an attempt to classify longitudinal patterns of intellectual development, as measured by the tests used (for the most part the Stanford-Binet).

Selection of this particular child was made on the basis of the slope of the I.Q. curve alone. It was desired that the curve did not, in its variation, differ markedly from those in the total group of curves. Yet, it seemed necessary to select a curve which would reveal *fluctuations,* and not simply a trend upward or downward. Finally, it seemed desirable that the child chosen for this analysis should not be one who for any reason (such as problem behavior) had come to the attention of the staff for special help.

All the case material here presented was extracted from records made by various observers and research workers and filed for future reference. These were interviewers, visitors to the home and to the school, observers in the nursery school and summer day camp groups for school-age children. Any one of these observers could be presumed to have had a general idea about the child's mental capacity but he was in no sense conversant in detail with his current or recent performance on a specific test occasion. The single exception to this might have been the administrator of the mental tests.[2] But even here, a high degree of control was operative; in her routine work the examiner purposely avoided familiarizing herself with the child's previous performance, devoting her attention to the present test-at-hand. Moreover, in the course of a year of the Fels study the examiner gives some five hundred tests. Thus, in extracting from the records material which may be pertinent to this synchronous analysis, we are examining material which has been accumulated quite independently of the variable to which it is here compared—the Stanford-Binet I.Q.

The case finally selected was that of a child whom we shall call Bobby James:

Bobby is the only child of parents who, intellectually and economically, are above average but not remarkably superior. The father is a college graduate, the son of a physician. With the Otis examination of mental ability he achieved an I.Q. of 127. He has been engaged principally in engineering work for public utilities organizations. The mother is the daughter of a business man, had some college training, and did secretarial work for a few years before her marriage; she attained on the Otis an I.Q. of 100. Bern-

[1] Fels Research Institute for the Study of Human Development, Yellow Springs, Ohio.

[2] Dr. Virginia L. Nelson.

reuter Inventory scores suggest a tendency away from *neuroticism* and toward *dominance* for both parents, while, on this inventory, the father appeared somewhat more self-sufficient than the mother.

The curve for all administrations of the Stanford-Binet test to Bobby is presented in Figure 1. It is seen that he was given the 1916 form at

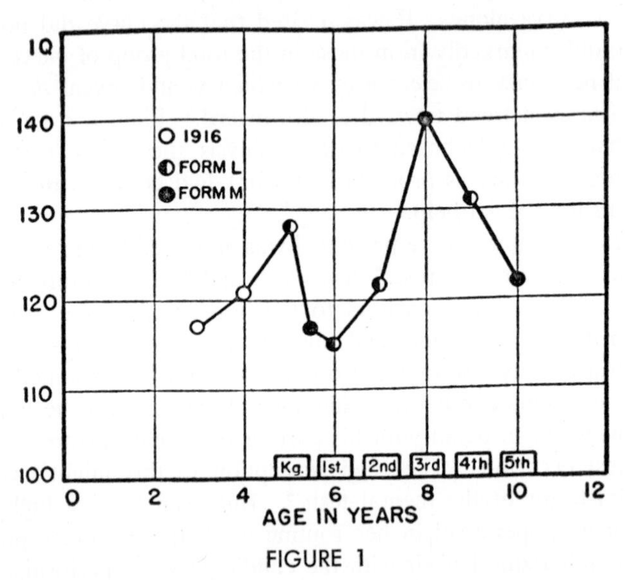

FIGURE 1

Stanford-Binet performance in terms of I.Q. of Bobby James at various points.

3 and 4 years, Form L of the Revised Stanford-Binet at 5, 6, 7, and 9, and Form M at 5½, 8, and 10. School grades are indicated in the boxes along the baseline.

There are four trends in the I.Q. curve: a rise of 11 points from 3 to 5 years; a drop of 13 points from 5 to 6; a rise of 25 points from 6 to 8 years; and a drop of 18 points from 8 to 10 years. For purposes of organization of the material in this report we shall refer at least in a loose way to these four periods.

BIRTH TO FIVE YEARS—PHASE 1

(I.Q. increase 11 points)

Medically, there was nothing remarkable about Bobby's birth. Breast feeding was discontinued at about two and a half months, bowel training was begun at six months, and toilet training was considered complete before three years. Since he was an only child, the household revolved, more or less, about Bobby. There is evidence of strong attachment to the mother during the preschool years.

So far as the usual signs and symptoms of maladjustment are concerned, the records made somewhat frequent mention of a tendency for Bob to pick his fingernails as far back as three years of age. There was also occasional reference to night terrors, and to an insistence, possibly compulsive, that his parents read to him nightly just before going to bed. Apparently a certain ritual was developed early in his childhood; when this reading had to be postponed or he slept elsewhere than at home he was quite upset.

Bob attended the Fels observational nursery school twice for brief periods. Here is a report from the observer during a period when he was three and a half:

> The outstanding thing about Bobby is his behavior of crying for his mother. Otherwise, he seems about average. He plays in the group, and alone; he has a good balance between cooperation and independence. He has a good use of language.
>
> He is absent much. The first day was his best—best-adjusted to his group—that is, he did not cry; he played alone and in the group. His mother expressed surprise that Bobby had been so good; she had thought that he would be the biggest crybaby. The next day Bobby turned up with a bad case of mother-sickness, and has shown it ever since.
>
> One day he told Miss N. (the head teacher) that he could cry whenever he wanted, etc. On two days he tried to persuade David to come to the gate and pretend to cry for their mamas. David refused and Bobby persisted intermittently for many minutes (15 to 30). But David only smiled superiorly and suggested, somewhat successfully, that they play something else.

Early records reveal Bob's close attachment to both parents. Evidence of the mother's conscientiousness and of her interest in Bobby's development was the daily record which she kept for one calendar year (largely Bob's fourth year). Almost every day she made some entry in this diary about his behavior, a performance on her part which was almost unique among the Fels mothers.

Throughout reports of contacts with Bobby and with his mother as written in his "black book" [3] there was frequent mention of Bobby's great admiration and respect for his father. It might be well to examine these comments in some detail to see whether or not they offer a longitudinal pattern.

> (8 months) Father plays with him about 15 minutes at noon, and 6:00 to 7:30. Mother won't let father play with him too much on Monday.

[3] The "black book" is a serial record of a variety of observations on the individual child.

He misses it. Father plays a little roughly with him, holds him up by the back. Despite father's playing with him, he is very much of a mama's boy. He will cry to come back to mother sometimes when father picks him up.

(25 months) Father spends one hour in the evening with Bobby. Bobby is not afraid of his father. Mother and father occasionally disagree in discipline. Father gets annoyed with child. Mother thinks he is too strict.

(27 months) The mother noted in her diary, "He said to his father, you are a nice, big man, Daddy." Here a home visit report describes the following incident—"Mr. James came home from the office to get ready for a hurried trip out of town. When upstairs, began opening drawers, and running water, etc. After a little while Bobby started up the stairs, calling to his father 'I'm coming up.' Mr. James said something in the form of a mild but unenthusiastic welcome, but Bobby went on and stayed up there until his father was ready to come down, apparently looking on without asking any questions. He started down the stairs, saying 'I'm going down first.' His father said 'Well, you'll have to hurry if you are going to get there first' and passed him on the stairs with no sign of emotion on Bobby's part. Bobby went to the door, saying 'I want to see daddy's car'."

Mother noted in her diary (when Bobby was about 32 months old) "Father has to read to Bob every night before he goes to bed. Bob always wants the same book of Eugene Field's poems." In his third year a home visit report gives the following incident: "Mr. James came in for a few minutes to bring home his new automobile license plates. Bob was delighted to see his father, and, starting to talk to him, got possession of the plates. He offered to put them on the mantle, climbed up to stand on the Chesterfield in order to reach. I remarked that he was a real help. Bob countered with 'I say so'; he asked his father 'You going back to work now. Pretty soon come home? Tonight?' As his father left he watched from the window and yelled 'Good bye'."

In the kindergarten which he entered before he was five years old, Bobby made a good adjustment and enjoyed it thoroughly. Some insight into the kindergarten itself is given by the home visitor's report of the mother's comments: "Mother chose Blaine School rather than Rockwood because she felt that *there was no point in sending Bobby to a progressive kindergarten for one year where he would learn to consider school a place of great freedom, since next year he would have to conform to the rather strict discipline of the public school.*" The inference here is, at least, that the kindergarten he attended was not progressive.

FROM FIVE TO SIX—PHASE 2
(a 13 point drop in I.Q.)

Bobby entered the first grade at five years and eight months. The reports of his teachers throughout this school year make frequent mention of his impulsiveness and boisterousness, but these were as often interpreted as enthusiasm and "boyishness" as really "bad" behavior. The mother commented to the home visitor, "Bobby is very pleased with school, considers it all play and greatly enjoys it; always getting ready to leave each day. The first two or three days of school he required punishment at home because he acted smart, but he has settled down to normal now. His teacher he likes but she is very strict."

In the reports of home visits during this fifth year, are found these comments—"attached to father, expects a great deal of attention . . ." "obeys both parents, but obeys father more promptly. Mother thinks this is due to father's more commanding voice and to the fact that he is with Bob so much less often." "Bobby, in relation to father, is fond and attached. On weekend trips father gives Bobby considerable care and attention." "Mr. James started a blueprint company in May [when Bob was 65 months old] which he carried in addition to his work with [a utilities company]. He spends an hour there immediately after work and then returns later in the evening, after Bobby is in bed. The work does not take every evening, as it has in the past. I [the home visitor] asked whether the heavy load of work seemed to affect Mr. James physically or temperamentally. Mrs. James remarked 'he would rather work than just sit around.' He and Bobby are congenial. Recently when Mrs. James was ill the two 'men' went for a hike to the Boy Scout Camp. Bob minds his father better than his mother, more obedient in general than he used to be."

Ratings of parent behavior when Bob was about 66 months old compared with the Fels group for that period of visits showed the following characteristics to deviate more than one sigma from the mean: *well-adjusted, democratic, little discord between parents, agreement regarding disciplinary policy, harmony, freedom, objectivity, rational and clear disciplinary policy, keen understanding of the child.*

FROM SIX TO EIGHT—PHASE 3
(the I.Q. rising 25 points)

In the middle of his first grade year, just after he became six, Bobby was transferred to a different teacher, Miss R. About her, the mother reported, "Bob likes her better because she is small and pretty." The Fels school visitor wrote: "She is a small lady of approximately 55, very orthodox and old school in her procedure, a stern disciplinarian, non-analytical. Thirty-five in the room, building modern, rooms large and pleasant." Bob continued with this teacher through the first semester of the second grade, then was switched to another room. Here he had as his teacher a friend of the family, Miss B., who, according to the mother "seems to be sympathetic with Bob's 'real boy' tendencies and not to hold it against him too much." In this connection, the Fels visitor, to whom the mother reported this, added: "I should expect Bobby to get on much better with Miss B. than he did with Miss R., partly because of Miss B.'s more modern understanding and tolerance, and partly because of her friendship with the family and interest in Bob. Miss R. seems to me to be the kind who would be largely annoyed by overactive and mischievous, though bright, children." Bobby continued with Miss B. through the third grade; in the middle of this grade he made his highest I.Q.

Notes from the interviewers, observations in day camp and otherwise are typically as follows:

(Day camp, age 6) "Easy-going, good-natured; not at ease with other children, but glad to cooperate with them." (Visit to Fels House, age 7) "This boy's interests seem usual, perhaps tending toward infantile side, but he is apparently very well-adjusted toward home and school and socially. A happy boy with few disturbances—so far."

(Rorschach test, age 7:1) "Characterized by considerable productivity with a quantitative practical bent rather than an organized creative tendency. Higher production in the last three cards, together with relative lack of movement, suggests an extratensive individual . . . brought out also in the free use of color on occasion. It was on the color cards that Bobby used movement, although this was animal and inanimate movement. On the achromatic cards he gave responses which were at times dysphoric: things were 'crushed,' there was a 'dead chicken,' etc. The general impression is that this is an individual who functions best under pressure, although in such situations he is somewhat tense and primitive. Left to his own devices, he is inclined to anxiety and depression, a tendency which is not, however, extreme."

(Day camp, age 7) "The 'all-American boy.' Miss S. (a staff observer) predicts a successful bond salesman some day. Very friendly, politic, conciliator, lazy, good-natured." (Winter visit, age 8) "Impression is of a boy who is genuinely popular with his friends and classmates, a boy who takes responsibility well. He conforms in certain respects without losing too much independence. Predict very good adjustment later for him."

These comments appear in the home visit reports: (age 6) "Bob attends movies occasionally. This afternoon he is going with his father to make up for being deprived of his company this morning due to his visit to Fels House. Bob respects his father and is more obedient to him than to his mother." During the six-year home visit, we find the following notation: "Mr. James has a heavy working schedule, has been very nervous and irritable recently—probably aggravated by a heavy cold and a siege of flu. He takes great interest in Bobby although his hours of work necessarily limit their interaction." Six months later: "Mr. James and Bobby are detached. Mr. James doesn't know how to get next to Bobby, even how to play with him. Mrs. James is worried about it. Has urged Mr. James to make more of an effort. Accordingly Mr. James has eliminated his night work and has taken Bobby to several shows and baseball games. Even now, however, Bobby always chooses his mother to accompany him to bed and to go with him to the bathroom. Bobby would rather be with his grandfather than either his father or his mother. Mr. James is discouraged about the future of his business and is thinking of dissolving the partnership." Following his seventh birthday appears the comment: "There is a ritual before bedtime, Bobby being carried upstairs by his father over his shoulder and mother putting him in bed and kissing him good-night." At age 7 years 2 months in home visit notes: "Bob is much closer to his father than he has been although he still relies on his mother more than he should, according to her. Mr. James has given up his evening blueprint job because of some difficulty with his partner and has been less tense and nervous. He had attacks of nausea recently which have not reappeared since Christmas when he gave up the blueprints. Mrs. James said that he was 'another man,' more thoughtful, easier to live with." (7 years 9 months) "Mr. James is spending more time with Bobby than he has in the past, has built him a large and elaborate table for his electric train in the basement. Mr. James plays with Bobby and the train every evening and told of their plans for future development."

Ratings of parent behavior for this period (actually when Bobby was a little beyond seven) placed the following characteristics at least one sigma above the mean: *well-adjusted, democratic, active, child-centered, acceleratory, sheltering, satisfying the child's curiosity, solicitous for the child, devoted, and affectionate.*

It is interesting to compare these ratings at seven years plus with the ratings made when the child was five and a half (while the curve was dropping). On the second rating, there was an increase by one sigma or more in *activeness in the home, child-centeredness, sheltering, approval, solicitousness for the child's welfare, devotion, affection,* and *more optimal suggestion.* There was a decrease by one sigma in *objectivity,* in the *severity of disciplinary penalties,* and *extensiveness of contact with the child.*

FROM EIGHT TO TEN—PHASE 4
(the I.Q. drops 18 points)

In the second semester of the third grade, after Bobby's eighth birthday, the school visitor commented in her notes that the school principal: "Just looked glum, at a school movie." Miss B., Bobby's teacher:

"looks tired and inactive compared with previous visits. She has little pep." At the end of this third grade year, it was noted that Miss B. had had a tumor removed from her face: "She said that it was high time she had it done, for it was making her nervous. This may be important in her classroom personality."

In the fourth grade, according to the home visitor's report "Bob's current teacher makes him toe the mark and Mrs. James approves of her severity. Today he had to stay after school to write out some spelling words." Comparing teachers, the mother commented: "Bobby's teacher last year (Miss B.) was too lenient with him." In December of the fourth grade year the school visitor wrote: "The teacher appeared tense and ill-at-ease, mentioned a recent operation, asked me to visit no longer than one hour and by appointment. Said such a visit was a strain; had no enthusiasm about record book,[4] but accepted it. . . ." "I returned a month later to receive a most cordial welcome. Late 30's, voice fairly high-pitched, clear speech, dominates room. Rather forced gaiety. Lets pupils participate in activities other than mere recitation, but always definitely directed by teacher. The gaiety and charm of this encounter were conspicuously lacking in the previous one."

In the fifth grade, Bobby had still a different teacher. (Comment made by mother to home visitor) "He has a very strict teacher this year, doesn't like her." (School visitor) "Whispering is not permitted. Mr. A called him out of dismissal line for being disorderly. The teacher's ideal child is doubtless one who moves about very little, speaks only when addressed, walks in a straight line and is always *neat and quiet*." A home visit report states, "Mrs. James attributes Bob's improvement in school to the teacher he has this year, the one she feels is the best in the school."

These are remarks concerning a Thematic Apperception Test given Bobby just after his eighth birthday: "Certain unusual themes pervade this total record of ten stories. A frequent one is that the hero is perplexed; he doesn't know what to do. Again he is sometimes sick or dizzy and often the stories end in his death. For a boy of eight it seems that the emphasis on themes of marriage and growing old is unusual. The male adult figure often seems to leave the marriage situation as a solution. However, you get the impression that the married state appears to Bobby an arrangement more convenient perhaps than any other. It is interesting that when the male figure is heading for disaster, such as prison or confinement of any sort, he is a negro."

On a questionnaire used at this point Bobby admitted a number of

[4] Asked of, and usually accepted with little or no comment, by most of the teachers of Fels children.

fears: of the dark, going into a dark room at night, deep water, being kidnapped, "scary dreams," and being told "scary things" by other people.

Day camp notes (age 8 years 6 months) show a decided shift in the impression he made:

Bobby has changed more dramatically than any of the other children here. He is less responsible, less of a leader, more unreasonable, harder to handle. He is extremely negativistic, never wanted to do what the rest of the gang wanted, difficult in the testing situation, very noisy, fresh, uninterested. He was a serious discipline problem. He wanted his own way impulsively and was unruly when he couldn't have it. At certain times he couldn't be reasoned with and had to be isolated. Complained about everything and everybody; a griper. He actually did not seem happy this year. He had some good times, but it was much more typical for him to be dissatisfied. His mother commented crossly one day that Bob was all for himself. She sounded as if he got on her nerves. He acted here as if something had gone wrong with his adjustment during the year."

A visit to Fels House the following year (when he was nine) suggests some recovery:

He seems rather a solid citizen, a little self-important, but quite natural in many ways. On the whole he is very friendly, very frank and open.

From home visit notes, the following are exerpts: (8 years 3 months)

He very much admires he-men, looks up to his father as a regular man. Bob's father has very little time for him; Bob's talking gets on his nerves, because there is a colleague of his at the office who talks constantly too. He seems to be unable to play at Bob's level although he will take him to movies and out for walks. Recently Bob asked his father to play a game with him. Mr. James said, "Heck, no." Mrs. James said, "If Bob said that to you, you'd whip him; Bob, I'll play with you." Mr. James then entered the game and fell asleep in the middle of it. Bob was heart broken. Mr. James is much more strict. (9 years 9 months) Mr. James is dissatisfied with his present utility company, and is taking a college course in electronics. The family is planning to move to another city. (10 years 4 months) The father is now working in another city, is home about every four weeks. Bob is restless, hard to handle. He is a different child on the days the father is at home, conforming and anxious to please.

A Rorschach test at ten revealed (according to evaluation by Marguerite Hertz):

A picture of a boy of superior ability, original in his thinking, independent in his judgment, who is emotionally immature, not yet adapted to his environment intellectually or emotionally. He is highly sensitive and cautious, has a tremendous drive to compensate for a feeling of insecurity and inadequacy.

A comparison of this Rorschach record with that attained earlier (when he was seven) shows a slight increase in number of responses (from 30 to 34). Figure 2 shows that there is a drop in pure form (F), accounted for, it seems likely, by the increase in movement of all sorts, but particularly animal movement (FM) and by the appearance

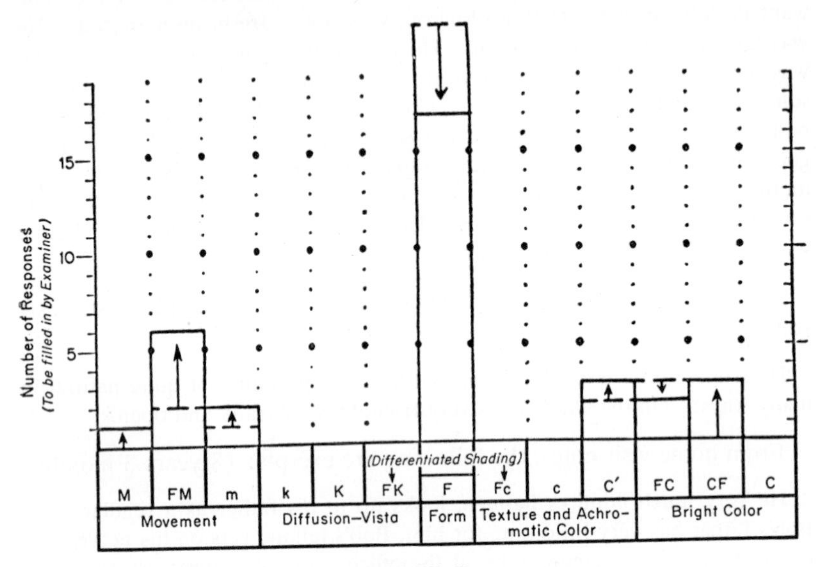

FIGURE 2

Rorschach performance in terms of determinants at age 7 years (dotted line) and at age 10 years (solid line).

of color-form (CF). Thus, he is more spontaneous at ten than at seven, but his spontaneity would be considered of an infantile, impulsive and over-reactive sort. The appearance of black and white shading response (C′) at seven, and its increased amount at ten suggest strongly that feelings of inadequacy and even morbidity are indeed prominent.

On the Thematic Apperception Test, given also at age ten, Bob was restrained. He was hesitant to identify himself with the figures in the pictures. A repeated theme was crime, of a sort not highly aggressive, but petty. Usually the culprit was eventually punished.

A comparison of the two performances with the Thematic Apperception Test (at 8 years and 10 years) shows certain changes. In general the later performance is much more constricted and less dynamic. Figure 3 presents in chart form the shift in terms of Aron's scoring of needs and press for self-identified heroes ("S") and other heroes ("O"). It is seen that in both records *manipulative needs* are prominent. These were, in particular, *n Acquisition* in both performances; in the earlier record *n Cognizance* and *n Construction* and the same needs but to a lesser extent in the later record. Note, however, that evidence of manipulative needs in characters other than the "self" increases over the ten year period. A similar tendency—that is, for decrease in the "self" character and increase in other characters—takes the place for Aggression Outward.

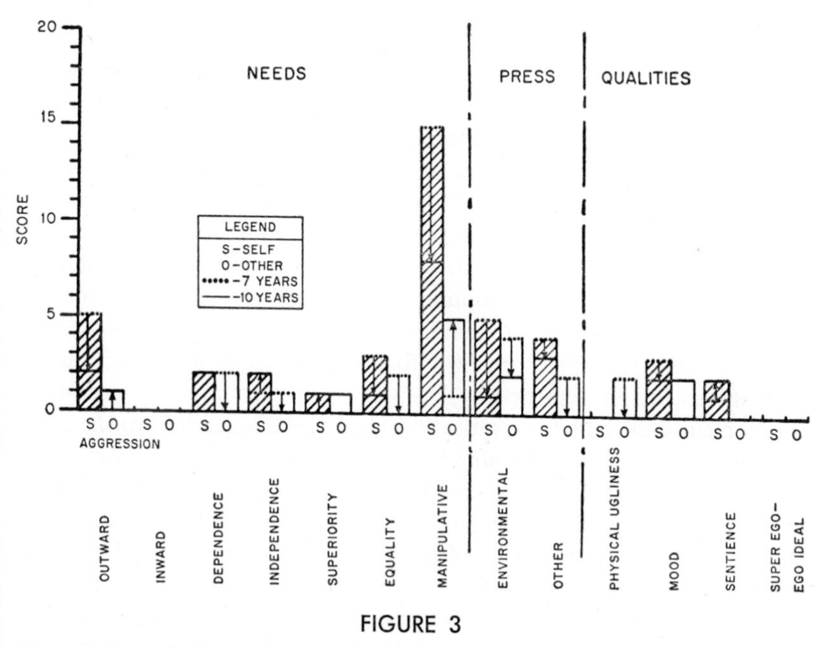

FIGURE 3

Assessment of needs, press, and other qualities in the TAT stories at 8 years (broken line) and 10 years (solid line).

A story of significance regarding Bob's relation to his father, at ten years, is as follows:

(Picture of an adult male figure lying in bed) "Looks like my daddy taking a nap. Looks like a man taking a nap. Must have stayed up late last night. He's sleeping on the bed. Looks like a comfortable chair in the room and a book on the table and a lamp and his pipe. [What happens?] Probably wakes up. If he's like my dad, I'll go up and wake him up. Probably woke up and goes out somewhere or . . . or reads a book. Comes home and goes to bed and starts another day all over again."

Parent behavior ratings for this period (made at the age of 9 years and 3 months) deviated from the mean by one sigma or more for *well-adjusted, democratic, vigilant,* and *child centered.* Compared with ratings made in the seventh year, the home was now (by one sigma difference) more *vigilant, disciplinary, penalties were more severe,* and there was greater *withholding of help to the child.* The home was less *active,* there was less *freedom,* less *concordance,* less *sheltering,* less *satisfaction of the child's curiosity,* less *devotion,* less *emotionality,* and less *affection.*

DISCUSSION

In 1940 Nancy Bayley published mental growth curves for several children together with data concerning the family and other background which made possible certain interpretations regarding "environment" of a general sort and subsequent test performance. In a later study, Despert and Pierce reported fluctuations in the mental test performance of nursery school children, as these seemed to accompany incidents (frustrating or otherwise) in the child's extracurricular life. These investigations, essentially attempting to correlate clinical with objective or experimental findings, are similar to the present study.

Harris and Thompson made a forthright attempt to show that the fluctuations in I.Q. reported by Despert and Pierce could be accounted for by chance deviation, or, more specifically, the regression-to-the-mean phenomenon; a trend governing human performance in such a way that —all other things being equal—the deviant will be found, upon re-examination, to be not so deviant and more like his fellows. Their calculations, based on the data of Despert and Pierce, showed that the means of later I.Q's coincided remarkably with those that could be predicted on the basis of the regression hypothesis alone, and their inference is that it is a violation of the law of parsimony to bring into the explanation for I.Q. changes phenomena (such as fluctuations in the child's life, etc.) of the sort given emphasis by Despert and Pierce.

Certain features of the present study seem to deserve emphasis. First of all, we are dealing with a boy of superior mental capacity (mean I.Q. 124). Secondly, the home, each time it was rated on the Parent Behavior Scales, was (by more than one sigma from the Fels mean) *well-adjusted* and *democratic.* We might infer that there was no apparent psychopathology in the parents or the home *in toto.*

Impressions from the notes made by various observers suggest that the following factors may have been significant as correlates of trends in the I.Q. curve.

1. The school situation (including the mother's concept of school) was formal, restrictive and disciplinary during Phases 2 and 4. During Phase 3 Bob seemed sensitive to the close personal relationship with Miss B. Unfortunately, the facial tumor which gradually developed seemed to affect Miss B.'s teaching; it was finally treated a few months beyond the point of highest and best test performance.

2. The home situation, particularly the role of the father, fluctuated considerably over Bob's ten years of life. In Phase 2 and Phase 4 the father's own adjustment seemed less integrated and purposeful, while during Phases 1 and 3, it seemed oriented toward a goal of advantage, at least to Bob.

3. While the home was rated always *well-adjusted* and *democratic,* there was an increase, in Phase 3, in those characteristics which make for warmth—child-centeredness, sheltering, approval, solicitousness, devotion, affection—and a decrease in disciplinary severity and in objectivity. In contrast, during Phase 4, penalties were more severe, there was less devotion, sheltering, emotionality, affection. While more vigilant, the parents were less in agreement and less active as parents.

CONCLUSION

On the basis of a single case, no generalizations can be made. It is our feeling, however, that the fluctuations in I.Q. presented by this child are not entirely fortuitous. They seem related plausibly to important characteristics of his current life situation.

---

28. *What Is an Aptitude?* *

JUST AS there is confusion about what intelligence really is, so is there uncertainty about the meaning of the term "aptitude." Students, knowing that aptitude tests exist, frequently expect to be able to assess their inborn capacities for different careers by means of such devices. The following discussion makes clear that "aptitude" measures involve prior experience and personality factors just as intelligence measures do. It helps us understand the real values of intelligence and aptitude tests by indicating the cautions we need to take in interpreting them.

* Alexander G. Wesman, "What is an aptitude?" *Test Service Bulletin* of The Psychological Corporation, No. 36 (August, 1948), pp. 2–3. By permission of the author and The Psychological Corporation.

AS INTEREST IN any technical field becomes increasingly widespread, it is perhaps inevitable that misconceptions concerning some of the relevant concepts and terminology should appear. This seems to be especially true of aptitude testing. That the misconceptions should refer to the basic understanding of the term "aptitude" itself is of serious import; clarification of the concept and resolution of differing meanings is vital, not only to aptitude testing but to the entire field of psychological measurement.

The definition of aptitude which Dr. Bingham prepared for Warren's *Dictionary of Psychology* is an excellent starting point for elucidation of the concept:

> APTITUDE. *A condition or set of characteristics regarded as symptomatic of an individual's ability to acquire with training some (usually specified) knowledge, skill, or set of responses, such as the ability to speak a language, to produce music. . . .*

A complete appreciation of this definition would do away with a number of misunderstandings which are prevalent. We may note, first, that nothing inherent in this concept assumes that aptitudes are hereditary. The expression "born that way" is a dangerous fallacy which still is heard even among educated people. On the other hand, one cannot undertake to make every average person into a genius. Fortunately for our present purpose, we really do not need to determine *how much* of an aptitude is hereditary and how much reflects environmental forces. Aptitude is the result of the interaction of heredity and environment. The infant is born with certain potentialities, and begins learning immediately. What he learns makes it possible for him to learn more. It is similar to the investment of capital which bears interest, the interest then becoming additional capital which also may be reinvested to earn still more interest.

A second important feature of the definition is that it is extremely broad. As conceived herein, aptitude embraces intelligence and achievement, personality and interests as well as any other abilities and skills which predispose to learning. The use of the term aptitude as being limited only to the specialized learning capacities for music or engineering or stenography is misleading. The familiar intelligence tests have found favor because they predict the student's ability to learn to read, or write compositions, or bisect an angle, or understand social trends. In other words, they are aptitude tests which describe the student's potentiality for learning in a number of academic subjects or vocational endeavors. This has been recognized in the healthy tendency to speak of scholastic aptitude tests rather than intelligence tests. A more sophisticated understanding of the nature of intelligence and aptitude has made this trend inevitable.

Many of us who have accepted the idea that intelligence tests measure aptitude have failed to recognize that achievement tests are also aptitude tests when used most purposefully. The most important function which an achievement test can serve is to make evident what the person has learned, either so that we can predict how well he will learn additional material of a similar nature, or to indicate whether he has the skills or knowledge required for future success in a particular profession or trade. The use of an achievement test score solely for recording a person's accomplishment is relatively sterile; only when it predicts, obviously or indirectly, is such measurement maximally useful.

The importance of interests and other personality traits for learning skills or acquiring knowledge needs no exposition. How well a person will acquire proficiency depends so much on his interest in the task, on his drives and his goals, that the layman appreciates these conditioning factors as thoroughly as does the psychologist. It is only when the term aptitude is too narrowly delimited that the contributions of interest and personality are overlooked as aspects of aptitude.

The total concept can perhaps be summarized by regarding aptitude as simply a capacity to learn. When we refer to stenographic aptitude, we mean the capacity to learn those skills which make for a successful stenographer. This is a relatively specific aptitude. When we refer to academic aptitude, we mean the capacity to complete successfully a more comprehensive curriculum. This is really a broader set of aptitudes, and we frequently use so-called tests of general mental ability to facilitate our prediction. It is noteworthy that the modern trend is away from single score intelligence tests in favor of tests which yield several scores—e.g., verbal, numerical, abstract, mechanical, etc. This is a recognition that for specific courses or jobs, the best prediction can be obtained from more specific measurement than is yielded by an undifferentiated single "intelligence" score or IQ.

The measurement of aptitude, then, is the assessment of knowledge, skill, and any other characteristics which serve to predict learning success. Usually test data are the most important bases for such prediction. Sometimes background data which reveal experience, interest or personality characteristics may be equally fruitful sources of prediction. Industry's use of the weighted application blank, for example, is based on solid experience with the value of biographical data.

What, then, is an aptitude test? It is any test which is used for prediction of some type of learning. Its validity as an aptitude test depends on the extent to which it will predict successfully. We probably shall continue to categorize tests as intelligence tests, achievement tests, interest tests, special aptitude tests, etc. as though there were no overlap in their functions. However, we must not let ourselves become confused by our own practical pigeon-holing. To avoid erroneous thinking about prediction, we need to keep constantly in mind the broad definition of aptitude.

---

29. Concerning the Nature and Nurture of Genius *

THE PROPER USE of our nation's intellectual resources may well be a decisive factor in national survival. Studies of intelligence seem to provide practical suggestions for a social policy designed to increase our reserves of this vital national resource. In this article, Dr. Pressey summarizes a variety of pertinent data and points out their implications in the light of present needs.

IT HAS BEEN well said that "in the present international tug of war, survival itself may depend upon making the most effective use of the nation's intellectual resources." Means of better identifying young people of superior intellectual capacities, and of getting more of them into present programs of advanced training, have been widely discussed. However, there has been relatively little consideration of whether present educational programs are best suited to the needs of our most brilliant young people. Superior abilities are now generally considered so predominantly a product of innate constitution that certain "educational" factors, possibly of very great importance in the growth of such abilities, are overlooked. It is sometimes well to get outside of current habits of thought and try to look at a topic in a reappraising way. This paper attempts so to do. It focuses attention on that most extraordinary type of very superior intellect—the precocious genius—as possibly exhibiting especially clearly both innate capacities and developmental influences involved in extraordinary accomplishment. It presumes to suggest that there may be ways by which many more "geniuses" might be not only discovered but even, to a substantial degree, *made* and brought to fruition.

* Sidney L. Pressey, "Concerning the nature and nurture of genius," *The Scientific Monthly,* LXXXI (September, 1955), 123–29. By permission of the author and the American Association for the Advancement of Science.

MAJOR FACTORS MAKING FOR PRECOCIOUS MARKED SUPERIORITY

An informal search for instances of marked precocity suggests that such cases have been especially frequent (or, at least, especially noted and featured) in certain fields and in certain localities at certain times. In the Europe of 100 to 200 years ago there were outstanding musicians of whom most were precocious. Handel played on the clavichord "when but an infant" and was composing by the age of 11. Haydn "played and composed at the age of 6." Mozart played the harpsichord at 3, was composing at 4, and was on a tour at 6. Chopin played in public at the age of 8; Liszt, at 9; Verdi, at 10; Schubert, at 12; and Rossini, at 14. Mendelssohn was playing publicly and also composing by the age of 9, as was Debussy at 11, Dvořák at 12, and Berlioz at 14. Wagner conducted one of his own compositions in public when he was 17.

Recently, and especially in this country, there have been many precocious athletes. Thus, Bobby Jones was state golf champion at 14. Marlene Bauer was playing notable golf at 13. Sonja Henie was figure-skating champion of Norway at 10 and world champion at 15. Barbara Anne Scott was Canadian figure-skating champion at 15. Vincent Richards was national tennis singles champion at 15, and Maureen Connolly was woman's singles champion at 16. Mel Ott was in big league baseball at 16; Feller, at 18. Eddie Lebaron was an intercollegiate football star at 16. Bob Mathias won an Olympic gold medal in track and field events at 17. The reader may doubt whether athletic champions are relevant to the topic of this paper but he can hardly question that they are very competent in their fields. Moreover, precocity in athletics and in musical performance might seem especially extraordinary because finger reach and dexterity on a musical instrument and strength, as well as skill and endurance, in athletic competition would seem especially to call for physical maturity.

An especially remarkable type of athlete must also be noted: the champion whose superiority emerged after great and persistent efforts to overcome a crippling handicap. Walt Davis, holder of a world's record in the high jump, was a former polio victim. Glenn Cunningham, the Olympic runner, was burned so severely in the legs when he was 8 years old that it was doubted that he would ever walk again. At the age of 8, Nancy Merki had polio and at 10 was more paralyzed, but at 13 she was high-point scorer in a national swimming meet. Other well-known athletes have had polio. In all these instances, the athletic prowess was the final result of very persistent (and usually expertly guided) efforts to overcome the handicap. There was no evidence before the injury or illness of notable athletic potential.

The first question, then, is why there should have been a rash of notable precocious musicians in the Europe of a century and more ago and a spate of youthful athletic champions in this country now. Certain major factors seem evident. In the Europe of that time, music was the major popular interest, reaching practically all social classes and all ages, and offering even to underprivileged youngsters the possibility of wide popular acclaim. Athletics is a similar interest in this country now. The second question is more specifically how, in such favorable total situations, have these prodigies come about. A study of their careers suggests that the following factors are important.

1. Precocious musicians and athletes usually had excellent early opportunities for the ability to develop and encouragement from family and friends. Mozart's father was a musician; his older sister was his companion in music; family and friends admired and encouraged the boy. Schubert's father was musical and fostered Franz's musical aptitude; soon Franz became a member of a string quartet with his father and two brothers. Of the athletes, Bobby Jones lived next to a golf course. When he was still a little boy, he was given small clubs and followed his father around the links. From early childhood, Barbara Anne Scott's skating was fostered by her father, and soon her whole life was so centered.

2. Usually individuals who developed precocious excellence had superior early and continuing individual guidance and instruction. From the age of 3, Mozart was taught, guided, and managed in his career by his father, who sought practically from the beginning to make his son an outstanding musician. Mendelssohn, also from the age of 3, was taught by his mother and other good musicians. Marlene Bauer's father, a golf professional, began to teach her the game when she was 3. Nancy Merki had an expert swimming coach.

3. Precocious individuals have had the opportunity frequently and continuingly to practice and extend their special ability and to progress as they were able. From the age of 3, Mozart practiced with his older sister; he had the opportunity to play the violin, the harpsichord, and the organ, to perform frequently in public, and a little later to conduct. From the age of 11, Maureen Connolly practiced tennis at least 3 hours a day. The climate of southern California made this possible at all seasons. She took on more able opponents and entered more important tournaments, as she was able. Nancy Merki was "in the water for hours at a time, just trying to master the trick of fluttering

her legs." Under the guidance of her coach she moved forward in her aquatic accomplishments as she was ready.

4. The special precocious ability usually brought a close association with others in the field, which greatly fostered the abilities of all concerned, and led to a still wider stimulating acquaintance. Mozart lived from early childhood in a world of musicians who listened to and watched one another, played together, cooperated, competed, raised levels of aspiration, and were keen in criticism and encouragement. His musicianship brought acquaintance with the great all over Europe, including the Austrian emperor. Bobby Jones lived largely in a golfers' world, which developed his skills at the same time that he raised golfing standards and increased the popularity of the sport. His friendships have indeed been wide, including President Eisenhower.

5. As a result of many opportunities for real accomplishment, within his possibilities but of increasing challenge, the precocious musician or athlete has had the stimulation of many and increasingly strong success experiences—and his world acclaimed these successes. It is well recognized that frequent failure and continued frustration may debilitate personality and competency, just as a disease does. But the opposite also seems true, although it is not generally appreciated: frequent, much-admired successes increase effort, build up psychosomatic vigor, make attempts more vigorous, and adequate, and better integrated, and build ability. The opinion is ventured that such "furtherance" is as important a phenomenon as frustration, and that systematic research regarding furtherance might well be as profitable as research on frustration has been.

At any age, development of any ability is fostered by a favorable immediate environment, expert instruction, frequent and progressive opportunities for the exercise of the ability, social facilitation, and frequent success experiences. Important advantages would seem to accrue from having these factors begin operation early. The physique may grow and adapt in congruence. As the young musician stretches out his hands and exercises needed muscles and coordinations, his skills may be not only learned but somewhat made part of his growth. This might be true, not for mechanical skills alone, but also for related integrations in the central nervous system, and for related percepts and concepts. So the precocious musicians played not only with skill but also with understanding, and they composed, notably and early. Possibly some integration of learning and growth might occur with abilities less closely related to a skill. Any ability, developing early, might benefit by having the great energies of childhood and youth devoted to it. Also, the child in the grip of a strong interest (as a hobby) seems often single-mindedly absorbed in it to an extent less common later, when problems of social status, economic responsibility, or the other sex may distract. If an interest is already well established when adolescence comes, the energies of that period may pour into it.

The thesis thus is that, in attempting to account for notable precocity in such fields as music and athletics, too much stress has been put on presumed extreme constitutional genius and too little on a concomitance of favorable factors, operating in the growth years. Instances of great athletic skill emerging from efforts to overcome a seemingly crippling handicap seem to emphasize the potency of these last factors. Presumably, the original physical potentials of these individuals were good, although not manifest, before the handicap struck; but the great potential of favoring circumstances seems especially evident. In this connection, Wechsler's argument may well be recalled—that the range of human physical traits, as in height, strength, and quickness, is really not great, and that the range in mental capacities may be less extreme than is usually supposed. Rather, superior original capacity, *growing under a favorable concomitance of circumstances,* develops into genius.

So far, the discussion has dealt primarily with outstanding precocious skills, in athletics and music. May the youthful organism not be capable of outstanding accomplishments more intellectual in nature? Here it should again be mentioned that notable musical performance would seem to involve keen musical understanding as well as dexterity (and outstanding athletic performance perhaps often involves more intelligence than is usually conceded). In youth, the famous precocious musicians not only performed but composed notably; and composing music is surely a highly intellectual activity.

But precocity has appeared in sundry other and clearly intellectual fields. John Stuart Mill began the study of Greek at 3. By the age of 8 he had read Xenophon, Herodotus, and Plato and had begun to study geometry and algebra. At 12 he began logic, reading Aristotle in the original. The next year he began the study of political economy; at 16 he was publishing controversial articles in that field. When he was 6 years old, John Ruskin wrote verse. Macaulay compiled a "universal history" at the age of 7. Published poems of William Blake, Thomas Chatterton, and Alexander Pope go back to their 12th years; poems of Robert Burns go back to his 14th year, and of Milton to his 15th year. Pascal wrote a treatise on acoustics when he was 12. Galileo made his famous observations of the swinging cathedral lamp when he was 17. Perkin discovered the first synthetic dye when he was 18. Farnsworth, at 15, "evolved an electronic means of sending pictures through the air." Recently, 11-year-old Italian Severino Guidi, 10-year-old Turkish Hasan Kaptan, and 11-year-old French Thierry Vaubourgoin have been mentioned as precocious painters. Norbert Wiener has written his sensitive account of his own precocity: college entrance at 11, Harvard doctorate at 18. However, as compared with music and athletics, precocity seems more rare in art, literature, and science, and especially so in this country. Why?

INFLUENCES HAMPERING THE PRECOCIOUS

There is a general belief, fostered in this country by most child psychologists and "progressive" educators during the past 25 years, that intellectual precocity is somehow not quite healthy, is almost always a hazard to good social adjustment, and should be slowed down rather than facilitated. In the home, the early-reading precocious child causes anxiety, in spite of the usualness of such precocity in Terman's gifted group and in biographies of famous men. The schools oppose entrance before the standard age of 6, in spite of the evidence, from some half-dozen experiments, that gifted tots admitted earlier have done well, both academically and adjustment-wise. The general public tends to regard the intellectually gifted small child as a freak. In short, there is usually none of the initial encouragement in the family, early fostering, and favorable general social climate that got many musical and athletic prodigies off to a flying start.

As a result of mass education and indifference to the needs of the gifted, there is almost none of the individualized guidance and instruction for excellence that was mentioned as an important element in the rapid development of precocity in music and athletics. A good music teacher is usually especially interested in finding and training pupils who are gifted musically. The athletic coach tries to find and bring to peak performance the ablest young athletes in his school. But the usual public school teacher does not have the time, the attitude, or the methods to do much, if anything, for another young Macaulay or Farnsworth in his classes.

In contrast to possibilities of continuing intensive practice and rapid progress in music or athletics, opportunities often are entirely lacking for a youngster to indulge intensively and continuingly an aptitude in such a field as a science, advancing as he is capable. A boy precociously interested in chemistry may have to await schoolwork in that subject until the regular course in his high-school junior year. He must then start and progress with his classmates, and in his senior year must take other subjects (intensive work in one field is frowned upon as interfering with a broad program) and not "hang around" the chemistry laboratory. Nor can the broadly gifted and precocious youngster advance in his total school program more rapidly than the average; acceleration is, in most schools, considered unwise.

Whereas the precocious young musician or athlete soon has an acceptance and a mounting status that is tremendously stimulating and educative for him, in musical or athletic groups—and these groups have status in school and community—the budding young scientist or scholar may be isolated or may associate only with a friend who is also considered "odd" or may belong only to an anemic subject club of no prestige in the community.

In contrast to the early and continuing successes of the young athlete or musician, possibly mounting to international acclaim, the young scholar or scientist may have no opportunities to make good except in class assignments and may obtain no evidence of success other than good marks. The teacher (perhaps made uncomfortable by keen questions) may even criticize his intense interest, and the other youngsters may call him sissy or odd. For him there is frustration, *not* the furtherance of cumulative success.

Suppose that Mozart or Bobby Jones had not been allowed to begin his music or his golf until the other children did, or to practice more or progress faster, or had had only the instruction of a school class in music or physical education. Suppose that they had been kept from playing with older children or adults in the fear that they might become socially maladjusted, kept from associating much with other musicians or golfers because that would be narrowing and undemocratic, kept from public performances or tournaments because that would be exploiting the poor child! It surely may be questioned whether they would then have reached the pre-eminence they did. Abuses in the afore-mentioned directions are, of course, possible. But it is also an abuse to withhold opportunities from precocious youngsters who are eager to advance and excel. The opinion is ventured that the last type of abuse is now, in this country, the more common one.

TOWARD MORE AND BETTER AMERICAN GENIUSES

The hypothesis thus is that a practicing genius is produced by giving a precocious able youngster early encouragement, intensive instruction, continuing opportunity as he advances, a congruent stimulating social life, and cumulative success experiences. In the instances given however, the circumstances have all been so superior as to seem somewhat out of reach. Moreover, there was sometimes imbalance or exploitation. In the average college or school, what steps might be possible that would move with reasonable caution and good sense in the directions indicated here and perhaps somewhat benefit a great many youngsters as well as occasionally help toward the production of a "genius"? Two steps would seem feasible and of great possible fruitfulness.

The first proposal is that there should be, in a college or a school system, a person who might be given the somewhat colorless title of coordinator of special programs, lest the more precise label of personnel specialist for superior students cause them embarrassment and antagonize parents of students not selected or served by him. Such a person in a college should scan each entering student's record to find high-school valedictorians, science-fair winners, and others with evidence of superior ability. He should watch for such evidence especially among students in the freshman year. He might even follow reports on high-school science fairs and the like and recruit promising youngsters for his college in the manner of a football coach. (If other colleges object to this, maybe competition among colleges for the intellectually superior might be a good thing!) As he locates such cases he should seek them out, encourage them, and bring them to the attention of appropriate faculty members. He should try to help these students in any problems they have, find opportunities for them on campus, and perhaps arrange summer work or travel opportunities. He should make a special effort to bring congenial members of his group together and to foster stimulating companionship and morale. He should see to it that his program receives publicity and that his youngsters receive recognition. He should guide and further any plans they have for professional or graduate training and for careers.

In a secondary school or school superintendent's office, a person similarly designated to find and foster the most able students would try to keep the elementary schools alert to discover especially bright children there. As these move on to high school, he could watch for them. He would have the high-school teachers inform him of outstanding students in their classes and keep alert for other evidences of talent, as in hobbies. He would become acquainted with all such youngsters, encourage them, and bring them into contact with appropriate teachers and into appropriate subject clubs or other groups. Educative trips with other youngsters might be arranged and perhaps summer work that would be both financially and educationally profitable. A local business or professional man might be enlisted to sponsor an outstanding youngster who needed such support. Contacts might be readied with a college or university.

If such guidance or personnel specialists for the most able were generally available in colleges and high schools or public school systems, it is believed that they could greatly increase the number of young people going into advanced training, select them better, and greatly improve the effectiveness of their education. Such a position might be only half time, for a student counselor or assistant principal, but it should be seen as his distinctive opportunity. If in a college, he would work with the ablest students, the best teachers on the faculty, and the best professional and graduate schools. If in a secondary school, he would deal with the finest students and the community leaders most interested in young people. He would try cumulatively to build community interest in and opportunities for these ablest young people, as through the local papers and service clubs. He would have mutually profitable relationships with the best colleges and universities. At regional and national meetings, as of guidance associations, these personnel workers at all levels would meet with others doing like work. Slowly, they might change public attitudes to interest in the intellectually, as well as the athletically, able. Surely no position could be more finely rewarding.

It is not enough, however, to provide special student personnel or guidance service for superior students. *In proportion as they are very able and especially as they have special talents, special adaptations of the usual curriculums are likely to be desirable.* The able youngster not yet sure of his special interests may wish to explore very widely. Once he has found that interest he may, legitimately, wish to push it hard. Before long, his accomplishments may warrant his admission into courses ahead of his status. (The sophomore may desire some course not usually available before the junior year.) Soon, he may be ready for an independent project under supervision of one of the ablest teachers, for an honors seminar, perhaps a project off campus or work experience in the field of his interest—first attempts at real accomplishment in that field. There should be readily usable administrative machinery—it might be called an honors program—making it possible for an able student, perhaps under the guidance of a person as mentioned in the previous paragraphs, and under the general direction of a faculty committee, to have certain curricular freedoms and special opportunities to foster best his potentialities.

It should be possible to adapt school and college programs to the needs of superior youngsters with regard to not only the nature of these programs but also their length. Occasionally a late start or an added year in school or college may be warranted. Far more often, an early start and rapid progress are desirable. Not only the occasional prodigy but most people of superior abilities show their superiority early and develop more rapidly than the average person. Moreover, impressive evidence indicates that intellectual creativity reaches its peak relatively early in adult life. The practically universal American educational policy, nevertheless, is the lockstep: every child must enter school at 6 (none more than a month or so earlier), progress a grade a year, and, if he seeks advanced training, continue his schooling often till around 30, which was the median age of receiving the doctorate in this country just before World War II. Now, military service may delay even more the completion of education. Yet numerous studies are practically unanimous in showing that able children can enter earlier and progress more rapidly than the average child, without harm and often with gain in regard to realized abilities and social adjustment. Outcomes have been thus favorable in spite of most common use of the *worst* methods for "acceleration"—grade-skipping in school and a lengthened year in college. Better methods—admission to the first grade on the basis of readiness for school rather than chronological age, replacement of the first three grades by a "primary pool" out of which children would move early or late depending on when they finish primary work, rapid-progress sections doing 3 years' work in 2 in junior and senior high school, and credit by examination in college—should permit each youngster to move through educational programs at his own pace, without being conspicuous if his rate is not that of the average.

Not only are accelerates usually successful and happy in school, but they are more likely to complete collegiate and advanced training. At Ohio State University, 50 per cent of the students entering when they were 16 years old graduated, but only 38 per cent of the 18-year-old entrants paired with them according to tested general ability at entrance and type of program. With selection for acceleration and guidance therein, outcomes should be even better. Of a group of students selected in their freshman year as capable of finishing a 4-year program in less time and guided in so doing 63 per cent graduated. Further, accelerates seem more often successful in their careers than individuals proceeding through their education at the usual pace. From 1880 to 1900, 29 per cent of those graduating from Amherst at 19 became nationally known, as compared with 12 per cent of those graduating at 22. Of those in Terman's gifted group who graduated from high school under the age of 15 years and 6 months, 16 per cent more graduated from college and 19 per cent more took one or more years of graduate work than did those who finished high school when they were 16 years and 6 months or older, although there was little difference between the two groups in general ability when they were tested in childhood.

(The average IQ's of the two groups at that time were 158 and 149, respectively.) Moreover, twice as many of the first group (42 per cent as compared with 19 per cent) were very superior in respect to career.

In short, simply to increase the number of bright American youngsters who "accelerate" should substantially increase the number obtaining technologic or other advanced training and make it easier for precocious genius to emerge. If it were possible for bright youngsters not only to move through school more rapidly but also in other ways to have their programs adjusted to their special needs, still more might be expected to complete such training, still more successfully, and with still more notable careers following. Moreover, they would finish their training and get into their productive careers sooner. And educational costs would probably be reduced! Thus it seems a reasonable estimate that every year there remain in the secondary schools around 300,000 students whom a reasonable program of acceleration would have graduated. Such a reduction in enrollment would involve substantial savings, which might more than provide for the suggested special counselors for the gifted.

To meet the needs for trained manpower mentioned at the beginning of this paper, greater efforts to interest bright students in collegiate and advanced training programs (as they are now), better guidance of students in those programs, and more scholarship or other financial aid, have been suggested. The suggestion is here ventured that special facilitated programs adapted to the needs of the gifted would be the best means of interesting them, that special guidance in such programs (as suggested here) would best keep these students in school, and that such facilitated and early-completed programs (often including paid work experience) would substantially reduce the need for financial aid to students. Finally, the proposed special measures should produce more "geniuses." To produce persons of notable accomplishment, educational efforts should be directed straight toward that goal, in the light of all that can be found out about such persons and their upbringing. Simply to increase the number of students in physical education classes would probably *not* very much increase the number of athletic champions!

VII

THINKING

THE LAYMAN is often surprised to discover how little space psychology texts devote to thinking as a topic. The reason for this apparent neglect is that much of the relevant material appears in discussions of other topics. Thus we find discussions of associations of ideas under *learning,* analyses of feelings and emotions under *motivation,* the attribution of meaning to experience under *perception,* fantasies and daydreaming under *personality.* Little, therefore, is left to the topic of thinking.

Most texts provide excellent discussions of the *processes* involved in thinking and in creativity. Three of the selections that follow are designed to supplement such discussions by reviewing recent researches on thinking *abilities,* suggesting the bases for developing practical methods for improving one kind of thinking (problem solving), and dealing with the existence of a *need* to think. In addition, one paper re-examines the nature of dreams, most often discussed in modern texts as an expression of wishes and needs, and suggests a different function, that of creative thinking. On this basis analysis of dreams should throw light on the individual's cognitive (intellectual) functioning rather than only his conative (striving) processes.

30. *Some Recent Findings on Thinking Abilities and Their Implications* *

AS WE HAVE LEARNED more about intelligence and other aptitudes, we have recognized the limitations of these concepts. We no longer

* J. P. Guilford, "Some recent findings on thinking abilities and their implications," *Informational Bulletin,* USAF Air Training Command, III (Fall, 1952), 48–61. By permission of the author and the *Instructors Journal.* Address given in the Contemporary Problems in Psychology series at San Diego State College, California, June 24, 1952.

assume naively that the quality of one's thinking depends on a unitary something called "intelligence," measure his I.Q., and believe that we are in a position to predict his performance in specific situations. Recent studies have revealed and analyzed the operation of specific abilities involved in different kinds of thinking. Here Dr. Guilford reviews the current status of this important forward-looking work.

THE FINDINGS contained in this article come primarily from studies that have been under way for three or four years at the University of Southern California. The general project has been known as the investigation of aptitudes of high-level personnel. High-level personnel are defined to include scientists, engineers, inventors, and persons in supervisory and administrative positions. For the financial support of these studies we have been indebted, first, to the U.S. Navy Electronics Laboratory here in San Diego, second, and primarily, to the U.S. Navy Office of Naval Research, and third, for one study, to the U.S. Air Force. The U.S. Air Force has also contributed generously the aid of its testing facilities. Without the aid from all these sources these investigations would not be possible.[1]

The findings have come through the application of the techniques of factor analysis and they throw considerable light on important aspects of intellectual abilities and functions. I shall have much more to say about the findings than about their implications. In our findings are suggestions about the nature of thinking and of intelligence that may eventually contribute to basic psychological theory. There are more direct implications for vocational psychology—for theory of aptitudes and for practices of selection, classification, and guidance. Very little psychological theory is without its implications in the field of education, hence our results should be of some interest to educators.

Although thinking is usually regarded as man's highest and most useful function, progress toward its understanding has been very slow. Progress in the understanding of any subject is indicated roughly by the number of useful and enduring concepts that have been invented to describe it. The terminology with which we describe phenomena of thinking is essentially that of our pre-scientific psychological ancestors. The vocabulary of commonly accepted terms is astonishingly small. The textbook terminology includes such terms as induction and deduction, abstraction and generalization, inference, and concept formation.

[1] The major contract is known as N6onr-23810. Neither the Navy nor the Air Force necessarily endorses our opinions or conclusions. A number of psychologists have been associated with me in these studies, among whom I should mention Andrew L. Comrey, Russell F. Green, Paul R. Christensen, and Robert C. Wilson.

Gestalt psychology added the concepts of closure and insight. Spearman, in developing his theory of cognition, proposed the concepts of *eduction of relations* and of *eduction of correlates.* By *eduction of relations* he meant that when we are presented with two objects we can see relations between them. By *eduction of correlates* he meant that when we are presented with an object plus a relationship we can think of a second object to complete the picture—two objects in relation. Neither the Gestalt concepts nor the Spearman concepts have gained much currency. Many other descriptive concepts that have been proposed have apparently fallen on stony ground.

One suspects that there must be something wrong with concepts, which, although well accepted, have made for so little progress. I think that there are several reasons why terms like induction and deduction have had their appeal and yet have failed to make for progress. They were inherited by psychology from logic and in that context they had about them a suggestion of clear-cut opposition which was deceiving. Even logicians now shy away from these terms, realizing that in application they do not represent clear opposites. The terms have served with enough descriptive value for psychologists, however, to keep them alive as working concepts. As the crudest sort of first approximations they have been moderately descriptive in both popular and psychological use where the user is not too demanding of accuracy.

From the standpoint of vocational psychology, the subject of thinking is most important because of its relationship to intelligence. Before Binet developed his famous intelligence scale, he had spent many years in research on thinking. Various types of thinking tests found their places in his scale. Terman has defined intelligence as the ability to do abstract thinking and evidently has been fully as sympathetic to thinking tests as was Binet. It is a curious turn of events, however, that factor analysis has revealed the chief component of most intelligence tests to be not a primary thinking ability but the primary ability known as verbal comprehension. The ability of verbal comprehension might be classified as a thinking ability, since it implies mastery of concepts, and concept formation is a form of thinking. Verbal comprehension is best measured by a vocabulary test, however, and one that does not necessarily call for very profound knowledge of word meanings. A reading knowledge seems to be all that is necessary. The verbal factor correlates very highly with most measures of school achievement. That is why it has gained such a prominent place in intelligence tests. Factorial studies have shown a wealth of thinking abilities that are but slightly touched by ordinary intelligence tests. This is one of the reasons factorial studies in the realm of thinking abilities are so important.

Perhaps it is desirable at this point to say why we may expect to determine anything about the nature of thinking abilities and functions by means of factor analysis. Factor analysis is a systematic procedure for summarizing intercorrelations of scores or other measures. Intercorrelations are measures of the covariations in behavior. Covariation is one of the most common evidences we have of order and system in nature. One could study the covariations by other methods than that of factor analysis. The story to be told by a table of intercorrelations could be ascertained by other methods, but as yet there is apparently no other as efficient or as searching as that of factor analysis. If one wanted to find the unique, independent measures of abilities, for example, he could keep hunting until he finds test that correlate zero with all other tests except those measuring the same ability. This would be an expensive and time-consuming procedure.

Once we have found measures of a unique ability, by whatever method we may use, what do we have? The practical vocational psychologist may be satisfied in having identified such an ability and in having determined what tests he needs to measure it. Some factor analysts would stop at this point. The average psychologist, however, would be dissatisfied with this limited outcome. He would be struck by the fact that here is some unitary and stable property of individuals that is characterized by tests of certain common features. He would interpret the factor and give it a psychologically meaningful name; one that tends to integrate the factor in the general body of psychological knowledge. There need be no implication that there is a corresponding bodily organ or even a psychological unity that underlies the hypothesized ability. The named primary ability is merely a label for the whole body of observed data that indicate some systematic fact about behavior of a certain character. Thinking is behavior and it is the business of psychologists to comprehend it. The discovery of the focal points of thinking activity should be a long step in the direction of this goal of understanding.

As a matter of fact, when it is properly applied to the study of any area of behavior, factor analysis by no means carries the entire burden; it is used merely as a helping tool. In an investigation aimed at the illumination of the basic abilities or functions in a certain area, it is used to test hypotheses we may have concerning those abilities or functions and to suggest new hypotheses where new hypotheses are needed. Much of the time of the investigator is spent in speculating about the nature of the separate abilities in that area, starting from anything he knows about it derived from any promising source. The analysis should give him some answers regarding the accuracy of his hypotheses. Such answers are never fully decisive but they rarely fail to add some light where light is needed.

Our investigations of thinking have not attempted to cover the whole realm of thinking abilities in any one analysis. The scope of that realm is entirely too large. For convenience we have approached each one of several domains separately—one domain comprised of reasoning abilities; one of creative-thinking abilities; one of evaluative abilities, including judgment; and one of planning abilities. After studying each one separately we will investigate them in combinations to see what they may have in common. We have completed two analyses of reasoning abilities and one of creative-thinking abilities and we are well on the way in a study of evaluative abilities.

Definitions are probably overdue. As defined in my *General Psychology* thinking is the broad term that includes all symbolic behavior. Symbolic behavior uses symbols as substitutes for perceived things. The symbols may be in the form of such things as muscular sets, images, or concepts. There can be objective evidence for the occurrence of any of these, though it must usually be indirect. Reasoning is defined as thinking directed toward the solution of a problem. Its common outcome is a conclusion or inference. Creative thinking is the production of new mental constructs that become evident in such things as scientific theories, novels, paintings, and musical compositions. Evaluation is critical thinking by which steps or end products are accepted or rejected. In evaluation, decisions are reached as to the relative merits of ideas or as to whether they measure up to some criterion. The concept of planning abilities follows the popular meaning of the term. The abilities found involved in planning activities may, after all, reduce to those also found in the domains of reasoning and creative thinking.

What was the situation with regard to the understanding of reasoning abilities, let us say, roughly, as of 1950? Binet, Terman, and Spearman regarded all tests of thinking, including reasoning, as measures of a single master ability, intelligence. In his first study of primary abilities, Thurstone distinguished three reasoning factors. One he called inductive reasoning and another deductive reasoning, thus adapting the traditional terminology for two of the factors. He defined inductive reasoning as the *discovering* of rules or principles and deductive reasoning as the *application* of rules. Inductive ability was found most loaded in tests involving the discovery of relationships. Deductive ability was found most loaded in syllogism tests of the true-false type. The third factor he hesitated to call reasoning at all. It was a prominent feature of an arithmetic-reasoning test. He defined it as reasoning under restrictive conditions, meaning by this that the arithmetic problem as given prescribed the boundaries for thinking. A number of subsequent studies from the University of Chicago laboratory have verified the so-called inductive and deductive factors but rarely the restrictive-reasoning factor.

In the wartime research in the AAF (Army Air Forces), the factor found prominent in an arithmetic-reasoning test repeatedly, became known as *general reasoning* because it also appeared in so many other types of tests. Two other reasoning factors were found but they could not be clearly defined as either inductive or deductive. There was no reason to expect Thurstone's deductive factor because no syllogistic tests were used. Briefly, this was the situation at the time we began our analyses of reasoning abilities. There is not time here to go into the planning of these studies. The chief efforts were to clear up the picture of both Thurstone's and the AAF factors. I can mention only the results briefly.

We are now quite satisfied that the general-reasoning factor of the AAF and Thurstone's restrictive-reasoning factor are one and the same. It continues to be baffling as to interpretation because of its appearance in so many different kinds of tests. The arithmetic-reasoning type of test continues to be its most faithful indicator. Our present conception is that it is an ability to structure a problem preparatory to its solution. It is necessary to relate two or more facts in doing so, and the likelihood of much trial-and-error thinking during the grasping of the problem seems to be a common feature.

It is interesting that the U.S. Employment Service, in selecting its primary abilities for vocational-testing purposes has called this factor *general intelligence*. It is undoubtedly of much general utility but the fact that it shows no relationship to many component parts of good intelligence tests should cause one to reject this name for it. Next to the verbal-comprehension ability this factor is probably the strongest contributor to the total variance of intelligence tests. One of my students has found a test of this factor significantly correlated with grades in most types of college-freshman courses, though usually correlating with them less than does a test of the verbal factor.

Among tests of the inductive type, we have found evidence for three factors, two of which came out in both analyses. The key to these factors is the examinee's discovery of something. To borrow Spearman's terminology we have called the discovery factors (1) eduction of *perceptual* relations, (2) eduction of *conceptual* relations, and (3) eduction of conceptual *patterns*. The AAF factor called "reasoning II" is probably identifiable with the first of these: eduction of perceptual relations. Thurstone's inductive factor is probably best identified with the second one: eduction of conceptual relations. The first inductive factor, eduction of perceptual relations, is characteristic of tests whose items are in the form of figures. The second, eduction of conceptual relations, is characteristic of tests in which the items are composed of numbers, letters, or words. The third, eduction of conceptual patterns, occurs in tests with both figural and non-figural content. The thing discovered is a system of relations.

Two of these inductive or discovery factors were verified in a second analysis and must therefore be given much credence—the eduction of perceptual relations and the eduction of conceptual relations. The separation of relation-seeing abilities along these lines is psychologically interesting. Gestalt psychology, especially, has emphasized the continuity of perception and thinking. This line of theorizing would lead to the belief that discovering relationships is the same function whether the things related are perceived figures or ideas or concepts. The separation of these two discovery factors indicates that this is not so. In general, this finding warns us not to assume too much generality for any ability or trait that we may hypothesize. It also demonstrates the importance of determining the degree of generality possessed by any trait, for our range of prediction of behavior is definitely limited by the scope or range of applicability of the trait.

In the area roughly known as deduction, we have found two factors. One of these is what Thurstone calls deduction, and, as usual, it is best measured by means of syllogistic types of tests. It should be pointed out that these tests have been of the true-false or multiple-choice form. The examinee may possibly draw his own conclusions from the facts given, i.e., he makes a deduction, but by the very nature of the test items, he has conclusions given to him and all that he has to do, essentially, is to decide whether they are consistent with the premises. It is possible, then, that the essence of this so-called deductive factor is not the ability to *draw* conclusions but the ability to *evaluate* conclusions; to decide whether they are logically consistent with the premises. We have consequently tentatively renamed the factor "logical reasoning," and have defined it as a sensitivity to logical consistency. The ability may belong rather in the domain of evaluation and we are making an intensive study of it in that connection. In order to determine whether there is another factor representing an ability to draw conclusions, we are including some syllogistic tests in *completion* form, in which the examinee will have to draw his own conclusion. He will, to be sure, also exercise some logical evaluation in deciding whether the answer he gives is a correct conclusion, and to that extent the syllogistic test in completion form would also measure the factor of logical reasoning. It remains to be seen whether there is in addition a genuine deductive or inference-drawing-ability factor as we have predicted.

The second factor in the deductive area we have called *eduction of correlates,* to borrow another of Spearman's terms. Spearman's armchair analysis of intelligence has proven to be better in many ways than his statistical analysis. He analyzed intelligence logically by stating three general principles of cognition, eduction of relations and eduction of correlates being the most important. He recognized that different kinds of relations exist, depending upon the kinds of objects presented. He was led to his logical analysis by observation of different kinds of tests that he thought to be the best measures of his universal *g* factor. Had he been less determined to find a *g* factor, his statistical analyses might also have led him to the discovery of important group factors separating along the lines of his logical analysis.

Let us now turn to the domain of creative thinking. In his preliminary research, Binet regarded imaginative thinking as an important aspect of intelligence, and he sprinkled a few tests requiring inventive thinking in his scale. Any unique variance that these tests may have contributed to the total determination of a mental age and an IQ was evidently completely overshadowed by variance in other abilities. This is true also of the Stanford Revision. In group tests of intelligence there is usually to be found none of it. And yet, of all the achievements of human intellect, those of greatest social importance have been of the inventive kind. Had the practical criterion of intelligence included creative production, we would have had quite different intelligence tests. Instead, the criterion has usually been docile grade-getting, which calls for measures of non-creative abilities to predict it.

In this connection I might refer again to the U.S. Employment Service battery of tests of primary aptitudes. I am definitely in sympathy with the general principle on which this battery is based, i.e., the use of several unique scores rather than the attempt to get along with one composite score. But, as the U.S. Employment Service itself recognizes, the aptitudes are much restricted to non-intellectual factors, which are important in skilled and semi-skilled types of labor but which do not begin to take care of the persons in professional types of work. The two aptitude scores representing verbal comprehension and general reasoning cover fairly well the variance in traditional intelligence tests, but they fall far short when it comes to distinguishing persons of good promise for professional and administrative functions. The extension of measurement to the reasoning factors I have mentioned should be a great help in this direction. For some purposes the extension should also include the creative abilities which I will now discuss. In this connection I will ask you to keep in mind that the findings here are from a single analysis and for the most part need verification.

With the research scientist particularly in mind, we hypothesized an ability to see problems, or to be sensitive to the existence of problems. How general this sensitivity might be we could not predict. It might include sensitivity to defects, deficiencies, gaps in our knowledge, incongruities, and even the odd and the unusual in general. The analysis showed a factor of this type but it appears to be limited to the sensitivity to defects of a practical nature, such as those in gadgets like the telephone or refrigerator or those in social institutions, such as elections. It was established, however, that the person who is likely to see defects in mechanical things is also likely to see them in social institutions. Two such tests correlate very substantially.

It was thought that all types of creative people have in common a fluency of ideas. In such people stimuli touch off a rapid flow of thinking responses. Previous to our study of creativity a number of fluency factors had been found and verified. We had the problem of determining whether these factors covered all types of fluency or whether there would be any new types discoverable. Our findings verify the three best-established types of fluency and reveal no new type. These three types are as follows: There is a word-fluency factor first discovered by Thurstone. This is apparently a rather superficial type of fluency, in which word meanings have no essential role. It is merely the ability to call up rapidly words with which one is very familiar. There is an associational fluency in which word meaning is an important condition. The ease with which one can think of synonyms or opposites or words meeting other specifications indicates the nature of the ability. The third factor in this area is ideational fluency, involving the speed with which one can call up ideas that are related to a given topic or that serve a certain purpose.

Concerning the social importance of these fluency factors we can readily speculate. It would seem that the word-fluency factor has little social significance. It should be useful in such games as cross-word puzzles, where words as letter patterns are emphasized, little more. It may be of some consequence in reading, but only under difficult conditions of illumination etc.

The associational-fluency factor is probably of considerable importance for writers and lecturers where one wants suitable words to be readily on tap. Whether accuracy of expression is facilitated by this ability is hard to say. But the descriptive writer who wants to liven his product by injecting variations of terminology should find the ability very useful.

Of the three fluency factors, that of ideational fluency is probably of greatest importance in the lives of creative people in general. When one is faced with a problem, in defining the problem he usually thinks of one hypothesis after another. The ease with which his store of potential hypotheses can be aroused will determine in part how quickly a good hypothesis comes along. After he has defined the problem, again, he thinks in quick succession of many possible solutions. The more rapidly he can call up possible solutions the more quickly he may reach one that will be accepted. In the process of evaluating either hypotheses or solutions, too, he needs to call up the implications of each one so that he can weigh it properly. Being able to see quickly the several consequences of one's proposed actions leads to a greater proportion of wise decisions.

We hypothesized that the creative person is a *flexible* thinker. He can break away from old habits of thinking and strike out in new directions. He is not rigid in a way that would make him stick to, or come back repeatedly to, wrong ideas or solutions.

Our findings show two flexibility factors. One of these appears in tests in which there is considerable freedom of response, as in a fluency test. In one fluency test we asked the examinee to name all the uses he could think of for a common brick and he was given eight minutes to do this. The fluency score was the total number of responses he gave. A flexibility score, based on the same responses, was the number of times he changed *classes* of uses. Some examinees confine their total list to one or two categories, such as the use of bricks in building or as a missile for throwing. Other examinees often change categories, giving few responses per category. The two scores are relatively independent. We have, then, a spontaneous type of flexibility, a lability of mental set, which in the extreme may entail a discursive type of thinking. In the pathological extremity we may have the manic flight of ideas or the circumstantiality of the senile. Those pathological conditions are worth studying from this point of view.

Spontaneous flexibility is probably not a great advantage to the creative person who must solve problems, such as the research scientist. In such connections there must be much goal-directed thinking. Too low a degree of the trait, however, might mean a rigidity that is inhibiting. This ability or trait is more likely to be of importance to writers like Gertrude Stein and to writers of comedy. I would expect the pun maker to stand high on this factor and in our next study of creativity there will be a pun-making test.

The second flexibility factor occurs in tests in which there is problem solving and in which the type of solution changes radically from problem to problem. In more general terms, the solution of each problem is facilitated by the ability of the examinee to break away from former habits of thinking and to do things in a new and unusual way. In one test, for example, he solves very simple numerical equations but under the instruction that a plus sign now means multiply and a division sign means add, and so on. A person who is bound to his habits will have difficulty in such tests. Such a person is probably not going to solve problems in life readily when new methods are required. I think it is with respect to this trait that our educational practices sometimes do much harm. We teach students to depend too much upon tried and successful methods taught in textbooks. They come to believe in the universal validity of those methods and ways of thought, with the consequence that where those methods and ways no longer work, as one often finds, he is sunk. The trail blazers in any field are those who are not habit-bound or custom-bound in their operations and outlooks in that field.

We are accustomed to think of the heart of creativity as being originality. Efforts were made in our investigation to approach the measurement of originality in quite a variety of ways. One approach was the scoring of responses by weighting them in proportion to their degree of statistical uncommonness in the population. This was in completion tests whose items were open-ended, i.e., the examinee could give any one of a very large number of responses, as in projective tests. The more unconventional his response, the less commonly it was given by others, the more weight it received. Another approach to the measurement of originality was by means of remote associations. The items of such tests called for the examinee to see far-fetched connections or rare and uncommon associations. In one test we asked for the listing of consequences of specified social changes, such as the repeal of all local and national laws. A fluency score was the total number of rather obvious consequences given. An originality score was the number of remote or indirect consequences given. A third approach to originality was in terms of ratings of the degree of *cleverness* of responses. In one fluency test the examinee was to name as many titles as he could for a short story. The responses were separated into two categories, clever and not-clever. The number of clever responses was taken as an originality score.

All three approaches proved to give measures of a single common factor that could be called originality. In view of the variety of scores developed for this purpose we should not have been surprised to find two or three factors in this area. The finding of only one and the discovery that there are so many ways to measure it was a very happy result, for some of the scoring methods are quite laborious and some are quite subjective and thus the better methods can be selected.

One very interesting finding with respect to the originality factor is its apparent bipolarity. By this we mean that some test scores were negatively related to it. High scores in some tests mean low originality and low scores mean high originality. When we examine these tests we find that as a group they are multiple-choice tests and that they are of the best-answer type. Furthermore, there is usually no one uncontestable right answer. The key is made up by decision of the test maker or by consulting the consensus of responses. In other words, the conventional response is the keyed response and it contributes to a higher score. The unconventional response is penalized by being called wrong. The examinee who gives an unconventional response may actually be doing a clever thing and if he could explain his reasons one might feel compelled to give him credit.

There is an important moral in this for educational practice, especially in connection with achievement examinations. Like many other teachers I have for years used the objectively scored type of examinations. I still believe that their virtues are many, but our finding that the original person may be penalized by this type of examination should give some pause for thought. I do not think that it is the multiple-choice form alone that sins in this respect. If one gave credit only for conventional responses to completion items the original person would also be penalized. One should not assume, either, that by contrast to multiple-choice examinations the essay examination is necessarily a measure of creativity. If the student knows or suspects, as he has good reason to suspect, that his examination paper will be graded on how well he repeats the ideas of the text or of his instructor, he will have little inducement to be creative in an essay examination. And if the one who marks the paper gives credit only for conventional statements, this form of measurement, too, will penalize the creative student. It is not the form of examination, then, that favors either the creative or the conventional student. It is the educational philosophy of the instructor and of the marker of examinations, the way in which the examination is written, and the way in which the scoring key is set up. One device I have used for several years in connection with multiple-choice items is to urge the examinee to write a brief explanation of his response if he has any doubts about its being the keyed one. He is given credit for a well-supported non-keyed answer. It might be good practice at times to *require* the examinee to explain every answer he gives, particularly in true-false tests, for I have a hunch that the creative student often feels so much confidence in a wrong answer that he does not attempt to explain it even when he has a chance.

One additional factor was found in the domain of creative thinking. From Gestalt psychology we derived the idea that an important quality of inventive people is the ability to re-define or to transform objects. Koehler's apes had to redefine the functions of sticks, boxes, and poles, in order to adapt them to their use as tools. Many a person in a practical situation has been able to solve his problem by adapting one object or a part of it to new uses. The story is told of a disabled military bomber landing in the wastes of the Arctic region. Of all the crew, one sergeant showed considerable facility for improvising. Using things at hand from the airplane, he set up a shelter complete with cooking and heating facilities. The apparent psychological element common to such improvising is the dropping away of old functions for things and the attaching of new ones. One might think that the factors of flexibility and originality would take care of this function. Our tests of improvising ability showed practically no relation to those factors, however, but had in common a separate factor which could be called *redefinition.*

What is the significance of these findings concerning reasoning and creative-thinking factors, for psychology, for vocational practices, and for education? As each factor was mentioned I have usually said something about its specific implications in one or more of these fields. Something remains to be said concerning the more general conclusions that we might draw in these connections.

Psychologists have not ordinarily looked to factor analysis to establish facts of a general or systematic nature. The factors found, usually in the study of individual differences, have as yet made little impression on the experimental psychologist who studies mental phenomena at closer range. In view of the power of factor analysis to turn up a wealth of hypotheses and to verify factors in repeated analyses, it is time that experimental psychologists paid more attention to factorial findings. There is no question about the ability of factor analysis to demonstrate confirmed unities in behavior through the study of its covariations. Closer examination into the nature of those unities calls for the employment of experimental techniques. It is true that we often introduce some features of an experiment into the planning of a factor analysis. For example, we vary certain properties of tests systematically and watch for effects on factor loadings. In the absence of tests of statistical significance, however, such effects cannot be assessed with the confidence one would like.

For vocational psychology the findings I have reported have a number of important meanings. For one thing, we need to enlarge once more our ideas concerning the probable number of aptitude factors that exist. Those who were brought up under the theory that there is but one aptitude and that aptitude is intelligence, may be appalled at the growing complexity of things. The belief in and use of a single measure of aptitude is certainly simple and comfortable. But it is also very restricting. If all I could know about the mental abilities of a person were a single score, I agree that it should be his IQ. But I should want to know how the factors are weighted in the particular IQ obtained. And I should realize that there are many things about this person's capabilities that I still did not know. I should know that under present methods of obtaining IQ's even much of intellect had not been touched. If I were a vocational counselor I should certainly want to know this person's scores in perhaps 20 different primary abilities, nonintellectual as well as intellectual. If I were called upon to distinguish his potentialities in professional and managerial occupations I should want his scores on many of the thinking abilities. This presupposes, of course, additional research which would demonstrate the importance of these factors for high-level personnel. In this direction we are starting validation studies with engineers, research scientists, and supervisory personnel. We believe it is important that factorial results be studied as soon as possible in connection with assessments of individuals from another source.

Educational practices are likely to be affected somewhat through changes in ideas about vocational aptitudes and in vocational practices. Our findings may thus indirectly affect education through their effects on vocational theory and practice. There should be more direct effects, however, on educational theory and practice.

For as many years as I can remember, it has been announced as an important aim of education to make students think and to train them in thinking habits. In view of how little we have known about the psychology of thinking this is a little like attempting to train a student in a sport concerning which no-one knows much about the rules. If we have succeeded at all in training students to think we have done it like the wrestler who proceeds on the catch-as-catch-can basis. Some students, fortunately, by dint of opportunities presented to them discover methods of thinking by a trial-and-error route. Others have good models to imitate or mentors to correct their errors. I believe that with more accurate knowledge of the thinking abilities we can do a much better job of teaching others how to think. Goals will become clearer. The kinds of exercises needed by the student to approach those goals will be more apparent.

The Thurstones have suggested that children be trained specifically in each primary ability by giving them exercises tailored for this purpose. Even first-grade children have been given exercises in several primary abilities, including the one they have called inductive thinking. I do not know whether well-controlled experiments have been conducted in this connection but the suggestion is interesting to the educator because in some respects it harks back to the days of belief in formal discipline. The chief differences are that today we have determined the primary abilities by empirical methods and that the type of discipline is more obviously designed for the purpose.

It may be that the natural consequence of the discovery of primary abilities is to promote their development or their usefulness in individuals by appropriate, specific exercises. This is something for educational theorists to consider and to explore. It may be assumed to start with that each primary ability or its utilization is something that can be improved by training. Until we have attempted to develop it by training of an appropriate sort we will never know whether it can or cannot be so developed. Educational theory and practice have generally steered between the belief in broad and general transfers as expected from the formal-discipline theory, at the one extreme, and the belief in no transfer as expected from the specific-skills theory, at the other extreme. It is important at this time to investigate the possible connections between areas of transfer and the primary abilities, a procedure that also avoids those extremes.

If we wish to train students to be creative producers, the creative factors should give us much to think about. Like most behavior, creative activity probably represents to some extent many learned skills. There may be limitations set on these skills by heredity, but I am convinced that through learning one can extend the skills within those limitations. The least that we can do is to remove the blocks that are often in the way. Everyone can be creative to some degree in many ways. Recognizing this simple truth is an important beginning. Knowing what the aspects of creative thinking are is another big step. The rest depends upon practice, practice, practice. Society's responsibility is to provide favorable environment and education and the appropriate rewards for creative production.

---

31. Can We Train Better Problem-Solvers? *

THE CONFLICT between effective training and personal initiative and creativity in thinking is a matter of concern to educators, industrial leaders, and men of affairs. As more and more problems arise in our complex, technological living, it becomes increasingly important to answer the question: Can people be trained to solve problems without indoctrinating them with a routine that makes independent thinking impossible? Dr. Hilgard discusses a number of significant researches that seem to suggest answers. The general response seems to be in the affirmative, although much work remains to be done on methods for bringing about the desired result.

WE HEAR on all sides that we need to train people to think independently, to solve the problems that they face. Whether we are talking about the "trouble-shooter" asked to find what is wrong with a piece of equipment that has failed, the commander faced with a strategic decision, or the scientist struggling with a research problem, we have the feeling that something ought to be done in our educational institutions and training centers to keep alive the sense of search, the distrust of conventional solutions, the willingness to be resourceful and inventive. Perhaps because flying equipment has changed so rapidly and so markedly, the Air Force has been particularly alert to problem-solving, and the Air Force ROTC program lays special emphasis upon the training of problem-solvers. If we are to succeed in training up a generation of problem-solvers, we have to know what we are about. We may legitimately ask the psychologists what they have been finding out that is useful to us.

Although psychologists have been working hard at the understanding of problem-solving and creativity, their findings are far from satisfactory. At the most interesting and important level—the level at which great inventions are made, or where great scientific discoveries arise—the issues are so complex as to resist scientific analysis. At the laboratory level, where the problems can be brought under better control, the problems worked on tend to become little games, and the results run the risk of being trivial. So the psychologist faces a dilemma. Should he work on the important problems and face almost certain failure, or should he work on small problems, and run the danger of missing what

* Ernest R. Hilgard, "Can we train better problem-solvers?" *Instructors Journal*, USAF Air Training Command, V (Spring, 1954), 15–21. By permission of the author and the *Instructors Journal*.

is most important? He does what all other scientists find it necessary to do: he works at once at several levels, knowing that not all of his experiments will pay off, but hoping that eventually through some of them he will find the generalizations that will prove to be most serviceable for the understanding of problem-solving, and most useful in the training of problem-solvers.

LEVELS OF ATTACK ON HOW MEN SOLVE PROBLEMS

In order to study problem-solving, we have to discover people who are good problem-solvers, and then see how they go about it. For convenience, we may think of four levels at which we can conduct our inquiry: the genius level, the research investigator level, the examination-passing level, and the laboratory level. Now for a word about each of these.

At the *genius level,* we look into the biographies of great scientists or inventors, to see what we can find out about their creative moments. If they are still alive, we may question them. For example, a number of accounts have been written about Einstein's discovery of the theory of relativity, based in part upon conversations with him. Two rather general conjectures arise about the origins of major new discoveries. One, the *great man* theory, says that the discoveries await the appearance of the great genius, the Galileo, Newton, or Einstein, whose appearance on the scene is in the hands of fate. The other, the *spirit of the times,* theory, says that the times get ripe for a discovery, and then some bright and well-trained person is almost sure to come along and make it. Those who hold to the second theory point to the large number of independent but simultaneous discoveries or inventions—logarithms, calculus, the structure of organic compounds, the theory of evolution —made when the time was ripe by men not in touch with each other. While we may learn something from the investigations at this level, the chance factors loom so large, and the opportunity to repeat observations is so remote, that we need to supplement what we can learn by data derived from other sources.

At the *research investigator level* we can select for study the scientists in any large research laboratory, such as those connected with industrial concerns, military establishments, or universities. Or we can study individual scientists nominated by their colleagues as creative workers. A number of such investigations are now going on. Dr. Anne Roe has recently published a popular book based on her careful study of high-level scientists among present-day physicists, biologists, anthropologists and psychologists. She conducted her study by interview and individual testing. Other such studies are being carried on under the direction of Professor J. P. Guilford at the University of Southern California, and Professor Donald W. Taylor at Stanford.

At the *examination-passing level* we think of the studies of how college students solve the problems set them in their courses. Some of Professor Guilford's work is done at this level, trying to find what kinds of abilities "hang together" in predicting creativity. Other studies compare the importance of the laboratory relative to the lecture, or the aid that comes by way of motion pictures. Here we are more concerned with the problem-solving abilities of the typical student, rather than confining attention to the high-level scientist.

At the *laboratory level* we are interested in the conditions leading to problem-solving rather than in the individual talents that make one person a better problem-solver than another. Sometimes laboratory tasks have to be chosen that are very simple ones in order to test special hypotheses about how problem-solving takes place. Because these experiments are conducted in the spirit of pure science, they are often somewhat remote from real life tasks. But this is the very nature of science, to simplify conditions so that casual factors can be brought under control. In what follows I wish to give some illustrations of laboratory studies, in order to show how these somewhat remote kinds of problem-solving furnish leads that may help us in practical situations.

SOME LABORATORY STUDIES OF PROBLEM-SOLVING

The three kinds of studies to be reported were designed to get at some general features of problem-solving that might be useful for those planning programs of training. We searched the literature of problem-solving and thinking to find some of the conjectures that seemed particularly "fertile," and then repeated and extended the earlier studies in order to firm up the generalizations from them.

1. *Rote memorization vs. learning with understanding.* We can learn by drilling on essentials, so that skills and information are readily available as habitual responses. Or we can learn by trying to understand principles, by making generalizations of wide applicability. As a final product of learning we want a skilled and informed person who knows what he is doing and can apply what he knows to new situations. Such disagreement as there is about appropriate training comes over the proper emphasis and order within training. If a child does not have automatic and habitual responses to 7×9 or to $56 \div 8$ he is hampered in learning long division. Perhaps in learning statistics we need to have acquaintance with a formula and its routine use, before learning

to derive the formula will bring us very much understanding. It is issues like this, of the interrelation between drill and understanding, that provide occasions for scientific study.

We have taken as our point of departure some experiments of Katona in which he contrasted rote learning with learning by understanding, in terms of (1) ease of learning, (2) accuracy of retention over time, and (3) transfer to new problems. While learning by rote often saves time in original learning, it is said to be at a disadvantage in both retention and transfer.

We used some simple card-trick problems first used by Katona. If you prearrange six ordinary playing cards in the order Red-Black-Black-Black-Red-Red, then you can perform a simple trick which gives the type of problem set by the more difficult tricks. You place the first card on the table face up. It is Red. Then you place one card on the bottom of the pack, and place the next card on the table, alongside the first. It is Black. Then you skip another card, and place the next face up. It is Red. By repeatedly skipping one card, the cards that turn up are alternately Red and Black. The gimmick in the trick is that some cards get used more than once, as they come up from the bottom of the pack, and the trick is of course solved if you can arrange the cards in the right order to begin with. You can either remember the right order, here R-B-B-B-R-R, or you can figure some systematic way to arrange the cards which will make it *unnecessary* for you to remember. (For an exercise in problem solving, you might try to figure out how to arrive at the arrangement. In the experiment, half the subjects are shown a way to do it.) Some subjects just memorize the order. Then they can do the trick. Other subjects learn how to construct the order. Then they, too, can do the trick. It takes longer to teach the "understanding" group, that is, those who have to learn how to construct the order.

Katona points out that results achieved by understanding are retained longer than those learned by rote. Over a shorter interval than he used (only a single day) our subjects who learned by rote did about as well at remembering the trick as those who learned by understanding so this is a limiting case for his generalization. But when it came to transfer, we agreed entirely with him. Those who learned by understanding were much better able to do other similar tricks, such as substituting even and odd for red and black, changing the length of the series, skipping two instead of skipping one, and so on.

One interesting by-product of our first experiments came out of the large number of failures of transfer in the understanding group. (These experiments were done with high school seniors.) Although better than the rote learning group, they were far from perfect, so that new problems were set by their failures. Some of the failures were evident. For example, having solved the problems by constructing the list, the subject sometimes converted the problem to a rote one by learning the final order and trying to reproduce it the next day instead of troubling to work it out again. Or the degree of understanding was very imperfect, so that the method used was in reality a formula learned by rote, and not really comprehended. Then there were the usual careless errors, made in haste. But even these errors had a somewhat systematic character which has led us to look into them further. We are convinced that there is no sharp dividing line between rote learning and understanding. This should be evident from what we know about the effect of meaningfulness within rote learning: meaningful materials are learned more easily by rote than nonsense ones, hence some role must already be played by understanding even in memorization by repetition. And understanding must itself have degrees, from the rather blind application of a formula, to the full appreciation of the relationships and principles involved.

The lesson to be learned from these studies is that the extra time and effort needed to learn by understanding pay off when it comes to dealing with new problems similar to but at the same time different from the ones used in training.

2. *"Functional fixedness": how what we know and do can reduce our flexibility*. While past learning often makes it easier to learn something new, most of us have at one time or another found old habits to interfere with new ones, as when we move from driving a car with conventional gear shift to one with automatic shift. An interesting illustration of such interference of prior knowledge in a problem involving situation was pointed out some years ago by Duncker. He showed experimentally that if you used something (say a pliers) in its familiar use (perhaps pulling a staple out of a board) then it becomes more difficult to convert the pliers to a novel use based on the requirements of a problem, such as using it for a pendulum-bob, or as a leg to support a small stand. When the pair of pliers was just lying around, and not previously used, subjects could more easily convert them to these new uses. This "freezing" the use-meaning of the object by making use of it in its familiar way was called by Duncker "functional fixation." This idea seemed to us to be sufficiently germinal to be worth restudying, both to confirm its generality, and to learn something more of its conditions. Parallels suggest themselves in familiar problems, when we get so "hipped" on one way of going at things that we fail to consider other possibilities. We lose flexibility because we have a course of

action that is plausible, and no longer look around. Dr. Adamson, then an assistant on the project, was able to show that Duncker's experiments are reproducible, so that we can accept the principle of functional fixedness as a genuine one: the pre-utilization of a tool or object in its normal use restricts its availability for novel uses by the subject who has just used it in the regular way.

The next step is to find some limiting conditions. One question asked (and answered) by Dr. Adamson, was the following: Does the inhibition against novel use decrease with lapse of time following the normal use of the tool or the object? In other words, is recency of normal use one of the conditions of functional fixedness? The answer came out in the affirmative: the more time that elapsed between the normal use and the novel use, the less the functional fixedness. This may help to explain why a baffling problem is sometimes solved upon our return to it after a time away from it. Perhaps during our vacation from the problem our "functional fixednesses" have declined.

Some suggestions for training problem-solvers come out of these experiments. We must be on our guard against "cook-book" kinds of instructions. ("When this happens, do the following things in one-two-three order—.") Routine, habitual ways of meeting problems may result in reduced flexibility in the face of the specific demands of crisis situations. The problem-solver needs to be good at doing things in unfamiliar ways, at improvising when standard tools are lacking. The experiments on functional fixedness do not tell us how to make good improvisors, but they do point up some of the conditions reducing flexibility in the approach to problems.

3. *Group problem solving: is it better than individual problem solving?* Many problems are solved in groups. That is, decisions are made in conference, by staff groups, by committees. Research workers often work in teams. We ought to know what we are about. Would it be better to send each of the problem solvers into his own cubicle to think about the problems, and then have them come together to report the outcome? Or, perhaps, does something happen in group deliberation that is superior to individual thinking about problems? This is a big order. Here we wish to talk about some experiments bearing on these problems, but reducing the problems to proportions manageable in the laboratory.

A beginning was made by using the game of "Twenty Questions." This is the familiar parlor-game, now somewhat common on television, in which the members of the group try by questioning to discover what the leader has in mind, the questions being of the sort that can be answered simply by "Yes" or "No." In a few questions the group arrives at answers such as "John Barrymore's profile" or "the second of the two birds in a bush." The game is fun enough that it is easy to get groups to work hard at it in the laboratory, and hence it has become a useful laboratory tool. Several findings from our first experiment (Taylor and Faust) are worth noting:

Arriving at the answer to the game of "Twenty Questions" is a problem solving skill that can be acquired. There is appreciable improvement in four sessions, in each of which four games are played.

When two people play the game at a time, they do better than one person working alone. When four people play, they likewise do better than one person at a time, but not better than two at a time. (These results depend in part on the measures used, but this is not the place for the detailed qualifications.)

There is no way to state with confidence which member of the group is most likely to get the answer: the one who asks the most questions, or the one who asks the least questions.

One of the observations that struck the experimenters in working at this game was the promptness with which the answers were reached (when they were reached at all). The highly specific answers can be reached in a few questions only if the guesses go far beyond chance. This points up a significant feature of social communication: there are concealed rules of the game, as though both experimenter and subject were using an agreed-upon code book to make the answers easier. To test this possibility, the game was simplified to that of guessing a number lying within given range. Here the logical solution requires successive division of the numbers into halves, one half in each case being rejected. It is found that it takes more questions to find a number between 1 and 50 than to find Abraham Lincoln among all people, living or dead! The point is that, in the concealed instructions, any number between 1 and 50 is "fair"; just anybody in the telephone book is *not* fair, but Abraham Lincoln is high among the "fair" choices. These social factors in the "Twenty Questions" game make it so complicated that it baffles analysis. While the Stanford experimenters are continuing with it, they have also turned to other types of problem solving to study the success of the individual relative to the success of the group.

These three investigations are but examples of the different levels at which we are finding it desirable to work. Which will pay off best we do not know. If we knew the answers, we would not have to do the experiments. It is pretty obvious, however, that clear answers from experiments such as these, done with rather simple laboratory problems, will give suggestions important for the training of problem-solvers. The tryout of these suggestions will have to be done systematically within training centers. That is, there will remain an "engineering" of these suggestions, just as the findings of any other science have to be "engineered" before they can serve practical purposes.

---

32. *A Cognitive Theory of Dreams* *

THE STUDY OF dreams has long fascinated man. In recent years there has been widespread acceptance of the Freudian theory of the dream. In this paper, Dr. Hall suggests a different approach. He identifies dreams as thoughts and offers an analysis in terms of the thinking processes. If proven valid by further investigation, this new approach should add much to our understanding and use of dreams and should enrich our concepts of thinking.

IN THE FINAL YEARS of the nineteenth century, Freud formulated a theory of the dream which has proved exceedingly useful to the clinical practitioner and to a lesser extent to the personality theorist for verifying propositions derived from dynamic theories of personality. Freud was very proud of his first original and independent achievement in psychological theorizing, so much so that he appears to have been reluctant to alter it as he did so many other discoveries of these early years. In a singularly mistitled lecture *Revision of the Theory of Dreams* published in 1933, Freud revises his original theory to the extent of adding the italicized word to the fundamental proposition, "the dream is an *attempted* wish-fulfillment." In this same essay, Freud observes that "the analysts behave as though they had nothing more to say about the dream, as though the whole subject of dream-theory was finished and done with." Freud must have had himself in mind as well as his colleagues when he made this observation for in his valedictory he abides by his original formulation, despite the fact that the psychoanalytic theory of the person had made great strides in the intervening 40 years. Probably the most noteworthy advances made by Freud in his later years were a revised theory of anxiety, a new theory of motivation, and the development of a far reaching ego theory. Of these three, ego theory has had the greatest impact upon current psychoanalytic theorizing.

What we should like to do in this paper is to bring dream theory

* Calvin S. Hall, "A cognitive theory of dreams," *The Journal of General Psychology,* XLIX (1953), 273–82. By permission of the author and The Journal Press.

within the context of ego psychology by defending the proposition that dreaming is a cognitive process. Before addressing ourselves to this thesis, let us define a dream. A dream is a succession of images, predominantly visual in quality, which are experienced during sleep. A dream commonly has one or more scenes, several characters in addition to the dreamer, and a sequence of actions and interactions usually involving the dreamer. It resembles a motion picture or dramatic production in which the dreamer is a participant-observer. Although a dream is an hallucination, the dreamer experiences it as he does any perceptual phenomenon. Scenes, people, objects, and actions are experienced as though they were impressing themselves on the senses from the external world. The world of dreams, it goes without saying, is a world of pure projection.

The principal thesis of this paper is that these images of a dream are the embodiment of thoughts. They are a medium by which a psychological process, cognition, is transformed into a form that can be perceived. Although images are the only means by which ideas find sensible expression in dreams, other media such as words, numbers, gestures, and pictures are employed in waking life for making one's thoughts known. When thought is made perceptible, it is said to be communicated. Unlike the communications of waking life, which may have an audience of millions, the audience of a dream consists of only one person, the dreamer himself. A dream is a highly private showing of the dreamer's thoughts.

In order to develop the thesis of this paper, it is necessary to say a few words about thinking. Thinking is a process of conceiving. The end-product of this process is a conception (idea). A conception is an item of knowledge, a formulation of experience which has meaning for a person. It is derived ultimately from experience but it is not dependent for its existence at any given moment upon the reception of sensory impressions from the external world or from one's body. In other words, conceiving is an autonomous process that requires no direct sensory data. It may be contrasted with perceiving, a process which is dependent upon direct stimulation of the senses. One *perceives* a wintry landscape when one looks out at a scene as it exists in the world and incorporates through the eyes a pattern of light waves which is the raw material for the formation of a perception.[1] One has a *conception* of winter when one thinks of it as being a time of cold weather, snow, short days, icy streets, and bare trees. One can conceive of winter at any

[1] It is doubtful whether a pure perception ever takes place. Perceptions are probably always acted upon and changed by autochthonous processes within the person, the chief of which may be conceiving.

time of the year, but one can only perceive winter during the winter. Although not a great deal is known about the process of conceiving, we are fairly well acquainted with its products, i.e., conceptions or ideas, since they are rendered perceptible in a variety of forms including dreams. An artist expresses his conceptions in visual terms, while writers and speakers use words to make their ideas public. Mathematicians employ numbers and symbols for conveying their thoughts, and musicians express themselves in patterns of tone, rhythm, intensity, and quality. A dancer embodies her ideas in physical movement, a sculptor in three dimensional forms, and an architect in buildings. The formulation and communication of ideas are the essence of all creative endeavors.

We return now to dreaming and dreams. If dreaming is defined as thinking that occurs during sleep, and if thinking consists essentially of generating ideas, then dreaming is also a process of conceiving and the resulting dream images may be viewed as the embodiment of conceptions. That which is invisible, namely a conception, becomes visible when it is transformed into a dream image. The images of a dream are pictures of conceptions. A dream is a work of art which requires of the dreamer no particular talent, special training, or technical competence. Dreaming is a creative enterprise in which all may and most do participate.

If dreaming consists of transforming conceptions into images, then dream interpretation reverses this process; images are translated into their referent ideas. How is this translation accomplished? It is accomplished by drawing inferences from material in the dream text, and by checking these inferences against other dreams of the person or against other information about the person. Although we cannot describe the methods of interpreting dreams within the limits of this paper, some general remarks regarding dream interpretation may be made here. To interpret a dream means, according to the theory presented in this paper, to discover the conceptions or conceptual systems of the dreamer. These conceptions may be inferred from a number of lines of evidence, some of which are as follows: (a) the actions and qualities of the dreamer in the dream, i.e., the rôle or rôles played by the dreamer, (b) the kind of characters introduced in the dream, (c) the actions and qualities assigned to them, (d) the nature of the interactions between the dreamer and these characters, and between the characters themselves, (e) the setting or dream scene, (f) transitions within the dream, and (g) the outcome of the dream. The final objective of dream interpretation is not to understand the dream but rather to understand the dreamer.

What kinds of conceptions are found in dreams? One is tempted to reply all kinds but this is not correct since many ideas seem to be excluded from dreams. Dreams are relatively silent regarding political and economic questions; they have little or nothing to say about current events in the world of affairs. I was collecting dreams daily from students during the last days of the war with Japan when the first atomic bomb was exploded, yet this catastrophe did not register in a single dream. Presidential elections, declarations of war, the diplomatic struggles of great powers, major athletic contests, local happenings that make the headlines, all are pretty largely ignored in dreams. A count of characters in a large sample of dreams reveals that the number of prominent people appearing in dreams is very small. Nor are intellectual, scientific, cultural and professional topics or the affairs of finance, business, and industry the subject matter of dreams.

What then is left? The whole world of the personal, the intimate, the emotional, and the conflictful remain. These are the ideas which register in dreams. For the sake of discussion, we shall present a classification of some common conceptions found in dreams.

a. Conceptions of self. A dream is a mirror that reflects the self-conceptions of the dreamer. Ideas of self are revealed by the repertoire of parts taken by the dreamer in a series of dreams. The repertoire may consist of a few rôles, or it may be extensive and varied. In one dream series, for example, the dreamer is pictured as a great general, a rich and influential man, and an important steel manufacturer. In each case, however, he loses his power by being disabled in vigorous combat with a superior force. Here we see that a self-conception of strength and potency cannot be maintained. A typical dream of strength turning into weakness is the following one.

> I was sitting knee deep in quarters in my room. People kept rushing into my room and stealing handfuls of money. I chased after them, grasping them violently and retrieving my money. But after a while so many people kept grabbing my money at once that I couldn't chase them all so I just sat there and cried.

This young man's conceptions of himself are disjunctive; he is both strong and weak, with weakness winning out over strength.

Perhaps no other medium gives us a more candid picture of what a person thinks about himself than do dreams. It was Ralph Waldo Emerson who wrote: "A skillful man reads his dreams for his self-knowledge."

b. Conceptions of other people. Dreams reveal what the dreamer thinks about his mother and father, his brothers and sisters, his spouse and children, and diverse other classes of people. These conceptions, like those of self, are embodied in the rôles played by the various characters. If the dreamer conceives of his father as a stern, demanding, autocratic person, the father is assigned a part that is in keeping with this conception. If he thinks of his mother as a nurturant person, she will perform some service in the dream to depict her nurturance. Young men commonly dream about being attacked by other men, thereby displaying a conception of enmity that exists in males for other males. Less commonly young men are friendly with other men. Women also conceive of men as attackers but their dreams reveal many other conceptions. In a single dream series, multiple conceptions of the same person or class of persons are the rule rather than the exception, which suggests that the average person has a network of conceptions regarding his mother, father, siblings, and various other individuals and classes with whom he interacts during waking life. These ideational or cognitive networks are conceptual systems, and it is one of the aims of dream analysis to delineate these conceptual systems.

c. Conceptions of the world. By the world is meant the totality of the environment, that which is not-self. In dreams as in poetic fancy the world may be invested with animistic qualities which reflect the dreamer's conceptions of the world. It may be viewed as benign, hostile, turbulent, sorrowful, lonely, or degraded depending upon the mood of the dreamer. These world-conceptions are often conveyed by the character of the dream setting. If the dreamer feels that the world presents a cold, bleak face, he may materialize this conception in the form of a cold climate and a bleak, rocky setting. A dreamer who feels that his world is one of turbulence and agitation, may dream of thunderstorms, raging seas, battles, milling crowds, and traffic jams. A feeling that the world is benign and peaceful can be scenically represented in dreams by serene natural settings.

d. Conceptions of impulses, prohibitions, and penalties. Since dreams are filled with impulse gratification, in particular those of sex and aggression, it is not surprising that Freud came to the conclusion that wish-fulfillment is the essence of dreams, and that the objective of dream analysis is the discovery of the wish which is fulfilled. It is hardly necessary, however, to consult dreams in order to learn that man seeks gratification of his urges. What dreams can tell us more profitably is how the dreamer conceives of his impulses, for it is these conceptions, not the impulses directly, that ordinarily elicit specific ways of behaving. Most people experience a sex drive, but they differ in respect to their conceptions of the sex drive. The sex impulse may be regarded variously as wicked, as unclean, as a mechanical pressure needing periodic release, as a natural force serving reproduction, as a way of expressing love and tenderness, or as a primitive and uncontrollable form of energy against which one wages a losing battle. Among our collection of nocturnal emission dreams, these and many other conceptions of this biological force appear. The following dream reveals a purely mechanical conception of sex.

> I got out of bed and went into the bathroom and attempted to turn on the water faucet. I turned and turned but no water came out. I then decided to call a plumber. Soon afterwards the door opened and an individual dressed in coveralls approached me. Upon closer examination I discovered the plumber was a female. I scoffed at the idea of a lady plumber, but unruffled she went to the basin, turned the faucet, and water immediately flowed. An emission occurred.

Dreams also show the person's conceptions of the obstacles that stand in the way of the gratification of his impulses. These obstacles are often prohibitions emanating from his conscience and may be represented in dreams by such obstacles as walls, curbs, and locked doors, by acts of restraint such as putting on the brakes of a car, or by the appearance of authority figures who interrupt the dreamer's pleasure. If an impulse is gratified, the dreamer may express his conception of the punishment that will be visited upon him for his transgression. He may be punished directly by another person, or he may be the victim of misfortune. In any event, the kinds of obstacles and the kinds of penalties which appear in dreams are interpreted in order to throw light upon the nature of the conceptual system which is called the superego. This conceptual system which is assumed to be detached from the ego contains the moral ideology of the person.

e. Conceptions of problems and conflicts. Perhaps the most important information provided by dreams is the way in which they illuminate the basic predicaments of a person as that person sees them. Dreams give one an inside view of the person's problems, a personal formulation that is not so likely to be as distorted or as superficial as are the reports made in waking life. Since it is the way in which a person conceives of his conflicts that determines his behavior, the inside view is a prerequisite for clear understanding of human conduct. As we have shown in another place, the delineation of a person's conflicts may be made by analyzing a dream series.

Of what value is it to know the conceptions of a person as expressed in his dreams? How does it help the psychologist to understand the person and thereby to predict and control his behavior? Of one thing we can be quite certain, namely that these conceptions are not dependable guides to objective reality; what one conceives to be true and what is actually true do not invariably coincide. A person may conceive of his father as a stern, autocratic, unreasonable person, when, in fact, his father does not possess these characteristics in the eyes of impartial observers. Dreams should not be read for the purpose of constructing a picture of objective reality.[2]

Our thesis is that dreams are one dependable source of information regarding subjective reality, and that knowledge of subjective reality is useful precisely because it does have effects in the conduct of a person. If a boy sees his father as an autocratic authority, he will react toward his father as though he really is that way. In other words, these personal cognitions are the real antecedents of behavior.

Parenthetically, we would like to observe that psychology may have been hampered in its development because it has tended to ignore subjective cognitions in favor of objective stimulus variables. Stimulus conditions are varied and the effects in behavior are noted, often without taking into consideration that the person's conception of the stimulus may be the decisive factor. People may react differently to the same stimulus because they have different conceptions of the stimulus or they may react in the same way to different stimuli because they have similar conceptions. This is a truism whose truth is too often forgotten in psychological experiments, although there are indications that the pendulum is swinging back in the direction of cognition variables.

Although this is not the place to develop fully our theory of *conceptual systems,* it is not inappropriate to mention briefly our view that the conceptions of a person are organized into interconnected networks. One network may consist of the conceptions that a person has of his family, and this network in turn may be interconnected with a network of ideas about government, or religion, or education. A recent study has demonstrated in a convincing manner how ideas about minority groups are intimately related with ideas about family, religion, government, and economics. It is the task of psychology, as we see it, to explore these conceptual systems or personal ideologies, to show how they are interrelated, to learn how they are developed, to demonstrate how they control and regulate conduct, and to discover how they may be changed. In order to do all of these things, it is necessary to devise

[2] The expression "objective reality" is used in contrast to "subjective reality." By the former, we mean those conceptions of reality which can be publicly demonstrated and repeatedly verified. By the latter, we mean those conceptions of reality which reside in a person's mind irrespective of whether these conceptions can be demonstrated and verified. Both kinds of conceptions are "real" inasmuch as they both have "effects."

methods of finding out what a person's conceptions are. Attitude-opinion questionnaire methods have reached a high level of development and are employed on a large scale to determine people's beliefs about everything under the sun. The value of such methods, although great, is nonetheless limited by several factors inherent in the methods. The respondent may not answer a question either because he does not want to or because he does not know the answer, or he may answer it untruthfully either intentionally or unintentionally. Moreover, the wording of the question is an important variable. At best, questionnaires get at the conscious and verbalizable conceptions of a person.

If one assumes, as the writer does, that the contents of personal ideologies are pretty largely unconscious or preconscious, then methods have to be used which will reveal these unconscious conceptions. Projective methods, especially of the picture-story type, lend themselves to the exploration of conceptual systems, although they have not been employed to any great extent for this purpose. Picture-story tests do have one drawback, however, and that is that the person's conceptions may not be fully laid bare by the collection of pictures used. Since the material obtained will be a function of the kind of pictures shown to the person, it is possible that those conceptions which are of greatest significance for him may not be tapped. This limitation does not apply to dreams. The dreamer makes his own pictures of those conceptions that are of greatest importance to him currently. Over a period of time, his dreams will depict the essential features of his conceptual systems. Moreover, dreams tap the unconscious and bring to the surface those prototypic conceptions around which conceptual systems are formed. It is our view that prototypic conceptions have their origin in early life and that they are more likely to express themselves in dreams than through any other medium. For these reasons, we feel that dreams constitute the best material for studying the conceptual systems of a person and that such knowledge is absolutely essential if we are to understand why people behave as they do.

We shall conclude by demonstrating how the views presented in this paper may be utilized in analyzing a dream. The following dream was reported by a young man.

I was at the blackboard in a school room doing a trig problem but I was having trouble with it because I could not remember the valence of nitrogen. I was about to give up on it when a girl came up to me and asked if I would like to dance. The music was good but very erratic, being very fast one instant and very slow the next; however, we were always exactly in step. She was an excellent dancer. When the music stopped we were both in the school shower but we still had our clothes on. I wanted to take hers off and make love to her but I had never done anything like that before so we just laughed and splashed water.

Then I was outside the school. It was night and lights shone in all the windows silhouetting a wild orgy of a party. I felt very lonely. I wanted to go inside but something seemed to hold me back. I heard chimes ringing in the church.

In the opening scene, we see the dreamer hard at work on a mathematical problem with which he is having difficulty. His self-conception is that of an industrious student engaged in a purely intellectual task for which he does not have the requisite knowledge. A girl appears and invites him to dance; that is, he conceives of the girl as a temptress and of himself as her victim. At her bidding, he leaves the hardships of intellectual activity for the pleasures of sensuality. Their sensuality stops short of complete fulfillment because he cannot conceive of himself as consummating the sexual act. The scene changes in line with a new conception. The dreamer now see himself as lonely outsider looking in on a wild orgy. He would like to go in, but he is held back by an unidentified force. The church bells, embodying as they do ideas of virtue and morality, suggest that the unknown force is his own conception of moral conduct.

This dream, then, reveals two opposing conceptual systems, one which contains the young man's conception of himself as a moral, industrious, and intellectual person, the other which contains his conception of himself as a sensual being. These disjunctive conceptions tend to inhibit one another. He cannot maintain a consistent conception of himself as being either moral or sensual. When he is doing the "right" thing, he is lured away by sexuality; when he is doing the "wrong" thing, he is pulled away by morality. A self-conception of inadequacy for either role is portrayed by his inability to solve the intellectual task or to fulfill his sexual wish. In this dream we see that it is not the sex drive per se that is of significance, but rather his conception of it as being forbidden to him.

Other dreams collected from this young man help to fill out the contents of his conceptual systems. In one dream, he does consummate the sex act, but only because the girl actively seduces him. This suggests that his conception of morality can be subordinated when he sees himself as the victim of external forces. Even in this dream, however, the dreamer feels ashamed because he is so easily excited. His personal ideology regarding women is an interesting yet not uncommon one. Women are of two types: aggressively sexual women who seduce men and pure women who are to be loved in a respectful manner but with whom sexual relations are forbidden prior to marriage.

We have spoken of the disjunctive nature of the dreamer's moral and immoral self-conceptions. In one dream he makes a partial fusion of these opposed views.

> I was studying for a test with my girl. We were lying on the bed in her room reviewing our notes and asking each other questions about them. As each topic would come up, instead of discussing the text, I would demonstrate a different point in making love to her. Although each type of love making seemed different, it never got beyond the kissing stage.

Work and sex are integrated, although the sex impulse is kept within bounds. The girl in the dream is one of the "nice" girls in the dreamer's life toward whom he would not be likely to have unrestrained sexual feelings.

CONCLUDING STATEMENT

The argument presented in this paper consists of the following assertions:

1. Dreaming is a cognitive activity, and a dream is a pictorial representation of the dreamer's conceptions.
2. Dream interpretation consists of discovering the conceptions that lie behind the dream images.
3. Conceptions represented in dreams usually fall into one of the following classes: (a) self-conceptions, (b) conceptions of other people, (c) conceptions of the world, (d) conceptions of impulses, prohibitions, and penalties, and (e) conceptions of conflicts.
4. Conceptions are organized into conceptual systems, and these systems are the antecedents of behavior.
5. Dreams provide excellent material for the analysis of conceptual systems since they portray unconscious and prototypic conceptions.
6. The theory presented in this paper represents an extension of ego psychology to include dreaming as a function of the ego.

---

33. Freedom and the Cognitive Need *

DR. TOLMAN applies some basic psychological principles to the question of academic freedom and develops the thesis that there

* Edward C. Tolman, "Freedom and the cognitive need," *The American Psychologist,* IX (1954), 536–38. By permission of the author and the American Psychological Association. This statement was originally presented as an address at a Special Convocation, McGill University, June 11, 1954.

exists in man a basic intellectual, or cognitive, drive to know, citing the influence of relevant factors on the implementation of this drive. Although he develops his thesis primarily from research done on animals, Dr. Tolman extends the principles to human functioning and applies them to contemporary society. This is another example of the relationship between the world of the laboratory, so often called "ivory tower," and the world of everyday living.

AN OCCASION such as this—a Convocation of a Great University in a great and intellectually free country, where scholars have gathered from many lands—testifies once again to the fact that science, reason, and the life of the mind are, and shall remain, international. There are no boundaries, national or otherwise, which can separate truth from truth. We "eggheads," to repeat an appellation meant to be opprobrious (but not perhaps inappropriate), pledge ourselves, each according to his talents, to seek, to investigate, and to report. It is by this pledge and its resultant commitments that each of us, insofar as he can, seeks to make his contribution to the general welfare. But we do this in all modesty. For what is truth today may prove but half truth tomorrow. But even such half truths are better than none—better than prejudice, better than hearsay, better than rumor, and better than the blind self-seeking in which we all indulge in our lower moments.

Especially crucial among the truths which we scholars and scientists search for are those of psychology and of the other social sciences. But it is these psychological and sociological truths or, it may be, only half truths which perhaps most often come into conflict with the prejudices and self-seeking of everyday men. If I were a dictator, I would banish psychology and its sister sciences. For psychology and sociology and anthropology and economics and political science, even though as yet still in their infancies, have already acquired enough truth to make men poor fodder for dictators. The truths which have been found are already forcing us out of our stereotyped, ethnocentric, jingoistic, and dangerous ways—ways which prove such a good soil for dictators to build upon.

But, you may ask, what can I, as primarily a rat psychologist who has spent most of his working hours observing how rats learn mazes or reading about how rhesus monkeys or chimpanzees learn more complicated mechanisms, what can I contribute in the way of useful or sound conclusions as to how real human beings solve real human problems? My answer is that I think there are certain fundamental features of rat behavior and of monkey and chimpanzee behavior which throw very considerable light upon how we human beings meet our problems.

It has been found, for example, that *nonhungry* rats learn best the "truth" that there is food in a given alley of a maze if they are not at the same time too thirsty or too frightened or too something else. Further, as has just recently been reported from the psychological laboratories here at McGill, rats will notice and investigate a new visual pattern even when they have no known practical motives for doing so and have food and water already at hand. Also it has been found that monkeys and chimpanzees will learn to operate quite complicated mechanical devices for what appears to be the mere cognitive pleasure of doing so. There are many such findings which suggest the operation of something like a pure cognitive or curiosity need in animals and also findings which indicate the nature of the dependence or the independence of this pure cognitive drive upon such more practical wants as thirst, hunger, sex, fear. Furthermore, we, or at any rate I, see these facts and relationships about cognitive needs more clearly when they have been observed in rats or apes than when they have been merely noted in a common-sense way in human beings.

I shall advance two main propositions. I shall claim that all *new* discrimination, *new* learning, or *new* problem solving requires, if it is to occur, the activity then and there of a pure cognitive or curiosity want to discriminate, to note, to see relationships. I shall also claim that the arousal of such a pure cognitive want at any given time will be dependent in several different ways upon the governing practical needs which may then also be present. And I shall present first three such types of dependence.

a. Any active, practical need or want such, for example, as that to get to food (when the animal is hungry) will, up to a certain intensity, tend to facilitate the arousal of a cognitive need or readiness relative to food itself and relative to such other objects as may prove means or paths for getting to the food. That is to say, a somewhat hungry rat is more apt to notice food and to discriminate the correct path to it than is a completely food-satiated rat, although, as we saw above, a completely nonhungry rat can under some conditions observe the presence of food in a maze alley and later remember where it was. And we also saw that completely nonhungry and nonthirsty rats will note the differences between visual patterns merely out of what would appear to be pure, disinterested curiosity. Nevertheless some moderate degree of practical needs such as hunger or thirst will, I believe, usually tend to increase the pure curiosity need.

b. When, however, a given practical need becomes too strong, too intense, the necessary, purely cognitive or curiosity want for observing and noting relationships seems to become less again. Thus, there is evidence that the very hungry rat is poorer about discovering the route to food than is the moderately hungry one.

c. Finally, when a given practical need is very strong, not only does it tend to interfere with cognitive curiosity for the finer details of the situation which would be relevant to this practical need itself, but such a very strong practical need also tends to interfere with any cognitive curiosity relative to other, perhaps then-and-there irrelevant features of the situation. Thus it was noted above that rats apparently did not note the presence or position of *food* when they were too thirsty.

Now let me suggest some human parallels. Suppose an individual, say a college professor, has been invited to make an address at a public meeting, perhaps a university convocation. What is his dominant practical need? I shall suppose (*merely for the sake of argument*) that his main need is a *thirst* for approval. That is, his immediate practical goal is that of writing a good speech because it will lead him to drink from the waters of approval, whether these waters be provided by himself or by his audience.

My first proposition, you will recall, was that all new learning or problem solving requires the arousal, at the time it takes place, of a pure cognitive or curiosity need (let us call it now the "truth" need) to discriminate, to note, and to observe relationships. In other words, this hypothetical professor will require at the time he is writing his speech the arousal of some pure cognitive or truth want if he is to discriminate his ideas objectively and to see the true relationships between them.

My second proposition was that the activation of this truth want will depend in three different ways upon any aroused practical need. (a) It was asserted that a moderately strong practical need would be better for releasing the pure truth want resulting in good discrimination and in the seeing of relationships than would no practical need at all. That is, if our professor were not motivated at all by the practical desire to make a good speech, he would do less cognizing, less noticing of the true relationships than if reasonably motivated to obtain approval. (b) It was also asserted that, if the dominating practical need were too strong, the pure cognitive need or readiness would become less. Our professor, if he were too motivated, too ambitious, too concerned about his own or the audience's reaction, would exhibit less pure truth seeking and would tend more to miss and slur over the finer distinctions, the true relationships, between his ideas than if he were only reasonably motivated. (This may well have been the case in the actual instance I have in mind.) (c) It was asserted thirdly that the presence of any overly strong practical need would interfere with the pure cognitive or truth want relative to other features of the situation not at the moment specifically related to the task at hand. The professor, if overmotivated, would become blind to other features of the total situation, such perhaps as notes on his calendar which should have reminded him of important engagements.

But now finally in order to give a complete account of our hypothetical professor we must assume a couple of still further principles. Suppose that, in addition to having a need to write a good speech, he is also driven by two other strong practical needs—a need to support his family and a need not to be rejected by his fellows. Suppose, in short, that he has a strong fear that his family may starve and a strong fear that what he says will lead him into conflict with the current climate of opinion. What will happen? Such strong fear needs will also decrease his pure cognitive appraisal of the ideas to be put into his speech. He will write a cautious, timid speech. In short, his fears will add another goal to his writing, and to achieve this secondary goal of playing safe his speech will be poorer and less objective. And as an aside I would also suggest that all his other activities will be similarly affected. He will not only write a poorer speech, but he will also become a poorer, more timid teacher, a blind type of research worker, and a neurotic committeeman. He will tend to fall down in all his activities. What I am saying is, in short, that any teacher, if he is to be what our liberal society "says" it wants him to be—namely, an open-minded, objective proponent of, and searcher for, truth—must then not be subjected to too strong economic fears or too strong social attacks.

And this, of course, is why we educators proclaim aloud the principles of Academic Freedom and Academic Tenure. Academic Freedom and its sister concept of Academic Tenure assert that if teachers are to think and teach freely, objectively, and critically, they must have reasonable economic security and a sturdy protection against temporary public pressures and public clamor. We teachers will not do our jobs well whenever we are made into wee, cowering, timorous beasties.

But this is, of course, only one side of the matter. If society is to grant us this somewhat specially privileged position, then we ourselves must take care not to abuse that position. Society must demand that each of us work and think and teach to the best of his ability. And it must also demand that, having so worked and thought and taught, we shall speak out and freely criticize only when in our considered opinion it is our duty to do so. In an ideal liberal society such procedures would be a matter of course. But, alas, we do not have an ideal society nor do we have ideal teachers.

What then are the characteristics of our actual society as we do have it today? Above all I would emphasize the rising tide of anti-intellectualism. This is due, I believe, to the fact that men today (and this means you and me and all of us, whether we dwell this side or that side of the iron or bamboo curtains) are largely dominated by fear. And when men are so dominated, a still additional psychological mechanism comes into play. This is the process known as scapegoating. As to this process, I have not learned much from rats or chimpanzees. The lower animals do not, to my knowledge, go in for scapegoating. But we human beings do (and I may say in passing it is one of our most disgusting and dangerous traits). When we are too afraid or too angry (usually a mixture of both), we want to take it out on somebody else. We want to believe that mother, father, teacher is to blame. In such moments we assert that it is the intellectuals, the scientists, who are doing us in. So we seek to attack and to destroy them. We say let's investigate them. Let's damn them as "eggheads." Let's prevent them from talking and continue in our good, old-fashioned, uninformed, selfish, jingoistic ways. Let us reject these leaders who try to make us think, close our eyes, and forget that we are headed for Armageddon.

What can be done? How can we mere mortals combat this terrible danger, this great divisiveness among us? How can society be made survive? Perhaps it cannot. But I think it can. For there is one still additional psychological mechanism which will work for us. It has been shown that if a human organism wants some positive goal and wants it passionately enough, then, though fear will get in the way and tend to narrow his cognitive functionings, will tend to lead him into distorted, narrowed perception and into scapegoating, such fear and scapegoating will not wholly prevail. Even rats will learn (and sometimes faster) how to get to food when there are fearful electric shocks along the way. Hence, if our need as human beings for a liberal society be passionate enough, if our demands for freedom, for fair play, for honesty, for open minds, and for simple human decency really be overwhelming (and basically I believe they are), then whatever our fears and distorting mechanisms we men will continue to seek the truth. Our liberal schools and colleges will survive, in spite of the recurring attacks upon them. They shall be neither Communized nor Nazified. For I assert that we, the people, all of us, intellectuals and nonintellectuals alike, still want the truth and nothing but the truth.

For in our hearts the words of the Nazarene still echo: "And ye shall know the truth, and the truth shall make you free."

VIII

SOCIAL BEHAVIOR

ALTHOUGH PSYCHOLOGY focuses on the individual, a complete understanding of the individual requires a knowledge of his interpersonal relationships. The selections in this section consider some of the basic problems concerning man's functioning as a social being. The first two papers deal with questions that have perplexed psychologists and philosophers alike, such as: What is the basis for social behavior? Is there an instinct of gregariousness? Are there biological factors that determine the quality of our social responses?

The following paper is concerned with the important practical problems involved in the individual's relationships with various groups of other individuals. It examines the stereotypes or images that are aspects of the way we think about people.

The fourth paper offers a detailed report on the functioning of a group of individuals under the impact of social change. The reader might try to identify the contributions of biological factors and specific experiences to the perception and thinking of the participants. This report gives us a chance to apply some of the concepts we have been developing to real-life problems which are being raised on a widening scale in the contemporary world situation.

34. The Basis of Social Behavior *

MANY interpret the common observation that man is a social animal to imply the existence of an inborn "gregariousness" motive. In

* William E. Blatz, *The Five Sisters* (William Morrow and Co., 1938), pp. 174–95. By permission of the author and the publisher.

this selection Professor Blatz challenges this interpretation. Basing his conclusions on a study of the world-renowned quintuplets, he explains social behavior in terms of the experience of the individual. His observational data call attention to variation in social behavior despite similar heredity and point up the need to examine the nature of the effective environment for the individual rather than simply its gross superficial aspects.

THE SOCIAL LIFE of human beings is so highly organized today that it is not to be wondered that the average individual believes human social needs to be as fundamental as hunger and thirst. It is difficult to understand or appreciate that social behavior is learned and not instinctive. We accept as commonplace and as necessities many of the attributes of social life which for generations we have used and enjoyed in our homes. Children brought up in urban centers look upon inside plumbing, elevators, telephones and public schools as integral parts of their lives just as they do the climate, and growth, and the sun and moon. A child growing up in a civilized community would look upon a house as a necessity, but early man did not fabricate a dwelling place, and perhaps the use of a cave came late in evolutionary history. It may be questioned why a house is mentioned in connection with social development; but perhaps the first use of a dwelling place, forcing individuals to live together, was the beginning of social behavior.

It is certainly far-fetched to assume that primitive man purposefully organized a group for communal living on the basis of the sharing of tastes for the good of the whole. It is more likely that even the custom of a family's living together was brought about by the accidental discovery that a shelter of some kind increased the comfort of an individual. And when more than one individual shared such a dwelling place, some interaction of a more or less personal nature was necessary. In the course of time the collection of individuals made it possible to satisfy some of the inherent needs which in the beginning were not, in any sense of the word, social. The development of an interest which depends on new and unique stimuli, and the response which the individual makes thereto, are more likely to be fostered when there are living organisms in the environment than when there are only inanimate objects. This is more fully understood when we consider that the more complex the situation, the more possibilities there are for new facts to be disclosed to the one who responds to it. Interest in an inanimate object is soon exhausted unless it changes its form through some activity of the individual. A lump of clay is interesting only when under the hands of the sculptor, whether professional or amateur, whether adult or child; it takes on a new shape, presents something new to hold the interest. Living objects, although they do not change their form, do continuously present new aspects—perhaps under the influence of the observer—because they are capable of moving, behaving and reacting. The more complex the organization of the living organism, the more interesting are its possibilities. And so the human being is more interesting than any other object in the universe.

Hence the social development of a child is not dependent upon the non-existing social instinct but rather upon the potentialities for maintaining and developing interest in the social environment that is provided for him. It would be a fascinating experience indeed if it were possible to relive with adult understanding the development in consciousness of an infant from the asocial outlook of the newborn to the accepted social activities of the youth, adolescent and adult. But we have all of us forgotten these early experiences—wherefore it is easy for us to assume that social experience was always part of our human heritage. Moreover, as it is impossible for us to examine directly this process of socialization in a growing child, we can only conjecture from observation of a child's behavior what is going on in the child's mind.

There are fundamental human needs which we have already discussed—the attitudes, the appetites, the emotions—and we must consider that the child's behavior from birth until death is directed towards their satisfaction. He will interpret the meaning of his surroundings in terms of the satisfaction he derives from each object. When we give a child an orange it already has a wealth of meaning for us; but to the child it means that for a moment a new color is presented and in its hands there is a new feeling and to its nose comes a new smell. Having exhausted these experiences, the child discards the orange. A spoon tapping on the table changes the auditory environment of the child as the playing of a symphony orchestra does for the adult.

The meanings grow with the child's experience. The wealth of meaning that has been attached to mothers and motherhood, parents and parenthood, are unknown to the child. The first meaning must necessarily be in terms of the gratification which the mother's ministrations supply. The baby's first smile is usually interpreted by the mother or father as recognition of their intimate status. But it must represent only the dawn of a meaning that the child derives from the repeated association of the mother with the satisfaction of some need. It is only after living in a social environment in which the implications of motherhood are repeatedly presented that the child derives this larger concept. In these early stages the mother is a source of satisfaction to the child; and any overtures he makes must be considered as lying no more within the social category than the response he makes to a new toy. In early infancy the child cries if he is not lifted. This is usually interpreted by the parents as a sign of affection. But in the light of cold analysis it can only be interpreted as a sign of growing experience, in that the child has learned that objects like mothers and fathers are more interesting than oranges and spoons.

The child at this stage is dealing with all his surroundings as objects, and he evaluates them wholly in terms of their capacity to satisfy the fundamental needs. It is when he begins to classify these objects in terms of his own capacity, to use them to serve his own purposes, that he begins to distinguish subtle but important differences. Some objects remain passive under manipulation; others, more plastic, readily change. Some, such as the orange and the spoon, which respond consistently to the child's manipulation, can be directly influenced. But then there is another class of objects, so he discovers, which must be dealt with in a different way if his purposes are to be fulfilled. The child at first undoubtedly smiles in imitation; but when he discovers that a smile can influence this object (the mother) to remain longer in an interesting situation than she will without the smile, then a new meaning has been added to experience, and from this early differentiation the child classifies his world into two major categories: those that are directly controlled and those indirectly controlled. The former are the inanimate and the latter the animate objects. Obviously this classification emerges only gradually—and a good many of the amusing incidents of early childhood are instances in which the child makes mistakes.

It is only when the child appreciates that he himself must be included as a special case in the animate category that social life and behavior can be said to have begun. Whether this profound meaning comes suddenly or gradually is a matter of conjecture because this too, as a childhood experience, is buried deep in the oblivion of early forgetfulness. When at the end of their first year the Quintuplets were placed in a playpen, it was obvious that each was classifying her sisters merely as objects of experience. To go from one side of the playpen to the other, Yvonne would thrust the interposing Annette nonchalantly out of her way as she would a teddy bear. Compare this behavior to that of an eighteen-months child, when Cecile would, with gestures, ask Marie for the doll with which Marie was playing.

Just as the child, by trying various methods, learns to shake a rattle or to put one block on top of another or to lift a cup to his lips, meeting many failures before ultimate success, so he learns the various indirect methods by which he can influence his social environment. A smile, a frown and a bleak glance, a cry, tears or a bellow are the first simple ingredients which the child mixes together to form the composite personality which is intimately and uniquely his own. Experience adds new ingredients. It is well to dwell for a moment upon this mechanism because to understand it is to clarify a great many of the factors which develop personality, and which heretofore have been considered the direct result of the inherent differences of protoplasm rather than the inevitable results of learning.

When a child first uses a smile as a deliberate device for controlling the behavior of another individual, the result of this attempt will obviously determine whether this smile will again be used or not. He must learn the circumstances under which a smile is effective. He will learn that a smile is more effective with one person than with another. This difference in individuals is an important aspect of the environmental situation. Furthermore, the reaction which the child makes towards the person who responds satisfactorily to the smile is different from that towards the person who does not. Thus the child is evaluating the social environment in exactly the same way as he evaluates the physical. And thus in a measure the child, through past experience and the development of habits of response, carries about with him virtually his own potential social environment. As this is dependent upon his experiences with others, it can readily be understood that this environment must be uniquely his own.

This is the explanation of the differences which arise in individuals because of the differences in the interactions which take place through contacts with other individuals. The child learns that by smiling he can persuade his mother to permit him to stay up for another five minutes, or that by being coy he can persuade his father to permit him to play with his watch; but when he tries this technique on the little boy next door who has a toy which he wants, he finds it ineffective. He may resort to direct methods by snatching, but the response of the little boy next door may discourage a repetition of this practice, and so he discovers that by praising some other object he may bring about a barter. This experience is one of the many steps in the development of personality, which only becomes crystallized when the community in which the child lives remains so stable that he is able to predict more or less infallibly the response which behavior on his part will elicit. A new member in the community disturbs the balance, and the learning process is resumed.

It was on the basis of the principles above discussed that investigations into the social development of the Quintuplets were founded. Obviously it was impossible to study their social behavior hour by hour and day by day; for although this would perhaps be the only method by which an accurate and complete delineation of a personality might be obtained, the Quintuplets could of course not be treated as guinea pigs. But it was thought that by taking samples of the social behavior of the children one could determine whether there were any differences between them, and whether these differences were greater than could be explained in terms of the slight difference in their common heredity.

The observations were begun prior to the emergence of true social behavior. Since at this stage in their development the only need which the sisters could satisfy in each other was the need for change (e.g., to be interesting), it was thought that a record of the frequency with which each child was interested in each one of the other children would be a measure of the capacity of each child to be interesting. This interest on the part of the first child could be manifested either by watching or by actually initiating a contact. Thus, if Yvonne looks at Annette and Annette behaves in such a way that Yvonne keeps looking at her, then Annette is obviously interesting to Yvonne. Furthermore, if Yvonne moves over to Annette and smiles at her or grasps her hand, then Yvonne is acting in such a way as either to enhance the interest or to influence Annette to continue the behavior. In order to study the effectiveness of the method or technique which each child used, a record was kept of the frequency with which each child responded to the overtures of the others. Thus if Marie tries to attract Emilie's attention without success and Cecile is successful, then obviously Cecile for the moment at least has been able to satisfy Emilie's interest while Marie has failed. These measures of social behavior, although in no sense an exhaustive analysis of the development of personality, make it possible, because of their simplicity, to measure the social attempts of the individual and their success.

The children were observed at regular intervals over a period of two years. From the values thus obtained it was possible to arrive at some measure of the early social habits of these five children. The values were represented in the form of ratios, of which three were obtained. The first might be called the "social success" ratio. This was computed by taking the number of times each child attempted to open negotiations with another child and the successes which this behavior elicited. This might be compared to the social success of a hostess in the community who sends out a great many invitations to a party, and who measures her popularity by the number of acceptances she receives. Or it might be compared to an individual at a tea party who measures her social success in terms of the number of people who seem to be interested in her conversation, as compared to the number who say "How do you do?" very politely and then immediately cross the room to someone else. The ratios for the five children were as follows:

Annette	1.3
Cecile	1.3
Emilie	.9
Marie	.9
Yvonne	1.8

Now what do these ratios mean? Obviously Annette had a return of 1.3 responses for every attempt she made at a social contact. Or in other words, if she sent out ten invitations she would get thirteen acceptances. That, on the face of it, appears rather ridiculous. But it must be remembered that often an attempt on the part of Annette to

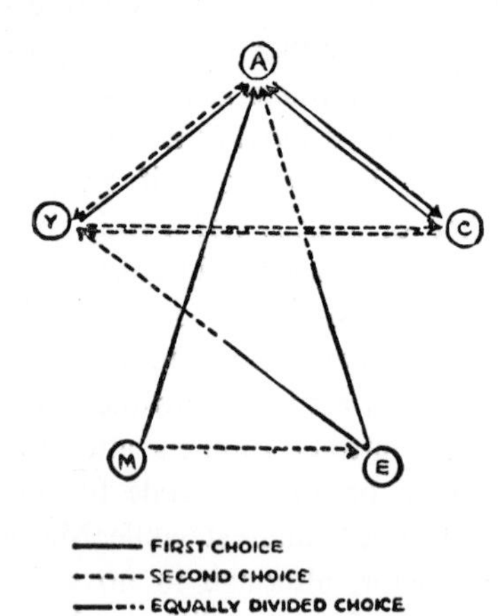

"Response" Social Contacts

This shows how frequently each child was *responded to* by her sisters. Annette received most responses from each of her four sisters, Yvonne followed, then Cecile. Emilie is Marie's second choice while Marie was responded to frequently by none.

arrange a social contact with one of the other sisters would be ignored, and that often, too, such an attempt would result in what is called a series, or chain, response. That is, Annette would go over to Yvonne, who was putting a teddy bear to bed, and help her to manage the bedclothes; and Yvonne would smile and ask her to bring another teddy bear. Annette would do this, and then Yvonne would take both teddy bears, ask Annette to rearrange the bedclothes, and so on. In other words this social gathering, initiated by Annette, would have resulted in several responses from Yvonne. (These chain responses, by the way, do not occur in the early stages of social development and are a sign of developing maturity.) Returning to the table of ratios, then, it is seen that Annette and Cecile are equal in their social successes; that Emilie and Marie also are equal, but much lower in the scale than Annette and Cecile, and do not receive a full return for their social attempts; and that Yvonne's ratio, 1.8, is highest of all. It is also interesting to note that Yvonne was the only one of the four others who was able to get a number of responses from Emilie greater than her initiated advances. Annette, Marie and Cecile did not succeed in stimulating Emilie to respond as often as they liked. It is well to mark this trait in Emilie because it has been noted all through the studies of her personality.

Now it is possible to study the children from another angle of their social behavior. Let us repeat the examples used above. The hostess who has sent out the invitations to her party may also measure her success by the number of invitations she receives in return for the hospitality she extended. Or to take the case of the guest at the tea party, she may feel that she is a successful member of the group in terms of the number of people who on their own initiative come up to her to pass the time of day. And so with these five children we may compute another ratio by comparing the number of times each child attempted to open social negotiation with another and the number of times each of the other children attempted to do the same towards her. This might be called the "social popularity" ratio, and is represented by the table:

Annette	.8
Cecile	1.2
Emilie	1.0
Marie	.7
Yvonne	1.6

It is easy to understand this ratio. If it is less than 1.0, the popularity of the individual might be questioned; and the amount above unity is an indication of the individual's popularity. It is to be expected that Yvonne would head the list, as she did in her "social success" ratio.

"Initiated" Social Contacts

This shows how frequently each child was *sought out* by her sisters. Annette was sought out frequently by all her sisters, Cecile followed, then Yvonne, while Marie was sought out most frequently by Emilie and Emilie herself by no one.

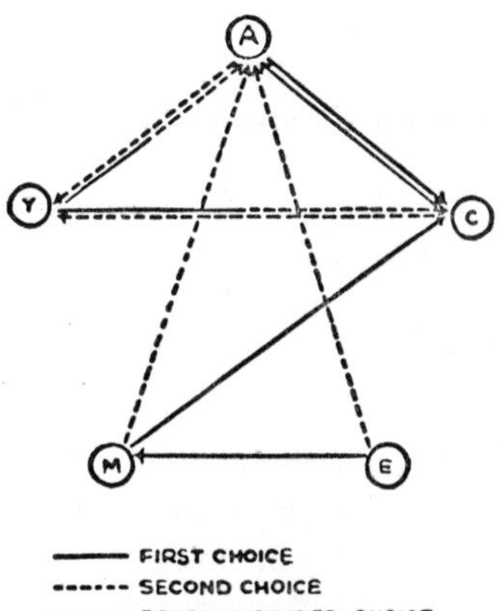

But it is rather surprising to find Annette with the ratio of only .8. This shows quite clearly that Annette is only half as popular as Yvonne. Again, it is in keeping with Emilie's personality to discover that her ratio is unity. Emilie meticulously pays her social debts but is not the least bit anxious to go one step further than is necessary. Cecile is next to Yvonne in popularity, largely because Cecile is unpredictable in her behavior and supplies that note of piquancy and originality which makes for social popularity. Marie is lowest in the scale because she is the smallest and therefore, at this stage, the least socially developed. A more detailed analysis of these values shows that Cecile, Yvonne, Annette, in this order, receive from Marie more overtures than these three initiate towards her, but that Emilie seeks out Marie oftener than Marie seeks her. This too is in line with Emilie's personality, suggesting comparison to the conduct of a dowager who, because of her social assurance, can afford to confer her social blessings without any expectation that they should be returned. Yvonne is the only one of the five sisters who receives more overtures from all four others than she confers. Since in the previous ratio Yvonne was the only one who not only received more responses but responded more to each of the other four, the present ratio of "social popularity" is definitely the result of Yvonne's own efforts and may be likened to the casting of bread upon the waters.

The third one, which might be called the ratio of "social interest," is computed by comparing the number of times each child watches each of the other four with the number of times she herself is watched by each of the others. Because watching or staring is frowned upon as socially immature, it is rather difficult to cite an example of this ratio in ordinary adult behavior. It can be likened to the social interest excited by a conversationalist who is able to hold the attention of a group, or perhaps better to that of the guest who can do parlor tricks or hold the center of the floor as an amateur magician. The values of these ratios for the five children are as follows:

Annette	2.7
Cecile	1.8
Emilie	.6
Marie	.4
Yvonne	1.0

Thus it can be seen that Annette is watched almost three times as often as she watches the others; Cecile is next in order, with Yvonne complacently at unity and Emilie and Marie at the bottom of the list. There is a difference between Annette's and Cecile's behavior. Annette can be compared to the guest with the parlor tricks and Cecile to the conversationalist who can hold the interest. Yvonne's placidity and serenity as the matron of the group is the explanation of the unity of her ratio. Emilie's ratio is low because she is really not very much interested in showing off; and Marie is the lowest of all because in this group of five sisters her performance in most of the skills has lagged behind that of the other four. It is noteworthy that Annette is watched by all four others more than she watches them; that Yvonne is more watched by three of her sisters, Cecile by two (Emilie and Marie), Emilie by one (Marie); and that Marie is watched by none of them as often as they each are watched by her.

"Watching" Contacts

This shows how frequently each child is *watched by* her sisters. Annette was watched by all her sisters, Yvonne followed, then Cecile. Emilie is Yvonne's second choice, while Marie was watched frequently by no one.

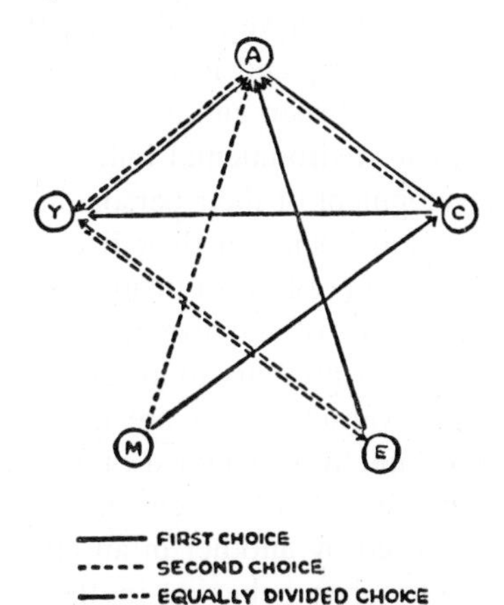

In summing up these three ratios and giving in a few words a picture of the divergent personalities of the five sisters, one must bear in mind that their physical inheritance is almost identical and that the variation in their physical characteristics is between 10 and 15 per cent. The variation in the extremes in these three ratios is 100 per cent, 130 per cent and 600 per cent. In other words, as they started out on their fourth year of life these children had already shown a degree of variation in their social behavior which might be considered an aspect of their personality far beyond what can be explained in terms of their biological inheritance. If we do not take our summary too seriously, we may attempt to describe these different personalities in everyday language. Annette is socially aggressive without marked success, perhaps due to the fact that she is trying too hard. Cecile is socially interesting, and for that reason is more successful than Annette in her appeal to her small community of four. Emilie is independent, self-assured and magnanimous. Marie is the "baby" of the group and may be looked upon as the younger sister. Yvonne is the most mature, the most serene, and gives the picture of the older sister. It will be interesting from time to time to notice the changes that will undoubtedly take place in the personalities of these five. Nothing, of course, is more certain than that the picture presented by these data is by no means crystallized. On the other hand, one can be equally certain that these values derived from actual observation of the five children represent valid and reliable differences.

The question arises, how did these differences emerge in a situation which, on the surface, presents so many common elements? Are these children not living in a common environment? From a superficial point of view they have lived under the same influences; with the same nurses and teachers, and in the same rooms; eating the same food, playing in the same garden and meeting the same people. But it is not this aspect of their environmental influences which has been most important in the development of their personalities. These have been, strangely enough, merely incidents in their lives. The continuous influence has been the interaction of four of them on each of the others.

A study of the five tables from which the above ratios have been computed presents more clearly than any description the infinite number of variables that are introduced in any social situation. The fact that Annette is watched more frequently than any of the other children definitely alters her behavior in every social situation. When one child is ignored by another in an attempt at a social overture, this experience modifies her behavior in the next. Multiply this by a number that represents the frequency with which these children have interacted one with the other, and one gets a picture of a variety of social influences that might reach astronomical proportions.

The fact that a child has been rebuffed is far more important in moulding personality than any rules, conventions or regulations. The emphasis in the development of personality has erroneously been placed upon the obvious and static aspects of the environment, and the dynamic and infinitely variable factors of social intercourse have been overlooked. It is not astonishing, with this view in mind, to observe and demonstrate the differences in these children, and also to anticipate that they will diverge more and more in their personalities. It would be far more astonishing to have discovered that even within the narrow limits of this social community of five, these sisters had resembled themselves as closely in their personalities as they do in their physical characteristics.

Later on in their development, because of the necessity to conform to rather rigid patterns of behavior when they learn the crystallized rules of manners and the social niceties, their *observable* behavior will appear to be almost identical. The mistake has been made of interpreting these crystallized behavior patterns as the true counterpart of personality. However, it is only when the individual is permitted an opportunity to express his wishes and desires, by means of his own initiative, through imaginative and creative endeavor, that the true differences in personality emerge. These always are potent in the innermost thoughts of individuals. At this stage, as indicated above, the Quintuplets have shown salutary differences because, aside from the necessary conformity in the routine, they have been unhampered in the development of individual personalities.

At the present time the five sisters form their own community. It will be interesting to follow their development. It can only be a source of gratification that, despite rather than because of their intimate blood relationship, their training has permitted them five separate individualities; and it would be a tragic circumstance if an attempt were made to incorporate into their training a rigid discipline of old-fashioned obedience and conformity.

---

35. Social Organization among Dogs of Different Temperaments, Terriers and Beagles, Reared Together *

MODERN DISCUSSIONS of human social behavior often minimize biological factors. Actually, their influence in man is difficult to trace. Man is relatively plastic and must respond to complex forces as he develops; moreover, his heredity and experiences are obscure and cannot be sufficiently controlled. With purebred dogs genetic background can be controlled and its influence on temperamental differences can be determined. This selection describes an interesting experimental study of the influence of hereditary and experiential factors on social behavior in animals. The extension of its findings to humans is, of course, highly speculative.

IN PREVIOUS STUDIES an analysis has been made of the social organization among dogs with emphasis mainly on dominance-submissive differences in food-taking situations. The experiments have dealt chiefly with the variations among the members of a litter of pure breed or

* W. T. James, "Social organization among dogs of different temperaments, terriers and beagles, reared together," *Journal of Comparative and Physiological Psychology*, XLIV (1951), 71–77. By permission of the author and the American Psychological Association.

The writer wishes to express appreciation to Dr. C. C. Little and Dr. J. P. Scott for the opportunity of working at the Jackson Laboratory. The work was done under a Research Grant from the Graduate School of the University of Georgia.

hybrid animals. There has been no previous attempt to study specifically the social order which forms when dogs of quite different temperaments are reared together from the time of birth. This report presents the data of an experiment dealing with the latter problem.

The present study had two objectives. First, to determine the dominance-submission order among the members of two litters of dogs of different breeds, and second, to determine whether there was a breed-preference order among the members of each group.

SUBJECTS

The animals consisted of two groups of dogs, each group containing both beagle and terrier puppies reared together since birth. One group of three beagles and two terriers was reared by a terrier mother. The second group of three beagles and three terriers was reared by a beagle mother. Both litters were born during the same week, and the puppies were exchanged while their eyes were still closed. In July, 1948, when the present study began, the dogs were one year of age and had been removed from the indoor kennels for about six months. Each group was confined in a rather large outside run which was surrounded by a blind fence, and for this reason their contacts with other dogs had been limited. These two groups of dogs therefore offered an excellent opportunity for studying the behavior of different types of dogs which had been reared together.

Even on casual acquaintance with these two breeds it becomes evident that they differ in temperament. The beagles are a typical hound type of medium size, weighing around 22 pounds. The body is short and muscular with a rather round and broad chest, a broad head, and a rather square, full muzzle. The coat is short and varies in color, containing red and white and, sometimes, black and white patterns. The terrier is a smaller breed, weighing on the average about 16 pounds. The body is thin and the head is rather thin and has a long thin muzzle. The body is more sagittal-shaped than round. The coat varies in mixtures of black and white, and the hair is of the stiff, wiry type. The terriers are highly active and excitable animals. They would invariably come forward as the experimenter entered the runs and begin to jump up as if trying to get attention. The beagles, on the other hand, would remain in the background and would seldom come within reach of the experimenter's hand. If the terriers were removed from the group, however, some of the most aggressive beagles would come within reach. Most of the beagles were difficult to catch. They would run to the far end of the kennel and would have to be cornered before the leash could be applied. When cornered they would take the passive defense attitude. They are definitely of a more inhibited type than the terriers.

EXPERIMENT I: DOMINANCE ORDER

Procedure

The method used in previous experiments to measure dominance was used in this experiment. The apparatus consisted of a food pan surrounded by a wooden frame with a lid over the pan which could be opened with a string by the experimenter. The hole over the pan was so small only one dog could eat at a time. The dogs soon learned that food was in the pan, and would run to the pan when it was placed in the kennel. During the experiments the dogs were fed first as a whole group and then later grouped in twos and threes to determine which animal would hold the pan and take the food. The positions of the dominant dogs are relatively easy to observe by this method. There is some difficulty in isolating the order among those of the mid-group and those at the bottom of the hierarchy. In the present case, however, the dominance order had been analyzed after 45 separate feeding experiments had been completed.

Results

A straight-line order of dominance had formed in both groups, with the terriers in the dominant positions. The dominance order of Group 1 ranged in series from high to low as follows: 576 ♂ Terrier, 577 ♂ Terrier, 580 ♀ Terrier, 618 ♂ Beagle, 615 ♀ Beagle, and 620 ♀ Beagle. The dominance order in Group 2 was as follows: 579 ♀ Terrier, 578 ♂ Terrier, 619 ♀ Beagle, 617 ♀ Beagle, and 616 ♂ Beagle. Those animals on the bottom of the hierarchy in each group, Beagles 620 and 616, were dominated by all members of their respective groups, and each animal gave the passive defense behavior when challenged by other dogs.

It has been emphasized in previous reports that there is little fighting between the dominant and the extremely submissive dogs. The same observations hold true in the present experiment. There was a great deal of conflict between the dominant terriers, but there was seldom an actual fight between terriers and beagles. This dominance order seems to be worked out in almost every case without any actual combat between the animals. As the dominant dog growls and challenges the position of the less dominant animal, the submissive dog retreats. Actual conflict occurs only among those which are about equal in dominance, or those rather close together in the hierarchy. There were many instances, of course, in which the terriers bit the less aggressive beagles, but in almost every case the beagle retreated without a fight.

In previous experiments we have reported that the dominant males of the group always sire the puppies. During these experiments four of the females, three beagles and one terrier, came into heat before the end of the summer. One beagle female was in Group 1, while two beagles and a terrier were in Group 2. In each case the dominant terrier male of the group sired the puppies. This evidence was based on observation of the matings and, also, on the form and coat color of the puppies. It was quite evident that the progeny of all beagles were F_1 hybrids while those of the terrier were pure breed.

EXPERIMENT II: BREED PREFERENCE

Since each litter was reared as a group isolated from contact with other dogs, there was opportunity to observe not only how the members of each group reacted to beagles and terriers from their own litter but, also, to the strangers of the second litter.

Procedure

An apparatus was constructed consisting of three compartments, A, B, and C, connected by alleys, as shown in Figure 1. The materials used were one-by-two inch boards and two-inch mesh wire. The cages were each 5 feet square, and the sides were 4 feet high. The alleys connecting the cages were 10 feet long. The animal to be tested was confined in Cage C, while decoys were placed in A and B. Since the sides of C were covered by heavy burlap bags, the dog confined there could not see the decoy animals until it was released through the sliding door into the alley. A wire framework was constructed around the doors of compartments A and B on the inside of the cages so that the test animal could enter the doors of compartments A and B and, at the same time, the animals confined there could not get out. In this manner the test animal was free to enter and make contact through the wire with the dogs in either A or B, but could not actually get into the cage with them. Each cage had a vertical sliding door which could be operated from the adjoining building by the use of strings. By means of these doors the animals could be inclosed in the cages in order to observe the reactions among the dogs for a longer period of time, if necessary. During the observation periods the observer was out of sight of the animals but could observe them from a window on the second

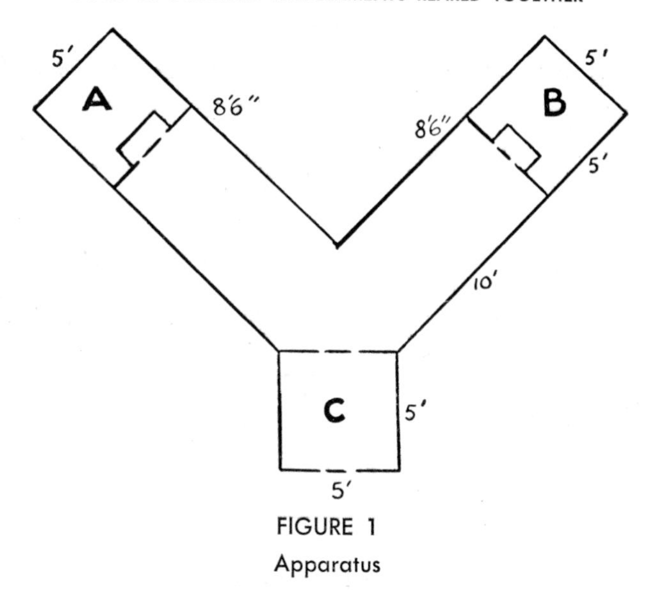

FIGURE 1

Apparatus

floor of the adjoining building. In this manner the dogs were free to react without being distracted by the experimenter.

During the experiment either a beagle or a terrier was confined in the starting compartment, C, while other animals, either strange or friendly beagles or terriers, were placed in A and B. The test dog was then released and observed for a period of 5 minutes with the positions of the animal noted on a record sheet every 15 seconds. If the animal remained either in or just before a compartment, nosing the dogs in the compartment or scratching on the wire for 75 per cent of the time, it was considered as having selected that particular group. On the other hand, if the animal spent the greater part of the time either running back from compartment A to B or remaining either in or near compartment C, it was considered as not having a preference for either group.

Results

Table 1 shows the summary of 21 choices beagles made to strange or friendly terriers and beagles, while Table 2 shows the summary of 21 choices terriers made to strange or friendly terriers or beagles. In the test situation the animal had three choices. It could either choose terriers or beagles or make no choice at all. In Table 1 the total number of times beagles were chosen by beagles was 11, while terriers were chosen 2 times and no choice was made 8 times. In comparing the observed results with those expected by chance, the value of chi-

TABLE 1

Reactions of beagles to strange and friendly beagles and terriers

Choice	No. Choices	Beagle Mates	Beagle Strs.	Terrier Mates	Terrier Strs.	No Choice
B. Strs. & T. Mates	5		2			3
T. Strs. & B. Mates	6	4				2
T. Mates & B. Mates	5	3		2		
B. Strs. & T. Strs.	5		2			3
Total	21	7	4	2	0	8

Chi-square = 6.25.

TABLE 2

Reactions of terriers to strange and friendly beagles and terriers

Choice	No. Choices	Beagle Mates	Beagle Strs.	Terrier Mates	Terrier Strs.	No Choice
T. Strs. & B. Mates	5	3				2
B. Strs. & T. Mates	7		3	3		1
B. Mates & T. Mates	4	4				0
B. Strs. & T. Strs.	5		4			1
Total	21	7	7	3	0	4

Chi-square = 10.5.

square was calculated for each group. The value of chi-square for the beagles was 6.25.

Of the 21 possible choices by the terriers, 14 were made to the beagles, 3 to the terriers, and 4 were of no preference. The value of chi-square for the terriers was 10.5.

From these data and the observations of the animals, there seems to be no doubt that the beagles were trying to avoid the terriers of each group, while the terriers were trying to reach the beagles of each group. This was possibly due to the strong differences in dominance among the members of the group. Since the beagles were dominated and frequently challenged by the terriers, they had developed a definite withdrawal attitude toward them.

EXPERIMENT III: REACTIONS TO MATES AND STRANGERS OF THE SAME BREED

Procedure

In Experiment II the animals had a choice between either terriers or beagles. Another short experiment was done in which the dogs had a choice between strangers and mates of one breed.

Results

Table 3 shows the summary of four choices the beagles made between beagle mates and beagle strangers, and here a chance value was obtained. It also shows eight choices the beagles made between their own

TABLE 3

Choices of beagles between two groups of beagles and two groups of terriers

Choice	*No. Choices*	*Beagle Mates*	*Beagle Strs.*	*Terrier Mates*	*Terrier Strs.*	*No Choice*
B. Mates & B. Strs.	4	2	2			
T. Mates & T. Strs.	8			3	1	4
Total	12	2	2	3	1	4

Chi-square B. mates and B. strangers = .666.
Chi-square T. mates and T. strangers = 1.69.

TABLE 4

Choices of terriers between two groups of beagles and two groups of terriers

Choice	*No. Choices*	*Beagle Mates*	*Beagle Strs.*	*Terrier Mates*	*Terrier Strs.*	*No Choice*
B. Mates & B. Strs.	4					4
T. Mates & T. Strs.	8			1	2	5
Total	12			1	2	9

Chi-square B. mates and B. strangers = 5.29.
Chi-square T. mates and T. strangers = 3.609.

terrier mates and terrier strangers, and in this case about a chance value was obtained. There appeared to be a tendency for the submissive beagles to avoid the strange terriers. This was especially observed in the case of 616. When this dog had a choice between two groups of terriers it would remain before compartment C and look toward A or B, but in no case did it enter either of these alleys. There was every indication that the dog was frightened by the terriers and remained away from them.

Table 4 shows the summary of four choices the terriers made to beagle mates and strangers and eight choices to terrier mates and strangers. In each case there was a significant chi-square value in regard to "no choice." When beagles were presented there were in a sense two stimuli of equal value, and the terriers ran from cage A to B barking at both groups. It is probable that there was a failure of choice in regard to terriers because of the high degree of conflict between the animals.

EXPERIMENT IV: TENDENCY TO PROTECT FEEDING AREA

Procedure

An attempt was made in a preliminary study to see if the dominant animals would protect a feeding area around the food pan as well as protect the pan. In 14 experiments cage A was made a feeding area with the food pan described above placed in A. During the experiments dominant and submissive animals were placed in the alleys of the experimental runs. A small amount of food was placed in the pan in area A and then the gate to the area was opened from the adjoining observation building. Since the animals had already become adjusted to the food pan they would compete to get into cage A and eat the food. Of the 14 experimental observations under these conditions, four cases consisted of beagles together, seven of terriers together, and three of beagles and terriers.

Results

The only observation of interest here was that in every case the dominant dog would take the food. These dogs would, as a rule, stand by the gate and, as it was opened, rush to the pan and begin eating. The less dominant dogs would stand aside. On four occasions Terrier 598, a dominant animal, was matched with Animals 578 and 580, and in each case 598 not only took the food, but kept the less dominant terriers out of area A. On two occasions Terrier 576 was matched with the less dominant terriers, 577 and 580, and 576 also kept these out of area A. When Terriers 576 and 577 were matched with less dominant beagles, the terriers not only took the food but kept the less dominant beagles out of area A. In the cases in which beagles were together, the dominant dog would eat, but there was less tendency to protect the area against the other beagles. These observations suggest that as the degree of dominance increases, the area of dominance becomes extended. This will have to be checked in further experiments, however, before any definite conclusions can be drawn.

SUMMARY

1. In this experiment with two mixed litters of terriers and beagles, the only social organization seemed to be based on the dominance-submissive differences among the dogs.

2. In each litter the terriers were dominant. They controlled the feeding situations as well as sired all pups born during the course of the experiment.

3. In the studies in which the beagles had a choice of terriers or beagles, the beagles chose beagles and avoided terriers, which dominated them.

4. The terriers, on the other hand, went to the beagles, which they dominated.

5. There was some tendency for terriers to avoid their aggressive terrier mates and strangers. This is probably due to the fact that, since there was a greater degree of dominance among the terriers, there was also greater conflict among them.

6. In a preliminary experiment in which one area of the experimental kennel was made a feeding area, there was some tendency for the dominant terriers not only to take the food presented but to keep the less dominant animals out of the area. This suggests that, as the dominance tendency increases, there is extension of the area dominated. Further studies are needed, however, before this is conclusive.

---

36. Pictures in Our Heads *

IMAGERY OCCUPIES an important place in the study of thinking, and stereotypes are mental images that play a significant part in social relations. In ordinary thinking the symbols we use differ widely and usually stem from our personal experiences. In intergroup relations, however, the stereotypes are shared by a large group of individuals and often represent socially standardized errors that interfere with optimal adjustments among peoples. In this selection Dr. Klineberg reviews a number of research studies of these barriers to clear thinking in intergroup relations.

ABOUT A YEAR AGO I was in London at the invitation of British psychologists and sociologists in order to lecture on "National Stereotypes." Throughout the preceding day, during which I was undoubtedly made more sensitive by my preoccupation with this topic, I kept running into examples of such stereotyped thinking.

In my hotel, I heard someone say, "Oh, she has that Scottish stub-

* Otto Klineberg, "Pictures in our heads," *The Courier,* VIII (September, 1955), 5–8. This article from the September, 1955, issue of *The Courier,* monthly publication of UNESCO, is reprinted by permission of the author and UNESCO.

bornness, you know." A book review in a newspaper used the phrase, "With true Gallic wit." At the theatre that evening, during the interval, I caught part of a conversation in which a pretty girl said to her escort, "I know that all Americans have a 'line' "; and in a mystery story that I read before retiring, there was a reference to "typical German thoroughness."

These are all instances of those "pictures in our heads" to which Walter Lippmann gave the name of stereotypes. They are typical of the ease with which most of us generalize about national or ethnic groups, usually without even stopping to think where such "information" comes from, and whether it represents the truth, the whole truth, or anything like the truth.

There are certainly very few, if any, among us who have not succumbed to the temptation to stereotype nations. One might almost describe the tendency as inevitable, or at least very nearly so. We *know* that Englishmen are reserved, and Irishmen pugnacious; we have heard it all our lives; besides most people agree with us. If we are asked, however, *how* we know, we would not easily find a suitable answer.

One of the earliest careful studies of this tendency was made by Katz and Braly, in 1932, in connection with the stereotypes held by Princeton University students. The technique was simple.

Each student was given a list of traits, and a list of nationalities; from the first list he chose the five traits which he regarded as characteristic of each national or racial group.

The results showed a fair degree of unanimity, e.g. out of 100 students, 78 described the Germans as "scientifically minded," and 65 described them as "industrious"; 53 students used the adjective "artistic" for the Italians; the same percentage described the English as "sportsmanlike"; 79 agreed that the Jews were "shrewd" and 54 stated that the Turks were "cruel"; 84 regarded Negroes as "superstitious," and 75 described them as "lazy."

We may summarize the results in a slightly different manner by indicating the three or four characteristics most commonly ascribed to each nationality. These included, for the Germans: scientifically-minded, industrious, stolid; the Italians, impulsive, artistic, passionate; Negroes, superstitious, lazy, happy-go-lucky, ignorant; the Irish, pugnacious, quick-tempered, witty; the English, sportsmanlike, intelligent, conventional; the Jews, shrewd, mercenary, industrious; the Americans, industrious, intelligent, materialistic, ambitious; the Chinese, superstitious, sly, conservative; the Japanese, intelligent, industrious, progressive; the Turks, cruel, religious, treacherous.

A recent study of the stereotypes of German students at the Free University of Berlin by Sodhi and Bergius showed a similar willingness to stereotype nations and, on the whole, comparable results. Americans, for example, were described as sportsmanlike, democratic, materialistic; the Italians as warmblooded, musical, light-hearted; the Chinese as poor, inscrutable, modest; the Germans as conscious of duty, loving their homeland, intelligent; the English as proud of their nation, bound by traditions, sportsmanlike. There were some variations between the German and the American stereotypes, but on the whole the overlapping is considerable.

On a more extensive scale, a study conducted in 9 countries under the auspices of Unesco in 1948 and 1949, showed that such stereotyped thinking could easily be elicited almost anywhere. In each country approximately 1,000 respondents, representing a cross-section of the population, were given a list of 12 traits, and asked to choose those which they thought were most applicable to themselves, to Americans, to Russians, and in some cases, to two or three other national groups as well. They could choose as many of the traits as they wished.

The British, for example, thought of Americans as primarily progressive, conceited, generous, peace-loving, intelligent, practical. The Americans regarded the British as intelligent, hard-working, brave, peace-loving, conceited and self-controlled. The Norwegians described the Russians as hardworking, domineering, backward, brave, cruel and practical. The full results can be found in the volume by Buchanan and Cantril, "How Nations See Each Other."

The "self-image" is also revealing. The British saw themselves as peace-loving, brave, hard-working, intelligent; the French saw themselves as intelligent, peace-loving, generous, and brave; the Americans saw themselves as peace-loving, generous, intelligent and progressive. All the groups agreed on one item: their own nation was the most peace-loving of all!

Few people realize how much the existence of stereotypes may colour our relations with other people, even to the extent of seeing them differently as a result. Psychologists have long known that our perceptions of the external world, and particularly of human beings, are determined not only by what is *out there,* but also by what is *in ourselves.* What we see is determined in part by what we expect to see. If we believe, for example, that Italians are noisy, we will have a tendency to notice those Italians who are indeed noisy; if we are in the presence of some who do not fit the stereotype, we may not even realize that they, too, are Italian. If someone points that fact out to us and says: "Look, those people are Italians, and they are not noisy," we can always dismiss them as exceptions.

Since there is no limit to the number of cases that can be so dismissed, we may continue to cling to the pictures in our heads, in spite of all the facts to the contrary. This does not always happen. Stereotypes do sometimes change in the light of new experience, and evidence for this is presented later. If we have had them for a long time, however, we surrender them with great reluctance.

A number of significant investigations have shown in a very dramatic manner how our stereotypes may determine our perceptions. Some years ago Allport and Postman, psychologists at Harvard University (Cambridge, USA) studied some of the phenomena associated with the spread of rumours, making use of a technique known as "serial reproduction," a very simple device which anyone can use with a group of friends in his own home. They showed a picture to one student, and he described to a second student what he saw in the picture. The second then told a third what the first had told him; the third told the fourth, and so on, through a series of 8 to 10 reproductions. Then a comparison was made between the final result and the original presentation.

One of the pictures used in this investigation showed a scene in a subway in which, in addition to a number of people seated, there were two men standing, one a white man, the other a Negro. The white man was dressed in working clothes, with an open razor stuck in his belt. It so happens that the stereotype of the Negro held by some people in the USA includes the notion that Negroes carry with them an open razor, of which they make ready use in an argument.

The psychologists were able to demonstrate that in half of the groups who served as subjects in these experiments, before the end of the series of reproductions had been reached, the razor had "moved" from the white man to the Negro. In some instances, the Negro was even represented as brandishing the razor violently in the face of the white man. This does not mean that half of the subjects in the experiment saw the Negro with the razor, since if only one person in the chain made this error, it would be repeated by those that followed. Interestingly enough, this did not occur when the subjects were Negroes (who rejected the stereotype), or young children (who had not yet "learned" it).

Another study conducted by Razran in New York points in the same direction. A group of college students in the USA were shown photographs of 30 girls, and asked to judge each photograph on a 5-point scale, indicating their general liking of the girl, her beauty, her intelligence, her character, her ambition, and her "entertainingness." Two months later, the same students were again shown the same photographs, but with surnames added. For some of the photographs Jewish surnames were given, such as Rabinowitz, Finkelstein, etc; a second group received Italian names, such as Scarano, Grisolia, etc; a third group Irish surnames, such as McGillicuddy, O'Shaughnessy, etc; a fourth, "old American" names like Adams and Clark.

The investigator was able to demonstrate that the mere labelling of these photographs with such surnames definitely affected the manner in which the girls were perceived. The addition of Jewish and Italian names, for example, resulted in a substantial drop in general liking, and a similar drop for judgments of beauty and character. The addition of the same names resulted in a rise in the ratings for ambition, particularly marked in the case of the Jewish surnames. It seems clear that the same photographs *looked different* just because they could now be associated with the stereotype held by these students.

If a great many people agree that a particular trait is associated with a particular nation, does that make it true? There is a fairly widespread theory to the effect that "where there's smoke there's fire"; or, in other words, that the very existence of a stereotype is, to some extent at least, an argument in favour of its truth. Otherwise, the argument runs, where does the stereotype come from? How would it come into existence?

There is, however, a good deal of evidence as to the possibility that stereotypes may develop without any kernel of truth whatsoever. We all know how widespread is the notion that intelligent people have high foreheads, yet scientific investigation in this field has failed to reveal any such relationship. The stereotype of the criminal as bearing in his features the mark of his criminality is widely accepted, but it is equally without foundation; the famous British criminologist, Sir Charles Goring, was able to demonstrate that a composite photograph, representing criminals in British gaols, bore no resemblance to the accepted stereotype of the criminal.

Stereotypes frequently change. In some cases it may be argued that this corresponds to a real change in the characteristics of the people; in others, however, it seems much more likely to be due to external circumstances which have little or nothing to do with the group concerned. The Dutch sociologist, Shrieke, has, for example, made a collection of some of the descriptive phrases applied to the Chinese during the course of their residence in the state of California, USA.

When the Chinese were needed in California, in order to carry on certain types of occupation, they were welcome there; during that period, newspapers and journals referred to them as among "the most worthy of our newly adopted citizens"; "the best immigrants in California"; they were spoken of as thrifty, sober, tractable, inoffensive, law-abiding. This flattering picture prevailed over a considerable period of time, but around 1860, presumably because economic competition had grown much more severe, there was a marked change in the stereotype of the Chinese. The phrases now applied to them included: "a distinct people," "unassimilable," "their presence lowered the plane of living," etc. They were spoken of as clannish, criminal, debased, servile, deceitful, and vicious.

This startling change can hardly be accounted for by any real modification of the characteristics of the Chinese population of California. The most acceptable explanation is that when it became advantageous to reduce the competition from the Chinese, the stereotype was altered in a direction which would help to justify such action. In this historical case it seems reasonable to conclude that the change in the characteristics ascribed to the Chinese throws doubt on the notion that stereotypes must necessarily contain some truth.

Another Dutch sociologist, Den Hollander, has studied the historical changes in the stereotype of the Hungarians in Europe. He points out that for centuries after the migration of Hungarians to Central Europe, they had a bad reputation, and were regarded as culturally different, and therefore inferior, to Europeans generally. During the 15th and 16th centuries, however, when they joined in the war against the Turks, they were pictured as a brave, devout, and chivalrous people.

By the second half of the 18th century their popularity had again declined, and they were described as savage, lazy, egotistical, unreliable, and tyrannous. This picture changed again a little later, when the Hungarians became romanticized and idealized. Den Hollander believes that the image followed the pattern of political interrelationships; it seems unlikely that there was sufficient transformation in the character of the people to justify the change in the national image.

One of the most amusing examples of a stereotype which has apparently developed without any kernel of truth emerges from an investigation by Schoenfeld on stereotypes associated with proper names. Here again the technique used was a simple one. The American students who served as subjects in this study were given a list of eight proper names and a list of eight adjectives; their task was to "match" or pair each name with the adjective regarded as most appropriate.

Since there were 120 students, and eight names, the results to be expected by chance alone, that is to say, if no stereotype existed, would be 120 divided by eight, or 15 for each name. The actual results showed that 63 out of the 120 judges matched Richard with "good looking"; 58 judged Herman to be "stupid"; 59 judged Rex as "athletic"; 71 associated Adrian with "artistic"; and 104 agreed that Cuthbert was "a sissy." In a similar experiment with American girls judging feminine names, 54 regarded Minnie as stupid; 60 saw Linda as sophisticated; 69 said that Mary was religious; 58 that Maisie was talkative; and 73 that Agatha was middle-aged.

Although this study was done with American students, it seems quite certain that comparable stereotypes would be found in languages other than English.

In any case, it can hardly be argued that Richard is really better looking than John, or Herman more stupid than Cuthbert. To return to ethnic stereotypes, one significant study may be cited which demonstrates the manner in which stereotypes may develop without any basis in truth. The American sociologist, La Piere, studied the attitudes of residents of California toward first and second generation Armenian immigrants in Fresno County in that State. There was almost complete agreement that these Armenians had more than their share of faults, and the general attitude toward them was relatively unfriendly.

La Piere proceeded to question non-Armenians as to the reasons for their antipathies, and he was able to classify the answers into three stereotypes. In the first place, it was stated that Armenians were treacherous, lying, deceitful. In actual fact, when measured by the criterion of business integrity, the Armenian merchants turned out to be equal and frequently superior to others. In the second place, they were alleged to be parasites, making excessive demands upon charitable organizations, free clinics, etc. Actually, such demands by them were less than half of what would be expected in terms of their proportion of the population.

Finally, it was said that they had an inferior code of morality, and they were always getting into trouble with the law. In fact, police records showed that they appeared in only 1.5 per cent of Police Court cases, although they constituted approximately 6 per cent of the population. La Piere concludes that all of these stereotypes have one factor in common, viz. that they are definitely false. This does not mean that stereotypes *never* contain any truth. It does mean that they *can* develop without any truth whatsoever.

There is, however, the possibility that a little truth may enter into a stereotype through the back door, so to speak. A Frenchman, with considerable experience of international meetings, once said that when he had occasion to address such a meeting he usually did so in a rather oratorical, flowery, "Latin" style. He said that otherwise his Anglo-

Saxon colleagues would be disappointed! When he was with other Frenchmen, he reverted to a quieter, more matter-of-fact, "un-Latin" manner, which really suited him personally much better.

In this case, the stereotype itself determined his behaviour under certain circumstances, and undoubtedly reinforced the conviction of the Anglo-Saxons that they really knew what Frenchmen were like. More rarely, the stereotype may operate in reverse. A member of a group with the reputation for frugality, may go out of his way to spend freely, and tip lavishly; if the stereotype calls for lack of punctuality, he may make it a point to arrive at his destination well before the hour specified. Since, in that case, as was indicated above, he will probably be regarded as an exception, the stereotype will still prevail.

Stereotyped thinking may be *almost* inevitable, but there is good evidence that it can at least be reduced, if not eliminated. Eighteen years after the Katz and Braly study, another psychologist (Gilbert) applied the same technique to a new generation of Princeton students. He found that there was some persistence of stereotypes, but also a very important change which he describes as "a fading effect."

There is much less agreement among the students in 1950 than in 1932; any specific trait is usually checked by a much smaller proportion of students in the later study. In 1932, for example, 84 per cent of the students described the Negroes as lazy; in 1950 the percentage had dropped to 31. The description of Italians as artistic drops from 83 to 28.

In London, a Unesco study conducted by H. E. O. James and Cora Tenen, showed how specific personal experiences might affect the nature and content of stereotypes. What they did was to obtain from schoolchildren their opinions of other ethnic groups, particularly of African Negroes, and then bring them into contact with two able African women teachers who spent a few weeks in the schools.

The "before and after" picture is very striking. As an example, a child before the experience stated that "I do not like black people; it's the *colour;* it makes me nervous; they might be savage . . . they are different in nature to us, more savage and cruel sometimes, so you don't trust them ever." The same child after the experience said: "Miss V. and Miss W. were nice people . . . there does not seem any difference between them and us except the colour. I think that Negroes are like that—just like us, except for the colour. I like them. They are nice people."

The authors give many examples of similar changes that occurred. Stereotypes cannot always be modified so strikingly nor so fast, but the fact that they can be changed at all as a result of experience is itself encouraging.

Sometimes just growing older helps. In a study sponsored by Unesco, Piaget and Weil report the results of a series of interviews with Swiss children of different ages. One interview with a little girl aged eight years ran as follows:

> Have you heard of foreigners?— Yes, there are Germans and French.— Are there any differences between these foreigners?— Yes, the Germans are bad, they are always making war. The French are poor and everything is dirty there. Then I have heard of Russians, but they are not at all nice.— Do you have any personal knowledge of the French, Germans, or Russians, or have you read something about them?— No.— Then how do you know?— Everyone says so.

On the other hand, a boy aged thirteen years, after having mentioned a large number of foreign countries of which he had heard, was asked, "Are there any differences between all those countries?" and his answer was, in part, "*you find all types of people everywhere.*" We are not all as "mature" as this thirteen-year-old boy, but perhaps we can move in that direction. Or is it possible that the Swiss are . . . ? Oh no! No stereotypes!

---

37. The Grocer and the Chief *

CONTEMPORARY SOCIETY is characterized by rapid changes in our ways of life. History has taught us, however, that not all innovations are accepted; even technological "advances" are often rejected by the people whom they might benefit. As one example, we might note how much controversy there has been about water fluoridation, although the Salk vaccine was accepted relatively easily. Social change apparently involves many interesting psychological problems. One way to study them might be to isolate the factors that determine individuals' responses. We might start, for example, in a particular situation and identify the innovators or accepters and the resisters. We might then try to find out what differentiates them as groups, aside from their responses to the precipitating situation.

In the following paper, Dr. Lerner gives us a detailed description of a small Turkish village and some of its key individuals at two

* Daniel Lerner, "The grocer and the chief," *Harper's Magazine,* CCXI (September, 1955), 47–56. By permission of Daniel Lerner, author and copyright holder.

different points in time—before and after a significant change affecting the whole community. His account provides an interesting case study for testing our thinking about the social and psychological dynamics of change. Thoughtfully analyzed, it may stimulate extensions of our thinking and offer additional enlightenment.

THE TURKISH VILLAGE of Balgat lies about five miles out of Ankara, in the southerly direction. It does not show on the standard maps and it does not figure in the standard histories. I first heard of it in the autumn of 1950 and most Turks have not heard of it today. Yet the story of the modern Middle East is summed up in the recent career of Balgat. Indeed the personal meaning of modernization in underdeveloped lands everywhere is traced in miniature in the lives of two Balgati—the Grocer and the Chief.

My first exposure to Balgat came while leafing through several hundred interviews that had been recorded in Turkey during the spring of 1950. One caught my eye because of the underlying tone of bitterness in the interviewer's summary of his impressions, his earnest sense of the hopelessness of place and people. I was moved by his five interviews in this village; even so, something in the perspective seemed awry. For one thing, the interviewer was clearly more sensitized to what he saw than what he heard. The import of what had been said to him, and duly recorded in his reports, had somehow escaped his attention. For another, in the interval between the interviews and my reading of them, there had been a national election in which, as a stunning surprise to everybody, practically all Turks over twenty had voted and the government had been turned out of office.

Nothing like this ever happened before in Turkey, possibly because universal suffrage with an opposition party in a fair election had never been tried before. The dazed experts who explain Middle Eastern events could only say of this epochal deed, while sparring for time, that the Anatolian villagers had done it. Since it would be hard to imagine Anatolian villagers of more standard pattern than the Balgati whose collected opinions were spread before me, I had it on top authority that during the summer of 1950 they had entered History. But it was not immediately obvious by what route.

Four years later, the Balgat interviews had become part of an oversized draft manuscript on the modernizing of the Middle East. To provide at least the internal satisfaction of having been "there," I went out to Turkey myself in the spring of 1954—an odyssey which terminated where my ideas began: in Balgat, on the eve of a second national election.

BALGAT PERCEIVED

The interviewer who recorded Balgat on the verge—his name was Tosun B.—had detected no gleam of the future during his sojourn there. "The village is a barren one," he wrote. "The main color is gray, so is the dust on the divan on which I am writing now." Tosun was a serious young scholar from Ankara and he loved the poor in his own fashion. He had sought out Balgat to find the deadening past rather than the brave new world. He found it: "I have seen quite a lot of villages in the barren mountainous East, but never such a colorless, shapeless dump. This was the reason I chose the village. It could have been half an hour to Ankara by car if it had a road, yet it is about two hours to the capital by car without almost any road and is just forgotten, forsaken, right under our noses."

Tosun also sought and found persons to match the place. Of the five villagers he interviewed, his heart went straight out to the village shepherd. "The respondent was literally in rags and in this cold wheather [*sic*] he had no shoe," wrote Tosun, in his own spelling, "but the mud and dirt on his feet were as thick as any boot. He was small, but looked rugged and sad, very sad. He was proud of being chosen by me and though limited tried his best to answer the questions. Was so bashfull [*sic*] that his blush was often evident under the thick layer of dirt on his face. He at times threw loud screams of laughter when there was nothing to laugh about. These he expected to be accepted as answers, for when I said 'Well?' he was shocked, as if he had already answered the question."

Tosun attributed to the Chief of Balgat his frustration in not getting more interviews. He reported that the Chief "imposed himself on me all the time I was in the village, even tried to dictate to me, which I refused in a polite way. I couldn't have followed his directions, as I would have ended up only interviewing his family." Tosun did succeed in talking privately with two Balgat farmers, but it is clear that throughout these interviews he was still haunted by the shepherd and bedeviled by the Chief. Not until he came to interview the village grocer did Tosun find another Balgati who aroused in him a comparable emotional response. Tosun's equal hostility to these very different men made me curious, and eventually convinced me of the notion that the parable of modern Turkey was the story of the Grocer and the Chief.

Aside from resenting the containment strategy which the Chief was operating against him, Tosun gave few details about the man. He reported only the impression that "the *Muhtar* is an unpleasant old man. Looks mean and clever. He is the absolute dictator of this little village." Nor did Tosun elaborate his disapproval of the *Muhtar's* opinions beyond the comment that "years have left him some sort of useless, mystic wisdom." But the main source of Tosun's hostility, it appeared, was that the Chief made him nervous. His notes concluded: "He found what I do curious, even probably suspected it. I am sure he will report it to the first official who comes to the village."

Against the Grocer, however, Tosun reversed his neural field. He quickly perceived that he made the Grocer nervous; and for this Tosun disliked *him*. His notes read:

> The respondent is comparatively the most city-like dressed man in the village. He even wore some sort of a necktie. He is the village's only grocer, but he is not really a grocer, but so he is called, originally the foodstuffs in his shop are much less than the things to be worn, like the cheapest of materials and shoes and slippers, etc. His greatest stock is drinks and cigarettes which he sells most. He is a very unimpressive type, although physically he covers quite a space. He gives the impression of a fat shadow. Although he is on the same level with the other villagers, when there are a few of the villagers around, he seems to want to distinguish himself by keeping quiet, and as soon as they depart he starts to talk too much. This happened when we were about to start the interview. He most evidently wished to feel that he is closer to me than he is to them and was curiously careful with his accent all during the interview. In spite of his unique position, for he is the only unfarming person and the only merchant in the village, he does not seem to possess an important part of the village community. In spite of all his efforts, he is considered by the villagers even less than the least farmer. Although he presented to take the interview naturally, he was nervous and also was proud to be interviewed although he tried to hide it.

All of this posed a weighty question: Why did the Chief make Tosun nervous and why did Tosun make the Grocer nervous? Looking for answers, I turned to the responses each had made to the fifty-seven varieties of opinion called for by the standard questionnaire used in Tosun's interviews.

The Chief, it became clear immediately, was a man of few words on many subjects. He dismissed most of the items on Tosun's schedule with a shrug or its audible equivalent. What interested him were questions having to do with the primary modes of human deportment. Only when the issues involved first principles of conduct did he consider the occasion appropriate for pronouncing judgment. Of the Chief it might be said, as Henry James said of George Eliot's salon style, *"Elle n'aborde que les grandes thèmes."*

The Chief has so little trouble with first principles because he desires to be, and usually is, a vibrant sound box through which the traditional Turkish virtues may resonantly echo. His themes are obedience, courage, loyalty—the classic values of the Ottoman Imperium reincarnate in the Ataturk Republic. For the daily round of village life these are adequate doctrine; and as the Chief had been outside of his village only to fight in two wars he has never found his austere code wanting. When asked what he wished for his two grown sons, for example, the Chief replied promptly: "I hope they will fight as bravely as we fought and know how to die as my generation did."

With his life in Balgat, as with the Orphic wisdom that supplies its rationale, the Chief is contented. At sixty-three his desires have been quieted and his ambitions achieved. To Tosun's question on contentment he replied with another question. "What could be asked more? God has brought me to this mature age without much pain, has given me sons and daughters, has put me at the head of my village, and has given me strength of brain and body at this age. Thanks be to Him."

The Grocer is a very different style of man and, though born and bred in Balgat, lives in a different world—an expansive world, populated more actively with imaginings and fantasies, hungering for whatever is different and unfamiliar. To Tosun's probe, the Grocer replied staccato: "I have told you I want better things. I would have liked to have a bigger grocery shop in the city, have a nice house there, dress nice civilian clothes." He perceives his story as a drama of Self *versus* Village. "I am not like the others here. They don't know any better. And when I tell them, they are angry and they say that I am ungrateful for what Allah has given me."

Clearly, from the readiness and consistency of his responses to most questions, the Grocer had in fact brooded much over his role. At one point in the interviews, after asking each respondent to state the greatest problem facing the Turkish people, Tosun was obliged by the questionnaire to ask what the person would do about this problem if he were the president of Turkey. Some were shocked by the impropriety of the very question. "My God! How can you say such a thing?" gasped the shepherd. "How can I . . . I cannot . . . a poor villager . . . master of the whole world."

The Chief, Balgat's virtuoso of the traditional style, summarized prevailing sentiment by his laconic reply to this question with another question: "I am hardly able to manage a village, how shall I manage Turkey?" When Tosun prodded him (by rephrasing the question to ask "What would you suggest for *your village* that you can not handle yourself?"), the Chief said he would ask for "help of money and seed for some of our farmers." When the turn of the Grocer came, he told what he would and would *not* do, if he were president of Turkey, without embarrassment or hesitation: "I would make roads for the villagers to come to towns to see the world and would not let them stay in their holes all their life."

To get out of his hole the Grocer even declared himself ready—and in this he was quite alone in Balgat—to live outside of Turkey. This came out when Tosun asked: "If you could not live in Turkey, where would you want to live?" The standard reply of the villagers was simply that they *would not* live anywhere else. When Tosun persisted by asking, "Suppose you *had* to leave Turkey?" the shepherd replied finally that he would rather kill himself.

The Chief again responded on this issue with the clear and confident voice of traditional man. "Nowhere," said the Chief, and then added, with a calm assurance that this was all the reason required, "I was born here, grew old here, and hope God will permit me to die here." To Tosun's further probe, the Chief responded firmly: "I wouldn't move a foot from here." Only the Grocer found no trouble in imagining himself outside of Turkey, living in a strange land. Indeed he seemed fully prepared, as a man does when he has already posed a question to himself many times. "America," said the Grocer, and, without waiting for Tosun to ask him why, stated his reason, "because I have heard that it is a nice country, and with possibilities to be rich even for the simplest persons."

The vivid sense of cash displayed by the Grocer was perhaps his most grievous offense against Balgat ideas of taboo talk. In the code regulating the flow of symbols among Anatolian villagers, cravings for blood and sex are permissible but not for money. To talk of money at all—possibly because so little of it exists—is an impropriety. To reveal a *desire* for money is—Allah defend us!—an impiety. The Grocer, with his "city-dressed" ways and his "eye at the higher places" and his visits to Ankara, provoked the Balgati to wrathful and indignant expressions of this code. But occasional, and apparently trivial, items in the survey suggested that some Balgati were talking loud about the Grocer to keep their own inner voices from being overheard by the Chief—or even by themselves.

As we were interested in knowing who says what to whom in such a village as Balgat, Tosun had been instructed to ask each person whether others ever came to him for advice, and if so what they wanted advice about. Naturally, the Balgati whose advice was most sought was the Chief, who reported: "Yes, that is my main duty, to give advice. [Tosun: *What about?*] About all that I or you could imagine, even about their wives and how to handle them, and how to cure their sick cow." But this conjunction of wives and cows, to illustrate all the Chief could imagine, runs the gamut only from A to B. Tosun discovered that some Balgati went for advice also to the disreputable Grocer. What did they ask his advice about? "What to do when they go to Ankara, where to go and what to buy, how much to sell their things. . . ."

The cash nexus, this suggested, was somehow coming to Balgat and with it a new role for the Grocer as cosmopolitan specialist in how to avoid wooden nickels in the big city. Also, how to spend the nickels one got, for the Grocer was a man of clear convictions on which coffee houses played the best radio programs for their customers and which were the best movies to see in Ankara. While his opinions on these matters were heterodox as compared, say, to the Chief's, they had an open field to work in, since most Balgati had never heard a radio or seen a movie and were not aware of what constituted orthodoxy with respect to them.

At the time of Tosun's visit, there was only one radio in Balgat, owned by no less a personage than the Chief. In the absence of a standard doctrine on radio inherited from the great tradition, the Chief —who was also of course the large landowner of Balgat—had bought a radio to please his sons. He had also devised an appropriate ceremonial for its use. Each evening a select group of Balgati forgathered in the Chief's guest room as he turned on the newscast from Ankara. They heard the newscast through in silence and, at its conclusion, the Chief turned the radio off and made his commentary. "We all listen very carefully," he told Tosun, "and I talk about it afterwards."

Tosun inquired of the Grocer, a frequent attendant at the Chief's salon, how he liked this style of radio session. Without complaining directly about the Chief's exclusive preoccupation with Radio Ankara news of "wars and the danger of wars"—which turned out in fact to be a rather single-minded interest in the Korean War to which a Turkish brigade had just been committed—the Grocer indicated that after all *he* had opportunities to listen in the coffee houses of Ankara where the audiences exhibited a more cosmopolitan range of interests. "It is nice to know what is happening in the other capitals of the world," said the Grocer. "We are stuck in this hole, we have to know what is going on outside our village."

The Grocer had his own aesthetic of the movies as well. Though the Chief had been to the movies several times, he viewed them mainly as a moral prophylactic: "There are fights, shooting. The people are brave. My sons are always impressed. Each time they see such a film they wish more and more their time for military service would come so that they would become soldiers too." For the Grocer, movies were more than a homily on familiar themes; they were his avenue to the wider world of his dreams. It was in a movie, he told Tosun, that he had first glimpsed what a *real* grocery store could be like—"with walls made of iron sheets, top to floor and side to side, and on them standing myriads of round boxes, clean and all the same dressed, like soldiers in a great parade."

This fleeting glimpse of what sounds like the Campbell Soup section of a supermarket had provided the Grocer with an abiding image of how his fantasy world might look. No petty pedantries obstructed his full sensory relationship to the movies; he delivered clear net judgments in unabashedly hedonist categories. "The Turkish ones," he said, "are gloomy, ordinary. I can guess at the start of the film how it will end. . . . The American ones are exciting. You know it makes people ask what will happen next?"

Here, precisely, arose the question that speculation could only rephrase but not answer. In Balgat, the Chief carried the sword, but did the Grocer steer the pen? When the Balgati sought his advice on how to get around Ankara, would they then go to see the movies that taught virtue or those that taught excitement? True, few Balgati had ever been to Ankara. But things were changing in Turkey and many more Balgati were sure to have a turn or two around the big city before they died. What would happen next in Balgat if more people discovered the tingle of wondering what will happen next?

BALGAT REVISITED

I reached Ankara last April via a circuitous route through the Middle East. The glories of Greece, Egypt, Lebanon, Syria, Persia touched me only lightly, for some part of me was already in Balgat. Even the Blue Mosque and Santa Sophia seemed pallid and I left Istanbul, three days ahead of schedule, for Ankara. I had saved this for last, and now here I was. I was half afraid to look.

I called a limousine service recommended by the hotel clerk and explained that I wanted to go out the following day, a Sunday, to a village some five miles south that might be hard to reach. As I wanted to spend the day, would the driver meet me at 8:00 A.M. and bring along his lunch?

While I waited for the car, next morning, my reverie wandered back through the several years since my first reading of the Balgat interviews. Was I chasing a phantom? Tahir S. appeared. With solitude vanished anxiety; confidently we began to plan the day. Tahir had been a member of the original interview team, working in the Izmir area. As Tosun had joined the Turkish foreign service and was stationed in North Africa, where he was conducting an inquiry among the Berbers, I had arranged in advance for Tahir to revisit Balgat with me in his place. Over a cup of sirupy coffee, we reviewed the questions that had been asked in 1950, noted the various responses and silences, decided the order in which we would repeat the old questions and interpolate the new ones.

As our plan took shape, Zilla K. arrived. She had had no connection with the original survey, but I had decided to take along a female interviewer who could add some Balgat women to our gallery while Tahir and I were working over the men. I had not seen Zilla before, but had "ordered" her, through a colleague at Ankara University, "by the numbers": thirtyish, semi-trained, alert, compliant with instructions, not sexy enough to impede our relations with the men of Balgat but chic enough to provoke the women. A glance and a word were enough to demonstrate that Zilla filled the requisition. The hall porter came in to say our car was waiting. We settled back for a rough haul, debating niceties of procedure. Twenty minutes later, the driver said briskly: "There's Balgat."

We looked puzzled at each other until Tosun's words of 1950 recurred to us: "It could have been half an hour to Ankara if it had a road." Now it did have a road. What was more, a *bus* was coming down the road, heading toward us from the place our driver had called Balgat. As it passed, jammed full, none of the passengers inside waved or even so much as stuck out a tongue at us. Without these unfailing signs of villagers out on a rare chartered bus to celebrate a great occasion of some sort, we could only make the wild guess that Balgat had acquired a regular bus service. And indeed, as we entered the village, there it was—a "bus station," freshly painted benches under a handsome new canopy. We got out and looked at the printed schedule of trips. "The bus leaves every hour, on the hour, to *Ulus* Station. Fare: 20 Kurus." For about 6 cents Balgati could now go, whenever they felt the whim, to the heart of Ankara.

The villagers were getting out of their holes at last.

Overhead wires were stretched along the road, with branch lines extending over the houses of Balgat. The village had been electrified. Alongside the road deep ditches had been dug, in which the graceful curve of new water pipe was visible. Feeling strange, we made our way along the erratic path through the old village, led and followed by a small horde of children, to the house of the Chief. Tahir knocked, an old woman with her head covered by a dark shawl appeared; the children scattered. We were led into the guest room.

The Chief looked as I had imagined. His cheeks a bit more sunken, perhaps, but the whole *présence* quite familiar. Tall, lean, hard, he walked erect and looked me straight in the eye. His own eyes were Anatolian black and did not waver as he stretched out a handful of long, bony fingers. *"Gün aydin, Bey Efendim,"* he said, "good day, sir, you are welcome to my house." I noted in turn the kindness which opens a door to strangers and the Chief responded that we honored his house by our presence. This completed the preliminary round of *formules de la politesse* and steaming little cups of Turkish coffee were brought in by the Chief's older son. The son was rather a surprise—short, pudgy, gentle-eyed, and soft spoken. He bowed his head, reddening slightly as he stammered, *"Lütfen"* (Please!) and offered the tray of demitasses to me. I wondered whether he had learned to fight bravely and die properly.

As the Chief set down his second cup of coffee, signifying that we could now turn to the business of our visit, I explained that I had come from America, where I taught in a university, with the hope of meeting him. There, in my own country, I had read about Balgat in some writing by a young man from Ankara who, four years ago, had talked at length with the Chief and other persons in his village. This writing had interested me very much and I had often wondered, as the years passed by, how things were going in the village of Balgat and among its people. When I had the opportunity to come to Turkey, I immediately decided that I would visit Balgat and see the Chief if I could.

The Chief heard me through gravely, and when he spoke I knew I was in. He by-passed the set of formulas available to him—for either rejecting or evading my implied request—and responded directly to the point. I was right to have come to see Balgat for myself. He remembered well the young man from Ankara. Much had changed in Balgat since that time. Indeed, Balgat was no longer a village. It had, only last month, been incorporated as a district of Greater Ankara. This was why they now had bus service and electricity and a supply of pure water that would soon be in operation. Where there had been fifty houses there were now over five hundred, and even he, the *Muhtar,* did not know any more all the people living here.

Yes, he had lived in Balgat all his life and never in all that time seen so much happen as had come to pass in these four years. "It all began with the election that year. The *Demokrat* men came to Balgat and asked us what was needed here and told us they would do it when they were elected. They were brave to go against the government party. We all voted for them, as the *Halk* men knew no more what to do about the prices then, and the new men did what they said. They brought us this road and moved out the *gendarmerie*. Times have been good with us here. We are all *Demokrat* party in Balgat now."

The Chief spoke in a high, strong, calm voice, and the manner of his utterance was matter-of-fact. His black eyes remained clear and his features retained their shape. Only his hands were animated, though he invoked only the thumbs and the index fingers for punctuation. When he had completed his statement, he picked his nose thoughtfully for a moment and then laid the finger alongside the bridge. The tip of the long, bony finger reached into his eye socket.

I explained then that the young lady had come with us to learn how such changes as the Chief mentioned were altering the daily round of life for the village women. Might she talk with some of them while Tahir Bay and I were meeting the men? The Chief promptly suggested that Zilla could speak with the females of his household. (We recalled Tosun's resentful remark that, had he followed the Chief's suggestions, "I would have ended up only interviewing his family," when Zilla reported on her interviews later that day. All had identified the biggest problem of Balgat as the new fashion of young men to approach girls shamelessly on the village outskirts—precisely what the Chief had told me, in answer to the same question.)

But if the Chief still used his containment tactics with the women, in other directions he had taken a decidedly permissive turn. Tahir and I, he said, could walk about Balgat entirely as we wished and speak with whomsoever it pleased us to honor—even, he added with a smile in response to my jest, some non-*Demokrat* party men, if we could find any. We chatted a bit longer and then, having agreed to return to the Chief's house, we set out for a stroll around Balgat. Our next goal was to find the Grocer.

After a couple of bends and turns, we came to a coffee house. Here was something new and worth a detour. We stopped at the door and bade the proprietor *"Gün aydin!"* He promptly rushed forward with two chairs, suggested that we sit outdoors to benefit of the pleasant sunshine, and asked us how we would like our coffee. (There are five ways of specifying the degree of sweetening in Turkish coffee.) Obviously, this was to be on the house, following the paradoxical Turkish custom of giving gratis to those who can best afford to pay. In a matter of minutes, the male population of Balgat was assembled around our two chairs, squatting, sitting on the ground, looking us over with open and friendly curiosity.

Top man among the group was one of the two farmers Tosun had interviewed in 1950. He too was tall, lean, hard. He wore store clothes with no patches and a sturdy pair of store shoes. His eyes were Anatolian black and his facial set was much like the Chief's. He sat with his chair tilted back and kept his hands calmly dangling alongside, as he ambled along in conversation, with no apparent terminus in view. Interrupting him, even long enough to steer his flow of words in another direction, was not easy. His voice was deep and harsh, with the curious suggestion of strangling in the throat that Anatolian talk has, and the content was elusive. He spoke from such a height to such a height, located somewhere in the space above my head into which he gazed steadily, that little of his discourse made concrete contact with my notebook.

As I review my notes on that hour of monologue-with-choral murmurs, he appears to have certified the general impression that great changes had occurred in Balgat during the four years past. But in his recital, these great events lost some of their luster. The tough old farmer did not look shining at new styles of architecture, nor did he look scowling, but simply looked. Under his gaze the new roofs in Balgat were simply new roofs; the wonder of there being new roofs *in Balgat* brightened other eyes and cadenced other voices.

These other voices were finally raised—either because he had exhausted the prerogative of his position (he had certainly exhausted Tahir S., whose eyes were glazed and vacant) or because the issue was grave enough to sanction discourtesy toward a village elder—when the quondam farmer undertook to explain why he was no longer a farmer. He had retired, over a year ago, because there was none left in Balgat to do an honest day's work for an honest day's lira. Or rather two lira (about 36 cents)—the absurd rate, he said, to which the daily wage of farm laborers had been driven by the competition of the voracious Ankara labor market. Now, all the so-called able-bodied men of Balgat had forsaken the natural work which Allah had intended men to do and swarmed off to the factories of Ankara where, for eight hours of so-called work, they could get five lira a day.

The protests that rose did not aim to deny these facts, but simply to justify them. Surprised, we asked whether it was indeed true that there were no farm laborers left in Balgat. "How many of you," we quickly rephrased the question, "work on farms now?" Four hands were raised among the twenty-nine present, and all of these turned out to be small holders working their own land. (These four were sitting together and, it later developed, were the only four members of the *Halk* party among the group.)

Galvanized by the intelligence now suddenly put before us (even Tahir S. had reawakened promptly upon discovering that there were hardly any farmers left in Balgat), we started to fire a battery of questions of our own. As this created a din of responding voices, Tahir S. —once again the American-trained interviewer—restored order by asking whether each man around the circle would tell us, in turn, what he was now working at and how long he had been at it. This impromptu occupational census was never quite completed. As it became clear that most of the male population of Balgat was now in fact working in the factories and construction gangs of Ankara—*for cash*—our own impatience to move on got the better of us.

How did they spend the cash they earned? Well, there were now over a hundred radio receivers in Balgat as compared to the lone receiver Tosun had found four years earlier. There were also seven refrigerators, four tractors, three trucks, and one Dodge sedan. Also, since there was so little farming in Balgat now, much of the food came from the outside (even milk) and had to be bought in the grocery stores (of which there were now seven in Balgat). Why milk? Well, most of the animals had been sold off during the last few years. What about the shepherd? Well, he had moved to a village in the east a year or so ago, as there were no longer any flocks for him to tend. How was the Grocer doing? *"Which one?"* The original one, the great fat one that was here four years ago? *"Oh that one, he's dead!"*

Tahir S. later told me that my expression did not change when the news came (always the American-trained interviewer). I asked a few more questions in a normal way—"What did he die of?" "How long ago?"—and then let the questioning pass to Tahir. I don't recall what answers came to my questions or to his. I do recall suddenly feeling very weary and, as the talk went on, slightly sick. The feeling got over to Tahir S. and soon we were saying good-by to the group of Balgati, relieved that the ritual for leave-taking is less elaborate than for arriving. We promised to return and said our thanks. *"Güle, güle,"* answered those who remained ("Smile, smile" signifying farewell).

"What a lousy break," growled Tahir in a tone of reasonable indignation as we started back toward the house of the Chief. He was speaking of the Grocer. I didn't know what to say by way of assent. I felt only a sense of large and diffuse regret, of which indignation was not a distinct component. "Tough," I agreed. As we came up to the Chief's house, I told Tahir we might as well return to Ankara. We had gathered quite a lot of information already and might better spend the afternoon putting it together. We could come back again the next day to interview the Chief. The Chief was agreeable to this plan and invited me to be his guest for lunch next day. We collected Zilla K. and our driver, and drove back to the city.

BALGAT REGAINED

I slept late the next morning and was tired when I awoke. While dressing slowly and ingesting a full-scale breakfast, I decided that the Grocer was—and, to face right up to it, had been right from the start —*my* man.

I recalled Tosun's unflattering sketch of him as a pretentious phony, as "the only unfarming person in the village . . . who is even less than the least farmer." But I had never minded this about the Grocer, nor Tosun's disgust that "he even wore some sort of a necktie." What had located all these details in a context I could understand, what had made the Grocer a man I recognized, was Tosun's acid remark: "He most evidently wished to feel that he is closer to me than he is to the other villagers and was curiously careful with his accent all during the interview."

There was something in this sentence that had sounded to me like History. Maybe it was the eighteenth-century field hands of England who had left the manor to find a better life in London or Manchester or Liverpool. Maybe it was the nineteenth-century French farm lad, who, wearied by his father's burdens of the *taille* and the *tithe* and the *gabelle,* had gone off to San Francisco to hunt gold and finding none, tried his hand as a mason, mechanic, printer's devil; though none of these brought him fortune, as he cheerfully wrote home (in a letter noted by the perspicacious Karl Marx), he was going to stay in this exciting new city where the chance to try his hand at anything made him feel "less of a mollusk and more of a man."

The Grocer of Balgat stood for some part of all these figures as he nervously edged his psyche toward Tosun, the young man from the big city. I'm like you, the Grocer might have been feeling, or I'd like to be like you and wish I could get the chance. It was harsh of Tosun, or perhaps only the antibourgeois impatience of a consecrated young scholar looking for the suffering poor in a dreary village, to cold-shoulder this fat and middle-aged man yearning to be comfortably rich in an interesting city. But the Grocer had his own sort of toughness. He had, after all, stood up to the other villagers and had insisted, even when they labeled him infidel, that they ought to get out of their holes.

This time I was going out to Balgat by bus instead of taxi, to see how the villagers traveled. The way the villagers traveled, it turned out, was in a shiny new bus from Germany that held three times as many passengers as there were seats. The bus was so new that the signs warning the passengers not to smoke or spit or talk to the driver (while the bus is moving) in German, French, and English had not yet been converted into Turkish. There was, in fact, a great deal of smoking (some Turkish tobacco is used *in* Turkey) and several animated conversations between the driver and various passengers occurred, in the intervals between which the driver chatted with a crony whom he had brought along for just this purpose.

In Balgat I reported directly to the Chief. He was out on his land but appeared after a few minutes, steaming and mopping his large forehead. He had been pruning some trees and, in this warm weather, such work brought the sweat to his brow. This was about the only work he did any more, he explained, as he had sold or rented most of his land in the last few years, keeping for himself only the ground in which he had planted a small grove of trees that would be his memorial on earth. The Chief agreed to show me his trees and as we strolled away from the house he resumed his discourse of yesterday.

Things had changed, he repeated, and a sign of the gravity of these changes was that he—of a lineage that had always been *Muhtars* and landowners—was no longer a farmer. Nor was he long to be *Muhtar*. After the coming election, next month, the incorporation of Balgat into Greater Ankara was to be completed and thereafter it would be administered under the general municipal system.

"I am the last *Muhtar* of Balgat, and I am happy that I have seen Balgat end its history in this way that we are going."

The new ways, then, were not bringing evil with them? "No, people will have to get used to different ways and then some of the excesses, particularly among the young, will disappear. The young people are in some ways a serious disappointment; they think more of clothes and good times than they do of duty and family and country. But it is to be hoped that as the *Demokrat* men complete the work they have begun, the good Turkish ways will again come forward to steady the people. Meanwhile, it is well that people can have to eat and to buy shoes they always needed but could not have."

And as his two sons were no longer to be farmers, what of them? The Chief's voice did not change, nor did his eyes cloud over, as he replied: "They are as the others. They think first to serve themselves and not the nation. They had no wish to go to the battle in Korea, where Turkey fights before the eyes of all the world. They are my sons and I speak no ill of them, but I say only that they are as all the others."

I felt at this moment a warmth toward the Chief which I had not supposed he could evoke. His sons had not, after all, learned to fight bravely and die properly. These two sons through whom he had hoped to relive his own bright dreams of glory had instead become *shopkeepers*. The elder son owned a grocery store and the younger one owned Balgat's first clothing store. As we turned back to the house, the Chief said we would visit the shops after lunch and his sons would answer all my questions.

That afternoon we went first to the elder son's grocery store, just across the road from the Chief's house and alongside the village fountain. The central floor space was set out with merchandise in the immemorial manner—heavy, rough, anonymous hemp sacks each laden with a commodity requiring no identity card, groats in one and barley in another, here lentils and there chicory. But beyond the sacks was a distinct innovation, a counter. What is more, the counter turned a corner and ran parallel to two sides of the square hut. Built into it was a cash drawer and above each surface a hygienic white porcelain fixture for fluorescent lighting. Along the walls was the crowning glory—a case of shelves running from "top to floor and side to side, and on them standing myriads of round boxes, clean and all the same dressed, like soldiers in a great parade." The Grocer's words of aspiration came leaping back to mind as I looked admiringly around the store. His dream house had been built in Balgat—in less time than even he might have forecast—and by none other than the Chief!

The irony of the route by which Balgat had entered history stayed with me as we walked in quartet, the Chief and I ahead, the sons behind, to the clothing store of the younger son. This was in the newer part of the village, just across the new road from the bus station. The stock inside consisted mainly of dungarees, levis, coveralls—all looking rather like U. S. Army surplus stocks. There was a continuous and growing demand for these goods, the Chief stated solemnly, as more and more men of Balgat went into the labor market of Ankara, first discarding their *shalvars* (the billowing bloomers of traditional garb in which Western cartoons always still portray the "sultan" in a harem scene). In a corner of the store there was also a small stock of "gentleman's haberdashery"—ready-made suits, shirts, even a rack of neckties.

The younger son, who maintained a steady silence in the presence of the Chief, replied to a direct question from me that he had as yet sold very few items from this department of the store. The Balgat males by and large were still reticent about wearing store-bought clothes. A few, however, had purchased in a *sub rosa* sort of way neckties which remained to be exhibited in public. But wearing them would come, now that several owned them, as soon as an older man was bold enough to wear his first. The owners of the neckties had only to get used to them in private, looking at them now and then, showing them to their wives and elder sons, and some one of them had to show the way. I remembered Tosun's rather nasty comment, as though this were his most telling evidence against the Grocer's preposterous pretenses, *"He even wore some sort of a necktie."* As one saw it now, the Grocer *had* shown the way, and it was now only a hop, skip, and jump through history to the point where most men of Balgat would be wearing neckties.

The Grocer's memory stayed with me all afternoon, after I had expressed intense satisfaction with the shops, wished the sons good fortune, thanked the Chief again and, with his permission, started out to walk among the alleys and houses of Balgat. On the way, I absently counted sixty-nine radio antennas on the roofs and decided that yesterday's estimate of "over a hundred" was probably reliable. And only four years ago, I reminded myself, there was but a single radio in this village. The same theme ran through my recollection of the numbers of tractors, refrigerators, and "unfarming persons." That was what Tosun had called the Grocer—"the only unfarming person in the village." Several of these newly unfarming persons, recognizing their interlocutor of yesterday's coffee-house session, greeted me as I strolled along. One stopped me long enough to deliver his opinion of the Turkish-Pakistani pact (strong affirmation) and to solicit mine of the proposed law to give Americans prospecting rights on Turkish oil (qualified affirmative).

Weary of walking, I turned back to the coffee house. The ceremony of welcome was warm and the coffee was again on the house, but the conversational group was smaller. Only eleven Balgati appeared to praise the weather and hear my questions. The group got off on politics, with some attention to the general theory of power but more intense interest in hearing each other's predictions of the margin by which the *Demokrat* party would win the elections next month. There was also general agreement, at least among the wiser heads, that it would be better to have a small margin between the major parties. "The villagers have learned the basic lesson of democratic politics," I wrote in my notebook.

The afternoon was about over before I got an appropriate occasion to ask about the Grocer. It came when the talk returned to the villagers' favorite topic of how much better life had become during the past four years of *Demokrat* rule. Again they illustrated the matter by enumerating the new shops in Balgat and the things they had to sell that many people could buy. "How are these new grocery shops better than the old grocery shop of years ago owned by the fat grocer who is now dead?" I asked. The line of response and the examples cited were obvious in advance, but the question served to lead to another. What sort of man had the Grocer been? The answers were perfunctory, consisting mainly of *pro forma* expressions of good will toward the departed. I tried to get back of these ritual references to the Grocer by indirection. How had he dressed? Why had he been so interested in the life of Ankara? The light finally shone in one of the wiser heads and he spoke the words I was seeking: "Ah, he was the cleverest of us all. We did not know it then, but he saw better than all what lay in the path ahead. We have none like him among us now. He was a prophet."

As I look back on it now, my revisit to Balgat ended then. I went back to the village several times of course, once to bring some gifts for the grandchildren of the Chief, another time with a camera (as he had coyly suggested) to take his picture. On these visits, I felt less tense, asked fewer questions, than during the earlier visits. The last time I went out with Ahmet Emin Yalman, publisher of a prominent Istanbul newspaper and then a devoted *Demokrat* man, who was eager to see the transformed village I had described to him over an endless series of "Screwdrivers" (Turkish vodka with orange juice) in the bar of the Ankara Palas Hotel.

He was enchanted with the Chief, the stores, the bus service and electricity, and other symbols of the History into which his party had ushered Balgat. He decided to write a feature story about it and asked permission to call it "Professor Lerner's Village." I declined, less from modesty than a sense of irrelevance. The Balgat his party needed was the suburb inhabited by the sons of the Chief. The village I had known for what now seemed only four short years was passing, had already passed. The Grocer was dead. The Chief—"the last *Muhtar* of Balgat"—had reincarnated the Grocer in the flesh of his sons. Tosun was in North Africa studying the Berbers.

IX

PERSONALITY AND ADJUSTMENT

THOUGH we now address ourselves specifically to the study of personality and the adjustment-maladjustment of the individual, we must not forget that we have really been studying personality all along. Motives, emotions, learning, perception, abilities, quality of thinking, and social behavior are all part of personality. When we focus on personality as such, however, we concentrate on the *organization* of these parts: we try to see how they integrate to form the totality we know as a person. Adjustment carries this emphasis on integration a bit further, as we examine the relation between the individual and the world about him.

When the layman refers to psychology, he usually means the study of personality and psychotherapy. Moreover, his recognition of names associated with this field is most often limited to Freud, Jung, and Adler. The many psychologists who have made important contributions to personality theory and psychotherapy are rarely known beyond the inner world of the specialists. However, even the beginning student should have some contact with the variety of sources that are contributing to this field.

The eight papers in this section have been selected from the many available publications largely because they offer material that is lacking in most texts. The first provides a theoretical formulation, integrating much empirical material, that might supplement the currently popular "dynamic" definitions, which concentrate almost exclusively on non-intellectual factors in development. The second provides a review of a number of specific studies revolving about one experiential factor that seems to have significance for personality development. Two papers deal with general cultural factors in personality formation: one is a general review; the other, a study of two specific societies. Adjustment and psychotherapy are discussed in three selections written by recognized psychotherapists. The last paper in the section deals with vocational selection and adjustment, an important applied problem in its own right and of special significance in the study of personality because of the importance of work tasks in our society.

38. The Organization of a Person *

THE AUTHOR of this article, the late Edward Lee Thorndike, was one of the giants of modern American psychology, a founder of the field of educational psychology, and a major contributor to the study of intelligence and learning and the analysis of mental abilities. In this recent formulation, he synthesizes a biological and psychological perspective and offers a framework for integrating the empirical material that has developed in psychological research and clinical reports.

DEFINITIONS

WHAT IS SAID in this article will, I hope, be true for any reasonable meanings of "person" and "organization." But the reader may be saved some confusion by a brief statement about these words.

History, biography, anthropology, law, and political science agree in considering a person to be what he would do, feel, and think in response to the situations of life. The biological sciences would accept this as far as it went, but might add that all that a person did or felt or thought was caused by the nature and arrangement of the cells composing his body, so that ultimately the person is those cells and what they do. Theology would add to the notion of a person as a set of probabilities or certainties of response to the situations of life in the natural world, a soul responsive also to certain supernatural events and forces.

Current psychology would accept the assertions of anatomy, physiology, and bio-chemistry, but would emphasize the fact that at present we know little about what a person's nerve-cells do except by what he does, feels, or thinks. It need not deny the existence of supernatural features of a person, but as a natural science it does not use them to explain persons as natural phenomena. It busies itself with getting more and better knowledge of acts, feelings, thoughts, and their probabilities

* E. L. Thorndike, "The organization of a person," *Journal of Abnormal & Social Psychology,* XLV (1950), 137–45. By permission of the American Psychological Association.

of occurrence in various important situations. It seeks especially knowledge of a person's abilities and proclivities.

History and law have rarely, if ever, used the word organization for facts within one person. Any opinions they have had about the matter need not concern us. For the biological sciences the organization of a person means the interrelations of his parts. Psychology pays special attention to the interrelations of those parts of a person which are called abilities, proclivities, impulses, wants, habits, skills, perceptions, memories and ideas.

GENERAL CHARACTERISTICS

The billions of cells in a person are differentiated and organized into tissues, organs, and systems. The relations between the activity of one cell, tissue, organ, or system and that of another vary from direct to indirect, close to loose, regular to casual, important to trivial. So also do the relations between one impulse, want, habit, skill, perception, memory, idea, ability, or proclivity and another.

In both the organization of a person's cells and the organization of his behavior the relation is often one of means to end. The survival of the species by the person's production of human genes and the gametes that carry them is the chief end. It does not however seem to be the chief end of such activities of a person as music, painting, science, and philosophy on the one hand or morbid appetites, cruelty, and superstition on the other. From the point of view of natural history the noblest achievements of civilization are a minor incident in a tiny bit of the evolution of living things. From the point of view of the survival of the human species they are perhaps less important than healthy action of the white blood corpuscles. And it must be admitted that if human genes perished, the products of civilization would serve as inferior food and shelter for rats and worms. But from the point of view of certain human wants they are the highest things a person can seek. They illustrate the general fact that activities which produce pleasures of one sort or another or otherwise satisfy a person's wants, become their own excuse for being. Each person thus has his own system of ends and means which may even oppose the basic system of survival and reproduction.

The fundamental organization of a person is determined by his genes, a collection of tiny organisms, comparable in complexity to the viruses, each able to produce approximate duplicates of itself, and together able to absorb food and grow into a human being, to which each contributes its peculiar share. This fundamental organization is modified and extended by what happens to the person the genes create. Thus the genes provide an organization for running and grasping, but environmental forces determine the organization for skating, dancing, drawing, or playing the violin.

Psychology is specially interested in the organization of a person as observer, thinker, learner, possessor of skills, well-spring of fear, anger, pride, shame, pity and other emotions and sentiments, favorer of some events and conditions, disfavorer of others, agent and patient in a human group as parent, neighbor, worker, etc., cause of conduct good, bad, and indifferent, and possible exhibitor of various unhealthy tendencies in mind or brain. The rest of this article will be restricted to persons thus defined and thereby devoid of some of their purely anatomical and physiological features; and further restricted by leaving very young children, aments, and dements out of consideration.[1]

PSYCHOLOGICAL ORGANIZATION

1. The organization of such a person is extremely complex, and permits almost any act, feeling, or thought of which the person is capable to be attached to almost any external situation to which he is sensitive or to almost any internal event in him. Habitual attachments are, however, the rule: over nine tenths of the behavior of the average person is routine.

2. The organization is to some extent hierarchical. A number of units of control, spheres of influence, sets of mind, or directing potencies commonly known as the self and better called the selves (self at school, self at home, self with intimate friends, self as lover, self as employee, etc.) usually survey and manage what the person thinks or does. Under the self at school rank the self as learner of French, the self as learner of Latin, the self as learner of chemistry, etc. Under the self at home rank the self as eater of meals, the self as payer of bills, the self as authority over children, etc. At still lower, narrower, and more subservient levels of the organization we have the learning of this or that vocabulary, the taking of this or that test, the preference for this or that food, the use of such and such table manners, the computing of this or that item of accounts, in which the "self as" may dwindle to become only a small fraction relevant to the particular behavior concerned. Finally there are at the bottom of the hierarchy items of knowledge, character, and skill so subservient that one can think of them as tools of a self rather than parts of it. Such are "an unexpected loud sound → startle," "sight of bread on your plate → eat it," "9 + 7 → 16," "see X →

[1] An infant is in process of becoming such a person; an idiot is only a part of one; a dement is only the ruins of one.

wave to her," "a customer's inquiry → polite deference in answering it."

It is often justifiable to think of a person as having, at the top of the hierarchy, a self of selves which can approve or veto choices made by lesser selves, harmonize their conflicts, and act for the interests of all with due consideration of the importance of each such interest to it and to them all. Approval by this self of selves is especially potent in a person; its guilt and shame make the deepest wounds.[2]

3. Besides the hierarchical organization, a person has two great layers or departments concerned respectively with (a) things, qualities, events, acts, feelings, and directly felt relations and (b) gestures, words or other symbols that *mean* things, acts, etc. The second layer parallels the first in obvious ways, but may transcend it, as in "$\sqrt{-1}$," "∞," "a soul that never had a body," or "an omniscient and omnipotent mind." The main link between these two departments is the acts of the throat and mouth parts in producing sounds. Spoken language develops from their babbling; and most, if not all, written symbols are based ultimately on speech. The mechanisms by which a person learns languages, sciences, and histories and arouses ideas in other men thus trace back to neurones that move the jaws and wag the tongue.

4. Besides the "vertical" organizations as a hierarchy of selves, components of selves, and tools of selves, there is a "horizontal" organization into abilities, proclivities, and other tendencies or "traits." The thousands of things a person can do are not equally closely related. Nor are his thousands of likes and dislikes, desires and aversions. A vast amount of labor has been devoted by psychologists to this "horizontal" organization of a person, and with important results, but the interrelations are not yet known completely or exactly.

THE ORGANIZATION OF ABILITIES

Knowledge is furthest advanced in the cases of cognitive abilities, such as to understand words, sentences, and paragraphs, to manage numerical facts, to supply missing parts in sentences or in pictures, to remember meaningless and meaningful material, and to discriminate lengths, weights, colors, or pitches.

If the observed relations between measurements of such abilities are properly corrected for attenuation by chance errors and by restricted

[2] The description of the hierarchy given here oversimplifies the facts. It is not a neat pyramid in which each situation → response item at the bottom has one proper place, and each group of tendencies at any higher level has only certain specified inclusions from below. On the contrary a given tendency may operate in many different settings; one of a person's selves may, as it were, intrude upon another, and may work with or against another in various ways.

ranges of persons a table of interrelations can be constructed that reveals the organization within this cognitive part of a person. It will show a substantial amount of specialization according to the form of the operation, or the data operated on, or both. The correlations will range from zero or near zero, as for discrimination of reds from greens with most or all other abilities, to near 1.00, as for ability to give the meanings of nouns with ability to give the meanings of verbs. This specialization remains in large measure after the observed abilities have been replaced by inferred factors. Either the factors found are themselves numerous or complex, or a large part of the variance is left to be accounted for by other more specific abilities. This is true of every factorial analysis of any large field of abilities from Spearman's first with its numerous and potent "specifics" to Thurstone's last. Thurstone writes of intellectual abilities, ". . . with further progress in this field we shall have a profile for each person with a very large number of columns."

Much work has been done also with motor abilities and with combinations of motor and cognitive abilities, as in mechanical skills, drawing, or music. There is more specificity in these than in the verbal and numerical abilities dealing with meanings and symbols, many of the intercorrelations being below .25.

Little work has been done with the organization of abilities to deal with animals and people. The interrelations of the abilities to deal with adults, children, men, women, friends, enemies, superiors, equals and inferiors, are not known.

THE ORGANIZATION OF TRAITS OTHER THAN ABILITIES

The organization of proclivities, emotions, and other features of character and temperament has been explored, though much less extensively and exactly than the organization of cognitive abilities. There are a few investigations by actual observations of behavior in instructive situations, as by May and Hartshorne. There are more using persons' testimony concerning their likes and dislikes, or other attitudes and habits, in fairly reasonable ways. There are some that use questionnaires and ratings prudently. There are some that use them recklessly, with little or no surety that the answerers are able and willing to give even approximately true answers or that the raters are able to give ratings free from very large errors, constant and variable.

Psychologists should, and probably will, in time progress from the traits of popular opinion to traits defined operationally by the actual behaviors used to identify and measure them. Two or more behaviors could then be averaged under one name if their correlations were near enough to 1.00.[3] Ratings could be used (with proper precautions) if the raters were familiar with the actual behaviors that identified the trait and rated persons for what they knew the behavior would be in the persons rated. We should then have traits that corresponded to actual behaviors identical or closely allied, and could be sure that we were relating realities in persons when computing correlations between "traits." This progress, however, involves much labor, and for the present we must do the best we can without it.

. . . . .

On the whole the following statements concerning the organization of traits other than abilities seem justifiable:

1. As with abilities, the intercorrelations of esteemed traits tend to be positive.[4]

2. Proneness to fear and proneness to anger may be due to different genes. Their correlation is near zero, and, if freed from the influence of a general tendency to manifest emotions, is probably slightly negative.

3. Proneness to sorrow rather than joy and to submissiveness and shyness rather than to domination and display are positively, but not closely, related to proneness to fear.

4. A sthenic-asthenic or strong-weak dimension of personality is real and important. How unitary it is remains to be discovered, as does its genetic basis.

5. Likings are positively related to the corresponding abilities, possibly to the extent of .70.

6. It has been customary to average measures of alleged manifestations of some trait such as honesty, neuroticism or introversion, and use the average as a measure of some supposed unitary constituent of a person. When the investigation goes far or deep enough, it is likely to reveal that the trait is not unitary, but a collection of more or less independent features of a person. For example, May and Hartshorne proved that honesty with money, honesty in school work, and honesty in games are somewhat independent features of a person. Objective studies of neuroticism have proved that it is complex.

Traits of character and temperament, like everything else in a person, are caused by the genes he inherits and the environment which acts upon them and upon the organism they create. Anyone who is familiar

[3] Ideally they should reach 1.00 if they are to be treated as the same trait; but practical considerations may justify certain leniencies.

[4] As Bronson Price has shown, this could have come about in both cases as a necessary consequence of assortative mating. The influence of a person's environment would also presumably favor the predominant acquisition of "good" traits or of "bad" traits more than the acquisition of equal numbers of "good" and "bad."

with the behaviors of different breeds of dogs knows that dog genes influence dog personalities; and Stockard's experiments in breeding dogs gave brilliant illustrations of this. Perhaps breeding men for pugnacity, timidity, activity, inertia, shyness, display, sociability, seclusiveness, etc., and later crossing of the breeds attained would show similar results.

Among the environmental facts especially important for a person's personality traits are the mores of his tribe, community, occupation, family and gang, his treatment by mother and/or nurse, the availability of certain means of getting a livelihood and entertainment, the restrictions set by status (*e.g.* slavery) at birth, dietary deficiencies, infections and accidents.

A person's fears, loves, joys and all other "personality traits" live together in him, sometimes in cooperation, sometimes in antagonism. They facilitate and reinforce certain behaviors and interfere with others. They may constitute a unified and consistent system, but they need not, their only necessary unity or consistency being such as the person's neurones require.

It remains to consider how the "unconscious cerebration" of older writers and the "unconscious" of Freud (or of Jung) are related to the more directly observed organization. Most psychologists will accept the following statements:

1. Habits, skills and all other probabilities that certain situations will evoke certain responses can exist unconsciously as conditions in the neurones.

2. This fact is general; even the selves at the top of the hierarchy may so exist, it being the rule rather than the exception that a person is, consciously, only one of his selves at a time.

3. The tendencies thus stored in the neurones vary in the ease with which they can be summoned to cooperate in the person's behavior.

4. Some of them are irrecoverable as separate entities, existing, if at all, only in their effects upon other tendencies.

5. The recovery of a past experience may vary from an hallucinatory reliving of it to a mere memory that it occurred. In healthy waking life the latter is many thousands of times as frequent as the former.

6. Inherited tendencies of which the person is not aware, and perhaps never has been aware, may persist in his neurones, so that, for example, in some frenzy he tears an animal limb from limb to eat it raw. A person may have by nature or by training likes, dislikes, prejudices, mannerisms, etc., of which he is not aware even though they may be apparent to others.

7. A part or parts of a person may be more or less dissociated from the rest of him, as in hypnosis, somnambulism, and hysteria.

8. "Unconscious cerebration" may do elaborate and difficult, even original, work, as in the case of the mathematician Poincaré. Freud's doctrine of the

repression into, and imprisonment in, the unconscious of certain intolerable experiences would be accepted by many psychologists. His doctrine that it contains also acquisitions from ancestral experiences would be accepted by very few.

THEORIES CONCERNING THE ORGANIZATION OF A PERSON

The complex and specialized organization, vertical and horizontal, which I have described is *sui generis,* comparable to nothing else in nature. Anybody is tempted to favor a theory of it that satisfies him rather than to labor to find one that satisfies all the facts. So a Freudian is satisfied by setting off an "id" at the bottom of a person and a "super-ego" at the top. So a faculty psychologist was content to divide a person into a body and a mind, the latter consisting of intellect, feeling and will. So a holist insists on a person's unity, and seems to think of him as a sort of ruler of behavior who allots responses to situations. So a too narrow connectionist can treat a person as a mere bundle of habits; a too narrow purposivist can treat a person as a mere bundle of purposes.

It is perhaps instructive to consider the analogy of forms of political, industrial and mercantile organization which do approach the complexity of a human brain. For example, a somewhat comparable organization is that of a great mail-order establishment which responds to a great variety of situations in millions of homes by supplying millions of combinations of articles to fit those situations. Such an establishment is obviously complex. It is characterized by arrangements of means to attain ends. Its personnel and equipment often show regnancy and subservience: thus the arrangement of stock is subservient to the finding and gathering of items of it. Much of it is hierarchical. It has an extensive "horizontal" organization of imperfectly correlated features such as upkeep of buildings, heating, lighting, fire-protection, insurance, selection of personnel, payrolls, cafeterias, lockers, bookkeeping, advertising, etc. Its typewriters, computing machines, conveyors and time-clocks may be likened to the minor habits and skills which are the tools of an ability. It lacks, however, traits corresponding to the emotions and attitudes of a person. It lacks clear correspondences with human genes and environmental influences, though the arrangements universal in the department stores of 1900 could be considered as paralleling human genes, and the experiences of the business since its beginning as paralleling events in a person's environment. It does not show the great division into directly perceived or felt things, qualities, events, emotions, etc., and gestures, words or other symbols that mean the things, qualities, etc., though there is a somewhat similar division into the articles sold and their catalogue names and numbers.

The afferent neurones of a person are paralleled by postal, telegraph and telephone services outside the company. The order slips correspond rather to the effects upon cerebral cells of stimuli from afferent neurones. The efferent neurones of a person are paralleled by parcel post, express and freight services outside the company; wrapping, addressing and forwarding correspond to cerebral functions.

---

39. Observations of Older Children Who Were Deprived in Infancy *

IN RECENT YEARS, evidence concerning the importance of early experiences for the course of human development has been mounting. Of all factors, the most dramatically documented is the individual's need for continuity of affection, care, stimulation, and contact with a stable personal environment in early childhood. Dr. Bowlby gives us an impressive review of the data supporting this conclusion.

SOME OF THE immediately bad effects of deprivation on young children and some of the short-term after-effects have now been discussed, and note taken that those without training in mental health are apt either to deny the existence of such responses or to waive them aside as of no consequence. In this chapter, the tremendous weight of evidence will be reviewed which makes it clear that those who view these responses with concern, so far from crying wolf, are calling attention to matters of grave medical and social significance.

During the late 1930s, at least six independent workers were struck by the frequency with which children who committed numerous delinquencies, who seemed to have no feelings for anyone and were very difficult to treat, were found to have had grossly disturbed relationships with their mothers in their early years. Persistent stealing, violence, egotism, and sexual misdemeanours were among their less pleasant characteristics.

* John Bowlby, "How we can study the harm done: II. Observations of older children who were deprived in infancy," *Child Care and the Growth of Love* (London: Penguin Books, Inc., 1953), ch. 3, pp. 33–49. Reprinted from *Child Care and the Growth of Love,* edited by John Bowlby, by permission of the editor and of Penguin Books, Inc.

One of the first cases recorded still stands as typical:

My first example is an eight-year-old girl who was adopted a year and a half before being examined. After an illegitimate birth, the child was shifted about from one relative to another, finally brought to a child-placing agency, and then placed in a foster-home for two months before she came to the adoptive parents. The complaints were lying and stealing. The parents described the child's reaction to the adoption as very casual. When they took her home and showed her the room she was to have all for herself, and took her on a tour of the house and grounds, she showed apparently no emotional response. Yet she appeared very vivacious and "affectionate on the surface." After a few weeks of experience with her, the adoptive mother complained to her husband that the child did not seem able to show any affection. The child, to use the mother's words, "would kiss you but it would mean nothing." The husband told his wife that she was expecting too much, that she should give the child a chance to get adapted to the situation. The mother was somewhat mollified by these remarks, but still insisted that something was wrong. The father said he saw nothing wrong with the child. In a few months, however, he made the same complaint. By this time, also, it was noted that the child was deceitful and evasive. All methods of correction were of no avail. . . . The schoolteacher complained of her general inattention and her lack of pride in the way her things looked. However, she did well in her school subjects, in keeping with her good intelligence. She also made friends with children, though none of these were close friendships. After a contact of a year and a half with the patient the adoptive father said, "You just can't get to her," and the mother remarked, "I have no more idea to-day what's going on in that child's mind than I knew the day she came. You can't get under her skin. She never tells what she's thinking or what she feels. She chatters but it's all surface."

Here, in brief, are many of the typical features:

- superficial relationships;
- no real feeling—no capacity to care for people or to make true friends;
- an inaccessibility, exasperating to those trying to help;
- no emotional response to situations where it is normal—a curious lack of concern;
- deceit and evasion, often pointless;
- stealing;
- lack of concentration at school.

The only item in this case which is not typical is the child's good schoolwork, as more often than not this is seriously interfered with.

Between 1937 and 1943 there were many papers on this subject, several of which originated independently and some of which were completed in ignorance of the work of others. The unanimity of their conclusions stamps their findings as true. With monotonous regularity each observer put his finger on the child's inability to make relationships as being the central feature from which all the other disturbances sprang, and on the history of long periods spent in an institution or, as in the case quoted, of the child's being shifted about from one foster-mother to another as being its cause. So similar are the observations and the conclusions—even the very words—that each might have written the others' papers:

> The symptom complaints are of various types. They include, frequently, aggressive and sexual behaviour in early life, stealing, lying, often of the fantastic type, and, essentially, complaints variously expressed that indicate some lack of emotional response in the child. It is this lack of emotional response, this shallowness of feeling that explains the difficulty in modifying behaviour.

> Early in the work a third group of girls was recognized who were asocial [*i.e.* unaware of obligations to others], but not obviously neurotic, and with whom no treatment methods seemed of any avail. Later it became clear that the feature common to them was an inability to make a real relationship with any member of the staff. There might seem to be a good contact, but it invariably proved to be superficial. . . . There might be protestations of interest and a boisterous show of affection, but there was little or no evidence of any real attachment having been made. In going over their previous history, this same feature was outstanding. . . . [These girls] have apparently had no opportunity to have a loving relationship in early childhood [and] seem to have little or no capacity to enter into an emotional relation with another person or with a group.

> All the children [twenty-eight in number] present certain common symptoms of inadequate personality development chiefly related to an inability to give or receive affection; in other words, inability to relate the self to others. . . . The conclusion seems inescapable that infants reared in institutions undergo an isolation type of experience, with a resulting isolation type of personality.

> Two special problems were referred to the ward from two child-placing agencies. One came from an agency [in which] there is a feeling that no attachment should be allowed to develop between the child and the boarding home, so that by the time the child is five years old, he has no attachment to anybody and no pattern of behaviour. . . . Another special group consisted of children placed in infancy [who] are given the best pediatric care . . . but have been deprived of social contacts and play materials. . . . These children are unable to accept love, because of their severe deprivation

in the first three years. . . . They have no play pattern, cannot enter into group play and abuse other children. . . . They are overactive and distractible; they are completely confused about human relationships. . . . This type of child does not respond to the nursery group and continues overactive, aggressive and asocial.

"Imperviousness and a limited capacity for affective relationships" characterize children who have spent their early years in an institution. "Can it be that the absence of affective relationship in infancy made it difficult or even unnecessary for the institution children to participate later in positive emotional relationships . . . ?"

These communications came from across the Atlantic: meanwhile quite independent observations by Dr. Bowlby in London led to exactly the same conclusions:

Prolonged breaks [in the mother-child relationship] during the first three years of life leave a characteristic impression on the child's personality. Such children appear emotionally withdrawn and isolated. They fail to develop loving ties with other children or with adults and consequently have no friendships worth the name. It is true that they are sometimes sociable in a superficial sense, but if this is scrutinized we find that there are no feelings, no roots in these relationships. This, I think, more than anything else, is the cause of their hard-boiledness. Parents and school-teachers complain that nothing you say or do has any effect on the child. If you thrash him he cries for a bit, but there is no emotional response to being out of favour, such as is normal to the ordinary child. It appears to be of no essential consequence to these lost souls whether they are in favour or not. Since they are unable to make genuine emotional relations, the condition of relationship at a given moment lacks all significance for them. . . . During the last few years I have seen some sixteen cases of this affectionless type of persistent pilferer and in only two was a prolonged break absent. In all the others gross breaches of the mother-child relation had occurred during the first three years, and the child had become a persistent pilferer.

Since these early papers there have been several careful "retrospective studies," namely, studies made by specialists who were called upon to treat nervous symptoms and disturbances of behaviour, who by working back into the children's histories, unearthed the common factors of lack of care—caused either by their being in institutions, or being posted, like parcels, from one mother-figure to another.

One doctor in a large New York hospital had some 5,000 children under her care from 1935 to 1944. She found that from 5 per cent to 10 per cent of them showed the characteristics which have already been described.

There is an inability to love or feel guilty. There is no conscience. Their inability to enter into any relationship makes treatment or even education impossible. They have no idea of time, so that they cannot recall past experience and cannot benefit from past experience or be motivated to future goals. This lack of time concept is a striking feature in the defective organization of the personality structure. . . .

Ten of the children referred to were seen five years later. They "all remained infantile, unhappy, and affectionless and unable to adjust to children in the schoolroom or other group situation."

Dr. Bowlby, writing of the children he dealt with in London, described how in some of their histories it was possible to find how the child had reacted to some startling and painful happening. He laid especial emphasis on the tendency of these children to steal. Dividing all the cases he had seen at a child guidance clinic into those who had been reported as stealing and those who had not, he compared a group of forty-four thieves with a control group, similar in number, age, and sex, who although emotionally disturbed did not steal. The thieves were distinguished from the controls in two main ways. First, there were among them fourteen "affectionless characters," while there were none in the control group. Secondly, seventeen of the thieves had suffered complete and prolonged separation (six months or more) from their mothers or established foster-mothers during their first five years of life; only two of the controls had suffered similar separations. Neither of these differences can be accounted for by chance. Two further points of great importance were that the "affectionless characters" almost always had a history of separation, and that they were far more delinquent than any of the others.

The results showed that bad heredity was less frequent amongst the "affectionless" thieves than amongst the others: of the fourteen children who came into this class only three could be said to have had a bad heredity (i.e. parents or grandparents with serious psychological ill-health), but twelve of them had histories of separation from their mothers. Thus there can be no doubting that for the affectionless thief nurture not nature is to blame.

Dr. Bowlby concludes:

There is a very strong case indeed for believing that prolonged separation of a child from his mother (or mother substitute) during the first five years of life stands foremost among the causes of delinquent character development.

Among the cases described is one of a boy who was believed to have had a good relation to his mother until the age of eighteen months, but who was then in hospital for nine months, during which time visiting by his parents was forbidden. Other cases suggest that hospitalization and changes of mother-figure as late as the fourth year can have very destructive effects in producing the development of an affectionless psychopathic character given to persistent delinquent conduct and extremely difficult to treat.

Other retrospective studies touch on this problem. Thus the record of some 200 children under the age of twelve seen at a child-guidance clinic in London during the years 1942–6, whose troubles seemed to have been caused or aggravated by the war, showed that in one-third of the cases the trouble had been caused by evacuation. Almost all the difficult and long treatment cases were due to evacuation, not, it must be emphasized, to experience of bombing. No less than two-thirds of the children who presented problems after evacuation had been under the age of five when first evacuated. Since the number of young children evacuated in proportion to older ones was small, the figures make clear the extent to which it is especially the young child who is damaged by experiences of this kind.

Again, studies of adult patients have often led their authors to the conclusion that love deprivation is the cause of their psychological condition. Writing of hysterical patients, one doctor puts forward the view that

> regardless of the nature of the individual's inborn tendencies, he will not develop hysteria unless he is subjected during childhood to situations causing him to crave affection.

Among such situations he lists the death of a parent and separation of child from parents. Another doctor who collected information on 530 prostitutes in Copenhagen, found that one-third of them had not been brought up at home, but had spent their childhood under troubled and shifting conditions.

> Three per cent were brought up by close relations, 3 per cent were boarded out or sent to a home, 27 per cent were raised under combined conditions, partly in homes or almshouses, partly in institutions for the feeble-minded or epileptics, partly at home or with relatives.

Sometimes they had three or four different foster-homes during the course of their childhood. Seventeen per cent of the total were illegitimate.

The objection to all these retrospective studies is, of course, that they are concerned only with children who have developed badly and fail to take into account those who may have had the same experience, but have developed normally. We now come to studies of especial value, since they take a group of children placed as infants in institutions and seek to discover how they have turned out.

One very careful investigation carried out by a New York psychologist, Dr. Goldfarb, was scientifically planned from the beginning to test the theory that the experience of living in the highly impersonal surroundings of an institution nursery in the first two or three years of life has an adverse effect on personality development. What he did was to compare the mental development of children, brought up until the age of about three in an institution and then placed in foster-homes, with others who had gone straight from their mothers to foster-homes, in which they had remained. In both groups the children had been handed over by their mothers in infancy, usually within the first nine months of life. Dr. Goldfarb took great care to see that the two groups were of similar heredity. The children most thoroughly studied consisted of fifteen pairs who, at the time of the examination, ranged in age from ten to fourteen years. One set of fifteen was in the institution from about six months of age to three and a half years, the other set had not had this experience. Conditions in the institution were of the highest standards of physical hygiene, but lacked the elementary essentials of mental hygiene:

> Babies below the age of nine months were each kept in their own little cubicles to prevent the spread of epidemic infection. Their only contacts with adults occurred during these few hurried moments when they were dressed, changed, or fed by nurses.

Later they were members of a group of fifteen or twenty under the supervision of one nurse, who had neither the training nor the time to offer them love or attention. As a result they lived in "almost complete social isolation during the first year of life," and their experience in the succeeding two years was only slightly richer. Dr. Goldfarb has gone to great pains to ensure that the foster-homes of the two groups are similar, and shows further that, in respect of the mother's occupational, educational, and mental standing, the institution group was slightly superior to the controls. Any differences in the mental states of the two groups of children are, therefore, almost certain to be the result of their differing experiences in infancy. We must remember that none of the children had had the advantage of a quite unbroken home life. All had been in their foster-homes for six or seven years. Yet the differences between the groups are very marked and painfully full of meaning.

The two groups of children were studied by a great variety of tests. In intelligence, in power of abstract thinking, in their social maturity, their power of keeping rules or making friends, the institution group fell far below those who had stayed with their mothers for some months and then gone straight to the care of foster-mothers. Only three of the fifteen institution children were up to the average in speech, whilst all fifteen of the others reached this level. This continuing backwardness of speech has been noticed by many other observers—it looks as though the art of speech must be learnt at the right time and in the right place.

Whilst it will be seen that in most respects Dr. Goldfarb's conclusions are much like those of other observers, it must be noted that in two respects they differ from Dr. Bowlby's. First, the New York children "craved affection" and the London ones are observed to be "affectionless." This contrast is probably more apparent than real. Many affectionless characters crave affection, but none the less have a complete inability either to accept or reciprocate it. The poor capacity of all but two of Goldfarb's children for making relationships clearly confirms other work. The fact that only one of this group of Goldfarb's institution children stole and none truanted is, however, surprising in view of Bowlby's findings. The difference is probably valid and needs explanation: perhaps it can be explained this way. All of Goldfarb's cases had been institutionalized from soon after birth until they were three years old. None of Bowlby's had—they were all products of deprivation for a limited period, or of frequent changes. It may well be that their stealing was an attempt to secure love and gratification and so reinstate the love relationship which they had lost, whereas Goldfarb's cases, never having experienced anything of the kind, had nothing to reinstate. Certainly it would appear that the more complete the deprivation is in the early years the more indifferent to society and isolated the child becomes, whereas the more his deprivation is broken by moments of satisfaction the more he turns against society and suffers from conflicting feelings of love and hatred for the same people.

Before we leave the subject of Dr. Goldfarb's writings, we must make it clear that we must not take it for granted that all infants and toddlers in institutions have similar experiences. Not only is it clear that they do not, but the more one studies all the evidence on the subject the more one becomes convinced that the outcome is to a high degree dependent on the exact nature of the psychological experience. If further research is to be fruitful, it must pay minute attention not only to the ages and periods of deprivation, but also to the quality of the child's relation to his mother before deprivation, his experiences with mother-substitutes, if any, during separation, and the reception he gets from his mother or foster-mother when at last he becomes settled again.

There are several other follow-up studies which, though far less thorough, show similar results. An American psychiatrist, Dr. Lowrey, studied a group of children comprising among others twenty-two unselected cases who, with one exception, had been admitted to an institution before their first birthday and had remained there until they were three or four, when they were transferred to another society for fostering. They were examined when they were five years of age or older. All of them showed severe personality disturbances centering on an inability to give or receive affection. Symptoms, each of which occurred in half or more of them, included aggressiveness, negativism (contrariness or obstinacy), selfishness, excessive crying, food difficulties, speech defects, and bedwetting. Other difficulties only a little less frequent included over-activity, fears, and soiling.

Both Dr. Goldfarb and Dr. Lowrey report 100 per cent of children institutionalized in their early years to have developed very poorly; other studies show that many such children achieve a tolerable degree of social adaptation when adult. Though this finding is in accordance with the expectations of the man in the street, it would be a mistake to build too much on it, since it is known that very many people who are psychologically disturbed are able to make an apparent adjustment for long periods. Moreover, these other studies show a large proportion of obvious mental ill-health which the authors regard as confirming the harmfulness of institutional conditions for young children.

As long ago as 1924, a comprehensive study was made in America of the social adjustment as adults of 910 people who had been placed in foster-homes as children. A particularly interesting comparison is made between ninety-five of them who had spent five years or more of their childhood in institutions and eighty-four who had spent the same years at home (in 80 per cent of cases in bad homes). Not only had all the children of both groups, later, been placed in foster-homes of similar quality and at similar ages, but so far as could be determined the heredity of the two groups was similar. The results show that those brought up in an institution adjusted significantly less well than those who had remained during their first five years in their own homes. Since the two groups were of similar heredity, the difference cannot be explained in this way. The fact that no less than one-third of the institution children turned out to be "socially incapable," of which nearly half were troublesome and delinquent, is to be noted.

It will be remarked, however, that, despite the institutional experience in the early years, two-thirds turned out "socially capable." So far as it goes this is satisfactory, but, as no expert examination was carried out, psychological troubles not leading to social incompetence were not recorded.

So far all the evidence has pointed in but one direction. It is now time to consider the three studies which present evidence which calls these conclusions in question. It may be said at once that none of them is of high scientific quality. One is a brief note, questioning the accuracy of Dr. Lowrey's 100 per cent bad results in some institutions, by another specialist who states that he has seen some sixteen children coming from the same institution and having had the same experiences as Lowrey's group, and that only two showed adverse features of personality. No details are given and there appears to have been no systematic investigation of the individual cases.

Another critic compares a group of 100 boys aged nine to fourteen years living in an institution with another 100 of the same age living at home in bad surroundings, where broken homes and family discords predominate. Using questionnaires, he shows that the two groups are similar in mental ill-health. Not only is a questionnaire an unsatisfactory way of measuring mental health, but no evidence is given regarding the age at which the children entered the institution.

The most recent of the three studies was carried out by a group of child-guidance workers in England. They compared the "social maturity" of two groups of fifteen-year-old children: fifty-one who had spent the previous three years or more in an institution, and a comparable fifty-two who had lived at home. They showed that, although the institution children have a lower score than the family children, when the cases are regrouped according to their heredity an exactly similar difference is to be seen. On the basis of these figures they conclude that the case of those who argue that any social or personal retardation is attributable exclusively or mainly to environmental influences is weakened, and that constitutional factors are at least as important as environmental factors in the growth of social maturity.

These conclusions are ill-judged and certainly cannot be sustained by the evidence presented. In addition to technical criticism of the methods used in the enquiry, it is pointed out that some of the institution children did not enter until they were quite old, the average age of admission being four years; while, even more serious, of the family children in the control group, no less than twenty-two had been evacuated from their homes during the war, the average length of time being one year and nine months. Work with so many shortcomings cannot be accepted as calling in question the almost unanimous findings of the workers already quoted.

There is one other group of facts which is sometimes quoted as casting doubt on these findings—that from the Jewish communal settlements in Israel known as Kibbutz (plural, Kibbutzim). In these settlements, largely for ideological reasons, children are brought up by professional nurses in a "Children's House." Babies are reared in groups of five or six, and are later merged at the age of three years into larger groups numbering twelve to eighteen. The emphasis is throughout on communal rather than family care. Is not this, it may be asked, a clear example that communal care can be made to work without damaging the children? Before answering this question it is necessary to look more carefully at the conditions in which the children are raised. The following account is taken partly from the report of an American psychiatric social worker who recently visited Israel, and partly from a personal communication from the Lasker Child Guidance Centre in Jerusalem. Both describe life in certain of the non-religious Kibbutzim. The former remarks:

> Separation is a relative concept and separation as it appears in the Kibbutz should not be thought of as identical with that of children who are brought up in foster-homes or institutions away from their parents. . . . In the Kibbutz there is a great deal of opportunity for close relationship between child and parents.

Not only does the mother nurse the baby and feed him in the early months, but, to follow the Lasker Centre's description:

> once the suckling tie between mother and child is abandoned, the daily visit of the child to the room of the parents becomes the focus of family life for the child, and its importance is scrupulously respected. During these few hours the parents, or at least one of them, are more or less completely at the disposal of the children; they play with them, talk to them, carry the babies about, take the toddlers for little walks, etc.

The time spent with the children "may amount to as much as two to three hours on working days and many more on the Sabbath."

Here, then, is no complete abandonment of parent-child relations. Though the amount of time parents spend with their young children is far less than in most other Western communities, the report makes it clear that "the parents are extremely important people in the children's eyes, and the children in the parents'." It is interesting to note, too, that the trend is steadily towards parents taking more responsibility. Formerly parents had to visit the children in the Children's House—now the children come to the parents' room and the parents even prepare light meals for them; feasts are now celebrated in the parents' room as well as communally in the Children's House; mothers are asserting themselves and demanding to see more of their children.

Finally, it is by no means certain that the children do not suffer from this regime. While both observers report good and co-operative development in adolescence, the Lasker Centre think there are signs of a somewhat higher level of insecurity among Kibbutz children than among others, at least until the age of seven years. They also point out that the strong morale and intimate group life of the Kibbutz are of great value to the older child and adolescent, and that these may offset some of the unsettlement of earlier years.

From this brief account it is evident that there is no evidence here which can be held to undermine our conclusions. The conditions provide, of course, unusually rich opportunities for research in child development, and it is to be hoped that these will not be missed.

OBSERVATIONS OF WAR ORPHANS AND REFUGEES

Evidence of the adverse effects on children of all ages of separation from their families was provided on a tragic scale during the Second World War, when thousands of refugee children from occupied lands in Europe were cared for in Switzerland and elsewhere. Owing to the scale of the problem, there was little time for systematic research, and in any case the children had been submitted to such diverse and often horrifying experiences that it would have been almost impossible to have isolated the effects of separation from those of other experiences. A summary of the findings of medical, educational, and relief workers emphasizes that "while the reports tell of disturbances in character resulting from war, they show also the fundamental part played in their causation by rupture of the family tie." Of experiences with refugee children at the Pestalozzi Village at Trogen, Switzerland, we read:

> No doubt remains that a long period without individual attention and personal relationships leads to mental atrophy; it slows down or arrests the development of the emotional life and thus in turn inhibits normal intellectual development. We have observed that acute psychical traumata [damaging experiences], however serious, do not result in such deep injury as chronic deficiencies and prolonged spiritual solitude.

In 1944 a small comparative study was made of ninety-seven Jewish refugee children in homes in Switzerland and 173 Swiss children of about the same age (eleven to seventeen years). All the children were asked to write an essay on "What I think, what I wish, and what I hope." From a scrutiny of these essays it appeared that for the refugees separation from their parents was evidently their most tragic experience. In contrast, few of the Swiss children mentioned their parents, who were evidently felt to be a natural and inevitable part of life. Another great contrast was the refugee children's preoccupation with their suffering past, or with frenzied and grandiose ideas regarding the future. The Swiss children lived happily in the present, which for the refugee was either a vacuum or at best an unsatisfying transition. Deprived of all the things which had given life meaning, especially family and friends, they were possessed by a feeling of emptiness.

Another psychologist also studied refugee children in Switzerland and others in a concentration camp. He describes such symptoms as bed-wetting and stealing, an inability to make relations and a consequent loss of ability to form ideals, an increase of aggression, and intolerance of frustration.

In the Netherlands after the war, a group of psychiatrists studied some thousands of children whose parents had been deported in 1942 and 1943 and who had been cared for in foster-homes, often from earliest infancy. They report that frequent changes of foster-home almost always had very adverse effects, leading the child to become withdrawn and apathetic. This was sometimes accompanied by a superficial sociability and, later, promiscuous sex-relationships. Some young children managed to weather a single change, but others could not stand even this, and developed symptoms such as anxiety, depression, excessive clinging, and bedwetting. Many of the children were still emotionally disturbed when examined after the war and in need of treatment. It was noted that those who had had good family relationships before separation could usually be helped to an adjustment, but that for those with a bad family background the outlook was poor.

Finally may be noted an extensive psychological and statistical study undertaken in Spain following the civil war on over 14,000 cases of neglected and delinquent children housed in the environs of Barcelona. Once again there is confirmation of the decisive and adverse role in character development played by the break-up of the family and the vital importance of family life for satisfactory social and moral development. Particularly interesting is the confirmation of Dr. Goldfarb's findings regarding impaired mental development. The intelligence levels of the neglected and delinquent children are much below those of a control group. Lessened capacity for abstract thought is also noted—the evidence, in the investigator's opinion, pointing to the existence of a strong link between the development of the abstract mental faculties and the family and social life of the child. He notes especially the following characteristics of the neglected and delinquent child:

> Feeble and difficult attention due to his great instability. Very slight sense of objective realities, overflowing imagination and absolute lack of critical ability. Incapacity for strict abstraction and logical reasoning. Noteworthy backwardness in the development of language. . . .

The similarity of these observations on war orphans and refugees to those on other deprived children will not fail to impress the reader.

---

40. Cultural Factors in Personality Adjustment of Children *

IT HAS BEEN well noted that if a fish were to inventory his environment, the last feature he would describe would be the water. Similarly, the influence on personality development that we would find most difficult to identify, in all likelihood, would be that of the culture in which we live. It is easier to get perspective on cultural influences if we draw material from cultures other than our own before we turn to the social world around us. In the following paper, Dr. Klineberg helps us to approach such objectivity most convincingly by referring to many cultures, and demonstrating repeatedly the impact of cultural influences under different cultural conditions.

IN A RECENT DISCUSSION of the accomplishments of the social sciences, Stuart Chase places high on the list the "discovery" of culture by the anthropologists. We may argue about the date of this discovery; we may even question whether it does not refer to something we have always known. The fact remains that emphasis on cultural factors in the development of personality, both normal and abnormal, is now standard equipment. We have all become culture-conscious; not only those of us who are identified with the traditional social sciences, but also psychiatrists, social workers, physicians, criminologists, educators, lawyers. Our writings and even our conversation show this anthropological sophistication; we are on terms of intimacy with Malinowski's Trobrianders and Mead's Mundugumor; a concern with culture has become *our* "pattern of culture."

Studies dealing specifically with children in different cultures could fill a library. Many anthropologists have brought back from their field work accounts of early childhood training, of relationships in the family, of the socialization process in general; they have supplied descriptions of basic personality configurations, their conclusions sometimes bolstered by Rorschach protocols or an occasional TAT. Much closer

* Otto Klineberg, "Cultural factors in personality adjustment of children," *American Journal of Orthopsychiatry,* XXIII (1953), 465–71. By permission of the author and the *American Journal of Orthopsychiatry.* Presented at the 1953 Annual Meeting in the Opening Session, "Orthopsychiatry and Education."

to home, culture has been "discovered" all over again in relation to the child-rearing practices of different socioeconomic classes (Davis and Havighurst), or in the behavior of our own adolescents (the "youth culture" of Parsons), as well as of children of different ages ("peer cultures"). This material is certainly known to most of you. I wonder whether it is not carrying coals to Newcastle or beer to Munich, to bring "culture" to the American Orthopsychiatric Association!

However, as I look at the data with which I am familiar, I see many blank spaces, many problems unsolved and questions neglected or inadequately answered. I hope I may be permitted to bring some of them to your attention.

We are told a great deal, for example, about the training procedures which adults direct *to* the child, but not always enough about their effect *on* the child. Perhaps the best illustration of this is to be found in reports concerning a form of discipline found among the Pueblos of the Southwest, particularly the Hopi and the Zuni. The Hopi father rarely if ever uses corporal punishment to socialize his child; he relies on precept, example and admonition. Occasionally a Hopi child refuses to be socialized. The father may then threaten him with the Katchinas, the masked dancers who are often of genuinely terrifying appearance, and who are interpreted to the child as being spirits or gods. Sure enough, if the child continues to misbehave, he is approached by a Katchina on the occasion of the next feast, and told that now he will be severely punished. The father "tries" to protect the child; he tells him to run away from the Katchina; or he may beg the Katchina not to hurt the child, promising that there will be no further trouble. The Katchina usually remains adamant, however, and the child is punished, sometimes severely. The child of course remains ignorant of the fact that it is the "protective" father himself who is directly responsible for the whole painful procedure.

From the point of view of parent-child relationships this seems to be a good system. The father remains the friend, the protector; there is no paternal punishment to threaten the friendly atmosphere; hostility comes from and is projected upon impersonal, supernatural beings; the oedipal reaction is attenuated. But what happens when the slightly older child makes the terrible discovery that the Katchinas are only men with masks? What does it do *to him* to become aware of his father's treason?

In the Hopi biography, *Sun Chief,* written by Leo Simmons, we find that the discovery of the real nature of the Katchinas may come as a devastating and disillusioning experience. Fred Eggan quotes a Hopi informant as saying: "I cried and cried when I found out that Katchinas were real people instead of gods." What we do not know is what all of this means to the child in terms of his later relationship to the father. The cultural facts alone need to be supplemented by what W. I. Thomas called "the definition of the situation," the experience as perceived by the principal actors in this recurring family drama, and more particularly, the situation as defined *by the child.*

A second, somewhat analogous problem is concerned with the relation between cultural factors in the life of the young child, and the personality of the adults in the community. The assumption is still commonly made that the early training procedures to which the child is subjected are, if not responsible for the adult personality, at least its reflection. (I shall return to the question of cause and effect later.) Are these necessarily congruent? Is the child inevitably and inexorably "the father of the man"? The literature is rich in references along these lines: to Japanese toilet training as related to later compulsive and obsessive characteristics, to Russian swaddling as reflected in later aggression, to Chinese "oral optimism" as related to later freedom from stress (before the days of Red China, however!), etc. I am not suggesting that there is no relationship; I am raising certain questions as to its nature, and as to the extent and the consistency of the assumed correspondence.

Ruth Benedict long ago made us familiar with the concept of "Continuities and *Discontinuities* in Cultural Conditioning." The line from childhood to adult personality is not always a straight line, and the assumption that it is, in cultures, if not necessarily in individuals, may land us in serious difficulties of interpretation.

Some specific adult traits may be introduced early into the life of the child, and developed consistently. This seems true, for example, of the trait of generosity among the Sioux; this was one of the cardinal virtues of the old Dakota society, and is still strong today. Macgregor writes: "Modern Dakota children are carefully trained in this tradition. . . . Children of five, six and seven give freely and pleasantly to their younger brothers and sisters. Small children learn the more formal type of giving by observing their elders. . . . Among the Sioux property does not have the high value associated with it in white society. This carries over into Dakota child-training in ways that are astonishing to white observers."

A similar example of continuity is to be found in the relative absence of competitiveness among the Hopi, young and old alike. Laura Thompson writes: "In marked contrast to the competitive norms of the general American culture, there is a strongly entrenched attitude among the Hopi against singling out one individual for special recognition or praise. A teacher who is herself a Hopi considers it undesirable to praise a child in the presence of other children. . . . Such a procedure, she says, leads to resentment but never to emulation. This teacher never singles out a child in class, either for praise or blame." Thompson cites a number of observations by Asch, who found the adult Hopi pattern in this respect reflected in the comparable behavior of children of five and six years of age.

We have a little more difficulty, however, with the description (by Davis and Havighurst) of child-training practices in the subcultures represented by socioeconomic class. Middle-class girls, for example, as contrasted with those of the lower class, are expected to help earlier at home with the younger children, with cooking, washing dishes, etc. It is not easy to see the direct relationship between these patterns of upbringing and the differential responsibilities of the two groups in later life.

Most striking, perhaps, is the problem raised by Kluckhohn's observations among the Navaho. Infants are well treated and well fed, weaning is late and gradual, toilet training is neither strict nor premature; "tension and its counterpart, anxiety, should have been but little developed in the first year of life." Kluckhohn goes on: "The most striking theoretical question which emerges from this consideration of some of the main aspects of Navaho infancy is this: how can this picture be reconciled with the facts on Navaho witchcraft, on the states of morbid melancholia and endemic uneasiness which have been well documented for adult Navaho? How can the anxiety level be so high among a people where infants are nursed whenever they want to be, where childhood disciplines are so permissive, where there is so much genuine affection for children? If the writings of certain psychoanalysts were literally true (and the whole truth), adult Navahos ought to have calm and beautifully adjusted personalities. However, this is certainly not the case. In spite of the fact that Navaho infants receive a maximum of protection and gratification, they tend to be moody and to worry a great deal when they become adults."

The explanation of such discontinuities represents a challenge which has not yet been met by those who insist upon finding in early childhood *all* the seeds of later growth and development.

The third problem to which I should like to draw attention is that of cause and effect. Does the child training determine adult personality? Or is it the other way around? Or both? It is not easy to determine whether the hostile and assertive behavior of Mundugumor women is the cause or effect of the relatively unfriendly treatment of children. It is not easy to know whether the insistence upon obedience within the German home is the origin (to follow Shaffner's analysis) or the reflection of the widespread emphasis on discipline and obedience allegedly characteristic of German culture.

In the theoretical scheme developed by Kardiner, it appears that patterns of child training (primary institutions) give rise to the basic personality structure, and this in turn becomes projected into the secondary institutions (for example, religious belief and practice). One of the major questions raised in connection with Kardiner's stimulating approach deals precisely with the *direction* of the causal relation. It is logical to assume that basic personality will also *affect* child training, and that religious attitudes may help to shape both the family relationships and the common traits of personality.

The usual way out of this difficulty is to assume a circular relationship. Newcomb, for example, states that "different practices in child training are *consequences* of differences both in culture and in personality," and that "different practices in child training also *lead* to differences both in culture and personality." This would appear to me to be the most acceptable, though not always the most clearly expressed position. It leaves a number of important questions unanswered, however. Does the circular relation mean that all aspects of the relationship are equally important? Which ones can be changed most readily? Is a change in one as significant as a change in the other? These become practically important problems in connection with the current interest in the human implications of technological change. What will new practices in child care do to the rest of the culture? What will the introduction of a factory do to parent-child relations? Such questions could be multiplied. The research now in progress and planned for the future in areas in which changes are being introduced on a rather broad scale may give us further insight into this relationship, if the human and social aspects of technological change are kept constantly in mind.

A fourth major problem arises in connection with the *absolute* as contrasted with the *relative* effect of cultural practices concerned with child development. An example should make this point clearer. Oscar Lewis in his *Life in a Mexican Village* writes as follows, in connection with the attitude of women toward having children: "Women for the most part 'accept' children fatalistically as a burden to be endured." And further, "It is common for women to complain at having to bear many children, which they believe to be a punishment of God." This sounds pathogenic, in terms of our usual standards; it implies a certain amount of maternal rejection, and I presume that most psychiatrists would not exactly regard such an attitude as the best preparation for a healthy mother and child relationship. I can now restate my problem more specifically. What is the effect (for example, in our own society) of a certain degree of maternal rejection on a child who sees *all around him* other children who are welcomed and wanted by their mothers? And how does this compare with the effect on the child when *all around him* he sees other children "rejected" to the same degree? These questions must be answered before we can assume that a causal relationship established between child training and adult personality in one cultural and social context can safely be extended to another. This is what I mean by the absolute and relative effects, respectively. The meaning to the individual of a certain amount of frustration will surely vary in relation to the amount of frustration to which he sees other individuals subjected.

This problem comes close to home, for many of us. It is a rare parent indeed in our society who has not heard from his child on more than one occasion: "Why can't I? Johnny Jones is allowed to, and he is even younger than I am." It is probably not so much the absolute as the comparative frustration which causes resentment. I was struck forcibly by this consideration when I first discovered the range of answers given by parents in a relatively homogeneous community in the Midwest to a query concerning the age at which they permitted their daughters to go out with boys unchaperoned. The spread was from about 14 to 20 years (Butterfield, *Love Problems of Adolescence*). Think of the frustrations of every one of these girls above the age of 14! There is undoubtedly a comparable range in connection with the hour at which teen-agers are expected home at night (the Cinderella complex!), the number of dates permitted, the night spots that one may visit, the use of the family car, etc. On several occasions I have suggested that the wear and tear upon both parents and children might be reduced if some code of standards could be adopted and accepted by both, in order to decrease this tremendous variation. This suggestion was recently the subject of two articles by Dorothy Barclay in the *New York Times* and has been rather actively debated.

I am not suggesting a national referendum, with the decision of the majority becoming the law of the land. Coercion of even a single individual or family would be out of place in a matter of vital personal concern. In any case, no general agreement could possibly be reached in a country as heterogeneous as ours; codes would have to be local, and advisory rather than binding. Rugged individualists may still force their daughters to come home earlier—or even to stay out later!—than the average. Finally, the code would have to be selective, and apply only to those items on which it is possible to reach an agreement. Research could help by way of surveying the relevant attitudes, and analyzing the nature of the difficulties which arise in individual families. If successful, this approach might well reduce many of the strains which are due to *relative* frustrations even in groups which in material terms might seem to have little cause for complaint.

This area is closely related to a further problem which requires much more investigation than it has so far received. I refer to the so-called "peer cultures," the standards of behavior laid down by children *for themselves,* with strong pressures toward conformity, often in conflict with the norms set by adults, and with definite sanctions against the dissenter. The phenomenon is particularly noticeable in the teens, and Talcott Parsons has labeled it "youth culture"; this includes "a set of patterns and behavior phenomena which involve a highly complex combination of age, grading, and sex role elements." These various peer cultures await the detailed analysis and description of the anthropologist, although the task of establishing the proper rapport with the needed informants may turn out to be more difficult than in the case of the Chavantes or the Kaffirs. To me, at least, many aspects of peer cultures remain a mystery. How do the culture patterns develop and how do they change? Why are certain boy-girl relationships acceptable one year and frowned upon the next? Who decides how much necking (if that is the correct term) should be permitted, and where the line must be drawn? What are the processes of invention, and of diffusion, or culture borrowing? How is it agreed that certain clothes must be worn by "all the girls," or at what age lipstick should be used; who determines when boys should drink beer or smoke a pipe? Certainly not the parents—at least not in all cases—since the standards they have for their children do not always coincide with those set by the children for themselves. The problem is an important one, since the child's adjustment to his peer culture may turn out to be at least as significant for his feelings of personal security and worth as the process of socialization to the world of adults.

Next on my list is the problem of culture conflict. We have become familiar with this area in connection with the process of assimilation of immigrants; there has been much discussion of the possibility that differences between old and new cultural norms may contribute to personal maladjustment, including delinquency and crime. Even within our own "American" culture, it has been suggested (the Lynds, Horney, and others) that our values contain within themselves many serious contradictions and conflicts; we expect of our children both independence and conformity; we believe in progress and also in the *status quo;* we glorify competition and at the same time advocate the Golden Rule.

These and similar conflicts have been interpreted as accounting for the "neurotic personality of our time." Children confronted by such conflicting norms may well find adjustment difficult. The question which I would raise, however, relates to the extent to which conflicts in the *culture* become conflicts in the *individual*. If we believe in progress in one field, or at certain times, or under certain conditions, we may perhaps *without conflict* still believe in the *status quo* when the context is different. Competitiveness and the Golden Rule may peacefully coexist within the individual if his compartments are sufficiently watertight. We will not know how important these cultural conflicts are in terms of personal adjustment until we have thoroughly examined them not only in society as a whole, but also in specific individuals.

Finally, a word about the problem of individual variations within the same culture. Some of us have been disturbed by the tendency among many students of culture to generalize too widely and too quickly. A significant corrective to this tendency is to be found in a number of recent studies (for example, Jules Henry on the Pilagá, Thompson and Joseph on the Hopi, Kluckhohn and the Leightons on the Navahos, Lewis on the Tepoztecans), in which the combination of psychological and ethnological techniques has restored the individual to his proper place. We need to extend this concern with the individual when we study cultural factors. In one sense the individual remains an enigma, in spite of all the research at our disposal. Two children, growing up in the same society in a similar family constellation, with equally protective mothers and understanding fathers, with comparable feeding and toilet training, etc., still somehow retain their own uniqueness. Many years ago Piéron spoke of the "semi-permeable membrane" surrounding each personality, letting some experiences in, keeping others out. Every individual makes his own choice and his own interpretation of what his culture offers him. Explanations in terms of glands, constitutional type, heredity, uterine environment, earliest training, have all so far proved unsatisfactory. Future research may be more fruitful if the attempt to discover the basis of individual variations is joined to the study of culture, instead of going its own separate way.

I have said little about what we know, and much more about what we need to know. A look at the past may be heartening, but there is a greater challenge in looking ahead. In the ranks of Ortho, with its truly interdisciplinary membership, are to be found the skills needed to bring us closer to the answers we are all seeking. It has been a privilege to be with you. I hope that at least at some points I have been fortunate enough, in expressing my own concerns, to have touched upon yours as well.

---

41. A Comparison of Socialization and Personality in Two Simple Societies *

Brief illustrations from many different cultures may suffice to demonstrate that culture influences personality, but to understand how these influences operate we need a closer and fuller look at culture in action. For this purpose, the following discussion offers a review of child-rearing customs and their effects among the Kaska Indians of western Canada and the rural children of southwestern Haiti. This review raises a number of questions concerning hypotheses about personality development based on data drawn only from one society, our own. Such questions show the need for cross-national and cross-cultural research for the development of a true science of human behavior.

INTRODUCTION

This paper presents infancy and childhood data from two societies. Those aspects of childhood are stressed which seem to be important in the formation of the more readily apparent personality qualities of the people studied. The conclusions, based upon a comparison of the materials, represent generalizations directed toward problems currently facing the field of personality development.

It is coincidental that the societies discussed offer direct contrasts in two significant aspects of personality development—discipline and the induction of emotionality. In the fall of 1944 a group of students, recently returned from the field, met at a discussion meeting of the Yale Anthropology Club to compare their notes on child development. The members of this group, with varying interests, had each gone to a different society. Nevertheless, the data brought back covered comparable categories of infancy and socialization. The diverse childhood pictures described for each society provoked inquiry into consequences for the adult personalities. This paper was written to show the rela-

* Frances W. Underwood and Irma Honigmann, "A comparison of socialization and personality in two simple societies," *American Anthropologist,* XLIX (1947), 557–77. By permission of the authors and the *American Anthropologist.*

tionship between patterns of child development and the adult personality. It is unfortunate that not all the groups originally discussed could be represented here.

Although extended knowledge of infancy and childhood is vital in understanding the adult personality in any society, the insight gained from such data alone is very partial indeed. A richer, more complete understanding of personality would depend upon a comprehensive knowledge of the total culture. Kardiner has made this point. He denies that personality formation can be predicted from life-cycle data alone. Rather "the indicators of what are the permanent effects of traumatic experiences in childhood are found in religion, folklore, and a host of other facts gathered from the description of the institutional set-up."

It is with this limitation in mind that the studies below are offered. Comprehensive ethnographies are being prepared for both the Haitians of Beaumont Plateau and the Kaska.

SOME ASPECTS OF PERSONALITY PATTERNING IN KASKA INDIAN CHILDREN

The Kaska Indians today inhabit the northern area of British Columbia and southern Yukon Territory from the Continental Divide on the west to the Rocky Mountains on the east. Climatically this area is in the polar continental zone of extremely cold winters and warm, even hot, summer days. Biotically it is in the forest belt of spruce, jackpine and poplar, a region hospitable to moose, bear, caribou and a number of smaller, fur-bearing animals.

Lower Post, the trading post for this region, is located at the confluence of the Dease and Liard Rivers, about 150 miles below the headwaters of the Liard. The settlement extends from the Liard River to the Alaska Highway, a distance of about a quarter of a mile, and is about a mile long. Three trading stores are the nucleus of the town, the merchant personnel, the policeman and the game warden constituting the permanent residents of the community. During the summer months, when the Indian families and white trappers return from the bush, the population swells to about 200 persons. Most of the Indians are Kaska. From about May to September the Indians remain in Lower Post. They trade their furs and then relax after the strain of the rigorous winter life. Before they leave they also stock up for the new trapping season, which begins in November after the first heavy snowfalls.

The data presented below were collected during a three months' stay in Lower Post, from June to September, 1944, and a six months' stay in 1945. June to August was spent in Lower Post, September to December at a winter settlement of Kaska Indians on the Upper Liard River. Rapport was such that at the trading post I exchanged visits with eight Indian women who had children, and in addition could observe the activities of other children and parents as they loitered around the trading stores. The presence of my own two children undoubtedly aided in establishing rapport. In the bush we were completely accepted as participant members of the small community and were fitted into the matrilocal set-up by being assigned appropriate native kinship terms. In spite of these advantages, however, it was not easy to obtain specific information by verbal communication. For one thing most of the culture patterns are highly unformalized, so that a mother could not say what general procedures people followed with relation to children. Also, although most of the Indians speak a simple English, they are extremely introverted and taciturn so that spontaneous discussions were limited. The most frequent Indian contribution to a conversation was "Yes" or "No." Most of my information, therefore, was gained through participant observation.

The hunting-trapping-trading economy of the Kaska Indians necessitates a long winter stay in the bush. Late in July families begin to pull out of Lower Post for their trapping areas. By the middle of September the last stragglers have rolled up their tents and are busy transporting their winter outfit to their trap lines. Trap lines are owned by individuals, usually the men, but occasionally by an unattached woman. Until spring a single family or a matrilocal group of three or four families lives in isolation in its winter cabins with only a rare visitor. Winters are long, dark and intensely cold. By October the rivers begin to freeze, not to run again until March. Winter temperatures average about 35 degrees below zero, Fahrenheit, occasionally dropping to 60 and 70 below. Daylight is at a premium during winter; in December there are days of almost 20 hours of darkness. This is balanced in June and early July when it is light almost 24 hours a day. On the trap line a woman may frequently remain home alone for days with her young children and daughters while her husband, sons and sons-in-law are visiting and setting traps. All Indian women interviewed said they liked the winter life with its work and isolation. The cabin in the bush is referred to as "home." But by winter's end the people are again eagerly looking forward to their summer's visit to the post, with its opportunities for sociability.

The atomic nature of the Indian community in Lower Post is quickly perceived. No attempt is made to set up a planned community. Each family pitches its tent where it pleases, usually at a spot near the river bank having sufficient trees and brush around to insure privacy from other dwellings. Occasionally, related families will set up adjacent tents.

Sociability takes the form of groups of men, women and children loitering in front of trading stores, exchanging visits, drinking and dancing together, participating in gambling games. Dances, gambling and drinking parties are eagerly anticipated and almost every night during midsummer one or another of these activities will take place. Nevertheless, unless stimulated by alcohol, social interaction is rarely intense. At a dance it may take an hour or even two before the ten or fifteen participants are sufficiently at ease with one another to venture onto the dance floor. There is somewhat more spontaneous interaction between adolescents, particularly of the same sex. Intrasexual chasing, tickling, hugging, wrestling is readily provoked and greatly enjoyed. Similar intersexual "horsing around" is more inhibited and usually initiated after dark, or after the ice between the sexes has already been broken by a dance or a few drinks.

The individualistic manner in which the Kaska participate in group activities can be illustrated in the following situations: Arrangements for a dance are made without prior planning and in a completely informal manner. On the spur of the moment someone will say, "Ask Pete to play fiddle tonight?" Word will get around that Pete is being asked "to make dance." At about midnight folks begin to drift toward an empty cabin usually used for dancing. Should Pete not feel like playing that night, the group disperses. Pete is under no compulsion to cooperate, although he usually does. In the same way anyone may leave the dance on impulse without any apparent thought as to how his absence will affect the party. Alcoholic beverages are prepared by individuals, on rare occasions by two individuals, who then invite a few friends to share them. This is in sharp contrast to the practice of the whites at Lower Post who cooperate in making brews, five or six individuals contributing supplies, money and services toward making liquor which may later be shared among ten persons.

Sanctions in this loosely knit Indian community are rarely severe. Although there is a nominal chief appointed by the Canadian government he exercises no authority whatsoever. Criticism is the strongest sanction. No matter how much a man's behavior may be disapproved of, barring actual endangering of the life of others, he will be accepted, respected and supported by his kin and friends, although they may tell him he is doing a bad thing, scold him and urge him to mend his ways in the case of severe misconduct, or simply gossip about his faults.

This was graphically illustrated with relation to sexual misbehavior. Promiscuity of the girls with visiting soldiers was severely disapproved of by the older people. Nevertheless the girls were not ostracized nor were they disrespected as individuals. They were lectured by one of the old men, criticized and gossiped about, but no one denied them friendship or hospitality. In general people prefer to avoid the resentment of others by minding their own business.

Rorschach tests interpreted for 28 Indians confirm the picture of introversion and emotional aloofness observable in much of Kaska behavior.

The Developing Personality

Children are wanted and welcomed by their parents. The actual birth is dealt with casually, no ceremonies marking the occasion. Some mothers are up and active in a week, some take it easy for about a month. The baby is wrapped in a velvet, embroidered "moss bag," now frequently modernized with the substitution of flannel for moss. The infant's legs are firmly bound, but its hands are usually free. I observed no restriction on thumb sucking. The baby is comforted whenever it cries, fed whenever it appears hungry. Babies are breast fed although some take a supplementary bottle. (It is not at all unusual to see a discarded whiskey bottle or cologne bottle used for this purpose.) The mother takes the baby with her wherever she goes, packing it in its moss bag. Around the camp the child is held in arms; on the trail it is packed on its mother's back, its face toward the mother. A baby rests contentedly on its mother's back and can sleep comfortably with its head nestled on her neck. An older baby has its legs free, but continues to be packed around by its mother or father until it can walk. It appears that the child's initial experiences in life are such as to foster a sense of security. Since the people are undemonstrative and emotionally aloof, however, there is not much open demonstration of affection.

Weaning usually occurs between one and three years of age and is a gradual process. The child is urged to stop suckling by being talked to and scolded. A persistent child, however, will be allowed to the breast till he stops the habit of his own accord. An older child goes to his mother's breast, undoes her dress and helps himself whenever he wants to.

Training for elimination control occurs at about two years and is not severe. The mother takes the child with her into the bush to indicate to him the expected behavior. Conformity is expected to come from the child. As one mother put it, "I never say nothing. He learn himself." Young boys from about a year and a half to about two years have a large hole slit in their pants for ease in self-training. Others wear no pants at all during this period. By three years most children go alone into the bush around the camp to eliminate in privacy. A child who persistently soils beyond this age is criticized and scolded.

A more severe attitude is taken with regard to masturbation. Such activity is discouraged with threats of insanity. It is important to note, however, that parents sincerely believe insanity to be a possible consequence of masturbation.

A child walks and talks when he is developmentally motivated to do so. He receives no pressure from others. The taciturnity of the parents offers little stimulation for a child to express himself verbally. My own young son was always a source of amusement to the little Indian children because of his constant stream of chatter.

When a child can walk he is left more and more to himself, a process of emotional weaning taking place. He fulfills his activities with little parental supervision. If he hurts himself he must go to his mother or father for comfort. Only in situations of immediate danger—if a child walks too close to the cut-bank above the river, or approaches too near the fire—will a parent interrupt the child's activity. The laissez faire attitudes of parents in many cases is not an active rejection of the child; "passive acceptance" would probably better describe the relationship. This is particularly so for the child living with both his true parents. The child living with but one true parent and a step-parent is more isolated emotionally since a step-parent usually considers his spouse's child by a former marriage to be out of his jurisdiction. One seven-year-old orphaned child presented a picture of very severe isolation. The boy exhibited attachment to no one, not even to his grandfather with whom he lived. He roamed around alone, usually failed to respond to his grandfather's requests, and frequently prepared his own meals from cans. When his grandfather nagged him to go to the summer missionary school he simply "disappeared," sleeping on a white trapper's porch and eating whatever left-over food he could find at our camp. Food was one of the few things this boy responded to with enthusiasm. About 10 per cent of the children live with at least one step-parent. Often a two-year-old can be seen walking alone, playing or crying out of sight and hearing of his parents. For example, I twice had to remove two-year-olds from the road to permit trucks to pass, the parents of the children being nowhere in sight. One two-year-old was sitting in the road howling while his parents were shopping in the trading store. Finally someone picked him up and brought him to his mother who then held him and patted him while she continued making her purchases. It is generally the case that if the crying child is brought to its mother, or if he goes to her, he will be picked up and quieted. A petulant child, hanging around his mother's skirts, is absently indulged so long as he hangs around.

Rather than directly refuse a child anything, the parent will use sly tricks to distract a child from an object. For example, a two-year-old wanted some of his mother's chewing gum. In her pocket the mother slipped the gum out of its wrapper and showed the child the empty wrapper, saying she had no gum left. Later when she wanted the gum for herself she pointed out an airplane to the boy and, as he looked up, popped the gum into her mouth. Being caught in a lie by the child did not appear to disturb this parent. Such experiences re-enforced the child's loss of faith in his parents.

The only temper tantrums that were observed occurred in children eighteen to twenty-four months of age. The child was either ignored or picked up and removed from the frustrating situation. That these temper tantrums may be an expression of resentment against the early emotional weaning is suggested by the fact that the ages of the two phenomena coincide.

It seems likely that being thrown on his own at so early an age involves a serious threat to the child's sense of security. Psychologists have pointed out for children in our own society that a very frequent reaction to lack and loss of love is a withdrawal from affectional relationships. The early emotional weaning experienced by the Kaska child may well be an etiological factor in the emotional isolation and introversion exhibited by these Indians. The childhood situation appears to offer some compensations to the child. Warm sibling ties develop; for sisters particularly, this warm tie is retained all through life. The child is also given ample opportunity to develop self-sufficiency and to acquire a sense of independence. These are qualities which permit at least conscious adjustment to a sense of aloneness.

A low energy level prevails among children, manifested in little gross motor activity. This is undoubtedly related to poor nutrition. A good deal of the time young children sit quietly close to their parents, who discourage too great boisterousness. Children who run about constantly, shout and are more aggressive toward their playmates are thought of as too wild.

Play groups are small, consisting of close-aged siblings or relatives. The structure of these groups is atomic. There is little cooperative play and even this is at a low level of organization. For example, a child may throw a toy boat to which a rope is attached into the river and another child will pull it in, entirely spontaneously and with no pre-discussion of roles. When the second boy tires of pulling it in, the first does his own pulling without comment. Cooperation is accepted but not expected. There is no formalized or organized group play. Predominantly there is parallel play. As an example take two or three boys, each sailing his own boat in the river with little reference to each other, outside of occasional comments or exclamations. A new child joining the group adds his presence and activity but leaves the structure of the group undisturbed. A child motivated to leave simply walks off without disturbing the activities of the others. Nevertheless children usually play in groups of twos and threes, apparently finding gratification and stimulation in the mere presence and exclamations of fellow mates.

From the foregoing it can be seen that the qualities of emotional aloofness and individualism also manifest themselves in the play relationships among children. Group interaction in play is weak and the child maintains his identity in group activity.

Sibling relationships are good. As stated above, close-aged siblings invariably play together. Indeed, being isolated in the bush for nine long winter months they are likely to see few children other than siblings and maternal parallel cousins until they return to the post. Physical aggression among children is infrequent. Cultural values are strongly oriented against aggression. An older child being beaten by his younger sibling smiles as he disengages himself from the onslaught. Should he fight back his parent will scold, "That's your brother. Don't hit your brother." Children may tease one another, for example by taking away another's pet toy.

Without strong positive pressure from adults and without formal education the young child readily learns cultural activities. A little two-year-old can occasionally be seen fetching water from the river in a small pot. The child's voluntary contributions to camp chores are accepted. Children are permitted to use sharp knives, scissors and axes as soon as their activities demand the need of these tools. A five-year-old was seen making a rolling toy for himself. He nailed the round top of a coffee tin to a thin pole, using the flat side of a sharp ax to pound the nail through. This same boy was playing with a fly hook at the river front. No one paid any attention to him till the hook got caught in my daughter's overalls. Then the boy was scolded for his carelessness.

Older children are expected to help around the camp. A girl of six or seven is asked to pack small wood into the house and attend to other routines commensurate with her abilities. A ten- or eleven-year-old girl is assisting in the bulk of the housework. In addition she sets and visits rabbit snares, assists in sawing and splitting wood. In winter she may set a few traps, the fur from which will become her own to sell. A boy's education for his economic role in the family begins at about ten years of age when he starts to accompany his father or brothers fishing, hunting and trapping, and watches them prepare the various manufactures needed by the family. He is also expected to haul, saw and split wood. Educational methods are extremely flexible and indirect. A child learns primarily by observing how a thing is done. So long as he can fairly well approximate the finished product, the steps whereby he managed to achieve it are not rigorously prescribed. For example a six-year-old child was asked to build a fire in the stove. No further instruction was offered. The child put the kindling on top of the heavy wood and consequently the fire failed to catch. Her guardian said nothing but rebuilt and set the fire herself.

No one in this society is bogged down with work. A girl contributing heavily to household chores still has a great deal of free time. During her leisure she is her own boss, although she is expected to return quickly to camp whenever her assistance is needed. A boy enjoys even more free time.

It appears to be not so much the pressure of other people that brings about socialization but more importantly the values inherent in the cultural patterns as answers to the problems that the individual will face growing up in his milieu. For example, a boy eagerly accompanies his father on the trap line. To subsist in the adult culture the boy needs trapping experience and knowledge. A good hunter and trapper is respected, has a definite prestige with girls and can reassure himself as to his self-sufficiency. Therefore, although trapping is an extremely rigorous business, the task has a strong enough positive valence to make the boy eager to begin it. On the other hand the boy who fails to become a good trapper and who, upon marriage, cannot support his wife and family does not face severe deprivation, for he will be assisted in supporting his family by his wife's family.

From the above it can be seen that socialization for the Kaska is a consistent process which steadily re-enforces the personality qualities which were initiated at the break between infancy and childhood.

Summary and Conclusions

Two cultural trends appear to influence Kaska personality development. The first trend makes its appearance with the early emotional weaning of the child. The parents, particularly the mother, withdraw themselves from any intensive emotional interaction with the two- and three-year-old. Their attitudes may be described as being compounded of passive affection and emotional indifference. The result in the child appears to be an emotional aloofness which later manifests itself in the withdrawn, taciturn adult personality which we have described as introverted. The impetus to strong social interaction having been removed from the developing individual, the child is thrown upon his own resources.

The second cultural trend influential in Kaska personality formation stems from the opportunities for independent development afforded by the atomic social structure of the community and society. Discipline is lax, frustrations are minimal, and social sanctions, such as aggression, scarcely elaborated. The individual developing in this milieu is stimulated along strongly individualistic lines, a development that is highly compatible with his emotionally aloof personality. Only the expectation of rewards like social approval, sexual opportunities, and economic independence instigate definite behavioral trends. Negative sanctions are far less effective as motives of behavior, since the atomic structure of the society makes such sanctions of minor importance to the strongly individualistic personality of the Kaska Indian.

PEASANT CHILD REARING IN RURAL SOUTHWESTERN HAITI [1]

The observations recorded below were made during the summer of 1944 in rural villages scattered over the Beaumont Plateau which lies approximately in the center (both north-south and east-west) of the mountainous southern peninsula of Haiti. They are not as complete as the author could wish, since rapport with peasant women was difficult, but it is hoped that such information as it is possible to give may help fill out gaps in our knowledge of this phase of life in simple societies.

The term "child" (*êfê*) [2] has two cultural meanings: (1) all subadults, and (2) individuals of age six months to five or six years. The first is a generalized meaning; the second's practicality in cultural terms is demonstrated by the acquisition of pants for boys and knee-length dresses for girls at the latter age, and by the economic fact that children of five or six are put to work in towns as domestics.

Within childhood, then, two categories are defined and recognized:

[1] The following villages were visited in the six-weeks' stay: Beaumont, Cassonette, Centre d'Avezac, Digotrie, Guinée, and Lachicotte Valley. Funds for anthropological research in Haiti were supplied through a grant to the Department of Anthropology at Yale University from the Viking Fund, Inc.

[2] Spelling of Créole words follows the official phonetic script adopted by the Haitian government. ^ indicates nasalization of the vowel. All vowels and consonants indicated are pronounced, and with the usual French qualities.

infants (*ti êfê,* or *bébé*), comprising babies from the day of birth to approximately six months, and children, or individuals from six months to approximately six years.

A word about the organization of this section is in order here. Young humans must make two types of adjustment to life, and society must solve two sets of problems in regard to new individuals. One is the result of the physiological weaknesses of the baby; the second is the result of societal living. These two aspects have, therefore, been set off as categories, and pertinent information subsumed under them. At the end a summary will be attempted.

Child Care

Feeding. Babies are breast fed, the hours seeming to depend on the child's needs and desires in the matter. During the nursing period some other forms of nourishment are given to babies. These are of the gruel type and made of corn meal, wheat flour, or manioc boiled in water.

Weaning. This takes place at fifteen to seventeen months, according to my informant, and children of two years or more were never seen breast feeding but were given solid foods, such as fruit or cassava cakes, when they asked for a bite. Presumably their regular meals correspond with the adult diet.

Teething. The baby's gums are massaged by the mother to soothe them, and she may let him chew on a lime or a piece of orange to aid the dental eruption.

Cleanliness. New babies wear a diaper arrangement to facilitate cleaning, but later (about four months) have one piece of clothing only —a little dress for a girl, a shirt for a boy—or nothing at all, a costume most practical and functional. From birth through the crawling stage few restrictions seem to be placed on the children, as they were observed urinating and defecating in the houses and on the porches with no one taking any notice except to clean the spot if it interfered with adult activities. Since the floors are of earth and lime, liquid is easily absorbed; every family owns a chamber pot which no doubt is utilized if the child is caught in time. In some cases, it was noticed that the baby was cleaned. Although no information was secured on the techniques of toilet training, with the exception of mild intrasibling ridicule among some upper class boys, the fact that after five years children are fully clothed in most instances would indicate that they are expected to have learned control by that time.

Frequency of bathing was not observed, but each peasant washes his face and mouth the first thing in the morning, using either fingers or a wooden stick to clean the teeth. Presumably these practices extend to the children.

Sleeping. Babies sleep with the mother at night. They nap during midday and during the first few months sleep much of the twenty-four hours. If the mother must be away during the day, the grandmother or other elder female relative will rest or sleep with the baby. An instance of this was observed in Cassonette one morning about eleven. The baby was lying on some rags within the curve of the old woman's arm. Both were peacefully asleep in the cookhouse near the banked fire.

Health. Attention to this varies with the individual family. For example, two cases of hernia in young boys were seen. One family is literate and expects to see that the child gets an operation; the other is of average peasant level and the child will probably go without help. Another factor enters here. The peasant does not like to spend money on children—it is with the greatest reluctance that he will buy clothes for them hence the preponderance of nudity in young children. Most of the minor ailments, however, have folk remedies which are applied when needed.

Clothing. Only for infants is clothing a protection. The climate is so mild and salubrious that clothing after infancy serves the functions of adornment and modesty. A new baby is clothed in a diaper, sometimes an undershirt, cap, and little dress, then wrapped in a cloth or blanket. The six-week-old girl I met my first day in the area was wrapped in a dirty, ragged cloth, with equally soiled cap and dress the only other items of clothing seen. Booties are optional. After three or four months, as mentioned before, this is changed to the single garment. From birth to death the average peasant is barefooted.

Crying. Children are not encouraged to cry; if they do so except when they have been punished, the nearest adult will attempt to soothe them; if they are in the hands of an older sibling, the latter will usually pick up the child and try to quiet it by cuddling or directing its attention elsewhere. The children observed seem to have a rather low frustration threshold. Even older children will cry if teased, and young ones will howl if someone accidentally pushes them or will not pick them up when they want it, or does not allow them whatever they wish at the moment. They always cry when disciplined, but in such case they get no attention—or if any, it is a sharp word to keep quiet.

Walking. No pressure to walk was observed; babies are put on the floor after a few months and allowed to crawl as much as they like. Presumably children imitate siblings or other youngsters who care for them. By two years of age they are walking.

Play. Babies' play is about half and half baby-adult and baby-child in composition. They enjoy peek-a-boo, patting or grasping at objects held for them, being jiggled, trying to participate in the activities of the older youngsters.

After the toddling stage, play is in sex-differentiated gangs. Frequently, however, a girl was seen attempting to join the boys. Most play after toddling is done on the way to or from an errand, or when the family has not assigned a task.

Favorite forms noticed include: tag, chasing each other in an apparently aimless fashion (this is confined to young children), teasing (verbal and otherwise), pretending activities of their elders, and practical joking. These are all child-and-child games. Verbal teasing is mainly confined to older children and was not so easily observed as the more active type. Every time a group of youngsters gathered at a water supply spot there was much splashing, screaming, and laughing, evidencing dousing. One youngster was observed teasing a playmate by practically wiping him with a kitten. Only one case of practical joking was observed. A group of her contemporaries set a puppy at the heels of the girl dwarf of Lachicotte Valley as she was on her way home with a water-filled bamboo stalk balanced on her head. Pretending ranges all the way from imitating the characteristics of relatives, strangers, and others to riding sticks with fiber tassels as horses.

Play with animals is fairly frequently to be seen, smaller children confining themselves to dogs and cats, while older ones love to ride every chance they get. The boys prefer horses for the speed.

Sex play. Masturbation is a prohibited form of behavior and my informant (R. Hs. Etienne) insisted he knew of no incidence of it or of a child trying it. My own observations agree with his, but the suspicion is that the children do attempt it, only to come up against one of the strongest cultural taboos. The way they are dressed (or undressed) would enable elders to inhibit its occurrence easily. The efficacy of training here is indicated by the fact that not once was a native boy seen with an erect penis.

About the age of puberty (fifteen) great interest in sex relations is manifest, and my informant is sure that there is considerable experimentation. Sex relations are not considered obscene or wicked, but fun; there are no taboos on speaking of the sex organs; work songs mention them, and sexual jokes are frequent. Also houses are small (mainly one or two rooms only) and members of the family have a minimum of privacy so that children must learn much of the sex act early.

Responsibility for care. The mother is primarily responsible in car-ing for the children. No one replaces her for feeding, but a relative (either sex and any age from two on) will watch a baby or child for her. These surrogates are permitted discipline privileges, but tend to be less severe than the parents.

Amount of care. Supervision and attention are continuous for children until the walking age. After that they are not under direct supervision, but parents can ask any villager going by the door and usually get an answer as to where the children are. Total impressions are that the culture follows physiological lines closely here as care is continuous until the child is talking and walking. Then, casualness replaces the previous pattern.

Training for Social Living

Talking. Since only upper-class Haitians were observed trying to encourage speaking in children, it is assumed that little pressure in this direction is exerted among the peasants who do, however, teach the talking baby mannerly address in short order. In addition another factor comes into play. Society is organized either in terms of a village which is relatively heterogeneous as regards lineages, or of a village composed of several lines within the same family tree. These units are high in daily interaction levels, so that a growing child would move in a very verbal world and probably be rewarded by forms of adult activity for intelligible speech.

Diet. Information on this point is negligible. Two meals a day are eaten by the peasants with snacks in between. Children of two were seen nibbling on cassava cakes between meals, and older ones eating bread or fruits, such as oranges or mangoes. Children attending the market ate rice and beans together with their mothers, so that the diet tends to approximate that of adults soon after weaning.

Clothing. Reference has been made previously to infants' and young children's apparel. After five or six, children always wear clothes: shirt and short trousers for boys until puberty; slip and dress for girls. After changing voice and other secondary sexual characteristics appear in a boy, he dons long pants, although two boys of seventeen were observed still wearing short ones. Generally two sets of clothing are maintained for each individual, the old ones being used for work or sleeping garments and being replaced when necessary. No shoes are worn, though sandals are now being used to a slight degree.

Work. At an early age children are given the responsibility of certain tasks. Girls and boys of two or more watch their younger siblings, and take care of them in the sense of providing companionship and entertainment as well as supervising how far they toddle, crawl, or otherwise motivate themselves. A boy of four was noticed walking with a younger brother and holding him by the hand to aid if he stumbled over a stone or depression in the ground; two girls of four and five were seen playing hide-and-seek, cuddling, and rolling about with three younger siblings. A little fellow of about three was frequently observed picking up his year-and-a-half-old sister whenever she cried or strayed. Other examples are found above under *Crying*.

The children are the water-getters; they are sent for it the first thing in the morning and the last thing at night, and as often in between as necessity and distance demand. They are also the family messengers. A little girl of about four carried a communication to me from her father, the total distance going and returning being about a mile.

After six or seven, children become economic cogs in the family wheel. At that age a child may be sent into town to work as a domestic, or, if he stays at home, he takes an active part in daily activities. Two young girls were encountered one day on their way from home in Cassonette village to Andre village where they were going to market the produce carried on their heads. A girl of eight was observed helping her mother with the exacting task of fixing manioc for cassava cakes. Boys will help the father cultivate, make saddles, run long errands, and so on. A six-year-old boy was seen one morning with a small mâchete on his head, on his way to join his father at cutting branches for the production of charcoal. Both sexes learn to ride early, but boys were more often seen playing at riding and more often in the saddle than the girls, even though the latter will grow up to ride donkeys to market.

Especially at a communal work project, like building a house or preparing coffee for market or doing a major farm task such as working the ground for cultivation, the children are pressed into service in many ways. At the gathering of a sosiété datribusiô to help a Centre d'Avezac man get his stored coffee ready to sell, young boys were playing the musical instruments to which the men sang and worked; young girls were carrying water and assisting in the cooking. In the same village, neighbors of another man were helping him build his new house. The little fellows carried stones to the site in company with adult males; little girls carried baskets of lime from the kiln and, together with the women, brought in water.

Sex differentiation. Distinction between male and female runs through every aspect of peasant culture and children are early made aware of it. Differentiation starts before birth, for boys are much more desired than girls since they are the ones who will bear the family name and be responsible for their elders in old age. This continues throughout life in the relationship between parents and children. Ambitions are had and planned for the son—more money will be spent on him; if any education is to be had, the son is given it.

Clothing, ornamentation, and hair style are differentiated after three months. In church, baby girls were seen with caps or hats and earrings. The heads of boys are shaved; the hair of the girls is parted in squares over the head and the hair in each square braided. Frequently bright ribbons or string are tied to the braids.

Distinction in tasks performed was not noticeable until five or six, when the dress of the children shows that they are now in a semi-adult category. Then girls are set to helping the mother to cook, bearing responsibility for youngsters in the family, and marketing goods. The boys at this age begin to operate within the adult male circle of activities —farming, musicianship, cock fighting, housebuilding, charcoal making.

In sleeping arrangements boys and girls are separated after they leave the mother's side (about six months?), so that siblings of the same sex sleep together. This division seems to have more than an incest-prevention function since it is carried so far back into childhood. Still wider chasms separate the home environments of boy and girl at puberty, because the peasant family in the majority of cases keeps the girls home at night as a check on their sexual life, while the boys are out late courting or trying to. Thus the ideal is for the girl to be virginal, but cultural allowance is made for experimentation by the boy in maturing.

Control measures. Treatment of infants and children up to two years is indulgent. By that age they are walking and saying some words, and real discipline begins here. The father is the primary disciplinarian because of his position as head of the family, and much of the discipline is directed toward teaching children the father's role and that they must always obey him. A mother may have to go and get a child after she has called it, but he will always appear when the father calls, though he may move slowly enough to show he resents being disturbed.

One could say that almost any adult may discipline a child, although there is a definite ranking in terms of authority. The godfather (*paren*) is obeyed and respected almost on a par with the natural father. The same is true of the grandfather.

The measures used for discipline which were observed are: (1) scolding; (2) sharp tone of voice; (3) withholding of affectionate behavior; (4) force, in the sense of picking a child up, dragging it, and so on; (5) force, in the sense of the use of pain, such as switching. Only one case of the latter was seen. Back of the market place one Tuesday (market day) a boy of about five was noticed crying; a few seconds later his mother appeared with a switch she had pulled from a nearby tree. She grabbed the boy roughly and switched his bare legs and back about a half dozen times, scolding during and after the performance. An instance of spanking was heard one evening before dusk. A little four-year-old boy had been shooed from our premises by my cook and a few minutes later was given two spanks on his buttocks by one of the farm workers. The child ran home screaming and crying. A father was seen to go across the street one morning in Beaumont, pull his crying daughter of four or five away from her playmates and back to her home, set her in a chair, go into the house, and come out with a horsewhip which he handed her with a lecture. During the whole time his voice was raised, loud, and angry.

As indicated above, the use of stern measures seems confined to immediate parents; surrogates will slap, speak sharply, or just take the child away from the spot of misbehavior, or, if possible, remove the cause. Naturally, individual parents vary in the application of discipline. One mother asked her young son to let his younger brother have a ride on the horse which the elder was galloping up and down the path. As an answer, the rider whipped the horse off down the lane. The mother just shrugged her shoulders and went her way, leaving the younger boy to get his ride as best he could.

Rewards for good performance by a child were observed as follows: (1) tokens of affection, such as caressing head, face, arms, shoulders, back, or legs by rubbing and stroking; hugging; kissing; cuddling or cradling in lap or arms or both; [3] (2) verbal praise; (3) verbal thanks; (4) food, such as a sweet, a fruit, cassava cake, and so on.

The learning situation. There are several interesting points to be considered in the learning situation of the peasant child on the Beaumont plateau.

One which contrasts strongly with our own is the lack of painful pressure surrounding the toilet and sex areas of the training process. Due to the "realistic" handling of these two problems, the potential psychological stresses involved are almost eliminated as factors. This is interpreted as contributing to the friendliness and openness noticeable in the personality of the people studied, since the child does not develop aggression toward his social environment at this time but receives cooperation and understanding.

On the surface it might seem that feeding could be added to the above list, but although mothers tend to feed children when they desire it, there is not much quantity of food so that a large proportion of the

[3] Public display of affection is reserved for children only.

youngsters are undernourished. It is suspected that nursing children fare a little better in this respect than their older brothers and sisters. This, plus the sudden change from indulgence to stern discipline at the walking stage, may be the important factors in the production of the low frustration threshold which characterizes these people. None of the indications of oral fixation was noted, with the exception of grass chewing by all ages and both sexes.

A more important aspect of conditioning is the radical variation in the social environment after a youngster has become intelligibly verbal and physically coordinated. The previous pattern, as outlined, was highly protective (stemming from the high infant mortality rate and the cultural pressure for large families), attentive, and coddling. The new one, on the other hand, is restrictive of the child's whims and desires, casual in attentive reaction, and rather oppressive where elders are involved. For it is at this time that the training for adult roles takes place and, presumably due to reasons of economics (both lack of adult time and a constant need for added labor) and of status (respect and obedience must be accorded all elders), this educational process is hurried along through the mechanism of strong discipline. Enforcement, moreover, is in the hands of volatile individuals. This means that the psychological atmosphere in which the child must learn is productive of insecurity and ambivalence in emotion.

Lastly, there is the structural aspect of the social environment of the child. Figures available on peasant families (Lachicotte Valley) show that they average five children per family, the range being from one (newly married couple) to thirteen. In addition, at least a third of the families are polygamous. Further, three of the six villages visited are what is known as *aglomerasiô de famiye* (Aux Pommes—part of Beaumont, Digotrie, and Guinée). This is the result of the sharing of the same area of land by several branches of the same family or several related families. In such communities one is struck by the African compound-like aspect they exhibit, the houses clustering around a central clearing. Still further, a set of godparents, with concomitant co-siblings, is added to the child's list of blood and affinal relatives. With all these facts in mind one can vision the continuity and density of social interaction affecting growing youngsters.

It is assumed by workers in the field of culture and personality that child-training patterns correlate directly with the adult personality configuration and the institutional emphases of a given culture. Therefore, in summary, we will briefly examine the validity of this assumption for Beaumont plateau.

Adult character structure in this culture has, as components, (1) extroversion (indicated by easy friendliness, openness, curiosity toward the novel, social initiative), (2) volatility, (3) relative aggressiveness, (4) relative individualism, and (5) relative insecurity. The possible role of non-painful toilet and sex training in contributing to elements of extroversion has been mentioned already. Other factors include the structure of the physical and social environments. In the case of the former, there are few dangers for the growing child. For example, houses are usually small, one-storied, with a minimum of furniture. An eating table, several rush-seated chairs of the straight-backed variety, water jug, a cabinet for the necessary eating equipment, and beds or mats comprise the average household articles. Lamps are hung or put out of reach of a child; mats and baskets are fairly easily replaced, so that a youngster moves in relative freedom about his or another home. His social environment is extended, rewarding (in terms of food, affection, and novelty [4]), and consistently group-oriented in every phase of life. Agricultural activity is carried on mainly by groups; relaxation is gained in group dances, sings, and pageants (such as the Kombit revues and Easter Rara festival); marketing is communal; death involves kinship and local-group participation; even laundry is frequently done in a group. Security is so strongly a function of group activity that only a few instances of solitary activity were noted during the six weeks. One was by a man who had been drinking; another was the singing, as he worked alone, by a man who had been a laborer in Cuba for several years. He was not an average member of the community.

Individualism is noticeable, however, in the personality of the plateau peasant. It is especially so in two spheres—political and emotional. By political is not meant reference to the Haitian government, but a say in the affairs of the community. One evening, while passing the house of the local policeman of Beaumont, a group of persons was seen gathered around him in what seemed to be a heated debate. It was discovered that a man had been accused of killing four goats which had wandered onto his property. It is perfectly permissible to kill one or two which have done damage, but to kill four was to be wantonly destructive of the meat resources of the village. Some of the individuals gathered to participate in the "trial" were owners of the animals killed; others were just interested members of the town. Anyone going by could have stopped and added his opinion and argument to the

[4] This term subsumes play, attentive interaction of other individuals in the group with the child, and the varied experiences offered a youngster in a community. The word is used in recognition of a social need (possibly with a physiological basis) which has been well outlined by Linton.

informal proceedings. Several had. Such an occurrence has analogies in many areas of village life.

Emotionally, the individual is allowed considerable freedom of expression, which not only adds to his individuality but is basic to the norm of volatility or excitability. Perhaps a convenient generalization would be that these people are emotional. They laugh easily, cry easily (at least as children), are angered easily and so on. This seems to be related to the sharp change in the character of child care from indulgence to strict discipline, the latter administered by adults whose self-control is weak.

This same constellation is responsible for an amount of insecurity noted among the inhabitants of Beaumont plateau and gives rise to aggressiveness. The latter can be dissipated culturally through gossip, teasing and joking, black magic (*via* the *bokor* or vodû priest), cock fighting and verbosity. Mistreatment of wives and children is common, as might be expected.

From the foregoing, there is seen to be a direct relationship between the patterns of child training in this section of Haiti and the adult character structure which supports and is implemented by the institutional life of the communities mentioned. Children become adults who find congeniality in the group activity which makes possible a better economic existence. The same groupings provide the necessary entertainment and relaxation to offset hard work and in-group tensions growing out of individual aggressiveness and excitability. Babies are well enough treated to support the cultural pressure for many of them; older youngsters, under the impact of relatively harsh discipline and loss of permitted willfulness, develop the tempermentality and aggressiveness which are characteristic of adult personality.

From the facts of child training presented in this paper, there is a temptation to predict great sibling rivalry and the presence of the Oedipus complex. Unfortunately insufficient data were gathered to support such predictions. More information would probably yield clues, at least, to their existence.

CONCLUSIONS

The existence of a causal relationship between the child-training process of a society and the adult character structure exhibited by its members is an accepted axiom in the social sciences. Data from simple human aggregates, however, have frequently been declared to offer an especially fertile field for insight into the various operative factors involved, and it is with the hope of thus adding further information on these forces that the present authors have undertaken to conclude with a qualitative and comparative analysis of the material presented in the foregoing sections.

Psychoanalysis has placed particular emphasis on the role of infant years of experience in the production of the mature personality on the thesis that initial handling of basic drives forms the ultimate source for the direction of adult character. It is interesting, then, that the Kaska personality norm is introvert and the Haitian extrovert, although in both societies babies are fed when they so desire, receive no pressure to control elimination, are comforted and handled when irritable or playful, and suffer no discipline for emotional willfulness. The indication is that other criteria than those associated with physiological urges are important in personality structuring, and moreover, that these may lie in the childhood rather than infant experiences, at least for the two societies under discussion.

Goldfrank, in an important recent article, has pointed out that the period beyond infancy may be the critical stage for molding adult character in some cases. On the basis of disciplinary policy, she sets up four categories: (1) societies where discipline is weak throughout infancy and childhood; (2) societies where it is severe throughout; (3) societies where it is severe in infancy and weak later; and (4) societies where infant discipline is weak and that of childhood is severe. Following her outline, the Indian group is seen to fall into class one, as lax discipline is continued into later years and the culture itself exhibits atomistic features of organization plus mild sanctions for non-normal behavior. The Negro communities of the Haitian plateau, on the other hand, fit into category four, since, after two years of permissive and indulgent treatment from its elders, a child is subject to increasingly stern and widespread discipline from these same persons. In other words, Kaska society offers continuity in this sphere, and Haitian peasant groups are characterized by discontinuity as between babyhood and childhood. It should be pointed out, however, that despite the fact that Kaska conditioning shows continuity in regard to the single feature of discipline, after infancy there is a demonstrable withdrawal of maternal warmth and affection which seems to have a qualitative effect upon the growing organism. Both societies, at the transition period between the helpless, unsocial, verbally uncommunicative baby and the coordinated, relatively socialized, talking child show a discontinuity in the affective relationship between the youngster and its parents plus/or surrogates, whether it be gradual withdrawal of overt emotionality or the imposition of rather harsh discipline. In either case, there appears to be a traumatic effect on the personality produced by the change itself (shown by temper tantrums among the Kaska and sullen malingering in Haiti). In addition, the new configuration is measured against an initial secure, pleasurable pattern of infancy, thus furthering its impact. We conclude, therefore, that a positive correlation exists here between the affective environment of an individual's formative years and his personality structure.

Within the total discipline picture, the mechanisms of reward and punishment may also offer further clues to character formation. Consistency in the agencies by which and the areas in which specific rewards and punishments are administered is thought to have quite different implications in personality development than lack of it. The Haitian peasant child entering the stage of sub-adult, but non-infant, is punished or rewarded according to the whims of the volatile elders of his family and community. He may be brutally spanked today when bawling because his mother had just quarreled with his father, or the same misdemeanor may be ignored tomorrow if his mother had made some extra money at the market. But the Kaska child can depend upon a minimum of discipline and a passively permissive parent. Thus, in Haitian plateau society, added to the discontinuity of discipline as a whole, inconsistency in dispensing punshments and rewards by adults with weak self-control is characteristic, while continuity of discipline policy and relative consistency in its mechanisms is an attribute of the Indian group.

Cultural bases for these opposite traits are readily observable. The Haitian pattern contributes to an ambivalence of feelings toward elders, which is exploited culturally to hurry the sub-adult into the period of maturity; the Kaska constellation permits the development of a self-reliant, independent individual who will maintain the atomistic social organization. This interaction may also be seen in the fact that the severe discipline of peasant society operates greatly as external pressure to take on cultural skills. At the same time the child loses the right of emotional spontaneity within the family, so that he is provided with an internal drive to regain a volatile state (adulthood) where these crafts will be utilized. Conversely, among the Kaska, there is a low degree of outside compulsion to acquire customary aptitudes, while the child's independence is supported by emotional withdrawal on the part of his parents. Thus, he receives progressive impetus toward self-reliance over the years, and due to lack of attention and direction by senior members in regard to traditional techniques, his learning is by a gradual process of imitation.

In summary, the data from Kaska and Beaumont plateau point up several possible elements in personality formation. Firstly, the total socialization process must be examined in attempting to understand the production of character type in any group. Secondly, we agree with Goldfrank and Benedict that where this continuum shows discontinuity over its course or inconsistency in its application, these in themselves can be important factors in personality development. Further, the imposition of a changed affective pattern may have a traumatic effect upon the organism. As a corollary of this latter fact, it is felt that additional support is given the thesis of a human need for affection. Still another inference to be drawn is that where a secondary period of disciplinary policy can be distinguished, its impact upon the personality of the individual is a function of the initial experiences of that individual.

Lastly, our examination of socialization in two simple societies shows that in addition to the handling of hunger, weaning, elimination, and sexuality, other diagnostics are to be looked for in explaining personality structuring. Those reaffirmed by analysis of Kaska and Haitian material are (1) affectional relationships, and (2) the nature of discipline and its administration.

---

42. *The Nature of Psychotherapy* *

ALTHOUGH THE COURSE of personality development does run smoothly for many people, situations arise for some people to which they cannot make effective adjustments. A variety of techniques have been developed by psychiatric and psychological specialists to help people who are experiencing trouble of this type. Here Dr. Kubie reviews the most commonly practiced methods of facilitating successful personal adjustment and suggests the specific uses of each.

PSYCHOTHERAPY is as old as medicine: indeed, it is nearly as old as religion; and a history of psychotherapy would be a history of human culture. Yet it is only the last half century that has brought scientific knowledge of its scope and limitations; and it is only in the last half century that anything new has been added to its techniques.

In the perspective of history, the term itself is young. Yet it has already acquired a meaning so vague and general as to be difficult to use with precision. It can include the mystical healing rites of a priest-

* Lawrence S. Kubie, *Bulletin of the New York Academy of Medicine,* second series, XIX (1943), 183–94. By permission of the author and the publisher.

physician of ancient Greece, or the drum-beating and the voodoo practices of a modern primitive, David strumming his lyre against Saul's melancholy or classes in rhythmic dancing in a modern psychiatric clinic, forced labor in an old prison asylum or the rhythm of a modern occupational class in basket weaving. As one witty patient described it, "under one, and over two, rest in a neutral environment."

In this loose sense, psychotherapy embraces any effort to influence human thought or feeling or conduct, by precept or by example, by wit or humor, by exhortation or appeals to reason, by distraction or diversion, by rewards or punishments, by charity or social service, by education, or by the contagion of another's spirit. This broadest possible use of the term would also include the temporary lift of spirit through music, art, or literature.

Such methods as these depend upon an artful blend of imagination, feeling, intuition, firmness and common sense; but it will be our thesis that as a science psychotherapy begins only where these leave off. It happens that it usually will be good common sense to give water to a thirsty man; but this is not science until we know the role of water both in the normal body and in its pathology. So too with all such simple psychotherapeutic sips of water as sympathy or advice or rewards and punishments: we use these with scientific precision only when we know their relationship to normal and disturbed functions of the mind. Therefore, our first task is to formulate a concept of psychological normality and to define the boundary line between normality and neurosis.

We will not be aided in this by any distinction between normal and neurotic which is based on the usual differential points. We are not concerned with the issue of whether a man knows the difference between right and wrong in the archaic and unrealistic legal sense, nor with the question of whether he believes that he knows what he is doing and why he is doing it, that is, whether he can rationalize his conduct. Nor are we concerned whether his conduct conforms to the social and cultural mores of any special time and place, or whether it is extravagant and fantastic or orderly and sedate. These are important aspects of behavior but not basic or constant in their implications. Thus it is normal to wash one's hands but not normal to have a handwashing compulsion, although there is nothing eccentric or anti-social or deviant from any culture in the mere act of handwashing. Similarly, to stand on your head in a tumbling act is normal, while to stand on your head in church is not; unless perhaps it is done to pay an election bet, or as a hazing stunt. Evidently the critical difference must be sought neither in the act nor in its setting, but in the determining mechanisms of the act. Behavior is normal or abnormal because of the nature of the inner forces which produce it.

What, then, are the characteristics of the inner determining forces which make any moment of thought, feeling, and action normal, and what are the characteristics which make it neurotic? The answer to this requires one further distinction—a distinction between forces which are within the range of our conscious perceptions, and those which are so deeply buried as to be inaccessible to any introspective knowledge of ourselves. It is as difficult for men who are unfamiliar with this field of phenomena to realize that unconscious yet psychologically powerful forces are constantly at work in everyone, as it was for the old scientist who had never looked through a microscope to believe in the microscopic objects which von Loevenhoeck described. Nevertheless it is one of the great achievements of modern science that the evidence for this has become incontrovertible. It is not possible to describe this evidence in detail; but it is important to note in passing that it is firmly based on a variety of different techniques applied to four fields of observation: to wit, experimental work with humans, clinical observations with psychoanalytic methods, clinical observation of animal behavior, and experimental work with the conditioned reflex. The weight of this varied evidence forces the psychiatrist to proceed from the premise that in every moment of human life the mosaic of thought, feeling and conduct which constitutes behavior is determined by confluent forces, that we can be aware of only a fraction of these forces at any time, and that we tend naively to overestimate the relative power of those of which we are aware even in events in which the unrecognized forces have played a determining role. To simplify our terminology, we can use a somewhat inaccurate foreshortened jargon and say that while we are conscious at any moment of some of the reasons for our conduct we are always unconscious of others.

But how does this help us understand the distinction between the normal and abnormal in behavior? Here we are on clear grounds. Whether "conscious" or "unconscious" forces play a major part in producing any moment of behavior is the most important single distinction in human psychology. This is because conscious motives are constantly molded by external realities, whereas unconscious forces pay no heed to the outside world. They are uninfluenced equally by the pain that they may cause the individual himself and by the pain which they may inflict on others. They are deaf to exhortation, argument, and reason, or to appeals to love or hate. They are so blind that the symptomatic acts which they engender do not succeed in satisfying even themselves. Their tensions remain undischarged. Therefore they are literally insatiable.

Consequently, the larger is their influence in any particular act, the more unrealistic do they make that act, and the more inflexible and the more endlessly repetitive it becomes. This is what has been called the "Repetitive Core of Neurosis" (Kubie), and this is why neurotic behavior is endlessly and ceaselessly repetitive, whether it appears in the form of overt neurotic symptoms or of neurotic life patterns disguised as ordinary behavior. This is what the layman means when he says that we learn so little by experience. It would be more accurate to say that the consciously organized normal aspects of man can learn by experience, but not that part of him which is unconsciously driven: because the unconscious neurotic mechanisms go on their way unsated by gratification and unaltered by experience.

It is precisely this repetitiveness which constitutes the essential challenge to psychotherapy and its most difficult problem. However, the approach to this ultimate stronghold is always preceded by less complicated preparatory maneuvers. These simpler psychotherapeutic expedients may be grouped under three main headings: (a) Practical support—consisting primarily of advice, guidance, and assistance in the management of life situations and environmental difficulties through social service aids, etc. (b) Emotional support—consisting essentially of sympathy, exhortation, admonition, encouragement, humor, art, recreation, companionship, etc. (c) Reorienting education—consisting primarily of efforts to alter the patient's habitual attitudes of guilt, fear, hate, and depression, by educating him to tolerate his own conscious and unconscious needs and cravings, his instinctual hungers, his familial jealousies and hates, etc.

The third of these groups requires extensive knowledge of unconscious psychological forces, and hides many subtle dangers which will be discussed below. The first two, however, can hardly be called a discovery of the psychiatrist. They are the homely non-specific, commonsense weapons of every wise parent and teacher. They must always be tried first. Indeed where they succeed alone, one may be sure that the maladjustment is more external than internal: since it is precisely their failure which reveals the rigid repetitiveness of behavior which is energized predominantly by unconscious internal forces, rather than by external environmental stresses. This again is why we say that psychotherapy as a science begins where the simple, rational methods fail.

Perhaps a banal example can make this clear. A child of three or four wakens at night, slips out of his bed, and comes pattering into the front room in search of his parents. On the first occasion he is picked up, hugged, and carried back to his room; and after his wants are attended to he is tucked in, kissed and left there. A few minutes later, however, he reappears. The same "medicine" is applied, perhaps a little more brusquely, but nonetheless kindly. Even if it didn't work the first time it might work now. But again the youngster appears. The parents try successively leaving the light on or the door open, a toy in his bed, cuddling, promises, bribes, scoldings, threats or punishments; but in spite of their versatile efforts the child appears over and over through the course of many evenings. This is a typical transient neurotic episode of childhood. The parents become distracted. They run through the whole gamut of human feelings, from affectionate patience to irritability, anger, and finally a panicky feeling that something is wrong. They feel that they have tried every possible sensible device, without success. They do not realize that their failure constitutes a thorough therapeutic test, demonstrating that the roots of the child's disturbed behavior lie deeply buried, on a level which is inaccessible to any surface manipulations.

What is true of the small child is also true of the adult. Rewards and punishments, discipline and education, argument and reason, the sensible manipulation of the environment, occupational therapy, comfort, solace and exhortation, these are all essential preliminary steps in the approach to any psychotherapeutic problem. They clear away external complications. They effect cures when the situation is sick rather than the individual. Thus they are at once the ante-chamber to deeper treatment, and a therapeutic test of its necessity. Where they work it is folly to go deeper: but where they fail it is even greater folly to persist with education, habit training, social service, work adjustment, etc., because, until he is already on the road to health, the neurotic patient cannot use such aids, no matter how badly he needs and craves them. For the neurotic, treatment must precede practical assistance: or the wisest guidance will be sabotaged by the neurosis.

But psychotherapy cannot always achieve or even aim at the eradication of causes. As in any other medical discipline, it must sometimes content itself with palliative measures.

Palliative psychotherapy consists primarily of an effort to teach patients how to live with some measure of comfort within the confines of their uncured neuroses. Of itself this can relieve much suffering. For instance, an agoraphobia may manifest itself first merely in an uneasy feeling in very large, open spaces. At this stage the neurosis will make little difference in a patient's life. Gradually, however, the anxiety will become more all-pervading, until the patient becomes unable to go out of doors at all, or even to go into a moderately large room. With each successive encroachment on his freedom, his life and that of his family become more circumscribed. Soon all who know him begin to pay with him the price of his neurosis. If the psychotherapist does no more than to keep the patient from succumbing to these successive restrictions, he will contribute greatly to the happiness of the patient and of his family. It is here that education, exhortation and endless ingenious manipulations of the environment can play a role of major importance.

If more than palliative treatment is to be attempted, the psychotherapist must attack the rigid, inflexible, automatic, repetitive core of the neurotic process. It will be seen that this challenge cannot be effectively met in the naive spirit which underlies the time-worn concept of "habit training."

It is not orthodox to place this rigid repetitive tendency at the very heart of our psychotherapeutic problem: yet I do so because I believe that this is the nucleus which is common to all neurotic processes, and that the customary emphasis on mood and content is an emphasis on secondary symptomatic manifestations. When the repetitive process manifests itself in certain recurrent ideas we speak of obsessions, in recurrent acts we speak of compulsions, in recurrent mood states we speak of anxieties, depressions, elations, etc., and in recurrent distortions in the patient's view of external reality we speak of delusions. These variegated secondary symptoms demand flexible temporizing care: but they are the branches and not the roots of the tree. It is towards the roots, i. e., the forces that make the disturbance recur, that our therapeutic efforts must be directed.

First, however, we must raise one more important preliminary question, namely, whether the repetitive pattern ever becomes so structuralized in the nervous and glandular organization of the individual as to be unalterable by experience on the psychological level; or whether the mechanism by which that force is mediated can be altered by means of psychological events. On the answer to this question hinges the future of all psychotherapy: yet the answer is not known. We know that the duration of a symptom is no indication as to its structuralization. For instance, as a result of purely psychological treatment I have seen a man of 57 lose symptoms which began when he was three years and ten months old: while in other cases, in spite of penetrating insight into buried forces, quite recent symptomatic manifestations may persist almost unaltered. We do not yet know why this is true. It is possible that in certain patients the nuclear repetitive phenomena may be the expression of an inherent organic inclination towards such repetitions. We know that repetitive phenomena occur universally and from infancy onward; but as yet no quantitative studies are possible of their incidence, of the factors which produce them, or of their correlation with later neurotic manifestations. In brain injuries and in certain experimental lesions repetitive phenomena may be produced; and Brickner has shown that the stimulation of a certain area in the brain can induce perseveration. This does no more than suggest the possibility that organic factors may play a role. It gives no information as to possible variations in the inherent inclinations of different brains towards the production of repetitive states under similar psychological stresses. Therefore, we are left with several alternative possibilities, which are not mutually exclusive. In the first place, there may be a greater inherent inclination toward stereotyped repetitive phenomena in one brain than in another. Secondly, certain types of gross or subtle injury to the brain may possibly enhance this tendency. Thirdly, psychological influences of varying severity can induce this phenomenon. Presumably if sufficiently intense they can induce the phenomenon in any central nervous system: but it is also possible, if not probable, that in certain nervous systems they can be induced more readily than in others, and that once they arise in certain brains they may thereafter be more tenacious than in others. Finally, repetitive phenomena once induced may be mediated by reversible changes in one nervous system, and by irreversible or even progressive changes in another. It is particularly in such cases as this that lobotomy may be a rational procedure. Our knowledge of all of these matters waits upon the development of methods by which these hypothetical variables can be measured. In the absence of such methods in our pursuit of therapeutic weapons we are forced to rely upon the oldest device in medicine, the method of trial and error. Let us turn to the errors first, to dispose of them.

Throughout his life every psychiatrist learns one lesson over and over again, only to forget it, namely, that however much it may relieve his own feelings it does no good to a patient to call his illness names. When a patient comes with a frank symptom, such as a hand-washing compulsion, we know that it is a mere waste of breath to tell him solemnly that he suffers from a compulsion. The patient tells us that himself. Our technical nomenclature can help him neither to control his symptom nor to get rid of it. Nevertheless, when dealing with subtler compulsive patterns this is forgotten, and psychiatrists hopefully describe to patients their "neurotic trends." There is no parent who in layman's terms has not told his child the same thing, calling him lazy or good-for-nothing or disobedient. Scientific name-calling is not more effective than this: because scientific epithets can not alter the repetitive nucleus of a single neurotic manifestation. At worst they merely mobilize the patient's defenses. Jung and Adler and Rank all made that mistake. It is regrettable to see it recurrently repeated by others.

Many years ago William Allen White pleaded against this error, when he said that the hardest lesson a psychiatrist has to learn is to allow a patient to say that 2 plus 2 equals 5, until the patient discovers why he *had* to cling to this belief.

It is impossible to lay too much emphasis on the futility and dangers of naive confrontation; because this is the most frequent mistake of the immature psychiatrist, and of the well-intentioned general practitioner who has read psychiatric theory without having rigorous drill in its procedures. Superficial confrontations which merely describe the patient to himself without long and patient preparation, inevitably precipitate resentment and mobilize his defenses. Premature confrontations which reach to deeper levels, challenging the patient to recognize some of his deeper fears, yearnings and hates, must either be rejected as far-fetched or else they will precipitate the patient into unmanageable terror, guilt or depression. One learns slowly never to force a patient to look at a painful fact about himself until you are in a position to explain its origin in his history and its function in his present life. This may take patient exploration over many months.

So important is this that we must recognize that it may be dangerous to attempt to argue a patient out of cherished ideas and beliefs even about seemingly impersonal affairs, such as science or politics. Argument may be as dangerous as confrontation. If it succeeds in breaking down the defensive barrier of symptomatic ideas, all that can be achieved is a sudden eruption of overpowering emotions.

Thirdly, there may be danger even in reassurance or consolation. A patient said a few mornings ago, "I was in a panic. My sister telephoned me and assured me that her household were well. Then all of a sudden I found myself in such a depression that I stood at the window and thought of throwing myself out." It is not too much to say that the only safe thing to do with a patient is to listen to him, until one understands enough about him to be in a position to relate everything one says and does to *his* unconscious psychological processes.

And now we are ready at last to suggest a possible answer to the final question: namely, what is the nature of a psychological process that can influence the basic underlying repetitive patterns which characterize all neurotic phenomena? This may not be too difficult to understand if we recall that the repetitive pattern is a recurring effort to bring to a satisfactory completion a painful, forgotten, and incomplete experience which has been left hanging in air. Thus the child who wakens in the midst of a nightmare puts himself to sleep again by telling himself a happy ending. The man who has been worsted in an altercation goes down the street muttering all the fine things that he might have said had he only thought of them in time. Indeed we do this throughout life, the only difference being that most of our attempts to discharge the tensions left by past experiences are carried through without our knowing what we are doing.

In such experiences, moreover, the boundary line between reality and dream is never hard and fast, because each "experience" is a mosaic of fact, confusion, misunderstanding, and fantasy. The past which we try vainly to undo is half real and half imaginary: but the neurotic shadows which it casts on the present screen of life are real enough. The neurotic component in all of us is always the residue of just such incomplete experiences, nightmares which have not lost their emotional hold even after we have wakened, nor after we have forgotten the dreams themselves. It is as though we had wakened just as the villain was poised to strike. Then we "forget" the dream but not the feeling, and live out our waking lives through symptoms or symptomatic acts which are disguised and unsuccessful attempts to avert or avenge the fancied blow.

One characteristic form of the acute traumatic war neurosis gives us a clear picture of this process. Night after night the patient attempts self-cure. That is, he redreams his shattering experience, trying each time to dream it through to a happy ending. But as he dreams, his terror mounts to a point at which he is wakened prematurely at the very climax of danger. This leaves him shaken with terror, grief and rage. There is a point in the dream beyond which he cannot go, some mingling of reality and fantasy so highly charged that every time he tries to re-live it his mind shies away at the last moment like a horse that refuses just before the take-off. Just as this happens spontaneously in the war neurosis, so it occurs in the treatment of the neurotic patient. He, too, must shy away from deeply painful if less melodramatic early experiences, whenever the therapist tries to help him re-live them to a realistic conclusion, thus to free him from the endless, closed repetitive circles of his neurotic patterns.

This incessant struggle is the source of a state of constant inner tension, for which the most obvious therapy would be a discharge of the pent-up feelings. The process of discharge is often called "catharsis," and much is made of it in psychiatric literature. Therefore, it is important to know that catharsis is not enough. Furthermore, the concept is poorly understood and widely misused. Any discharge of emotional tension can give temporary relief, be it a temper tantrum or an uncontrolled outburst of crying and laughing. Even a painful symptom gives momentary relief. The patient with a compulsion neurosis discharges tension in the moment in which he executes his compulsion. In fact, every act and thought and feeling discharges tension in some measure;

and all of this is catharsis. Unfortunately, however, most of these acts rapidly recreate as much tension as they discharge, and sometimes more. In a somewhat more lasting sense, however, it is cathartic to help a patient to express pent-up feelings which he has previously been afraid or ashamed to face. A man who has never been ready to admit that he hated some member of his own family may find marked relief when the psychiatrist's non-critical attitude encourages him to acknowledge this feeling. But even here, a fresh up-welling of guilt or anxiety can exact a heavy price for the catharsis, and precipitate the patient into graver depression and terror. Thus, no mere discharge of feeling, either from the surface or from the depths, can accomplish lasting benefits unless it is preceded and accompanied by an eradication of the source of the feelings. Without this, the feelings inevitably recur.

A psychotherapy which aims at the eradication of etiological sources must recover the content of the forgotten dreamlike "experiences," since it is these which give rise to the feelings which produce symptoms. They are the links in the chain of conditioning experiences. Therapy must complete the dream, in order to dispel the haunting moods which flow from it. It must find the happy ending which the child in us seeks incessantly. And in order to recover that which was forgotten it must penetrate the mists which shroud the past, and enable the patient to re-live vividly the acutely painful and confused experiences which make up the "dream."

All of the defensive forces of the patient's personality are mobilized against any such effort to penetrate into the forgotten areas of experience, because they have been "forgotten" not by accident, but as an obligatory defense against the pain of the original experience. Therefore, every technical advance in psychotherapy has been in the direction of finding ways around these defensive barriers.

This whole matter is widely misunderstood. The question is asked, "Does the rediscovery of past events automatically dissipate feelings which had their roots in those particular events?" Or in another form the question is asked, "Does the discovery of a secret purpose, yearning, or desire automatically dissipate that purpose?" In reality these are not two questions but one. It is not merely the recovery of an event which releases the patient, nor merely the recovery of the event plus the feelings and desires which derive from that event. It is the discovery of the totality of the purposes, the hopes, the fears, the loves, and the hates which animated the individual at the moment of the event, plus what that event did to those purposes, loves and fears and hates, and how these were deviated by that event from their initial pathway onto another. This, and not less than this, is the potent discovery. If at a certain moment in the life of an individual the bank of a river assumed a terror-laden significance and if that moment and all of its attendant circumstances were subsequently "forgotten," then the terror becomes isolated, like a station with no railroad tracks leading to or from it. The terror can be experienced but only about substitutes; and can never be discharged. And the recovery of the memory of the moment when for the first time the bank of the river acquired a nightmarish quality allows the whole structure to be dissipated, until the bank of the river again becomes only a bank of a river and nothing more. The recovery of facts thus is merely a necessary part of the total process of undoing experience, of deconditioning the human animal. This is why "habit training" is a naive and empty concept.

All highly charged symptoms acquire many meanings through the course of life. Consequently, in retrospect one must trace its evolution through a series of discoveries, each of which gives temporary relief and then a disappointing recurrence of pain. This has led some theorists to the easy conclusion that the discovery of the genetic experiences is unimportant. This is equivalent to saying that it is unimportant to discover the bacterial organism which causes an infection if you cannot always prepare a powerful antitoxin from it.

A full consideration of the methods of recovering the past would involve us in difficult technical details concerning the handling of various types of resistances and transference phenomena. It is not possible to do justice to these problems here; but it may be useful to emphasize that the strength and power of the patient's defenses constitute the final reason why blunt confrontation is worse than useless, usually serving merely to increase the patient's opposition, and throw him into panic, and from panic into rage. In turn, this is why all short-cuts are dangerous.

During recent years various methods have been developed by which this goal is pursued. The most important of these is psychoanalysis; not because it is a perfect instrument, but because it is still the pathfinder. Hypnotism, which once was used naively as a magic wand with which to order symptoms to disappear, has more recently been used as a method to assist in the recovery and re-living of the past. It is used both in combination with and as an extension of psychoanalytic technique. In turn, both of these have been used in combination with medications of various kinds; and experiments are under way in their use in combination with hypnagogic states. Finally, even the various forms of shock treatment come into consideration in this connection, because they sometimes render material accessible which is otherwise hidden behind the repetitive patterns of thought and behavior. Shock treatment can be used, therefore, not merely as a crude way of disrupting temporarily the associative pathways, but also to render accessible to investigation the life experiences which lie buried behind those patterns.

Not one of these methods has as yet established beyond argument its own territory of assured pre-eminence, nor its own limitations. Each is in the developing, testing and formative stage. Few psychiatrists would agree to any formulation of the indications or contraindications of any one of them. Under these circumstances, little would be gained by putting forward my own views of the moment: especially since they, too, will undoubtedly change with the experiences of tomorrow. However, if we have succeeded in making clear the basic principle and goal which underlie all of them, and if we have brought the concept of psychotherapy into harmony with scientific medical attitudes on the relationship of therapy to etiology, then I will feel that the main purpose of this paper has been achieved.

---

43. What Is a Neurosis? *

THE TERM "neurotic" has been widely used and much abused in recent years. As we learn more about how men function, we begin to think that everyone is somewhat neurotic and wonder where normality leaves off and neuroticism begins. In this discussion, Dr. Ivimey, from her years of experience as a psychiatrist, offers a clarification of the nature of neuroses that should prove helpful in making the distinction.

KAREN HORNEY FOCUSES on the total character of the neurotic personality. Psychic being or personality has its own forces for survival, its own dynamics of development and growth and fulfillment. Neurosis is the expression of inhibited and distorted development of the whole self.

With this focus, a psychology emerges clear and distinct, unconfused

* Muriel Ivimey, "What is a neurosis?" Pamphlet of the Auxiliary Council to the Association for the Advancement of Psychoanalysis, 1946. Abridged from the chapter "What Is a Neurosis?" by Muriel Ivimey in *Are You Considering Psychoanalysis?* edited by Karen Horney, M.D., copyright 1946 by W. W. Norton & Company, Inc., New York. By permission of W. W. Norton & Company, Inc., and the Association for the Advancement of Psychoanalysis. This article is one of a series on psychoanalytic subjects, printed individually in pamphlet form. Information and copies, at 10¢ each, may be obtained from ACAAP, 220 West 98th St., New York 25, N.Y.

with issues relating to organic, instinctual considerations as basic factors in the understanding of man's nature, sick or well.

Neurosis originates in disturbances in human relations. The crucial period in personality development is early childhood; the child is malleable and at this period human environment is the decisive factor in character formation. In view of the factual immaturity and relative weakness of the child, his strongest needs are consistent and unwavering personal warmth, reliability, and regard for his immaturity. As his judgment and reasoning develop he needs understanding, respect, justice. These qualities and capacities in those who take care of him mean genuine love for him which he can appreciate and understand. These conditions would be the ideal psychic environment for the development of a strong, healthy personality.

What are unfavorable psychic conditions in the early environment? The closest and most influential relationship in the child's early life is with his parents. Relatives, nurses, guardians, institution authorities, etc., in intimate contact with the child, also influence his development. The most potent adverse influences are the shortcomings of such persons —their inexperience and inability to give genuine love to the child for himself alone, with no ulterior or spurious aims. Such shortcomings and failures are shown in excessive "love" and adoration; unreliability and inconsistency in regard to understanding, guidance and rational discipline; overindulgence; oversolicitude; favoritism; capriciousness; unpredictability and injustice when the spoiled child runs wild.

Parents sometimes demand expressions of love and devotion which the child does not feel and cannot give. He thus fails to live up to exorbitant expectations of his parents and is rejected and made to feel wanting and guilty. Active antagonism from adults is obviously frightening, as are humiliations, ridicule, contempt, inappropriate use of authority and too rigid or cruel discipline. Undue psychological discipline cramps, frustrates and crushes the child's feeling of his value as a human being. Overemphasis on conventional social behavior and school performance give the child a feeling that he is no good as he is, but can only be worthy if he comes up to arbitrary standards. Inattention, coldness, and remoteness in parents are likely to set up a feeling of vagueness and eeriness in the child's feeling about himself. He gets no feeling of the reality of his existence as a person if he does not see himself as real and important in the eyes of others.

In addition to these adverse psychological conditions, many parental attitudes bear the imprint of general cultural prejudices and distortions of human values common in the community, state, country or civilization at large. For instance, the following attitudes are frequently communicated through parents: a preference for boys and a prejudice against girls or vice versa; attaching special values to personal appearance and physical development; intense competitive strivings for popularity, dates, high marks at school, educational accomplishment; the possession of money, fashionable clothes, material things that are the criteria of "belonging"; pernicious political ideologies; dishonesty, cynicism, decadence, which may taint a whole culture or civilization.

These attitudes and prejudices are not always mediated by parents, but may be encountered outside the home. They are likely to affect the child's sense of his own worth if emotional factors in the home have already contributed to an inner sense of precariousness. But if relationships in the home have contributed to the development of a strong and secure inner core of personality, the child may not be much affected by adverse conditions from cultural sources outside.

Since there is no such thing as perfect understanding or pure essence of love for a child, inferiority feelings are probably very common in childhood. Those that persist have their origin in a sense of real danger to the self. The child feels helpless, abandoned, alone, isolated; he feels there is no one to go to who can be trusted and the whole world is hostile to him. He inevitably develops a sense of hostility to the world. The state of feeling helpless, isolated and hostile is called *basic anxiety.* Basic anxiety is the motivating force that starts the neurotic process going. In order to allay basic anxiety, the child mobilizes his resources and energies, and his attitudes and behavior toward others are modified in the interest of insuring his safety.

There is a deep human need to orient oneself in relation to other human beings. We are beginning to discern phenomena in human relationships that express this need and that are manifested in three kinds of movement in relation to others: (1) Tendencies to go toward others—expressed in being friendly and considerate, in being in close affectionate rapport, in trusting people, asking for help when it is needed, giving help, in yielding to others when it is appropriate; (2) Tendencies to go against others—expressed in standing up to others, insisting on one's own rights, pushing one's own claims, competing with others with the aim of forwarding one's own legitimate interests, protesting and fighting if necessary when one is ill-used, being alert and on guard against insidious attack; (3) Tendencies to move away from others—expressed in withdrawing and maintaining personal privacy. These satisfy natural interests in self-sufficiency and independence, natural needs for solitude, respite from the impact of the outer world, contemplation necessary for maintaining contact with oneself and for developing one's own creative capacities.

A child who has a sense of inner precariousness or basic anxiety has to regulate his movements in human relationships according to his need for safety, and the natural movements in relation to others become invested with forces and energies necessary to attain it. When he moves toward others, he is driven by intensified needs for affection, needs to find someone to cling to in undue dependence, to be excessively compliant, appeasing, placating, conciliatory. When he moves against others, he feels he must dominate, override, get the best of others, and fight for supremacy. Movement away from others is expressed in extreme withdrawal, pulling away, covering up, and hiding. These are called *neurotic trends*. They are neurotic because they are provoked by an inner state of trepidation and alarm, and because they are imbued with excessive tensions and are carried out with an excessive amount of energy in striving for the particular goal of each trend, which in each case means safety. A little paraphrase of the term *neurotic* would be "full of nervous tension."

Neurotic trends are characterized by constant and intense preoccupation with the goal of the trend and with the means to achieve it, and they are pursued with relentless tenacity. This is the quality of compulsiveness. They also have the quality of indiscriminateness, that is, the individual must get *everyone* to like him, or he must be defiant and aggressive on *all* occasions, or he must protect himself by withdrawing *as a blanket policy*. And finally, when the individual is frustrated in his neurotic aims and activities, he feels unsafe, anxious or panicky. He may not feel anxiety as such but it may be transmuted into a depression, or an outburst of rage, or a state of paralyzing blankness, or disorders of bodily function.

We see different types of solution of the problem of anxiety in childhood—in the approval-seeking, obedient, submissive child; the rebellious, defiant child; and the quiet, withdrawn child. Later developments show that no matter which general type of reaction first emerges, neurotic trends of the other two categories have also developed although they may not be in evidence.

In the course of time there is a great expansion of needs. All people with whom the neurotic individual comes in contact take on the aspect of "prospects" for the satisfaction of neurotic needs, and all situations represent mainly a potential field in which to operate on these terms. The neurotic person will behave in the same compulsive way regardless of the relative importance of situations—whether making a trivial purchase or pursuing his life-work.

Each trend is implemented, in time, with special strategies, tactics and maneuvers appropriate to it. These are seen more clearly in persons in whom trends of one category predominate, and in whom trends of other categories are kept out of sight or repressed. With time and experience, the predominantly compliant individual develops endearing, flattering and cajoling methods. He goes to great lengths to be submissive, self-effacing, and never to put forward claims for himself. The predominantly aggressive individual develops special alertness to the weaknesses, flaws and sensitivities of others in order to increase his advantage. He cultivates the arts and skills of the fighter, and callously overrides the rights and interests of others. Inattention, coldness, great guardedness in respect to approaches of others, extreme independence and self-sufficiency are cultivated by the predominantly detached individual.

Associated with each neurotic trend are special sensitivities, fears, inhibitions and values. People with strong compliancy trends are especially sensitive to displeasure or anger in others, are fearful of anything approaching an argument or fight, and are unable to be demanding or aggressive. Those who are mainly compulsively aggressive are wary of affectionate, considerate behavior and treatment and are generally inhibited in any expression of softer feelings. People who are predominantly detached are extremely uncomfortable when it is necessary to be in close contact with others; they dread anything which threatens their independence and self-sufficiency, and they are quite strictly limited in respect to real personal intimacy.

The neurotic individual evolves special falsely rationalized values for neurotic trends in order to justify them and in order not to see them in their true light. For if he did, he would have to realize that they are indefensible. He comes to regard them as sensible, logical, necessary, unavoidable, attractive, praiseworthy and superior to other ways. And conversely, he regards natural healthy ways as inferior, impractical, senseless or positively immoral.

In the pursuance of neurotic aims and the practice of neurotic ways, the individual has not developed natural, appropriate ways of dealing with life. Hence, when his neurotic devices fail him he has nothing else and is really helpless. He is then exposed to his worst terror—being completely at the mercy of the world. His expectations of danger are enhanced because his impulses are supercharged.

His very safety devices, while warding off dangers, constitute at the same time a threat to safety. Compliancy trends lead to being exploited; aggressiveness stirs up counterattack and alienates affectionate people; and detachment tendencies lead to ostracism. But the neurotic individual does not realize that what happens to him is to a large extent the result of his own behavior and activities; nevertheless, he suffers from these consequences.

In addition, the simultaneous existence in the individual of neurotic trends belonging to these three categories leads to the generation of more anxiety from internal sources. He has three means of achieving safety, all of which are at variance with each other. Getting approval and establishing clinging, dependent relationships constitute attempts to achieve safety by means that are diametrically opposite to rebellious, offensive, and aggressive tactics. And these means which bring him into close contact with others, one in excessive friendliness, the other in enmity, are at variance in turn with his compulsive needs to withdraw and isolate himself. Isolation frustrates the needs for affection and aggression.

If impulses from discrepant and incompatible sources arise simultaneously, they can create a most serious dilemma, the dilemma of *conflict*. The individual has no choice of compulsive means to insure safety since the forces involved in all his compulsive ways are equally strong. When drives aiming at different goals are felt in full force, the individual has the experience of being torn apart, of going to pieces. Conflict felt less acutely precipitates confusion and anxiety. The individual feels threatened with the breakdown of his defense system and the penalty for such a breakdown is total vulnerability in a hostile world.

The neurotic individual must avoid such a calamity at all costs. He must create the illusion of integrity, harmony, or unity in order to maintain his equilibrium and avoid the threat of disintegration.

We identify four main ways in which the neurotic individual attempts to solve inner conflicts: (1) predominance of one set of major neurotic trends; (2) externalization of internal problems; (3) construction of an idealized image of the self; (4) detachment from emotional relationship with others.

In the first instance, the predominance of one set of major neurotic trends, the individual admits neurotic trends of one category into consciousness, though without a true appreciation of their significance, and represses contradictory trends. He can thus think of himself as one kind of person and establish a feeling of unity, of not being divided. Inhibitions are the chief clues to repressed trends. The person in whom compliance and dependency predominate will be unable to stand up for himself and fight; the aggressive type of person is unable to yield and seek the good graces of others. Both types are frequently unable to contain themselves in solitude. The withdrawn type of person is unable to establish intimate personal relationships with others either for approval or in aggressive action. Repressed trends also find expression in slips of the tongue, inadvertent remarks, forgetting and absent-mindedness (revealing tendencies by the person unknown and unacknowledged); and in phantasies and dreams. Furthermore, the rationalized values for the predominating trends are greatly reinforced, and the repressed trends are devaluated to the point of abhorrence.

Externalization of inner problems means that the individual manages to remain unaware of his neurotic trends and conflicts by focusing on other people's difficulties, their troubles, their weaknesses. He usually feels that his environment is in a turmoil, that the world is out of joint. He may take a morbid satisfaction in such matters. He tends to interfere, criticize, advise, instruct, apparently helpfully. But there is always a quality of indiscriminateness, indiscretion, and tactlessness that is the clue to a driven need to avoid awareness of problems within himself. He tends to put the blame for whatever he suffers in consequence of his own inner conflicts upon external conditions, and he may feel helpless and swamped by them.

He looks to the outside for the solution to his difficulties—a change of location, a different wife, a devoted friend who would understand him —and he busies himself manipulating and changing the external circumstances of his life. Such an individual never looks into himself to figure out his responsibility and to discover how he himself could bring about constructive changes.

Creating an idealized image of himself to solve conflicts means that the person tries to dismiss his inner difficulties by constructing a glorified version of himself in which all his contradictions are reconciled. One woman patient saw herself as "a benevolent business woman with a broad social outlook." Analysis revealed her intense needs for approval and compulsive tendencies to submit to others. She was overconsiderate, self-sacrificing, exaggeratedly helpful and overindulgent to others. This was her "benevolence." She also had strong hostile aggressive tendencies expressed in exploitive business practices and subtly sadistic attitudes. This was the "business woman." She also tended to be an onlooker in human affairs, unduly independent, a manifestation of withdrawal trends. Taking traits from each of her neurotic trends, she had harmonized them all as virtues—in her own estimation —and thus saw herself as "a benevolent business woman with a broad social outlook."

Avoiding all emotional involvement with others is the fourth main way in which the neurotic individual attempts to eliminate conflict. This constitutes an attempt to ignore or deny contradictory trends by seeing to it that no occasion arises in which emotions would come into play.

For instance, if there are very strong needs for affection, the individual may adopt sexuality as the basis of relationships with others. In this he maintains *emotional detachment,* satisfies needs for closeness to others, and has the illusion that he is participating in a love relationship. Or an individual may limit himself strictly to intellectual interests with others or practical affairs as a common ground, making them the whole point of contact.

Although neurotic solutions of conflict are devised for the purpose of holding the personality together and maintaining equilibrium, they in turn constitute defenses that must be maintained, else the individual feels endangered and upset. A variety of secondary defenses function as additional insurance against becoming aware of conflict. These are the cultivation of blind spots by which the individual can remain blissfully unaware of contradictions and discrepancies; rationalization, by which he explains away inconsistencies by plausible but spurious justifications.

He also compartmentalizes his thinking, that is, he is able to avoid seeing his inconsistencies by behaving and acting one way in private, another way in public; one way toward members of the family, another way toward friends and acquaintances outside the family; one way toward social equals, another way toward those he does not consider his social equals, etc. Other common defenses are to claim arbitrary and unquestioned rightness for all he thinks and does, including his inconsistencies; to attempt to protect himself from awareness of uncontrollable impulses by maintaining an iron control over feelings; to reduce everything to total inconsequentiality by being cynical or flippant; or to avoid all issues by being elusive.

In general, the development and the upkeep of neurotic patterns consumes a prodigious amount of energy which could otherwise be used in the development of real capacities and gifts, in the cultivation of good human relationships, and in the enjoyment of life. This wasteful expenditure of energy brings about a sense of futility, a feeling that one is not getting enough out of life or a vague, sometimes acute discontent. There are also likely to be pervasive feelings of strain and fatigue, and a need for more rest and more sleep than is required by the average healthy person.

The powerful crosscurrents underlying unresolved conflicts result in inertia, ineffectualness, and indecision. The individual is unable to settle on a course in life and exert his best efforts in some definite, consistent direction. Spontaneous initiative and sustained action are extremely difficult. If initiative is not paralyzed, it is short-lived and shifting. The individual tends to avoid constructive effort. It takes so much out of him since he has to reckon with the exhaustive intensity with which he applies himself and with the counterpull of opposite impulses.

At the core of every neurotic personality there is more or less hopelessness. This stems from being caught in conflicts that cannot really be resolved in view of the individual's deep feelings of helplessness, isolation and hostility. Besides, his rigid patterns in human relations and in whatever he undertakes always brings about the same frustration, so he is likely to feel doomed to failure. Neurotic development takes him further and further away from himself, so that he becomes shadowy and unreal to himself. He has no real hold on the direction of his life and no notion of what he really wants, for he is in the grip of forces driving him toward the goal of safety only.

Despair may be so abysmal that he may succumb to complete resignation, settle down quietly, and even feel somewhat at peace. He "accepts" his fate but forfeits the fullness of his real capacities and the real richness of his nature. But hopelessness, despair and resignation may lead to bitterness and rage against fate which may be focused on those who are participating in life and enjoying it. In an attempt to reclaim or salvage some feeling of self, the individual turns destructive and sadistic in revenge. Sadistic tendencies are directed not only toward others in overt subtle ways but also toward the self.

As further consequences of unresolved conflicts there are many fears, some of them diffuse, some of them specific and sharply focused. The individual feels vaguely fearful whenever a safety device is threatened, when a compromise solution is in danger of failing him, or when defenses are jeopardized. He fears the loss of neurotic satisfactions, as for instance in any disturbance of his idealized image and the gratifications he gets from it in his imagination. He fears exposure of his false claims, for to him this would mean certain ridicule and humiliation in the eyes of others and in his own eyes. Since his equilibrium is usually shaky, and requires constant support and stabilization, he is always afraid of being upset. Some sharply focused inner fears are externalized in outer situations. The dread of being in high places and of falling is usually connected with fear of falling from a pinnacle of perfection one has arrogated to oneself, fear of collapse of one's illusions, of falling into the abyss of self-degradation. These fears do not have one simple direct derivation but may be compounded of fears arising from several sources. Such fears may force the individual to extreme precautions expressed in compulsive handwashing or bathing, avoiding contact with certain things for fear of contamination.

The sense of being helplessly caught in conflicts and the resultant feeling of impotent rage are, generally speaking, the components of depressions. Rage may be quite deeply repressed; the depression is then diffuse and unfocused and the individual is lost in feelings of abysmal self-pity. When rage and despair are more openly in play, depressions may bring the individual to ruminations on suicide or to an actual attempt at self-destruction.

Other outspoken neurotic manifestations are general inhibitions such as inability to think, to concentrate, to make decisions, to embark on fresh enterprises, to learn something new.

Frequently symptoms are directly connected with relationships with others, such as inability to get along, feeling always an outsider who is excluded by others, intense shyness, uncontrollable aggressiveness; terrible, frightening impulses to harm others, undue dependence on others, inability to love, inability to hate. In this category are specific disturbances in sex life such as frigidity and painful intercourse in women, impotence and premature ejaculation in men, compulsive sexual promiscuity, aversion to sex relationships with the opposite sex and a preference for relationships with persons of one's own sex, and undifferentiated sexuality, sometimes called bisexuality.

Many of the physical symptoms of neurosis are the expression of tensions precipitated by repressed anxiety or rage such as flushing or pallor, sweating, palpitation, high blood pressure, low blood pressure, muscular tensions of all sorts, severe cramping pains, especially around the neck and shoulders and lower back, lump in throat, shortness of breath, sinking feelings, fainting, excessive sleepiness, gastrointestinal upsets, constipation, diarrhea, nausea, headache, migraine attacks and some functional disorders of the reproductive organs.

You will notice that I have used a few of the familiar diagnostic terms. Thinking in terms of symptoms does not offer any real guide to understanding and treatment. Our interest lies in attempting to understand the character structure as a whole, its development, and the dynamics of the neurotic process in their present form and complexity. By this route we get light on the meaning of the particular manifestation in the individual character structure.

44. *Possibilities of Self-Analysis* *

STUDENTS OF psychology naturally raise questions about self-analysis. In their desire for self-improvement, they often forget what they have learned about defense mechanisms, about the way our motives influence our perceptions, about functional fixedness and other obstacles to clear thinking. Self-analysis seems to be possible for some people and under some conditions, but the requirements for a successful outcome have not been completely or systematically demonstrated. In this selection, Dr. Hirsh reviews the nature of psychoanalysis and neurosis and discusses the possibilities and values of self-analysis within this framework. Tentatively, she identifies four groups of people who fulfill the prerequisites for successful self-analysis.

HUMILITY AND HOPE, Karen Horney says, are required while considering the possibilities of self-analysis. This topic is challenging because of its far-reaching implications. What it amounts to is: Can we learn to analyze ourselves and thereby live more productively? Can we, when in distress, get relief by analyzing ourselves? This question has broader meanings, which I am affirming, for we can increasingly learn to know and to help ourselves by learning through living. In this broader connotation self-analysis is feasible, desirable and accessible to all of us. We learn through joy and through pain, sometimes without being aware of it, sometimes with conscious intent. Inherent in this belief in our ability to learn through living is the belief in a core of integrity within us, and in our incentive to contact it. This constructive endeavor is essentially different from neurotic introspection, which intensifies, rather than relieves, stress.

I am aware of numerous difficulties in attempting a discussion of self-analysis, yet I feel that the advantage of bringing into the open some of the problems involved and coming to tentative conclusions outweighs the difficulties. The number of people in need of help is large. Many who could benefit from psychoanalysis cannot under-

* Ada C. Hirsh, "Possibilities of self-analysis," Summary of Lecture No. 73 delivered before the Auxiliary Council to the Association for the Advancement of Psychoanalysis, copyright 1953. By permission of the author and the Association for the Advancement of Psychoanalysis. This article is one of a series on psychoanalytic subjects, printed individually in pamphlet form. Information and copies, at 10¢ each, may be obtained from ACAAP, 220 West 98th St., New York 25, N.Y.

take it for various reasons, yet might gain help from self-analysis. Approaching our topic I feel a clearer understanding of what is involved may be gained by a discussion of the following questions: What is neurosis? What is psychoanalysis? What is self-analysis? What are their objectives, and how are they pursued?

I will first outline the concept of neurosis. A healthy plant, growing in adequate soil, becomes a strong specimen. If the soil lacks important ingredients, the growth of the plant is impeded. The soil for the child is the atmosphere of its environment, with a healthy atmosphere providing love and consistency. In it the child feels secure; he learns to contact himself and others, and thereby grows stronger. Many parents cannot give these essentials to their child because of their own neurotic involvement. The child then feels anxious, insecure, and often hostile. He is compelled to seek safety in his relationships with those people who are closest to him. These relationships become distorted. The sum total of these devices and their consequences make up neurosis. Thus, inherent in neurosis is a disturbance in human relationships, and an abandonment of the self.

Psychoanalysis is a specific medical treatment of neurosis. The one factor most responsible for its increasing efficiency is a change of emphasis and of direction. The treatment is concerned with the person as a whole, rather than his symptoms. His character shows the neurotic disturbance and his genuine qualities, the latter being more or less accessible.

Psychoanalysis is a process in which the patient and the analyst work together, the participation of the patient gradually increasing. The work consists of identifying the patient's behavior, including unconscious processes, with the purpose of learning to understand his difficulties and, equally important, his resources. Through understanding, which includes experiencing and changing, his psychic health improves. He learns to contact it and to use it, in fighting against neurosis and for the development of his potentialities.

Inherent in psychoanalysis is a human relationship. Since neurosis is a disturbance in relationships, the work done with another person, centering on the patient's behavior, comes to be a telling example of those relations. It is also an opportunity to experience a close relationship and to change attitudes and values under favorable conditions. In psychoanalysis, as in self-analysis, we learn to evaluate our life, present and past, and to search for a direction in which we want to go. The person undertaking self-analysis attempts to cover, more or less, the work of the patient and of the analyst which I shall specify later. This venture we could call a systematic self-analysis. In its broader meaning, as mentioned, self-analysis implies helping ourselves by learning through life experiences.

What are the goals of neurosis, psychoanalysis and self-analysis? The goal of neurosis, a neurotic goal, consists of pacifying anxiety, which has been caused by conflict, through maintenance of the neurotic structure. Neurotic processes are largely kept out of awareness, which contributes to securing their continuity. Thus we are unaware of losing ourselves. The following is an example of the tenacity of the neurotic structure, which the patient could detect: She related a dream in which she was riding in a bus driven by a teen-ager. The bus collided with another bus, similarly manned. Here the dream ended. She was struck by the thought, "If I would give up any of my neurotic trends, I'd be as foolhardy as those teen-agers. I'd get hurt." Yet she realized that she was getting hurt again and again because she clung to her neurotic trends with such tenacity.

In a discussion of the goals of psychoanalysis and of self-analysis, it is helpful to distinguish between immediate and long-term goals. Immediate goals indicate the direction in which the work is going at a given moment. An immediate goal may be that of alleviating anxiety. Thus a patient paralyzed by anxiety desperately reached out for help. I tried to convey to him the reality of health within him. He was startled, as he had considered only his weakness, and contempt for that weakness intensified his anxiety. That he could learn to rely on himself was comforting. His strength has been steadily increasing. I have chosen this example because it leads to the long-term goal of psychoanalysis and also because this patient made considerable progress through working on himself between sessions. The long-term goal can be expressed by enumerating a multiplicity of goals: an increase in vitality, sincerity, wisdom, in the ability to enjoy life, to tolerate pain and to improve relationships. Also, this goal can be designated by a symbol—finding our real self (Horney). In this goal there are two components: a movement, a reaching out for something that we want, which is the process of finding, and the goal itself, the real self. We can think of it as of the essence of our aliveness.

Getting ready for self-analysis is inherent in the goal of psychoanalysis. Self-analysis is a lifelong process. Offhand this may be frightening, but realizing that it can become an integral part of a better way of living, we can accept it as a challenge. To the degree that we are neurotic, the picture we see of ourselves is distorted into one that is both idealized and degraded. In all neurotic processes a drive toward the absolute is the main and most destructive characteristic. The goal of self-analysis, as of psychoanalysis, then, lies in the acceptance of human and individual limitations as a basis for striving toward sincerity and self-realization.

How do neurosis, psychoanalysis and self-analysis go about pursuing their goals? The severe neurotic does it indiscriminately. His drive toward perfection is so compelling, the threat of experiencing anxiety so great, that his ways can be likened to those of a desperado, who does not care how he achieves his ends, so long as he does and is not found out. The aim of neurosis is attained by blotting out of awareness as much as possible both health and the reality of sickness, and by idealizing the trends that constitute neurosis. Thus, by doing away with reality and by glorifying unreality, the person is largely unaware of both processes.

How is awareness of health precluded? For one thing, the concept of health is often unclear. Lack of clarity is an important factor in this blotting-out process. Neurosis operates with confusion and distortion, as well as haziness. Achievements and difficulties are exaggerated, minimized or distorted. The exaggeration of difficulties leads to hopelessness. The sum total of neurotic processes increases suffering, alienation from our feelings, and distortion of feelings about others.

I have described the ways of neurosis—compulsive ways, which are predominately unconscious and in their character misleading and destructive—to show what psychoanalysis and self-analysis are up against in pursuing their goal. How do they go about it?

In her book, *Self-Analysis,* Horney enumerates five main activities of the analyst: observation, understanding, interpretation, help in resistance and general human help. The three main activities of the patient are expressing himself as freely as possible, becoming aware of his unconscious forces and changing.

Observation is indispensable in analytic work, and includes testing reality, adhering to it, and acting upon it; all these steps are important. For example, if there is a fire in our house, we may observe smoke. Going at it immediately, testing our observation as to reality, adhering to it, locating its focus, realizing the danger, we are able to deal with the fire effectively. If we do not observe smoke, or discard the observation, its verification, location and danger, we cannot act effectively. Serious damage may be done to our house. It may burn down.

Serious damage occurs again and again to severe neurotics who cannot observe what is going on in themselves—actually what they are doing to themselves. Such observation would be too great a threat to their shaky equilibrium. In psychoanalysis it is possible to gradually see the damage, because the analyst times interpretations, which are suggestions as to possible meanings. He gives them at a time when the patient can take them and in such a way that he can gradually accept them.

The work of the patient, and of the person analyzing himself, consists of learning to express himself as sincerely as he can, by free association. Ideally, it consists in saying everything that is thought, felt and visualized. Its function is to provide the material for investigation. This material indicates what is being experienced. Not only content, but also spirit, sequence and total behavior are revealing. Thus it is possible, to a considerable degree, to identify specific manifestations of health and the patient's attitude to them, as well as to identify neurotic manifestations and the patient's attitude to these, specifically, and to his illness in general.

A second major activity of the patient and of the person analyzing himself is becoming aware of the reality of his constructive and destructive unconscious processes. Accepting them intellectually does not suffice; their language has to be experienced and re-experienced before their lessons are learned. The analyst conveys this language, characteristic of each person, to the patient. For instance, one patient may go into a coughing spell during excitement, another may jump from the couch when the situation is hot. This individual language enhances understanding, mainly when the patient is eager to learn it. As neurotic pride decreases, we learn to accept unconscious processes by repeatedly experiencing their validity.

The third major task is changing. How can we learn to change? Living means changing—either moving closer to what we can become or moving away from it. Both directions are operating. The resulting direction which we take depends on their relative strength. What interests us is the influence we can learn to exert on the direction and tempo of changing aside from unconscious processes. The following steps occur, overlapping, while we are moving toward health: allowing ourselves to see the reality of changing, experiencing it as an inherent part of living, recognizing neurotic trends with their implications, intensity and conflict, experiencing their compelling and negative character, seeing that we can change by feeling the struggle between health and neurosis. The ability to change increases as pride and fear diminish. While facing and fighting pride, contempt, anxiety, conflict,—while experiencing health—our self-confidence increases.

There may be considerable fear of progress. As one patient put it, "I know I am getting better. I am afraid of it. I don't want it. Yet I *do* want it." Note the fast swings, indicating conflict. For this patient, "I know I am getting better," meant experiencing health, "I am afraid of it," experiencing the pull of neurosis, "I don't want it," identifying with neurosis, "yet I *do* want it," taking a stand for health. He recognized this struggle and fought for himself.

The person analyzing himself encounters difficulties which, oversimplified, spring from two main sources: the absence of the human and professional help of the analyst and the person's alienation from himself. Psychoanalysis is not a clear-cut division of labor between patient and analyst, but a mutual undertaking. Let me compare it with a complicated research project at which two people are working in separate areas which overlap. While working they help each other. The person analyzing himself can be compared to the research worker going ahead in the absence of his colleague. He can do it if he knows the job of his coworker, or if he can learn it. However, his work will be less efficient and slower. Similarly, the person analyzing himself is at a disadvantage. He deals with intricate psychological processes of which he is largely unaware. He is unaware of the intensity of his neurotic need not to succeed.

He may find it difficult to analyze himself because he is indifferent to his welfare. He may feel unworthy of the undertaking, or he may feel that his self-knowledge is excellent, although he really knows little about himself. He has difficulty accepting himself as he is, as a person with responsibilities, with assets and with shortcomings. In analysis he gradually feels that the analyst accepts him. This may be his first experience of feeling accepted—in fact, of being accepted by another person. It helps him to learn to accept himself. In self-analysis this advantage is missing. Therefore, he may lack the ability to give himself the human help—the kindness—which is indispensable in such an arduous undertaking. Then he cannot sufficiently replace the human help of the analyst.

Substituting other relationships for that with the analyst presents handicaps. The person may lack a friend who is understanding. He may find it difficult to reveal himself and in his relationships to learn to know himself and others, because he cannot evaluate his share in difficulties that arise. It may be hard for him to center on what he can do at a given moment, and to derive satisfaction from achievement. It may be hard to evaluate a fact—for example, to distinguish a mistake from his reaction to it. If he feels threatened or hopeless, difficulties can arise in the free flow of association, in the acceptance of unconscious processes and in the accuracy of observation. His observation may not deepen to the quality of understanding. He may not proceed to interpretation when insights are threatening or fear of change is too great.

The extent to which a systematic self-analysis can be successful depends in essence on the degree to which a person can identify and fight resistance. Horney enumerates five main limitations: profound resignation, neurotic solutions which are too successful, a predominance of destructiveness, too extensive loss of self and strong secondary defenses. Out of these difficulties the following may arise: A person may give up working because of resignation, suffering or hopelessness. He may misuse self-analysis for self-punishment. There may be a striking discrepancy between apparent insight and change, because of extensive evasion. Intellectualization may be taken for experience. The person may take pride in his findings instead of evaluating them. However, as Horney pointed out, he is not entirely at a disadvantage. He lives in his own world. He has a wider scope of observation—if he can make use of it. Externalization onto the analyst is absent, as are his errors. The liberating joy of coming closer to truth, of having conquered obstacles on his own, increases the incentive to proceed. It is well not to generalize, but to remember the valid work done by severely handicapped people.

Considering the objectives and pursuits of neurosis and self-analysis, and the difficulties mentioned, what are the prerequisites for a systematic self-analysis? Foremost is a profound desire to analyze oneself, a strong incentive to make the initial effort and to pursue it, despite suffering, anxiety, conflict, doubt, setbacks, and progress. This is possible if self-analysis is meaningful to the person; it can be successful only to the degree that he is in it with his entire being, as much as he is able. Thus he is affirming life, especially his own life. In line with these assets is necessary a degree of health substantial enough and sufficiently available to enable the person to contact it, to contact his feelings and to search for a truer understanding of himself; likewise, to accept to a considerable degree his difficulties—his human and individual limitations. Equally important is the acceptance of the possibility of changing, the wish to do so, and the ability to think logically and psychologically. It is essential to be able to accept the reality of unconscious processes. Final prerequisites are an open mind and courage.

It is implied in the above that a systematic self-analysis is not feasible for all people. Through my experience with myself and others, I have arrived at certain tentative conclusions. There are people gifted for self-analysis; they have the above mentioned qualities to a substantial degree. In general, I feel that the following groups qualify:

1. People, not in need of psychoanalysis, who are stimulated to analyze themselves by satisfaction derived from creativity. For example, a writer may feel that his work is benefited by an awareness of

well-being. He may wish to enhance the depth of this experience by finding out how he arrived at it and what prevented its occurrence.

2. People, likewise not in need of psychoanalysis, who want to analyze themselves because they are aware of disturbances in their dealings with life. They feel that factors within themselves are responsible for their difficulties. Their dissatisfaction shows interest, an ability to evaluate. This healthy dissatisfaction is essentially different from self-accusation.

3. People who have successfully terminated formal psychoanalysis. The question arises, can people in need of psychoanalysis learn to analyze themselves? The answer depends on the degree of the need, and the latter on the diagnosis. How is a diagnosis of neurosis arrived at? Horney worked out very valid criteria, which consist of drawing the balance between forward-moving and retarding forces, including the current behavior and the history. Examples of constructive factors are good functioning in certain areas—for example, in work, an ability to maintain more or less close relationships over longer periods, the wish to understand oneself and to grow. Retarding factors are incapacitating anxiety and conflict, hopelessness, cynicism, dependency, sadism and resignation. No single constructive or retarding factor is decisive, but their combination—the person as a whole.

Statistics on psychoanalysis, certainly on self-analysis, are lacking. We are in the investigative stage; thus venturing is permitted, even asked for. A person belonging to one of the three groups I have mentioned, who is aware of the hard work he would be undertaking, and who appears able to stand anxiety and pain for the sake of greater sincerity, joy and wisdom, can be encouraged to embark on self-analysis. Considering the seriousness of the undertaking and the difficulty in evaluation, I feel it is important to discuss the question of feasibility with an analyst. Also the work would be less arduous and more successful if it were initiated and followed up by analytic sessions. I would encourage self-analysis mainly under such conditions. I would not advise it for a person in need of psychoanalysis, unless the need is minor. It is highly important that circumstances be evaluated. They often are colored by neurotic needs. This may seem pessimistic, but I don't think it is. I have experienced the intrinsic value of psychoanalysis and of self-analysis with myself and others. I like thinking of the work as walking along a broad road with an outlook of sunshine and beauty in the distance. As we walk we come closer to this goal. Again and again we lose ourselves in sidetracks. They are dark. The going is difficult. We may not know where we are. What counts is finding our way forward to the main road and toward our goal.

The analyst helps the patient proceed when he feels caught in the sidetracks of neurotic entanglement. I have described their tenacity and trickiness to show that it may be impossible to do that alone. However, we can learn to do it. Thinking in terms of learning, of process, of movement, is a valuable approach which Dr. Harold Kelman has been using for years. It is hopeful. In the frame of process thinking our limitations of today can become our possibilities for tomorrow. We can think of them as fences which we move forward while progressing. Thus, self-analysis, although difficult, can be undertaken. Or it can be worked toward within psychoanalysis.

Self-analysis has an important place within psychoanalysis. There is a great difference in the work of a patient who feels compelled to come and leaves the rest to the analyst, and that of the patient who wants to learn and is productive. There is the patient, who, after closing the treatment door behind him, forgets analysis until he re-enters. Others leave and continue working. They progress faster, go deeper, and are ready sooner for self-analysis on their own.

A heartening experience with successful self-analysis within psychoanalysis has been that of a patient who lived at a distance from New York. As he was very sick when he started, I felt there was danger in his isolation and suggested he go to a doctor in his home community; he declined. Part of my help was correspondence between sessions. This patient has fought remarkably well, has faced despair, panic, hopelessness, and has come out wiser. Instead of feeling himself pulled in too many directions, he saw one direction in which he wanted to go.

Finally the question: is self-analysis desirable? Self-knowledge, acclaimed by great people throughout the ages, is desirable, if it is put into the service of becoming more integrated. In her last book, *Neurosis and Human Growth,* Horney calls the work at ourselves not only a prime moral obligation, but also a prime moral privilege. It is an obligation and a privilege to move in the direction of health, foremost for our own fulfillment. Only then can we make a contribution to others. We can do this to the degree that we contact our real self. Do we need self-analysis to this end? Not necessarily. Life is our greatest teacher, if we are ready to learn its lessons. What psychoanalysis and self-analysis do is to help us learn them more successfully.

Summarizing, I have discussed the concept, aims and process of neurosis, psychoanalysis and self-analysis. We are in the investigative stage of self-analysis. Conclusions arrived at can be only tentative. The prerequisites for self-analysis are a substantial degree of psychic health, a desire to come closer to the truth about ourselves, a belief in the ability to change, an ability to think logically, psychologically and with an open mind, and finally courage.

The following groups, I feel, fulfill the prerequisites: (1) People, not in need of psychoanalysis, who have experienced the joy of creativity and want to enhance this experience. (2) People, likewise not in need of psychoanalysis, who are dissatisfied in their dealings with life. (3) People who have successfully terminated formal psychoanalysis. (4) People in need of analysis, where the need is minor, and if circumstances do not permit psychoanalysis. It is desirable that an analyst advise as to the feasibility, and that the work be initiated and followed up by analytic sessions.

If the prerequisites are fulfilled, I feel self-analysis may well be encouraged for it can help toward the relief of suffering and toward a truer expression of ourselves. Let us remember that a systematic self-analysis entails as the most potent factor an increasing desire and ability to help ourselves. This we can all do. As we progress in this very human endeavor, living becomes easier, better, and more meaningful.

---

45. A Theory of Vocational Development *

SELECTING A CAREER today is often a hit-or-miss affair. Children do not follow precisely in their fathers' footsteps, and the apprenticeship system has disappeared in this country. Choices are made long before the individual has had enough experience to know fully what is available, and before he has matured sufficiently to know himself. In recognition of this situation educational programs are being adjusted to deal realistically with students, and guidance specialists have developed procedures to aid individuals of different ages in making their choices. Here Dr. Super outlines the general process of vocational development, the theory and assumptions underlying the work of the guidance specialist, and suggests some of the factors an individual ought to consider in making his choice if he is not relying on a guidance specialist.

TWO AND ONE-HALF YEARS AGO a colleague of mine at Columbia, Dr.

* Donald E. Super, "A theory of vocational development," *The American Psychologist,* VIII (1953), 185–90. By permission of the author and the American Psychological Association. Presidential address at the annual meeting of the Division of Counseling and Guidance, American Psychological Association, Washington, D.C., September 1, 1952.

Eli Ginzberg, an economist, shocked and even unintentionally annoyed many members of the National Vocational Guidance Association by stating, at the annual convention, that vocational counselors attempt to counsel concerning vocational choice without any theory as to how vocational choices are made. A year later Dr. Ginzberg published his monograph on *Occupational Choice,* in which he stated:

> Vocational counselors are busy practitioners anxious to improve their counseling techniques . . . the research-minded among them devote what time they can to devising better techniques. They are not theoreticians working on the problem of how individuals make their occupational choices, for, though they have no bias against theory, they have little time to invest in developing one.

Ginzberg continues, apropos of the fields of psychology and economics:

> . . . there are good reasons why the problem [of how occupational choices are made] has not been a focus of investigation for psychology or economics. . . . The process has roots in the interplay of the individual and reality, and this field is only now beginning to be included in the boundaries of psychological inquiry. The obverse formulation applies to economics, which as a discipline concentrates on a detailed analysis of reality forces and satisfies itself with a few simplified assumptions about individual behavior.

These conclusions were based partly on a review of the research literature which I did at his request, and partly on a number of discussions in which he, his research team, and I participated. Consequently, I have a feeling of responsibility, not for the conclusions which he drew, but for drawing my own conclusions and for sharing them with my colleagues in psychology and guidance.

Basis of Ginzberg's criticisms. It may help to point out that Ginzberg's conclusions were based on a review of the research literature which was designed to provide answers to specific questions asked by his research team in order to help them plan their own research project. What synthesizing of results I did was undertaken to answer these questions. I did not attempt to answer the question "What theories underlie the principles of vocational guidance now generally accepted by practitioners?"

But I do agree with his analysis of the situation with regard to theory construction: we have done relatively little of it, and for the reasons he has suggested. However, this does not mean that we have operated without theory. It is the principal purpose of this paper to set forth a theory of vocational development, a theory inherent in and emergent from the research and philosophy of psychologists and counselors during the past two decades. But first I should like, as a help in formulating a more adequate theory, briefly to present the theory of occupational choice put forth by Ginzberg and his associates, to show how each of its elements had already been set forth by psychologists doing research in this field, and to point out some of its limitations.

THE GINZBERG THEORY

As Ginzberg, Ginsburg, Axelrod, and Herma summarize their theory of occupational choice, it contains four elements:

1. *Occupational choice is a developmental process which typically takes place over a period of some ten years.* This theory of Ginzberg's, it should be noted, is one of the points made by the official statement of the *Principles and Practices of Vocational Guidance,* first formulated by the National Vocational Guidance Association 25 years ago; it is a point stressed by Kitson in his *Psychology of Vocational Adjustment,* published in 1925; and, in 1942, in my own *Dynamics of Vocational Adjustment* several pages are devoted to a discussion of the fact that "choosing an occupation . . . is a process which . . . may go on over a long period."

2. *The process is largely irreversible:* experience cannot be undone, for it results in investments of time, of money, and of ego; it produces changes in the individual. This second theory of Ginzberg's is clearly implied in Charlotte Buhler's 20-year-old theory of life stages, in Lehman and Witty's equally old studies of play interests, in Pressey, Janney, and Kuhlen's 13-year-old discussion of adolescent and adult development, and in my own 10-year-old text on vocational adjustment.

3. *The process of occupational choice ends in a compromise between interests, capacities, values, and opportunities.* This third theory of Ginzberg's is well illustrated in the practices of individual diagnosis developed by the Minnesota Employment Stabilization Research Institute 20 years ago and described by Paterson and Darley; it was further demonstrated and described by the Adjustment Service experiment 17 years ago; and it is basic to presentations of the use of diagnostic techniques in texts such as Bingham's and mine, both of which appeared before the completion of Ginzberg's study. In fact, Frank Parsons, in 1909, discussed vocational counseling as a process of helping the individual to study both himself and possible occupational opportunities, and to work out a compromise between his abilities, interests, and opportunities. He called this last process "true reasoning."

4. Ginzberg's final theoretical formulation is that *there are three*

periods of occupational choice: the period of *fantasy* choice, governed largely by the wish to be an adult; the period of *tentative* choices beginning at about age 11 and determined largely by interests, then by capacities, and then by values; and the period of *realistic* choices, beginning at about age 17, in which exploratory, crystallization, and specification phases succeed each other. Those who are acquainted with Lehman and Witty's early research in the change of interest with age, with Strong's more searching work in the same area, with Sisson's research in the increasing realism of choice with increasing age, with Charlotte Buhler's research in life stages, and with the use made of these data by Pressey or by me, will find these three choice periods familiar. The special contribution of Ginzberg and his associates is the postulation of the successive dominance of interests, capacities, and values as determinants of choice before reality begins to play a major role.

It is easy, and perhaps even rather petty, thus to take a theoretical contribution and demonstrate its ancestry, showing that there is nothing particularly original about it. This is, undoubtedly, the normal reaction to claims of originality. But originality is more generally the result of a rearrangement of the old than the actual creation of something new: the rearrangement is original because it brings out details or relationships which have been missed or points up new applications. Ginzberg's theory is indeed an important contribution: this seems clear to me, at least, as I recollect the struggle I had in writing parts of my *Dynamics of Vocational Adjustment* (a struggle which resulted from the lack of a theoretical structure and from inadequate research), and as I work on its revision in the light, among other things, of Ginzberg's theoretical formulation and the thinking which it has stimulated. I have used this critical approach to Ginzberg's work in order to demonstrate that we have not entirely lacked a theoretical basis for our work in vocational guidance, and to show that the elements of theory on which we have based our practice have been sound, at least in that they have foreshadowed the elements which one group of theorists used when they went about constructing a theory of occupational choice.

LIMITATIONS OF GINZBERG'S THEORY

But this is not the whole story. Ginzberg's theory is likely to be harmful because of its limitations, limitations other than those of research design and numbers in his basic study.

First, it does not build adequately on previous work: for example, the extensive literature on the nature, development, and predictive value of inventoried interests is rather lightly dismissed.

Second, "choice" is defined as preference rather than as entry or some other implementation of choice, and hence means different things at different age levels. To the 14-year-old it means nothing more than preference, because at that age the need for realism is minimized by the fact that the preference does not need to be acted upon until the remote future. To the 21-year-old student of engineering, on the other hand, "choice" means a preference which has already been acted upon in entering engineering school, although the final action will come only with graduation and entry into a job. No wonder that reality plays a larger part in choice at age 21, when, unlike choice at age 14, it is by definition a reality-tested choice!

A third defect in Ginzberg's theory emerges from these different meanings of the term "choice" at different ages: it is the falseness of the distinction between "choice" and "adjustment" which he and his research team make. The very fact that choice is a continuous process going on over a period of time, a process rather far removed from reality in early youth but involving reality in increasing degrees with increasing age, should make it clear that there is no sharp distinction between choice and adjustment. Instead, they blend in adolescence, with now the need to make a choice and now the need to make an adjustment predominating in the occupational or life situation.

Finally, a fourth limitation in the work of the Ginzberg team lies in the fact that, although they set out to study the process of occupational choice, and although they properly concluded that it is one of compromise between interests, capacities, values, and opportunities, they did not study or describe the compromise process. Surely this is the crux of the problem of occupational choice and adjustment: the nature of the compromise between self and reality, the degree to which and the conditions under which one yields to the other, and the way in which this compromise is effected. For the counseling psychologist's function is to help the individual to effect this compromise. He must not only know the factors which must be compromised and how these have been compromised in the experience of others, but also the dynamics of the compromising process, so that he may facilitate this process in his counselee with constructive results.

ELEMENTS OF AN ADEQUATE THEORY OF VOCATIONAL DEVELOPMENT

An adequate theory of vocational choice and adjustment would synthesize the results of previous research insofar as they lend themselves to synthesis; it would take into account the continuity of the development of preferences and of the differences in the stages, choices, entry, and adjustment; it would explain the process through which interest, capacities, values, and opportunities are compromised. The second part of this paper will be devoted to a sketch of the main elements of such a theory of vocational development as they appear in the literature, and the third and final part will consist of an attempt to synthesize these elements in an adequate theory. The term "development" is used rather than "choice," because it comprehends the concepts of preference, choice, entry, and adjustment. There seem to be a dozen elements to a theory of vocational development: they are taken up in sequence.

Individual differences. One of the basic elements of a theory of vocational development has been the theory of individual differences, a cornerstone of modern educational and vocational psychology. Kitson based much of his early *Psychology of Vocational Adjustment* on this theory and on the findings on which it was based. It was essential to the work of the Minnesota Employment Stabilization Research Institute. It is surely unnecessary to document the fact of individual differences in aptitudes, interests, and values, or the significance of these differences for vocational development.

Multipotentiality. A second basic element of theory has been the concept of the occupational multipotentiality of the individual. It was first documented for intelligence by Army psychologists in World War I, and was stressed by Kitson in his early textbook. It was documented for interests by Strong's work on the classification of occupational interests. It is a well-established fact and a basic assumption of vocational counseling that each person has the potential for success and satisfaction in a number of occupations.

Occupational ability patterns. The existence of occupational ability patterns, that is, the fact that abilities and interests fall into patterns which distinguish one occupation from another, was established by the Minnesota Employment Stabilization Research Institute and has been confirmed in other studies, particularly those of the United States Employment Service. People have been found to prefer, enter, remain in, like, and succeed most consistently in occupations for which they have appropriate patterns of traits. The theory of the patterning of aptitudes and interests within individuals and within occupational families and the significance of this patterning for choice, entry, and adjustment are widely accepted and applied by counselors and psychologists today.

Identification and the role of models. Much has been made of the importance of identification with parents and other adults in individual development by psychoanalytically oriented writers, and this concept is widely used by counseling psychologists regardless of orientation. It has been little documented, however, in psychological research in the vocational choice and adjustment process. The work of Friend and Haggard and a study by Stewart do, however, provide some objective basis for the theory that the childhood and adolescent identifications play a part in shaping vocational interests, and also provide role models which facilitate the development and implementation of a self-concept, provided that the required abilities and opportunities are present.

Continuity of adjustment. The continuity of the adjustment process was stressed by Kitson in his 1925 textbook as a result of his analysis of the careers of men whose success was attested to by being listed in *Who's Who in America.* The fact that adolescents and adults face a succession of emerging problems as they go through life, and that some of these problems are peculiar to the various life stages, was brought out by the studies of life stages made by Charlotte Buhler and by those of occupational mobility conducted by Davidson and Anderson, Strong, and Miller and Form. And theories of the development of interests have been formulated by Carter and by Bordin, theories which I modified slightly in my book on testing and upon which I drew in describing the process of vocational choice and adjustment in a speech first made at Ft. Collins, Colorado, in 1949, revised several times, and later published in the journal *Occupations,* under the title of "Vocational Adjustment: Implementing a Self-Concept." These formulations are drawn on again as the cement for the various elements which need to be brought together in a theory of vocational development and as an explanation of the process of compromise between self and reality.

Life stages. The work of psychologists and sociologists in describing the stages through which growth and development proceed, and in showing how these stages bear on the process of vocational choice and adjustment, has already been referred to. It was drawn on heavily in the text by Pressey, Janney, and Kuhlen, in my own first text, in Ginzberg's research, and in a recent text on *Industrial Sociology* by Miller and Form which is as important for its original contribution and synthesis as it is annoying for its bias against anything that does not conform to sociology as they conceive of it. Buhler's theory of development through the exploratory, establishment, maintenance, and decline stages is translated into occupational terminology by Miller and Form, who also documented the theory for American careers, while Ginzberg, Ginsburg, Axelrod, and Herma have developed in more detail the phases of the exploratory stage. This latter theory needs confirmation with a larger sample and more objective procedures, in view of Small's recent failure to confirm it with a somewhat different adolescent sample, but the general theory of life stages is basic to vocational guidance and will be drawn on heavily in my attempt at synthesis.

Career patterns. The formulation of a theory of career patterns resulted from the occupational manifestations of life stages first documented by Davidson and Anderson, added to for a select group by Terman's genetic studies of gifted persons, and then pointed up by Ginzberg and his associates and by Miller and Form. Career pattern theory appears to be a key element in the theoretical basis of vocational guidance, for it gives the counselor basic assumptions concerning the social, educational, and occupational mobility of his counselees, and it enables him to foresee types of problems which a given client is likely to encounter in establishing a career.

Development can be guided. Another basic element in a theory of vocational development is the theory that development through the life stages can be guided. Although there is ample evidence that ability is to some extent inherited, and that personality too has its roots in inherited neural and endocrine make-up, there is also good evidence that manifested aptitudes and functioning personality are the result of the interaction of the organism and the environment. It is a basic theory of guidance as we know it today that the development of the individual can be aided and guided by the provision of adequate opportunities for the utilization of aptitudes and for the development of interests and personality traits.

Development the result of interaction. That the nature of the interaction between the individual and his environment is by no means simple has been brought out by a variety of investigations ranging from studies of the effects of foster homes and of education on intelligence to evaluations of the effects of occupational information and of test interpretation on vocational plans and on self-understanding. The realization of this fact and the acceptance of this principle have led to a greater humility in our claims for counseling and to a greater degree of sophistication in our use of guidance techniques.

The dynamics of career patterns. The interaction of the individual and his environment during the growth and early exploratory stages, little understood though the process actually is, has been much more adequately investigated than has this same process during the late exploratory, establishment, and maintenance stages. We still know relatively little about the dynamics of career patterns. Terman's work tells us something about the role of intelligence, Strong's about interests, and Hollingshead's about social status, but no adequate studies have been made of the interaction of these and other factors in determining whether the individual in question will have a career pattern which is typical or atypical of his parental socioeconomic group. It was partly with this objective that an investigation known as the Career Pattern Study was launched in Middletown, New York, last year.

Job satisfaction: individual differences, status, and role. Early theories of job satisfaction stressed the role of intelligence and interest in adjustment to the occupation or to the job, building on studies of the relationships between these traits and occupational stability such as those made by Scott and by Strong. More recently other investigations such as the Hawthorne and Yankee City studies, anticipated in this respect by Hoppock's work and by a minor study of mine in job satisfaction, have played up the importance of the status given to the worker by his job, status both in the sense of group membership or belongingness and of prestige.

While researchers interested in the role of one kind of factor or another have tended to emphasize the signal importance of that type of factor, there is nothing inherently contradictory or mutually exclusive in these findings. They can all be included in a comprehensive theory of job satisfaction or work adjustment. This is the theory that satisfaction in one's work and on one's job depends on the extent to which the work, the job, and the way of life that goes with them, enable one to play the kind of role that one wants to play. It is, again, the theory that vocational development is the development of a self concept, that the process of vocational adjustment is the process of implementing a self concept, and that the degree of satisfaction attained is proportionate to the degree to which the self concept has been implemented.

Work is a way of life. This leads to a final theory, one that has been more widely accepted and stressed by sociologists than by psychologists, but familiar to most counselors and considered basic by some writers in the field. This is the theory that work is a way of life, and that adequate vocational and personal adjustment are most likely to result when both the nature of the work itself and the way of life that goes with it (that is, the kind of community, home, leisure-time activities, friends, etc.) are congenial to the aptitudes, interests, and values of the person in question. In the estimation of many, this is a basic element in a theory of vocational development.

A THEORY OF VOCATIONAL DEVELOPMENT

Now that we have surveyed the diverse elements of a theory of vocational development, there remains the final task of organizing them into a summary statement of a comprehensive theory. The theory can be stated in a series of ten propositions:

1. People differ in their abilities, interests, and personalities.
2. They are qualified, by virtue of these characteristics, each for a number of occupations.
3. Each of these occupations requires a characteristic pattern of

abilities, interests, and personality traits, with tolerances wide enough, nowever, to allow both some variety of occupations for each individual and some variety of individuals in each occupation.

4. Vocational preferences and competencies, the situations in which people live and work, and hence their self concepts, change with time and experience (although self concepts are generally fairly stable from late adolescence until late maturity), making choice and adjustment a continuous process.

5. This process may be summed up in a series of life stages characterized as those of growth, exploration, establishment, maintenance, and decline, and these stages may in turn be subdivided into (a) the fantasy, tentative, and realistic phases of the exploratory stage, and (b) the trial and stable phases of the establishment stage.

6. The nature of the career pattern (that is, the occupational level attained and the sequence, frequency, and duration of trial and stable jobs) is determined by the individual's parental socioeconomic level, mental ability, and personality characteristics, and by the opportunities to which he is exposed.

7. Development through the life stages can be guided, partly by facilitating the process of maturation of abilities and interests and partly by aiding in reality testing and in the development of the self concept.

8. The process of vocational development is essentially that of developing and implementing a self concept: it is a compromise process in which the self concept is a product of the interaction of inherited aptitudes, neural and endocrine make-up, opportunity to play various roles, and evaluations of the extent to which the results of role playing meet with the approval of superiors and fellows.

9. The process of compromise between individual and social factors, between self concept and reality, is one of role playing, whether the role is played in fantasy, in the counseling interview, or in real life activities such as school classes, clubs, part-time work, and entry jobs.

10. Work satisfactions and life satisfactions depend upon the extent to which the individual finds adequate outlets for his abilities, interests, personality traits, and values; they depend upon his establishment in a type of work, a work situation, and a way of life in which he can play the kind of role which his growth and exploratory experiences have led him to consider congenial and appropriate.

X

PERSPECTIVE

At the conclusion of a program of study it is often useful to take stock: to review what has gone before and attempt to look ahead. By relating psychology as a science to human values, Dr. Cantril places this field of study in perspective, thereby helping the student to consolidate what he has learned and to consider future possibilities.

46. Toward a Humanistic Psychology *

A chronic problem confronting students of psychology is the question of values. Students often assume that a scientific approach to the study of man means a denial of values, that it requires an impersonal acceptance of fact, denying the validity of any concept of right or wrong, good or bad. In this selection, Dr. Cantril outlines an approach to the study of values within the framework of systematic transactional psychology that should be reassuring to the reader who feels the need to combine a scientific approach with a system of values. In addition, this paper offers an opportunity for further contact with a relatively new approach in psychology.

In a recent discussion of "The Task Before Us," the physicist P. W. Bridgman has lamented the humanistic interest of many American universities as merely a "return to" without any "notable revitalization of these humanities themselves in the light of our recent intellectual ex-

* Hadley Cantril, "Toward a humanistic psychology," *ETC.: A Review of General Semantics,* XII (1955), 278–98. Copyright 1955 by International Society for General Semantics. By permission of the author and *ETC.: A Review of General Semantics.*

periences." Bridgman continues, "It seems to me that in this cry for a 'return' there is grave danger that we shall turn our backs on a job which not only is not finished but which is hardly begun. This job is to assimilate into our whole intellectual outlook, and in particular into our relation to social problems, the lesson implicit in scientific experience." We should perhaps bear in mind throughout the discussion an important differentiation between the humanistic and scientific approaches: that the latter is developmental and additive, attempting to build on increasing data to reach more adequate conceptualizations. But just because of this, there is no reason why the "humanist" need feel apologetic, modest, or in any way be on the defensive for his insights and expressions.

The problem is nicely posed in the recent *Dialogues of Alfred North Whitehead* as recorded by Lucien Price. Whitehead is asked the question, "Why should science be able to take such leaps, as it has done in the last century, even the last forty years, when the humanities advance so slowly? Are we really much ahead of Plato and Aristotle there?" To which Whitehead's reply was, "In the eighteenth century (I speak of England where I know what I am talking about) you could follow Rome and Greece of their best ages. The social structures were similar enough for historical precedents to be of some practical value: you still had the mob and the aristocrats. If it was a question of governing a colonial empire, India, you could still follow your Roman model; if a colonial governor was brought to trial for maladministration —Warren Hastings—you had Cicero's orations against Verres for his rapacious governorship in Sicily. . . . Even in the nineteenth century the Graeco-Roman model would still be fairly closely patterned after. But now, in the twentieth, this new technology has so altered the moral values, or the social relationships, that a much more searching and subtle readjustment of the traditional classic models to modern needs is wanted. . . . We are sending out as colonial administrators men trained not in the old humanistic tradition, but products of the scientific schooling. They are just as good intellects, but is their training as happy? I doubt if they will bring as sensitive an understanding to the emotional set-up of the peoples they must rule."

I should like to take the liberty here to spell out a point of view which a group of us are developing and which we have labeled "Transactional Psychology," borrowing the term "transaction" from John Dewey. It is my hope that a brief discussion of the main premise of this point of view may serve as a catalyst for discussion among general semanticists. For it does seem to me that the way in which we are now trying to look at "experience" and "behavior" includes the possibility, indeed the necessity, of taking into account in any psychology that pretends to be adequate those problems which are common problems to the humanist and the true scientist.

The ultimate goal of psychology is the understanding of human living so that individuals can live more effectively. The psychologist's aim is that of formulating a set of constructs which will enable him conceptually to "understand," "explain," and "predict" the activities and experiences of the functional union we call a behaving person.

A prerequisite for psychological research is an understanding of what an individual is aware of from his unique behavioral center in any occasion of living. The word "center" is used here in the dictionary sense of "the point toward which any force, feeling or action tends or from which any force or influence takes its origin; as a storm center" (*Webster's Collegiate,* 5th ed.).

The psychologist interested in understanding the process of living must start from naive experience in the phenomenal area. For only then will he be able to undertake investigations that will disclose the nature of the processes playing a role in behavior which the experiencing individual is taking account. The words "experience" and "behavior" are used here as *interdependent* abstractions man has created, neither of which would be meaningful except for the other.

As anyone knows, the task of starting with naive experience and formulating systematic constructs on the basis of naive experience is a particularly difficult undertaking. For the very essence of living is its unity and flow. Yet in order to get any grasp of his most complicated subject matter and to communicate his understanding to others, the psychologist is forced to break up into distinguishable parts what really constitutes an indivisible, functional aggregate; he is forced to consider separately the various aspects of living which are all interrelated and interdependent and none of which would function as they do except for all the others. The various aspects of living that are experienced are never separate from each other but fuse together to form this living. And the psychologist must try to orchestrate into a single symphony the harmonious or discordant sounds with motifs, themes, phrases, accents, and repetitions related to the separate notes played by the many instruments.

If the psychologist, then, is to be faithful to his subject matter, he must always bear in mind that living is an orchestration of on-going processes and that any process he may choose to differentiate out of this aggregate of on-going processes of living can be understood only if it is recognized as referring to a phase of man's orchestrated functioning. It is, for example, a commonplace of philosophical and psychological thinking that "cognitive" and "motor" processes are themselves distinctions that can be misleading unless there is full cognizance of the fact that there can be no "knowing" without "doing," just as there can be no "person" except for an "environment," nothing "subjective" except for what is "objective," nothing "personal" except for what is "social," nothing experienced as existing "out there in its own right" except for the organizations and significances to an individual of the happenings going on in the world around him which he associated with light waves, sound waves, etc., as instruments of explanation.[1]

It is important in any consideration of "moral ideas" to re-emphasize this point, to indicate some of the different experiential aspects into which the process of living may be abstracted, to show how each aspect plays a functional role in the congregation of experience and cannot be regarded as a single mechanistically-caused variable.

A necessary part of our consideration is, of course, that the conceptual abstractions we use are several steps removed from our primary data, namely, naive experience. In order to bridge the gap between naive experience and conceptual abstractions, the psychologist must consider areas of complexity and abstraction that become progressively further removed from his first-order data. It is imperative that any investigator be aware of the level of abstraction at which he operates. For there is always the danger that anyone, especially the scientist, may tend to mistake the conceptual abstraction for what it refers to, embrace it

[1] This is, of course, by no means a new emphasis. It runs through William James and was clearly expressed by John Dewey in his memorable address in 1896: "The older dualism between sensation and idea is repeated in the current dualism of peripheral and central structures and functions; the older dualism of body and soul finds a distinct echo in the current dualism of stimulus and response. Instead of interpreting the character of sensation, idea and action from their place and function in the sensory motor circuit, we still incline to interpret the latter from our preconceived and preformulated ideas of rigid distinctions between sensations, thoughts and acts."

In giving a list of ideas he rejects, Korzybski names, among others, "elementalism" which he defines as "the assumed sharp division of 'senses' *and* 'mind,' 'precept' *and* 'concept,' 'emotions' *and* 'intellect,' etc." He proposes instead a "non-elementalistic theory of meanings" based on a "psycho-physiological theory of semantic reactions" of the "organism-as-a-whole."

The same point of view has been more recently elaborated by Dewey and Bentley, who used the term "transactional" to refer to the relationship between the processes involved in human behavior in contra-distinction to "interaction" and "self action" which have so affected much psychological thinking. While we have also used the term "transactional" as it is commonly employed in everyday life with reference to our interpersonal dealings, it is hardly inclusive enough for our purposes, chiefly because it leaves out the novel aspects of living. But for psychological description, however, the term "transactional" does seem useful in referring to the variables we describe below that are involved in the orchestration of man's experience and except for which there would be no real "transaction of living."

eagerly because of the feeling of security it affords, forget that it obscures uniqueness and differences, that it is a function of some human purpose and is at best partial and tentative.

Any such approach to the study of man's values and ideas is automatically denied us if we follow certain current "schools" of psychology which, stemming from the scientific tradition set by Descartes, attempt to explain the nature of man entirely in terms of a mechanistic determinism. This does not in the least, of course, imply that we turn our backs on the results of rigid scientific experimentation. Indeed, the most rigorous of these as found in modern physics support the conclusion that our traditional conceptions of matter are due for serious revision and, further and more important for us here, the conclusions of modern physics as well as modern biology deny any complete determinism and indicate that what makes up the universe, including man, is ceaseless activity, continual flow from form where the spirit of man plays a creative role.

DIFFERENT WAYS OF VIEWING EXPERIENCE

It may be helpful for us in setting the stage if we differentiate between four different ways in which experience may be viewed, four differentiable areas of complexity.

On-going, Naive Experience

This is the level of immediate, "pure" experience as experienced—unanalyzed, unconceptualized, unmediated, and with no concern on the part of the experiencing individual to describe, analyze, conceptualize, or communicate his experience. This on-going, naive experience is what Korzybski called "first-order" or "objective level" or "un-speakable" experience. He writes: "Thus we *handle* what we call a pencil. Whatever we *handle* is un-speakable; yet we *say* 'this *is* a pencil,' which statement is unconditionally false to facts, because the object appears as an absolute individual and *is not* words." This is perhaps what the poet Wordsworth had in mind when he said, "We murder to dissect."

As has been frequently pointed out, any attempt to describe or analyze experience immediately alters that experience. When we are trying to describe or analyze experience or any aspect of it, we are functionally organized quite differently than when we are participating in a process of living and are not describing or analyzing it. Our experiences in the occasions of living are dependent upon and characterized by processes involving, for example, overtones of satisfaction or dissatisfaction, a sense of involvement and responsibility, a sense of intent or aim, commitment through activity, a sense of worry, frustration, or urgency, a sense of despair, hope or faith, etc., depending upon the particular orchestration going on in a particular unique occasion of living. The obvious complexity of the orchestration that any on-going experience *is* makes the process of isolating aspects of it particularly difficult. But if the psychologist ignores any significant aspects of experience in an attempt to isolate easily manipulable variables, he is bound to fail in his attempt to understand that experience.

Description

Verbalization and communication, either retrospectively or simultaneously with the occurrence of some experience, may be distinguished methodologically from naive experience itself because of a form of awareness on selected aspects of experience. For some focusing, categorization, and coding are operating in the process of dealing consciously or verbally with any selected experiential aggregate. It is as if with any such focusing, awareness is shifted from the full orchestration as a whole to the role of a particular instrument in the orchestra.

As stated by Korzybski: "Animals may 'feel,' and 'suffer,' but they cannot *describe*. Humans differ in this respect; the given person may feel pain, the pain is very *objective* to the given individual, but it is *not words* (*objective level*); but we can describe it, this description being valid on the *descriptive level,* a higher order abstraction than the objective level (which is un-speakable for the given individual). If we *ascribe* this process to others, this is no longer a description but an inference, or a still higher order abstraction. . . ."

It is important for psychologists using descriptive material of any kind never to lose sight of the fact that reports of experience are not to be equated with experience itself. Such "protocol" data, however, do provide the psychologist with valuable raw material. This is not limited to introspective reports obtained in the laboratory or to clinical material. Some of the most penetrating descriptions of experience have been given us by poets, novelists, composers, and religious prophets. From this point of view, the psychologist concerned with an understanding of the full range of human experience can enormously benefit by sensitizing himself to the insights found in the "humanities."[2] The

[2] Henry A. Murray has pointed out that: "Until theory has been much further developed we would be inclined to favour the use of clear literary language, despite the current tendency among American psychologists to become suspicious whenever there appears in the writings or speech of a fellow-scientist the slightest trace of aesthetic feeling. A psychologist who believes that he can tell the truth without being 'literary' has only to try writing a case history or biography, and then compare what he has done to a character sketch by any novelist of the first order. We

humanists, on the other hand, as already indicated, should be able to profit by keeping in touch with the psychologist who, in his self-appointed capacity as scientist, must try to systematize the intuitive portrayals of humanists and formulate constructs of general validity.

Focused Analysis and Conceptualization

Instead of focusing on a selected phenomenon in an experience of living we may, in the midst of that living, try to "figure out" conceptually what is going on. We do so for some purpose. Perhaps we are trying to resolve some personal problem, perhaps we are delving into our own experience in the hope of discovering hunches or clues that will provide us with some hypothesis, or perhaps we are only obeying the instructions of some experimenter in the psychological laboratory. Analysis of any occurrence for whatever purpose is a very different experiential aggregate than purposive behavior itself or focused aspects of it.

This area of complexity described as "focused analysis and conceptualization" also includes our attempt to understand the behavior and purposes of other people as we try to carry out our own purposes in social situations. Such understanding will usually be successful insofar as we are able to bring to an occasion appropriate sets of abstractions derived from our own experience. Our ability to "put ourselves into another's position" and to "share" his experience vicariously seems generally to depend upon the similarity of our experiential backgrounds, our purposes, our standards for sensing satisfaction, our values, etc. In other instances, where there may be little similarity of experiential background, our understanding of others may increase if the situation is such that we develop with those others some community of interest through the repeated sharing of new experiences.

No matter how close the correspondence may be between all the factors involved in giving us an awareness of another person's experience under certain circumstances, we still have to interpret their experiences in terms of our own experience. And no matter how closely-knit the person may feel in the social group, no matter how great the correspondence may be between his experiential background, his needs, his purposes or values with those of other members of the group, his experience of participation with the group is still uniquely his own. Complete understanding of another person is an unobtainable ideal.

Yet our understanding of another person (or his understanding of us) may be more accurate than his own understanding of himself since our

---

academic psychologists have yet to discover how much can be learnt from the realists of literature. A little humility here would add to our stature."

"explanation" of his behavior may be taking more factors into account, may give very different priorities to different aspects that constitute the aggregate experience, may differentiate or abstract out of his process of living as we observe it more intrinsically reasonable aspects so that we are more aware of the processes playing a role in his behavior than he is himself. Thus an experienced physician will be able to tell us why we are tired or suffer certain aches or pains; an experienced psychiatrist may be able to point out to us what purposes that we are unaware of seem to be guiding our actions; a wise friend may be able to point out contradictions in our value-standards, etc.

Abstracting for Scientific Specification

The scientist's attempt to understand the nature of human living is ultimately an attempt to distinguish components, to choose those by means of which he will be able to define and interpret the significance of any process of living, and to describe the variables on which the singularity of any process depends. If the abstracting a scientist makes can be effectively related to his presuppositions, then he will have an instrument to render communication more accurate and to enable others to understand the abstractions without reference to any particular item of behavior that might illustrate it. This point is discussed at length by Korzybski in his treatment of "higher inferential levels" in his chapters "On Abstracting," "On the Structural Differential," and "On 'Consciousness' and Consciousness of Abstracting."

Such scientific abstractions are not affected by individual behavior and are not altered when conceptualized from the point of view of different persons. If they were so affected or altered, they would prove useless; it is their static quality that gives them the utility they have in understanding the significance of concrete behavioral situations. This does not mean, of course, that such scientific abstractions never change. They are, on the other hand, constantly evolving and being modified by scientists themselves to increase their usefulness. The creative scientist tests his abstractions by their performance, not by their consistency, realizing that any abstraction is highly tentative. In describing William James, Whitehead wrote, "His intellectual life was one protest against the dismissal of experience in the interest of system." What we mean by the "static quality" of an abstraction is simply that scientific abstractions would be operationally useless if their significances were not "fixed."

But it should be emphasized again that when we are dealing with this fourth area of complexity which makes scientific communication possible, we are necessarily violating phenomenal data. The psychologist's awareness of this fact and of some of the omissions involved in operating in this area should help give him perspective to increase the usefulness of his abstractions.

Two points should be noted in passing with respect to this fourfold differentiation: (1) whichever way a process of living is considered will depend upon one's purposes, and, (2) no matter which way a process of living is considered, the consideration is still yours, is still a process in which you cannot be detached, is still a transaction involving what Bridgman has called the "personal equation" from which no scientist can escape. All experiences are from a personal behavioral center.

A major task, then, for anyone trying to work through an adequate understanding of human nature is to describe what a transaction of living *is* in all of its aspects from any personal behavioral center. Since experience is "real" only insofar as it is "yours," we must try to make an approximate description of a transaction of living that will appear intrinsically reasonable and verifiable in terms of your own experience and behavior. Such a description, of course, must be derived from an analysis of your own experience and behavior, which is all you have to base it on. This means that we must work out from what is given in a transaction of living rather than work in toward a transaction of living from some arbitrary outside starting point, such as any pre-established abstractions or any pre-established methods borrowed from another discipline.

The psychologist cannot avoid his responsibilities merely by becoming insensitive to the compelling aspects of human experience which defy neat systematization or the use of picturesque models which can be quantitatively described. If, for example, we take the more traditional, "scientific" point of view alone and try to account for another person's experience and behavior, we are likely to over-emphasize the aspects of any transaction of living which have been determined in the past. For from this point of view—e.g., from the past—since we are *outside* the personal behavioral center which is our object of understanding, we ourselves cannot possibly participate as another individual is himself participating in what is to him a "now" or "present" where *he* must make *his* choices in order to carry out *his* purposes in a situation that impinges upon *him* and in which *he* initiates some action that is, in part, pushed by a determined, repeatable past and in part pulled by an undisclosed, uncertain future. Likewise, from the "objective," "outside" point of view we may entirely neglect the experiential background and the past interpersonal relationships that bring to an occasion of living a determined set which affects the direction that occasion of living will take. We then land in the complete situational determinism "outside of us," a metaphoric "field" theory and cannot account for the consistency of behavior, the apparently directed flow of living, or the value overtones without which any transaction of living would not be what it is.

It is perhaps especially worth noting in a discussion of the ways in which "experience" can be viewed that, as William James long ago emphasized, the range of our awareness is most restricted. Your awareness is an attribute of a transaction of living which refers to a very limited and particular range of "things" (objects, people, happenings, ideas, etc.) at any time. Your awareness is of what "concerns you now" together with the sense of obligation or responsibility you experience at any given time as related to what concerns you at that time. You are by no means aware of all the determinants of your awareness—that is, all the aspects involved in a total transaction of living except for which you would not have the awareness you do.

You can become intellectually aware that your experience at any time is an almost infinitesimal drop in the bucket of what you might be potentially aware of and is even more limited with respect to all the happenings and stimulus-excitations going on within and around you—what Harry Stack Sullivan labeled "selective inattention." Through analysis you can see that what you are aware of at any given time, that your "selection" of possibilities for awarenesses is made on the basis of what is of importance, worth, or value to you relative to your immediate purposes whether these concern the retention of your psychological "form," structure or set or the effective participation in novel situations, or both. You can become intellectually aware that there is no *at*tention without *in*tention. As expressed by Horace Kallen, "Consciousness is attention between divergencies which decision temporarily relieves by bringing one to dominance."

To state the matter somewhat differently, you can understand intellectually the difference between what you are "aware of" and what you are "taking into account" in any transaction of living. This was expressed by Mr. Justice Holmes as "an intuition of experience which outruns analyses and sums up many unnamed entangled impressions which may be beneath consciousness without losing their worth." You can understand intellectually that you become aware of certain factors you are now taking into account, but had previously been unaware of when your behavior was incomplete because you had not experienced the consequences you expected from your behavior—i.e., as when a front tire on your car blows out and you suddenly swerve; when you go up in a fast elevator and become aware of your gravitational adjustment; when you underestimate the magnitude of some task you have set out to accomplish; when a trusted friend disappoints you; when some institution or ideology "fails" to give you expected satisfactions, etc. You can be intellectually aware of the legal concept that a person is guilty only if he had a certain "intent" in his awareness at the time the particular act was committed.

At any one time, then, there is a multiplicity of happenings potentially available for awareness, together with a multiplicity of previous happenings available for recall and a multiplicity of possible future happenings available for expectancies. Of all the phenomenal aspects of any transaction of living which we are taking into account during that transaction of living, we are aware only of those aspects which we are in the process of giving meaning or significance to in order to experience the consequences of the purposeful behavior we are trying to participate in or trying to initiate. From the psychologist's point of view, then, "awareness" as a quality of any transaction of living is not merely an adornment of nature but itself plays a functional role.

From the point of view of our present discussion, this fact must be especially borne in mind since our behavior in everyday life seems to involve an implicit adherence to value and moral standards of some kind which basically pattern our behavior.

DIFFERENTIATION OF THE SIGNIFICANCES WE EXPERIENCE

In order better to understand where valuings and moral ideas fit into the total orchestration of human experience, it may be helpful to differentiate between what we might term various "matrices" of experience. In making such differentiation, however, we must recall that each matrix is interdependent upon all other matrices and that no one would exist except for the others.

Our Perception of the World around Us

Here we refer to our experience of objects and people as these seem to exist in a world outside of ourselves and seem to have attributes and characteristics of their own that can be placed in the space-time continuum. It can be demonstrated that the attributes which we assign to the "things" outside of ourselves—whether objects, people or societies—are significances which we build up in the course of our experience, are learned. Insofar as our subjective perceptual experience corresponds to what we encounter in the environmental situation, then our perceptions are judged by us as correct or accurate. From this point of view we may say that the world as we experience it is the creation of our perception and not the cause of it. "Naked sense impressions simply do not occur, and the traditional analysis of our conscious experience into naked sensations as building blocks is palpably bad description." This does not imply, of course, any variety of solipsism since we would not have our normal perceptions except for impingements from the outside environment. It should be particularly stressed that from this point of view our perceptual awarenesses are only probabilities—guesses or hunches that we make, based on our previous experience, as to what the attributes of "things" are. This parallels Korzybski's conception that there is no such thing as a raw "reality" but only that which we evaluate in terms of our values–fears–past-history, etc.

Our Awareness of Sequential Significances

Here we refer to our assumptions that a certain event will be followed by another event, that events take place in sequences. When we are able to predict with considerable reliability what the sequential order of events will be, we experience a sense of surety. On the other hand, we become apprehensive when we cannot predict consequences.

From the point of view of the relationship between the sciences and the humanities, it is important to stress that all of man's scientific inquiry and the ingenious applications man makes from this inquiry are concerned either with extending the range of man's perceptual and motor processes (radar, television, airplanes, etc.) or with improving the reliability with which he will be able to predict and manipulate sequential events. Man has already created a bewildering variety of artifacts which he seems to have designed for the purpose of insuring that certain sequential events will follow other events in a direction which he can reliably predict. The important point to bear in mind here and to be elaborated later is that scientific inquiry as such does *not* concern itself with the problem of rightness or wrongness, the goodness or badness, of these sequential events which the scientist tries to understand and to control.

We stated above that our perception is only a probability. It is a probability for *action* or some potential action which we might undertake. Perception, then, has reference to the future as well as to the past. We act in order to experience some consequences from our actions, in order to achieve what we call some "purpose." The purpose which we intend to achieve may be immediate or it may be a long-range goal.

The purpose which we set out to achieve, the consequence which we hope will result from our action, is obviously not a purpose that exists in a vacuum or that is determined entirely by whim or the circumstances of the moment. Purposive action seems to have as its ultimate goal the experience of *value satisfaction* which may take the form of the rudimentary attempts to preserve our physiological organism or, particularly characteristic of human beings, the more basic and ultimate satisfaction of experiencing some *emergence,* some novelty that we characterize as "richer," "higher," "better." As I have stated elsewhere, "the outstanding characteristic of man is his capacity to participate in the creation of emergent value attributes which enrich the quality of his experience." It would appear that if we do not root our conceptual scheme in this value matrix characteristic of man, then all the other matrices tumble since their function appears to be to *serve* man in his ceaseless striving for value satisfactions.

SOME INFERENCES RELATED TO HUMANISTIC INQUIRY

I have taken the liberty to outline the point of view expressed above in the hope that it will provide in bold relief a background against which to consider what seem to me important aspects involved in the development and function of moral ideas. The genetic development of moral ideas has been brilliantly traced by Jean Piaget, as well as by numerous psychologists and social scientists in the United States and England. From the data so far gathered by these investigators and from our own analysis of what seems to be an intrinsically reasonable account, I should like to call attention here to at least five aspects or characteristics of human experience that are related to the development and function of man's moral ideas: purposive behavior, hitches or obstructions, choice, inquiry, and the reality of faith.

Purpose

When you do something, you nearly always do it because of some intent, aim, or purpose. You are generally only aware of a single intent, aim or purpose. And in doing this something—for example, reading this paper—you sense that "you" are involved in directing the doing because of "your" decision or intuition as to what will be the best thing to do under the particular circumstances, what will bring about a sense of worthwhileness and satisfaction, or, in other instances, what it is necessary to do in order to maintain life, to carry on, etc. The intent, aim, or purpose you have in mind when you do something is experienced with varying degrees of conflict or lack of conflict concerning its "goodness," "rightness," "efficacy," etc.

You can realize intellectually that while your naive, on-going, unanalyzed experience is of some single and particular purpose—that is, a desire for the coming-about in your awareness of some particular consequence—if this purpose is to be carried out, a number of intermediate purposes will also be involved. For example, while your purpose at the moment may be to read this, you are also involved in the intermediate purposes of maintaining your equilibrium in a chair, holding this paper, focusing your eyes, etc. Furthermore, you are not reading this simply for the purpose of reading it but because such reading is presumably related to other, "higher" valueful purposes having to do with your basic standards of what is worthwhile and what will bring about a sense of personal satisfaction, development, etc.

In any transaction of living there is a multiplicity of purposes involved. These require differentiation and a choice of the satisfactions to be derived from various possibilities of what behavior is *for* anyway, what the value standards for this behavior "should" be. An individual's "sensed values"—that is, his own feeling of what is "important," "worthwhile," or "satisfying"—are ultimately the impelling aspects of living that lead to any behavior at all. In any transaction of living it appears that the purposeful aspect of the transaction can be further differentiated into three factors: the first involving and insuring the preservation of physiological and psychological processes, the second "directing" action and sensed as the "purposive" accent in experience, the third involving a sense of the consequences the action will have once it is initiated. Each of these three factors has its own felt significance and no one of them would be experienced except for the felt importances of the other aspects. A "purpose" therefore becomes a weighted average of multiple purposes.

Hitches or Obstructions

The process of living involves participation in situations which you do not by any means sail through without experiencing some obstruction, some obstacle, or some problem. You experience some sense of frustration, which may be great or small, ephemeral or relatively enduring. This frustration may come about either from a difficulty in carrying out effective behavior that will lead to some pre-determined goal, or, it may result from your concern as to what goal is the proper one for you to pursue anyway. Your sense of frustration in these respects is characterized by what you call "worry," "inferiority," "guilt," "struggle," "indecision," "anxiety," etc., depending upon the circumstances of the particular occasion.

On analysis you can be aware of the fact that no matter how annoying or upsetting the hitches or problems you encounter may be, these are almost inevitable aspects of living in a cosmos where the future is undisclosed and where you, as a participant, must play a role in determining that future. Furthermore, you can become intellectually aware that it is only insofar as you encounter illusions, surprises, disappointments or other varieties of obstacles and problems that you yourself "learn" something, that you yourself have an opportunity to test out new choices, hunches, and formulations by experiencing the consequences they lead to in action. Problems of "how" to achieve a predetermined end challenge and hold the possibility of clarifying and enlarging your value standards, that is, your own code of ethics, morality, or worthwhileness.

A transaction of living involves in more or less degree a set of conditions that present a problem for choice or action. The ability to meet the problem depends upon the adequacy and appropriateness of the pattern of assumptions we bring to bear on the occasion and only by "working through" the problems can we build up more inclusive and more appropriate assumptions for future occasions.

Choice

You sense, sometimes vaguely, sometimes intensely, that what you do involves the choice you make of alternatives and possibilities; the hunch you have that your intended actions will result in the intended consequences with their intended satisfactions. You have a sense of greater or less surety concerning the probable effectiveness of your choice; a sense of more or less conflict between alternatives involved in making your choice. And in the process of choosing and carrying out selected behavior resulting from choice, you have a sense of more or less personal responsibility.

You can be intellectually aware that you have no absolute control over future occurrences and that chance is likely to play a greater or less role in your behavior. You can become intellectually aware of many of the factors you are taking into account in the process of choosing. You can observe that many of your choices concerned with long-range goals involve the selection of alternatives and possibilities which you feel will lead to further alternatives and possibilities that will make future choices more effective.

Since what we call the "future" is made up of non-repeatable, undisclosed happenings, a transaction of living involves in some degree the aspect of choice with the corollary aspects of personal responsibility and anxiety concerning the consequences of that choice. "Choosings are seen to be processes of the normal consciousness, each a present passage to an anticipated future having no guarantees and contingent on 'faith' and 'fortune' as well as on the energies and intellect of the chooser."

Inquiry

As you participate in a transaction of living, you sense that you are more or less figuring out how to do what you want to do, or, that you are making some evaluation of what is most worthwhile doing, what you "should be" doing.

On analysis, we can become intellectually aware that insofar as our behavior is completely reliable, certain, and effective we will go on to further behavior which will lead us to further desired consequences, but that when we run up against some obstacle, some difficulty, some sense of inadequacy, we become aware of this and must undertake some inquiry. If the difficulty encountered is one of *how* to achieve a predetermined goal, we make use of rational, logical inquiry involving conceptual abstractions which in its most highly developed form can be labeled "scientific inquiry." On the other hand, if a difficulty involves a choice of goals, a lack of surety with respect to *what* goals we "should" pursue, then we undertake a different kind of inquiry: instead of indulging in rational and intellectual processes alone, we undertake what we refer to as "mulling things over," "reflecting," "meditating," in which we try to weigh the reliability of different value standards. We can sense that associated with inquiry of the former type is the collection of facts, the accumulation of knowledge, the attainment of skills, the use and development of artifacts, the development of "know how," the proper use of scientific method, etc. Associated with the latter type of inquiry are the less tangible but equally "real" experiences concerned with the development of faith, the acceptance of things past, the cultivation of charity, the broadening of love, etc.

In any transaction of living there is a multiplicity of alternative possibilities with respect to what goals an individual may pursue and a multiplicity of alternative possibilities with respect to how he may best realize any intended goal.

It is with respect to the form of inquiry involved when we must decide *why* we should do one thing rather than another (or possibly why we should do anything at all) that the psychologist still has to create some method of investigation. And it is in this area especially where he can learn from the humanists, skilled in description or portrayal, how individuals have learned to sensitize themselves to value inquiry. For, as already stated, the process involved in such value inquiry is totally different from the processes involved in the inquiries necessary for solving procedural difficulties. We remember that Aristotle said in his *Ethics,* "The end cannot be a subject of deliberation." Value inquiry is intensely personal and unique. You always feel it as yours. It involves what is the "me" built up from the past facing the transition of the present into the future as "I."

The function of this "value inquiry" is to provide us with a value judgment that will serve as a compass, a directive for action. In "value inquiry" we are seeking standards of rightness, wrongness, more right than, goodness, badness, beauty, ugliness, etc., which will serve as signs or clues and which will indicate to us the nature of the probable consequences we will experience by following a particular course of action. The standards we use and question in "value inquiry" concern our duties, loyalties, and responsibilities. Hence the value judgments we reach through "value inquiry" involve "conscience," "charity," "humility," etc.

The role of "value inquiry" is symbolized by the Hindu custom of marking one's self between the brows with ashes each day in order to be reminded of the "inner vision" provided by a "third eye"; it is reflected in the hymn which says, "Lead, kindly light, amid the encircling gloom."

Descriptions of value inquiry are almost necessarily best given us by poets. A revealing description by a modern poet is found in Christopher Fry's *The Lady's Not for Burning.* In the excerpts which follow, Jennet, who had been accused of being a witch and is to be burned the next day, is wondering whether or not to accede to the request of Humphreys that he enter her cell at night and sleep with her, in return for which favor Humphreys will have her sentence revoked because of his official position. Her decision not to accede to his request is a value judgment. Jennet soliloquizes:

> Don't speak, contemptible boy,
> I'll tell you: I am not. We have
> To look elsewhere—for instance, into my heart
> Where recently I heard begin
> A bell of longing which calls no one to church.
> But need that, ringing anyway in vain,
> Drown the milkmaid singing in my blood
> And freeze into the tolling of my knell?
> That would be pretty, indeed, but unproductive.
> No, it's not that . . .
>
> I am interested
> In my feelings. I seem to wish to have some importance
> In the play of time. If not,
> Then sad was my mother's pain, sad my breath,
> Sad the articulation of my bones,

Sad, sad my alacritous web of nerves,
Woefully, woefully sad my wondering brain,
To be shaped and sharpened into such tendrils
Of anticipation, to feed the swamp of space.
What is deep, as love is deep, I'll have
Deeply. What is good, as love is good,
I'll have well. Then if time and space
Have any purpose, I shall belong to it.
If not, if all is pretty fiction
To distract the cherubim and seraphim
Who so continually do cry, the least
I can do is to fill the curled shell of the world
With human deep-sea sound, and hold it to
The ear of God, until he has appetite
To taste our salt sorrow on his lips.
And so you see it might be better to die.
Though, on the other hand, I admit it might
Be immensely foolish.[3]

Christ and Gandhi may be taken as examples of individuals who were trying to create an environment in order to act on the "what for" value judgments emerging from their value inquiry. In order to indulge in the necessary value inquiry, Christ went to the top of the mountain and Gandhi had his day of silence.

Most of us, at times, have wanted to be alone so that we could "mull things over." We apparently need to insulate ourselves in this way from immediate here and now conditions as we weigh those standards that are not bounded by time and space considerations. Such insulation allows our conscious and subconscious processes of mentation and feeling the widest possible range.

And some such insulation also allows us to make a more accurate distinction between (a) those feelings and emotions related to our physiological bodily activity and the conditions at the moment of which we are a part and (b) those overtones of feeling which derive from the standards for value that have become a part of our assumptive world and that are not dependent on a specific set of conditions or actions in the here and now. It is these value standards that sustain us between one doing and the next. Insofar as we feel sure of these value standards, we can weather frustration and deprivations; if we have no such value standards, then we feel lost.

We use our value standards to give us the most reliable bets for obtaining a repetition of some experience that has been satisfying. And it is

[3] Christopher Fry, *The Lady's Not for Burning.* New York, Oxford University Press, 1950, © 1950 by Christopher Fry, pp. 82 f. By permission of the publisher.

especially characteristic of human beings also to use value standards as springboards for obtaining some new satisfactions they feel will emerge in the flow of the present from the past into the future.

The value standards each of us uses are the consequences of our action in the past that have been registered, and have become a part of our assumptive world insofar as they have proved to be good bets for further judgment and action. This registration is not of an intellectual nature. It is a change, a confirmation, or a denial of the weight to be given different assumptions concerning the "worthwhileness," the "goodness," the "rightness" of any action. Thus our complex of standards serves both as our criterion of satisfaction and as our best guide for effective action.

The process involved in "value inquiry" is one of trying to expand the range of the cues we can include. We attempt to increase our value specifications. These are bounded neither by the space-time considerations of any immediate situation nor by conceptual specifications. Hence, if a person accepts as absolute and inviolable any variety of ideology, the clues he uses in his value inquiry will be restricted, and the directive for action indicated by his inquiry will lack the reliability it might otherwise have. For the reliability of the directives reached through value inquiry is directly related to the adequacy of the cues taken into account. The point was made by Hayakawa: "People who are not accustomed to distinguishing between attitudes institutionally arrived at and those extensionally arrived at are capable of real self-deception. In a real sense, they don't know which of their opinions are simply a parrot-like repetition of institutional opinions, and which are the result of their own experience and their own thinking. Lacking that self-insight, they are unable to arrive at realistic self-concepts; they are unable to map accurately the territory of their own personalities."

In cases where we have resolved a "what for" hitch and have arrived at a value judgment or decision, we may conceptualize this decision to ourselves or feel emotionally that it is good and proper. However, it is important to bear in mind that this conceptualization or feeling can be experienced only because of a large background of value standards which constitute an important aspect of each of our assumptive form worlds.

If this is not recognized, we are apt to make the mistake of believing that our purposive decision in and of itself is of a final or ultimate nature and justifies any action that may lead to its accomplishment. Furthermore, these value standards are largely on the silent, non-verbal level. By and large we are quite unaware of them and, except in rare cases, have never "thought them through" or systematized them. Yet they are the standards against which we measure our feelings of pleasure, happiness, our sense of well-being, our sense of self-esteem, our "ought I" judgments.

Thus it becomes "wrong" to act on the basis of the adage, "The end justifies the means" insofar as the consequences of our actions will not ultimately lead to what we expected. The glib rationalizations and conceptualizations of a particular "end," together with the action we take to achieve it, may prevent the realization of those unconceptualized, unconscious value standards without which the specific end we have in mind would not exist. There is a marked contrast between the ease with which most of us can rationalize why we have set a particular goal and the tortuous, soul-searching type of rationalization in which Lincoln indulged.

Rational inquiry, while not excluded in the resolution of difficulties on the *why* level, is only of secondary importance. In "what for" purposive inquiry, we keep expanding our reference base. This extension cannot go on freely, as indicated before, if an individual is disturbed by impingements from his senses. Apparently the function of our senses is to give us a standpoint in time and space so that we *can* act *after* we have decided *why* we should act.

Thus to return to Gandhi as an example, the function of prayer for him, and one of the functions of some of his fasts, was to sensitize himself to cues that could be taken into account in the process of value inquiry in order to achieve the most reliable and satisfying value judgment. He was trying to take into account a synthesized phenomenon which he could feel, rather than abstracted aspects of a phenomenon he could grasp intellectually. It was only *after* what Gandhi called his "instinct" had shown him a course of action was right that he tried to determine intellectually why it was right.

The resolution of a difficulty encountered on the *why* or *what for* level, and the consequences of action that follow, more likely than not involve some modification of our previous assumptions, some revision of our assumptive form world. Decisions involving purpose are peculiarly our own, since the value standards that compose so crucial a part of our assumptive form world constitute a complex of value assumptions unique to each of us. These decisions, therefore, involve both responsibility and opportunity. These interdependent responsibilities and opportunities are highly personal. They are products of our unique biological equipment participating in the culture unique to our own life history.

Judgments concerning *what for* and *why* are often disturbing or painful because the resolution of "what for" or "why" difficulties does involve a modification or revision of our assumptions. Hence, we may try to delay them or temporarily rationalize the dilemma away.

Practically all of us at times try to avoid—and usually unconsciously—many hitches on the purposive level of "what for." We do this by keeping ourselves busy, by pursuing only the means involved in earning a living, or by escape through over-indulgence in entertainment, by over-concern with what we eat or wear, by escape through drink, or by rationalization. In some such cases, we are making the false assumption that solving hitches in the means will bring personal development. In other instances, we may be deliberately marking time in the hope that things will change and we can renew our pursuit of goals. Or in order to obtain some relief from the anguish of making such decisions, we may let other people make the decisions for us, possibly leaving the responsibility to God or to some charismatic leader. A prolonged inability of individuals to make these "what for" decisions themselves provides the psychiatrist with many of his patients and the political or religious leader with followers who are blindly devoted.

We get satisfaction in our experience only insofar as *we* are involved in *action* as well as in *judgment*. If there is no participation, no action on our part, there is no real satisfaction, no value attribute to our experience. It is our action only that can be registered in us and that can give some stability to or cause some revisions in our assumptive form world. And it is only through action that our value judgments have the possibility of being registered beyond ourselves, as was pointed out long ago in the parable of the Good Samaritan.

If our satisfaction is to be genuine, our action must be related to a "what for" reason. Otherwise, there is no assurance at all for the very existence of value standards. Real pioneers in any field seem to sense this. For example, Charles Edison reports, "After an invention became a commercial success, father simply lost interest in it."

All our means of "how-to-do's" are related to some purpose, some "what for's," even though in many cases we may be quite unconscious of the purposive assumptions involved. It would seem that insofar as a person can obtain insight into the purposes that lie behind the means, he can experience what we label personal development, a "richer" life, emergent values.

If value standards are continually disregarded, then the means may become goals in themselves with a consequent "lowering" in the satisfyingness of experience, a "lowering" for which the experiencing individual may not be able to account. We can see examples of this in those who fish to win a prize, those who earn more money than they need to satisfy their wants simply in order to become rich, those who try to get a college degree for the sake of a degree, those who strive to live on a reputation after achieving some position that has prestige in their particular social group.

There is a submergence of an individual's capacity to make value decisions involving purposes insofar as he is coerced to do anything, insofar as force is a factor he must heed. Compulsion restricts the free flow of value inquiry. This necessarily means that the quality of satisfaction obtained in living will be "lower." Under compulsion a person is forced to worry about means, about "how-to-do's" and his consideration of purposes becomes dulled or restricted by fear, insecurity, intimidation, or the uncertainty that comes from being unable to test his own decisions in action.

As we have already said, value judgments are intensely personal and unique. Hence, freedom exists only insofar as an individual makes decisions on his own responsibility. This is an inalienable right, rooted in the very biological organization that characterizes human beings. If the possibility to make one's own choice does not exist, there is not true liberty but, rather, some degree of enslavement.

Also, insofar as an individual is freed from frustrations, for example by being protected by parents and others from encountering difficulties, he will be unable to experience personal growth in the sense of progressing from one value judgment to another value judgment that is more satisfying because it is more inclusive and provides a better bet for effective action in new situations.

A problem for every individual, or for every group or society or ideology, therefore, appears to be the problem of clarifying purposes and simplifying means. Clarification of purposes in terms of creating value standards that serve as effective and satisfying guides for action can be a never-ending process. And it is such for individuals who themselves surmount the continuing hitches or frustrations brought about by changing conditions. The process of value inquiry they engage in and test by action gives them increasingly adequate value judgments. Insofar as an individual becomes complacent and static in his own value judgments, then living becomes repetitious, loses its zest, and changing conditions bring increasing puzzlement or new searches for escape.

And it appears that only insofar as an individual "raises" the level of his purposes can he minimize the annoyances of life. Only then can discrimination be improved and means become simplified by being judged in terms of more inclusive purposes. In the *Bhagavad-Gita* there is a verse: "The wise should perform tasks without attachment, yet with as much ardor as the foolish, who are bound up in the results of their deeds—thus to the world shall they set an example."

The Reality of Faith

While it may be easy enough for us to realize intellectually that all of our own perceptions of objects and people, our prehension of the sequences which events may take, our purposes and our values are only probabilities, in everyday life we cannot possibly act only on the basis of what might "probably" happen. We must, as Vaihinger noted, act *als ob.* We must make fixed assumptions, have certainties and beliefs. For example, as we carry on the process of living we have to assume that the chair which we are about to sit in *is* a chair; we have to assume that certain people *are* trustworthy; we have to assume that certain actions *are* the right actions to take. Throughout the whole process of living, then, we are continually engaged in the business of making certainties out of probabilities in order that we can act effectively to attain some value satisfactions. Thus objects and people become realities for us. Causal effects become realities for us. Purposive behavior becomes a reality for us. Our values and moral codes become realities for us. All of these become realities in concrete situations and must become such if we are to act at all. While our action in such concrete situations takes place in a milieu bounded by time and space, the values which carry us through this action transcend time and space. Yet they become real in our experience only insofar as we transact—as unique and responsible individuals endowed with the capacity to choose—within the environment around us.

In the same way, the symbols man has created to conceptualize his awarenesses and the behavioral patterns, such as rituals and ceremonies that he sustains in order to "feel" value relationships, are realities from the point of view of the individual acting in his unique behavioral situation. Apart from the behaving individual acting in a concrete situation, these realities would not exist as such. But to deny them from the point of view of the experiencing person can lead only to chaos and ineffectual action. The individual, then, becomes the focus of reality. And in creating our patterns of value and our moral codes, we seem constantly to be attempting to integrate more and more specific purposes which are themselves unconceptualized and undetermined.

CORRELATION TABLES AND INDEX

CORRELATION OF THIS BOOK WITH ELEMENTARY TEXTS

Hilgard *Introduction to Psychology* Harcourt, Brace, 1953		Kimble *Principles of General Psychology* Ronald Press, 1956	
Ch. nos.	*Related articles*	*Ch. nos.*	*Related articles*
1	1, 2	1	2
2	3, 4, 34, 41	2	1
3	23, 39	3	—
4	6, 7	4	26, 28
5	5, 21	5	6, 27, 29
6	22, 24	6	8
7	23, 35	7	9
8	22	8	10, 11, 12, 13, 14
9	11, 25	9	3, 4, 5, 7
10	15, 16, 17	10	15, 17
11	20	11	16
12	18, 19	12	20, 30, 31, 32, 33, 46
13	8, 9, 10, 14	13	18, 19
14	30, 31, 32	14	22, 23
15	28	15	21, 24
16	26, 27	16	25, 35
17	29	17	34, 36, 37, 38, 40, 41, 45
18	38, 40	18	39, 42, 43, 44
19	42, 43, 44		
20	45		
21	28		
22	13, 37		
23	12, 33, 36		
24	46		
25	—		

CORRELATION OF THIS BOOK WITH ELEMENTARY TEXTS—*continued*

Morgan *Introduction to Psychology* McGraw-Hill, 1956		Munn *Psychology: The Fundamentals of Human Adjustment,* 3rd ed. Houghton Mifflin, 1956	
Ch. nos.	*Related articles*	*Ch. nos.*	*Related articles*
1	1, 2	1	1, 2, 36, 37
2	3, 4, 6	2	3, 4, 6, 7
3	5, 21, 22, 34	3	26, 27, 29
4	7, 24, 25	4	5, 21, 22, 35
5	15, 16, 17, 18, 19, 20	5	7, 24, 39
6	30, 31, 32, 33	6	23, 25, 32
7	10, 11, 12, 13, 14	7	34, 38, 40, 41, 42, 43, 44
8	—	8	15, 16, 17
9	38, 40, 41	9	19, 20
10	23, 39	10	18
11	42, 43, 44	11	30, 31, 32, 33
12	34, 35, 41	12	10, 11, 12, 13, 14
13	37	13	9
14	36	14	8
15	26, 27, 29	15	—
16	28, 45	16	28, 45, 46
17	14		
18	9		
19	8		
20	46		
21	—		
22	—		
23	3, 16, 17, 35		

CORRELATION OF THIS BOOK WITH ELEMENTARY TEXTS—*continued*

Ruch *Psychology and Life,* 4th ed. Scott, Foresman, 1953		Wickens and Meyer *Psychology* Dryden Press, 1955	
Ch. nos.	*Related articles*	*Ch. nos.*	*Related articles*
1	1, 2	1	1, 2
2	34, 38, 41	2	15
3	3, 4, 5	3	16, 17
4	6, 7, 26, 27, 28, 29	4	18, 19, 20
5	21, 22	5	21, 22, 23
6	24, 35	6	25, 45
7	23, 25, 39	7	24
8	40, 42, 43, 44	8	10, 14
9	8, 9	9	11, 12, 13
10	10, 11, 12, 13, 14	10	30, 31, 32, 33
11	15, 16, 17	11	3, 4, 5, 6, 7
12	18, 19, 20	12	26, 27, 28, 29
13	30, 31, 32	13	34, 35, 36, 37
14	33, 34, 37	14	38, 39, 40
15	45	15	41, 42, 43, 44
16	36, 46	16	—
		17	8, 9
		18	—
		19	—
		20	46

INDEX

R